THE
CUSTER
COMPANION

THE
CUSTER
COMPANION

A Comprehensive Guide to
the Life of George Armstrong Custer
and the Plains Indian Wars

THOM HATCH

STACKPOLE
BOOKS

Published by
STACKPOLE BOOKS
5067 Ritter Road
Mechanicsburg, PA 17055
www.stackpolebooks.com

Cover design by Caroline M. Stover

Cover illustration: "Custer's Last Stand," by Edgar S. Paxson. Courtesy of The Buffalo Bill Historical Center, Cody, Wyoming.

Printed in the United States of America

10 9 8 7 6 5 4 3 2 1

FIRST EDITION

Library of Congress Cataloging-in-Publication Data

Hatch, Thom, 1946–
    The Custer companion : a comprehensive guide to the life of George Armstrong Custer and the Plains Indian wars / Thom Hatch.— 1st ed.
        p.   cm.
        ISBN 0-8117-0477-7
        1. Custer, George Armstrong, 1839–1876.   2. Generals—United States—Bibliography. 3. United States. Army—Biography.   4. United States—History—Civil War, 1861–1865— Campaigns.   5. Indians of North America—Wars—1866–1895.   6. Indians of North America— Wars—West (U.S.).   7. Custer, George Armstrong, 1839–1876—Bibliography.   I. Title.

E467.1.C99 H38   2002
973.8'2092—dc21
[B]
                                                                            2002018907

*To my wife, Lynn,
and daughter, Cimarron*

Contents

CHAPTER THREE: On the Plains

CHAPTER FOUR: The Winter Campaign of 1868–69

CHAPTER FIVE: The Yellowstone Expedition

CHAPTER SIX: Into the Black Hills

CHAPTER SEVEN: Custer's Last Stand

CHAPTER EIGHT: The Reno-Benteen Hilltop Fight

CHAPTER NINE: After Little Bighorn

Maps

Introduction

Although the bibliographies of George Armstrong Custer and the Plains Indian Wars—the battle of the Little Bighorn in particular—are among the most voluminous in American history, the book in your hands is a unique and beneficial addition to that list.

The *Custer Companion* is intended to serve as an easy-to-use, comprehensive guide to assist the serious researcher or casual reader in better appreciating and placing in perspective the military campaigns; the vast number of colorful characters; the significant social, political, cultural, and historical events; and other relevant information associated with the life of George Armstrong Custer and the conflicts between the U.S. Army and the Indian tribes that occurred on the Great Plains from the late 1700s to the late 1800s.

Each chapter offers an informative overview of the subject matter that provides a clear and concise synopsis of the time period. In-depth biographies of notables, as well as others who may be less known but deserve recognition, are arranged alphabetically and run throughout each chapter along the outside column of each page. Related sidebars that explain pertinent aspects of the material—fact, theory, and speculation—are featured in the main body of text and appear after each chapter's overview. Following nearly every overview, biography, and sidebar is an exhaustive list of suggested reading on the topic, with summaries and critiques of the most credible and valuable sources available. Finally, quotes from Custer himself, interspersed throughout most chapters, allow the man to speak for himself.

In other words, *The Custer Companion* will complement and enhance the enjoyment and understanding of every other book you may find pertaining to this stirring era, as well as open up new areas of interest for you to explore. It also can stand alone as a highly readable and fascinating account of the nineteenth-century Western military frontier—and of this country's most enigmatic and controversial soldier and the history in which he participated and, indeed, had a hand in writing.

CHAPTER ONE

Early Life

OVERVIEW

George Armstrong Custer was born on December 5, 1839, in the back room on the first floor of a house in New Rumley, Harrison County, Ohio, the first child of Emanuel Henry and Maria Ward Kirkpatrick Custer. Although he was formally named George Armstrong, the family simply called him Armstrong. As he learned to talk, "Autie," his childlike way of pronouncing his name, became his nickname.

Both of Armstrong's parents had lost a spouse and each had brought two children to their marriage, which was beset by tragedy in the early years. Within five months of his marriage to Maria in February 1836, Emanuel's three-year-old son, John, died. The first two children born to the couple died in infancy, before five healthy children, beginning with the yellow-haired George Armstrong, survived. Following Armstrong were three more sons—Nevin Johnson (July 1842), Thomas Ward (March 1845), and Boston (October 1848)—and a daughter, Margaret Emma (June 1852).

The Custer family was not by any means well-to-do, but Emanuel and Maria compensated for the lack of material possessions by creating a home full of love and family unity. The children from the three families bonded together with loyalty and affection, and the Custer household was said to be always in a happy uproar.

From an early age, Autie enjoyed hanging around his father's blacksmith shop, listening to the friendly banter and watching his father work. The boy test-rode the newly shod horses, which enabled him to develop an early skill in horsemanship. Young Autie also attended militia musters and parades, always wearing the little uniform his mother had made for him and carrying a toy musket or a wooden sword. Emanuel enjoyed showing off his son to his military companions, having Autie execute the manual of arms.

The Custer children attended school in New Rumley, and Autie became known as "a wide awake boy full of all kinds of pranks and willing to take all kinds of chances." The teacher's son added that Autie "was a rather bad boy in school, but one thing would be said of him, he *always* had his lessons, yet he was not considered an unusually bright lad."

"I never wanted for anything necessary. You and Mother instilled into me principles of industry, self-reliance, honesty. You taught me the value of temperate habits, the difference between right and wrong. I look back on the days spent under the home-roof as a period of pure happiness, and I feel thankful for such noble parents."

—CUSTER IN A LETTER TO HIS FATHER ABOUT CHILDHOOD AT HOME

Cadet George Armstrong Custer, West Point, 1861. *Courtesy Little Bighorn Battlefield National Monument.*

✺ Margaret Emma "Maggie" Custer Calhoun
Sister

Maggie was born on January 5, 1852, in New Rumley, Ohio, the fifth child and only daughter born to Emanuel and Maria Custer. Her education at Young Ladies' Seminary and Collegiate Institute, commonly referred to as Boyd's Seminary, Libbie Custer's alma mater, was made possible by the generosity of her brother, George Armstrong, who arranged to pay her tuition. He also paid for her voice and music lessons, and Maggie became an accomplished pianist.

Maggie became a frequent guest of Armstrong and Libbie at their various frontier posts. On one such visit to Fort Leavenworth in 1870, she met a young infantry lieutenant named James "Jimmy" Calhoun, with whom she became romantically involved. Custer used his influence to gain a transfer for Calhoun to the 7th Cavalry. Maggie and Jimmy were married at the Methodist Church in Monroe, Michigan, on March 7, 1872. She accompanied her husband to his duty stations whenever possible and, along with sister-in-law Libbie, was at the center of a close-knit group good-naturedly referred to as Custer's "royal family." When the Custers rented a piano in St. Paul and had it delivered to Fort Abraham Lincoln, Maggie was in much demand as a pianist.

On May 17, 1876, when the 7th Cavalry rode out of Fort Lincoln en route to the Valley of the Little Bighorn, Maggie and Libbie accompanied the regiment as far as the Heart River and returned later that first day with the paymaster. Maggie was present in Libbie's parlor to receive the officers who brought word of the tragic death of their husbands. As the officers departed, Maggie ran after them and cried, "Is there no message for me?" There was no message. She had lost not only a husband, but three brothers and a nephew as well. Later, a member of Gen. Alfred Terry's staff presented her with some cartridge casings fired from her late husband's revolver.

On July 30, Maggie returned to Monroe with Libbie and Annie Yates, widow of Capt. George Yates, on a special train provided by the Northern Pacific Railroad. The three women, along with Annie's three small children, remained for a time in seclusion at the Custer home. On August 13, a memorial service was held for the fallen men, conducted in part by Rev. James Venning, the minister who had united Maggie and Jimmy in marriage. In November, she received $510 from

(continued on following page)

In 1849, Emanuel sold his shop in town and moved his family to an eighty-acre farm on the outskirts of New Rumley, where Armstrong began attending Creal School. For reasons unknown—perhaps financial—Armstrong was soon apprenticed to a furniture maker in Cadiz. This arrangement did not work out, and the boy was sent to live with his half-sister, Lydia Ann Reed, and her husband in Monroe, Michigan. Ann became a surrogate mother and trusted confidant to Custer, a relationship that continued throughout his life.

Armstrong attended New Dublin School, then Alfred Stebbins's Young Man's Academy in Monroe. According to his deskmate at the academy, Armstrong had a penchant for sneaking adventure novels into class and reading them instead of his textbooks. His favorite titles included *Tom Burke of Ours, Jack Hinton,* and *Charles O'Malley, the Irish Dragoon.*

The young man was hardly a bookworm, however, but a spirited and fun-loving youngster who was a natural born leader. He was remembered by the minister of the Methodist Church in Monroe as the main instigator of mischief and minor disruptions during services.

At age sixteen, Armstrong returned to New Rumley and attended McNeely Normal School in Hopedale, where he became "quite a favorite" with the young ladies. One classmate remembered that Custer "was kind and generous to his friends; bitter and implacable towards his enemies."

Armstrong interrupted his own education in 1856 to teach at the Beech Point School in Athens Township for $28 a month. The young teacher was known as a "big-hearted, whole-souled fellow," which made him extremely popular.

Armstrong, however, did not intend to teach forever and wanted to further his education. But because of his family's poor economic situation, he felt that he needed some sort of assistance. To that end, he wrote to the district's Republican representative, John A. Bingham, and requested an appointment to the U.S. Military Academy at West Point.

———— ◆ ————

"I've seen and kissed that crimson lip
With honied smiles o'erflowing.
Enchanted watched the opening rose,
Upon thy soft cheek flowing.
Dear Mary, thy eyes may prove less blue,
Thy beauty fade tomorrow,
But oh, my heart can ne'er forget
Thy parting look of sorrow."

—POEM WRITTEN BY CUSTER TO
MARY JANE "MOLLIE" HOLLAND IN 1856

———— ◆ ————

This audacious act demonstrates the undaunting determination that would be Custer's lifelong hallmark. The odds that a son of an outspoken Democrat such as Emanuel could gain political patronage from a Republican were beyond comprehension.

Many stories have been written about why Armstrong Custer was even considered for such a prestigious appointment from a man whose politics were contrary to those of the staunchly Democratic Custer family. Bingham later related—after Custer had become famous—that the honesty of the young man's letter captivated him. Perhaps that was true, but another story appears to have gained more credibility.

Historians have speculated that the father of a girl with whom Custer was romantically involved used his influence with the congressman in order to remove Custer from his daughter's life.

While Armstrong had been teaching in Cadiz Township, he had boarded with a farm family and was said to have fallen in love with the farmer's daughter, Mary Jane "Mollie" Holland. The attraction was apparently mutual, and the two began spending quite a bit of time together.

Mary's father, Alexander Holland, however, frowned upon a relationship between his daughter and this young man with the Democratic father—if not for other reasons as well. Holland was evidently familiar with the rule that West Point cadets were forbidden to marry and persuaded his old friend Congressman Bingham to seriously consider an appointment for Custer.

Custer's Boyhood Homes

donations collected by the *Army and Navy Journal* from its readers for the widows of the battle.

Maggie's curiosity compelled her to write to 7th Cavalry officer Capt. Myles Moylan later that year requesting information about the death of her husband. Moylan wrote back in December that he had observed Jimmy's body and that he had been scalped but not terribly mutilated. In truth, however, Calhoun's body could be identified only by his teeth, which would indicate that he indeed had been badly mutilated.

Maggie, who had been ill with migraine headaches and feverish and dizzy spells since returning to Monroe, was advised by her physician not to travel the following August to Fort Leavenworth for the reinterment of her husband's remains. She decided, however, that her place was at her husband's gravesite and, ignoring her doctor's wishes, attended the ceremony on August 3, 1877.

Maggie remained close friends with Libbie Custer throughout her life. In September 1884, she was residing with Libbie in the Stuyvesant Apartment Building at 3rd Avenue and 18th Street in New York when a fire broke out shortly before daybreak one morning. The two women and their maid fled the building, and the flames were soon extinguished. When they returned to their apartment, Maggie, much to her dismay, discovered that someone had stolen a gold watch and chain that had belonged to her brother Tom. Libbie had lost a purse containing a small amount of money.

In 1887, Maggie, who had participated in winter theatricals at Fort Lincoln, embarked on a career as a professional elocutionist. She went on tour and received rave reviews. One reviewer stated: "Her graceful bearing and commanding presence, her entire self-possession, her masterly interpretation of her subjects, and her impersonation of the characters she assumed, combined to claim her master, or rather mistress, of the situation." Maggie performed from coast to coast but eventually tired of the constant traveling. In 1891, she accepted the position as Michigan state librarian, a post she held until 1893, when she returned to her first love, dramatic reading.

On July 2, 1903, Maggie married John Halbert Maugham at Onteora Park in New York's Catskill Mountains. The couple honeymooned in Mexico. Maggie had converted to the Christian Science faith, and when she discovered that she had cancer, she turned to the prayers of healer Wentworth Bryan Winslow to restore her health. She at first improved, but then died unexpectedly on March 22, 1910.

✹ Boston "Bos" Custer
Brother

On October 31, 1848, in New Rumley, Ohio, Boston became the fourth child born to Emanuel and Maria Custer. His year of birth has also been listed as 1850. On an August 1862 Civil War reconnaissance, Armstrong captured a "splendid double-barrelled" shotgun, which he sent home as a present for his little brother.

Boston Custer. *Courtesy Little Bighorn Battlefield National Monument.*

Boston apparently was intent on following his brother into the military service. On January 15, 1868, he wrote a letter to George Armstrong, who was stationed at Fort Leavenworth, stating that he wanted to continue his education and "go to that Naval School." He also vowed that he was "going to try to live a Christian life, God being my helper, and you don't know how much better I feel, and if I have done anything to your feelings or wronged you in any way, I ask your pardon for all and will try to do better." Evidently Boston had undergone a religious conversion and desired to wipe the slate clean with his older brother—if there indeed had been any animosity between them, which was unlikely.

Bos, as he was known, never made it to that naval school, but he was asked to accompany his brother as a forage master for the Black Hills Expedition of 1874. It was his first trip west, and he quickly became the butt of his older brothers' good-natured teasing and practical jokes. Tom presented Bos with a rock that he claimed was a "sponge-rock" and if placed under water would transform into a sponge. Bos soaked the rock for a few nights, much to the delight of his brothers, until realizing that he had been taken in. Another, more inventive, prank was played on Bos when he paused on the march to pick a rock from one of his horse's shoes. Armstrong and Tom galloped ahead and hid, then fired shots over Bos's head when he appeared, which sent the young man racing to spread the alarm of an Indian attack.

Bos was hired as a citizen guide at $100 a month for the Little Bighorn campaign—regardless of the fact that he could not recognize one trail from another. He wrote to his mother on June 21, 1876, from the 7th Cavalry's camp at the confluence of the Yellowstone and Rosebud:

> My Darling Mother—The mail leaves to-morrow. I have no news to write. I am feeling first-rate. Armstrong takes the whole command, and starts up the

(continued on following page)

Regardless of the circumstances, in January 1857, seventeen-year-old George Armstrong Custer received notification that he had been awarded an appointment to West Point that would take effect in June.

Armstrong's pending admission became a matter of family discussion. His mother, who had wanted her son to become a minister, voiced her opposition. She worried that war was on the horizon and military training would place her son in the thick of the fighting. The other family members viewed the appointment as an opportunity for Armstrong that could not be ignored. Maria was outvoted by the others and finally acquiesced. Emanuel mortgaged his farm in order to raise the $200 necessary to pay for his son's expenses and admission fee.

On July 1, 1857, Armstrong Custer and sixty-seven other plebes reported for duty as the Class of 1862 at the U.S. Military Academy at West Point, New York.

📖 In addition to the biographies listed on page 5, see *Custer Genealogies,* edited by John M. Carroll and Donald Horn (Bryan, TX: Guidon Press, n.d.); Milton Ronsheim's *The Life of General Custer* (Monroe, MI: Monroe County Library System, 1991); *Custer's Ohio Boyhood: A Brief Account of the Early Life of Major General George Armstrong Custer,* by Charles B. Wallace (Freeport, OH: Freeport Press, 1978); *General Custer and New Rumley, Ohio,* by John M. Carroll (Bryan, TX: privately printed, 1978); "Custer's First Romance Revealed," by Thomas E. O'Neil, *Newsletter, Little Big Horn Associates* 28, no. 2 (March, 1994); and Lawrence A. Frost's *Custer Legends* (Bowling Green, OH: Bowling Green University Popular Press, 1981).

SIDEBARS

🐎 Custer Biographies

Surprisingly, given the amount of information written about George Armstrong Custer and the famous battle, there are few notable biographies available. Minor and major points in Custer's life are the subjects of countless books and essays, and the most relevant of these are contained in the "Suggested Reading" listings within the chapters.

Rather than start with the best biography, the first one published still deserves attention. That would be *A Complete Life of Gen. George Armstrong Custer,* by Frederick Whittaker (New York: Sheldon and Co., 1876). Whittaker, who was a British expatriate and Civil War brevet captain in the 6th New York Cavalry, had met Custer at the offices of Sheldon and Company, where he worked as a dime novelist during the time when Custer published his *My Life on the Plains; or, Personal Experiences with Indians* with that firm (see "Custer's Literary Career" on page 69). Libbie Custer provided Whittaker with Custer's personal correspondence, and the book was released within six months of Custer's death. The biography was an instant success and played a major role—second only to that of Libbie—in transforming Custer into a national hero.

That portrayal went unchallenged until 1934—one year after Libbie's death—when Bobbs-Merrill published Frederic Van de Water's *Glory Hunter: A Life of General Custer.* In this iconoclastic work, Van de Water, an admirer of Sigmund Freud, attempted to delve beyond the deeds and into the mind of Custer. Van de Water concluded that Custer was a deeply flawed man, a perpetual adolescent, addicted to fame, driven and destroyed by ambition, and responsible for the defeat at Little Bighorn.

A compelling, if not rather unusual, biography is *The Custer Story: The Life and Letters of General George A. Custer and His Wife Elizabeth,* by Marguerite Merington (New York: Devin-Adair, 1950). Hundreds of excerpts from letters, the majority written by Custer and Libbie, provide a unique, intimate insight into the subject. Merington, who was a close friend of Libbie Custer in later life, adds a narrative that fills in the blanks and puts the letters in proper perspective. This "first-hand" account stands as one of the better portrayals of Custer, Libbie, and their life and times.

"I would not leave this place for any amount of money because I would rather have a good education and no money, than to have a fortune and be ignorant."

—Custer to his half-sister, Ann Reed, after his first year at West Point

---

Sweet Briar on an Indian trail with the full hope and belief of overhauling them—which I think he will, with a little hard riding.... I hope to catch one or two Indian ponies with a buffalo robe for [brother] Nev, but he must not be disappointed if I don't.... Now don't give yourself any trouble at all as all will be well.... Goodbye my darling Mother.

Bos was detailed to the rear with the pack train on Custer's June 25 approach into the Little Bighorn Valley. He hurried forward to join his brothers when word of the impending fight was received. His body was found, along with those of his brothers and nephew Autie Reed, among the forty on Custer Hill.

Boston was initially buried on the battlefield. His body was exhumed in 1878 and reinterred in the family plot at Woodlawn Cemetery in Monroe, Michigan. His obituary appeared in the January 11, 1878, edition of the *Monroe Commercial.*

📖 *Letters from Boston Custer.* Thomas E. O'Neil, ed. (Brooklyn, NY: Arrow and Trooper, 1993).

✹ Emanuel Henry Custer
Father

Emanuel Custer entered the world on December 10, 1806, in Cresaptown, Allegany County, Maryland, the oldest of seven children born to John and Catherine (Valentine) Custer. Emanuel's namesake grandfather, who was of German descent, had served as a member of the Philadelphia County Militia in the Revolutionary War, and his great-grandmother was a cousin of the mother of George Washington.

Evidently the Custer men had worked for generations as blacksmiths, and Emanuel was no exception, learning the trade from his father or an uncle. Another uncle, his father's brother Jacob, had earlier moved to Ohio and apparently requested that Emanuel come to work for him. In 1824, Emanuel traveled to the tiny village of New Rumley, Ohio, which was about eleven miles from Cadiz, the county seat of Harrison County. Within a year, Jacob Custer decided to move to a farm outside of town and at that time handed his business over to Emanuel. He was now the town smithy, and his shop became a gathering place for those with time on their hands who had a propensity for debating the issues of the day.

On August 7, 1828, Emanuel married Matilda Viers, the daughter of New Rumley's justice of the peace. Two years later, Emanuel became justice of the peace, a post he held for twelve years. The couple had three children: a daughter, Hannah, who died within a year, and two sons, Brice and John.

(continued on following page)

On July 18, 1835, Emanuel suffered another loss when Matilda died of unknown causes.

Emanuel soon began courting Maria Ward Kirkpatrick, the daughter of a tavern owner who had lost her husband in March 1835 and had been widowed with two small children, David and Lydia Ann. On February 23, 1836, Emanuel and Maria were married, and the combined families moved into the home she had shared with her late husband.

Emanuel regarded his loyalty to the Democratic party, which could be called nothing less than militant, to be as sacred as his church ties. Although raised Presbyterian, he had helped found the New Rumley Methodist Church and was deeply committed to that faith. Emanuel was also a prominent member of the New Rumley Invincibles, the local militia.

Emanuel acted like a big kid when he was around his children, romping, wrestling, and playing as aggressively as any of them. He also made them the target of practical jokes and dodged their mischief in return, which became a lifelong practice between them.

In early 1849, Emanuel sold their house and blacksmith shop and bought an eighty-acre farm three miles out of town. He did not abandon blacksmithing but used the trade to supplement his income while attempting to eke out a living from the land. In 1857, Emanuel put up the farm as collateral when he borrowed $200 to pay for George Armstrong's admission fee to West Point. Four years later, Emanuel moved his family to an eighty-acre farm on the Tontogony Creek in Washington Township, Wood County, Ohio, near his son Nevin, who lived just north. In 1863, in order to be closer to Lydia Ann, the daughter from Maria's first marriage, who had married David Reed and moved to Monroe, Michigan, Emanuel—without selling his farm—borrowed $200 from David Reed and bought a house on the corner of Cass and Third Streets in Monroe. Finances were tight, and the Custer family depended on money sent by George Armstrong to survive. Emanuel finally sold the farm in August 1865, realizing a profit of about $1,000.

In 1866, when Armstrong was stationed in New Hempstead, Texas, Emanuel was hired to serve as a forage master for the division, a job with "little to do and fine pay." The extended family had a grand time riding and hunting and playing practical jokes on each other. On one occasion, Emanuel was reading the newspaper when his boys set off fireworks beneath his chair. On another, while Emanuel was at the dinner table immersed in a political tirade against the Repub-

(continued on following page)

The next biography of note was *Custer: The Life of General George Armstrong Custer,* by Jay Monaghan (Boston: Little, Brown and Co, 1959). This book, which is favorable without exception to Custer, highlights his Civil War career but fails to provide a completely satisfying account of the Little Bighorn battle. Also, myths about Custer are treated as fact.

One biography barely worth mentioning is D. A. Kinsley's two-volume *Favor the Bold* (New York: Holt, Rinehart and Winston, 1967–68), which offers little of value other than being well written.

Crazy Horse and Custer: The Parallel Lives of Two American Warriors, by Stephen E. Ambrose (Garden City, NY: Doubleday and Co., 1975), presents the story with intelligent speculation where facts are absent. This intriguing book reconstructs a period in history through the eyes of two notable participants by one of the country's premier historians, and that in itself makes for a good read. It does, however, perpetuate too many myths.

One book of borderline biography is Charles K. Hofling's *Custer and the Little Big Horn: A Psychobiographical Inquiry* (Detroit: Wayne State University Press, 1981). As the title suggests, this speculative work delves into the deeper recesses of Custer's mind and therefore is not recommended for the beginner.

One of the best biographies is Evan S. Connell's *Son of the Morning Star* (San Francisco: North Point Press, 1984). Connell restores Custer's reputation as a heroic figure and does so not in chronological order of his life, but by wandering off on research tangents into aspects of white-Indian relations and culture that some have found enlightening but others have deemed maddening. There are several drawbacks to this work, however. One is the brief treatment of certain aspects of Custer's life in order to concentrate on events pertaining to Plains history and characters. Another is the lack of documentation, which, considering the diversified subject matter, would have been quite helpful for the researcher. Also, the index is relatively sparse, which often requires the reader to leaf through the pages when seeking specific material. Nevertheless, this book is utterly fascinating.

The best biography for the beginner or casual reader—and not to exclude the serious student—is Robert M. Utley's *Cav-*

"You cannot imagine how sorry I will be to see this happen as the majority of my friends and all my roommates except one have been from the South."

—CUSTER TO ANN REED WHEN SOUTHERN CADETS VOWED TO RESIGN FROM WEST POINT WHEN THEIR STATES SECEDED

"It is useless to hope the coming struggle will be bloodless or of short duration. Much blood will be spilled and thousands of lives, at the least, lost. If it is to be my lot to fall in the service of my country's rights I will have no regrets."

—CUSTER TO ANN REED ABOUT THE IMPENDING WAR

---

alier in Buckskin: George Armstrong Custer and the Western Military Frontier* (Norman: University of Oklahoma Press, 1988). One area that might have been of some concern with this book is the lack of footnotes and documentation, except for the fact that Utley is a historian without peer and brought a lifetime of knowledge and perspective to this biography. This is without question the first book one should read when delving into the life of Custer.

One "specialty" biography that deserves mentioning is *The Custer Album: A Pictorial Biography of General George A. Custer,* by Lawrence A. Frost (Norman: University of Oklahoma Press, 1990). This volume not only tells the story in an inspiring narrative by one of the foremost Custer scholars, but also, as the title suggests, is chock-full of photographs and drawings that depict just about everyone and everything associated with Custer.

Another book that does not snugly fit into the category of biography but should be noted is *The Custer Reader,* edited by Paul Andrew Hutton (Lincoln: University of Nebraska Press, 1992). Beginning with the Civil War, the reader is presented with a series of articles by Custer, his contemporaries, and noted historians that portray Custer's personality, career, and the many myths surrounding his life.

Perhaps the best overall biography to date is Jeffry D. Wert's *Custer: The Controversial Life of George Armstrong Custer* (New York: Simon & Shuster, 1996). This meticulously researched, well-written study covers every aspect of Custer's life in a balanced and thoughtful manner. Wert did not fall victim to the myths and legends perpetuated by earlier biographers; rather, he carefully analyzed each claim to present the most factual portrayal possible and backed up his findings with ample documentation.

Custer's closest living relative, Brice C. Custer, provides interesting family anecdotes and admirably defends his great-great-uncle in *The Sacrificial Lion George Armstrong Custer: From American Hero to Media Villain* (El Segundo, CA: Upton & Sons, 1999). This book not only offers a clear view of Custer's life, but also challenges critics of the general who have failed to properly research their subject.

licans, his son Tom covertly spirited away his plate of food and ate it, returning the empty plate. Emanuel was quite befuddled when he concluded his lecture and noticed that his dinner was gone.

At the June 1876 Little Bighorn battle, the man who valued family over everything else in his life lost three of his beloved sons, Armstrong, Tom, and Boston; a son-in-law, James Calhoun; and a step-grandson, Autie Reed. Emanuel was left with his daughter, Margaret; step-daughter, Lydia Ann; and two boys, Nevin and Brice, his son by his first marriage, who was a bridge inspector living in Cleveland. Libbie Custer arranged for Emanuel to have Armstrong's horse, Dandy, and for years he proudly rode his son's favorite mount in parades.

Maria died in 1882, and Emanuel eventually went to live on son Nevin's farm three miles west of Monroe. He passed away on November 27, 1892, two weeks before his eighty-sixth birthday. He was remembered by townspeople as a man of strong religious and political convictions. He had once been asked, "Don't it shake your faith in Democracy in general, Father Custer, to know that most clergymen are Republicans?" Emanuel replied, "No, it don't shake my faith in Democracy, but it does make me rather suspicious of their religion."

Libbie Custer reflected on her father-in-law in the December 11, 1892, edition of the *Detroit Free Press:*

> His warmest friends, his genuine admirers, were half of them opposed to his politics, but he loved dearly to have them oppose him; he challenged their thrusts and then invited them to a country dinner of fatted turkey after Michigan went Democratic to show them how he valued their society in spite of what he thought their mistaken views.

📖 In addition to the sources listed at the end of the narrative, further information as well as amusing anecdotes about Emanuel Custer can be found in *General Custer's Libbie,* by Lawrence A. Frost (Seattle: Superior Publishing Co., 1976).

✹ Maria Ward Kirkpatrick Custer
Mother

Maria was born in 1807 in Burgettstown, Washington County, Pennsylvania, to James and Catherine Ward, who were of Scotch-Irish descent. In 1816, the Ward family relocated to New Rumley, Ohio, where James opened an unlicensed tavern, which was illegal. He was fined for his crime and subsequently obtained a license for a legal establishment. James Ward built a two-story log home with attached kitchen on a corner lot across

(continued on following page)

from the town square and opened for business. The tavern, however, was far from being a friendly neighborhood watering hole. Ward and his two sons, James, Jr., and Joseph, were involved in frequent fights with local citizens, which would indicate the rowdy nature of the establishment where Maria was raised.

One particular patron of the tavern was a twenty-seven-year-old merchant named Israel R. Kirkpatrick. He began courting fifteen-year-old Maria, and the two were married on January 8, 1823. Maria gave birth to a son, David, later that year and a daughter, Lydia Ann, in 1825. Her father died in 1824, her mother in about 1829, and with her death the tavern was closed. The Kirkpatricks moved into the tavern and made it their family home. On March 6, 1835, Israel Kirkpatrick died, and Maria was left with two small children.

Maria was probably already acquainted with Emanuel Custer, the local smithy, who lost his wife in July 1835, leaving him with two young sons, Brice and John. Emanuel soon began courting Maria, and the couple married on February 23, 1836. The combined families moved into the home that she had shared with her late husband, where they had five healthy children of their own. Maria, a Lutheran, and her husband, a Presbyterian, both embraced the Methodist faith and became devout worshipers.

The Custers moved on several occasions, finally settling in Monroe, Michigan. Maria was opposed to Armstrong entering West Point, primarily due to the threat of an impending war, but finally acquiesced and placed his care in God's hands. After the Civil War, Armstrong wrote to his parents to express his admiration for their efforts in raising him with proper values and principles. Maria was moved to write in reply:

> My loveing [sic] son—When you speak about your boyhood home in your dear letter I had to weep for joy that the recollection was sweet in your memory. Many a time I have thought there was things my children needed it caused me tears. Yet I consoled myself that I had done my best in making home comfortable. My darling boy, it was not for myself. I was not fortunate enough to have wealth to make home beautiful, always my desire. So I tried to fill the empty spaces with little acts of kindness. Even when there was a meal admired by my children it was my greatest pleasure to get it for them. I have no doubt I have said some things to you and my other children that was not always pleasant, but I have no regrets about that. You, my son, have more than compensated your mother for all she has done for you. It is sweet to toil for those we love.

(continued on following page)

EPILOGUE

Armstrong Custer's record at West Point can be summed up in a statement he later wrote:

> My career as a cadet had but little to commend it to the study of those who came after me, unless as an example to be carefully avoided. The requirements of the academic regulations, a copy of which was placed in my hand the morning of my arrival at West Point, were not observed by me in such a manner at all times as to commend me to the approval and good opinions of my instructors and superior officers. My offences [sic] against law and order were not great in enormity, but what they lacked in magnitude they made up in number.

The blue-eyed Armstrong Custer stood nearly six feet tall, weighed about 170 pounds, and was called "Fanny" by his classmates due to his wavy, blond hair and fair complexion. Students were organized into sections according to their academic abilities, and Armstrong found himself for the most part among the Southerners and Westerners, who were generally inferior to the New Englanders. Therefore, Custer's closest friends were those with Southern roots—Kentuckians William Dunlop and George Watts, Mississippian John "Gimlet" Lee, Georgian Pierce M. B. Young, and Lafayette "Lafe" Lane, a Southern sympathizer from Oregon. Custer's best friend was Texan Thomas L. Rosser, who roomed next door.

His fun-loving nature was immediately at odds with the strict academy code of conduct, which was calculated by a system of demerits—called "skins" by the cadets—issued for various offenses. One hundred skins in a six-month period would be grounds for dismissal from the academy.

At the end of his first year, Fanny Custer ranked fifty-second in mathematics and fifty-seventh in English—in a class of sixty-two. His placement was due in part to the fact that he had accumulated 151 demerits, the highest number in his class. His less-than-glowing academic record was not the result of a lack of intelligence on his part, but of his propensity for pranks and devil-may-care attitude. Fellow cadet Peter Michie wrote: "Custer was always in trouble with the authorities. He had more fun, gave his friends more anxiety, walked more tours of extra guard, and came nearer to being dismissed more often than any other cadet I have ever known."

Although his "boyish, but harmless frolics kept him in constant hot water," Custer excelled in popularity and leadership. "He was beyond a doubt," one cadet wrote, "the most popular man in his class." Another reported:

> West Point has had many a character to deal with, but it may be a question whether it ever had a cadet so exuberant, one who cared so little for its serious attempts to elevate and burnish, or one on whom its tactical officers kept their eyes so constantly and unsympathetically searching as upon Custer. And yet how we all loved him.

Custer, however, was disciplined enough when his total of demerits reached levels of dismissal to behave for long periods of time or to work off minor infractions by walking extra guard duty. Also to his credit, he was never assessed a skin for fighting or an altercation with another cadet throughout his West Point career.

A check of his four-year record reveals, among other offenses, making a boisterous noise in his sink, talking and laughing in class, throwing snowballs outside, throwing bread in the mess hall, being late for parade, swinging his arms in formation, not keeping his eyes to the front, throwing stones on post, not properly carrying his musket during drill, having cooking utensils in the chimney, and gazing about in ranks.

Armstrong's second year showed little improvement over the first. He accumulated 192 demerits—only 8 short of the 200 that would have resulted in his dismissal. His class standing was fifty-sixth out of sixty. He did, however, prove his skill as a horseman by, according to tradition, executing the highest jump of a hurdle ever at the academy while slashing at a dummy with his saber.

Custer's third year at West Point was another poor performance. He earned 191 demerits, one less than the preceding year, and ranked at the bottom of his class.

For the 1860–61 academic year at the academy, Congress voted to reduce the school term from five to four years because of the threat of war between the North and the South; new officers might be required to fight to preserve the Union. And, indeed, the Southern cadets vowed to resign from West Point when their states seceded. "You cannot imagine," Custer wrote to Ann Reed, "how sorry I will be to see this happen as the majority of my friends and all my roommates except one have been from the South."

The formation of the Confederate States of America in February 1861 had a profound effect on the cadets. This separation of loyalties became evident at the academy with impromptu good-natured contests of regional pride. As winter turned into spring, however, these rivalries more often than not escalated into arguments that resulted in blows being exchanged.

"My class numbered upon entering the Academy about one hundred and twenty-five. Of this number only thirty-four graduated, and of these thirty-three graduated above me. The resignation and departure of the Southern cadets took away from the Academy a few individuals who, had they remained, would probably have contested with me the debatable honor of bringing up the rear of the class."

—CUSTER ON HIS CLASS STANDING AT WEST POINT

Maria, who was in ill health or invalid most of her life, developed a special bond with her oldest son—an invisible umbilical cord that was never severed. Libbie Custer wrote:

> The hardest trial of my husband's life was parting with his mother. Such partings were the only occasions when I ever saw him lose entire control of himself. . . . She had been an invalid for so many years that each parting seemed to her the final one. The general would rush out of the house, sobbing like a child, and then throw himself into the carriage beside me, completely unnerved.

Maria was understandably grief-stricken following the deaths of her three sons, a son-in-law, and a grandson in the Little Bighorn battle. She lamented, "How can I bear it? All my boys gone." Apparently, for reasons unknown, she did not attend the ceremony at West Point when her oldest son was reinterred on October 10, 1877. Maria passed away in January 1882.

📖 See *The Ancestry of Maria Ward Custer, 1807–1882,* by Raymond Martin Bell. (Washington, PA: Raymond Martin Bell, 1992.)

✹ Nevin Johnson "Nev" Custer
Brother

This second son of Emanuel and Maria Custer was born on July 29, 1842, in New Rumley, Ohio. At the outbreak of the Civil War, Nevin, who was somewhat frail as a child, reported to the recruiting office in Cleveland to volunteer for military duty but was physically disqualified due to chronic rheumatism. Nev, as he was known, took up farming, married, and had five children. He was the only member of Custer's generation to marry. His son James Calhoun Custer was the only one of those children to have children to carry on the family bloodline.

In early 1871, George Armstrong sold some mining stock (see "The Stevens Lode Mine" on page 105) and sent Nev a down payment on a jointly purchased farm three miles west of Monroe, Michigan, on the north side of the River Raisin that would permit his brother to remain close to their aging parents, who had moved from Ohio to Monroe. Apparently Nevin's new farm did not prosper. Libbie wrote Armstrong in late August 1873: "Mother Custer is in low spirits. She worries about Nevie. His poor crops, his poverty, his increasing family." After the death of Armstrong, Libbie sold her portion of the farm, 114 acres, to Nev for $775, although another man had offered $1,000 more.

On February 10, 1915, Nevin died suddenly from an attack of gastritis. The occasion of his funeral was the final time that Libbie visited Monroe.

✺ Thomas Ward Custer
Brother

Tom was born on March 15, 1845, in New Rumley, Ohio, to Emanuel and Maria Custer, the third of five children. At the outbreak of the Civil War, he attempted to enlist in the army from his home in Monroe, Michigan, but was thwarted when Emanuel notified the recruiter that his son was only sixteen and therefore too young for service. Tom, however, would not be denied. He crossed the border to the town of his birth, New Rumley, Ohio, and on September 2, 1861, was sworn in as a private in Company H of the 21st Ohio Infantry. He fought as a common foot soldier for the next three years, participating in such battles as Shiloh, Stones River, Chickamauga, Missionary Ridge, Chattanooga, and the Atlanta campaign. His distinguished service gained him duty as escort for Generals James Negley, Ulysses S. Grant, George Thomas, and James Palmer. He was promoted to corporal on January 1, 1864.

Tom, however, craved the excitement and notoriety that the cavalry had provided for his famous brother. On October 23, 1864, he accepted an appointment as second lieutenant, Company B, 6th Michigan Cavalry, and was soon detailed as an aide-de-camp to his older brother. Armstrong showed Tom no favoritism and often chose him for extra assignments—which evoked grumbling from the sibling, who swore it was not fair. Nevertheless, the hardened veterans of the unit were skeptical of their commanding officer's sibling—until early April 1865, when Tom, in the tradition of his brother, made some history of his own.

On April 3, 1865, Gen. Robert E. Lee, with 80,000 men, was retreating west through the Appomattox River Valley and happened to pass just north of General Custer's campsite. Custer followed until reaching Namozine Creek, where the bridge had been destroyed. Rebel fortifications could be observed across the river, and Custer, not knowing he was greatly outnumbered, ordered one detachment to outflank the position while men with axes were detailed to remove fallen trees from the creek in order to permit the remainder of his troops to charge across. Tom Custer became impatient, however, and spurred his horse to brazenly streak across the creek toward the enemy position. His action inspired the other troops to follow, and the Rebels quickly broke under the surprise pressure. Tom chased the retreating enemy and unhesitatingly charged directly into a skirmish line near Namozine Church. When the smoke had cleared, Tom presented his brother with a Confederate battle flag, which at that time was considered quite a prize, and fourteen prisoners, including three officers. Maj. Gen. Philip Sheridan recommended that Tom be breveted to major and awarded the Medal of Honor for his bravery.

Three days later, when Lee's exhausted army inadvertently split into two columns, General Custer's opportunistic cavalrymen plunged into them at a place called Sayler's Creek. Tom Custer was at the front of the 3rd Brigade when it led the charge against enemy fortifications. The Rebels once again broke but continued to fight as they withdrew. Tom spotted an enemy standard-bearer and was about to capture another prized flag when the Confederate soldier fired point-blank at the charging Custer's head. The bullet struck Tom in the cheek and exited behind his ear, knocking him backward against his horse's rump. His face was blackened with powder, and blood poured from the severe wound. Tom righted himself, coolly drew his pistol, shot the standard-bearer, and grabbed the coveted banner. Col. (later general) Henry Capehart had witnessed the scene and later said, "For intrepidity I never saw this incident surpassed." Tom wheeled his horse and raced to show his trophy to his brother. The general took one look at Tom's face and ordered him to the rear for medical attention. Tom refused, stating that he would not leave the field until the battle was over. Armstrong Custer placed his younger brother under arrest and had him escorted to the surgeon who had set up a hospital at a nearby plantation. For this demonstration of courage, Tom was breveted lieutenant colonel and awarded his second Medal of Honor.

Thomas Ward Custer became the first person in history to be distinguished with two awards of our nation's highest military medal and was the only double honoree during the Civil War.

Tom served with his brother in Texas until being officially mustered out on April 24, 1866. After a brief appointment as second lieutenant, 1st Cavalry, he accepted an appointment to first lieutenant, 7th Cavalry, effective July 28, 1866.

During the 1867 Hancock expedition, Tom was involved in the shooting of deserters and his brother's mad dash across Kansas, which led to the elder Custer facing a court-martial (see "Custer's Mad Dash across Kansas" on page 63). The following year, he participated in the battle of the Washita, where he was slightly wounded in the right hand and assumed command of Company C when Capt. Louis Hamilton was killed.

Tom, who worshiped his older brother, endeared himself to Libbie Custer and was a prominent member of the Custer "royal family" at the various frontier posts where the 7th Cavalry was garrisoned. He was, however, a wild and reckless youth, who had an affinity for playing cards and was known to habitually drink to excess. It has been rumored that he had fathered several children in Ohio. He apparently was prepared at some point to marry a New Jersey woman named Lulie Burgess, but she died before the union took place, and Tom remained a bachelor for the rest of his life.

His impetuous traits were instrumental in an episode in Hays City, Kansas, in 1869, when he found himself on the wrong side of William Butler "Wild Bill" Hickok (see "Wild Bill's Showdown with Tom Custer" on page 67).

Tom's company was stationed in South Carolina and Mississippi during Reconstruction duty, then participated in the Yellowstone expedition of 1873 and the Black Hills expedition the following year. He was involved with the arrest of the Sioux warrior Rain-in-the-Face at Standing Rock Agency in January 1875 for the murders of two men during the Yellowstone expedition. The incensed warrior at that time vowed to someday cut out Tom's heart and eat it (see "The Arrest and Revenge of Rain-in-the-Face" on page 129).

(continued on following page)

Capt. Thomas W. Custer, wearing his two Medals of Honor, 1870. *Courtesy Little Bighorn Battlefield National Monument.*

Tom was appointed captain effective December 2, 1875. He rode out on the 1876 Little Bighorn campaign as commander of Company C, but it has been speculated that at some point during the June 25 battle, he was detailed as an aide-de-camp to his brother. Regardless, Tom's body was found beside that of his brother on Custer Hill. He had been singled out for the most brutal of mutilations. His body had been repeatedly stabbed, slashed, crushed beyond recognition, and riddled with arrows. He was identified only by his tattoos: an American flag, an eagle with outspread wings, and the initials "T. W. C." Some have speculated that Rain-in-the-Face had exacted vengeance, but that likely was not the case, as Tom's heart was intact.

Tom was temporarily laid to rest where he fell beside his brother. His remains were exhumed in July 1877 and reinterred on November 3 at the Fort Leavenworth National Cemetery.

✳ Harry Armstrong "Autie" Reed
Nephew

Autie, as he had been nicknamed after his famous uncle, was born in Monroe, Michigan, on April 27, 1858, to David and Lydia Ann Reed. He was eighteen years of age when he headed west to accompany his uncle on the 1876 Little Bighorn campaign. Autie had initially been hired as a herder with the cattle herd, but at the time of the battle, he was without an assignment. On June 25, he was killed alongside his three uncles on Custer Hill and temporarily buried on the field. His body was later exhumed and reinterred in Woodlawn Cemetery in Monroe in January 1878. His name on the battle monument is listed as "Arthur Reed."

Harry Armstrong Reed. *Courtesy Little Bighorn Battlefield National Monument.*

📖 "Autie Reed's Last Letters," by Thomas E. O'Neil, ed. *Newsletter, Little Bighorn Associates* 28, No. 3 (April 1994).

On April 12, when Southern artillery opened up on Fort Sumter in Charleston Harbor, thirty-seven cadets, including Custer's best friend, Tom Rosser, departed the academy to offer their services to the Confederacy. In spite of his friendship with Southern classmates, Custer vowed to honor the oath of allegiance he had sworn upon entering West Point and offer his services to the governor of Ohio.

The Class of 1861 was graduated early on May 6. Custer's class, which was subjected to an abbreviated curriculum that would supplant the final year of studies, was scheduled to graduate on June 24.

Though it may have seemed amazing to many instructors and fellow cadets, Fanny Custer had satisfactorily completed his studies and was commissioned a second lieutenant. He had racked up an additional 192 demerits during the year, which gave him an impressive four-year total of 726. Nevertheless, the class clown who excelled in horsemanship and athletic prowess but lagged behind in academics had overcome his own outrageous antics to qualify for graduation from West Point.

Perhaps predictably, Custer's military career was in trouble before the ink had dried on his diploma. On June 29, he was officer of the guard when a fist fight broke out between two

BIOGRAPHIES

✳ Lydia Ann Kirkpatrick Reed
Half-sister

Ann, as she was known, was born in 1825 in New Rumley, Ohio, to Israel and Maria Ward Kirkpatrick. On December 1, 1846, Ann married David Reed and moved to Monroe, Michigan, where her husband had a drayage business, a farm, and dabbled in real estate. The couple had three children.

Perhaps due to the ill health of Maria Custer, Ann held a special place in the life of George Armstrong Custer as a second mother. He went to live with the Reeds for two years, beginning when he was ten years old, and was treated like a son. Ann was the recipient of countless letters from Armstrong throughout his life, which told her about his current duties, details of battles, and the personalities of those with whom he served; occasionally complained about something or other; discussed family business; and chatted about social events. Over the years, he visited the Reeds whenever possible.

Another major impact of Ann on Armstrong's life came when he was in Monroe on sick leave in 1862. Custer had spent the evening at the tavern and had imbibed to excess. He staggered home, only to be greeted by a horrified Ann. The deeply religious woman made him pledge before God that he would never drink again. Her primary evangelistic concern, however, was Armstrong's salvation, and her prayers were answered in early 1865, when Custer publicly professed his faith (see "Custer's Oath of Temperance and Religious Conversion" on page 19).

In 1876, Ann's eighteen-year-old son, Harry Armstrong "Autie" Reed, who was a civilian accompanying the 7th Cavalry on the Little Bighorn campaign, was killed alongside his famous uncle on Custer Hill. David Reed departed for Fort Abraham Lincoln the moment the news arrived and escorted home the Monroe ladies—Libbie, Maggie Calhoun, and Annie Yates, wife of George Yates.

Lydia Ann Reed, who had so much influence on Custer's life, died in 1906 at the age of eighty-one.

"Too far off to exchange verbal adieux, I responded by bringing my musket to a 'present.'"

—CUSTER REMARKING ABOUT HIS ACTIONS WHILE ON GUARD DUTY WHEN TWO SOUTHERN FRIENDS DEPARTED THE ACADEMY TO SERVE IN THE CONFEDERATE ARMY

---

cadets—one of whom was William Ludlow, who would be chief engineer on Custer's Black Hills expedition of 1874. Inexplicably, Custer disregarded his duty to break up the fight, and instead told the assembled crowd, "Stand back, boys; let's have a fair fight."

The officer of the day, 1st Lt. William B. Hazen, a West Point instructor and future Custer critic, happened along and placed Custer under arrest. While his classmates departed the academy and proceeded to Washington for further orders, Custer was detained to await a court-martial, which would convene on July 5.

On that date, nine officers listened to evidence pertaining to charges of neglect of duty and "conduct to the prejudice of good order and military discipline." Custer was found guilty on both counts. His punishment, however, was the ruling that he only be "reprimanded in orders."

Under normal circumstances, Custer probably would have been dismissed from the service. "Custer's Luck," the term that Custer and others would employ to characterize the favorable events that occurred to him throughout his life, had saved his military career. He was now free to apply the lessons that he had learned at the academy on the battlefields of the Civil War.

📖 In addition to the biographies listed on page 5, *The Class of 1861: Custer, Ames, and Their Classmates after West Point,* by Ralph Kirshner (Carbondale: Southern Illinois University Press, 1999), provides an interesting insight into Custer and his contemporaries at West Point. See also *"Skinned": The Delinquency Record of Cadet George Armstrong Custer U.S.M.A. Class of June 1861,* by W. Donald Horn (Short Hills, NJ: W. Donald Horn, 1980); Register of Delinquencies, 1856–61, United States Military Academy Archives, West Point, New York; *Regulations for the U.S. Military Academy at West Point, New York* (New York: John F. Trow, Printer, 1857); *Custer and His Times: Book Two,* edited by John M. Carroll (Fort Worth, TX: Little Big Horn Associates, 1984); *Four on Custer by Carroll,* by John Carroll (New Brunswick, NJ: Guidon Press, 1976); *The Spirit of Old West Point, 1858–1862,* by Morris Schaff (Boston and New York: Houghton, Mifflin Co., 1907); and Special Orders, no. 21, U.S. Military Academy Archives.

CHAPTER TWO

The Civil War

OVERVIEW

The historic image and reputation of George Armstrong Custer have been unfairly established from the events of one day in his life—the day he died, of which very little is actually known. Every other aspect of his career has been overshadowed by that lone Indian fight on the frontier.

In his time, however, Custer was not a symbol of defeat, but a national hero on a grand scale due to his amazing achievements in the Civil War. He captured the first enemy battle flag taken by the Union army and accepted the Confederate white flag of surrender at Appomattox. In between those notable events exists a series of intrepid acts of almost unbelievable proportion as he personally led electrifying cavalry charges that earned the flamboyant general the admiration of his men and captured the fancy of the newspaper reporters and the public.

It is impossible to adequately chronicle the true scope of Custer's record in the limited space available here. The reader is highly encouraged to delve into one or more of the volumes listed at the end of this narrative in order to better appreciate the brilliance of Custer's battlefield leadership and the fame he attained during his extraordinary service.

Custer's military career had a somewhat inauspicious beginning, but nevertheless, his ambition and flair for being in the thick of the fight were always evident.

On July 21, 1861, just three days out of West Point, Second Lieutenant Custer rode out to join Company G, 2nd Cavalry, at Bull Run. In his only action of the battle, he was cited for bravery when he turned an every-man-for-himself retreat, which had blocked a bridge across Cub Run, into an orderly formation.

Because of his West Point education, Custer was subsequently assigned to the staffs of several minor generals while new army commander Maj. Gen. George B. McClellan attempted to mold raw recruits into a capable fighting force. Although serving as aide-de-camp, he constantly sought out opportunities to see action.

In early May 1862, during the siege of Yorktown, Custer served as a military observer from a hot-air balloon. He would ascend with field glasses, map, and notebook and count enemy

"I had often heard the sound made by cannon balls while passing through the air during my artillery practice at West Point, but a man listens with changed interest when the direction of the balls is toward instead of away from him."

—CUSTER UPON COMING UNDER ENEMY ARTILLERY FIRE AT BULL RUN

Bvt. Maj. Gen. George Armstrong Custer, 1865. *Courtesy Little Bighorn Battlefield National Monument.*

✳ Elizabeth Clift Bacon "Libbie" Custer
Wife, Author

Elizabeth "Libbie" Bacon Custer, 1874. *Courtesy Little Bighorn Battlefield National Monument.*

Libbie was born in Monroe, Michigan, on April 8, 1842. Her father, Daniel Stanton Bacon (December 12, 1798–March 18, 1866), was a descendant of the Plymouth colony and at one time or another had been a farmer, schoolteacher, member of the Territorial Legislature, losing candidate for Michigan lieutenant governor in 1837, probate judge, and director of a bank and railroad. In September 1837, at the age of thirty-eight, Judge Bacon married twenty-three-year-old Eleanor Sophia Page of Grand Rapids by way of Rutland, Vermont, the daughter of a nursery owner who had been educated in one of the finest seminaries in the East.

Daniel and Sophia, as she was known, had four children. Two girls, Harriet and Sophia, died in infancy, and a boy, Edward, born on June 9, 1839, died of a childhood disease at the age of eight. That left little Libbie to be doted upon. She was raised in an idyllic traditional American setting, living in an imposing white house with green shutters surrounded by a well-kept lawn, guarded by a white picket fence, and towered over by stately elm trees.

When Libbie was twelve, her mother passed away from a disease that, according to Judge Bacon, the "physicians were unacquainted with." One source lists the cause of death as dysentery. The judge had promised his wife on her deathbed that he would properly care for their daughter. To that end, he enrolled Libbie in the Young Ladies' Seminary and Collegiate Institute, commonly known as "Boyd's Seminary" after its

(continued on following page)

campfires while sketching the locations of gun emplacements and tent positions.

On May 5, he was serving on the staff of Gen. Winfield Scott Hancock, whose troops were engaged with Confederate soldiers at Williamsburg. The Union soldiers had been formed on a skirmisher line, and when the Rebels came within striking distance, a bayonet charge was ordered. Hancock's troops hesitated—until Custer spurred his horse and burst from their midst. The Union soldiers obediently followed this gallant one-man charge, which resulted in routing the Confederates into retreat. Custer returned to friendly lines after single-handedly capturing an enemy officer, five enlisted men, and—the real trophy—the first Confederate battle flag taken in the war by the Army of the Potomac.

Later that month, Custer participated in a daring daylight reconnaissance along the Chickahominy River by guiding a raiding party to its objective. According to the official report, he "was the first to cross the stream, the first to open fire, and one of the last to leave the field." His heroic actions came to the attention of General McClellan, who requested Custer's presence. At that time, he accepted a position on McClellan's staff with the brevet rank of captain effective June 5.

McClellan came to depend greatly on the adventurous Custer, who was already a McClellan admirer, and their relationship flourished. "His head was always clear in danger," McClellan later wrote, "and he always brought me clear and intelligible reports." McClellan, however, was critical of the policies established by the Lincoln administration and was removed from his role as army commander on November 7, 1862.

Custer, who was devastated by the move, returned to Monroe, Michigan, to await further orders. This respite from the war provided him the opportunity to become acquainted with Monroe resident Libbie Bacon, with whom he fell in love. He courted her relentlessly, charging through obstacles in his pathway in true cavalry fashion, until finally winning her hand in marriage in February 1864 (see "The Custers' Courtship and Marriage" on page 25).

On May 6, 1863, Custer was assigned as aide-de-camp to Gen. Alfred Pleasonton, the commander of a cavalry division. The Custer-Pleasonton relationship developed into mutual admiration, with Custer claiming, "I do not believe a father could love his son more than Genl. Pleasonton [*sic*] loves me."

At this time, Custer commenced an effort to gain a colonelcy of one of the regiments of the Michigan Cavalry Brigade. His application, although endorsed by various prominent generals, was denied by the Republican governor of Michigan, who considered that Custer was a Democrat and, worse yet, a "McClellan man." McClellan had continued to criticize the Lincoln administration and was rumored (rightly so) to be the Democratic nominee in the 1864 presidential election.

At the June 9 Brandy Station battle—the first and largest true cavalry engagement of the war—Custer, as a personal representative of Pleasonton, rode in the spearhead of the surprise attack. Legend has it that he distinguished himself that day by assuming *de facto* command of a detachment.

Eight days later at Aldie, Custer was credited with a daring charge when his horse bolted and carried him through and around enemy lines, which required him to slay two Rebel cavalrymen in order to extricate himself. The press dismissed Custer's protestations that he was simply a rider on a runaway horse and embellished the tale, to the delight of the public.

On June 29, 1863, to the surprise of everyone, including himself, twenty-three-year-old George Armstrong Custer—upon recommendation from Pleasonton—was unexpectedly promoted to brigadier general. Additionally, he was assigned command of the Michigan Brigade, which was part of the first division under Hugh Judson Kilpatrick, a man Custer would come to detest due to his recklessness. Custer had attempted to become colonel of one of the Michigan regiments; now he commanded them all. Pleasonton silenced critics of the promotion by saying, "Custer is the best cavalry general in the world." (See "Custer's Promotion to Brigadier General" on page 20.)

Brigadier General Custer made a memorable debut as a commander several days later at the battle of Gettysburg. On July 3, the third day of the battle, Custer, in a most heroic performance, prevented an overwhelming number of Confederate cavalrymen under legendary commander J. E. B. Stuart from reaching the Union rear in coordination with Pickett's decisive charge. Custer personally led two spectacular charges into the heart of Stuart's determined troopers that afternoon on the Hanover Road east of Gettysburg, in a little-known conflict that may have turned the tide of that bloody battle. The final charge drove Stuart's troopers from the field and denied them access to the Union rear.

Civil War officers were expected to motivate and inspire their troops under fire by example—bravery was contagious. George Armstrong Custer, however, had elevated that responsibility to a higher level. Custer had proven during the Gettysburg campaign that, contrary to those who had questioned Pleasonton's judgment in promoting the twenty-three-year-old to brigadier general, he was quite capable of commanding a brigade. In addition, he had gained the admiration of his men with his propensity for leading charges rather than simply directing movements from a safe position in the rear. This one distinct trait had instilled within his troops a confidence that if Custer, a general, had the nerve to charge into the blazing guns of the enemy, there was no reason not to believe that if they followed, victory would be within their grasp.

founder, Rev. Erasmus J. Boyd. Libbie graduated in the spring of 1862, the valedictorian of her class. At this time she was perhaps the prettiest young lady in Monroe, standing five feet, four inches tall, with chestnut brown hair and light blue-gray eyes, and did not want for suitors.

George Armstrong Custer, an occasional resident of Monroe, aggressively courted the popular Libbie and eventually won her heart and the permission of her father for the couple to marry. On February 9, 1864, Armstrong and Libbie were married in a storybook wedding at the First Presbyterian Church of Monroe (see "The Custers' Courtship and Marriage" on page 25).

Throughout the years, Libbie was a model army wife, faithfully following her husband to his duty stations whenever possible, enduring the sacrifices and hardships of the Civil War and frontier life without complaint—satisfied to be at the side of the man she loved. Custer in turn adored his wife and even stood a court-martial for an unauthorized visit with her at the conclusion of the Hancock expedition of 1867. Libbie was a deeply

(continued on following page)

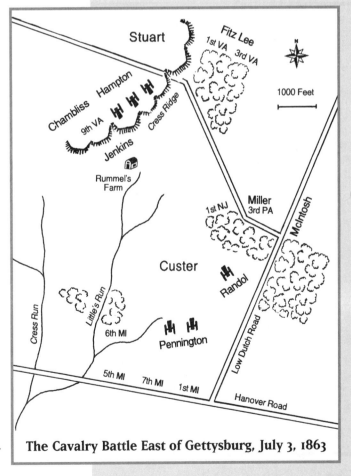

The Cavalry Battle East of Gettysburg, July 3, 1863

religious woman, and her efforts, along with those of Lydia Ann Reed, led her husband to become a born-again Christian (see "Custer's Oath of Temperance and Religious Conversion" on page 19). The marriage of Armstrong and Libbie Custer, although childless, was truly one of history's great love stories.

On Sunday, June 25, 1876, while the battle of the Little Bighorn raged, Libbie and other wives had gathered as usual at Fort Abraham Lincoln to sing hymns. It was not until 7 A.M. on July 6 that several officers visited the Custer residence to inform Libbie of the tragedy that would change her life forever. Although devastated by her loss, she bravely accompanied the officers as they broke the news to other wives who were now widows.

"I would forsake everything and follow him to the ends of the earth. I would lay down my life for him. I would fight anyone who would say a word against him"

—Custer commenting about new army commander George B. McClellan in March 1862

Libbie was thirty-four years old when her husband was killed in the Little Bighorn battle. She returned to Monroe and contemplated her future. Her life's mission was soon decided when a debate ensued over Custer's actions during that battle. Libbie worked tirelessly to protect the image of her beloved husband and vigorously defended him against those who brought criticism. Her first act was to assist Frederick Whittaker in his writing of his 1876 *A Complete Life of Gen. George A. Custer* by putting personal correspondence at his disposal. This favorable portrayal of Custer would be the predominant view for many years to come (see "Custer Biographies" on page 5).

In the summer of 1877, Libbie moved to New York to better her opportunities. She had been faced with considerable family debt that had exhausted her funds and, with only a $900 donation raised by the *Army and Navy Journal* and a $30-a-month pension (raised to $50 in 1882), needed to find work to support herself. She also began raising money that would eventually pay for monuments honoring Custer in Michigan and at West Point.

(continued on following page)

Edwin Havens of the 7th Michigan described Custer in a letter dated July 9, 1863: "He is a glorious fellow, full of energy, quick to plan and bold to execute, and with us has never failed in any attempt he has yet made." Another proud Wolverine praised: "Our boy-general never says, 'Go in, men!' HE says, with that whoop and yell of his, 'Come on, boys!' and in we go, you bet." Capt. S. H. Ballard of the 6th Michigan said: "The command perfectly idolized Custer. When Custer made a charge, he was the first sabre that struck for he was always ahead." Another said that Custer "was not afraid to fight like a private soldier . . . and that he was ever in front and would never ask them to go where he would not lead." Lieutenant James Christiancy wrote to Custer's future father-in-law, Daniel Bacon, that "through all that sharp and heavy firing the General gave his orders as though conducting a parade or review, so cool and indifferent that he inspired us all with something of his coolness and courage."

The Michigan Brigade was so impressed that they had whipped Jeb Stuart at Gettysburg that they began to emulate their commander by adopting Custer's trademark scarlet neckties, which he wore to make himself conspicuous to his troops during a battle (see "Custer's Uniform" on page 22).

The young, dashing Boy General with the yellow curls and outlandish uniform certainly made for excellent copy. Newspaper and magazine correspondents saw a rising star, and the Custer legend was born.

Eleven days later, at Falling Waters, Custer's brigade nipped at Lee's retreating heels and captured 1,500 prisoners and three battle flags. An admiring private from the 5th Michigan, describing the hand-to-hand combat in that affair, marveled when he saw Custer "plunge a saber into the belly of a rebel who was trying to kill him. You can guess how bravely soldiers fight for such a general." Custer continued to distinguish himself throughout 1863, particularly at Culpeper, where he received his lone war wound—shrapnel in the foot.

Maj. Gen. Philip Sheridan had assumed command of the cavalry and persuaded Grant to change the mission of the cavalry from support to active operations. May 1864 saw Custer victories in the Wilderness, at Beaverdam Station, and at Yellow Tavern, where on May 11 he personally led the charge that resulted in the death of Jeb Stuart. Sheridan, who would be Custer's mentor throughout his army career, was compelled to say, "Custer is the ablest man in the Cavalry Corps."

Custer's momentum was somewhat slowed the following month at Trevilian Station, when he was surrounded and compelled to fight his way out, leaving behind his headquarters wagon in the hands of his West Point best friend, Confederate general Tom Rosser (see "Custer and Confederate Friends" on page 27).

In August, Sheridan was dispatched to the Shenandoah Valley to face Lt. Gen. Jubal A. Early's Confederate army. Custer continued to reap glory and respect for his brilliantly executed charges and field generalship during this campaign, time and again exploiting the enemy's weaknesses with snap decisions—particularly at Winchester, where he brazenly led 500 of his Michigan "Wolverines" against 1,600 entrenched Confederates and emerged with 700 prisoners. On September 30, 1864, he was awarded his second star and command of the 3rd Cavalry Division.

On October 9, Custer gained revenge on Tom Rosser by humiliating his friend at Tom's Brook (see "Custer and Confederate Friends" on page 27). One officer boasted, "With Custer as a leader we are all heroes and hankering for a fight."

Custer's cavalrymen fought on, and ten days later at Cedar Creek, they captured forty-five pieces of artillery, thirteen battle flags, and swarms of prisoners. One reporter wrote of that victory, "Custer, young as he is, displayed judgment worthy of Napoleon." In March 1865 at Waynesboro, he crushed the remnants of Early's forces, capturing 1,600 prisoners, 11 artillery pieces, over 200 wagons laden with supplies, and 17 battle flags.

Custer received his third star as a major general on March 29, 1864. He then led his division to decisive victories at Dinwiddie Court House, Five Forks, Namozine Church, and Sayler's Creek before arriving at Appomattox.

On the morning of April 9, 1865, Custer had pushed within sight of Appomattox Court House when a Confederate major arrived at his headquarters under a flag of truce, with a request from Robert E. Lee to suspend hostilities. The Civil War had ended on Custer's doorstep (see "The Surrender Flag Controversy" on page 30).

The words of Horace Greeley perhaps best sum up the Civil War legacy of Custer:

Future writers of fiction will find in Brig. Gen. Custer most of the qualities which go to make up a first-class hero and stories of his daring will be told around many a hearth stone long after the old flag again kisses the breeze from Maine to the Gulf. . . . Gen. Custer is as gallant a cavalier as one would wish to see. . . . Always circumspect, never rash, and viewing the circumstances under which he is placed as coolly as a chess player observes his game, Gen. Custer always sees 'the vantage of the ground' at a glance, and, like the eagle watching his prey from some mountain crag, sweeps down upon his adversary, and seldom fails in achieving a signal success. Frank and independent in his demeanor, Gen. C unites the qualities of the true gentleman with that of the accomplished and fearless soldier.

The traditional favorite book covering Custer's Civil War career is *Custer Victorious: The Civil War Battles of General George Armstrong Custer,* by Gre-

One setback in her effort to promote the truth about her husband came when the final report of the 1879 Reno Court of Inquiry was released and failed to place the blame for the defeat on the actions of Maj. Marcus Reno, the man whom Libbie believed was responsible (see "The Reno Court of Inquiry" on page 266).

Libbie was the author of three memoirs—each of which became quite popular with the public—that related her adventures on the frontier and further shaped the heroic image of her husband. *"Boots and Saddles"; or, Life in Dakota with General Custer* (New York: Harper and Brothers, 1885) recounted the story of how her marriage survived the frustrations, dangers, and hardships of living on frontier posts, and concludes by blaming the corrupt Indian policy for the tragedy at the Little Bighorn. *Tenting on the Plains; or, General Custer in Kansas* (New York: Harper and Brothers, 1887) addresses duty in Texas, where a near mutiny occurred, as well as duty in Kansas, including those events pertaining to Custer's 1867 court-martial. *Following the Guidon* (New York: Harper and Brothers, 1890) refutes criticism over the 1868 Washita battle. These fascinating books stand as several of the best ever written about that period in history.

(continued on following page)

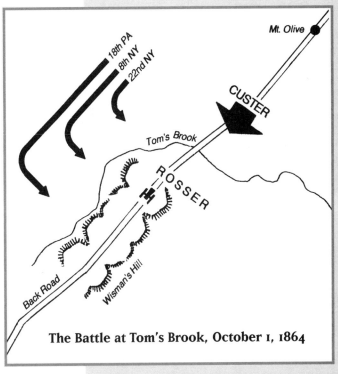

The Battle at Tom's Brook, October 1, 1864

Libbie also wrote "Custer's Favorite Photo of Himself," *Tepee Book* 1 (July 1916); "The General Custer Statue," *Michigan Historical Commission Historical Collection* 39 (1915); "General Custer and the Indian Chiefs," *Outlook Magazine* (July 1927); "Home Making in the American Army," *Harper's Bazaar* (September 1900); "An Out-of-the-Way 'Outing,'" *Harper's Weekly,* July 18, 1891; "Where the Heart Is: A Sketch of Women's Life on the Frontier," *Lippincot Magazine* (February 1900); and "A Beau Sabreur," in *Uncle Sam's Medal of Honor: Some of the Noble Deeds for Which the Medal Has Been Awarded, Described by Those Who Have Won It, 1861–1886,* edited by Theodore F. Rodenbough (New York: G. P. Putnam's Sons, 1886).

Libbie, who remained unmarried for the rest of her life and lived most of the time in a Park Avenue apartment, traveled the world and was

(continued on following page)

Custer's Notable Engagements, July 21, 1861–April 8, 1865

gory J. W. Urwin (East Brunswick, NJ: Associated University Press, 1983). Minor drawbacks to this exciting and well-written work is that some have claimed that it is too pro-Custer, with too much cheerleading, and that it—as the title suggests—concentrates on the battles when Custer was a general and fails to adequately chronicle his first two years of service and associated aspects of his career. Setting aside those minor criticisms, this book is a great read that will stir the reader's imagination.

Clashes of Cavalry: The Civil War Careers of George Armstrong Custer and Jeb Stuart, by Thom Hatch (Mechanicsburg, PA: Stackpole Books, 2001), offers a complete and balanced view of Custer's entire rags-to-riches story, from birth through the Civil War. This work provides details about little-known operations, skirmishes, and controversies; debunks myths; and chronicles each battle and heroic act with a full account.

Custer's own words, in *Custer in the Civil War: His Unfinished Memoirs,* edited by John M. Carroll (San Rafael, CA: Presidio Press, 1977), provide an insightful glimpse into his early career, and the book would have been a major work had it been completed for the period beyond May 1862. This volume also includes all of the official reports written by Custer and provides an extensive bibliography that cites every Civil War book the editor could locate at that time that mentions Custer.

Another notable book is *Custer and His Wolverines: The Michigan Cavalry Brigade, 1861–1865,* by Edward G. Longacre (Conshohocken, PA: Combined Publishing, 1997), which focuses on the "Wolverines" with and without Custer.

The best memoir is *Personal Recollections of a Cavalryman with Custer's Michigan Brigade in the Civil War,* by James H. Kidd (Grand Rapids, MI: Black Letter, 1969), written by one of Custer's officers, who had an excellent eye for detail and offers a fascinating portrayal of Custer and his exploits.

Other notable sources include *Last Hours of Sheridan's Cavalry: A Reprint of War Memoranda,* by Henry Edwin Tremain (New York: Bonnell, Silver and Bowers, 1904); *East of Gettysburg: Stuart vs. Custer,* by David F. Riggs (Bellevue, NE: Old Army Press, 1970); *From Winchester to Cedar Creek: The Shenandoah Campaign of 1864,* by Jeffry Wert (Carlisle, PA: South Mountain, 1987); and *The Union Cavalry in the Civil War,* vol. 1: *From Fort Sumter to Gettysburg, 1861–1863,* and vol. 2: *The Union Cavalry in the Civil War in the East, from Gettysburg to Appomattox, 1863–1865,* by Stephen Z. Starr (Baton Rouge: Louisiana State University Press, 1979, 1981).

SIDEBARS

ᔑ Custer's Oath of Temperance and Religious Conversion

In early October 1862, Armstrong Custer was stricken with a mysterious illness and was granted a leave of absence. He returned home to the Reed household in Monroe, Michigan, and also visited his parents at their newly purchased eighty-acre farm in northeastern Ohio. Custer was greeted in Monroe as a local war hero and enthusiastically immersed himself in the social scene. He could be found on most nights romancing an adoring young lady or carousing with friends and other soldiers on furlough at any one of the establishments that served alcohol and provided the merriment of music. This behavior led to an episode that greatly affected his future—negatively in the short term, but positively for the remainder of his life.

On this particular occasion, Custer had imbibed to excess at a local tavern. He and an army companion staggered through the streets of Monroe on their merry way to Armstrong's half-sister's house. The soldiers created quite a ruckus as they loudly laughed and sang without regard for those within hearing distance of the boisterous serenade.

The two revelers happened to pass the Bacon residence, where they were observed by Judge Daniel Bacon and his nineteen-year-old daughter, Libbie, who later that year became the object of Custer's affections. But because of the improper behavior that the young man had displayed on that winter day, Judge Bacon forbade any contact between his daughter and the raucous cavalry officer (see "The Custers' Courtship and Marriage" on page 25).

On his return home, Custer's half-sister, Ann Reed, a woman of deep religious convictions, was appalled by her brother's condition. With Bible in hand, she took Armstrong into her bedroom, delivered a temperance lecture, and made him promise before God that he would never touch another drop of intoxicating beverage. Her efforts were successful. From that day forth, Custer never again touched alcohol, not even wine at formal dinner parties.

Ann Reed's other primary concern, along with that of his wife, Libbie, once the couple had married, was saving the spiritual soul of George Armstrong. She had taken him to Sunday school at the Methodist church as a boy and attempted over the years to influence him to become a born-again Christian.

Custer was aware of the efforts of the two most important women in his life to convert him. He wrote to Libbie on May 1, 1864:

> I suppose my little one has been to church today. Among the traits of her character that I first learned to love was her religious earnestness. . . . It may seem strange to you, dear girl,

in much demand as a public speaker. The issues she embraced ranged beyond maintaining her husband's image to include the women's suffrage movement and other feminist causes. She invested her money wisely and purchased property in Bronxville, Westchester County, New York, where she spent her later years. Libbie died of a heart attack on April 4, 1933—four days short of her ninety-first birthday—and was buried beside her husband two days later at the U.S. Military Academy at West Point, New York. Her obituary appeared in the *New York Times* on April 5, 1933.

The most interesting biography is *General Custer's Libbie* (Seattle: Superior, 1976), by Custer scholar and Libbie admirer Lawrence A. Frost. Another biography of note is the meticulously researched and well-written *Elizabeth Bacon Custer and the Making of a Myth*, by Shirley A. Leckie (Norman: University of Oklahoma Press, 1993). *Touched by Fire*, by Louise Barnett (NY: Henry Holt, 1996) contains much information about Libbie following Custer's death.

> *"Some were quite young and boyish, and looking at their faces I could not but think of my own younger brother. . . . As he lay there I thought of the poem: 'Let me kiss him for his mother . . . and wished his mother were there to smooth his hair.'"*
>
> —Custer at the burial of members of his unit after an April 1862 skirmish

---

Excerpts from a sample of Libbie's correspondence, some of which was donated to the Little Bighorn Battlefield National Monument, can be found in *The Custer Story: The Life and Intimate Letters of General George A. Custer and His Wife Elizabeth* (New York: Devin-Adair, 1950), by Marguerite Merington, an acquaintance of Libbie's in later years who also provides an excellent narrative of the Custers' life together.

Other letters and manuscripts of Libbie's are housed at the Detroit Public Library, Lincoln Memorial University, Monroe County Historical Museum, U.S. Military Academy at West Point, and Yale University.

(continued on following page)

See also *A Life within a Life: The Story and Adventures of Libbie Custer,* by Pat Kines (Kroshka Books, 2001); "Sidesaddle Soldier: Libbie Custer's Partnership in Glory," by Stephen E. Ambrose, *Timeline* 7 (August–September 1990); "Mrs. General Custer at Fort Riley, 1866," by Minnie Dubbs Millbrook, *Kansas Historical Quarterly* 40 (Spring 1974); "The Girl He Left Behind: Elizabeth Custer and the Making of a Legend," by Michael Tate, *Red River Valley Historical Review* 5 (Winter 1980); "Elizabeth Bacon Custer in Japan: 1903," by Susan Wabuda, *Manuscripts Magazine* 35 (Winter 1983); *The Civil War Memories of Elizabeth Bacon Custer,* by Arlene Reynolds. Austin: University of Texas Press, 1994.

"I must say that I shall regret to see the war end. I would be willing, yes glad, to see a battle every day during my life."

—CUSTER TO HIS COUSIN ON OCTOBER 9, 1862, WHILE SERVING AS AN AIDE-DE-CAMP TO MCCLELLAN

❀ Hugh Judson "Kilcavalry" Kilpatrick
Major General, Army of the Potomac

Judson Kilpatrick was born into a farming family in Deckertown, New Jersey, on January 14, 1836. He entered the U.S. Military Academy at West Point in 1856 and graduated five years later, ranked nineteenth in a class of forty-five. Three days thereafter, he was promoted to captain in the 5th New York Zouaves, and one month later, he became the first Regular army officer wounded in the Civil War when he was hit at Bethel, Virginia, on June 10, 1861. Kilpatrick returned to duty in September as a lieutenant colonel in the 2nd New York Cavalry. He rose to colonel in December 1862 and brigadier general in June 1863, when he assumed command of the 3rd Cavalry Division.

Kilpatrick, who was known as a smooth talker, was an excellent politician, but his camps were said to lack discipline and good order, and he had a propensity for allowing the presence of women of questionable virtue.

In July 1863, newly appointed general George Armstrong Custer was given command of the Michigan Brigade, which was part of Kilpatrick's division. Fortunately for Custer, his command

(continued on following page)

that I, a non-professing (tho not an unbeliever) Christian, should so ardently desire you to remain so. . . . I have never prayed as others do. Yet, on the eve of every battle in which I have been engaged, I have never omitted to pray inwardly, devoutly. Never have I failed to commend myself to God's keeping, asking Him to forgive my past sins, and to watch over me in danger . . . and to receive me if I fell, while caring for those near and dear to me. After having done so all anxiety for myself, here or hereafter, is dispelled. I feel that my destiny is in the hands of the Almighty.

Ann Reed continued her quest for Custer's salvation, and wrote to him in August 1864: "O my dear brother I think of you every day. I do wish you a good Christian. I have often thought that was the only thing you needed to make you a perfect man. I want to meet you in heaven."

The prayers of the two women were finally answered on Sunday evening, February 5, 1865, when Custer publicly professed his faith. The Custers had attended a service at the Monroe Presbyterian church, and Armstrong accepted Jesus Christ as his savior. He wrote in a letter dated February 19 to Rev. D. C. Mattoon, who had assisted with their wedding:

It was about this very hour two weeks ago tonight that I knealt [*sic*] with you and your family circle in Monroe. . . . In your presence I accepted Christ as my Savior. . . . Years of reflection and study had convinced me that I was not fulfilling the end of my Creator if I lived for this world alone. . . . I feel somewhat like the pilot of a vessel; who has been steering his ship upon familiar and safe waters but has been called upon to make a voyage fraught with danger. Having in safety and with success completed one voyage, he is imbued with confidence and renewed courage, and the second voyage is robbed of half its terror. So it is with me.

📖 Accounts of Custer's temperance and religious conversion can be found in most biographies of him. Also see *General Custer's Libbie,* by Lawrence A. Frost (Seattle: Superior, 1976).

🐎 Custer's Promotion to Brigadier General

Maj. Gen. Alfred Pleasonton sought an audience with Gen. George Meade on June 28, 1863, the afternoon of the new commander's first day at the office, to suggest a reorganization of the cavalry corps. Pleasonton also recommended the promotions to brigadier general of three officers: Capt. Elon Farnsworth, whose uncle, Congressman John Farnsworth, was a political ally; capable Capt. Wesley Merritt; and the twenty-three-year-old lieutenant, brevet captain, George Armstrong Custer. Meade ordered that the appointments be made with June 29 as the official date of rank.

More legend than fact surrounds how Custer received and reacted to the astounding news of his promotion. In one of the more popular and amusing accounts, Custer had returned to his tent following an inspection tour of pickets, to be greeted by a tentmate who announced, "Gentlemen, General Custer!" The banter continued with phrases such as "You're looking well, general," and "How are you, General Custer?" Custer was somewhat embarrassed and rebutted that they may laugh now, but someday he *would* be a general.

He was then directed to an envelope addressed to "Brigadier General George Armstrong Custer, U.S. Vols." Custer was allegedly mortified, chagrined, and on the verge of tears.

Whether the above account contains any truth is a matter of conjecture. More than likely, Pleasonton, who regarded Custer as a surrogate son, would have desired to personally break the news. In a letter to Isaac Christiancy dated July 26, 1863, Custer wrote that he had been summoned to cavalry headquarters at 3:00 on the afternoon of Pleasonton's meeting with Meade. It was at that time that the announcement was made that stunned Custer and confounded and infuriated veteran officers.

At the tender age of twenty-three, Custer was now the youngest general in the Union army. Bugler Joseph Fought described the reaction to the promotion: "All the other officers were exceedingly jealous of him. Not one of them but would have thrown a stone his way to make him lose his prestige. He was way ahead of them as a soldier, and that made them angry." Pleasonton responded to any criticism of his choice by saying: "Custer is the best cavalry general in the world and I have given him the best brigade to command."

Not only was the promotion remarkable, but the accompanying assignment was almost equally astonishing. Pleasonton placed his new general in command of the 2nd Brigade of Brig. Gen. Hugh Judson Kilpatrick's 3rd Cavalry Division. This brigade consisted of the 1st, 5th, 6th, and 7th Michigan Volunteer Cavalry Regiments. Whereas Custer had earlier exercised every possible act within his power to be appointed colonel of any one of the Michigan regiments, he now had charge of them all.

It was not only fellow officers who were surprised and baffled by Custer's promotion. The Monroe, Michigan, *Commercial,* Custer's hometown newspaper, was initially skeptical, saying in its July 23, 1863, issue:

> Upon the first appearance of the report that Captain Custer had been made a brigadier general of Cavalry, we were in some doubt as to its genuineness: but it proved to be a bona-fide appointment. He had fairly earned his promotion to this position, and it is an honor which Monroe citizens should be proud of. He will no doubt prove fully capable and efficient.

📖 The official record of Custer's promotion can be found in *The War of the Rebellion: A Compilation of the Official Records of the Union and Confederate Armies,* 70 vols. (Washington,

was on detached duty serving under Gen. David Gregg during the Gettysburg battle. On the third day of that battle, Kilpatrick goaded Brig. Gen. Elon Farnsworth, who had received his appointment on the same day as Custer, into leading a reckless, meaningless charge, which resulted in the death of Farnsworth and most of his men. The action cast doubts on Kilpatrick's ability to command and struck fear in his men, who worried that they too could be called upon to charge the cannon's mouth for little or no reason. This needless slaughter gained Kilpatrick the nickname "Kilcavalry."

Kilpatrick's recklessness also elicited uncharacteristic criticism from General Custer during the October 1863 Bristoe campaign. In a ten-day period, Custer's brigade lost over 200 men killed, wounded, or captured, and he bitterly blamed Kilcavalry's tactical blunders for the losses.

"I was never in better spirits than I am at the moment. . . . In case anything happens to me, my trunk is to go to you. Burn all my letters."

—CUSTER TO HALF-SISTER ANN REED ON THE NIGHT BEFORE THE JUNE 1863 BRANDY STATION BATTLE

Kilpatrick attempted to restore his sagging reputation in the spring of 1864 by staging a bold raid against Richmond that was designed to liberate Union prisoners. Custer's brigade did not participate in the raid but acted as a diversion into enemy territory to keep Confederate cavalry general Jeb Stuart at bay, which was successful. The Kilpatrick-Dahlgren raid, however, was a disaster when Kilpatrick lost his nerve on the doorstep of Richmond. The ensuing action resulted in the death of Col. Ulric Dahlgren and the death or capture of a great number of troops. Kilpatrick once again became the subject of widespread criticism for his lack of good judgment. One member of General Meade's staff called Kilpatrick "a frothy braggart without brains and not overstocked with desire to fall on the field."

Kilpatrick was relieved of his command in April 1864, when Gen. Philip Sheridan assumed leader-

(continued on following page)

ship of the Cavalry Corps. He was transferred to Gen. William T. Sherman's Army of the Cumberland, which was engaged in the Atlanta campaign, and assigned as commander of a cavalry division. His unit was mainly dispatched on raids behind Confederate lines, and on one such foray at Dalton, Georgia, Kilpatrick was seriously wounded. He returned to duty in time to participate in Sherman's March to the Sea and through the Carolinas.

After the war, Kilpatrick resigned his major general's commission and accepted an appointment as minister to the Republic of Chile, a diplomatic post he held until 1868. He returned to the United States and in 1880 became a losing candidate for Congress. Soon thereafter, he was appointed to a second term as minister to Chile and married a Chilean women—his first wife had passed away in November 1863. Kilpatrick died on December 4, 1881, in Santiago, Chile, and was eventually buried at West Point.

"I had not the remote idea that the president would appoint me, because I considered my youth, my low rank and what is of great importance at times & recollected that I have not a single 'friend at court.' To say I was elated would faintly express my feelings."

—CUSTER TO ISSAC CHRISTIANCY, JULY 26, 1863, FOLLOWING CUSTER'S APPOINTMENT TO BRIGADIER GENERAL

✸ George Brinton McClellan
General, Army of the Potomac

McClellan was born on December 3, 1826, in Philadelphia, the son of a prominent physician from an old and distinguished family. In 1840, at age thirteen, he enrolled at the University of Pennsylvania. Two years later, McClellan transferred to the U.S. Military Academy at West Point, where he graduated ranked second in the Class of 1846. He served as an engineer officer in the Mexican War and was twice breveted for distinguished service. After the war, McClellan was involved in construction and surveying work for the army—building forts, mapping railroad routes, and improving

(continued on following page)

DC, 1880–1901), vol. 27, pt. 3, p. 373. The amusing myth about Custer's initial reaction to the promotion began with Frederick Whittaker's *A Complete Life of Gen. George A. Custer* (New York: Sheldon, 1876) and was perpetuated in biographical works by Jay Monaghan, Gregory J. W. Urwin, and Stephen Ambrose. Custer's own version of the promotion is contained in a letter he wrote to Judge Christiancy, July 26, 1863, which is located in the Christiancy-Pickett Papers, U.S. Army Military History Institute.

🐎 Custer's Uniform

The first order of business for the fashion-conscious, newly appointed Brig. Gen. George Armstrong Custer was to properly display his new rank. He had a flashy uniform, but locating a pair of stars would be a challenge. He dispatched bugler Joseph Fought on a scavenger hunt. Finally, late in the night, Fought found and purchased two silver cloth stars from an army sutler. He sewed on the stars to complete Custer's uniform. Properly adorned, Custer rode out in the early morning of June 29, 1863, to assume his command of the Michigan Brigade.

Perhaps the best description of Custer and his uniform was written by Capt. James M. Kidd of the 6th Michigan Cavalry in his *Personal Recollections of a Cavalryman with Custer's Michigan Cavalry Brigade in the Civil War* (Grand Rapids: Black Letter, 1969). Upon seeing his new commander for the first time on June 30, 1863, Kidd wrote:

> Looking at him closely, this is what I saw: An officer superbly mounted who sat his charger as if to manor born. Tall, lithe, active, muscular, straight as an Indian and as quick in his movements, he had the fair complexion of a school girl. He was clad in a suit of black velvet, elaborately trimmed with gold lace, which ran down the outer seams of his trousers, and almost covered the sleeves of his cavalry jacket. The wide collar of a blue navy shirt was turned down over the collar of his velvet jacket, and a necktie of brilliant crimson was tied in a graceful knot at the throat, the long ends falling carelessly in front. The double rows of buttons on his breast were arranged in groups of twos, indicating the rank of brigadier general. A soft, black hat with wide brim adorned with a gilt cord, and rosette encircling a silver star, was worn turned down on one side giving him a rakish air. His golden hair fell in graceful luxuriance nearly or quite to his shoulders, and his upper lip was garnished with a blonde mustache. A sword and belt, gilt spurs and top boots completed his unique outfit.

This would be the distinctive uniform by which the dashing General Custer would be known for the remainder of the war. His scarlet necktie became the defining element of the uniform and made him known by sight to every news correspondent, Confederate soldier, and more important to him, his men.

James E. Taylor, an artist for *Frank Leslie's Illustrated Newspaper,* wrote in *The James E. Taylor Sketchbook: With Sheridan up the Shenandoah Valley in 1864. Leaves from a Special Artist's Sketch Book and Diary* (Dayton, OH: Morningside House, 1989) that the necktie served "as an emblem of bravado and challenge to combat—with like Motion of the Toreador flouting the Crimson cloth to infuriate and lure the Bull to his doom." Taylor also observed that each member of Custer's Michigan Brigade wore his own version of the conspicuous red necktie like a badge of honor.

Not everyone, however, fully appreciated Custer's uniform. One Union officer on Meade's staff, who was impressed with Custer's conduct and bravery in September 1863 at Culpeper Court House, wrote:

> This officer is one of the funniest-looking beings you ever saw, and looks like a circus rider gone mad! He wears a huzza jacket and tight trousers, of faded black velvet trimmed with garnished gold lace. His head is decked with a little, gray felt hat; high boots and gilt spurs complete the costume, which is enhanced by the General's coiffure, consisting in short, dry, flaxen ringlets! His aspect, although highly amusing, is also pleasing as he has a very merry blue eye, and a devil-may-care style!

When asked why he would wear such an outfit that would make him a target on the field, Custer replied that it was a matter of leadership. He wanted his troops to recognize him when they were under fire and thereby be reassured by his presence along the battle line.

🦌 Custer's Promotion to Brigadier General in Jeopardy

While Libbie Bacon prepared for a February 1864 wedding, Custer was informed by General Pleasonton of a rumor that dampened a portion of his happiness. Pleasonton, who professed his own shock, had heard that Custer's official confirmation as brigadier general was being opposed by Republican senator Jacob M. Howard of Michigan, who was a member of the Military Affairs Committee.

Howard had questioned Custer's youth and the fact that the Ohio native was not a *"Michigan Man."* More than likely, however, the real reason was that Custer was a "McClellan Man," and Howard feared McClellan was out to sabotage the policies of the present administration. Pleasonton told Custer that "it would be a lasting disgrace on the part of the government to allow such injustice" and advised Custer to exert whatever influence he could muster to fight this action by Howard and other unnamed political enemies.

Custer speculated that Gov. Austin Blair and the former commander of the Michigan Brigade, Joseph Copeland, were "at the bottom of this attempt." He took action that night by writing to Senators Jacob Howard and Zachariah Chandler

harbors—before being sent overseas in 1855 as an observer of the Crimean War. He also invented a comfortable and practical cavalry saddle that bears his name. In 1857, Captain McClellan resigned his commission to serve as chief engineer, then vice president, of the Illinois Central Railroad in Chicago. In 1860, he became president of the Ohio and Mississippi Railroad.

At the outbreak of the Civil War, McClellan was appointed a major general of the Ohio Volunteers and gained national attention for several minor victories in western Virginia. On July 27, 1861, President Lincoln placed McClellan in command of the Union army. "Little Mac," as he was known, quickly employed his innovative organizational skills to create a fighting force he dubbed the "Army of the Potomac," which earned him the admiration of his troops. However, the relationship of this commander with Democratic ties and the Republican administration—Secretary of War Edwin M. Stanton in particular—was contentious, to say the least. He would not divulge his plans to civilians in authority and even once refused to see the president. Lincoln was forced to order McClellan to begin campaigning, and the general responded in March 1862 by organizing an ambitious amphibious invasion up the Virginia Peninsula.

In May, McClellan was informed of the actions of 2nd Lt. George Armstrong Custer during a raid on the Chickahominy River and requested the presence of the heroic officer. McClellan remembered seeing Custer for the first time: "He was then a slim, long-haired boy, carelessly dressed [his uniform was likely dripping water and covered with mud from the field]. I thanked him for his gallantry, and asked him what I could do for him. He replied very modestly that he had nothing to ask, and evidently did not suppose that he had done anything to deserve extraordinary reward." McClellan asked if Custer would be interested in serving as an aide-de-camp on his personal staff. Custer accepted, and with that, the former West Point class clown had been chosen to assist the man whom he swore to "follow to the ends of the earth." That admiration and devotion would soon became mutual. McClellan wrote: "In those days, Custer was simply a reckless, gallant boy, undeterred by fatigue, inconscious of fear. His head was always clear in danger and he always brought me clear and intelligible reports of what he saw under the heaviest fire. I became much attached to him."

McClellan failed to seize the initiative in his Peninsula campaign, however, and although victo-

(continued on following page)

rious in a series of battles, he chose to withdraw his army in early July. In August, Lincoln removed McClellan from command in favor of Maj. Gen. John Pope, but after Pope's defeat at Second Bull Run, McClellan was restored. In September, McClellan successfully repelled Lee's invasion of Maryland, but when he failed to gain the upper hand, he was once again removed from command—this time for good. At that time, Custer returned to Monroe, Michigan, without an assignment until McClellan summoned him to New Jersey to assist the general in writing his final reports.

McClellan was the Democratic party's nominee for president in 1864, but he won only three states—Delaware, Kentucky, and New Jersey—21 of 233 electoral votes. He subsequently traveled extensively, pursued business ventures, and remained in politics, being elected governor of New Jersey in 1878 for a three-year term. McClellan died in Orange, New Jersey, on October 29, 1885.

His autobiography is *McClellan's Own Story: The War for the Union* (London: Sampson, Low, Marston, Searle & Rivington, 1887). See also *George B. McClellan and Civil War History: In the Shadow of Grant and Sherman,* by Thomas J. Rowland (Kent, OH: Kent State University Press, 1998); and *General George Brinton McClellan: A Study in Personality,* by William S. Myers (New York: Appleton-Century, 1934).

✹ Alfred Pleasonton
Major General, Army of the Potomac

Pleasonton was born on July 7, 1824, in Washington, D.C. He attended the U.S. Military Academy at West Point and graduated in 1844, ranked seventh in a class of twenty-five. He was a lieutenant of dragoons in the Mexican-American War and received one brevet for his service. Pleasonton then served at a number of frontier posts, including action in the Third Seminole War and in Kansas during the conflict known as "Bleeding Kansas."

Pleasonton was serving as a captain in the 2nd Cavalry in Utah at the outbreak of the Civil War and led his unit to the nation's capital for duty in the fall of 1861. He was promoted to major in February 1862 and fought in the Peninsula campaign, where he distinguished himself during the retreat to the James River. This earned him a promotion in July to brigadier general of volunteers and command of a cavalry brigade. He fought in various engagements, including Antietam, Fredericksburg, and Chancellorsville, where he exaggerated his role in his official report by inaccurately claiming to have singlehandedly thwarted an

and Congressman F. W. Kellogg, requesting that they "look after my interests." In a letter to Isaac Christiancy, Custer wrote: "I have addressed this letter to you with the hope that you could and would bring influence to bear with both Howard and Chandler which would carry their votes in my favor. If my confirmation was placed in the hands of the army I would not expect a single opposing vote."

Christiancy replied with assurance that he would contact the senators on Custer's behalf. He added his opinion that Custer, as the son of a Democrat and former member of McClellan's staff—and now a general in the army—was subject to the bitter political infighting that ruled Washington. The views of a general about such matters as the Emancipation Proclamation could be as influential as his exploits in combat.

At the same time, Custer received a reply from Senator Howard, which requested answers to questions about whether the Boy General was indeed a "McClellan Man" or a "Copperhead." Copperheads were those Democrats who were more conciliatory toward the South—Peace Democrats—and represented primarily midwestern states, which included their leader, Clement L. Vallandigham of Ohio, Custer's native state. They wore a copper penny as an identification badge, hence the name. The Copperheads, a strong and vocal minority in Congress, accused the Republicans, who were mostly from the Northeast, of provoking the war for their own interests and asserted that military means would fail to restore the Union. And George B. McClellan, whom Custer was known to worship, was being touted as their presidential candidate to oppose Lincoln in the next year's election.

Custer was pleased about the opportunity to state his case rather than being labeled by others without recourse. He wrote to Senator Howard and established his position as a loyal supporter of the policies of his commander-in-chief, Abraham Lincoln. The president, Custer affirmed, "cannot issue any decree or order which will not receive my unqualified *support.* . . . All his acts, proclamations and decisions embraced in his war policy have received not only my support, but my most hardy, earnest and cordial *approval.*" Custer

---

"For a moment, but only for a moment, that long, heavy column stood its ground; then, unable to withstand the impetuosity of our attack, it gave way to a disorderly rout, leaving vast numbers of dead in our possession. I challenge in the annals of warfare to produce a more brilliant or successful charge of cavalry."

—CUSTER COMMENTING ABOUT THE CHARGE AGAINST STUART

(continued on following page)

also addressed his position on the Emancipation Proclamation by declaring that his friends "can testify that I have insisted that so long as a single slave was held in bondage, I for one, was opposed to peace on any terms. . . . I would *offer* no compromise except that which is offered at the point of the bayonet."

Custer privately had blamed Lincoln and Secretary of War Stanton for the dismissal of George McClellan as commander of the Army of the Potomac and had at that time shared the general's opinion regarding the conduct of the war. The beliefs stated to Howard in this most important letter, however, can be judged as sincere rather than simply a contrived, hypocritical performance presented in order to gain confirmation of his promotion. Custer was no longer a wandering aide-de-camp, but a brigadier general whose leadership had been tested under fire, and that in itself had a way of maturing and altering youthful impressions. To add further credence to the issue, Custer had previously pledged his loyalty to the Lincoln administration in a letter to Judge Bacon—and his future father-in-law was known to despise Lincoln.

Howard and his Republican colleagues were satisfied that Custer was a loyal "Lincoln man," and the Senate readily confirmed his nomination to brigadier general. Custer was relieved that he had escaped becoming a victim of politics, and he took pains in the future to curry favor with the power elite in Washington rather than rely merely on his battlefield prowess.

📖 The best version of this controversy can be found in *Custer: The Controversial Life of George Armstrong Custer,* by Jeffry D. Wert (New York: Simon & Schuster, 1996). Also see *Civil War Echoes: Character Sketches and State Secrets,* by Hamilton Gay Howard (Washington, DC: Howard Publishing Co., 1907).

🐎 The Custers' Courtship and Marriage

If first impressions were lasting impressions, Libbie Bacon, the beautiful daughter of Judge Daniel Bacon, a leading citizen of Monroe, Michigan, certainly never would have become involved with George Armstrong Custer. She and her father had witnessed an episode in October 1861 when Custer and an army companion, both drunk and boisterous, had staggered past their house (see "Custer's Oath of Temperance and Religious Conversion" on page 19). And although they had not been acquainted at that time, "that awful day," as she called it, was to affect their future relationship.

Custer had been an occasional resident of Monroe, but due to their differing social levels, the refined Miss Bacon and the son of the town smithy had not met as children. Their formal meeting came at an 1862 Thanksgiving party at Boyd's Seminary, from which Libbie had graduated the previous spring. Custer was instantly smitten with Libbie and courted her

effort by the Rebels to strike the Union rear. His story, however, was accepted by army commander Joe Hooker, who later introduced Pleasonton to President Lincoln by exclaiming, "Mr. President, this is General Pleasonton, who saved the Army of the Potomac the other night!"

In the tradition of a cavalryman, Pleasonton was a self-confident man and a fastidious dresser, and perhaps more importantly, he had the advantage of being politically well connected. His ambition was no secret to anyone and compelled some to observe that he had already risen beyond the level of his field competency. Rumors about his lack of bravery under fire were also commonplace. He became known for embellishing his own role in a battle or blatantly taking credit for actions in which he did not participate. Postwar writers dubbed him the "Knight of Romance" on account of his dispatches, which were said to be full of "sound and fury, signifying nothing."

Nevertheless, on June 7, 1863, Hooker rewarded Pleasonton by making him commander of the Cavalry Corps. At that time, Pleasonton requested that George Armstrong Custer join his staff as an aide-de-camp. Custer at first refused, out of loyalty to McClellan, but reconsidered and transferred his fierce allegiance to his new commander, whom he termed "an excellent cavalry officer." Pleasonton responded to Custer's fidelity with what could be called a paternal affection. Custer began to emulate Pleasonton in dress and mannerisms—studying in particular the art of self-promotion—and became known as "Pleasonton's Pet."

To his credit, Pleasonton initially proved his critics wrong when his troopers attacked Jeb Stuart's cavalry at Brandy Station on June 9 in the largest true cavalry engagement of the war. The Union horsemen held their own against an enemy that had up to that point been decidedly superior. On June 22, Pleasonton received a promotion to major general of volunteers.

On June 28, Gen. George Meade replaced Hooker as commander of the Army of the Potomac. Pleasonton sought an audience with Meade on the afternoon of the new commander's first day at the office to recommend a reorganization of the Cavalry Corps, as well as several promotions to brigadier general, including his favorite aide-de-camp, twenty-three-year-old brevet captain George Armstrong Custer.

Pleasonton subsequently failed to duplicate his earlier success and was perceived as lacking aggressiveness. On March 25, 1864, he was relieved of command of the Cavalry Corps in

(continued on following page)

favor of Gen. Phil Sheridan and was transferred to the Department of the Missouri to serve as second in command to Maj. Gen. William S. Rosecrans. When Confederate general Sterling Price and 10,000 troops invaded Missouri in October 1864, Pleasonton's command distinguished itself by repulsing Price at Jefferson City as well as in pursuit of the retreating Rebels. Pleasonton's subsequent actions were instrumental in the defeat of Price's force. In March 1865, he was named the department's chief of cavalry.

After the war, Pleasonton reverted to the rank of cavalry major and was assigned to the District of Wisconsin. He had refused the rank of infantry lieutenant colonel and as a result was junior to a number of officers whom he had previously outranked and even commanded. Pleasonton requested retirement at his volunteer rank, which was denied. He became bitter about these indignities and resigned his commission in January 1868.

In civilian life, Pleasonton lived in Washington, D.C. and received several federal appointments, including that of internal revenue collector. He was retroactively retired from the army in 1888—but at the rank of major. He died on February 17, 1897.

✺ Thomas Lafayette Rosser
Major General, Army of Northern Virginia

Rosser was born into a farming family on October 15, 1836, in Campbell County, Virginia. The family moved to Panola County, Texas, thirteen years later, from whence Rosser entered the U.S. Military Academy at West Point in 1856. Among his classmates was George Armstrong Custer, who roomed next door. Tall, swarthy Rosser, with his jet black hair and piercing black eyes, and slender Custer, with wavy, blond hair and fair complexion, became inseparable friends. This close relationship sadly ended in late April 1861—two weeks before graduation—when Rosser resigned from the academy to join the Confederate army.

Confederate general Thomas Rosser, Custer's best friend at West Point.
Courtesy Virginia Historical Society.

Rosser was commissioned a lieutenant and assigned duty as an instructional officer with the Washington Artillery. He was in command of a company of that unit three months later at the first battle of Bull Run and was promoted to captain two months later. Rosser distinguished himself while commanding the battery during the

relentlessly. Libbie, however, was not too certain about him—after all, she was not exactly wanting for suitors. Judge Bacon noticed Custer's growing interest and decided to put an end to the relationship by making Libbie promise not to see Custer again or write to him after he returned to duty in the Civil War. He did not desire his daughter to marry a common military man, especially one who had demonstrated such a display of drunkenness as he had witnessed in October 1861.

Custer, nevertheless, pledged his undying love for her. Libbie rebuffed him but later wrote in her diary:

> He is noble, brave and generous and he loves, I believe, with an intensity that few know of or as few ever can love. . . . He tells me he would sacrifice every earthly hope to gain my love and I tell him if I could I would give it to him. . . . Oh, Love, love, how many are made miserable as well as happy by all the powerful influence.

Meanwhile, Armstrong Custer had been promoted to brigadier general and was gaining national fame as commander of the Michigan Brigade. Libbie had obeyed her father's wishes and refused to see or accept mail from Custer. But Annette "Nettie" Humphrey, a friend of Libbie's and the future wife of Custer's adjutant, Jacob Greene, emerged as a go-between to pass information between the two.

Libbie gradually fell in love with the gallant General Custer, and at a masquerade ball at the Humphrey house on September 28, 1863, she promised to marry him if he could gain her father's consent. Custer composed the most important letter of his life, apologizing for his drunken episode and professing his temperance, and asked that he simply be permitted to correspond with Libbie. The judge relented—no doubt partially due to Custer's growing fame—and granted Libbie permission to write. Her first letter began: "My more than friend—at last—Am I a little glad to write you some of the thoughts I cannot control?"

The romance escalated to the point that Custer wrote to Judge Bacon in late 1863 asking for Libbie's hand in marriage. The judge replied that he might ponder the matter for "weeks or even months." Custer persisted with a frontal assault worthy of any cavalry charge and finally received the judge's blessing. He then persuaded Libbie to marry him at the soonest possible moment, when he could be granted a furlough.

At 8 P.M. on February 9, 1864, George Armstrong Custer and Elizabeth Clift Bacon were united in marriage at the First Presbyterian Church (which still stands) in a storybook wedding with a standing-room-only congregation of witnesses. Rev. Erasmus J. Boyd, who served as principal at the seminary where Libbie had attended school, performed the ceremony,

(continued on following page)

assisted by Rev. D. C. Mattoon. Custer, with hair cut short and wearing his dress uniform, chose his adjutant Jacob Greene as best man. Libbie wore a traditional gown, described by her cousin, Rebecca Richmond, as "a rich white rep silk with deep points and extensive trail, bertha of point lace; veil floated back from a bunch of orange blossoms fixed above the brow." Libbie was given away by her father, who later boasted, "It was said to be the most splendid wedding ever seen in the State." The judge also said: "Elizabeth has married entirely to her own satisfaction and to mine. No man could wish for a son-in-law more highly thought of."

The wedding party was whisked away in sleighs with bells jingling for a reception in the Bacon parlor that was attended by more than 300 guests. The judge provided a generous buffet of delicacies that featured tubs of ice cream.

At midnight, the bridal party—four couples—boarded a train and arrived in Cleveland at 9 the following morning. After an afternoon reception and an evening party hosted by friends, Armstrong and Libbie traveled to Buffalo, then on to Rochester, where they attended a performance of *Uncle Tom's Cabin*. The honeymoon continued with a visit to Libbie's upstate New York relatives, then a trip down the Hudson River to visit West Point. Next they traveled to New York City, and finally to Washington, D.C., where they dined with Michigan members of Congress and other dignitaries.

Custer then returned to duty to command a diversionary force during the ill-fated Kilpatrick-Dahlgren raid on Richmond.

🐎 Custer and Confederate Friends

Armstrong Custer maintained unswerving loyalty to the Union, but at times during the war he demonstrated great compassion and generosity toward Southerners—especially his former West Point classmates who had chosen to join the Army of Northern Virginia. He also exhibited an aggressive spirit of competition when facing any of them across the field of battle, his best friend, Tom Rosser, in particular.

One of the Confederate prisoners taken at Williamsburg in May 1862 was Armstrong Custer's former classmate and friend, Capt. John "Gimlet" Lea, who had been badly wounded in the leg. Upon seeing Custer, Lea cried and hugged him. The two young men then exchanged information about classmates on both sides of the conflict. Custer received permission to remain with Lea for two days, and upon leaving, he gave Lea much-needed stockings and some money. Lea reciprocated by writing in Custer's notebook that if captured, Armstrong should be given good treatment by the Southerners. "God bless you old boy," Lea said in parting.

Later that month, Custer happened upon Lt. James B. Washington, another Confederate taken prisoner after the

Peninsula campaign and the Seven Days' battles. He was wounded in May 1862 at Mechanicsville—the first of nine wounds he would suffer during the war. He was promoted to lieutenant colonel of artillery while he recovered from his wound, and when he returned to duty, he was promoted by Maj. Gen. Jeb Stuart to colonel of the 5th Virginia Cavalry. In May 1863, Rosser married Betty Winston. He came under fire for excessive drinking said to be caused by being away from her while he was in the field. He blamed Stuart when passed over for a promotion, but the War Department, which was aware of his drinking, was actually the culprit.

"Often I think of the vast responsibility resting on me, of the many households depending on my discretion and judgment—and to think that I am just leaving my boyhood makes the responsibility appear greater."

—CUSTER TO ANNETTE HUMPHREY IN OCTOBER 1863 UPON HIS RETURN TO DUTY AFTER RECUPERATING FROM HIS WOUND

Rosser, however, worked to earn a reputation as a capable, often brilliant, commander, and on September 28, 1863, he was promoted to brigadier general and assumed command of the Laurel Brigade. Six days later, he led his brigade at the battle of Raccoon Ford. He followed that with the second Brandy Station, where he was again wounded. His brigade was in constant action, including the May 11, 1864, battle at Yellow Tavern, where General Stuart was killed.

Rosser faced his friend Custer as opposing generals on the field of battle on several occasions, with Custer generally—with one exception at Trevilian Station—gaining the upper hand (see "Custer and Confederate Friends" on page 27).

Throughout the war, Rosser did his best, but his depleted ranks presented little challenge to the Union horsemen. In spite of the lack of success, he was promoted to major general on November 1, 1864, and remained in the valley until March 1865, when he joined the main army. Rosser became the subject of controversy at the March

(continued on following page)

31–April 1 battle of Five Forks—another Custer victory—when he was enjoying dinner while his command was attacked. Rosser surrendered to Union authorities in May 1865.

After the war, Rosser and his wife moved to Baltimore, where he briefly studied law and was superintendent of the National Express Company. He soon accepted the position as an assistant engineer in the construction of the Pittsburgh and Connellsville Railroad. Rosser left that position in the spring of 1870 for the Northern Pacific Railroad. In February 1871, he was appointed chief engineer of the Dakota Division at Fargo. Rosser was survey chief for the Yellowstone expeditions of 1871 and 1872, and assumed the same position for the following year's expedition, in which Custer and his 7th Cavalry also participated. Eight years had passed since Rosser and Custer had met as enemies on the battlefield, and both men were thrilled to be together. Custer wrote in his July 1876 *Galaxy Magazine* article, "Battling with the Sioux on the Yellowstone":

"Oh, could you but have seen some of the charges that were made! While thinking of them I cannot but exclaim 'Glorious War!'"

—CUSTER TO ANNETTE HUMPHREY IN OCTOBER 1863, DESCRIBING HOW, ALTHOUGH HE WAS SHOT OFF TWO HORSES, HIS SURROUNDED TROOPS MANAGED TO PUNCH A HOLE THROUGH JEB STUART'S CAVALRY NEAR CULPEPER COURT HOUSE AND ESCAPE

Scarcely a day passed, during the progress of the expedition from the Missouri to the Yellowstone, that General Rosser and I were not in each other's company a portion of the time as we rode in our saddles, "boot to boot," climbed together unvisited cliffs, picked our way through trackless canyons, or sat at the same mess table or about the same campfire. During the strolling visits we frequently questioned and enlightened each other as to the unexplained or but partially understood battles and movements in which each had played a part against the other.

At one point during a feud between Custer and Col. David Stanley, Rosser interceded with Stanley to permit Custer's cavalry to return to its rightful place at the head of the column.

(continued on following page)

Seven Pines–Fair Oaks battles. Washington, who had once called Custer "the rarest man I knew at West Point," sat for a photograph with his friend. Custer gave Washington some money before the prisoner was removed to the rear.

When Custer arrived in Williamsburg in August 1862 with McClellan's staff, he learned that Gimlet Lea, who was on parole and recuperating in that town, was about to marry a young woman who had nursed him back to health in her family's home. Custer, dressed in his blue uniform, served as groomsman during the ceremony, and proudly stood beside his gray-clad friend. Lea would be exchanged in November 1862, and according to Custer "fighting for what he *supposes* to be right!" Lea was wounded at Chancellorsville and again at Third Winchester.

On September 26, 1862, after the battle of Antietam, Custer escorted a group of paroled Confederate soldiers across the Potomac under a flag of truce and met several of the enemy who had been classmates or friends. The gregarious Custer and his Rebel acquaintances "had an hour's social chat, discussing the war in a friendly way."

Custer lost a West Point classmate when Alabaman major John Pelham, Jeb Stuart's gallant artillery commander, was struck in the back of the head by fragments of a bursting shell on the morning of March 17, 1863, at Kelley's Ford and died the following afternoon.

General Custer, in command of the Michigan Brigade, first met his West Point best friend, Confederate general Tom Rosser, who was part of Jeb Stuart's cavalry, on the field in May 1864 at the Wilderness battle. A brazen charge by Custer pushed the Rebels back and eventually forced a retreat.

The following month, it was Rosser who bested Custer at the June 11–12 battle of Trevilian Station. Custer's brigade became trapped between two Rebel divisions—"on the inside of a living triangle"—and were struck from behind by Rosser. Custer eventually fought his way out but left behind in Rosser's possession his adjutant, his cook, and the trappings of his headquarters—wagon, bedding, field desk, clothing, cooking outfit, spare horse, his commission to general, his letters from Libbie, and an ambrotype of her.

At Winchester in September 1864, Custer's Michigan Brigade charged into entrenched Rebel riflemen commanded by another West Point friend, Gen. Stephen D. Ramseur, and sent them into retreat. Then, in October at Cedar Creek, Custer, now commanding the 3rd Division, executed a daring charge that split the enemy in half. The Rebels began a hasty retreat, with Custer's command nipping at their heels and inflicting heavy casualties. One severely wounded captive was Stephen Ramseur, whom Custer rushed to Sheridan's headquarters for medical attention. Ramseur, the youngest West Pointer to attain the rank of major general in the Confederate army, died the next morning.

"It is confidently believed that, considering the relative numbers engaged and the comparative advantage held on each side, the charge just described stands unequaled, valued according to its daring and success, in the history of war."

—Custer commenting about his brazen charge that turned the tide in the September 1864 Winchester battle

In early October 1864, Rosser's brigade was ordered to the Shenandoah Valley, and he was dubbed the "Savior of the Valley." At Tom's Brook on October 9, however, Custer exacted revenge on his friend. Custer with 2,500 horsemen faced Rosser's 3,500 troops, who were entrenched on the high ground. When all was ready for battle, Custer—in an act of bravado of which legends are made—rode out in front of his command, where he could be observed by both sides. He removed his broad-brimmed hat and swept it across himself in a salute as if to say, "May the best man win." Rosser was not particularly amused by the showmanship and said to his staff: "You see that officer down there? That's General Custer, the Yanks are so proud of, and I intend to give him the best whipping today that he ever got!"

Custer charged with eight regiments to the front and three in a surprise attack on Rosser's left flank. Rosser's men could not withstand the pressure and were forced into a disorganized retreat. Custer's horsemen chased the fleeing Rebels for ten to twelve miles. Rosser had not simply been defeated; he had been humiliated. He later admitted that it was the worst defeat he had ever suffered. To add insult to injury, Custer had captured Rosser's headquarters wagon. Custer got back the ambrotype of Libbie that had been captured at Trevilian Station and appropriated a pet squirrel that had belonged to Rosser. That night in camp, he adorned himself in Rosser's baggy, ill-fitting uniform and treated his men to a good laugh. He later added to Rosser's humiliation by writing and asking that his old friend advise his tailor to shorten the coattails for a better fit.

Custer also briefly faced Rosser later that month at Cedar Creek and on a November raid at Lacey's Springs, where each commander suffered more than 100 casualties without settling the matter. The following March, at the battle of Waynesboro, Custer scored a smashing victory over Jubal Early—with Rosser's cavalry in support—that effectively destroyed the Confederate army in the Shenandoah Valley. One month later, on April 1, Rosser, this time with Gen. George E. Pickett, was once again routed by Custer's troops at Five Forks.

In April 1874, Rosser persuaded Custer to write a public rebuttal to remarks made by Col. William Hazen about the worthlessness of land along the railroad's route (see "The Custer-Hazen Feud" on page 135).

Shortly after the 1876 Little Bighorn battle, Rosser engaged in a brief newspaper literary duel with Maj. Marcus Reno with respect to Reno's actions during the battle, which Rosser sternly condemned.

In 1881, Rosser moved on to become chief engineer of the Canadian Pacific Railroad. In 1885, he returned to Charlottesville, Virginia, and became a gentleman farmer. At the outbreak of the Spanish-American War in 1898, Rosser was appointed brigadier general in the army and trained three regiments of infantry that did not see action. In 1905, he became postmaster of Charlottesville. He died on March 29, 1910.

📖 See *Fightin' Tom Rosser, C.S.A.*, by Millard K. Bushong and Dean McKain (Shippensburg, PA: Beidel Printing House, 1983). Portions of Rosser's Civil War career are also chronicled in such books as *Bold Dragoon: The Life of J. E. B. Stuart*, by Emory M. Thomas (New York: Harper & Row, 1986); *I Rode with Jeb Stuart: The Life and Campaigns of Major General J. E. B. Stuart*, by Maj. Henry B. McClellan (Bloomington: Indiana University Press, 1958); and *Custer Victorious: The Civil War Battles of General George Armstrong Custer*, by Gregory J. W. Urwin (Rutherford, NJ: Associated University Presses, 1983).

Rosser and Custer on the Yellowstone expedition, in addition to biographical material on Rosser, is covered in *Custer's 7th Cav and the Campaign of 1873*, by Lawrence A. Frost (El Segundo, CA: Upton & Sons, 1986). The correspondence involved in the Rosser-Reno feud has been reprinted in *The Custer Myth: A Source Book of Custeriana*, by W. A. Graham (Harrisburg, PA: Stackpole, 1953).

✸ Philip Henry Sheridan
Lieutenant General, U.S. Army

Sheridan was born on March 6, 1831—that much is known. On various occasions, he mentioned his place of birth as Boston, Somerset, Ohio, and Albany, New York, although he also may have been born in Ireland or at sea during his parents' emigration to the United States. It is known that Sheridan received his early education in Somerset and entered the U.S. Military Academy at West Point from that town in 1848 after lying about his age. His career as a cadet got off to a shaky start when Sheridan, who was known for

(continued on following page)

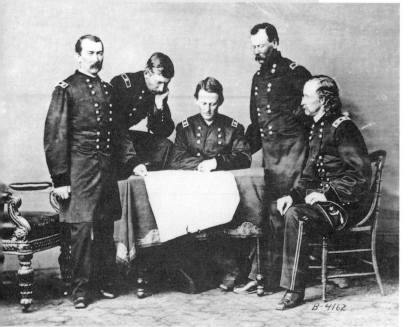

From left: Gens. Philip H. Sheridan, James Forsyth, Wesley Merritt, Thomas C. Devin, and George Armstrong Custer.
Courtesy Little Bighorn Battlefield National Monument.

his hair-trigger temper and nicknamed "Little Phil" due to his shortness—he stood five feet, five inches tall, with a huge torso and short, bandy legs—assaulted an upperclassman, which resulted in his suspension for a year. He graduated in 1853, ranked thirty-fourth in a class of forty-nine.

Sheridan was commissioned a second lieutenant in the 1st Infantry and assigned to duty fighting hostile Indians along the Rio Grande in Texas. In 1854, he joined the 4th Infantry and moved on to Oregon to participate in a futile campaign against the Yakima Indians. Sheridan narrowly escaped death in March 1856 when he led forty dragoons against Cascade Indians, who had captured a blockhouse near the Dalles on the Columbia River. He spent the next five years on the Grande Ronde Indian Reservation, living most of the time with a Rogue River Indian girl.

At the outbreak of the Civil War, Sheridan was called east to serve as a captain in the 13th Infantry in southwest Missouri. He soon joined the staff of Maj. Gen. Henry W. Halleck as regimental quartermaster and commissary, and accompanied the general on his ill-fated advance on Corinth, Mississippi. The feisty Sheridan, however, was not particularly suited for staff duty and craved action. In late May 1862, he was appointed colonel of the 2nd Michigan Cavalry, and just over

(continued on following page)

The April 6, 1865, battle of Sayler's Creek, in which Custer played a major role, had been a smashing victory for the Union. Over 9,000 Confederates had been taken prisoner—more Americans than had ever before or after been captured at one time on this continent. Custer formed his division the following morning for the march just as a long line of Confederate prisoners straggled past on their way to the rear. In a show of respect for his vanquished enemy, Custer ordered the band to play "Dixie" for these brave men, which evoked cheers from the Southern boys.

Custer could be found either out in the yard or on the porch of Wilmer McLean's house on April 9, 1865, renewing acquaintances with his Confederate friends while Lee formally surrendered to Grant.

Custer and Rosser, who became chief engineer of the Northern Pacific Railroad, spent many hours together reliving their war experiences during the Yellowstone expedition of 1873.

📖 *The Class of 1861: Custer, Ames, and Their Classmates after West Point,* by Ralph Kirshner (Carbondale: Southern Illinois University Press, 1999) offers information about those cadets who departed West Point early to join the Confederate army.

🦌 The Surrender Flag Controversy

After the disastrous battle at Sayler's Creek, Confederate general Robert E. Lee was desperate to seek an escape route through the Union line. At daybreak on April 9, Palm Sunday, Rebel cannons commenced firing volleys, and gray-clad cavalry appeared from the dense fog to attack Custer's dismounted troopers. This last-ditch effort by Lee was thwarted when Yankee infantry roared forward to reinforce the position and push the Rebels back. Custer mounted his men and moved them south with the intention of striking the Confederate flank.

"Custer took the road at a gallop," recalled a member of the 1st New York Cavalry. "It was a glorious sight to see that division as it dashed along, with sabres drawn, the gallant Custer leading, and the Confederate army on a parallel road, only three hundred yards distant, vainly endeavoring to escape." Custer was readying his regiment for a charge when a lone Confederate staff officer rode forward carrying a stick with a towel attached.

Maj. Robert Sims of Gen. James Longstreet's staff was received by Custer and stated that General Lee requested that hostilities be suspended. Custer replied that he was not the commander on the field and would attack unless Lee agreed to an unconditional surrender. He then sent word back to

Sheridan and dispatched his chief of staff, Lt. Col. Edward W. Whitaker, to accompany Major Sims to obtain an answer to his surrender demand.

The Civil War was about to end on Custer's doorstep—that much can be documented. The precise circumstances surrounding Custer's actions in this surrender entreaty, however, have become a matter of controversy.

Eyewitness accounts—primarily a questionable remembrance by Longstreet written thirty-one years after the incident—suggest that after dispatching Whitaker, Custer crossed the Confederate line and was presented to Longstreet. Custer demanded that Longstreet surrender his army. Longstreet allegedly was irritated by the brash young general and refused, citing the fact that he was not the commander. In addition, Longstreet was said to have taunted Custer by boldly professing that the Rebs were not beaten and that Custer could attack if he damn well pleased. He then ordered Custer out of his lines. Longstreet claimed that Custer meekly retired, asking for an escort to safely return to friendly lines.

In another account, Major Sims confirmed Longstreet's basic version. Sims entered Union lines carrying a flag that he said was "a new and clean white crash towel, one of a lot for which I had paid $20 or $40 apiece in Richmond a few days before." He had braved Federal pickets that fired upon him and requested to see Sheridan but was told that only Custer was available. Sims relayed his message to Custer, who replied that nothing less than an unconditional surrender would be accepted. Sims departed with Whitaker to report back to Longstreet. Sims wrote that when he arrived at Longstreet's headquarters:

> I found General Custer and he [Longstreet] talking together at a short distance from the position occupied by the staff. Custer said he would proceed to attack at once and Longstreet replied: "As soon as you please," but he did not attack. Just after I left Custer came in sight of our lines. He halted his troops and, taking a handkerchief from his orderly, displayed it as a flag and rode into our lines. He was surrounded by some of our people and was being handled a little roughly when an old classmate of his recognized him and rescued him.

Although Custer without question would have relished the glory associated with being the officer who accepted the Confederate surrender, he was West Point educated and would have understood protocol in such matters. If he had indeed crossed the lines, it was perhaps out of concern for Whitaker's well-being. Longstreet's challenge to attack would not have been taken seriously. The Rebels were whipped, and Custer, a man of action, would certainly have welcomed another fight.

📖 The various accounts can be found in the *New York Times,* April 10, 1865; the *National Tribune,* June 25, 1896; James Longstreet's *From Manassas to Appomattox: Memoirs of the*

a month later, he distinguished himself during a raid at Booneville, Mississippi. The army desperately needed aggressive officers, and Sheridan was rewarded for the ability that he had demonstrated with an appointment to brigadier general and command of an infantry division in Buell's Army of the Ohio. He earned accolades once again in the October 8 battle at Perryville, Kentucky, and was credited with saving the army of Maj. Gen. William S. Rosecrans at Murfreesboro, Tennessee, in December by repulsing stiff Confederate attacks. In March 1863, Sheridan—at the age of thirty-two—was promoted to major general of volunteers to rank from December 31, 1862.

Sheridan, as commander of XX Corps, Army of the Cumberland, campaigned in central Tennessee with Rosecrans throughout the remainder of 1863, which culminated in the Chattanooga campaign. At the November battle of Chattanooga, Sheridan led his forces—without orders—on a gallant charge up the steep terrain of Missionary Ridge and successfully captured the heights, which greatly contributed to the defeat of Gen. Braxton Bragg.

This latest act of bravery under fire brought "Little Phil" to the attention of Lt. Gen. Ulysses S. Grant, who made Sheridan—although most of his background was in infantry—chief of cavalry in the Army of the Potomac, which included three divisions of about 10,000 horsemen.

"I'm going to charge if I go alone!"

—Custer challenging his troops to seize a vital artillery implacement near Appomattox in April 1865

In appearance, Sheridan did not by any means portray the prototype image of a cavalryman. President Lincoln wryly described him as "a brown, chunky little chap, with a long body, short legs, not enough neck to hang him, and such long arms that if his ankles itch he can scratch them without stooping." But what the Irishman lacked in physical presence was offset by his demeanor on the field of battle. "In action," one officer noted, "or when specially interested in any subject, his eyes fairly blazed and the whole man seemed to expand mentally and physically. His influence on his men was like an electric shock."

(continued on following page)

Brig. Gen. George Armstrong Custer, commander of the Michigan Brigade, first met his new boss on the evening of April 15 and remarked that the general "impresses me very favorably . . . from what I learn and see [he] is an able and good commander and I like him very much." Custer became one of Sheridan's most trusted lieutenants throughout the remainder of the war, and the two men established a warm friendship that endured until Custer's death.

Sheridan quickly overhauled the cavalry from its traditional mission of battlefield support into a mobile, hard-hitting strike force. The horsemen responded in battles at the Wilderness, Todd's Tavern, Spotsylvania Court House, and Cold Harbor. Sheridan, however, targeted legendary Confederate general Jeb Stuart's nearly invincible cavalry for destruction. Sheridan's cavalry met Stuart at Yellow Tavern on May 11, 1864, and in the ensuing battle, Stuart was killed in a charge led by George Armstrong Custer. The Union cavalry went on to destroy vital communication lines, tear up the Virginia Central Railroad, and capture stores and supplies around Richmond.

In August 1864, Sheridan was assigned command of the Army of the Shenandoah, with orders to wreak havoc upon this valley that had been the main source of supplies for the Rebel army. A strategy known as "total war," a reign of terror on the civilian populace designed to deny the enemy army comfort and sustenance, was implemented with great success. On October 19, when Jubal Early surprised his army at Cedar Creek, Sheridan became famous for riding from Winchester to the front and rallying his troops—including Custer—to a resultant victory. He was awarded the coveted Thanks of Congress for his heroic actions and became the subject of a popular poem, "Sheridan's Ride," by Thomas Buchanan Read.

Sheridan resumed his raiding tactics into the spring of 1865, and by April, the Army of Northern Virginia had been for all intents and purposes beaten into submission—with much of the glory showered upon the efforts of the cavalry. The war ended on April 9, when Robert E. Lee formally surrendered to Grant at Appomattox, and Sheridan emerged as one of the most famous and revered Union commanders. He purchased the table on which the surrender was signed and presented it to Libbie Custer in honor of her husband (see "Sheridan's Presentation of the Surrender Table to Libbie Custer," right).

Immediately following the war, Sheridan was dispatched in command of more than 50,000

Civil War in America (Bloomington: University of Indiana Press, 1960); *To Appomattox: Nine April Days,* by Burke Davis (New York: Rinehart & Company, 1959); *A Civil War Treasury of Tales, Legends and Folklore,* edited by B. S. Botkin (New York: Promontory Press, 1981).

🐎 Sheridan's Presentation of the Surrender Table to Libbie Custer

On the afternoon of April 9, 1865, General Lee presented himself to General Grant at the home of Wilmer McLean to surrender his army. The two commanders retired inside to McLean's parlor and signed the surrender document. George Armstrong Custer was not present inside the McLean home during the signing; rather, he has been placed on the porch or in the yard renewing acquaintances with Southern friends from their days at West Point.

When the ceremony had concluded, the small, oval-shaped pine table upon which Grant had written the terms of surrender was purchased for $20 in gold by Gen. Phil Sheridan. The next day, the cavalry commander handed the table to Custer as a gift to Libbie. Sheridan enclosed a note, which read:

> My dear Madam, I respectfully present to you the small writing table on which the conditions for the surrender of the Army of Northern Virginia were written by Lt. General Grant—and permit me to say, Madam, that there is scarcely an individual in our service who has contributed more to bring about this desirable result than your gallant husband.

Libbie Custer treasured the table for the remainder of her life. After her death, the surrender table was added to the collection of the Smithsonian Institution.

📖 This subject is covered in most Custer biographies. Also see *General Custer's Libbie,* by Lawrence A. Frost (Seattle: Superior, 1976); and *The Custer Story: The Life and Letters of General George A. Custer and His Wife Elizabeth,* by Marguerite Merington (New York: Devin-Adair, 1950).

EPILOGUE

In June 1865, Lt. Col. George Armstrong Custer was assigned duty in Louisiana and Texas, once again under the command of Gen. Phil Sheridan. More than 50,000 troops had been dispatched along the Rio Grande as a show of force to the French, who had invaded Mexico. Custer would head a division of 4,000, organized in Alexandria, Louisiana, and later stationed in Texas.

(continued on following page)

Custer immediately encountered severe disciplinary problems with these veteran troops who had fought in the Civil War and wanted to return home. It was the first time that he commanded troops who did not worship him, which compelled him to face a rumored assassination attempt and to squelch a near mutiny. In August, the unit moved to Hempstead, Texas, and by November, it was headquartered at the Blind Asylum in Austin.

Although Custer and his troops remained at odds, he enjoyed his duty in Texas on a personal basis. He had been accompanied by Libbie, brother Tom, and his father, Emanuel, who was employed as a forage agent. The local society was extremely cordial, and the Custer clan occupied their time riding, hunting, playing practical jokes on each other, and catching up on life after the wartime separation. This assignment ended in February 1866, when the Custers traveled to New York City, with a side trip to Monroe to attend the funeral of Daniel Bacon, Libbie's father, who had passed away on May 18 of cholera.

While in New York exploring possible civilian endeavors, Custer was offered the position of adjutant general of the Mexican Army, which was in a struggle with Emperor Maximilian, the French puppet. The position commanded a salary of $16,000 in gold—twice his major general's pay. Although highly recommended by President Grant, Secretary of War Stanton, and Phil Sheridan, both Libbie and Sheridan counseled Custer against accepting the offer. The matter was settled, however, when Secretary of State Seward, who thought France might be offended if an American officer directed soldiers against French troops, refused to allow Custer a leave of absence.

In September 1866, Custer and Libbie were members of an entourage that toured with President Andrew Johnson in an attempt to win support for the president's Southern policy. Johnson likened the Union to a circle that had been broken and required mending, and therefore called his tour "Swinging Round the Circle." Custer's participation was not well received by the Northern press, which attacked him vehemently for associating with traitor Southerners. Even in Custer country—Michigan, Ohio, and Indiana—the reception was unpleasant at best. The Custers decided to leave the presidential party before the completion of the trip in order to escape the protesters and bad publicity.

On July 28, 1866, Congress authorized four new cavalry regiments, including the 7th Cavalry, which would be formed at Fort Riley, Kansas. Custer would have preferred a colonelcy and command of one of the regiments, but with the influence of Phil Sheridan, he was appointed a lieutenant colonel—second in command—of the 7th Cavalry. He accepted the commission and made plans to travel with Libbie to their new duty station on the Great Plains, where he would resume his business of fighting, this time against hostile Indians.

Confederate general J.E.B. Stuart. Custer gained glory against Stuart at Gettysburg, then led the charge during which Stuart was killed at Yellow Tavern. *Courtesy the Museum of the Confederacy.*

troops along the Rio Grande in Texas as a show of strength to the French, who had invaded Mexico. He was convinced that this action persuaded the French to subsequently abandon that country. Sheridan then commanded the 5th Military District, encompassing Texas and Louisiana, on Reconstruction duty. He said of the area, "If I owned both Hell and Texas, I'd rent out Texas and live in Hell." His harsh treatment of the populace inspired the hatred of Southerners and compelled President Andrew Johnson to relieve him of that command.

In the meantime, Sheridan helped George Armstrong Custer, who had served with him in Texas, obtain the lieutenant colonelcy of the 7th Cavalry. He also graciously offered the Custers use of his personal quarters at Fort Leavenworth when Custer was suspended for a year after an 1867 court-martial.

In February 1868, Sheridan assumed command of the Department of the Missouri and became responsible for enforcing peace among the numerous hostile Plains Indian tribes. He implemented his "total war" strategy (see "Total War" on page 83) in the winter campaign of 1868–69 against the Southern Cheyenne, Kiowa, and

(continued on following page)

Comanche. Sheridan recalled Custer early from his suspension to lead the campaign, which was successful in driving those tribes onto reservations. At about that point in time, Sheridan was said to have made the statement "The only good Indian is a dead Indian," but it is unlikely that he originated this common sentiment.

In 1869, when Gen. W. T. Sherman was made general-in-chief of the army, Sheridan was promoted to lieutenant general and assumed command of the Military Division of the Missouri, which extended from the Mississippi River west to the Rocky Mountains and north to south from border to border. In 1871, he served briefly as an observer during the Franco-Prussian War. Sheridan went on to direct and coordinate the so-called Red River War of 1874–75 and did much of the planning for the Great Sioux War of 1876–77, which included the battle of the Little Bighorn. He also directed the final operations that forced the surrender of Chief Joseph and his Nez Perce tribe in 1877.

Sheridan became general-in-chief of the army in November 1883 when Sherman retired. In that capacity, he brought the bloody period of American Indian wars to an end with the capture of Geronimo in 1886.

Sheridan was made a four-star general shortly before he died in office at the age of fifty-seven on August 5, 1888, in Nonquitt, Massachusetts. He was survived by a wife, a son, and three daughters.

📖 Sheridan's *Personal Memoirs of P. H. Sheridan, General. U.S. Army,* 2 vols. (New York: Charles Webster, 1888), was completed three days before his death. See also *Phil Sheridan and His Army,* by Paul Andrew Hutton (Lincoln: University of Nebraska Press, 1985); *Border Command: General Phil Sheridan in the West,* by Carl Coke Rister (Norman: University of Oklahoma Press, 1944); *Sheridan's Troopers on the Borders: A Winter Campaign on the Plains,* by De B. Randolph Keim (Williamstown, MA: Corner House Publishers, 1973); and *Sheridan: The Life and Wars of General Phil Sheridan,* by Roy Morris (New York: Crown Publishers, 1992). The Philip H. Sheridan Papers are in the Library of Congress.

"With profound gratitude toward the God of battles, by whose blessings our enemies have been humbled and our arms rendered triumphant, your commanding general avails himself of this his first opportunity to express to you the admiration of the heroic manner in which to-day resulted in the surrender of the enemy's entire army. . . . When the war is ended and the task of the historian begins; when those deeds of daring which have rendered the name and fame of the Third Cavalry Division imperishable, are inscribed upon the bright pages of our country's history, I only ask that my name be written as that of the commander of the Third Cavalry Division."

—Custer from his April 9, 1865, tribute to his division

📖 Custer's activities during this period of time are covered in the following: *Tenting on the Plains; or, General Custer in Kansas and Texas,* by Elizabeth B. Custer (New York: Harper and Brothers, 1887); *Custer in Texas: An Interrupted Narrative,* by John M. Carroll (New York: Sol Lewis, 1975); "The Boy General and How He Grew," by Minnie Dubbs Millbrook, *Montana: The Magazine of Western History* 23 (Spring 1973); and "A Better Time Is in Store for Us: An Analysis of the Reconstruction Attitudes of George Armstrong Custer," by William L. Richter, *Military History of Texas and the Southwest* 11 (1973), and "Custer's Texas Home," by Denise E. Shannon. *Texas Highways* 33, no. 2 (February, 1986).

CHAPTER THREE

On the Plains

OVERVIEW

Lt. Col. George Armstrong Custer, wife Libbie, and their cook, Eliza Brown, reported for duty at Fort Riley, Kansas, on the evening of November 3, 1866. Custer, however, soon traveled to Washington to appear before an examining board and did not participate in the training of the unit until his return just before Christmas. In February 1867, commanding officer Col. A. J. Smith departed to head the District of the Upper Arkansas, and Custer assumed *de facto* command—a position he would hold until June 25, 1876.

Custer experienced Indian fighting for the first time during the spring and summer of 1867 on what would be called the Hancock expedition. The Cheyenne, Sioux, Kiowa, Comanche, and Arapaho Indians had been roaming western Kansas, incessantly menacing homesteaders and workers on the Kansas Pacific Railway. It was determined that a military force commanded by Maj. Gen. Winfield Scott Hancock would be sent into the field to demonstrate the might of the U.S. Army and punish these Great Plains marauders for their crimes.

In late March, more than 1,400 soldiers—including eight companies of Custer's 7th Cavalry—marched down the Santa Fe Trail to the Arkansas River (see "Table of Organization and Distribution of the 7th Cavalry for the Hancock Expedition of 1867" on page 42). The troopers were kept busy along the way staging aggressive battle exercises that were intended to intimidate and impress the unseen Indian observers. This show of force convinced Custer that the Indians would "accept terms and abandon the war-path."

Two members of the expedition were famed Civil War illustrator Theodore R. Davis and newspaper correspondent Henry M. Stanley, who would later gain fame as the discoverer of the lost Livingstone in Africa. Davis and Stanley were the first correspondents to accompany an army campaign against the Plains Indians. Stanley, when writing about the prospects of engaging the Indians, said: "Custer is precisely the man for that job. A certain impetuosity and undoubted courage are his principal characteristics."

On April 12, Edward W. Wynkoop, the former Fort Lyon commander who now served as an Indian agent for the Cheyenne and Arapaho, invited several Cheyenne and Sioux chiefs—

"I wrote a letter recently against an Indian War. . . . I regard the recent outrages as the work of small groups of irresponsible young men eager for war."

—CUSTER TO LIBBIE, MAY 1867

George Armstrong Custer. *Courtesy Little Bighorn Battlefield National Monument.*

✸ Isaac Taylor Coates
Medical Officer, 7th U.S. Cavalry

Coates was born on March 17, 1834, in Coatesville, Chester County, Pennsylvania. He taught school in Delaware County, which enabled him to afford medical school at the University of Pennsylvania, where he received his M.D. in 1858. He served as ship's surgeon on a packet ship and made several trips to England. Coates settled briefly in Louisiana but headed north at the outbreak of the Civil War. He was appointed surgeon on a steamship in the South Atlantic Blockading Squadron. He later served on a frigate and a gunboat until receiving a commission to join the 77th Pennsylvania Volunteers at Victoria, Texas, where he remained until mustering out with his regiment. On March 22, 1865, Coates married Mary Penn-Gaskell, a descen-

(continued on following page)

including Tall Bull and Pawnee Killer—to Fort Larned for a parley with General Hancock. Hancock professed his desire for peace but made it clear that the chiefs must live up to the provisions of their treaties and cease hostilities. The general then decided to march his men twenty-one miles up the Pawnee Fork to the village of the Indians and resume talks at that location. The apprehensive chiefs—as well as Wynkoop—requested that Hancock keep his distance from the village. Their protests fell on deaf ears, however, and Hancock commenced his march.

The Indians responded by painting themselves for war and riding back and forth in front of the army column to indicate their intention to defend their village. Hancock countered by ordering his men into battle formation.

Halfway to the Indian encampment, Hancock, Wynkoop, and a handful of officers rode forward to meet with the chiefs. Both sides agreed to avoid a battle, if possible. As a show of good faith, Hancock promised that his men would not enter the village or in any way molest the inhabitants. The Indians

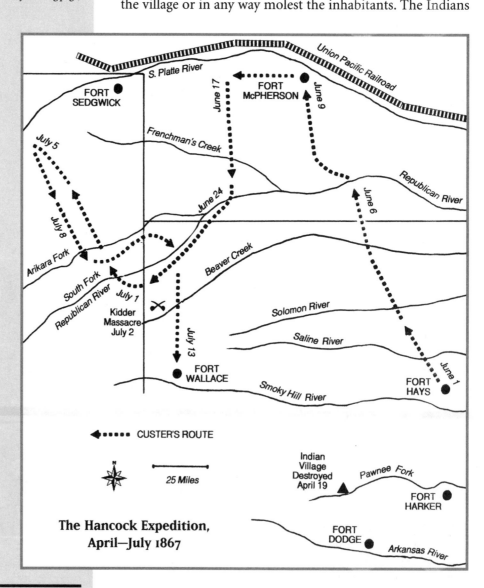

The Hancock Expedition, April–July 1867

retired to their village with Hancock's column following and eventually halting to camp 300 yards away.

That pledge by Hancock to avoid the village apparently held little credence with the Indians. When the command arrived at its destination, scouts informed Hancock that while the chiefs had been delaying the troops, the women and children had fled the village. Hancock believed that he had been tricked and, in a council with the chiefs, demanded that the women and children be returned. Instead, scouts later observed the warriors also preparing for flight.

Hancock awakened Custer around midnight and ordered that his cavalrymen surround the village. Custer arrived to discover that the nearly 300 lodges had been abandoned. The inhabitants had departed in such haste that they had left behind most of their personal belongings. To Hancock's way of thinking, this insulting action signified war. At dawn on April 15, Custer and his eight companies were dispatched to pursue the Indians.

Custer chased his prey for some thirty-five miles but discovered that the escaping Sioux and Cheyenne had split into numerous smaller groups and had simply vanished into the rugged landscape.

On the second day out, Custer rode ahead of his column and, disregarding an order from Hancock, engaged in a personal buffalo hunt—one that almost turned disastrous. While aiming at his quarry, he accidentally shot and killed his own horse. Custer was now afoot, alone in the open prairie in hostile country. Fortunately for Custer, his troops happened upon him before the Indians. (see "Custer, the Sportsman" on page 132)

At the same time, Hancock was contemplating whether to employ Civil War standards of warfare and destroy the Indian village on Pawnee Fork. His men already had been disobeying orders by ransacking the lodges and looting for souvenirs. Hancock's mind was made up when a courier from Custer arrived to report that the Indians had been attacking stagecoaches and stations along the Smoky Hill Road. On the morning of April 19—against the advice of agent Wynkoop and Col. A. J. Smith—the troops burned the village and its contents to the ground, a declaration of war to the Indians.

In the meantime, Custer continued down the Smoky Hill Road to camp near Fort Hays, where he had expected to find forage and supplies. Instead, the supply trains had been delayed, and he would be forced to endure an undetermined period of waiting. The weather had turned cold and rainy, disgruntled troopers were deserting in great numbers, and Custer, a man of action, became deeply depressed by his inability to resume his march and punish the hostiles. His only solace was the presence of Libbie, who visited for two weeks. Also during this respite from the march, Custer had the opportunity to continue his ongoing discussions about the culture and customs of the Plains tribes with James Butler

dant of William Penn. The couple had three children, two of whom died in infancy.

Coates served as acting assistant surgeon with the U.S. Volunteers in Atlanta, Georgia, from April to July 1866. On March 7, 1867, he signed a "Contract with a Private Physician" with the U.S. Army and was assigned to the 7th Cavalry at Fort Riley, Kansas, as assistant surgeon.

Coates accompanied Custer in the field on the Hancock expedition of 1867 and was the only doctor in the column on July 7 when several cavalrymen—one of whom later died—were shot while deserting. Coates later testified about his version of events that day at Custer's court-martial, which reflected favorably on Custer. On December 31, 1867, Coates was transferred to Fort McRae as post surgeon.

"Whether the buffalo was dumbfounded by the changed aspects of affairs, and looked upon the lofty tumbling he had just witnessed as a new and dangerous kind of tactics [sic]*, with which he would do well not to trifle, or considered my condition then and there as being sufficiently helpless and humiliating, I know not."*

—CUSTER AFTER ACCIDENTALLY SHOOTING HIS HORSE WHILE HUNTING BUFFALO ALONE ON THE PLAINS

The military career of Dr. Coates ended under rather unusual circumstances. He had signed the death certificate attesting to the suicide of Maj. Wickliffe Cooper during the Hancock expedition in June 1867, a ruling that prevented Cooper's widow from obtaining a survivor's pension. The widow's lawyer contacted Coates, and the doctor—apparently willing to help Mrs. Cooper—subsequently returned a signed, blank pension form, which was a violation of army regulations. For that reason, in March 1869, Coates was involuntarily dismissed from the service and his name placed on a list of physicians not to be contracted again.

Coates practiced medicine in Chester, Pennsylvania, before accepting the position as medical

(continued on following page)

director on a Peruvian railway in 1871. He made the first recorded ascent of the volcano El Misti in 1873 and explored much of South America before returning to Chester in 1876. Two years later, he traveled through Brazil and Bolivia as surgeon on a railway expedition. Coates went into private practice in 1881 in Colorado and later in New Mexico, where he died in Socorro on June 23, 1883.

📖 *On the Plains with Custer and Hancock: The Journal of Isaac Coates, Army Surgeon,* by W. J. D. Kennedy, the husband of Coates's great-granddaughter (Boulder, CO: Johnson Books, 1997), provides an insight into this relatively obscure but interesting figure. Although Coates's actual journal covers only the early stages of the Hancock expedition of 1867 and ends before the events that led to Custer's court-martial, the author has provided a comprehensive narrative that documents the entire expedition. Included is Coates's testimony at Custer's court-martial, which can also be found in *The Court-Martial of General George Armstrong Custer,* by Lawrence A. Frost (Norman: University of Oklahoma Press, 1968). Custer recounts several interesting anecdotes about Coates in *My Life on the Plains; or, Personal Experiences with Indians* (Norman: University of Oklahoma Press, 1962).

"We witnessed one of the finest and most imposing military displays, prepared according to the Indian art of war, which it has ever been my lot to behold."

—CUSTER REMARKING ABOUT THE SIGHT OF THE INDIANS WHO PROTESTED HANCOCK'S APRIL 1867 MARCH TO THE VILLAGE ON PAWNEE FORK

❀ William Averill Comstock
Scout

This grandnephew of James Fenimore Cooper was born on January 17, 1842, at Comstock, Michigan, and raised in Kalamazoo; Corning, New York; and perhaps Wisconsin. He headed west at age fifteen, and by eighteen, he was working with an Indian trader in Cottonwood Springs, Nebraska, and had possibly ridden for the Pony Express. Comstock

(continued on following page)

"Wild Bill" Hickok, who had gathered valuable knowledge from years of experience.

Throughout the last week of April, Hancock, now at Fort Dodge, met with various tribal chiefs, including Kicking Bird, Little Raven, and Satanta. Hancock was impressed by the unanimous declarations of peace, but his talks failed to produce positive results. The raiding increased during the month of May. Stagecoach service along the Smoky Hill Road at times was suspended, and no mail station or white traveler was safe.

On June 1, Custer and six companies—about 350 men, guided by William "Medicine Bill" Comstock and Moses "California Joe" Milner—finally marched. The raiding had by then shifted from the Smoky Hill Road to the Platte Road in Nebraska, the principal route to Colorado and California. Custer headed northward toward Fort McPherson with orders to clear out the hostiles in the area between the Republican and Platte Rivers. The 215-mile march was uneventful, however, other than the death of Maj. Wickliffe Cooper, who was said to have committed suicide.

Near Fort McPherson on about June 16, Custer held a parley with Pawnee Killer, who pledged peace and accepted gifts of coffee, sugar, and other goods. Custer believed that the chief was sincere, but he was later chastised for his position by Gen. William T. Sherman, who arrived the following day. Sherman was of the opinion that Pawnee Killer should have been detained and sent Custer out on the improbable mission of locating the chief and persuading him to move his village closer to the fort, where his actions could be monitored.

Custer's orders called for him to scout south to the forks of the Republican River, turn northward toward Fort Sedgwick, which had access to the Union Pacific Railroad, where he could replenish supplies and perhaps receive orders from Sherman, then sweep the plains along the Republican to the South Platte. Four days later, Custer went into camp along the forks of the Republican without finding any sign of Pawnee Killer.

Sherman had made vague mention about Libbie Custer perhaps joining her husband at some point at Fort McPherson. Custer, however, wrote to his wife and requested that she travel to Fort Wallace, the westernmost post in Kansas, and he would send an escort. Presumedly for that reason, Custer chose not to report to Fort Sedgwick. Instead, on June 23, under the cloak of darkness, Maj. Joel Elliott and a small detail were dispatched to Fort Sedgwick to check for orders. At the same time, 1st Lt. William W. Cooke led a forty-eight-man wagon train south to Fort Wallace to requisition supplies—and possibly escort Libbie back to her husband.

At dawn the following day, an Indian raiding party attempted to stampede Custer's horses but was driven off, with only the sentry being wounded. The Indians formed on a nearby hill, and Custer requested a council. To his surprise, the raiders were led by Sioux chief Pawnee Killer. Custer refused to issue supplies, and the parley ended without resolution.

Meanwhile, a small Indian decoy party invited pursuit, and Custer obliged by sending Capt. Louis Hamilton and two companies after them. The sturdy Indian ponies easily outdistanced the heavier army mounts, and the Sioux attempted to lure the cavalrymen into an ambush. Disaster was averted when Hamilton recognized the potential danger and dismounted his men to drive off the warriors.

On June 26, Lieutenant Cooke's fifty-man resupply detachment was attacked by an estimated 600 to 700 Sioux warriors on its return trip from Fort Wallace. Cooke formed the wagon train into two parallel columns, and a running battle ensued. The Indians were fought off on a direct assault, then commenced circling the steadily moving wagons. The warriors exhibited great horsemanship skills by racing at full speed, and leaning low to hide and fire from behind their ponies while the cavalrymen expended most of their ammunition. This tedious battle lasted for more than three hours until, surprisingly, the Sioux abruptly withdrew. Custer had, without being aware of the circumstances, prudently ordered two companies—those of Myers and West—to ride out and reinforce the detail. The approach of this column was sighted by Indian scouts, and just like in the movies, it had arrived in the nick of time to rescue Cooke's beleaguered command.

To Custer's relief, his letter to Libbie had never reached its destination, or her life would have been in peril riding with the wagon train. Standing orders had been issued for officers to shoot any white women should an Indian attack appear overwhelming, to save them from capture.

Cooke reached camp on June 27, and Major Elliott returned the following day—without any new orders. Those orders had arrived the day after Elliott had departed and likely would have been available had Custer reported to Fort Sedgwick as ordered. The dispatches were then placed in the care of 2nd Lt. Lyman S. Kidder and a ten-man detail. While Kidder scoured the area attempting to locate Custer, he was discovered by Pawnee Killer on July 2. The mutilated bodies of Kidder and his men were subsequently discovered by scout William Comstock strewn across the plains near Beaver Creek, where each had fallen in a desperate running battle with the Sioux.

Custer, complying with his original orders, resumed his sweep of the headwaters of the Republican, his route curiously leading away from locations where the Indians were known to be operating. The march into Colorado across a desolate, waterless terrain spotted only with cactus and rife with ravines under the scorching July sun proved torturous for both troopers and horses. Relief from this demanding march—as well as the prospect of riches in Colorado's mines—became a temptation that many of the troopers could not resist. The column was depleted by a mass desertion.

had a passing interest in the "Pikes Peak or Bust" gold rush, then lived with Arapaho and Cheyenne Indians on the Republican River, which was where he learned Indian culture and gained the nickname "Medicine Bill" for his superstitions. He briefly served as post guide at Fort Halleck, Wyoming, in 1865, then moved on as a guide and scout at Pond Creek Station, Kansas, until early 1866, when he took up residence at Fort Wallace while that post was being constructed and garrisoned.

George Armstrong Custer heard about Comstock's attributes from Capt. Myles Keogh, who commanded I Troop at Fort Wallace. Keogh wrote that Comstock was "an eccentric genius and an ardent admirer of everything reckless and daring. He is of great service." With that glowing recommendation, Custer requested Comstock for the Hancock expedition of 1867. The scout, who proved himself highly skillful throughout the campaign, became a favorite of Custer's. He accompanied Lt. William Cooke on his perilous resupply wagon train to Fort Wallace, and in July, he located the mutilated bodies of Lt. Lyman Kidder and his ten-man detail, all of whom had been killed in a running battle with Sioux chief Pawnee Killer.

In January 1868, "Medicine Bill" killed a wood contractor in a dispute at Fort Wallace; he was subsequently cleared of murder charges. That summer, legend has it that Comstock and William F. Cody engaged in a buffalo-shooting duel to determine which one deserved the title "Buffalo Bill." Apparently Cody won.

On August 16, 1868, Comstock was scouting under Lt. Frederick H. Beecher when he and scout Abner S. Grover entered a Cheyenne Village west of Fort Hays on the headwaters of the Solomon River to gather information about hostiles. The two scouts were initially welcomed, but later both were removed from the camp and shot. Comstock was killed, his body never recovered; Grover escaped by playing dead.

📖 "Will Comstock—The Natty Bumppo of Kansas," by John S. Gray, can be found in the Chicago Westerners *Brand Book* 18, no. 12 (February 1962). Custer recounts several of Comstock's episodes on the Hancock expedition in *My Life on the Plains; or, Personal Experiences with Indians* (Norman: University of Oklahoma Press, 1962), as does illustrator-writer Theodore Davis in "A Summer on the Plains," *Harper's New Monthly Magazine* 36, no. 213 (February 1868).

BIOGRAPHIES

✷ William Winer Cooke
First Lieutenant, 7th U.S. Cavalry

1st Lt. William W. Cooke, 1875. *Courtesy Little Bighorn Battlefield National Monument.*

Cooke was born into a prominent family on May 29, 1846, in the hamlet of Mount Pleasant, a few miles south of present-day Brantford, Ontario, Canada, where his ancestors—British loyalists—had fled after the American Revolution. At the age of fourteen, he moved to Buffalo, New York, to live with relatives. In 1863, he lied about his age to join the 24th New York Cavalry in Niagara Falls as a recruiter, and he was commissioned a second lieutenant on January 26, 1864. Cooke was wounded on June 17 of that year at Petersburg and returned to duty a month later as unit quartermaster. He was promoted to first lieutenant on December 14, and in March 1865 he assumed command of Company A and participated in battles at Five Forks, Dinwiddie Court House, and Sayler's Creek. He received brevets of captain, major, and lieutenant colonel for his service. When honorably discharged on June 25, 1865, he returned home to Canada.

Cooke's father encouraged his son to form a cavalry unit in Canada, but he instead chose the U.S. Army. He was commissioned a second lieutenant in Company D in the newly formed 7th Cavalry and reported for duty on November 16, 1866. (His name at times has been listed as "Cook" due to administrative error.) Cooke served as regimental adjutant from December 1866 to February 1867, and again from January 1871 until his death at Little Bighorn.

He became known by the nickname "the Queen's Own" and had the reputation as one

According to regimental records, over 120 cavalrymen had already deserted since April 19. Then, on the morning of July 7, 34 more men disappeared. Theodore Davis noted that "this out of a force of less than three hundred was a serious misfortune." The readiness of the command in the event of an Indian attack had been severely compromised.

Shortly after noon that same day, thirteen troopers—seven on horseback—brazenly deserted in full view of the command. Custer ordered Elliott, Tom Custer, and Cooke to give chase and stop the fleeing cavalrymen by whatever means necessary. Six of the deserters were subsequently returned to camp, three shot and wounded, one of whom, Pvt. Charles Johnson, eventually died. Custer loudly ordered that the wounded not be given medical attention but quietly directed Dr. Isaac Coates to offer them care, which commenced within a half hour of the column moving out.

On July 13, the exhausted command—without any additional desertions—went into camp near Fort Wallace. Both men and mounts were in poor condition and could not return to the field until rested and resupplied. Custer rode to the fort—which was presently under the command of Capt. Myles Keogh and Company I—to learn that mail and dispatches had not been able to get through on the Butterfield Overland Stagecoach Line due to the hostile Indian presence along the Smoky Hill Road.

General Hancock had recently passed through from Denver on his way east to the comforts of Fort Leavenworth but had not left behind any orders for Custer. Custer was also informed that Capt. Albert Barnitz and his Company G, which had ridden to Pond Creek Station, had been attacked on June 26 by Roman Nose's Cheyenne and sustained six killed and six wounded.

On July 15, Custer impulsively assembled three officers—Hamilton, Tom Custer, and Cooke—and seventy-two men with the best stock available and headed east toward Fort Hays, a distance of about 150 miles. The detail—minus a number of deserters and two men killed by Indians near Downer's Station—completed the forced march in fifty-five hours, an extraordinarily short time. Custer, his brother, Cooke, and writer Theodore Davis traveled another sixty miles from Fort Hays to Fort Harker, where he thought Libbie awaited, arriving there at 2 A.M. on July 19 (see "Custer's Mad Dash across Kansas" on page 63). Libbie, however, was at Fort Riley. Custer boarded the morning train and was finally reunited with his wife. Later that day, Custer received a telegram from Col. A. J. Smith ordering him to report back to Fort Harker.

The inability of Hancock to carry out his mission had allowed the Indians to remain free to terrorize settlements and travelers along the Smoky Hill, Platte, and Arkansas Rivers,

(continued on following page)

which compelled western governors to resume their appeals to Washington for relief. That disappointing result would without question require a scapegoat to blame for the failure.

Upon reporting to Fort Harker, Custer learned that he would stand a court-martial for his recent actions. It was perhaps a fitting conclusion to an expedition that had become a series of miscalculations and breakdowns of military discipline.

📖 Perhaps the most interesting account of the Hancock expedition, although decidedly biased, was written by George Armstrong Custer in *My Life on the Plains; or, Personal Experiences with Indians* (Norman: University of Oklahoma Press, 1962). Another excellent choice would be *The Court-Martial of George Armstrong Custer,* by Lawrence A. Frost (Norman: University of Oklahoma Press, 1968), which includes a detailed narrative followed by the transcript of Custer's court-martial.

A well-researched reconstruction of events covering the years 1866–67 can be found in two fine articles by Minnie Dubbs Millbrook: "The West Breaks in General Custer," *Kansas Historical Quarterly* 36 (Summer 1970), which has been reprinted in Paul A. Hutton's *The Custer Reader* (Lincoln: University of Nebraska Press, 1992); and "Custer's First Scout in the West," *Kansas Historical Quarterly* 39 (Spring 1973).

Editor Brian W. Dippie's footnotes in *Nomad: George A. Custer in Turf, Field and Farm* (Austin: University of Texas Press, 1980) provide valuable information, and Custer's own story about his adventurous buffalo hunt is included in his first "letter" of that volume.

Views by two participants—a cavalry officer and the only doctor accompanying Custer—are also significant: *Life in Custer's Cavalry: Diaries and Letters of Albert and Jennie Barnitz, 1867–1868,* edited by Robert M. Utley (Lincoln: University of Nebraska Press, 1987); and *On the Plains with Custer and Hancock: The Journal of Isaac Coates, Army Surgeon,* by W. J. D. Kennedy (Boulder, CO: Johnson Books, 1997).

Two representatives of the press who accompanied the expedition documented their observations: illustrator Theodore R. Davis, in "A Summer on the Plains," *Harper's New Monthly Magazine* 36 (February 1868); and Henry M. Stanley of the New York *Tribune,* who later wrote *My Early Travels and Adventures in America and Asia* (Lincoln: University of Nebraska Press, 1982).

A highly critical assessment of Hancock's expedition from an Indian point of view is included in *The Fighting Cheyennes,* by George B. Grinnell (Norman: University of Oklahoma Press, 1956). Sources for the Kidder massacre can be found following the biography of Kidder.

Other notable sources include *Custer, Come at Once! The Fort Hays Years of George and Elizabeth Custer, 1867–70,* by Blaine Burkey (Hays, KS: Thomas More Prep, 1976); *The Bat-*

of the best shots and fastest runners in the regiment. His appearance was also quite distinctive. He wore long "dundreary" sidewhiskers, named after Lord Dundreary, a character in the play *Our American Cousin,* which was playing at Ford's Theater the night President Lincoln was assassinated.

Cooke was involved in a particularly perilous resupply mission to Fort Wallace during the Hancock expedition of 1867 and took part in the incident in which several deserters were shot—one of whom later died. Civil charges for murder were placed against Cooke and Custer in the shooting but were subsequently dropped. He also participated in Custer's mad dash across Kansas that led to Custer's standing a court-martial (see "Custer's Mad Dash across Kansas" on page 63).

In the winter campaign of 1868–69, which included the battle of the Washita, Cooke commanded a battalion of sharpshooters. On March 15, 1869, he put his life on the line when he and Custer alone rode unannounced into a hostile village at Sweetwater Creek, Texas, on March 15, 1869, to confirm the presence of white captives (see "The Rescue at Sweetwater Creek" on page 96).

"The hasty flight of the Indians and the abandonment of, to them, valuable property, convinces me that they are influenced by fear alone, and it is my opinion that no council can be held with them in the presence of a large military force."

—CUSTER UPON FINDING THE VILLAGE ON PAWNEE FORK VACATED

Cooke was on leave for the Yellowstone expedition of 1873, but he served in the Black Hills expedition of 1874 and became regimental adjutant in December 1874. He delivered Custer's order to Maj. Marcus Reno that commenced the June 25, 1876, battle of the Little Bighorn and later scribbled Custer's last message imploring Capt. Frederick Benteen to "Come On." Cooke died alongside Custer, who considered his adjutant a close family friend. Cheyenne Indian Wooden Leg claimed that he had scalped the whiskers from one side of

(continued on following page)

Cooke's face and presented the unusual "scalp" to his wary grandmother, who discarded it two nights later at a dance.

Cooke's body was removed from the battlefield in 1877 and reinterred in Hamilton, Ontario.

📖 *Custer's Forgotten Friend: The Life of W. W. Cooke,* by Steve Arnold (Howell, MI: Powder River Press, 1993). Arnold's "Cooke's Scrawled Note: Last Word from A Doomed Command," can be found in *Greasy Grass Magazine* 14 (May 1998), published by the Custer Battlefield Historical & Museum Association. There are numerous references to Cooke by Custer in *My Life on the Plains; or, Personal Experiences with Indians* (Norman: University of Oklahoma Press, 1962).

✳ Wickliffe Cooper
Major, 7th U.S. Cavalry

Cooper was born on October 19, 1831, in Lexington, Kentucky, and attended two years at Dickinson College in Pennsylvania before being commissioned a second lieutenant in the 20th Kentucky Infantry at the outbreak of the Civil War. He fought at Shiloh and Corinth, and was captured in the August 1862 battle of Richmond, Kentucky, but was later exchanged. He was commissioned lieutenant colonel with the 4th Kentucky Cavalry in March 1863 and promoted to full colonel a month later. He distinguished himself commanding his regiment at Chickamauga in September 1863, and in March 1865, he participated in Gen. James Wilson's raid into Alabama.

Cooper was rewarded for his war record by receiving a commission in 1866 as second major of the 7th Cavalry. His service, however, was marred by an addiction to alcohol. On June 8, 1867, during the Hancock expedition, Cooper allegedly committed suicide in a fit of delirium tremens by shooting himself in the head with his pistol. He left behind a pregnant wife. George Armstrong Custer called Cooper "another of rum's victims," saying, "But for temperance Col. Cooper would have been a useful and accomplished officer, a brilliant and most companionable gentleman." Custer ordered all of his officers to view Cooper's body as a reminder of the consequences of excessive drinking.

Cooper's wife, in an attempt to obtain a pension through friends in Congress, made an effort to change her husband's cause of death to an accident, which was at that time denied. Dr. Isaac Coates, who had signed the death certificate, subsequently promised to assist in this endeavor and sent a signed, blank pension form to Mrs. Cooper's lawyer, a violation of army regulations

(continued on following page)

tle of the Washita: The Sheridan-Custer Indian Campaign of 1867–69,* by Stan Hoig (Garden City, NY: Doubleday & Co., 1976); *Tenting on the Plains; or, General Custer in Kansas and Texas,* by Elizabeth B. Custer (New York: Harper and Bros., 1887); and "The Hancock and Custer Expedition of 1867," by Lonnie J. White, *Journal of the West* 5, no. 3 (1966).

SIDEBARS

Table of Organization and Distribution of the 7th Cavalry for the Hancock Expedition of 1867

Field and Staff
Lt. Col. George Armstrong Custer, commanding
Maj. Wickliffe Cooper
Maj. Joel H. Elliott
Dr. Isaac Coates, assistant surgeon
1st Lt. Myles Moylan, adjutant
2nd Lt. Charles Brewster, acting quartermaster
2nd Lt. William W. Cooke, acting commissary

Company A	Capt. Louis Hamilton
Company D	1st Lt. Samuel M. Robbins
Company E	Capt. Edward Myers
Company F	2nd Lt. Henry J. Nowlan
Company G	Capt. Albert Barnitz; 2nd Lt. Henry Jackson
Company H	1st Lt. Thomas W. Custer (from Troop A)
Company K	Capt. Robert M. West
Company M	1st Lt. Owen Hale; 2nd Lt. James T. Leavy

At Fort Dodge: Company B Capt. William Thompson

At Fort Lyon: Company C 1st Lt. Matthew Berry

At Fort Morgan: Company L Capt. Michael V. Sheridan; 1st Lt. Lee P. Gillette; 2nd Lt. Henry H. Abell

At Fort Wallace: Company I Capt. Myles W. Keogh; 2nd Lt. James M. Bell

Detached Service: Col. A. J. Smith; Maj. Alfred Gibbs; Capt. Frederick W. Benteen; 1st Lt. Thomas B. Weir

Under Arrest: Capt. William P. Robeson

🐎 Major Hostile Indian Tribes on the Great Plains

ARAPAHO

The Arapaho was an Algonquin tribe that was thought to have migrated to the Great Plains from the headwaters of the Mississippi in the late seventeenth or early eighteenth century. At that time, the five subtribes, or bands, gave up agriculture to become nomadic hunters. One band split away to become the Gros Ventre of the Northwest; the other four lived separately in the winter, gathering for hunts or ceremonies. Each band had a chief, but there was no principal chief for the entire tribe. The name *Arapaho* was derived from a Pawnee word that meant "he who trades," reflecting the role of the Arapaho as middlemen in trades between Northern and Southern Plains tribes.

Around 1835, the Arapaho divided into two groups: The Northern Arapaho settled just east of the Rocky Mountains along the headwaters of the Platte River in Wyoming; the Southern Arapaho settled along the Arkansas River of Colorado. By 1840, the Southern Arapaho had become friendly with the Kiowa and Comanche, and occasionally joined these other tribes on raids into Texas and Mexico. In 1866, Northern Arapaho warriors joined Lakota Sioux chieftain Red Cloud in the fight over the Bozeman Trail, which led to the Fort Laramie Treaty of 1868.

At about the same time, the Southern Arapaho, with their Cheyenne and Kiowa allies, were menacing work crews on the Kansas Pacific Railway in Kansas and skirmished with the 7th Cavalry during the Hancock expedition of 1867. The Arapaho signed the Medicine Lodge Treaty of 1867 and agreed to share a reservation with the Cheyenne (see "The Medicine Lodge Treaties" on page 65). Their raiding resumed, however, when provisions of the treaty proved unworkable.

Gen. Phil Sheridan initiated his winter campaign of 1868–69 in an effort to force hostiles onto the reservation. During the battle of the Washita, Arapaho camps were located downstream from Black Kettle's village, and warriors came to the assistance of their beleaguered brethren.

Sheridan was successful in persuading the Southern Arapaho to move onto the reservation at Fort Cobb. The Northern Arapaho, after participating in the Great Sioux War of 1876, were eventually settled on the Wind River Reservation in Wyoming with their former enemy, the Shoshon.

📖 See *The Arapahoes, Our People*, by Virginia Cole Trenholm (Norman: University of Oklahoma Press, 1973); *Arapahoe Politics, 1851–1978: Symbols in Crises of Authority*, by Loretta Fowler (Lincoln: University of Nebraska Press, 1982); and *The Arapaho Way: A Memoir of an Indian Boyhood*, by Althea Bass (New York: Clarkson N. Potter, 1966).

that resulted in his dismissal from the service. Finally, after almost twenty years, the War Department amended Cooper's record in 1885 to show that he had "died by hand of person or persons unknown."

📖 Custer's version of events can be found in a letter to Libbie dated June 8, 1867, and his notes from the same day as well as June 10, 1868, in *The Custer Story: The Life and Letters of General George A. Custer and His Wife Elizabeth*, by Marguerite Merington (New York: Devin-Adair Company, 1950). Other helpful sources include *Life in Custer's Cavalry: Diaries and Letters of Albert and Jennie Barnitz, 1867–69*, edited by Robert M. Utley (Lincoln: University of Nebraska Press, 1987); and *The Court-Martial of General George Armstrong Custer*, by Lawrence A. Frost (Norman: University of Oklahoma Press, 1968). Also see *On the Plains with Custer and Hancock: The Journal of Isaac Coates, Army Surgeon*, by W. J. D. Kennedy (Boulder, CO: Johnson Books, 1997).

---◆◆◆---

"I encouraged peace propositions and have sturdy hopes of a successful and satisfactory settlement with the Sioux which will leave us only the Cheyennes to deal with."

—CUSTER TO LIBBIE, JUNE 1867

---◆◆◆---

✸ Theodore Russell Davis
Illustrator and Writer

Davis was born in Boston in 1840. At age fifteen, he moved to Brooklyn. His talent as an artist was evident, and while studying under Henry W. Herrick, an engraver, Davis held his first public exhibition in 1856 at the American Institute. He joined the staff of *Harper's Weekly* in 1861 and covered the Civil War as a correspondent and illustrator. It has been said that Davis, who was twice wounded, produced more field sketches of that conflict than any other combat artist.

In 1865, Davis was sent west by *Harper's Weekly* to depict the mining camps and boom towns in Colorado. While traveling on a stagecoach bound for Denver, Indians attacked near the Smoky Hill spring station. Davis and the other passengers held off the hostiles until rescued by the army.

(continued on following page)

On February 17, 1866, *Harper's Weekly* published Davis's full-page illustration of this incident, which became the prototype of an Indian stage attack later shown on modern motion picture and television screens.

Gen. Winfield S. Hancock invited Davis to accompany his expedition on the plains in 1867. Davis attached himself to George Armstrong Custer and rendered hundreds of sketches of events and skirmishes with the Indians, including an illustration of the massacred remains of Lt. Lyman Kidder and his detail, which was reproduced in Custer's *My Life on the Plains; or, Personal Experiences with Indians* (Norman: University of Oklahoma, 1962). Davis accompanied Custer on his mad dash across Kansas (see "Custer's Mad Dash across Kansas" on page 63), and at that time boarded an eastbound train at Fort Harker and returned to New York.

Davis remained with *Harper's* until 1884, when he retired and turned to free-lancing material, including Western scenes—apparently drawn from memory, since he made no further trips west—and became known as the most accomplished combat artist of his generation. He died on November 10, 1894, in Asbury Park, New Jersey.

"Come as soon as you can. 'Whom God hath joined . . .' I did not marry you for you to live in one house, me in another. One bed shall accommodate us both. . . . You remember how eager I was to have you for my little wife? I was not as impatient then as now. I almost feel tempted to desert and fly to you."

—CUSTER TO LIBBIE, MAY 1867

📖 Work published by Davis that covers the Hancock expedition of 1867 includes "Indian War Scenes," *Harper's Weekly* 11 (May 11, 1867); "Our Indian War Sketches," *Harper's Weekly* 11 (June 29, 1867); "Gen. Custer's Command, *Harper's Weekly* 11 (August 3, 1867); "Indian War Scenes," *Harper's Weekly* 11 (August 17, 1867); and "A Summer on the Plains," *Harper's New Monthly Magazine* 36,

(continued on following page)

CHEYENNE

At some point in the seventeenth century, the Cheyenne, an agricultural Algonquin tribe, tired of constant warfare with the Sioux and Ojibway in Minnesota and began migrating to the Great Plains to become nomadic hunters. In about 1832, the tribe split into two distinct bands: The larger group became the Southern Cheyenne and established residence along the upper Arkansas River; the Northern Cheyenne, who settled around the North Platte River in northern Nebraska, assumed a lifestyle similar to that of their allies, the Sioux. The tribe had seven military societies, of which the Dog Soldiers was regarded as the most aggressive and feared, and constantly waged war on Indian enemies.

In 1858, the "Pikes Peak or Bust" gold rush in Colorado incited violence between the Southern Cheyenne and white intruders onto their traditional land. Provisions of the Fort Wise Treaty of 1861 resulted in the removal of the tribe to eastern Colorado, where they were neglected and compelled to raid white settlements in order to survive. Colorado governor John Evans responded by encouraging civilians to take up arms against the marauding Indians. In 1864, Evans decided that friendly tribes would be protected by settling at designated sites. Chief Black Kettle accepted this offer, and his 600 Cheyenne camped for the winter of 1864 along Sand Creek, about forty miles from Fort Lyon. On November 29, Col. John Chivington and the 700-man 3rd Cavalry attacked, killing more than 150 men, women, and children (see "The Sand Creek Massacre" on page 104). The Cheyenne and their allies stepped up their raids, forcing the February 1865 abandonment of the town of Julesburg, Colorado.

In 1866, the Northern Cheyenne aligned themselves with Sioux chief Red Cloud and participated in a war against the U.S. Army over the Bozeman Trail. The resultant Indian victory led to the Fort Laramie Treaty of 1868 (see "The Fort Laramie Treaty of 1868 and the Black Hills Expedition" on page 158).

In 1867, attacks by the Southern Cheyenne on work crews from the Kansas Pacific Railway, as well as on white travelers along the Smoky Hill, Arkansas, and Platte Roads, compelled the army to form the Hancock expedition for the purpose of punishing these hostiles. Custer's 7th Cavalry pursued the Cheyenne under Tall Bull and their Sioux allies throughout Kansas, Nebraska, and Colorado but failed to deter the raids. In hopes of peace, the Medicine Lodge Treaty of 1867, which the Cheyenne signed, provided for a reservation shared by the Cheyenne and Arapaho (see "The Medicine Lodge Treaties" on page 65). The treaty provisions were unworkable, however, and raiding by the Cheyenne resumed. In September 1868, warriors under Roman Nose attacked Maj. George Forsyth in what became known as the battle of Beecher Island (see "The Battle of Beecher Island" on page 98).

In an effort to force the Cheyenne and their allies onto the reservation, Gen. Phil Sheridan launched his winter campaign of 1868–69. On November 27, 1868, Custer's 7th Cavalry attacked Black Kettle's village on the Washita River and killed nearly 100 Cheyenne, including Black Kettle. The campaign continued with a sweep of the plains, which encouraged many bands to submit to their reservation. Free-roaming Southern Cheyenne under Tall Bull were defeated by Maj. Eugene Carr at the July 11, 1869, battle of Summit Springs, an action that effectively ended hostilities on the southern plains when most of the Cheyenne and their allies submitted to the reservation at Fort Cobb (see "The Battle of Summit Springs" on page 101).

The Northern Cheyenne and their Sioux allies were targeted by the U.S. Army in what would be known as the Great Sioux War of 1876, which included the battle of the Little Bighorn. Following the November 1876 Dull Knife Fight, in which Col. Ranald Mackenzie defeated Northern Cheyenne under Dull Knife and Little Wolf, the tribe was settled on a reservation with their Southern Cheyenne brethren in Indian Territory (present-day Oklahoma), far removed from their traditional homeland in Montana. In September 1878, some members of the tribe, led by Dull Knife and Little Wolf, fled the reservation, heading north toward their former Tongue River homeland. More than 10,000 soldiers and civilians pursued and eventually apprehended the escaping Cheyenne. In the early 1880s, the Northern Cheyenne were finally granted their wish for a Tongue River Agency.

📖 Many excellent sources are available, including *The Fighting Cheyennes*, by George B. Grinnell (Norman: University of Oklahoma Press, 1956); *The Southern Cheyennes*, by Donald J. Berthrong (Norman: University of Oklahoma Press, 1963); *The Northern Cheyennes*, by Verne Dusenberry (Helena, MT: Montana Magazine 1955); *The Cheyennes: Indians of the Great Plains*, by E. Adamson Hoebel (New York: Holt, Rinehart and Winston, 1970); *Cheyenne Memories*, by John Stand-in-Timber and Margot Liberty (New Haven, CT: Yale University Press, 1967); *Cheyenne Autumn*, by Mari Sandoz (New York: McGraw-Hill, 1953); and *Conquest of the Southern Plains*, by Charles J. Brill (Oklahoma City: Golden Saga Publishers, 1938).

COMANCHE

It has been speculated that the Comanche separated from other Shoshonean-speaking peoples in the Great Basin and western Wyoming, and migrated southeastward. By the late seventeenth century, the Comanche had reached the southern plains, assuming a range spanning northern Texas, eastern Oklahoma, southwestern Kansas, southeastern Colorado, and eastern New Mexico. Perhaps the most skilled horsemen on the plains, this warring tribe battled Indian enemies and mounted raids into Mexico to steal slaves, horses, and women.

In the late eighteenth century, they allied with the Kiowa and together skirmished with the Spanish, effectively halting that country's expansion. The Texas Rangers engaged in many

no. 213 (February 1868), which is the most extensive work. His articles include "General Sheridan's Personality," *Cosmopolitan* 13 (June 1892); and "How a Battle Is Sketched," *St. Nicholas Magazine* 16, no. 9 (July 1889).

Artwork by Davis can also be viewed in *Artists and Illustrators of the Old West, 1850–1900*, by Robert Taft (New York: Charles Scribner's Sons, 1953); *Artists of the Old West*, by John C. Ewers (Garden City, NY: Doubleday & Company, 1965); and "A Special Artist in the Indian Wars," by Edgar M. Howell, *Montana: Magazine of Western History* 15, no. 2 (April 1965).

✪ Joel H. Elliott
Major, 7th U.S. Cavalry

Elliott was born on October 27, 1840, in Centerville, near Richmond, Wayne County, Indiana. His military career began in August 1861, when he enlisted as a private with Company C, 2nd Indiana Cavalry. He subsequently fought in engagements at Shiloh, Perryville, and Stones River. In June 1863, Elliott received a commission as captain. He was wounded twice—once left for dead when shot through the lungs at White's Station—while serving in the command of Gen. A. J. Smith and Col. Frederick W. Benteen. In the spring of 1863, he commanded a regiment that accompanied Col. Benjamin H. Grierson on his famous raid from Memphis through Mississippi to Vicksburg.

Following the war, Elliott served with George Armstrong Custer in Texas on Reconstruction duty. At that time, he applied for a commission in the Regular army, which was "heartily" endorsed by Custer: "Capt. Elliott is a natural soldier improved by extensive experience and field service." While he waited, Elliott briefly taught school and was the superintendent of the Toledo public schools. Although field qualified as a captain, Elliott scored well enough on a mental examination taken before the Casey Board of Examiners to be appointed—with assistance from the governor of Indiana—third major in the 7th Cavalry in March 1867.

Three months later, during the Hancock expedition, Elliott distinguished himself as commander of an eleven-men detail by delivering dispatches a distance of 200 miles through hostile territory. The next month, he was involved in one of the incidents—the shooting of deserters—that led to Custer's court-martial and subsequent suspension. In August 1867, Elliott assumed command of the 7th Cavalry in Custer's absence.

It was events during the winter campaign of 1868, however, that caused his name to be indelibly stamped in the history of the 7th Cavalry. On

(continued on following page)

November 27, as the battle of the Washita raged, Elliott—without notifying Custer—called for volunteers to follow him downstream and chase Indians escaping from the village. When Custer prepared to depart, Elliott's detachment of perhaps sixteen or seventeen men could not be located. A search turned up no sign of the missing men, and Custer, under pressure from assembling warriors, was obliged to leave without them. On December 10, Sheridan and Custer discovered the mutilated bodies of Elliott and his volunteers downstream from the battlefield. Captain Benteen, Elliott's friend and former Civil War commander, blamed Custer for "abandoning" the missing men. This controversy created dissension among the officers of the 7th Cavalry that continued long after Custer's death (see "The Joel Elliott Controversy" on page 90).

Elliott was buried at Fort Arbuckle, Indian Territory.

✴ Alfred Gibbs
Major, 7th U.S. Cavalry

Gibbs was born on April 22, 1823, into a prominent scientific and political Long Island family. He attended Dartmouth College before entering the U.S. Military Academy at West Point, from which he graduated in 1846. He participated in the Mexican War as a second lieutenant in the Mountain Rifles and earned brevets up to captain. He then served on frontier duty in Texas, New Mexico, and California, where he chased deserters who had fled to the goldfields. In March 1857, Gibbs pursued eight Mimbres Apache who had stolen mules near Robledo, New Mexico. He caught up with them near Cooke's Springs, killing six, but suffered a lance wound that would plague him throughout his life.

Gibbs entered the Civil War and was promoted to captain in May 1861. He was captured by Texas Confederate troops in July of that year at St. Augustine Springs, New Mexico, but was soon exchanged. Gibbs then served as colonel of a New York regiment until October 1864, when he was promoted to brigadier general of volunteers. He then commanded a cavalry brigade under Phil Sheridan in the Shenandoah and Appomattox campaigns, earning brevets up to major general for his distinguished service.

Gibbs was appointed first major in the newly formed 7th Cavalry in July 1866 and was acting commander when Custer arrived to relieve him in November. His poor health—attributed to the wound received in 1857—kept Gibbs for the most part in garrison, but he nonetheless made his mark on his unit. Although Custer's relationship

(continued on following page)

bloody battles with the Comanche. In fact, the primary mission of the Rangers—from formation during the Texas Revolution until 1875—was to contain the Comanche. In November 1864, famed frontiersman Kit Carson battled a combined force of Comanche and Kiowa at Adobe Walls on the Texas Panhandle and managed to burn much of the tribe's winter stores. In 1865, the Comanche and Kiowa agreed to settle on a reservation south of the Arkansas River, but they were relocated in 1868 to Fort Sill, which was not to their liking.

During the Hancock expedition of 1867, Custer's 7th Cavalry fought a number of skirmishes against the Comanche in southwest Kansas. The tribe agreed to the Medicine Lodge Treaty of 1867, which provided for a shared reservation with the Kiowa and Kiowa-Apache, but many warriors resumed raiding when the government failed to fulfill the treaty provisions. Gen. Phil Sheridan initiated his winter campaign of 1868–69 to clear the plains of hostiles. Some Comanche were camped downstream from Black Kettle's village on the Washita when Custer attacked, and they came to the aid of the Cheyenne. This decisive action, however, persuaded more Comanche to submit to the reservation. The hostile elements aligned themselves with Kiowa chief Satanta and moved farther south into Texas. During the Red River War of 1874–75, the Comanche fought under Chief Quanah Parker, whose mother was a white captive. In September 1874, Col. Ranald Mackenzie defeated the Comanche at Palo Duro Canyon and destroyed their pony herd and village. The following year, Parker led his destitute refugees into Fort Reno and Fort Sill, ending Comanche hostilities. Parker helped develop the present-day Native American Church, which advocates the use of the hallucinogen peyote.

📖 *The Comanches: Lords of the South Plains,* by Earnest Wallace and E. Adamson Hoebel (Norman: University of Oklahoma Press, 1952); *The Comanche Barrier to South Plains Settlement,* by Rupert N. Richardson (Glendale, CA: William D. Clark, 1933); and *United States–Comanche Relations: The Reservation Years,* by William T. Hagan (New Haven, CT: Yale University Press, 1976).

KIOWA AND KIOWA-APACHE

The Kiowa and their kinsmen, the Kiowa-Apache, migrated south from the headwaters of the Yellowstone and Missouri Rivers, arriving in the region of the Red and Arkansas Rivers—present-day Oklahoma, Texas, New Mexico, Kansas, and Colorado—by the early eighteenth century. The Kiowa had seven mainly autonomous bands, one of which was the Kiowa-Apache, each electing its own chief and limiting marriage between bands. The various bands camped apart during the winter but came together for hunts and ceremonies. By the late eighteenth century, the Kiowa had allied with the

Comanche, and the two tribes, both skilled horsemen and warriors, fought against common enemies.

The Kiowa story from this point in time mirrors that of the Comanche, as the two tribes united to offer resistance to white emigration (see Comanche section, above). Kicking Bird, who advocated peace, and Satanta and Lone Wolf, who advocated war, became notable Kiowa leaders during the Plains Indian war years of the 1860s and 1870s.

📖 *Bad Medicine and Good: Tales of the Kiowas,* by W. S. Nye (Norman: University of Oklahoma Press, 1962); *The Kiowas,* by Mildred Mayhall (Norman: University of Oklahoma Press, 1962); *Satanta and the Kiowas,* by F. Stanley (Borger, TX: Jim Hess Printers, 1968); *Plains Indian Raiders: The Final Phases of Warfare from the Arkansas to the Red River,* by Wilbur S. Nye (Norman: University of Oklahoma Press, 1968); *Our Red Brothers and the Peace Policy of President Ulysses S. Grant,* by Lawrie Tatum (Lincoln: University of Nebraska Press, 1970); and *Carbine and Lance: The Story of Old Fort Sill,* by Wilbur S. Nye (Norman: University of Oklahoma Press, 1969).

LAKOTA SIOUX

The Teton, or Lakota, Nation of Sioux, along with their brethren the Dakota and Nakota Sioux, had migrated from the South in the sixteenth century to settle the headwaters of the Mississippi in northern Minnesota. Over time, the three groups split into distinct nations, each speaking a different dialect and occupying their own territory, although they were collectively known as Sioux. That title, however, a French interpretation of the Chippewa word *Nadoue-is-iw,* meaning "enemy," served only as a generic name for the three separate nations. In the late eighteenth century, the Lakota Sioux became the final major group of Indians to arrive on the Great Plains; the Dakota and Nakota Sioux remained in Minnesota.

The emigrating Lakota Sioux believed that the Black Hills region, a wilderness area along the South Dakota–Wyoming border, was sacred land, a place where spirits dwelled, and for three-quarters of a century they rarely made camp out of sight of this place they called *Paha Sapa,* "Hills That Are Black" (see "The Lakota Sioux and the Black Hills" on page 152). There were seven principal autonomous Lakota tribes—the Blackfeet (not to be confused with the Blackfoot tribe to the north, related to the eastern Algonquin), Brule, Hunkpapa, Minniconjou, Oglala, Sans Arc, and Two Kettle—each of which established its own territory throughout Montana, Wyoming, Kansas, Nebraska, and the Dakota Territory but would come together for hunts and annual ceremonies (see "The Seven Principal Lakota Sioux Bands" on page 154). The Lakota enjoyed greater numbers than their rivals due to this supportive alliance, and with their aggressive nature, they became the strongest and most feared tribe on the Great Plains.

with Gibbs was at times somewhat contentious, Libbie Custer recalled that "his influence in shaping our regiment in social as well as military affairs was felt in a marked manner." Gibbs, who was known as "General Etiquette," was also instrumental in creating the regimental band.

Gibbs was at Fort Leavenworth when he passed away suddenly of "congestion of the brain" on December 26, 1868. He was interred at Portsmouth, Rhode Island.

📖 Gibbs is the subject of numerous references in *Life in Custer's Cavalry: Diaries and Letters of Albert and Jennie Barnitz, 1867–69,* edited by Robert M. Utley (Lincoln: University of Nebraska Press, 1987).

"Volume after volume might be filled in recounting the unprovoked and merciless atrocities committed upon the people of the frontier by their implacable foe, the red man."

—CUSTER AFTER DESCRIBING IN DETAIL THE DEPREDATIONS SUFFERED BY TWO WHITE FAMILIES AT THE HANDS OF KIOWA AND CHEYENNE INDIANS

✸ Louis McLane Hamilton
Captain, 7th U.S. Cavalry

Hamilton was born into a historically notable family on July 21, 1844, in New York City and was raised on Long Island and in Poughkeepsie, New York. His father, Judge Philip Hamilton, was the son of Alexander Hamilton, a founding father of the United States and member of Washington's cabinet who was killed in a duel with Aaron Burr. Hamilton was named after his maternal grandfather, Louis McLane, who was a U.S. senator and secretary of the treasury and of state in President Andrew Jackson's cabinet.

In September 1862, at the age of eighteen—with assistance from influential friends—Hamilton was commissioned as a second lieutenant in the 3rd Infantry. He commanded a company at Fredericksburg, won brevets at Chancellorsville and Gettysburg, and fought at Petersburg and Appomattox. He was promoted to first lieutenant in May 1864.

(continued on following page)

Sioux Camp on the Tongue River, 1870s. *Courtesy Little Bighorn Battlefield National Monument.*

In July 1866, Hamilton became the youngest captain in the Regular army when he joined the 7th Cavalry and was assigned to command Fort Lyon, Colorado. He was an able and ambitious troop commander who was well liked by his fellow officers. His leadership skills under fire were admirably displayed on June 24, 1867, during the Hancock expedition. While in command of a small detachment, Hamilton averted an Indian ambush and repulsed forty-five attacking Sioux near the forks of the Republican River while pursuing Sioux under Pawnee Killer. He later commanded a detachment that followed Custer east during the incident that led to Custer's court-martial.

Hamilton's ambition, however, led to his death at the battle of the Washita on November 27, 1868. Hamilton, who had been assigned officer of the day and detailed to guard the pack train in the rear, arranged to trade places with 1st Lt. Edward Mathey. He was commanding a squadron on the initial charge into Black Kettle's village when killed instantly by a bullet through the heart. Dr. Henry Lippincott noted that the "ball entered about five inches below left nipple, and emerged near inferior angle of right scapula. Death was instantaneous." Hamilton was buried with full

(continued on following page)

During the mid-nineteenth century, the white advance encroached on Lakota territory, and in an effort to prevent trouble, the Fort Laramie Treaty of 1851 was signed. Hostilities exploded in 1854, however, when a Lakota warrior killed an ox from a wagon train, which resulted in the massacre of twenty-nine soldiers (see "The Initiation of Warfare between the Plains Indians and the U.S. Army" on page 49). The army retaliated by destroying an Indian village near Ash Hollow. This action caused hostilities to simmer; they finally boiled over in 1866 upon the creation of the Bozeman Trail, a shortcut to the Montana goldfields that passed through traditional Lakota hunting ground. In what is known as Red Cloud's War, Lakota chief Red Cloud became the only Indian ever to force the U.S. government to grant treaty demands through acts of violence (see "Red Cloud's War" on page 68). The Fort Laramie Treaty of 1868 provided for the Great Sioux Reservation, which was composed of most of present-day South Dakota west of the Missouri River (see "The Fort Laramie Treaty of 1868 and the Black Hills Expedition" on page 158). Red Cloud and many of his people retired to this reservation. The younger warriors, including Crazy Horse, Rain-in-the-Face, and Gall, led by Chief Sitting Bull, continued to fight western settlement by whites.

The Lakota harassed Custer and his 7th Cavalry on the Yellowstone expedition of 1873, an army mission to protect surveyors for the Northern Pacific Railroad. But it was Custer's Black Hills expedition of 1874, which was an intrusion and perhaps a treaty violation into their sacred Black Hills, that most threatened them.

Gold deposits were discovered in the Black Hills on this expedition, which brought a horde of prospectors onto Lakota land. The U.S. government entreated the Lakota to sell their sacred land. Most reservation tribe members were willing to sell, but dissidents led by Sitting Bull and Crazy Horse refused and began attacking the miners, wagon trains, and white settlements.

In late 1875, runners were dispatched by the U.S. government with a message to the Lakota and their Cheyenne allies that were camped in the area of the Yellowstone, stating that they must submit to the reservation by January 31, 1876, or the army would march against them. This edict led to the Great Sioux War of 1876–77, a series of skirmishes and battles, including the battle of the Little Bighorn, that resulted in the eventual submission of most Lakota. Sitting Bull and a small band of followers fled to Canada, where they remained until 1881.

In 1877, following the Great Sioux War, the U.S. Congress passed an appropriation bill that denied the Lakota rations and goods until they signed away ownership of the Black Hills. In order to save their starving people, the chiefs touched the pen to the treaty and lost forever their sacred Black Hills.

Lakota resistance flared up once more in 1890, when the tribe embraced a new religion called the Ghost Dance. This uprising led to the killing of Sitting Bull in October and the massacre of nearly 150 Lakota men, women, and children on December 29 at Wounded Knee Creek.

📖 *Red Cloud's Folk: A History of the Oglala Sioux Indians,* by George E. Hyde (Norman: University of Oklahoma Press, 1937); *Spotted Tail's Folk: A History of the Brule Sioux,* by George E. Hyde (Norman: University of Oklahoma Press, 1957); *My People the Sioux,* by Luther Standing Bear (Boston: Houghton Mifflin, 1928); *The Sioux: Life and Customs of a Warrior Society,* by Royal B. Hassrick (Norman: University of Oklahoma Press, 1964); *Lakota Society,* by James R. Walker, edited by Raymond J. DeMallie (Lincoln: University of Nebraska Press, 1982); *War-Path and Bivouac; or, The Conquest of the Sioux,* by John F. Finerty (Norman: University of Oklahoma Press, 1961); *The Last Days of the Sioux Nation,* by Robert M. Utley (New Haven, CT: Yale University Press, 1963).

🐎 The Initiation of Warfare between the Plains Indians and the U.S. Army

By the early 1850s, tension between the Plains tribes and the white man had been drawn progressively taut as a bowstring. Disease, hunger, despair, and uncertainty were prevalent among the tribes—the direct result of the increasing white civilian invasion and the threatening presence of army troops.

military honors near Camp Supply and later reinterred at Poughkeepsie, New York.

After George Armstrong Custer's remains were exhumed from the Little Bighorn battlefield in July 1877, they were stored in a Poughkeepsie, New York, vault owned by Louis's father, Philip. A flag belonging to Louis Hamilton adorned Custer's casket when the general was reinterred at West Point on October 10, 1877 (see "Interment and Reinterment of Little Bighorn Dead" on page 232).

📖 Custer's personal tribute to Hamilton can be found in "In Memoriam: Louis McLane Hamilton, Captain 7th U.S. Cavalry," *Chronicles of Oklahoma* 46, no. 4 (Winter 1968–69). Hamilton is the subject of numerous references in *Life in Custer's Cavalry: Diaries and Letters of Albert and Jennie Barnitz, 1867–69,* edited by Robert M. Utley (Lincoln: University of Nebraska Press, 1987); and *My Life on the Plains; or, Personal Experiences with Indians,* by George Armstrong Custer (Norman: University of Oklahoma Press, 1962).

◆━━◆━━◆

"I was never so anxious in my life."

—CUSTER RELATING HIS CONCERN THAT LIBBIE MIGHT BE A PASSENGER ON COOKE'S WAGON TRAIN, WHICH WAS ATTACKED BY AN OVERWHELMING NUMBER OF SIOUX

◆━━◆━━◆

✹ Winfield Scott Hancock
Major General, U.S. Army

"Hancock the Superb" as he would be hailed by Civil War–era newspapers, was born in Montgomery Square, near Norristown, Pennsylvania, on February 14, 1824. He graduated from the U.S. Military Academy at West Point in 1844 and distinguished himself in the Mexican War, winning brevets at Contreras and Churubusco, before serving in various quartermaster capacities. Hancock served in the Third Seminole War in the 1850s, the 1857 Utah expedition, and was appointed brigadier general in the Union army on September 23, 1861.

2nd Lt. George Armstrong Custer served as a volunteer aide to corps commander General Hancock on May 5, 1862, in an engagement near Williamsburg when the first battle flag taken by the Union army was captured. Hancock became a bona fide hero at Gettysburg when, in command

(continued on following page)

of the II Corps, he held the Union center against Pickett's charge, although badly wounded. He was formally thanked by Congress for his bravery, but he never fully recovered from his wounds received in that battle. Within six months, however, he was back commanding his corps in Virginia until November 1864, when his poor health compelled him to accept recruiting duty in Washington.

Hancock was appointed commander of the Department of the Missouri in 1867 and that year led an expedition in Kansas for the purpose of punishing Plains Indian tribes that had been raiding throughout the area. His operation, however, became a series of miscalculations, tactical errors, and breakdowns of military discipline—most of which could be blamed on Hancock—and ended in miserable failure. Hancock apparently urged Col. A. J. Smith to prefer charges against Lt. Col. George Armstrong Custer, branding him the scapegoat for this blot on the general's otherwise exemplary military career.

Hancock commanded various departments and divisions, including Louisiana and Texas, the Dakota, Atlantic, and the East, until 1886—with one exception. In 1880, he was the Democratic nominee for president but lost a close election to James A. Garfield. The general died at Governor's Island, New York, on February 9, 1886, and was buried at Norristown, Pennsylvania.

📖 *Reminiscences of Winfield Scott Hancock, by His Wife,* by Almira R. Hancock (New York: Charles L. Webster & Co., 1887); *The Life of Winfield Scott Hancock,* by D. X. Junkin (New York: Appleton, 1880); and *Winfield Scott Hancock: A Soldier's Life,* by David M. Jordan (Bloomington: Indiana University Press, 1988).

✳ James Butler Hickok
Army Scout, Gunfighter, U.S. Marshal

James "Wild Bill" Hickok was born on May 27, 1837, on a farm in Homer (later Troy Grove), La Salle County, Illinois. He assisted his father in running an underground railroad until his father died when Hickok was fifteen. Hickok then helped support the family by driving a wagon and hunting wolves for the bounty money. He headed west to Kansas at age eighteen after mistakenly believing he had killed a man in a fight, and he found work as a wagon and stagecoach driver. While recuperating after being badly mauled by a bear, Hickok shot and killed three men following a dispute, an act that was later greatly exaggerated but initiated his reputation as a handy man with a gun. In 1858, he briefly served as constable in Monticello, Kansas.

The initial volley of armed hostility between the Plains Indians and the U.S. Army was fired on August 17, 1854, when an ox from a wagon train of Mormon emigrants was killed by an arrow shot from the bow of a Lakota Sioux warrior named High Forehead. The precise reason for this rash act by High Forehead is more or less unknown. The ox, portrayed in various accounts as lame and worn out or crippled and having been left by the wayside, had strayed close to a Lakota camp near Fort Laramie and was apparently considered fair game. The audacious Sioux archer most likely was showing off for friends and killed the animal out of mischief rather than hunger. Relations between the U.S. Army and the Plains tribes by this point had degenerated to the extent that both parties derived great pleasure from provoking one another.

The indignant Mormons reported the incident to Fort Laramie and demanded satisfaction. Lakota chief Brave Bear was summoned by Lt. Hugh B. Fleming, the post commander, and informed about the intolerable act. Brave Bear deemed the incident inconsequential and readily offered to make restitution. Fleming, however, demanded that High Forehead be delivered to the fort for disposition.

Brave Bear refused, reminding Fleming that to surrender the warrior was in violation of the Fort Laramie Treaty of 1851, which provided for each tribe to punish their own guilty parties in crimes against whites. That argument failed to sway Fleming, who warned that troops would be dispatched the following morning to arrest the culprit if he did not turn himself in by then.

The thought of surrendering to the army clearly terrified High Forehead. The white man's practice of arrest and incarceration was alien to the Plains Indians, and the hot-tempered warrior feared that he would be murdered if removed from his people. The ox killer's cause was embraced by his brethren, who gathered to sing motivational songs and paint themselves for war.

One officer at the post, a recent West Point graduate named 2nd Lt. John L. Grattan, had yet to hear a shot fired in anger but had been known to brag that his primitive enemy would be no match for the might of the U.S. Army. Grattan persuaded Fleming to permit him to command the detail assigned to arrest this killer of the incapacitated Mormon oxen. The green lieutenant set out in the morning with a detachment of twenty-nine troopers.

Grattan, who some reports say had bolstered his courage with drink, approached his objective to find some 1,200 Lakota warriors swarming around the village like bees protecting their hive. When brief negotiations with Chief Brave Bear failed to deliver High Forehead, Grattan ordered his men to ready their weapons—perhaps in an attempt to rattle sabers and compel the surrender.

(continued on following page)

The tactic backfired. It has not been determined which side fired first, but within moments, the air was thick with bullets and arrows as the soldiers and the warriors opened fire on each other. Brave Bear fell in the first volley. When the smoke had cleared, every soldier had been killed. Grattan was found with twenty-four arrows piercing his body, his skull crushed beyond recognition.

The riled Lakota raided a nearby fur trading house and threatened a trading post, but were finally persuaded by their chiefs not to assault Fort Laramie. Instead, the triumphant warriors packed up their lodges and departed to participate in their annual fall buffalo hunt.

The Eastern press reported with great passion and embellishment the massacre of Grattan and his men to an inflamed public that demanded revenge. The man selected to punish the Indians for their treachery was Brig. Gen. William S. Harney, who would assemble his troops at Fort Leavenworth and prepare to take to the field.

In anticipation of Harney's arrival, runners were dispatched to the various Indian camps to advise the chiefs that all friendly Indians were to report to Fort Laramie, where they would be protected and provided with rations. Otherwise, they would be considered hostile and could expect the army to pay them an inimical visit. This edict was taken seriously by most tribes, and by early September, hundreds of lodges had gathered on the Laramie Fork, thirty-five miles above the fort.

One Lakota band, led by Brule Lakota chief Little Thunder, which was composed of forty lodges—about 250 people—remained camped on Bluewater River, a tributary of the Platte, about six miles northwest of Ash Hollow and 100 miles east of Fort Laramie. Little Thunder had always been considered friendly and had dismissed any notion that he would be attacked.

On September 3, 1855, General Harney with 600 troops arrived on Little Thunder's doorstep and, after a brief parley, proceeded to assault the village. In the ensuing massacre, eighty-six Lakota were killed and another seventy women and children taken prisoner. The village and its valuable contents were destroyed, and the pony herd was captured. Revenge for Lieutenant Grattan had been exacted.

The destruction of Little Thunder's camp was a catastrophe of proportions previously unheard of in the annals of Lakota warfare. Never before had an enemy killed so many of them or captured their wives and children in such great numbers, and never before had a village been so thoroughly ravaged.

The gauntlet had been thrown down in challenge. Many Lakota chiefs appealed for conciliation, but the army was convinced that Harney's action confirmed that the only way to deal with Indians was brute force. Those Indians who refused to submit to the reservation would be marked for death and

At the outbreak of the Civil War, Hickok, an opponent of slavery in an area of the country torn apart by the issue, signed on with the Union army at Fort Leavenworth and was in charge of supply trains. During this time, he gained further notoriety as a dangerous gunfighter—exploits later greatly exaggerated by writers of dime novels. The first gunfight of note came in July 1861, with David McCandles, which was described with great embellishment by George Ward Nichols in *Harper's Magazine*, making "Wild Bill" nationally famous. He participated in the August 1861 battle of Wilson's Creek, the battle of Pea Ridge the following year, then became involved in spying and scouting for the army in western Missouri and southern Kansas. In July 1865, he shot and killed Dave Tutt in a famous duel waged in the public square of Springfield, Missouri. He was arrested and turned over to civilian authorities by future 7th Cavalry officer Maj. Albert Barnitz but was eventually found not guilty by a jury.

Hickok served for a year as deputy marshal of Fort Hays, Kansas, and signed on as a guide for Gen. William T. Sherman on the general's first visit to the West. He quit law enforcement to scout for the army during the Hancock expedition of 1867, where he became acquainted with George Armstrong Custer. Wild Bill was extremely knowledgeable about the Plains Indians, and Custer spent quite a bit of time as his student. Hickok remained through the winter campaign of 1868–69, scouting for both the 5th and 7th Cavalries but not taking part in any notable battles. While carrying dispatches to Fort Lyon in early 1869, he was wounded in the leg in an attack by a Cheyenne war party.

Following that campaign, Hickok returned to Hays City, Kansas, as a U.S. marshal and spent much time as a spectator enjoying his favorite sport—baseball. At about this time—according to the lady's unsubstantiated claim—he married Martha Jane Cannary ("Canary"), the infamous Calamity Jane. While serving as marshal, he was involved in an incident with Tom Custer that resulted in Hickok's hopping a freight train and leaving town in a hurry, headed for Abilene (see "Wild Bill's Showdown with Tom Custer" on page 67).

In 1871, Hickok became marshal at Abilene, Kansas—a rowdy cow town at the end of the Chisholm Trail—where he was said to have encountered such notorious peers as John Wesley Hardin and Ben Thompson. By this time, he was losing his sight and habitually wore dark glasses. He was dismissed as marshal in December 1871

(continued on following page)

and moved to Georgetown, Colorado. William F. "Buffalo Bill" Cody, a longtime friend, coaxed the now-famous Hickok to join his traveling Wild West show, and he remained with the troupe through the 1872–73 season. For several years, he participated in stage productions of one kind or another.

On March 5, 1876, he married circus owner Agnes Lake, who was also an actress, high-wire walker, and lion tamer of some reknown. Within a month of his marriage, Hickok took part in the gold rush to the Black Hills of Dakota Territory. On August 2, he was in the town of Deadwood playing cards in the Sixty-Six Saloon—holding a hand of aces and eights—when shot in the back by Jack McCall. Hickok's body was initially buried at Ingleside, on a nearby mountainside, then on August 3, 1879, was exhumed and reinterred in Mount Moriah Cemetery. Calamity Jane, by the way, was later buried some twenty feet from Hickok's grave.

📖 Joseph Rosa compared Hickok to Custer in his excellent biography, *They Called Him Wild Bill: The Life and Adventures of James Butler Hickok* (Norman: University of Oklahoma Press, 1964), when he wrote: "Like George Armstrong Custer he came of a reckless breed; excitement and wanderlust were in his blood. An ancient General Custer or Wild Bill Hickok would be unthinkable. Maybe fate felt that way too." Rosa was also the author of *Wild Bill Hickok: The Man and His Myth* (Lawrence: University Press of Kansas, 1996). Another notable biography is *Wild Bill Hickok,* by Richard O'Connor (Garden City, NY: Konecky & Konecky, 1959).

Custer wrote about his relationship with Hickok in *My Life on the Plains; or, Personal Experiences with Indians* (Norman: University of Oklahoma Press, 1962). Libbie Custer, who greatly admired the swashbuckling Hickok, added her thoughts about him in *Following the Guidon* (Norman: University of Oklahoma Press, 1966).

The period of time during which Custer and Hickok were acquainted has been documented in *Wild Bill Hickok, the Law in Hays City,* by Blaine Burkey (Hays, KA: Thomas More Prep, 1975). Hickok is the subject of many interesting stories in the biography of his friend and fellow scout Moses "California Joe" Milner, whose own murder has been blamed on his exposing the true reason why Wild Bill was killed: *California Joe: Noted Scout and Indian Fighter,* by Joe E. Milner and Earle R. Forrest (Caldwell, ID: Caxton Printers, 1935).

compelled to defeat the mighty United States of America if they were to preserve their culture and territorial rights. This was the beginning of the tactic known as "Total War" (see "Total War" on page 83).

📖 Details of the Grattan massacre and subsequent events can be found in transcripts of interviews with Indian and white residents of the time, along with letters, newspapers clippings, and comments by Judge Daniel Ricker in the Ricker Tablets, Nebraska State Historical Society. More convenient sources include *Spotted Tail's Folk: A History of the Brule Sioux,* by George E. Hyde (Norman: University of Oklahoma Press, 1957); *Crazy Horse: Strange Man of the Oglala,* by Mari Sandoz (Lincoln: University of Nebraska Press, 1942); *Frontiersmen in Blue: The United States Army and the Indian, 1848–1865,* by Robert M. Utley (New York: Macmillan, 1973); *Red Cloud and the Sioux Problem,* by James C. Olson (Lincoln: University of Nebraska Press, 1965); *The Lance and the Shield: The Life and Times of Sitting Bull,* by Robert M. Utley (New York: Henry Holt, 1993); and "The Grattan Massacre," by Lloyd E. McCann, *Nebraska History* 37 (1956).

🐎 The 7th U.S. Cavalry

The creation of the 7th Cavalry was authorized by an act of Congress on July 28, 1866. The new unit was assigned the duty station of Fort Riley, Kansas. Enlisted recruits arrived at the fort throughout the summer and fall and were formed into companies by Maj. John W. Davidson of the 2nd Cavalry, until he was relieved in October by Maj. Alfred Gibbs.

By the end of the year, over 800 troops were joined by most of the officers, including Lt. Col. George Armstrong Custer, who made his first appearance with wife Libbie on November 3. Custer, however, soon returned to Washington to appear before an examining board for his new commission and remained away until late December.

The commanding officer, Col. Andrew Jackson Smith, arrived several weeks after Custer but departed in February 1867 to head the District of the Upper Arkansas. At that time, Custer—whose name would become synonymous with the regiment—assumed *de facto* command, a position he would hold until June 25, 1876.

The enlisted cavalryman of Custer's era was a volunteer who was paid $13 a month. Quite a number of them were immigrants from Ireland, Italy, Germany, and England, and many were Civil War veterans. The cavalryman learned how to ride and care for his mount and how to fight on horseback or dismounted. His normal daily routine in garrison, however, was not very exciting. He endured months of isolation, monotony, and rigid discipline, interrupted only by the occasional brief action against his enemy, the Plains Indians.

Reveille typically blew at 5:30, with the first drill commencing at 6:15. That was followed by stable call, guard mount, construction, woodcutting, water details, inspections and dress reviews, and various forms of drill. Taps sounded at 8:15, when the men retired to crude bunks fashioned with pole or board slats and straw ticks. In some cases during warm weather, they preferred to sleep outside.

The cavalryman wore a gray shirt, a dark blue blouse, sky blue trousers, black boots, and a wide-brimmed hat of either army-issue blue or white straw during the summer months. His uniform was crisscrossed with leather straps that held certain necessities, such as cartridge pouches and his three-pound, seven-ounce light cavalry saber. He was initially issued a seven-shot .56/.50-caliber Spencer repeating carbine and a .44-caliber Colt or Remington percussion revolver, and later a .45-caliber Springfield Model 1873 single-shot breech-loading carbine and a six-shot .45-caliber Colt single-action revolver (see "Weapons Carried by the Cavalrymen" on page 195).

The cavalryman's campaign outfit consisted of his weapons, a shelter half, haversack, poncho, canteen, mess kit, blanket, extra clothing, extra ammunition, a feedbag, fifteen pounds of grain, a picket pin and lariat, personal items, and several days' rations—usually greasy salt pork and hardtack washed down with bitter coffee.

The primary mission of the newly formed regiment was to protect work crews on the Kansas Pacific Railroad from hostile Plains Indian tribes, which had been incessantly raiding. Regimental headquarters remained at Fort Riley with Companies A, D, H, and M, while individual companies were assigned to garrison various posts along the Santa Fe and Smoky Hill Trails: Companies B and C were sent to Fort Lyon, Colorado Territory; E to Fort Hays, Kansas; F and G to Fort Harker, Kansas; I to Fort Wallace, Kansas; K to Fort Dodge; and L to Fort Morgan, Colorado Territory. The first action by the 7th Cavalry as a unit came during the Hancock expedition of 1867, which resulted in a frustrating, futile search for hostiles.

After remaining in garrison throughout the winter of 1867–68—without Custer, who was serving a one-year suspension—the 7th Cavalry saddled up under Maj. Joel Elliott to accompany Gen. Alfred Sully on a brief operation in September 1868 intended to punish the Indians. It was an embarrassing failure when Sully proved unfit for rigorous campaigning. Custer was called back to duty early and led the 7th on Gen. Phil Sheridan's winter campaign of 1868–69, which included the victorious battle of the Washita and moderate success at encouraging hostiles to submit to the reservation.

Following a period of rather mundane garrison duty, the unit was split up in 1871 and assigned in small detachments

7th Cavalry Regimental Standard. *Courtesy Little Bighorn Battlefield National Monument.*

✵ Kicking Bird
Kiowa

Kicking Bird (Tene-angpote, meaning "Eagle Striking with Talons," or Watohkonk, meaning "Black Eagle"), whose grandfather was a Crow Indian captive, was born about 1835 and soon adopted into the Kiowa tribe. He gained respect in his youth for his bravery as a warrior and married a woman named Guadalupe. In time, however, he arrived at the conclusion that peace with the white man was the only solution to hostilities. To prove his peaceful intentions, in 1865 he signed the Little Arkansas Treaty at Wichita, the first agreement to accept a reservation. The following year, when his tribe prepared to choose a new chief, Kicking Bird represented the peace faction in opposition to Satanta, who advocated war. In a compromise, the tribe settled on Lone Wolf, but the division of loyalties remained. In 1867, Kicking Bird signed the Medicine Lodge Treaty, which placed his tribe on a reservation in present-day Oklahoma, where he remained during the subsequent hostilities. Three years later, at a Sun Dance, he was accused of cowardice—called a "woman"—by his fellow tribesmen, and to disprove the charge, he participated in a raid into Texas. Kicking Bird led 100 warriors into battle against 54 cavalrymen and

(continued on following page)

demonstrated his courage by charging into the enemy and killing one with his lance. His flanking strategy was successful in defeating the outnumbered cavalry, which restored his reputation.

In 1872, Kicking Bird was one of the spokesmen of a delegation that traveled to Washington. When Lone Wolf joined the Comanche to fight the Red River War of 1874–75, Kicking Bird was tempted to fight but instead led most of his band to the reservation at Fort Sill. For that act, he was designated principal chief of his tribe by the Indian agent and persuaded authorities to build a school for his people. Following hostilities in Texas, he was assigned the task of determining which of his fellow Kiowa should be exiled to Florida. One of his choices was Lone Wolf, which infuriated many of his tribe. Less than a week later, on May 3, 1875, Kicking Bird was dead. It was said that he died from the magical powers of a medicine man, but more than likely he was poisoned with strychnine. He was interred, with Christian rites, in the Fort Sill cemetery—known as Indian Arlington.

For more about Kicking Bird, see "Kicking Bird: A Chief of the Kiowas," by Morris F. Taylor, *Kansas Historical Quarterly* 38 (Autumn 1972); *Bad Medicine and Good: Tales of the Kiowas,* by Wilbur S. Nye (Norman: University of Oklahoma Press, 1962); *Plains Indian Raiders: The Final Phases of Warfare from the Arkansas to the Red River,* by Wilbur S. Nye (Norman: University of Oklahoma Press, 1968); *The Kiowas,* by Mildred P. Marshall (Norman: University of Oklahoma Press, 1962); *Our Red Brothers and the Peace Policy of President Ulysses S. Grant,* by Lawrie Tatum (Lincoln: University of Nebraska Press, 1970); and *Carbine and Lance: The Story of Old Fort Sill,* by Wilbur S. Nye (Norman: University of Oklahoma Press, 1969).

Lyman Stockwell Kidder
Second Lieutenant, 2nd U.S. Cavalry

Kidder was born on August 31, 1842, in Braintree, Orange Country, Vermont, the second of four children. His father, Jefferson P. Kidder, was a teacher, lawyer, delegate to Vermont's constitutional convention in 1843, state's attorney from 1843 to 1847, state senator from 1847 to 1849, and lieutenant governor of Vermont from 1853 to 1854. In 1857, the Kidder family moved to St. Paul, the capital of Minnesota Territory, where Lyman's father was involved in real estate and politics.

On November 1, 1861, Kidder enlisted as a corporal in Company K, Brackett's Cavalry Battalion, a part of the 5th Iowa Cavalry. The unit formed at Fort Snelling, Minnesota, and was soon transferred to Benton Barracks, Missouri, where it began oper-

around the South—Kentucky, Tennessee, and South Carolina—for the inglorious purpose of monitoring the activities of the Ku Klux Klan and moonshiners.

The 7th Cavalry reassembled in Memphis in the spring of 1873, then traveled to Fort Rice, Dakota Territory. In June, the regiment marched from that post to provide security for the Northern Pacific Railroad on the Yellowstone expedition of 1873. The troops returned in September to garrison their new duty station at Fort Abraham Lincoln, near Bismarck, Dakota Territory.

In July 1874, Custer and ten companies of the 7th marched out to explore the Black Hills, a wilderness region along the South Dakota–Wyoming border. The expedition found gold on land that had been given to the Lakota Sioux under the provisions of the Fort Laramie Treaty of 1868. The cavalrymen returned to Fort Lincoln and settled in for the harsh winter, while a gold rush ensued that brought a flood of miners into the Black Hills, to the ire of the Sioux.

In the spring of 1876, the 7th Cavalry participated in the Little Bighorn campaign, which was intended to persuade elements of hostile Indian tribes to submit to the reservation. On June 25, Custer and more than 250 of his cavalrymen were killed by Sioux and Cheyenne warriors in the battle of the Little Bighorn.

The newly manned 7th Cavalry fought in the Nez Perce campaign of 1877 and participated in the 1890 Wounded Knee Ghost Dance uprising. The regiment bravely answered the call in ensuing wars and conflicts, and continues to proudly serve its country.

The best account of the 7th Cavalry is *Of Garry Owen in Glory: The History of the 7th U.S. Cavalry,* by Melbourne C. Chandler (Annandale, VA: Turnpike, 1960). Three fascinating books flavored with amusing anecdotes written by Libbie Custer, who followed the 7th Cavalry's guidon, offer an insight into post life and personalities: *"Boots and Saddles"; or, Life in Dakota with General Custer* (New York: Harper and Brothers, 1885); *Tenting on the Plains; or, General Custer in Kansas and Texas* (New York: Harper and Brothers, 1887; and *Following the Guidon* (New York: Harper and Brothers, 1890).

For the years 1867–69, an excellent account is given by George Armstrong Custer in *My Life on the Plains; or, Personal Experiences with Indians* (Norman: University of Oklahoma Press, 1962). A volume that covers the Custer years in detail is *Custer's 7th Cavalry: From Fort Riley to the Little Bighorn,* by E. Lisle Reedstrom (New York: Sterling Publishing, 1992). The 7th Cavalry is also well represented in Robert M. Utley's *Frontier Regulars: The United States Army and the Indian, 1866–1891* (New York: Macmillan, 1973).

(continued on following page)

For a look at the trials and tribulations of a cavalryman, see *The Troopers: An Informal History of the Plains Cavalry,* by S. E. Whitman (New York: Hastings House, 1962); and *Forty Miles a Day on Beans and Hay: The Enlisted Soldier Fighting the Indian Wars,* by Don Rickey (Norman: University of Oklahoma Press, 1966). A description of the weapons, dress, equipment, horses, and flags of the 7th Cavalry in 1876 can be found in *Boots & Saddles at the Little Bighorn,* by James S. Hutchins (Ft. Collins, CO: Old Army Press, 1976).

Biographical sketches of 7th Cavalry members include *They Rode with Custer: A Biographical Directory of the Men That Rode with General George A. Custer,* edited by John M. Carroll (Bryan, TX: J. M. Carroll, 1987). A revised edition of the above is *Men with Custer: Biographies of the 7th Cavalry,* by Ronald H. Nichols (Hardin, MT: Custer Battlefield Historical & Museum Association, 2000).

🦌 Military Forts on the Central and Southern Plains

Most frontier military posts failed to live up to the imaginations of modern-day television and screen writers, who never let go of that image of the wooden picket stockade of Colonial times. Great Plains forts were essentially a group of buildings constructed by the troops utilizing available local materials—timber, logs, stone, or adobe—and laid out in a quadrangle around a parade ground. The crude forts, the appearance of which resembled a small village more than a military installation, were intended to be in service for only a short duration. The Indians held out longer than expected, however, and living conditions deteriorated as the years passed. It was well into the 1880s before adequate accommodations were provided for the troops, who only partially in jest would remark that they could find better conditions in a military prison or national cemetery.

📖 General-interest sources on the forts include *Forts of the West: Military Forts and Presidios and Posts Commonly Called Forts West of the Mississippi to 1898,* by Robert W. Frazer (Norman: University of Oklahoma Press, 1965); *A Guide to the Military Posts of the United States, 1789–1895,* by Francis Paul Prucha (Madison: State Historical Society of Wisconsin, 1964); *Outline Descriptions of the Posts in the Military Division of the Missouri,* by Philip H. Sheridan, facsimile edition (Fort Collins, CO: Old Army Press, 1972); "The Army Fort of the Frontier," by Raymond L. Welty, *North Dakota Historical Quarterly* 2 (April 1928); and "The Military Fort as a Factor in the Frontier Defense of Kansas, 1865–69," by Marvin H. Garfield, *Kansas Historical Quarterly* 1 (November 1931).

ations in Kentucky and Tennessee. Kidder participated in skirmishes at Paris, Tennessee, and Fort Henry, but for the most part, his unit was assigned duty scouting and protecting telegraph lines.

On May 18, 1863, Kidder was appointed first lieutenant in the 1st Regiment of the Minnesota Mounted Rangers, which had been organized to protect against the hostile Sioux Indians. In July, he distinguished himself at the battle of Big Mound by leading a charge that routed Indians that were attempting to steal livestock, and he later participated in battles at Buffalo Lake and Stony Mound. He returned to Fort Abercrombie in September and joined a treaty expedition to the Chippewa. Kidder was discharged from the Minnesota Rangers at Fort Snelling on November 28, 1863.

"No historian will ever chronicle the heroism which was probably here displayed because no one is left to tell the tale, but from the evidence and circumstances before us we can imagine what determination, what bravery, what heroism must have inspired this devoted little band of martyrs, when, surrounded and assailed by a vastly overwhelming force of blood-thirsty barbarians, they manfully struggled to the last, equally devoid of hope or fear. Believe me Sir, although a stranger to you, and unknown to your son, I deeply sympathize with you and yours in this most sad and lamentable bereavement."

—From an August 1867 letter to Judge J. P. Kidder, the father of 2nd Lt. Lyman S. Kidder

Following nine months working as a civilian clerk, Kidder enlisted on August 26, 1864, as a private in Company E of Maj. Edwin A. C. Hatch's Independent Cavalry Battalion, which had been organized to assist Maj. Gen. John Pope's frontier Indian-fighting army. Within a week, Kidder was

(continued on following page)

promoted to first sergeant, but he saw no action other than that found on occasional patrols and garrison duty until his discharge in May 1866. Kidder returned to the family home, which was now in Vermillion, South Dakota, where his father served as an associate justice of the Supreme Court of Dakota Territory and worked as a printer.

Almost immediately, Kidder attempted—with the assistance of his father's political influence—to be appointed a first lieutenant in one of the newly organized cavalry regiments. Finally, on February 8, 1867, he was appointed second lieutenant in the 2nd U.S. Cavalry, and he reported on June 16 to Fort Sedgwick.

On June 29, he received the following orders:

> Proceed at once with an escort of ten (10) men of Company 'M' 2nd U.S. Cavalry to the forks of the Republican River, where you will deliver to General Custar [sic] the dispatches with which you will be

(continued on following page)

CAMP SUPPLY, INDIAN TERRITORY

Camp Supply was a stockaded supply depot established in November 1868 by Capt. John H. Page, 3rd U.S. Infantry, under orders from Lt. Col. Alfred Sully, to support Sheridan's winter campaign of 1868–69. It was located where Wolf and Beaver Creeks join to form the North Canadian River. Custer marched from Camp Supply to attack Black Kettle's village on the Washita and celebrated his victory there upon returning. Although it was never intended as a permanent installation, Camp Supply was used to supervise the Cheyenne-Arapaho Reservation, created under the Medicine Lodge Treaties, and to garrison troops that participated in the Red River War of 1874–75. It was designated a fort in 1878 and finally abandoned in 1895. The Western State Hospital for the mentally ill was built on the site.

📖 *Fort Supply Indian Territory: Frontier Outpost on the Plains,* by Robert C. Carriker (Norman: University of Oklahoma Press, 1970).

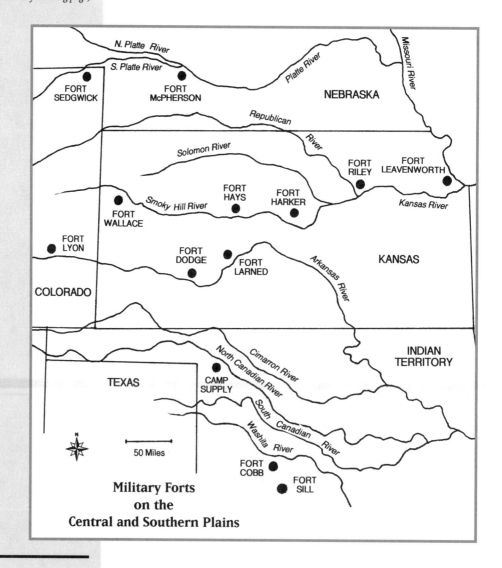

Military Forts on the Central and Southern Plains

FORT COBB, INDIAN TERRITORY

Fort Cobb was named for nearby Cobb Creek, which empties into the Washita River. This adobe fort was initially established in 1859 by Maj. William H. Emory, 1st U.S. Infantry, to garrison troops contending with Comanche and Kiowa raiding parties, but it became more of an agency providing rations and supplies to the nearby Indian reservations, as mandated by the Medicine Lodge Treaties. Fort Cobb, also named after Secretary of the Treasury Howell Cobb of Georgia, served as Phil Sheridan's base for much of the winter campaign of 1868–69. It was here that Black Kettle came prior to the Washita battle and convinced Col. William Hazen that his tribe was peaceful. Custer's subsequent crushing defeat of Black Kettle's Cheyenne encouraged other tribes to seek sanctuary at Fort Cobb. Upon completion of Fort Sill in 1869, most Indians were moved from Fort Cobb to that location on Medicine Bluff Creek.

📖 "A History of Fort Cobb," by Muriel H. Wright, *Chronicles of Oklahoma* 34 (Spring 1956).

FORT DODGE, KANSAS

Fort Dodge, located on the north bank of the Arkansas River, was established in April 1865 by Capt. Henry Pierce, 11th Kansas Cavalry, with orders from Maj. Gen. Grenville Dodge, who had selected the site as his camp while chasing both Indians and guerrillas toward the end of the Civil War. The fort was intended to protect travelers on the Santa Fe Trail, which forded the river twenty-five miles to the west at Cimarron Crossing. It was named by General Dodge—later chief engineer of the Union Pacific Railroad and a U.S. congressman from Iowa—either for himself or for Col. Henry Dodge, 1st U.S. Dragoons.

General Hancock delivered one of his war-or-peace ultimatums to Plains chiefs at Fort Dodge during his expedition of 1867. The following year, Custer assembled his troops at the fort to train in preparation for Sheridan's winter campaign. In 1874, Col. Nelson A. Miles marched southwest from Fort Dodge to commence his operations in the Red River War of 1874–75. The post was abandoned in 1882 as the town of Dodge City grew up nearby. Buildings that remained are part of the state soldiers' home.

FORT HARKER, KANSAS

Fort Harker was established in 1864 by 2nd Lt. Allen Ellsworth, under orders from Maj. Gen. Samuel R. Curtis, on the north bank of the Smoky Hill River about three miles east of present-day Ellsworth. It was intended to protect travelers on the Santa Fe Trail. Originally named Fort Ellsworth, it was moved one mile east in 1867 and renamed in honor of Brig. Gen.

entrusted; should General Custar have left that point you will take his trail and overtake him! After delivering your dispatches return to this post. Until you reach General Custar you will travel as rapidly as possible.

Kidder's presence on the open plains was discovered on July 2 about a half mile north of Beaver Creek by Sioux Indians led by Pawnee Killer. In a running battle, Kidder and his men were all killed and brutally mutilated. On July 12, Custer scout Will Comstock, riding ahead of the main column, found the bodies. A burial detail was formed, and graves were dug.

Kidder's father was determined to remove his son's remains for proper burial. In early March 1868, he accompanied an expedition led by 1st Lt. Frederick H. Beecher, which successfully recovered the bodies. Kidder was buried on March 19, 1868, in Oakland Cemetery in St. Paul.

A monument has been erected about twenty miles north of Goodland, Kansas, where State Route 28 crosses Beaver Creek, the site of what has become known as the Kidder massacre.

📖 The best source about Kidder and the massacre is *A Dispatch to Custer: The Tragedy of Lieutenant Kidder* (previously self-published under the title *Find Custer! The Kidder Tragedy*), by Randy Johnson and Nancy Allan (Missoula, MT: Mountain Press, 1999). This volume contains some very interesting correspondence written by those involved—including George Armstrong Custer—as well as excellent photos and maps. Custer's narrative of events is given in *My Life on the Plains; or, Personal Experiences with Indians* (Norman: University of Oklahoma Press, 1962).

See also "The Kidder Massacre," by E. A. Brininstool, *Hunter-Trader-Trapper* (December 1932); "Custer and the Kidder Massacre," by Lawrence A. Frost, *Westerner* (September 1970); "The Kidder Massacre: The Tragedy on Beaver Creek, Kansas, in 1867, as Told in Contemporary News Dispatches," compiled by Lawrence A Frost, *Chicago Westerners Brand Book* 19 (August 1962); and "Lieut. Lyman S. Kidder and the Tragedy on Beaver Creek," by Doane Robinson, *Monthly South Dakotan* 4 (November 1901).

✺ Little Raven
Southern Arapaho

Little Raven (Hosa) was born to a chief somewhere between 1810 and 1820 along the Platte River in Nebraska. At some point, he married a Kiowa-Apache woman, and in 1840, he acted as an intermediary for his people at a gathering near Bent's Fort when the Arapaho, Southern Cheyenne,

(continued on following page)

Kiowa, Comanche, and Kiowa-Apache tribes agreed to a peace treaty among themselves. Little Raven was known as an aggressive warrior in his youth, and when his father died in 1855, he became principal chief of his tribe. It was said that by 1859, he had seven wives and many children.

In 1861, he signed the Treaty of Fort Wise, but he participated in a number of raids when whites ventured onto tribal lands and refused to visit Washington with a delegation of chiefs in 1863. Little Raven joined Black Kettle's Cheyenne at Sand Creek in the fall of 1864 but did not trust the word of Colorado territorial governor John Evans and departed just before Chivington's massacre (see "The Sand Creek Massacre" on page 104). He signed the Little Arkansas Treaty of 1865 and the Medicine Lodge Treaty of 1867, but instead of settling on the reservation, he set up camp in the Wichita Mountains.

In January 1869, George Armstrong Custer and a detachment of sharpshooters located Little Raven's sixty-five lodges and persuaded him to submit to the reservation. He toured the east in 1871 and became known for his oratorical abilities. Little Raven, by then a proponent of peace at all costs, managed to keep most of his warriors from fighting in the Red River War of 1874–75. He died in the winter of 1889 at Cantonment, Oklahoma, and was succeeded as principal chief by Left Hand.

   See *The Arapahoes, Our People,* by Virginia Cole Trenholm (Norman: University of Oklahoma Press, 1973); and *Chief Left Hand: Southern Arapaho,* by Margaret Coel (Norman: University of Oklahoma Press, 1981).

✴ Pawnee Killer
Oglala Sioux

Pawnee Killer, whose date and place of birth are unknown, received his name due to his courageous exploits against the Pawnee, who were traditional enemies of the Sioux. This war leader, who was never a chief, migrated south into the Platte River Valley of Colorado and Nebraska during the 1850s and allied his band with the Cheyenne and Arapaho. Angry over the Sand Creek massacre, he participated in the attack on Julesburg, Colorado, on January 7, 1865. Pawnee Killer then moved north and was involved in the December 1866 Fetterman massacre, which was part of Red Cloud's War (see "Red Cloud's War" on page 68).

In 1867, Pawnee Killer became a thorn in the side of George Armstrong Custer by outmaneuvering the cavalrymen during the Hancock expedition—striking when opportunity arose and talking when it served his purpose. He and his band were

(continued on following page)

Charles G. Harker, who had been killed in the June 1864 battle of Kennasaw Mountain. The post protected the Smoky Hill Trail and workers on the Kansas Pacific Railroad, and it was the base of operations for the Hancock expedition of 1867. Famed correspondent Henry M. Stanley provided an apt description of the fort when he wrote that it looked "like a great wart on the surface of the plain." Fort Harker was abandoned in April 1872 upon completion of the railroad to Denver.

   "Memories of Old Fort Harker," by Mrs. Henry Inman, *True West Magazine* 11, no. 4 (March–April 1964).

FORT HAYS, KANSAS

Fort Hays, originally named Fort Fletcher in honor of Missouri governor Thomas Fletcher, was initially established in October 1865 near the mouth of Big Creek in central Kansas. After a June 1867 flood, it was moved to a site selected by Maj. Alfred Gibbs seventeen miles upstream near a railroad crossing. Renamed in honor of Brig. Gen. Alexander Hays, who was killed in the May 1864 battle of the Wilderness, the post saw considerable action during 1867 to 1870, while providing protection for workers on the Kansas Pacific Railroad. The Custers were occasional residents and enjoyed spending the summers camping at nearby Big Creek, where they hunted, fished, and picnicked. Fort Hays was garrisoned until 1889, when it was leveled and the land turned into a golf course. The surviving buildings—mainly a blockhouse and guardhouse—have been preserved in a state park, with part of the site presently the campus of Fort Hays State College.

   The flood and other reminiscences about the Custers' tenure at Fort Hays can be found in Libbie Custer's *Tenting on the Plains; or, General Custer in Kansas and Texas* (New York: Harper and Brothers, 1887). See also "Old Fort Hays," by James H. Beach, *Kansas Historical Collections* 11 (1909–10).

FORT LARNED, KANSAS

Fort Larned, initially known as Camp on Pawnee Fork and later Camp Alert, was established in October 1859 at the confluence of Pawnee Creek and the Arkansas River for the purpose of protecting travelers on the Santa Fe Trail. In May 1860, it was renamed in honor of Gen. Benjamin F. Larned, the paymaster of the army. The following year, Fort Larned became an Indian agency and distribution point for Cheyenne and Arapaho annuities, and it remained in that capacity until 1868. During the Hancock expedition of 1867, it was the first location where General Hancock met with Sioux and Cheyenne chiefs—and from where he subsequently marched to destroy their village on the Pawnee Fork. The fort was abandoned in July 1878 and passed through private ownership to the National Park Service as a national historic site.

📖 "The Story of Fort Larned," by William E. Unrau, *Kansas Historical Quarterly* 23, no. 3 (August 1957).

FORT LEAVENWORTH, KANSAS

Fort Leavenworth, the keystone of the western military fort system, was established in May 1827 by Col. Henry Leavenworth, who directed its construction on the west bank of the Missouri River. Initially intended as a base to protect the Santa Fe Trail and later the Oregon Trail, Fort Leavenworth served mainly as a supply depot for the Rocky Mountain region. It was the location where Gen. Stephen W. Kearny organized his army for the Mexican War, and it also played a part in operations in Bleeding Kansas before and during the Civil War. In 1866, the fort became the headquarters for the Department of the Missouri and supported the campaigns against the Plains Indians. Fort Leavenworth was the site of Custer's court-martial in 1867, and it was where he and his wife waited out his suspension during the winter of 1867–68 in quarters loaned to them by Gen. Phil Sheridan. The fort, which remains operational, is the oldest surviving post west of the Mississippi.

📖 *Fort Leavenworth, 1827–1927,* by Elvid Hunt (Fort Leavenworth, 1926).

FORT LYON, COLORADO

Fort Lyon, which was established in August 1860 on the north bank of the Arkansas River near present-day La Junta, had been known as Bent's New Fort, Fort Fauntleroy, and Fort Wise—honoring Virginia governor Henry A. Wise—before being renamed in 1862 to honor Brig. Gen. Nathaniel Lyon, the first Union general to die in the Civil War. The Fort Wise Treaty of 1861, which provided for a Cheyenne and Arapaho reservation, was signed here. It was from this location that Col. John Chivington marched in November 1864 to attack Black Kettle's village in what became known as the Sand Creek massacre. In June 1867, because of flooding, the fort was moved twenty miles upstream to a location two miles below the mouth of the Purgatoire River. Frontiersman Kit Carson died here on May 23, 1868. Later that year, Maj. Eugene A. Carr and his 5th Cavalry were based at Fort Lyon for Sheridan's winter campaign of 1868–69. It was abandoned in October 1889 and later became a veterans hospital.

FORT MCPHERSON, NEBRASKA

Fort McPherson was established by Maj. George M. O'Brien, 7th Iowa Cavalry, in September 1863 on the south bank of the South Platte River some eight miles from its confluence with the North Platte for the purpose of protecting travelers on the Oregon Trail and work crews from the Union Pacific

at that time responsible for much of the raiding and depredations in western Kansas, including the massacre of Lt. Lyman Kidder and his ten-man detachment on Beaver Creek, but successfully eluded capture. The following year, Pawnee Killer was said to have fought in the September 1868 battle of Beecher Island (see "The Battle of Beecher Island" on page 98), and in July 1869, he survived the battle of Summit Springs, where Tall Bull was killed and Cheyenne hostilities on the Plains were for all intents and purposes ended (see "The Battle of Summit Springs" on page 101).

Apparently in an act of letting bygones be bygones, Pawnee Killer was an invited member of the entourage—along with Custer—that entertained Russian grand duke Alexis on a Nebraska buffalo hunt in January 1872 (see "The Russian Grand Duke's Buffalo Hunt" on page 107). His band eventually settled on the Red Cloud Agency in Nebraska, but apparently Pawnee Killer was not among them for long and at that time vanished from the pages of history.

📖 See *Red Cloud's Folk: A History of the Oglala Sioux Indians,* by George E. Hyde (Norman: University of Oklahoma Press, 1937); *The Southern Cheyennes,* by Donald J. Berthrong (Norman: University of Oklahoma Press, 1963; *Life of George Bent Written from His Letters,* by George E. Hyde (Norman: University of Oklahoma Press, 1968).

✸ Red Cloud
Oglala Sioux Chieftain

Red Cloud (Mahpiua Luta, Makhpiya-luta, or Makhpia-sha, meaning "Scarlet Cloud") was born about 1822 near the forks of the Platte River in north-central Nebraska. He had a twin brother named Roaring Cloud, about whom nothing is known. Red Cloud gained the reputation as a fierce warrior who time and again proved his bravery and leadership skills in battle—he counted over eighty coups and once returned from a fight against the Crows with an arrow in his body. His individual accomplishments—including participation in the 1854 Grattan massacre (see "The Initiation of Warfare between the Plains Indians and the U.S. Army" on page 49)—led to his election as chief of the Oglala band.

In the 1860s, in what became known as Red Cloud's War (see "Red Cloud's War" on page 68), Red Cloud and other Lakota bands attacked travelers along the Bozeman Trail and eventually forced the U.S. government to grant treaty demands. The Fort Laramie Treaty of 1868 (see "The Fort Laramie Treaty of 1868 and the Black Hills Expedition" on

(continued on following page)

page 158) established a Great Sioux Reservation, and Red Cloud settled on this territory reserved for his people. In 1870, he traveled with a delegation to Washington to meet with President Grant.

Custer's expedition of 1874 discovered gold deposits in the Black Hills, and miners flooded onto Indian land in violation of the treaty. Red Cloud was a member of a delegation invited to Washington in the summer of 1875 for a meeting thought to be about agency business. Instead, the U.S. government pressured the chiefs to sign over title to the Black Hills. The chiefs refused, saying they had no authority. Red Cloud returned to the reservation and continued to advocate peace. But the young warriors, led by Crazy Horse and Sitting Bull, once again waged war with the army. The soldiers prevailed, and the Black Hills became the property of the United States (see "The Lakota Sioux and the Black Hills" on page 152). During this conflict, Red Cloud was accused of aiding the hostiles and was removed as principal chief of the Indian agency bearing his name.

He moved his people to Pine Ridge Reservation in 1878. Over the years, Red Cloud had five children and at least six wives. His health slowly declined, and he became blind. Prior to his death on December 10, 1909, he was baptized into the Roman Catholic Church.

The *Autobiography of Red Cloud: War Leader of the Oglalas,* edited by Eli R. Paul (Helena: Montana Historical Society, 1998), contains Red Cloud's insightful reminiscences about his life. The manuscript, which lay dormant in the Nebraska State Historical Society for many years, was the work of journalist and Pine Ridge postmaster Charles Allen, who transcribed the first-person narrative with assistance from a French Canadian trader named Sam Deon. Another excellent volume is *Red Cloud's Folk: A History of the Oglala Sioux Indians,* by George E. Hyde (Norman: University of Oklahoma Press, 1967).

Other notable sources include: *Red Cloud: Warrior-Statesman of the Lakota Sioux,* by Robert Larsen (Norman: University of Oklahoma Press, 1997); *Red Cloud and the Sioux Problem,* by James C. Olson (Lincoln: University of Nebraska Press, 1965); *I Have Spoken: American History through the Voices of the Indians,* edited by Virginia Irving Armstrong (Chicago: Swallow Press, 1971); *Fighting Indian Chiefs,* by E. A. Brininstool (New York: Bonanza Books, 1953); *Sioux Indian Leaders,* by Mildred Fielder (Seattle: Superior Publishing, 1975); and *The Bozeman Trail,* by G. R. Hebard and E. A. Brininstool (Cleveland: Arthur H. Clark, 1922).

Railroad. The fort underwent several name changes—Cantonment McKean, Post of Cottonwood, and Fort Cottonwood—until January 1866, when it was named in honor of Brig. Gen. James B. McPherson, who had been killed in the Civil War. During the Hancock expedition of 1867, Custer met with Gen. William Sherman at this fort to discuss strategy. Maj. Eugene A. Carr and his 5th Cavalry marched from the fort on the 1869 Republican River expedition, which resulted in the battle of Summit Springs. The fort played host to Grand Duke Alexis of Russia during his 1872 buffalo hunt on Red Willow Creek, some sixty miles away. In 1873, the burial ground at Fort McPherson was declared a national cemetery, and it remains such. The post, however, was abandoned in 1880.

📖 *Fort McPherson,* by Louis A. Holmes (Lincoln: University of Nebraska Press, 1963).

FORT RILEY, KANSAS

Fort Riley was established in May 1853 by Capt. Charles S. Lovell, 6th U.S. Infantry, under orders from Col. Thomas T. Fauntleroy, 1st U.S. Dragoons, on a high plateau on the north bank of the Kansas River at the junction of the Republican and Smoky Hill Rivers. It was originally named Camp Center for its geographic location near the center of the United States, but it was renamed soon after construction began to honor Col. (Bvt. Maj. Gen.) Bennett Riley, who had recently died. The purpose of the fort was to protect the Oregon and Smoky Hill Trails, and it played a vital role in this endeavor throughout the Plains Indian wars. It was the post where, in September 1866, the twelve companies of the 7th Cavalry were formed and commenced training for frontier duty. Custer, accompanied by his wife, reported for duty on the evening of November 3, 1866. Through the years, Fort Riley remained an important training center and housed the Cavalry School until 1946. The post is presently operational.

📖 *The History of Fort Riley,* by W. F. Pride (Fort Riley, 1926); "History of Old Army Posts—Fort Riley," by Donald A. Young, *Recruiting News,* March 1, 1923. See also Elizabeth B. Custer's *Tenting on the Plains; or, General Custer in Kansas and Texas* (New York: Harper and Brothers, 1887).

FORT SEDGWICK, COLORADO

Located on the South Platte River a mile east of Lodgepole Creek near present-day Julesburg, Fort Sedgwick was established in May 1864 by Col. Christopher H. McNally, 3rd U.S. Volunteer Infantry, under orders from district commander Brig. Gen. Robert B. Mitchell. It was named in honor of Maj. Gen. John Sedgwick, who had been killed while superintending the placement of artillery in preparation for the May 1864 battle of Spotsylvania. The purpose of the fort was to protect travelers on the Platte Road (the old Oregon-California Trail) as well as work crews from the Union Pacific Railroad. In July 1869, Maj. Eugene A. Carr marched to Fort Sedgwick following his decisive defeat of Tall Bull's Cheyenne at Summit Springs. The post was abandoned in May 1871.

📖 "Old Julesburg and Fort Sedgwick," by Mrs. C. F. Parker, *Colorado Magazine* 7 (July 1930).

FORT SILL, INDIAN TERRITORY

Gen. Phil Sheridan established Fort Sill in January 1869 at the confluence of Cache and Medicine Bluff Creeks at the eastern edge of the Wichita Mountains. The site was chosen by Col. Benjamin H. Grierson, whose 10th Cavalry—Buffalo Soldiers (see "Buffalo Soldiers" on page 99)—constructed the fort. The first encampment was known as Camp Wichita, but officers of the 7th Cavalry argued in favor of naming it Fort Elliott in memory of Maj. Joel Elliott, who had been killed the previous November during the Washita battle. Sheridan, however, chose to honor his former West Point classmate Brig. Gen. Joshua Sill, who had been killed while leading one of Sheridan's brigades at the December 1862 battle of Stone River. Agency Indians, including the Kiowa bands of Satanta, Lone Wolf, and Kicking Bird, were soon moved from Fort Cobb to reservations near Fort Sill and remained under the supervision of Col. William B. Hazen. This was one of the posts at which Secretary Belknap and his wife were accused of selling tradership rights in the 1876 scandal. Due to the number of interments of reservation residents, the cemetery at Fort Sill has been called "the Indian Arlington." The fort is presently operational.

📖 *Carbine and Lance: The Story of Old Fort Sill*, by W. S. Nye (Norman: University of Oklahoma Press, 1969).

FORT WALLACE, KANSAS

Fort Wallace, the westernmost post in Kansas, was established in 1865 and named in honor of Brig. Gen. William H. L. Wallace, who was killed at the April 1862 battle of Shiloh. The fort was located at the junction of Pond Creek and the South Fork of the Smoky Hill River. Its purpose was to protect stagecoaches, wagon trains, settlers, railroad surveyors, and work crews in the vicinity of the Smoky Hill Road. Conditions at Fort Wallace were nothing less than horrendous—no flowing water and rations of such poor quality that scurvy was commonplace—a situation made worse due to the lack of a telegraph line and the responsibility of covering a large territory with an inadequate number of troops. During the late 1860s, Fort Wallace was under constant siege by Cheyenne and Sioux warriors. The fort, under the command of Capt. Myles Keogh

✸ Roman Nose
Southern Cheyenne

Roman Nose (Woquini, Waquini, or Wokini, meaning "Hook Nose"), was born about 1830. He became a member of the Crooked Lance Society, a leading Dog Soldier Society. It is unknown whether he was ever a chief of his tribe, but he became so prominent as a warrior that he was accused of nearly every raid along the Bozeman Trail and on the southern plains in the 1860s. He became known for his famous warbonnet with eagle feathers and a single horn, made for him by White Buffalo Bull, which he always wore into battle. Roman Nose attended a council at Fort Harker in August 1866 to protest the construction of the Union Pacific Railroad and led numerous raids against survey and work crews.

Roman Nose agreed to meet with General Hancock at Fort Larned in the spring of 1867 and came away convinced that Hancock wanted war. Unknown to Hancock, Roman Nose had planned to kill him at that meeting but was dissuaded by others. He resumed his militancy by attacking wagon trains and railroad work parties, remaining one step ahead of Custer's 7th Cavalry during that summer's Hancock expedition. Roman Nose attended preliminary talks leading to the Medicine Lodge Treaty of 1867 but refused to participate in the council or sign the treaty.

On September 17, 1868, Roman Nose's Cheyenne joined Tall Bull's band and Pawnee Killer's Sioux to trap fifty-one soldiers under Maj. George Forsyth on a tiny island on the Arikaree Fork of the Republican River, which became known as the battle of Beecher Island. Roman Nose fully expected to die that day. He believed that the "medicine" had been removed from his warbonnet—an ornament that was so long it nearly touched the ground. On the previous night, either a woman had touched his warbonnet or he had eaten with metal utensils, both of which were considered taboo and meant death, and there had been no time for a purification ceremony. That afternoon, Roman Nose was shot through the spine; he died that evening (see "The Battle of Beecher Island" on page 98).

📖 See *Indian Fights and Fighters,* by Cyrus T. Brady (Lincoln: University of Nebraska Press, 1971); *The Southern Cheyennes,* by Donald J. Berthrong (Norman: University of Oklahoma Press, 1963); *The Fighting Cheyennes,* by George B. Grinnell (Norman: University of Oklahoma Press, 1956); and *Life of George Bent Written from His Letters,* by George E. Hyde (Norman: University of Oklahoma Press, 1968).

✸ Satanta
Kiowa

Satanta (Set-tainte, meaning "White Bear Person") was born on the northern plains about 1830. Gua-ton-bain or "Big Ribs," as he was known as a boy, rose in stature as a warrior while raiding in Texas, Mexico, and along the Santa Fe Trail during the Civil War—including the famous November 1865 battle of Adobe Walls. Nonetheless, he signed the treaty of the Little Arkansas in 1865.

By the 1860s, Satanta, so famed for his eloquence that he became known as the "Orator of the Plains," had established himself as a leader of the war faction within his tribe. When a new chief was to be chosen, he represented the warriors in opposition to Kicking Bird, who led the peace faction. In a compromise, Lone Wolf became principal chief, and Satanta resumed his raiding.

He agreed to meet with General Hancock in the spring of 1867. Hancock was so impressed with Satanta's declaration of peace that he presented the Kiowa warrior with a major general's dress uniform. Satanta later wore the uniform when his band raided the horse herd at Fort Dodge. Satanta signed the Medicine Lodge Treaty of 1867 but refused to submit to the designated reservation.

Satanta was camped downstream from Black Kettle's village when Custer attacked on November 27, 1868. Later, the dead bodies of Clara Blinn and her son were discovered in his abandoned village (see "Indian Captives Clara Blinn and Her Son" on page 84). Sheridan and Custer tracked down Satanta, who had secured a document from Col. William Hazen that proclaimed him a peaceful Indian. Nevertheless, Sheridan seized Satanta and Lone Wolf, and threatened to hang them unless their people moved onto the reservation. The chiefs were saved when their people finally straggled to Fort Cobb.

In May 1871, Satanta was convicted of murder for his part in the massacre of seven people in a wagon train belonging to a government contractor in Texas. He and his cohort Big Tree were sentenced to be hanged, but this punishment was commuted to life in prison. In October 1873, in spite of public outcry, Gov. Edmund Davis paroled Big Tree and Satanta.

Satanta fought in the Red River War of 1874–75 and was once again captured and sent to prison in Huntsville, Texas. He committed suicide on March 11, 1878, by jumping out of a second-story window in the prison hospital. His remains were removed from Texas in 1963 and reinterred at Fort Sill, Oklahoma.

(continued on following page)

and Company I, 7th Cavalry, played a major role in the Hancock expedition of 1867. The following year, Maj. George A. Forsyth marched from Fort Wallace on an expedition that led to the battle of Beecher Island. The post was abandoned in May 1882.

📖 "Fort Wallace and Its Relation to the Frontier," by Mrs. Frank C. Montgomery, *Collections of the Kansas State Historical Society* 17 (1928).

🐎 The Kansas Pacific Railway

Construction of a transcontinental railroad had become a national obsession that had unified the post–Civil War country with a purpose. The Union Pacific and Central Pacific were rushing to rendezvous from the West and East respectively when, in 1865, a young railroad entrepreneur named William Jackson Palmer convinced investors that they could turn worthless land into expensive real estate by building a separate railroad line from Kansas City through the Great Plains to California.

Palmer, the future founder of Colorado Springs and better known for his Denver and Rio Grande Railroad, had traveled to Europe at age nineteen to study how coal burned in locomotives, then worked as secretary to the president of the Pennsylvania Railroad. He had commanded one of Phil Sheridan's brigades in the Civil War, for which he achieved the rank of brigadier general and later received the Medal of Honor. With such credentials, Palmer had little trouble raising the necessary cash for his new railroad.

By the spring of 1866, the line—known as the Union Pacific Railway Company, Eastern Division—stretched for about 115 miles from Kansas City to Manhattan, but its progress had been delayed by frequent attacks from marauding Plains Indians, with an estimated 6,000 warriors.

The army had been given the responsibility of protecting surveyors and work crews from these hostiles. This task was heartily embraced by General Sheridan, whose responsibility as commander of the Department of the Missouri included Palmer's railroad, which traced the route of the Smoky Hill Road. This area was guarded by about 1,400 infantry troops and 1,200 cavalrymen—including the newly formed 7th Cavalry, which had companies garrisoned for that purpose along the Smoky Hill Road at Forts Harker, Hays, and Wallace.

The Hancock expedition of 1867 had been formed to punish and discourage those Indians that had been harassing railroad workers, but with the failure of the campaign, work on the railroad came to a grinding halt. In order to better oversee military operations, Sheridan moved his headquarters in the summer of 1868 from Fort Leavenworth to Fort Hays, which was at that time the railhead of the Kansas railroad.

By making protection of the railroad the number-one priority, the army's efforts soon permitted workers to lay tracks in relative safety. In March, the railroad officially became known as the Kansas Pacific Railway. By the summer of 1869, the Kansas Pacific had steadily progressed toward its destination, which was now the city of Denver. George Armstrong Custer, in recognition of his service to the Kansas Pacific, was one of the dignitaries aboard when the first train pulled into the Mile High City in September 1870.

The Kansas Pacific began advertising that passengers could actually shoot buffalo while the train moved along the tracks, and the thousands of carcasses that littered the nearby landscape attested to that fact. The train brought many dignitaries, such as congressmen, wealthy businessmen, and even P. T. Barnum, to Fort Hays, each desiring to say they hunted buffalo with the famous General Custer before that beast became extinct. In January 1872, while heading east toward St. Louis aboard the Kansas Pacific, Russian grand duke Alexis, accompanied by Custer and Sheridan, climbed atop the baggage car and claimed six buffalo kills from the train, which was moving at about twenty miles per hour.

The Kansas Pacific Railway eventually built tracks connecting Denver with the Union Pacific at Cheyenne, Wyoming.

📖 Custer described his inaugural excursion to Denver in the October 7, 1870, edition of *Turf, Field and Farm,* which has been reprinted in *Nomad: George A. Custer in Turf, Field and Farm,* edited by Brian W. Dippie (Austin: University of Texas Press, 1980).

General sources include "When the Union and Kansas Pacific Built through Kansas," by Joseph W. Snell and Robert W. Richmond, *Kansas Historical Quarterly* 32 (Summer and Autumn 1966); *The Story of the Western Railroads: From 1852 through the Reign of the Giants,* by Robert Edgar Riegel (Lincoln: University of Nebraska Press, 1964); *New Tracks in North America,* by William A. Bell (London: Chapman and Hall, 1869); and *Trails, Rails and War,* by J. R. Perkins (Indianapolis, Bobbs-Merrill, 1929).

Two notable works about railroad and land speculator William Jackson Palmer are *Rebel of the Rockies: A History of the Denver and Rio Grande Western Railroad,* by Robert G. Ahearn (New Haven, CT: Yale University Press, 1962); and *A Builder of the West,* by John S. Fisher (Caldwell, ID: Caxton Printers, 1939).

🐎 Custer's Mad Dash across Kansas

The Hancock expedition had basically fizzled to an end when Custer and his weary troops went into camp near Fort Wallace in July. Custer's controversial decision to immediately

📖 See *Satanta and the Kiowas,* by F. Stanley (Borger, TX: Jim Hess Printers, 1968); *Satanta,* by C. M. Robinson III (Austin, TX: State House Press, 1998); *Bad Medicine and Good: Tales of the Kiowas,* by Wilbur S. Nye (Norman: University of Oklahoma Press, 1962); *Plains Indian Raiders: The Final Phases of Warfare from the Arkansas to the Red River,* by Wilbur S. Nye (Norman: University of Oklahoma Press, 1968); and *The Kiowas,* by Mildred P. Marshall (Norman: University of Oklahoma Press, 1962).

⚙ William Tecumseh "Cump" Sherman
General, U.S. Army

Sherman, who was named in part after Shawnee Indian leader Tecumseh, was born on February 8, 1820, in Lancaster, Ohio. He was one of eleven children, and his younger brother John later served in Congress, was secretary of treasury and state (known for the Sherman Anti-Trust Act), and ran unsuccessfully for president on three occasions. His father, a jurist and lawyer, died suddenly in 1829, and Sherman was raised in the family of Thomas Ewing, a U.S. senator and cabinet member. Through the efforts of his foster father, he received an appointment to the U.S. Military Academy at West Point in 1836. He graduated four years later, ranked sixth in a class of forty-two.

Sherman served briefly in the Second Seminole War and was promoted to first lieutenant in 1842. He participated in the Mexican War of 1846–48 as an aide-de-camp and saw little action. Following that war, Sherman was made adjutant general of the newly created Pacific division in San Francisco. In 1850, he married Ellen Ewing, the daughter of his foster parents, in Washington, D.C.

In 1853, Sherman resigned his commission as captain and returned to San Francisco, where he worked for a St. Louis–based banking firm. Although his efforts at managing the bank's money during the 1857 financial crisis were admirable, the bank failed. At that time, Sherman moved to Fort Leavenworth, Kansas, and opened a law and real estate office. In 1859, he became superintendent of the Louisiana State Seminary of Learning and Military Academy near Alexandria, which later became Louisiana State University. In 1861, when Louisiana seceded from the Union, Sherman declined an invitation to join the Confederate army and instead accepted the presidency of a St. Louis streetcar company. In May 1861, he rejoined the Union army as colonel in the newly organized 13th Infantry.

(continued on following page)

Sherman greatly distinguished himself during the Civil War, initially serving as U. S. Grant's lieutenant at Shiloh, Vicksburg, and Chattanooga. After Grant was summoned east, Major General Sherman was appointed supreme commander of the western armies. In 1864, he launched his Atlanta campaign and March to the Sea, which proved decisive in defeating the Confederacy. By war's end, Sherman had twice received the prestigious Thanks of Congress and was regarded as a national hero.

Sherman's postwar assignment was as commander of the Division of the Missouri, with headquarters in St. Louis, which made him responsible for military assistance in the construction of the transcontinental railroad and campaigns of the Great Plains against hostile Indians. At that time, he, along with Gen. Philip Sheridan, implemented a policy against the Plains Indian tribes known as "Total War," which both men had applied with great success during the Civil War (see "Total War" on page 83). Sherman's policy in dealing with hostile Indians perhaps was best summed up in an October 15, 1868, message to Sheridan:

As brave men and as soldiers of a government which has exhausted its peace efforts, we, in performance of a most unpleasant duty, accept the war begun by our enemies, and hereby resolve to make its end final. If it results in the utter annihilation of these Indians it is but the result of what they have been warned again and again, and for which they seem fully prepared. I will say nothing and do nothing to restrain our troops from doing what they deem proper on the spot, and will allow no mere vague general charges of cruelty and inhumanity to tie their hands, but will use all the powers confided to me to the end that these Indians, the enemies of our race and of our civilization, shall not again be able to begin and carry on their barbarous warfare on any kind of a pretext that they may choose to allege.... You may now go ahead in your own way and I will back you with my whole authority, and stand between you and any efforts that may be attempted in your rear to restrain your purpose or check your troops.

When Grant was inaugurated president on March 4, 1869, Sherman was promoted to four-star general-in-chief of the army, relinquishing his plains command to Sheridan and moving to Washington. Sherman retired in 1883, turned down the opportunity to run for president, and died in New York on February 14, 1891.

📖 The best source for Sherman's influence on the frontier is *William Tecumseh Sherman and the*

(continued on following page)

head east to Fort Hays—a distance of over 150 miles—then 60 more miles to Fort Harker, where he expected to find his wife, has been the subject of much conjecture over the years.

The facts show that Custer ordered his six company commanders to each provide him with a dozen men with good mounts. On the evening of July 15, after assigning Maj. Joel Elliott the command, Custer, accompanied by seventy-two troopers, three officers—Hamilton, Tom Custer, and Cooke—and *Harper's Weekly* illustrator Theodore Davis, rode out on the Smoky Hill Road heading east.

Along the way, the detail met a wagon train containing forage, commanded by Capt. Frederick Benteen, which unknowingly carried cholera germs that would infect Fort Wallace. Later, two mail stages were stopped by Custer in a futile effort to find a letter from Libbie.

Just east of Downer's Station, a trooper disappeared, and Custer ordered Sgt. James Connelly and six men to chase after this deserter. The missing man was captured, but the party was attacked by Indians on the way back, suffering one man killed and another wounded; the rest took refuge at the station. Connelly reported the incident to Custer, who—even at the urging of Captain Hamilton—refused to delay his march to rescue the beleaguered men, who were only about three miles away. An infantry detail later found the victims, and the wounded man survived.

Custer and the exhausted cavalrymen arrived at Fort Hays on the morning of July 18. Custer, his brother Tom, Cooke, and Davis immediately departed Fort Hays with four government mules and an army ambulance, and proceeded sixty miles to Fort Harker, where Custer expected to find his wife. They arrived at 2 A.M. on July 19, but Libbie had returned to Fort Riley. After informing Col. A. J. Smith of his presence, Custer boarded a train headed to Fort Riley. The next morning, Smith sent a telegram to Custer ordering him back to Harker and had him placed under arrest for deserting his post at Fort Wallace.

Exactly why did Custer act like a man possessed—surely aware that he risked a court-martial? His defense, which was presented at his court-martial and documented in his book *My Life on the Plains; or, Personal Experiences with Indians* (Norman: University of Oklahoma Press, 1962), and also repeated in *The Court-Martial of General George Armstrong Custer,* by Lawrence A. Frost (Norman: University of Oklahoma Press, 1968), offers questionable reasons: He was seeking new orders, securing supplies at Fort Harker (although Fort Wallace was well stocked), and obtaining medical supplies to treat cholera victims (the cholera epidemic had not as yet reached Fort Wallace).

Stories have circulated that Custer embarked upon his mad dash in a fit of jealous rage after hearing that his wife and Lt.

Thomas Weir were becoming an item. This theory may have been more credible had it not been brought to light by Capt. Frederick Benteen, the notorious Custer critic, and to a lesser degree Lt. Edward Mathey many years later. No verifiable supporting evidence exists to indicate that Libbie engaged in anything more than a flirtatious passing interest in Weir—a common event on frontier posts.

The answer for Custer's actions, however, may lie in the words of his wife. Libbie later wrote of her husband's surprise visit to Fort Riley: "There was in the summer of 1867 one long, perfect day. It was mine, and—blessed be the memory, which preserves to us the joys as well as the sadness of life!—it is still mine, for time and eternity." She also wrote about the incident to her cousin when explaining the reasons for the court-martial: "He took a leave himself, knowing none would be granted him. When he ran the risk of a court-martial in leaving Wallace he did it expecting the consequences . . . and we are quite determined not to live apart again."

Why did Custer make his mad dash across Kansas? Only he knows for certain. But it would not be too far-fetched, not too much of a romantic notion, given the evidence and the character of the man, to consider that Custer jeopardized his career simply because he desperately desired to see the woman he loved.

📖 The best version of Custer's dash across Kansas can be found in "The West Breaks in General Custer," by Minnie Dubbs Millbrook, *Kansas Historical Quarterly* 36 (Summer 1970), which has been reprinted in *The Custer Reader,* edited by Paul Hutton (Lincoln: University of Nebraska Press, 1992). *The Custer Story: The Life and Letters of General George A. Custer and His Wife Elizabeth,* by Marguerite Merington (New York: Devin-Adair Co., 1950) contains Libbie's letter and other interesting observations. Also see Libbie's *Tenting on the Plains; or, General Custer in Kansas and Texas* (New York: Harper and Brothers, 1887), as well as the Frost and Custer works mentioned above. Benteen's theory is related in John M. Carroll's *Custer: From the Civil War to the Big Horn* (Bryan, TX: John M. Carroll, 1981); Mathey's account was told in an interview with Walter M. Camp, October 19, 1910, CP, box 6, folder 5, Harold B. Lee Library.

🦌 The Medicine Lodge Treaties

While Red Cloud and the Lakota Sioux remained defiant toward the U.S. government, Southern Plains tribes were willing to discuss peace treaties.

In late October 1867, more than 5,000 members of the Kiowa, Kiowa-Apache, and Comanche tribes gathered at

Settlement of the West, by Robert G. Athearn (Norman: University of Oklahoma Press, 1956). Also see the two-volume *Memoirs of General William T. Sherman: Written by Himself* (New York: D. Appleton, 1875). His papers can be found in the Library of Congress.

⚙ Andrew Jackson Smith
Colonel, 7th U.S. Cavalry

Andrew Jackson Smith, later known as "Old A. J.," was born on a farm in Buckingham Township, Pennsylvania, on April 28, 1815, and named after his father's commander at the battle of New Orleans. He graduated from West Point in 1838 and rose to the rank of major while serving at frontier posts—including participation in the Mormon battalion's march from Fort Leavenworth to California by way of Santa Fe in 1846–47—and in the Mexican War prior to the outbreak of the Civil War. In 1861, he became colonel of the 2nd California Cavalry, but he resigned that post in November to serve as chief of cavalry in Missouri. Smith was promoted to brigadier general in March 1862 and commanded a division in the Vicksburg campaign and at Nashville. He received an appointment to major general in May 1864 and held the rare distinction of defeating the legendary Confederate general Nathan Bedford Forrest on July 14, 1864, at Tupelo, Mississippi.

On July 28, 1866, Colonel Smith was appointed commanding officer of the newly formed 7th Cavalry, and he reported for duty later that year. He had a preference for administrative duty, which permitted Custer to become commander of the regiment in the field. Smith commanded the 7th Cavalry until May 6, 1869, when he resigned his commission to become postmaster of St. Louis, Missouri. He was serving in that capacity, as well as city auditor and commander of a militia brigade, when he died on January 30, 1897.

⚙ Sir Henry Morton Stanley
Explorer and Journalist

Stanley's early life could have been the subject of a novel by Charles Dickens—at least, according to his autobiography. As best as can be determined, he was born on January 28, 1841, near Denbigh Castle in North Wales and christened John Rowlands. His father, also named John Rowlands, was a farmer and his mother an unmarried woman. He was abandoned to a workhouse at age four, ran away when he was fifteen, and lived with various relatives for three years until taking a job as cabin boy on a ship from Liverpool to New Orleans. In

(continued on following page)

Louisiana, he found work and a home with a cotton broker named Henry Stanley and assumed the man's name. In 1861, Stanley decided to fight for the Confederacy in the Civil War. He was captured the following year at Shiloh and obtained his release from prison by changing sides and enlisting in the Union army, but he was soon discharged due to a severe case of dysentery. Stanley served briefly in the U.S. Navy before landing a reporter position with the *New York Herald*.

The young adventurer headed west to cover the Indian wars for the *New York Tribune* and *Weekly Missouri Democrat* as part of the Hancock expedition of 1867. Following Hancock's early discussions with Indian chiefs, Stanley candidly offered the opinion that the general had been deceived by the Indians. This statement allegedly encouraged Hancock to destroy the Indian village on Pawnee Fork. The reporter later estimated that it would take 3,000 buffalo to replace the loss. Stanley also contended that the provisions of the Medicine Lodge Treaties had never been fully read or explained to the Indians.

"The effect was all that could be desired. There was not another desertion as long as I remained with the command."

—CUSTER ABOUT HIS DECISION TO ORDER DESERTERS WHO HAD FLED IN PLAIN SIGHT OF THE COLUMN SHOT

In 1868, he accompanied a British expedition to Abyssinia (modern-day Ethiopia). He was on assignment in Madrid in late 1869 when he received the opportunity of a lifetime—to locate Dr. David Livingstone, a Scottish missionary explorer who was thought to be lost in central Africa. After an eight-month search, Stanley uttered those famous words, "Dr. Livingstone, I presume," upon meeting the doctor at Ujiji in November 1871. He remained to explore with Livingstone, and later on his own, becoming the third person in history to have crossed Africa, while opening a vast territory to British colonization.

In the late 1880s, after years of exploring, Stanley settled in England. He married Dorothy Ten-

(continued on following page)

Medicine Lodge Creek, Kansas, a traditional Sun Dance location about seventy miles from Fort Larned, to negotiate with representatives of the United States. After several days of discussion, feasting, and receiving presents, the Kiowa, Kiowa-Apache, and Comanche chiefs made their marks on the paperwork. The Cheyenne and Arapaho were wary about attending due to lingering animosity over Hancock's destruction of the village on Pawnee Fork. The dissident tribes, however, eventually wandered in—perhaps tempted by the promised gifts—and their chiefs also signed the treaty.

Provisions of the treaties provided for two large reservations in western Indian Territory. The Kiowa, Kiowa-Apache, and Comanche would share one; the Cheyenne and Arapaho the other. No whites, other than teachers, doctors, instructors, or other authorized visitors, would be permitted on these reservations. The government would furnish every adult with agricultural equipment and seed, and teach them the rudiments of farming. Clothing and other essential supplies would be issued by army representatives each year for the next thirty years.

In return, the Indians agreed to relinquish all territory beyond these specified reservations—except in the case of buffalo hunting south of the Arkansas River. They would also promise to cease attacks on the railroad, military posts, and white settlements and travelers outside of reservation boundaries.

The tenets of the Medicine Lodge Treaties were designed to be the example of how kindness and assistance rather than force would be the guidelines for the future of interracial relations. In other words, the Plains Indians would be removed from the pathway of Western expansion and, by eliminating their own culture, taught how to live like whites.

But these Indians, whose traditional lifestyle had never been anything other than that of nomadic hunters, would find it difficult to abandon their inherent nature in favor of settling down as common farmers. Adding to that was the fact that Congress failed to speedily enact the provisions of the treaty, which delayed sufficient rations reaching the reservations. Therefore, in order to hunt for food, most Indians ignored the treaty and roamed their accustomed territories, which resulted in continuing violent encounters with the U.S. Army.

📖 The best source on this subject is *The Treaty of Medicine Lodge: The Story of the Great Treaty as Told by Eyewitnesses*, by Douglas C. Jones (Norman: University of Oklahoma Press, 1966). (Jones also wrote the fictional work *The Court-Martial of George Armstrong Custer* [New York: Charles Scribner's Sons, 1976], a courtroom drama based on the premise that Custer alone survived the battle of the Little Bighorn.) The text of the treaties can be found in *Indian Affairs: Laws and Treaties,* by Charles J. Kappler, 2 vols. (Washington, DC, 1904). Government policy is outlined in *The Movement for Indian Assimilation, 1860–1890,* by Henry E. Fritz (Philadelphia: University of Pennsylvania Press, 1963).

Conquest of the Southern Plains: Uncensored Narrative of the Battle of the Washita and Custer's Southern Campaign, by Charles J. Brill (Oklahoma City: Golden Saga, 1938), makes the case that Sheridan's winter campaign of 1868–69 would never have been necessary had the government properly equipped the reservations in a timely fashion.

Other notable sources include "The Treaty Held at Medicine Lodge," by William E. Connelly, *Kansas State Historical Collections* 17 (1928); "The Medicine Lodge Peace Council," by Alfred A. Taylor, *Chronicles of Oklahoma* 2 (June 1924); and former 7th Cavalry officer Edward S. Godfrey's "Some Reminiscences of the Medicine Lodge Peace Treaties," *Cavalry Journal* 37 (January 1928).

🐎 Wild Bill's Showdown with Tom Custer

Wild Bill Hickok has been the subject of so many tall tales and dime novel exaggerations that it is often difficult to separate fact from fiction. One of those colorful stories concerns Tom Custer, George Armstrong's younger brother, while the 7th Cavalry was stationed at Fort Hays, Kansas, in 1869 and Hickok was the marshal of nearby Hays City.

Tom Custer was a wild and reckless young man, who frequently drank to excess. On one of those inebriated occasions, Tom was said to have ridden through Hays City shooting out lights and windows, then urging his horse into a crowded saloon, which caused considerable damage. This apparently had not been the first time Tom had sent the patrons of a saloon scrambling with his horse. Although Wild Bill was a friend of the elder Custer, enough was enough. Tom was promptly dragged off his mount by Wild Bill, hauled before a justice of the peace, and fined for his rash act. Tom was incensed with Hickok over the arrest and vowed revenge.

On New Year's Eve, Tom returned to Hays City with three burly soldiers and hung around the saloon to wait for Hickok. When Wild Bill strolled into the establishment, the soldiers cornered and disarmed him, and it appeared that physical revenge for Tom's arrest was about to be exacted. A friendly bartender, however, tossed a loaded pistol (or shotgun) to Wild Bill, and he commenced firing. The result was that the three soldiers lay sprawled on the barroom floor, wounded but still very much alive. Tom Custer lit out for Fort Hays to seek the assistance of his brother.

nant on July 12, 1890, resumed his British citizenship in 1892, and served in Parliament from 1895 to 1900. In 1899, he was knighted. Five years later, on May 10, 1904, he died of a stroke in London.

📖 Henry Stanley's observations of the Hancock expedition can be found in *My Early Travels and Adventures in America and Asia,* 2 vols. (New York: Charles Scribner's Sons, 1905).

✸ Tall Bull
Southern Cheyenne

Tall Bull (Hotoa-qa-ihoois), who was born about 1830 (or 1815, according to some accounts) to a Cheyenne father and Sioux mother, became a principal leader of the Dog Soldier warrior society on the southern plains in the 1850s and 1860s. He was persuaded in 1867 to sign the Medicine Lodge Treaty but ignored its provisions and encouraged hostilities against whites. Tall Bull met with General Hancock at Fort Larned in 1867 and at that time was described by George Armstrong Custer as "a fine, warlike-looking chieftain." The chief accepted Hancock's presents, but then resumed raiding. When his warriors attacked the Kaw Indians at Council Grove, Kansas, officials refused to distribute arms and ammunition among the Cheyenne for hunting purposes. Tall Bull retaliated by raiding white settlements along the Sabine and Solomon Rivers in Kansas and participating in a series of bloody skirmishes with the U.S. Army, including the battle of Beecher Island in September 1868 (see "The Battle of Beecher Island" on page 98).

In the spring of 1869, Tall Bull decided to move north of the Platte and join the Sioux, and he was pursued by Maj. Eugene A. Carr and his 5th Cavalry. On July 11, 1869, Carr attacked and destroyed Tall Bull's camp at Summit Springs. In the battle, Tall Bull was shot and killed, either by "Buffalo Bill" Cody or scout Frank North. This victory by the army and the death of Tall Bull marked the end of Cheyenne resistance on the southern plains (see "The Battle of Summit Springs" on page 101).

📖 See *The Southern Cheyennes,* by Donald J. Berthrong (Norman: University of Oklahoma Press, 1963); *The Fighting Cheyennes,* by George B. Grinnell (Norman: University of Oklahoma Press, 1956); and *The Summit Springs Battle,* by Fred H. Werner (Greeley, CO: Werner Publications, 1989).

BIOGRAPHIES

✷ Thomas Benton Weir
Captain, 7th U.S. Cavalry

Weir was born on either September or November 28, 1838 (likely the former), in Nashville, Ohio, but soon moved to Albion, Michigan. In 1858, he enrolled in the University of Michigan. He departed during August of his junior year to enlist in Company B, 3rd Michigan Cavalry. Weir served as an enlisted man until being appointed a second lieutenant on October 13, 1861, while serving in campaigns and expeditions, including New Madrid, the siege of Corinth, and battles at Farmington, Iuka, Coffeeville, and second Corinth. He was promoted to first lieutenant on June 19, 1862—seven days before being taken prisoner. He was released on January 8, 1863. While held prisoner, Weir was appointed captain on November 1, 1862, and eventually received brevets up to lieutenant colonel for his Civil War service. His regiment was assigned to Reconstruction duty in Texas in 1865, and as a Regular army brevet of major, he served on the staffs of Generals Custer and Gibbs. On July 28, 1866, Weir was appointed a first lieutenant in the newly formed 7th Cavalry, and he was promoted to captain on July 31, 1867.

Weir remained at Fort Hays, Kansas, and did not participate in the Hancock expedition of 1867. At that time, it is possible that his relationship with Custer's wife, Libbie, might have come under scrutiny. Weir served as Libbie's escort in Custer's absence, a normal practice for officers at frontier posts. In this case, however, it has been alleged that rumors circulated that the two were becoming an item, which may have contributed to Custer's mad dash across Kansas (see "Custer's Mad Dash across Kansas" on page 63).

He participated in the November 1868 Washita battle and assumed command of Company A when Capt. Louis Hamilton was killed. Weir, a heavy drinker, was recommended for discharge upon the reduction of the army in 1869, but he

Capt. Thomas Weir. *Courtesy Little Bighorn Battlefield National Monument.*

George Armstrong Custer, however, had departed for Fort Leavenworth to spend the holiday. Tom then sought out Gen. Phil Sheridan, who ordered the arrest of Hickok.

Word of the impending arrest reached Wild Bill before the soldiers that Sheridan had dispatched. Hickok thought it prudent to vanish for the time being and hopped a freight train headed for Ellsworth and Abilene until cooler heads prevailed.

📖 This incident is related by Richard O'Conner in *Wild Bill Hickok* (New York: Konecky & Konecky, 1959), and also in an article titled "Tom Custer: In the Shadow of His Brother," by E. Lisle Reedstrom, *True West Magazine* 41, no. 11 (November 1994).

🐎 Red Cloud's War

While George Armstrong Custer was chasing Indians around the Kansas plains, another conflict was being waged to the north. In 1862–63, explorer John Bozeman had pioneered a route to the Montana goldfields that passed directly through prime Sioux buffalo hunting grounds. In 1865, the government built a road from Fort Laramie, Wyoming, to Montana along this Bozeman Trail. Oglala chief Red Cloud and other Lakota Sioux bands retaliated by attacking miners, army patrols, and wagon trains that trespassed onto this land that had been promised them under terms of the Fort Laramie Treaty of 1851.

In 1866, the army attempted to negotiate a nonaggression treaty but balked at Red Cloud's demand that no forts be built along the Bozeman. In fact, the army commenced construction on two new forts—Phil Kearny in Wyoming and C. F. Smith in Montana—and reinforced Fort Reno in Wyoming.

Red Cloud responded by intensifying hostilities. He masterminded hit-and-run tactics to harass the soldiers with his 2,000 warriors—including ambitious young braves Crazy Horse, Gall, and Rain-in-the-Face—which kept Fort Phil Kearny under constant siege.

On December 21, 1866, Capt. William J. Fetterman, who had once boasted that he "could ride through the entire hostile nation with eighty good men," commanded a detachment of eighty men from Fort Kearny as escort for a woodcutting wagon train. Crazy Horse and a band of Sioux appeared and pretended to flee from the soldiers. When Fetterman took the bait and chased after this decoy, he and his men were ambushed and annihilated.

On August 1, 1867, Crazy Horse and a group of warriors estimated at 500 to 800 strong attacked a detachment of nineteen soldiers and six civilians that were guarding a haycutting detail near Fort C. F. Smith. In the ensuing three- to four-hour battle—known as the Hayfield Fight—two soldiers and one

(continued on following page)

civilian were killed and two soldiers wounded before troops from the fort arrived and the Indians broke contact. Indian casualties are unknown—the army claimed that eight were killed and thirty wounded, but this was likely an exaggeration.

The following day, Company C of the 27th Infantry was guarding a woodcutting detail about six miles from Fort Kearny when attacked by warriors under Crazy Horse. In what became known as the Wagon Box Fight, the soldiers took refuge in a corral crudely constructed from wagon beds. The Indians alternated sniping and charging for a period of about four hours before reinforcements arrived from the fort to drive them away. The soldiers lost 6 killed and 2 wounded; Indian losses were 6 killed and 6 wounded, although the army estimated 60 killed and 120 wounded.

Red Cloud's constant harassment made the soldiers virtual prisoners in their forts, and safe travel along the Bozeman Trail was impossible. The U.S. government finally yielded to Red Cloud's demands, and the Fort Laramie Treaty of 1868 was drawn up to end hostilities. The army agreed to abandon the three forts and to provide the Sioux a reservation that encompassed nearly all of present-day South Dakota west of the Missouri River, as well as other concessions. Whites were expressly forbidden to trespass on Indian land. More than 200 chiefs and subchiefs signed the treaty at Fort Rice on July 2, 1868. Red Cloud, however, waited until November 6 to sign—when the three forts had been abandoned and burned to the ground.

📖 The best sources include *Red Cloud's Folk: A History of the Oglala Sioux Indians,* by George E. Hyde (Norman: University of Oklahoma Press, 1937); *Fort Phil Kearny: An American Saga,* by Dee Brown (New York: Putnam & Sons, 1962); *The Bozeman Trail: Historical Accounts of the Blazing of the Overland Route into the Northwest and the Fights with Red Cloud's Warriors,* 2 vols., by E. A. Brininstool and G. R. Hebard (Cleveland: Arthur H. Clark, 1922); *The Fetterman Massacre,* by Dee Brown (Lincoln: University of Nebraska Press, 1971); *Indian Fights and Fighters,* by Cyrus T. Brady (Lincoln: University of Nebraska Press, 1971); *Red Cloud and the Sioux Problem,* by James C. Olson (Lincoln: University of Nebraska Press, 1965); *Indian Fights: New Facts on Seven Encounters,* by J. W. Vaughn (Norman: University of Oklahoma Press, 1966); and *My Army Life and the Fort Phil Kearny Massacre,* by Francis C. Carrington (Philadelphia: Lippincott, 1910).

⚞ Custer's Literary Career

One of Custer's classmates at West Point, J. M. Wright, wrote that the "greatest surprise in Custer's whole career in life was that he should turn out to be a literary man. If any one had

was given a reprieve by higher authorities and remained as commander of D Troop.

At the Little Bighorn battle, Weir's company was attached to Capt. Frederick Benteen's scout. When Benteen arrived at the bluff where Maj. Marcus Reno had taken refuge, Weir demanded that they march to the sound of firing to the north, which, unknown to them, was Custer under attack. He was refused permission. Following a heated argument with Reno, Weir disobeyed orders and advanced his company forward to a promontory now named Weir Point. His unit was soon forced back to the bluff by approaching warriors.

Following the battle, Weir wrote to Libbie Custer, a woman whom he probably loved, stating that he could vindicate accusations against Custer. But before he could make a promised trip to visit her with whatever information he perceived as relevant, Weir, who was in advanced stages of alcoholism, died of congestion of the brain on December 9, 1876, while on recruiting duty in New York City. He was buried on Governors Island. His obituary was printed in the *New York Herald* on December 10, 1876.

📖 Numerous references to Weir's personal relationship with the Custers can be found in *The Custer Story: The Life and Intimate Letters of General George Armstrong Custer and His Wife Elizabeth,* by Marguerite Merington (New York: Devin-Adair, 1950); and *Elizabeth Bacon Custer and the Making of a Myth,* by Shirley A. Leckie (Norman: University of Oklahoma Press, 1993). References with respect to Weir's actions at the Little Bighorn appear in *The Custer Myth: A Source Book of Custeriana,* edited by W. A. Graham (Harrisburg, PA: Stackpole, 1954). See also "Tribute to Colonel Weir," *Bismarck Tribune* (January 3, 1877); and "Death of Tom Weir," *Army and Navy Journal* (December 27, 1876).

✹ Robert M. West
Captain, 7th U.S. Cavalry

West was born on September 16, 1834, in Newton, New Jersey. In 1856, he enlisted in the Regiment of Mounted Riflemen. He served in that capacity for five years before entering the Civil War with the 1st Pennsylvania Light Artillery. Within a year, West had become a full colonel and commander of his unit. In 1864, the 1st Pennsylvania became the 5th Pennsylvania Cavalry, which was involved in some of the bloodiest battles of the war. West distinguished himself enough to earn a volunteer brevet of brigadier general.

In November 1866, West joined the 7th Cavalry as captain of K Troop. His fellow officers considered him a capable troop commander—when he was sober. West could not control his drinking, however, and was incapacitated for duty in the field on more than one occasion.

At some point, West became disenchanted with Custer. Perhaps a feud was initiated in May 1867 when West, as officer of the day, was ordered by Custer to shave the heads of six men as punishment for an unauthorized visit to the store. Then in June, two of the deserters ordered shot by Custer during the Hancock expedition were members of West's troop. West retaliated by preferring supplementary charges at Custer's court-martial. On January 3, 1868, he placed a civil murder indictment against Custer and 1st Lt. William W. Cooke for the same incident. Those charges were thrown out of court.

Custer brought charges of drunkenness against West in early 1868, and West was suspended from duty for two months. When Custer returned that fall from his own suspension, he was warmly greeted by his command but refused to shake West's hand. West perhaps read the writing on the wall and resigned his commission on March 1, 1869. General Sheridan promised him the sutlership at the new Fort Sill, but before he could open for business, West died near Fort Arbuckle on September 3, 1869.

said in the four years before the Civil War that Cadet Custer would in fifteen years be a scholar of artistic tastes and writer of graphic contributions to the magazines, the prediction would have been derided."

To consider that this devil-may-care cavalier could gain fame as an author may have seemed preposterous, given his lack of attention to academics, but Custer did indeed turn out to be a literary man, and an accomplished one at that.

Custer's initial foray into the publishing world was with a New York–based weekly sportsmen's journal called *Turf, Field and Farm,* which suited his taste for horses, hounds, and hunting. His first article or "letter," which he wrote under the pseudonym "Nomad," was submitted on September 9, 1867—just six days before his court-martial convened at Fort Leavenworth. In spite of the pseudonym, readers knew that "Nomad" was actually the famous General Custer. He wrote a total of fifteen letters describing his adventures to this publication between September 1867 and August 1875. Those letters have been reprinted in *Nomad: George A. Custer in Turf, Field and Farm,* edited by Brian W. Dippie (Austin: University of Texas Press, 1980). This book offers more than merely Custer's work. Dippie has provided extensive notes that place events in proper perspective, an addition that stands alone as fascinating reading.

Custer, convicted by court-martial, served out much of his one-year suspension with wife Libbie while residing in Phil Sheridan's quarters at Fort Leavenworth. It was during this period that he began work on his Civil War memoirs. Six years later, at Fort Lincoln, Custer was still working on this task. Unfortunately, he never finished these memoirs, completing only the period from his reporting for duty at Bull Run in July 1861—three days out of West Point—to the May 5, 1862, battle of Williamsburg, where he was said to have captured the first battle flag taken by the Union army. These unfinished memoirs, which make for excellent reading, have been published as *Custer in the Civil War: His Unfinished Memoirs,* edited by John M. Carroll (San Rafael, CA: Presidio Press, 1977). In addition to the Custer memoirs, the book contains perhaps even more valuable information with the reprinting of the reports Custer wrote as a general describing the actions of his commands, which Carroll compiled from the 130-volume *War of the Rebellion: A Compilation of the Official Records of the Union and Confederate Records* (Washington, DC, 1880–1901). Another feature is a bibliographic checklist of every book Carroll could locate that mentioned any aspect—no matter how insignificant—of Custer's Civil War career.

In 1872, while stationed at Elizabethtown, Kentucky, Custer began writing a series of articles for a magazine called *Galaxy.* In 1874, Sheldon and Company, the owners of the magazine, published selected articles in book form entitled *My Life on the Plains; or, Personal Experiences with Indians,* which

Custer and wife Libbie in their study at Fort Abraham Lincoln, November, 1873. *Courtesy Little Bighorn Battlefield National Monument.*

remains in print today (Norman: University of Oklahoma Press, 1962). The book, which detailed his activities on the Great Plains from 1867 to 1869, established Custer as a respected author.

Newspapers were another outlet for Custer's literary prowess. Upon returning from the Yellowstone expedition of 1873, Custer's entire official report was published in both the *New York Tribune* and the *Army and Navy Journal.* An article that he wrote pertaining to that expedition, "Battling with the Sioux on the Yellowstone," which was first published in the July 1876 issue of *Galaxy,* has been reprinted in *The Custer Reader,* edited by Paul A. Hutton (Lincoln: University of Nebraska Press, 1992).

The following year, Custer sparred in print with Col. William B. Hazen about the prospects of the Northern Pacific Railroad (see "The Custer-Hazen Feud" on page 135). He also was known to write speculative political pieces without a byline for leading Democratic papers, such as the *New York World,* and for his friend James Gordon Bennett, publisher of the *New York Herald.* In the summer of 1876, Bennett expected to receive anonymous articles from Custer about the Little Bighorn campaign.

Perhaps the most entertaining and revealing, if not informative, writings by Custer are his letters to Libbie and others. Marguerite Merington culled highlights from many letters contained in various collections and published them as *The Custer Story: The Life and Letters of General George A. Custer and His Wife Elizabeth* (New York: Devin-Adair, 1950).Other

✸ Edward Wanshear Wynkoop
Army Officer and Indian Agent

Wynkoop was born in Philadelphia on June 19, 1836. He emigrated to Kansas in the mid-1850s, and in 1858, he was part of the "Pikes Peak or Bust" Colorado gold rush. He remained in that state to become one of the founding fathers of Denver, serving as sheriff in 1859 and as first lieutenant in the Denver cavalry. In 1861, Wynkoop married Louise Wakely, an actress, with whom he had eight children.

In 1862, he was commissioned a major in the 1st Colorado Volunteers, and he fought as a company commander against the Confederate attempt to invade New Mexico in the battles of Apache Canyon and Glorieta Pass. As commander of Fort Lyon in 1864, Wynkoop was the officer who resettled Black Kettle and his Cheyenne at Sand Creek, which resulted in their massacre by Col. John Chivington (see "The Sand Creek Massacre" on page 104). In 1865, he became commander of the Veteran Battalion of the Colorado Cavalry and chief of cavalry for the District of the Upper Arkansas.

(continued on following page)

Wynkoop did not share the philosophy of genocide concerning Indians embraced by Chivington and most of his fellow Coloradoans, believing instead that hostilities could and should be prevented. This opinion made him a most hated man in Colorado, where Chivington was considered a hero. In July 1866, he resigned his commission and became an Indian agent for the Cheyenne and Arapaho, vigorously defending his charges whenever they were accused of depredations. Wynkoop could not, however, prevent the army—whose officers and men had little respect for him—from waging war. He accompanied the Hancock expedition of 1867 and was outraged by General Hancock's aggressive actions, in particular the destruction of the Cheyenne village on Pawnee Fork. Finally, to protest the killing of Black Kettle at Washita, he resigned his post as Indian agent in November 1868 (see "Public Reaction to the Washita Battle" on page 88).

Wynkoop returned to Pennsylvania, but after failing in an iron-making business, he headed back out west in 1874 to participate in the Black Hills gold rush—where he fought Indians with the local ranger unit under Capt. Jack Crawford, the so-called poet scout. He then worked in various positions, including adjutant general of New Mexico Territory and warden of the territorial penitentiary. Wynkoop died in Santa Fe of kidney disease on September 11, 1891.

📖 References to Wynkoop can be found in most books and articles associated with the Sand Creek massacre and Sheridan's plains campaigns of 1867–69. His early years on the frontier are covered in his unfinished autobiography, *The Tall Chief: The Unfinished Autobiography of Edward Wynkoop, 1856–1866,* edited by Christopher B. Gerboth (Denver: Colorado Historical Society, 1994). His son, Edward E. Wynkoop, wrote a biographical sketch of his father that appears in *Kansas Historical Collections* 13 (1913–14). See also "The Controversial Career of Edward W. Wynkoop," by Thomas D. Isern, *Colorado Magazine* 56 (Winter–Spring 1979).

writing by Custer, including personal letters and orders, can be found in collections at the Little Bighorn Battlefield National Monument; University of Michigan; Monroe, Michigan, County Library System; Monroe County Historical and Museum Association; New York Public Library; Rochester, New York, Public Library; U.S. Army Military History Institute; U.S. Military Academy at West Point; and Yale University.

EPILOGUE

The court-martial of George Armstrong Custer convened at Fort Leavenworth at 11 A.M. on September 15, 1867.

Col. A. J. Smith—at the urging of General Hancock—had charged Custer with "absence without leave from his command," for traveling from Fort Wallace to Fort Hays at a time when his command was expected to be engaged with hostile Indians, and "conduct to the prejudice of good order and military discipline," by completing a long and exhausting march when the horses were in unfit condition, neglecting to recover or bury the body of the trooper killed at Downer's Station, and procuring two ambulances and four mules belonging to the United States without proper authority. An additional charge was preferred by Capt. Robert W. West, who accused Custer of "conduct prejudicial to good order and military discipline" for ordering that the deserters from the column be shot down without a trial and for denying the wounded proper medical attention.

Custer pleaded not guilty to all charges. He had prepared his defense with the assistance of his counsel, Capt. Charles C. Parsons, a former West Point classmate. The trial lasted until October 11, concluding with Parsons reading a lengthy rebuttal written by Custer that answered each charge and specification.

The court, however, was not swayed by Custer's explanations or plea for acquittal. He was found guilty on all counts but cleared of any criminality regarding the ambulances and the treatment of the wounded deserters. His sentence was suspension from rank and command for one year, and to forfeit his pay for that period. Custer hoped that the reviewing officer might overturn the verdict, but on November 18, General Sherman issued a statement that the "proceedings, findings and sentence . . . are approved by President Grant."

Custer and wife Libbie were of the opinion that he had been the scapegoat for the failure of the Hancock expedition. Some vindication came when Phil Sheridan, who sided with Custer, graciously offered the Custers the use of his quarters at Fort Leavenworth. Sheridan's offer was accepted, and the couple enjoyed the winter social season at that post before leaving for Monroe, Michigan, in the spring.

There were, however, two episodes of nasty business stemming from the court-martial. Custer charged Captain West of

*"All of whom I have conversed deem the verdict
not sustained by the evidence. . . ."*

—Custer writing to a friend in November 1867
about the results of his court-martial

drunkenness on duty, for which West was found guilty and suspended for two months. West retaliated by preferring charges of murder in a civil court against Custer and 1st Lt. William W. Cooke for the death of trooper Charles Johnson. On January 18, 1868, the judge cited a lack of evidence and dismissed that case.

Further vindication for Custer came two months short of the end of his suspension, when he was summoned back to duty for Sheridan's winter campaign of 1868–69.

📖 *The Court-Martial of General George Armstrong Custer,* by Lawrence A. Frost (Norman: University of Oklahoma Press, 1968), provides an excellent narrative of the Hancock expedition and a verbatim account—testimony and exhibits—of Custer's court-martial proceedings. Two other notable sources are "The Custer Court Martial," by Robert A. Murray, *Annals of Wyoming* 36 (October 1964); and "The Court-Martial of Brevet Major General George A. Custer," by Milton B. Halsey, Jr., *Trail Guide* 13 (September 1968).

The Custers' point of view can be found in Armstrong's *My Life on the Plains; or, Personal Experiences with Indians* (Norman: University of Oklahoma Press, 1962); and Libbie's *Tenting on the Plains; or, General Custer in Kansas and Texas* (New York: Charles L. Webster & Co., 1889).

The subject is also covered from various angles in every biography of Custer, but none comes close to matching Frost's work, which allows readers to form their own conclusions regarding Custer's actions and subsequent punishment.

CHAPTER FOUR

The Winter Campaign of 1868–69

OVERVIEW

In the summer and fall of 1868, the southern plains were being terrorized by incessant attacks from Cheyenne, Kiowa, and Arapaho Indians. Raids by marauding hostiles against white settlements, soldiers, the railroad, and stage lines were so prevalent that the government was forced to find a solution. Indian policy had vacillated between the tolerance advocated by Eastern humanitarians and shows of military force demanded by Westerners, which included the U.S. Army.

Finally, in a victory for the army, Lt. Gen. Philip Sheridan was directed to take whatever measures were necessary to force the hostiles onto reservations and punish those responsible for the atrocities. Total war had been declared against the Plains Indians (see "Total War" on page 83).

In August, Sheridan established an elite force of scouts under the command of Maj. George A. "Sandy" Forsyth with orders to guard the railroad up the Smoky Hill Road. On September 17, Forsyth and his fifty-one men were attacked by Indians. They were pinned down for nine days until rescued by the 10th Cavalry in what would be called the battle of Beecher Island (see "The Battle of Beecher Island" on page 98).

Sheridan's next move was to dispatch Col. Alfred Sully and his 3rd Infantry, bolstered by eight companies of the 7th Cavalry under Maj. Joel Elliott, to hunt down the Cheyenne that had been raiding south of the Arkansas River. Sully, who had distinguished himself fighting Sioux in the Dakotas, had apparently grown timid and, much to the disgust of Sheridan, returned empty-handed after just one week in the field.

Sheridan, however, was well acquainted with an officer who had the tenacity to implement his strategy of total war. A telegram was sent to summon Lt. Col. George Armstrong Custer, who was serving out his suspension in Monroe, Michigan. An elated Custer was on the train the following morning and reported to Fort Hays on September 30 to prepare for a winter campaign.

Before firm plans had been developed, a debate ensued over the practicality of a cold-weather operation, which could pose potential health dangers for the troops and present difficulty in keeping a supply line open. No less of an authority than Jim Bridger arrived from St. Louis to argue against the cam-

"Some of the officers think this may be a campaign on paper—but I know Genl. Sheridan better. We are going to the heart of the Indian country where white troops have never been before."

—CUSTER TO LIBBIE, NOVEMBER 1868

Lt. Col. George Armstrong Custer during the Winter Campaign of 1868–69. *Courtesy Little Bighorn Battlefield National Monument.*

BIOGRAPHIES

✹ Albert Barnitz
Captain, 7th U.S. Cavalry

Barnitz was born on March 10, 1835, in Bedford County, Pennsylvania, but moved to Ohio shortly after his birth. He attended Kenyon College and the Cleveland Law College but was for the most part a self-educated man. Barnitz toured the Midwest, conducting classes in elocution and performing dramatic readings, and in 1857, he published a volume of poetry. He married Eva Prouty in 1859, but the next year she and their infant daughter died during childbirth.

At the outbreak of the Civil War, Barnitz enlisted as a sergeant in the 2nd Ohio Volunteer Cavalry, earned second lieutenant in June 1862, and was appointed senior captain early the following year. In June 1864, Barnitz was wounded during a skirmish at Ashland Station. That fall he returned to his unit, which operated until the end of the war in the Shenandoah Valley under the command of Brig. Gen. George Armstrong Custer in the 3rd Cavalry Division. He was promoted to major and brevet lieutenant colonel before mustering out in September 1865.

Barnitz was appointed a captain in the 7th Cavalry in November 1866 and two months later married Jennie Platte. He participated in the Hancock expedition of 1867, and at that time, his opinion of George Armstrong Custer, which had been quite high after the Civil War, deteriorated. "I am thor-

(continued on following page)

paign. But Sheridan was won over by Custer's argument that their only chance for success was to locate and engage the Indians at the time of year when they were relatively immobile and therefore vulnerable.

On November 12, Custer and eleven companies of his 7th Cavalry, under the command of Colonel Sully with his five infantry companies, marched south from Cavalry Creek to a supply base on the North Canadian River appropriately named Camp Supply. On the way to Camp Supply, Custer discovered the trail of an Indian war party estimated at seventy-five warriors. Custer was anxious to follow, but Sully refused permission until reinforced by the 19th Kansas Volunteer Cavalry, which was en route to Camp Supply (see "The 19th Kansas Volunteer Cavalry" on page 94).

Custer was furious. When Sheridan arrived on November 21, he complained about Sully's typical passivity. Sheridan resolved the tug-of-war over command by sending Sully back to Fort Harker. Custer now had the freedom to pursue the Indians.

Two days later, Custer and the 7th Cavalry—800 men—marched south toward the Washita River Valley, where it was believed that large bands of Indians, perhaps as many as 6,000, were camped for the winter (see "The Table of Organization and Casualty Report of the 7th Cavalry at the Washita Battle" on page 81). On November 26, Major Elliott and the command's Osage Indian scouts came across a fresh trail near Antelope Hills made by hundreds of warriors presumedly returning from a raid in Kansas. Custer dispatched Elliott to follow the trail while he marched the main column forward through the deep snow. The troops were eventually halted on a ridge over-

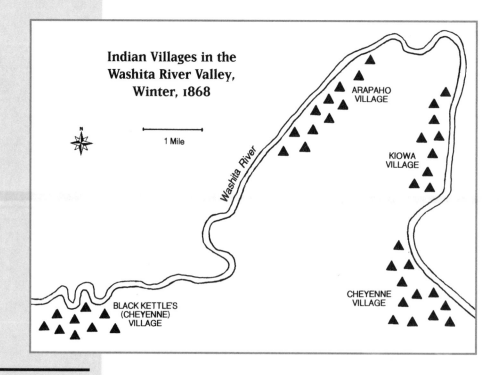

Indian Villages in the Washita River Valley, Winter, 1868

looking the Washita River where below was situated a village of fifty-one lodges under Cheyenne chief Black Kettle.

Custer sounded officers' call to detail his plan of attack. The regiment would be separated into four detachments. Major Elliott would attack from the northeast with Companies G, H, and M; Capt. William Thompson would lead Companies B and F from the south; Capt. Edward Myers with Companies E and I from the west; and Custer with two squadrons commanded by Capt. Louis Hamilton and Capt. Robert West, along with Cooke's sharpshooters, from the north. Eighty men under quartermaster 1st Lt. James M. Bell would remain with the wagon train.

At dawn on November 27, 1868—as a shot rang out from within the village—the buglers sounded the charge, and the 7th Cavalry swept into the unsuspecting village. Bullets peppered the air, and most of the Indians fled their lodges to take refuge in the nearby timber or ravines or raced for the river. Black Kettle and his wife tried to flee on his pony but were shot down at the river.

In the opening moments, Captain Hamilton was shot through the heart, and Capt. Albert Barnitz was critically wounded. Thompson was late in arriving on the field, creating a gap between his command and that of Elliott, which permit-

oughly <u>disgusted</u> with him!" Barnitz wrote about Custer to his wife on May 15. "He is the most complete example of a petty tyrant that I have ever seen." Perhaps that attitude could be partially blamed on the fact that Barnitz had been arrested for discarding forage and not feeding his horses.

On June 26, Barnitz and his Company G, which had ridden to Pond Creek Station, were attacked by Cheyenne Indians under Roman Nose. Barnitz and his men fought off the determined warriors but sustained six killed and six wounded. Later that day, he came upon the wagon train commanded by Lt. William Cooke, which was besieged by at least 600 Sioux for a period of three hours, until the approach of Capt. Robert West with reinforcements. Barnitz's fight against Roman Nose, the first notable skirmish by the 7th Cavalry, gained him accolades from his superiors and coverage by the press.

At the November 1868 battle of the Washita, Barnitz's company was part of Elliott's battalion on the charge into the village. He was severely

(continued on following page)

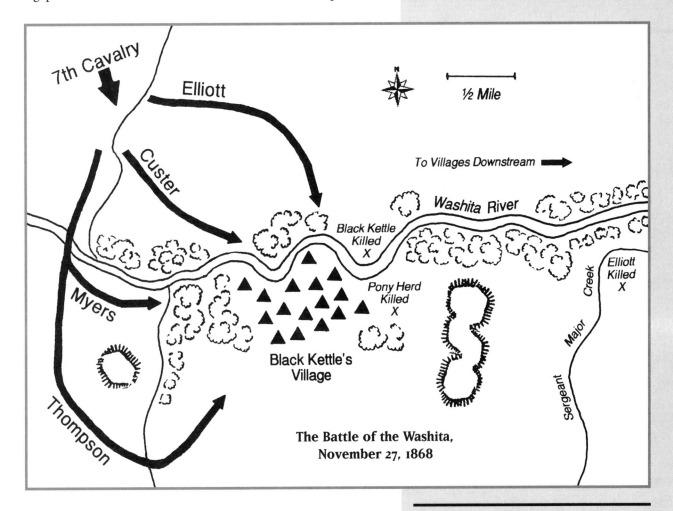

**The Battle of the Washita,
November 27, 1868**

wounded while engaged in a personal duel with a Cheyenne warrior whom he killed but from whom he received a bullet in the abdomen. At the time, the wound was believed fatal, but Barnitz miraculously recovered and in 1870 was retired from the service on medical disability. He became a newspaperman until his death on July 18, 1912, which came as the result of a growth around the wound he had received at Washita.

Barnitz is notable not necessarily for his service with the 7th Cavalry, although that was certainly meritorious, but for his recording of his unit's history during the years 1867–68. The diaries and letters of both Albert and Jennie Barnitz have provided rich insight into frontier life, as well as the operations, personnel, and controversies of the 7th Cavalry. An early admirer of Custer, Barnitz later painted a rather unflattering portrait of his commander.

📖 Excerpts from the Barnitz diaries and letters have been edited within an informative narrative by Robert M. Utley in *Life in Custer's Cavalry: Diaries and Letters of Albert and Jennie Barnitz, 1867–68* (Lincoln: University of Nebraska Press, 1977).

"Don't tell Mother but I was overjoyed to get back to the post again and the big house never seemed so welcome. I experienced a home feeling here in garrison that I cannot find in civil life."

—CUSTER TO LIBBIE, OCTOBER 1868, UPON HIS RETURN TO DUTY FROM SUSPENSION

✳ Frederick H. Beecher
First Lieutenant, 3rd Infantry

Beecher, the nephew of well-known clergyman Henry Ward Beecher, was born in New Orleans on June 22, 1841, and raised in Massachusetts. His military career began after graduation from Andover and Maine's Bowdoin College in August 1862 as a second lieutenant with the 16th Maine Volunteer Infantry. He was wounded at Fredericksburg, fought at Chancellorsville, and was wounded once again—this time more severely— at Gettysburg. The nature of this leg wound, in which a shell severely damaged his right knee,

(continued on following page)

ted a number of Indians to escape. Without Custer's knowledge, Elliott led a detachment of sixteen to nineteen volunteers downriver to chase those fleeing warriors.

Custer gained control of the village within ten minutes of his charge and spent the remainder of the morning eliminating small pockets of resistance—103 Indians were killed, according to Custer's report (see "Indian Casualties of the Washita Battle" on page 86). At one point, the overzealous command of Captain Myers, contrary to explicit orders issued by Custer, was observed firing into a group of women and children.

Custer dispatched scout Ben Clark to order Myers to stop shooting and instead capture all noncombatants. Fifty-three women and children were subsequently taken prisoner, including a girl named Mo-nah-se-tah, who acted as an interpreter throughout the remainder of the campaign and later became the subject of controversy in Custer's personal life (see "Custer and Mo-nah-se-tah" on page 92).

Custer then ordered that the entire village be destroyed. Bonfires soon blazed, and every possession belonging to the Cheyenne was thrown onto the flames. The pony herd was rounded up and also destroyed. (See "Total War" on page 83 for an estimate of property loss.) While sorting through the contents of the village, Custer's men found mail, daguerreotypes, clothing, and other items taken from white settlements.

Around noon, swarms of Indians from the villages downstream began massing to fire from the surrounding bluffs, which placed Custer in a precarious position. Lieutenant Bell bravely fought his way through the Indians with a critical resupply of ammunition, and Custer formed his men into a defensive perimeter while the burning of the village was completed.

Additional warriors continued to arrive—perhaps as many as 1,500 now rimmed the bluffs, surrounding the cavalrymen. It was approaching dusk, and Custer realized that he must withdraw. Major Elliott and his men had not returned, however. Custer dispatched Captain Myers to scout for Elliott. Myers reported that he had ridden two miles downriver without finding any sign of the missing party.

Custer mounted his troops and, in a bold tactical move, ordered the band to play "Ain't I Glad to Get Out of the Wilderness" while marching down the valley toward the downstream villages. When the surprised warriors fell back to defend their families, Custer, with darkness as an ally, countermarched his command and escaped to the supply train. Two days later, the 7th Cavalry arrived triumphantly at Camp Supply.

In early December, Sheridan and Custer, reinforced by the 19th Kansas Volunteer Cavalry, returned to the Washita battlefield. On December 10, some miles downstream from the site of Black Kettle's village, they found the mutilated bodies of Maj. Joel Elliott and his detachment. Elliott's death created an enduring controversy within the 7th Cavalry, provoked by the notorious Custer critic Capt. Frederick W. Benteen, who claimed that

Custer had abandoned Elliott (see "The Joel Elliott Controversy" on page 90).

Farther downstream, they found the bodies of white captives Clara Blinn and her son in an abandoned village reportedly belonging to Kiowa chief Satanta (see "Indian Captives Clara Blinn and Her Son" on page 84).

Sheridan and his 700-man force continued to follow the Indian trail for another seventy-five miles, until they happened upon a large band of Indians. The chief of these Kiowa, none other than Satanta, rode out to display a message from Colonel Hazen—who had the unenviable task of determining the status of Indians—indicating that he and the other chief present, Lone Wolf, were friendly and should not be molested. Sheridan challenged Satanta to demonstrate his tribe's friendliness by accompanying him to the reservation at Fort Cobb. When Satanta hesitated, Sheridan seized the two chiefs and threatened to hang them if the tribe did not submit to the reservation. Most of the Kiowa grudgingly complied to save the lives of their chiefs.

In January 1869, Custer swept through the Wichita Mountains with a detail of only forty sharpshooters and persuaded an Arapaho village of sixty-five lodges under Chief Little Raven to surrender.

compelled a transfer to the Veteran Reserve Corps, where he served for the remainder of the war with the Freedman's Bureau in Raleigh, North Carolina. He received his regular army commission as a second lieutenant in the 3rd Infantry in November 1865 and was promoted to first lieutenant the following year at Fort Riley.

In 1867, Beecher was post quartermaster at Fort Wallace, which he helped construct despite being under constant siege by hostile Indians. He served in early 1868 as a roving scout and liaison between Phil Sheridan and civilian scouting patrols. In early March 1868, Beecher led an expedition that recovered the bodies of 2nd Lt. Lyman S. Kidder and his detail, who had been killed the previous summer during the Hancock expedition.

His wounds from the Civil War, which had rendered him somewhat lame, caused him great pain, and he sought a transfer to the Quartermaster Department. Before those orders could be issued, however, he was assigned as second in command in a detachment of elite scouts under the command of Maj. George A. Forsyth, which had been organized in the fall of 1868 to patrol the Smoky

(continued on following page)

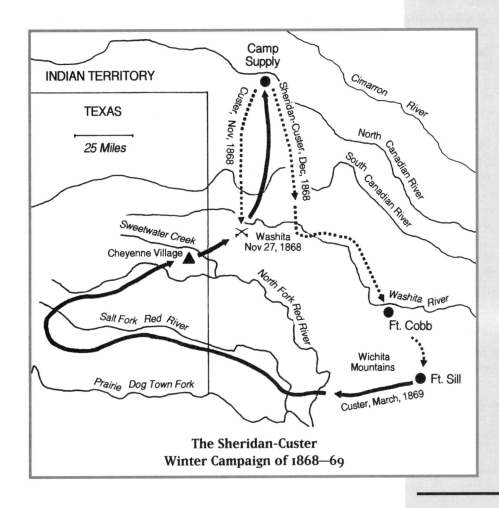

The Sheridan-Custer Winter Campaign of 1868—69

Hill Road. In mid-September, the frontiersmen were besieged by Cheyenne on an island on the Arikaree Fork of the Republican River. Beecher was killed—reportedly suffering seven wounds—on September 17, 1868, in the battle at Beecher Island, so named in his honor (see "The Battle of Beecher Island" on page 98). He was buried near the place of his death, but when the grave was later opened by soldiers, Beecher's body was missing.

✹ James Montgomery Bell
First Lieutenant, 7th U.S. Cavalry

Bell was born on October 1, 1837, at Williamsburg, Pennsylvania, and earned a master's degree from Wittenburg College in 1862. He was mustered into the 13th Pennsylvania Cavalry as a captain in October 1863 and participated in sixteen major engagements, including the Wilderness, Spotsylvania, North Anna, White Oak Road, and Coggins Point, where he was wounded.

He was appointed a second lieutenant in the 7th Cavalry on July 28, 1866, and promoted to first lieutenant in April of the following year. Bell served as quartermaster from 1867 to 1869 and became a friend and frequent social guest of the Custers. During the November 1868 Washita battle, he was in charge of the advance supply train and distinguished himself by fighting through a superior force of Indians to reach Custer with a critical resupply of ammunition.

Bell married Emiline "Emily" Mary Hones on March 12, 1872, at Trinity Church in Pittsburgh. The couple did not have any children. Maj. Marcus Reno stood a court-martial in May 1877, in part for making improper advances to Emily Bell—a charge Reno denied, claiming that she had been the aggressor. Nevertheless, Reno was found guilty.

Bell did not participate in the Yellowstone or Black Hills expeditions, as he was on detached service with the Northern Boundary Survey (see "The Northern Boundary Survey" on page 121). He missed the Little Bighorn campaign while on a leave of absence and received his captaincy as a result of the death of George Yates. He served in the West for the next twenty years, receiving a brevet to lieutenant colonel for the 1877 battle of Canyon Creek against the Nez Perce.

Bell served as escort for Northern Pacific Railroad construction crews during the summers of 1880–82. Bell was appointed major in April 1896, and in 1898, he commanded a regiment in the Cuban campaign of the Spanish-American War. In 1899, as brigadier general of volunteers, he led a brigade in the Philippines. He retired as a Regu-

(continued on following page)

On March 15, Custer, reinforced by the 19th Kansas Volunteer Cavalry, located two villages with a combined 260 lodges under Chiefs Little Robe and Medicine Arrow at Sweetwater Creek, Texas. The Kansans believed that these Cheyenne were holding two women who had been captured from their state. Custer, with help from Mo-nah-se-tah, his guide, confirmed that suspicion but refused to attack, a decision that incensed the Kansas volunteers. Instead, Custer was able to secure the release of the white women without firing a shot (see "The Rescue at Sweetwater Creek" on page 96). Custer also gained assurances that these Indians would move onto the reservation as soon as their ponies grew stronger.

The participation of the 7th Cavalry in the winter campaign quietly concluded on March 28, 1869. At that point, not all Cheyenne had submitted to the reservation. On July 11, however, the 5th Cavalry under Maj. Eugene Carr defeated Tall Bull's Cheyenne at the battle of Summit Springs, which broke the will of the Indians and finally accomplished Sheridan's mission of clearing all hostiles from the area between the Platte and Arkansas Rivers (see "The Battle of Summit Springs" on page 101).

📖 The best overall account of the winter campaign can be found in Stan Hoig's *The Battle of the Washita: The Sheridan-Custer Indian Campaign of 1867–69* (Garden City, NY: Doubleday, 1976). Another excellent choice is *Phil Sheridan and His Army,* by Paul A. Hutton (Lincoln: University of Nebraska Press, 1985).

For a compilation of the official documents, see *General Custer and the Battle of the Washita: The Federal View,* edited by John Carroll (Bryan, TX: Guidon Press, 1978). An eyewitness perspective from a reporter who accompanied the campaign is *Sheridan's Troopers on the Borders: A Winter Campaign on the Plains,* by De B. Randolph Keim (Lincoln: University of Nebraska Press, 1985). The classic *Indian Fights and Fighters,* by Cyrus T. Brady (Lincoln: University of Nebraska Press, 1971), includes a notable version of the Washita battle.

Edward Godfrey, one of Custer's officers, adds interesting details in "Some Reminiscences, Including the Washita Battle, November 27, 1868," *Cavalry Journal* 37 (October 1928). Godfrey's article also appears in Paul A. Hutton's *The Custer Reader* (Lincoln: University of Nebraska Press, 1992). Custer's view of events is included in his memoirs, *My Life on the Plains; or, Personal Experiences with Indians* (Norman: University of Oklahoma Press, 1962). Libbie Custer provides her insight in *Following the Guidon* (Norman: University of Oklahoma Press, 1966).

Another work of merit is "Custer on the Washita," by Reginald S. Craig, *Brand Book of the Denver Westerners* 10 (1965). Two of the more critical assessments are Charles J. Brill's *Conquest of the Southern Plains: Uncensored Narrative of the Battle* of the Washita and Custer's Southern Campaign (Oklahoma City: Golden Saga Publishers, 1938); and *Custer's Battle of the Washita and a History of the Plains Indian Tribes,* by Jess C. Epple (New York: Exposition Press, 1970).

See also "Battle of the Washita," by Paul Nesbitt, *Chronicles of Oklahoma* 3, no. 1 (1924); "The Battle of the Washita," by Tahan, *Chronicles of Oklahoma* 8, no. 3 (1930); and "Winter Campaigning with Custer and Sheridan," by Lonnie J. White, *Journal of the West* 6, no. 1 (1967).

SIDEBARS

Table of Organization and Casualty Report of the 7th Cavalry at the Washita Battle

Custer's Detachment (approximately 300 men)

Field and Staff:
Lt. Col. George Armstrong Custer,
    commanding regiment
1st Lt. Myles Moylan, adjutant
1st Lt. James M. Bell, quartermaster
1st Lt. Samuel M. Robbins, engineer
2nd Lt. Algernon E. Smith, commissary
2nd Lt. Henry Lippincott, asst. surgeon
2nd Lt. William C. Renick, acting asst. surgeon
Sgt. Maj. Walter Kennedy (killed in action)
Regimental Band
2nd Lt. Edward G. Mathey, commanding pack train

Cooke's Sharpshooters:
1st Lt. William W. Cooke
40 men, no casualties

Hamilton's Squadron:
Capt. Louis M. Hamilton, commanding (killed in action)

Troop A	1st Lt. Thomas W. Custer	
	60 men, 1 officer wounded (Custer), 2 enlisted wounded	
Troop D	Capt. Thomas Weir	
	2nd Lt. H. Walworth Smith	
	60 men, 1 enlisted wounded	

West's Squadron:
Capt. Robert M. West, commanding

Troop C	1st Lt. Matthew Berry	
	60 men, no casualties	
Troop K	1st Lt. Edward S. Godfrey	
	2nd Lt. Edward Law	
	60 men, no casualties	

lar army brigadier general in 1901 to Pasadena, California, and died in Hermosa Beach on September 17, 1919. Bell was buried in San Francisco National Cemetery.

✸ Frederick William Benteen
Captain, 7th U.S. Cavalry

Capt. Frederick W. Benteen. *Courtesy Little Bighorn Battlefield National Monument.*

Benteen was born in Petersburg, Virginia, on August 24, 1834. He moved to St. Louis at age seven, where he attended a private academy and began working alongside his father painting houses and signs. Surprisingly for a young man with Virginia roots, he turned his back on the South and entered the Civil War in September 1861 as a first lieutenant in Bowen's Battalion, which later became the 10th Missouri Cavalry. His slave-owning father, Theodore C. Benteen, was furious at this betrayal by his son and, in addition to disowning Fred, was alleged to have said, "I hope the first bullet gets you!"

Benteen's "defection" was probably not entirely due to philosophical reasons, but encouraged by a young Unionist lady from Philadelphia named Catherine Norman, whom he married on January 7, 1862. The Benteens lost four children to spinal meningitis and raised one son, Fred, who later became a major in the army.

Benteen, who was promoted to captain on October 1, 1861, distinguished himself in actions at West Glaze, Wilson's Creek, Bolivar, Milliken's Bend, and the battle of Pea Ridge; skirmishes at Springfield, Sugar Creek, Batesville, Cotton Plant,

(continued on following page)

Kickapoo Bottom, and Greenville; and the defense of Helena.

While Benteen fought for the Union cause, his father was employed as chief engineer on a Mississippi steamboat called the *Fair Play,* which supplied the Confederacy. On August 18, 1862, Captain Benteen's company was part of a Union flotilla that captured his father's boat. The civilian crew members were soon released, except for T. C. Benteen, who, perhaps on account of his son's influence, was imprisoned for the duration of the war.

Benteen was appointed major in December 1862, and the following year, he fought in skirmishes at Florence and Cane Creek, the siege of Vicksburg, Iuka and Brandon Station, and the capture of Jackson. He was appointed lieutenant colonel in February 1864 and placed in command of the 4th (Winslow's) Brigade of General Pleasonton's Cavalry Division. He led his brigade in actions at Bolivar and Pleasant Hill, engagements on the Big Blue and Little Osage Crossing in Missouri, and the assault and capture of Selma and the raid on Columbus. During the October 1864 Federal pursuit of Confederate general Sterling Price, who had invaded Missouri, Benteen's brigade spearheaded the decisive charge at the battle of Mine Creek that shattered the Rebel lines. On June 6, 1865, he was recommended for the brevet rank of brigadier general, but the recommendation was not accepted. Benteen was mustered out in Chattanooga on June 30, 1856.

After the war, Benteen was appointed colonel of the 138th U.S. Colored Volunteers and served in that unit from July 1865 to January 1866. He received his Regular army commission as a captain in July 1866 and was assigned to the 7th Cavalry.

Benteen took an immediate dislike to George Armstrong Custer, who was younger in age yet senior in rank and nationally famous, and has become notorious as Custer's most outspoken critic. One public confrontation between the two officers occurred following the battle of the Washita, when Benteen, in an anonymous letter, accused Custer of the abandonment on the field of Maj. Joel Elliott, who had been Benteen's friend and subordinate officer during the Civil War (see "The Joel Elliott Controversy" on page 90).

Custer, to his credit, never spoke or wrote in a disparaging manner about Benteen. In fact, in *My Life on the Plains; or, Personal Experiences with Indians* (Norman: University of Oklahoma Press, 1962)—which Benteen referred to as "My *Lie* on the Plains"—Custer related an incident during the Washita battle that was quite complimentary

(continued on following page)

82

Elliott's Detachment (180 men)
Maj. Joel H. Elliott, commanding (killed in action)

Troop G	Capt. Albert Barnitz 60 men, 1 officer wounded (Barnitz), 2 enlisted wounded
Troop H	Capt. Frederick W. Benteen 60 men, 5 enlisted killed
Troop M	1st Lt. Owen Hale 2nd Lt. Thomas J. March 60 men, 1 officer wounded (March), 7 enlisted killed, 1 enlisted wounded

Myers's Detachment (120 men)
Capt. Edward Myers, commanding

| Troop E | 1st Lt. John M. Johnson
60 men, 3 enlisted killed,
1 enlisted wounded |
| Troop I | 1st Lt. Charles Brewster
60 men, 2 enlisted killed,
2 enlisted wounded |

Thompson's Detachment (120 men)
Capt. William Thompson, commanding

| Troop B | 1st Lt. David W. Wallingford
60 men, 2 enlisted killed |
| Troop F | Capt. George W. Yates
2nd Lt. Francis M. Gibson
60 men, 1 enlisted wounded |

Detached Service: Col. Andrew J. Smith; Maj. Alfred Gibbs; Capt. Michael V. Sheridan; Capt. Myles W. Keogh; Capt. Lewis M. Dayton; 1st Lt. Henry Jackson; 2nd Lt. Oliver W. Longan

Leave of Absence: Maj. Joseph G. Tilford; 2nd Lt. John F. Weston; 2nd Lt. Bradford S. Bassett

At Fort Lyon: Company L under 1st Lt. Henry H. Abell; 2nd Lt. J. Henry Shellabarger

At Camp Supply: Capt. Lee P. Gillette; 1st Lt. Henry J. Nowlan

Sick: 2nd Lt. Donald McIntosh

Undergoing Suspension: 2nd Lt. William B. Clark

Appendix D in Stan Hoig's *The Battle of the Washita: The Sheridan-Custer Indian Campaign of 1867–69* (Garden City, NY: Doubleday, 1976) presents a comprehensive listing of officers and enlisted men killed or wounded at Washita. The "Remarks" column furnishes notes about the condition of the bodies from Dr. Henry Lippincott's report, File F, 421, Old Military Records, National Archives, that are quite graphic in nature—those of Elliott's command in particular.

Elliott's entry, for example, reads: "Two bullet holes in head, one in left cheek, right hand cut off, left foot almost cut off, penis cut off, deep gash in right groin, deep gashes in calves of both legs, little finger of left hand cut off, and throat cut." Lippincott's descriptions also appear in Custer's *My Life on the Plains; or, Personal Experiences with Indians* (Norman: University of Oklahoma Press, 1962); and *Sheridan's Troopers on the Borders: A Winter Campaign on the Plains,* by De B. Randolph Keim (Lincoln: University of Nebraska Press, 1985).

🐎 Total War

During George Armstrong Custer's absence from duty, government policy with respect to the "Indian problem" had been the subject of fierce contention between two diverse factions. The Eastern humanitarian groups combined with the Indian Bureau to favor a policy of tolerance, generosity, and fair treatment for the Indians, which they believed would encourage them to respond in kind. Westerners allied with the army to scoff at what they considered an idealistic and impractical notion. The only manner in which to deal with the Indians, according to Westerners, was by a demonstration of military might—punishment and supervision.

Both sides, however, agreed that all Plains Indians should be removed from the pathway of westward expansion between the Platte and Arkansas Rivers and resettled onto reservations north of Nebraska and south of Kansas. To that end, a peace commission was created by Congress, and the Medicine Lodge and Fort Laramie Treaties were negotiated. Due to cultural differences and miscommunication, peace was elusive, and before long Cheyenne and Sioux warriors were raiding across Kansas, attacking settlements as well as detachments of the army that had been dispatched to subdue the hostiles.

The army, under Generals William T. Sherman and Phil Sheridan, was called upon in the fall of 1868 to embark on a major winter campaign designed to restore peace on the plains. The two men had decided that a new ruthless measure was required to punish the Indians and implemented the concept of "total war," which had been pioneered by Brig. Gen. W. S. Harney against the Lakota Sioux in 1855 (see "The Initiation of Warfare between the Plains Indians and the U.S. Army" on page 49).

Total war meant subjecting the civilian populace, not just the enemy fighting force, to a reign of terror. By invading the enemy's homeland and mercilessly destroying property—lodges, food stores, and ponies—the will to fight would be broken. Rarely could these nomadic Indians be caught in the summer, but a winter campaign would find them vulnerable—camped along some waterway, ponies weakened from lack of forage, caches of food barely sufficient to last until spring. Sherman and Sheridan held the view that the torch was as effective a weapon as the sword, that poverty would bring about peace more quickly than the loss of human life.

to Benteen (see "Benteen's Battlefield Duel" on page 103).

Benteen, as commander of Company H, participated in the Yellowstone expedition of 1873 and the Black Hills expedition the following year.

At the June 1876 battle of the Little Bighorn, Benteen was on a reconnaissance with about 125 troops when he received Custer's last message, written by Adj. William W. Cooke, which read: "Benteen. Come on. Big Village. Be Quick. Bring [ammunition] Packs. W. W. Cooke. P. bring pacs." Instead of hurrying to rescue Custer, Benteen lollygagged along the way, which in the opinion of many scholars constituted a disobedience of orders. Had he acted immediately, it has been theorized, he could have reached the battlefield in time to assist Custer. To be fair, statements made by orderly John Martin, who had delivered the message, were of a reassuring nature, which might have convinced Benteen that the situation was well in hand.

"We are as certain to find Indians as you are to finds ducks in the Monroe [Michigan] marsh."

—CUSTER TO A HOMETOWN FRIEND, NOVEMBER 1868

Also, Benteen stated at the 1879 Reno Court of Inquiry that he believed it would have been tantamount to suicide to follow Custer's order. "We were at their hearth and homes," he said, referring to the Sioux, "their medicine was working well, and they were fighting for all the good God gives anyone to fight for." Perhaps that was the case when Benteen finally arrived near the scene of the battle. Had he "come on" and been "quick," the presence of his 125 troopers might have made a difference in reducing the fighting spirit of the enemy.

Custer's last message, by the way, has survived. In a letter to his wife on July 4, Benteen quoted the message and said, "I have the original, but it is badly torn and it should be preserved." He brought it to Reno's Court of Inquiry and later gave it to a friend in Philadelphia, who sold it to a New Jersey collector. At some point, Col. Charles Bates, author of several Custer-related books, noticed the message advertised for sale at an auction. Bates

(continued on following page)

arranged with the owner to have it secured by the U.S. Military Academy at West Point.

Benteen slowly moved his battalion toward the valley and, upon hearing firing and claiming to have observed at least 1,500 Indians, turned his command and headed for the bluffs where Reno had fled. His battalion joined Reno's troops to form a perimeter, and Benteen distinguished himself by apparently assuming *de facto* command in place of Reno, who was said to have been incapacitated. Benteen bravely rallied the troops throughout the two-day siege, in which he received a wound to his thumb.

Benteen, true to form, also held the opinion that Custer had disobeyed the orders of General Terry and thereby sacrificed his command (see "Did Custer Disobey Orders?" on page 208).

Benteen fought against the Nez Perce at Canyon Creek in 1877, for which he received a brevet to colonel. In 1882, he was promoted to major and transferred to the 9th Cavalry. While serving as commander of Fort Duchesne, Utah, in 1886, Benteen, who had a fondness for alcohol, faced a court-martial and was found guilty of various offenses ranging from "drunkenness on duty" to "using obscene and profane language" and "exposing his person." His punishment, dismissal from the army, was later amended by President Cleveland to a one-year suspension in respect for Benteen's long and honorable service.

Benteen established his residence in Atlanta and requested that he be retired on disability following his suspension, which took effect July 7, 1888. Two years later, he received a brevet of brigadier general for his actions at Little Bighorn and against the Nez Perce. Benteen died on June 22, 1898, from paralysis following a stroke. He was initially buried in Westview Cemetery in Atlanta but was reinterred in November 1902 in Arlington National Cemetery.

One volume, *The Benteen-Goldin Letters on Custer and His Last Battle,* edited by John M. Carroll (New York: Liverright, 1974), best reveals the true personality of the sarcastic and critical Frederick Benteen. Bitter and vindictive in his old age, Benteen's hatred of Custer and contempt for most of his old comrades literally blisters the pages of these letters to a former 7th Cavalry private named Theodore Goldin and others. He occasionally rattled his saber by alluding to great crimes or misdeeds committed by Custer, but he failed to provide evidence and instead merely repeated camp gossip spiced with his rancorous conjectures. *The Custer Myth: A Source Book of Custeriana,* by W. A. Graham (Harrisburg, PA: Stackpole

(continued on following page)

And if noncombatant lives happened to be lost, that would simply be a regrettable but excusable tragedy of war.

The total war concept, however, required a leader undeterred by the discomforts of winter campaigning, one with the capacity to tenaciously carry out orders. When Col. Alfred Sully proved too timid for the task, Sheridan summoned his trusted subordinate from the Shenandoah Valley, George Armstrong Custer, to command the 7th Cavalry on the winter campaign of 1868–69.

Custer indeed implemented total war to perfection on Black Kettle's village. In addition to 103 killed and 53 women and children taken prisoner, the property loss was devastating. The pony herd, estimated at 875, was destroyed, and everything in the entire village—every lodge, 1,100 buffalo robes, 210 axes, 140 hatchets, 47 rifles, 35 revolvers, 90 bullet molds, 535 pounds of powder, 75 spears, 35 bows and quivers, 4,000 arrows, 470 blankets, large quantities of dried meat and food stores, 300 pounds of tobacco, and clothing—was either confiscated or burned to the ground.

The debate about the "Indian problem" is described best in *Uncle Sam's Stepchildren: The Reformation of the United States Indian Policy, 1865–1887,* by Loring Benson Priest (New York: Octagon Books, 1969); and *American Indian Policy in Crisis: Christian Reformers and the Indian, 1865–1900,* by Francis Paul Prucha (Chicago: University of Chicago Press, 1977). A discussion of the concept and execution of "total war" demonstrated during the winter campaign of 1868–69 can be found in *William Tecumseh Sherman and the Settlement of the West,* by Robert G. Athearn (Norman: University of Oklahoma Press, 1956); *Personal Memoirs of Philip Henry Sheridan, General United States Army,* 2 vols., by Philip H. and Michael V. Sheridan (New York: S. Appleton and Company, 1904); *Phil Sheridan and His Army,* by Paul A. Hutton (Lincoln: University of Nebraska Press, 1985); *General Custer and the Battle of Washita: The Federal View* by John M. Carroll (Bryan, TX: Guidon Press, 1978); Robert M. Utley's *Cavalier in Buckskin: George Armstrong Custer and the Western Military Frontier* (Norman: University of Oklahoma Press, 1988); *Sheridan's Troopers on the Borders: A Winter Campaign on the Plains,* by De B. Randolph Keim (Lincoln: University of Nebraska Press, 1985); and Stan Hoig's *The Battle of the Washita: The Sheridan-Custer Indian Campaign of 1867–69* (Garden City, NY: Doubleday, 1976).

Indian Captives Clara Blinn and Her Son

While preparing for the winter campaign of 1868–69, Phil Sheridan was bothered by the number of settlers, especially white women, who had fallen into the hands of the hostile Indians raiding across Kansas. One case that particularly haunted Sheridan, and later, George Armstrong Custer, was that of a young woman named Clara Blinn.

Richard and Clara Blinn and their infant son, Willie, had been traveling by wagon train to Franklin County, Kansas, when they were attacked on the Colorado plains by Arapaho or Cheyenne warriors. During the ensuing skirmish, Clara and Willie were taken captive. The circumstances surrounding the abduction are unknown; the wagon train was said to have been carrying eleven armed men, only one of whom was wounded, and no other members were killed or captured—including Blinn's husband.

Clara soon managed to smuggle a letter out of an Indian camp. Addressed to "Kind Friend," the message read:

> Whoever you may be, if you will only buy us from the Indians with ponies or any thing, and let me come and stay with you until I can get word to my friends, they will pay you well; and I will work for you also, and do all I can for you. If it is not too far to this village, and you are not afraid to come, I pray you will try. The Indians tell me, as near as I can understand, they expect traders to come, to whom they will sell us. Can you find out by the bearer, and let me know if they are white men? If they are Mexicans, I am afraid they will sell us into slavery in Mexico. If you can do anything for me, write, for God's sake! to W. T. Harrington, Ottawa, Franklin County, Kansas—my father. Tell him we are with the Kiowahs, or Cheyennes; and they say when white men make peace we can go home. Tell him to write to the Governor of Kansas about it, and for them to make peace. Send this to him, please. We were taken on the 9th of Oct. [1868] on the Arkansas below Fort Lyon. I can't tell whether they killed my husband or not. My name is Mrs. Clara Blinn. My little boy Willie Blinn, he is two years old. Do all you can for me. Write to the Peace Commissioners to make peace this fall. For our sake do all you can, and God will bless you for it! If you can let me hear from you, let me know what you think about it. Write to my father. Send him this. Good-by!
>
> Mrs. R. F. Blinn
>
> P.S.—I am as well as can be expected, but my baby, my darling, darling little Willie, is very weak. O, God, help him! Save him, kind friend, even if you can not save me. Again, good-by.

Sheridan learned of Clara Blinn's captivity when he received a letter from her father, W. T. Harrington, who pleaded with Sheridan to rescue his daughter and grandson. Col. William Hazen had been in the process of attempting to negotiate their release, but Sheridan halted that effort, writing: "After having her husband & friends murdered, and her own person subjected to the fearful bestiality of perhaps the whole tribe, it is mock humanity to secure what is left of her for the consideration of 5 ponies." The ultimate mission of Sheridan's winter campaign, however, had now taken on a more personal chivalrous purpose—if not rescuing Clara Blinn, then protecting others from suffering the same fate.

Books, 1953), dedicates a full chapter to a sampling of Benteen's writings on various topics.

Benteen was the subject of a rather sympathetic biography, *Harvest of Barren Regrets: The Army Career of Frederick William Benteen, 1834–1898*, by Charles K. Mills (Glendale, CA: Arthur H. Clark, 1985). His softer yet no less sarcastic side is revealed in *Camp Talk: The Very Private Letters of Frederick Benteen of the Seventh U.S. Cavalry to His Wife, 1871–1888*, edited by John M. Carroll (Bryan, TX: J. M. Carroll, 1983).

Other notable sources include *Gray Head and Long Hair: The Benteen-Custer Relationship*, by Karol Asay (New York: John M. Carroll, 1983); *Cavalry Scraps: The Writings of Frederick W. Benteen*, edited by John M. Carroll (East Stroudsburg, PA: Guidon Press, 1979); *Benteen's Ordeal and Custer's Field*, by Barry Johnson (London: Johnson-Taunton Military Press, 1983); and *The Court Martial of Frederick W. Benteen, Major, 9th Cavalry; or, Did General Crook Railroad Benteen?* edited by John M. Carroll (Bryan, TX: Privately printed, 1981). The Frederick W. Benteen Collection, which consists of three boxes of material, is located in the University of Georgia Library.

"Huh, all I am afraid of is we won't find half enough. There are not Indians enough in the country to whip the Seventh Cavalry."

—Custer responding to an inquiry from an officer on the eve of the battle about the potential strength of the Cheyenne camped on the Washita River

---

✹ Black Kettle
Southern Cheyenne

This prominent chief (Moke-ta-ve-to), who was born in the Black Hills about 1803, proved himself in his youth to be a fierce warrior against his tribe's enemies. By the early 1860s, however, he had become an advocate of peace between his people and whites. Black Kettle signed the 1861 Treaty at Fort Wise and two years later was said in many accounts to have been part of a delegation that traveled to Washington to meet President Abraham Lincoln. His participation in that trip to

(continued on following page)

Washington in 1863, however, has been a matter of contention. He likely did not visit Washington.

Despite his peaceful intentions, the Cheyenne chief was the victim of two disastrous attacks by military forces.

The first tragedy occurred in 1864, when Black Kettle accepted protection from the army and at the direction of military authorities moved his camp to a designated place at Sand Creek, Colorado Territory, to spend the winter. On November 27, he barely escaped with his life when the Colorado militia led by Col. John Chivington launched a surprise attack on the Sand Creek camp and slaughtered at least 150 Cheyenne—most of them women and children (see "The Sand Creek Massacre" on page 104).

Black Kettle continued to advocate peace in spite of this betrayal. At the request of his friend, Indian agent Edward Wynkoop, he attended the council at Medicine Lodge and signed the 1867 treaty. Violations of this treaty were commonplace; therefore, Black Kettle moved his tribe to a location on the Washita River that he believed would allow them to avoid any conflict with the army.

In November 1868, Black Kettle met with Col. William B. Hazen, who had the unenviable task of determining which Indian tribes were friendly or hostile. Hazen was convinced that Black Kettle was peaceful but advised the Cheyenne chief to make peace with General Sheridan, who had initiated an offensive against hostiles. Before Black Kettle could locate Sheridan, the 7th Cavalry, led by George Armstrong Custer, had tracked some renegade hostiles to Black Kettle's village on the Washita and attacked at dawn on November 27, 1868. Black Kettle and his wife were shot and killed near the icy water of the Washita as they attempted to escape. His death sparked an outrage among both Indians and whites and initiated a debate about whether the attack by Custer was a battle or a massacre similar to Sand Creek (see "Public Reaction to the Washita Battle" on page 88).

Black Kettle has never been the subject of a biography. His story is best told in *The Fighting Cheyennes*, by George Bird Grinnell (Norman: University of Oklahoma Press, 1956); *The Southern Cheyennes*, by Donald J. Berthrong (Norman: University of Oklahoma Press, 1963); *The Peace Chiefs of the Cheyennes*, by Stan Hoig (Norman: University of Oklahoma Press, 1980); *Cheyenne Memories*, by John Stand in Timber and Margot Liberty (New Haven: Yale University Press, 1967); and *Life of George Bent, Written from His Letters*, by George E. Hyde (Norman: University of Oklahoma Press, 1967).

On November 27, 1868, Custer attacked and destroyed Black Kettle's camp on the Washita River. In early December, Sheridan and Custer returned to examine the battlefield. Downstream, at the site of another village determined to be Kiowa under Satanta, they encountered a grisly discovery—the bodies of Clara Blinn and her son, Willie. Mrs. Blinn had been shot twice in the forehead from point-blank range, her skull crushed, and her scalp taken. Willie, who had been reduced to skin and bones, had likely been picked up by the feet and bashed against a tree. It was speculated that the two captives had been killed at about the same time that Custer had charged into Black Kettle's village, perhaps because the Indians, as Custer reported, feared "she might be recaptured by us and her testimony used against them."

Custer agonized over his failure to rescue the two captives, but he had learned a valuable lesson that he applied the following March at Sweetwater Creek, Texas. Instead of charging into an Indian village known to hold captives, Custer—despite accusations of cowardice—successfully negotiated their freedom (see "The Rescue at Sweetwater Creek" on page 96).

Clara Blinn's message is on display at the National Frontier Trails Center in Independence, Missouri, and has been reprinted in Carl Coke Rister's *Border Captives: The Traffic in Prisoners by Southern Plains Indians* (Norman: University of Oklahoma Press, 1940), which details the incident. W. T. Harrington's letter to Sheridan dated November 8, 1868, is located in the Records of the U.S. Army, Box 16, Division of the Missouri, Special File, RG 393. For an excerpt of the incident from Custer's official report, see *My Life on the Plains; or, Personal Experiences with Indians*, by George Armstrong Custer (Norman: University of Oklahoma Press, 1962). This edition also includes an argument by Col. William B. Hazen with respect to the identity of the Indians who were responsible for the death of Mrs. Blinn.

Other notable sources include *The Battle of the Washita: The Sheridan-Custer Indian Campaign of 1867–69,* by Stan Hoig (Garden City, NY: Doubleday, 1976); *Cavalier in Buckskin,* by Robert M. Utley (Norman: University of Oklahoma Press, 1988); *Sheridan's Troopers on the Borders: A Winter Campaign on the Plains,* by De B. Randolph Keim (Lincoln: University of Nebraska Press, 1985); and *Phil Sheridan and His Army,* by Paul A. Hutton (Lincoln: University of Nebraska Press, 1985).

Indian Casualties at the Washita Battle

Rarely, if ever, have Indian casualties from a battle been accurately reported. Commanders throughout history have tended to exaggerate enemy "body counts" to embellish the significance of their victories or minimize their losses. Eyewitnesses—on both sides—have often related contradictory estimates, which may or may not be based on personal prejudices, hearsay, or failing memories in old age. The battle at the Washita River is no exception.

In his official report, George Armstrong Custer reported the number of Indian dead at 103 and claimed that an exact body count was taken on the field after the battle, but he contradicted the statement in his memoirs by relating that his figures were calculated the following day by asking his officers for estimates. Custer later amended that total when he wrote in a report dated December 22, 1868, that "the Indians admit a loss of 140 killed, besides a heavy loss of wounded. This, with the Indian prisoners we have in our possession, makes the entire loss of the Indian in killed, wounded, and missing not far from 300." (Senate Executive Document No. 40, 40th Congress, 3rd Session, 1869.)

Black Kettle's village was composed of fifty-one lodges, which, if Custer's last figure is to be believed, would mean that just about every person in the village was killed or captured.

A sampling of eyewitnesses and other interested parties provides a wide disparity in casualty totals.

Capt. Henry Alvord, a representative of Indian agent Col. William B. Hazen, set the figure at five chiefs and distinguished braves, including Black Kettle, and about seventy-five ordinary fighting men. (House Executive Document No. 18, 41st Congress, 2nd Session, 1869.)

George Bent, who was married to Black Kettle's niece, claimed that eleven Cheyenne warriors, two Arapaho warriors, twelve women, and six children were killed. (*Life of George Bent: Written from His Letters,* by George E. Hyde, Norman: University of Oklahoma Press, 1968.)

James S. Morrison, a scout formerly in the employ of Indian agent Edward W. Wynkoop, quoted John Poysell and Jack Fitzpatrick, two of Custer's scouts, when he wrote on December 14, 1868, that the 7th Cavalry killed twenty warriors and about forty women and children. (*Conquest of the Southern Plains,* by Charles J. Brill, Oklahoma City: Golden Saga Publishers, 1938.)

Custer scout Ben Clark was quoted in the May 14, 1899, edition of the *New York Sun:* "I estimate the Cheyenne loss at seventy-five warriors and fully as many women and children killed."

Cheyenne chief Little Robe related in April 1869 that thirteen men, sixteen women, and nine children had been killed. ("Report of the Commissioner of Indian Affairs," *Report of the Secretary of the Interior,* Washington, 1869.) This estimate was confirmed verbally by Kiowa chief Black Eagle to Colonel Hazen at Fort Cobb several days after the battle.

Any total must take into consideration the inclusion of an undetermined number of noncombatants. It is known that during the battle, Custer was informed that Capt. Edward Myers's command, despite orders to the contrary, was firing into a group

✺ Eugene Asa Carr
Major, 5th U.S. Cavalry

Carr was born on March 20, 1830, in Concord, Erie County, New York. He entered the U.S. Military Academy at West Point in 1846 and graduated four years later, nineteenth in a class of forty-four. Carr was assigned to the Mounted Riflemen, which became the 3rd Cavalry, and served on the frontier for the next ten years. In October 1854, he was severely wounded by an arrow in a skirmish with Apache Indians near present-day Limpia, Texas, and was subsequently promoted to first lieutenant, 1st Cavalry Regiment. In 1855, Carr began serving in Kansas and Nebraska, protecting emigrant routes from hostile Sioux and worked for a time as aide-de-camp to Kansas governor Robert J. Walker. He was promoted to captain in 1858 and transferred to Indian Territory to battle Kiowa and Comanche.

At the outbreak of the Civil War, Carr was assigned to Brig. Gen. Nathaniel Lyon's command in Missouri. He distinguished himself in the August 10, 1861, battle of Wilson's Creek, which six days later gained him an appointment to colonel of the 3rd Illinois Cavalry. At the March 1862 battle of Pea Ridge, Arkansas, Carr suffered three wounds but refused to leave the field, electing instead to have his wounds treated as he remained astride his horse. He was promoted to brigadier general on the first day of that battle and later awarded a Medal of Honor for his bravery. Carr assumed command of the Army of the Southwest in 1862 and commanded a division during the Vicksburg campaign. He was promoted to brevet major general of volunteers on March 13, 1865. That same year, he married Mary P. Maguire, with whom he had two children.

After the war, Major Carr commanded an army detachment in North Carolina from March 1866 to April 1867. He received a brief staff assignment in Washington, D.C., before rejoining the 5th Cavalry in Kansas in 1868. Carr participated in Sheridan's winter campaign of 1868–69 and on July 11, 1869, was in command when his unit routed Tall Bull's Cheyenne at Summit Springs, Colorado, in one of the army's most decisive victories against the Indians (see "The Battle of Summit Springs" on page 101).

Carr was promoted to lieutenant colonel in 1873 and commanded the 5th Cavalry at the Slim Buttes battle of September 9, 1876, where numerous items belonging to the 7th Cavalry were found. As colonel of the 6th Cavalry in 1879, he was sent to Arizona and participated in cam-

(continued on following page)

paigns against the Apache, including the affair at Cibicu Creek in August 1881, when he put down a mutiny of his Apache scouts. His regiment was transferred to New Mexico in 1883 and sent north to Wounded Knee for the 1890 uprising. Carr was appointed brigadier general in July 1892 and retired in February 1893.

He died in Washington, D.C., on December 2, 1910, and was buried at West Point.

📖 James T. King's biography, *War Eagle: A Life of General Eugene A. Carr* (Lincoln: University of Nebraska Press, 1963), provides an excellent look into the career of this man who has been described as "perhaps the most famous and experienced Indian fighter . . . following the Civil War." The Eugene A. Carr Papers are located at the U.S. Army Military History Research Collection at Carlisle Barracks, Pennsylvania. Other notable sources include those associated with the Summit Springs and Slim Buttes battles, as well as *General Crook and the Sierra Madre Adventure,* by Dan L. Thrapp (Norman: University of Oklahoma Press, 1972); and Thrapp's *Victorio and the Mimbres Apaches* (Norman: University of Oklahoma Press, 1974).

✹ Ben Clark
U.S. Army Scout

Clark was born in St. Louis on February 2, 1842. At age thirteen, he traveled to Fort Bridger, Wyoming, where he served as post courier. In 1857, he enlisted in a battalion of volunteers under Col. Albert S. Johnston in the so-called Mormon or Utah War. He was mustered out the following year. During the Civil War, Clark served with the 6th Kansas Cavalry, which patrolled the borders of Arkansas, Missouri, and Indian Territory. After the war, he managed pack trains for Indian traders and married a Cheyenne woman, who bore him eleven children—seven of whom survived infancy. Some of his children graduated from the Carlisle Indian school. Clark, who became fluent in native languages—Cheyenne in particular—and sign language was respected by both Indians and whites, which served him well as a go-between.

He signed on as an army scout in 1868 and became a valuable asset to Sheridan and Custer during the winter campaign of 1868–69. As Custer's chief scout, Clark and three other scouts reconnoitered the vicinity of Black Kettle's village on the Washita and reported precise information regarding terrain to Custer, who could then formulate his attack plan. During the battle on November 27, Clark reported to Custer that Myers's command—in disregard of Custer's

(continued on following page)

of women and children, and scout Ben Clark was dispatched to order Myers to stop and instead take them prisoner.

Regardless of opinions and circumstances, the number of Indian dead that has withstood the test of time as the accepted figure—and has been inscribed on historical markers—is 103.

📖 In addition to the above references, other sources include *The Battle of the Washita: The Sheridan-Custer Indian Campaign of 1867–69,* by Stan Hoig (Garden City, NY: Doubleday, 1976); *General Custer and the Battle of the Washita: The Federal View,* edited by John M. Carroll (Bryan, TX: Guidon Press, 1978); and Paul A. Hutton's *Phil Sheridan and His Army* (Lincoln: University of Nebraska Press, 1985).

🐎 Public Reaction to the Washita Battle

The battle of the Washita was considered a great victory in the estimation of the military establishment. Eastern humanitarians, however, called the action a massacre. Newspaper editorials and a deluge of letters criticized the army and condemned Custer—comparing him to Colonel Chivington of Sand Creek fame—for the killing of innocent women and children. Interested parties decried in particular the death of Black Kettle, whom they called a fine example of a peace-loving Indian.

Indian agent Edward W. Wynkoop resigned his post in protest over the killing of the Cheyenne chief and likened the slaughter to Sand Creek by claiming that "Black Kettle had proceeded to the point at which he was killed with the understanding that it was the locality where all those Indians who were friendly disposed should assemble."

Peace commission member Maj. Gen. W. S. Harney wrote, "I know Black Kettle was as good a friend of the U.S. as I am." Superintendent of Indian Affairs Thomas Murphy wrote that Black Kettle was "one of the truest friends the whites have ever had among the Indians." Another peace commission member, Samuel F. Tappan, demanded an "immediate and unconditional abandonment of the present war policy."

Division commander Gen. William T. Sherman summed up the army's sentiments in a letter to General Sheridan dated December 3, 1868:

> This you know is a free country, and people have the lawful right to misrepresent as much as they please—and to print them—but the great mass of our people cannot be humbugged into the belief that Black Kettle's camp was friendly with its captive women and children, its herds of stolen horses and its stolen mail, arms, powder, etc.—trophies of war.

Sheridan went on the offensive to refute the assertion that Black Kettle was on a reservation at the time of the attack and blamed the wanton raiding of the Indians for the army's retaliation. He listed as evidence items found in the village, such as mail—including a military dispatch carried by one of Sheridan's couriers who had been killed—daguerreotypes, bedding, and other domestic goods taken from settlers' cabins.

The contention that Black Kettle was a proponent of peace was very likely true, however. The day before the attack, the chief had returned from a meeting at Fort Cobb with Col. William B. Hazen, who had the unenviable task of determining which Indians were hostile and which were friendly. Hazen was convinced that Black Kettle was indeed peaceful but advised the chief to personally make peace with Sheridan to ensure his safety. The general could not be readily located, and Black Kettle simply went home. Nevertheless, that endorsement by Hazen does not absolve Black Kettle of any blame. He made a mistake by harboring hostiles that had participated in recent raiding parties and paid for it with his life.

The battle of the Washita was without question a one-sided affair, but it does not by any means fit the definition of a massacre. Black Kettle had been warned prior to the attack by Hazen that his safety could not be guaranteed unless he surrendered to Sheridan, which he failed to do. The village contained captives and items taken by resident armed warriors who had recently skirmished with the soldiers and had been on raiding parties against white settlers, which was evidenced by the fact that Custer's Osage scouts tracked them to Black Kettle's doorstep.

Furthermore, Custer did not order a slaughter, but issued specific orders to spare noncombatants. In fact, Custer followed his orders from Sheridan to the letter: "To proceed south, in the direction of the Antelope hills, thence towards the Washita river, the supposed winter seat of the hostile tribes; to destroy their villages and ponies; to kill all warriors, and bring back all women and children."

The inability of the army to catch the Indians on the open plains and the failure of the government to clearly state specific hunting grounds in the provisions of the peace treaty at Medicine Lodge made necessary the implementation of "total war," and the battle of the Washita was the tragic result.

📖 The most balanced debate can be found in Paul A. Hutton's *Phil Sheridan and His Army* (Lincoln: University of Nebraska Press, 1985.) One of the better arguments for the humanitarian position is covered in detail in chapter 12, "A Quarrel of Conscience," in Stan Hoig's *The Battle of the Washita: The Sheridan-Custer Indian Campaign of 1867–69* (New York: Doubleday, 1975). Ironically, although Hoig concluded that the battle was a massacre, he provides more than enough evidence to dispute that finding. Custer reacts to the criticism in *My Life on the Plains; or, Personal Experiences with Indians* (Norman: University of Oklahoma Press, 1962). For a reporter's eyewitness point of view that at times both supports and refutes the army's presentation of events and evidence, see

orders—was shooting into a group of women and children. He was dispatched to order Myers to cease and instead take them prisoner.

Clark later implied that—without naming the girl—Custer had formed an intimate relationship with Mo-nah-se-tah, a Cheyenne captive from Black Kettle's village who had served as a mediator for the remainder of the winter campaign of 1868–69. Some historians tend to regard his statement as suspect, inasmuch as Clark blamed Custer for his dismissal as an army scout (see "Custer and Mo-nah-se-tah" on page 92).

Clark was appointed post interpreter at Camp Supply in 1869 and to the same position at Fort Reno in later years. He took leaves of absence to scout for General Miles in the Red River War of 1874–75, serve with General Crook during the Little Bighorn campaign, and participate in the Dull Knife campaign of 1878. Ben Clark died on July 24, 1914, and was buried beside his wife, who had passed away the previous year, in the Fort Reno, Oklahoma, cemetery.

📖 Clark, with the assistance of William G. McDonald, wrote a manuscript called "Legends of the Cheyenne and Arapahoe Indians," which contains interesting information about Plains Indian ethnology and customs. A copy can be found in the Fred Barde Collection of the Oklahoma Historical Society. An interview of Clark by historian Walter Camp can be found in Field Notes, Folder 4, Box 2, Walter Camp Papers, Lily Library, Indiana University. Also see "Ben Clark: The Scout Who Defied Custer," by Kevin Thomas, *Oldtimers Wild West* (February 1980).

❂ William Frederick "Buffalo Bill" Cody
Scout and Showman

Cody was born in 1846 at LeClaire, Scott County, Iowa (near Davenport). In 1854, his family moved to Salt Creek Valley, near Fort Leavenworth in Kansas Territory. Cody's father, Isaac, established a trading post, and young Bill Cody learned the ways of the local Kickapoo Indians. Three years later, Isaac, who was antislavery, died from complications of a stab wound received during an argument. Bill's mother, Mary, maintained the family business while he helped out by working as a mounted messenger. In 1860, at age fourteen, Bill secured a job riding for Major's and Russell's Pony Express.

At the outbreak of the Civil War, Cody returned to Kansas and served with an irregular "jayhawker" militia company dedicated to stealing horses for the Union army from Confederate sympathizers. He enlisted in the 7th Kansas Volunteer

(continued on following page)

From left: Sioux Chief American Horse, William F. "Buffalo Bill" Cody, Sioux Leader Red Cloud. *Courtesy Little Bighorn Battlefield National Monument.*

Cavalry as a guide in 1864 and participated in skirmishes with the Confederate-allied Kiowa and Comanche. He met Louisa Frederici while on duty in St. Louis and married her in 1866. The couple returned to Salt Creek Valley, where Cody went into the hotel business. When that enterprise failed, he headed west. In 1867, he contracted to supply buffalo meat for workers on the Kansas Pacific Railway. It was at that time that he was bestowed with the nickname "Buffalo Bill."

In 1868, Gen. Phil Sheridan hired Cody as chief of scouts for the 5th U.S. Cavalry. Cody was said to have taken part in sixteen Indian fights, including the decisive July 1869 battle of Summit Springs—where a controversy ensued over whether Cody or scout Frank North was the killer of Cheyenne chief Tall Bull (see "The Battle of Summit Springs" on page 101). His Indian fighting exploits were glorified in greatly embellished dime novels written by "Ned Buntline" (E. Z. C. Judson), and Cody became a living legend. In 1872, he served as guide for the royal buffalo hunt of Russian grand duke Alexis and, along with George Armstrong Custer, assisted Alexis in bringing down his first buffalo (see "The Russian Grand Duke's Buffalo

(continued on following page)

Sheridan's Troopers on the Borders: A Winter Campaign on the Plains, by De B. Randolph Keim (Lincoln: University of Nebraska Press, 1985). Sheridan's orders to Custer appear in the works by both Hoig and Keim.

Other sources, for the most part sympathetic to the Indians, include *The Fighting Cheyennes,* by George B. Grinnell (Norman: University of Oklahoma Press, 1956); *Our Indian Wards,* by George W. Manypenny (Cincinnati: Robert Clarke Co., 1880); *Conquest of the Southern Plains: Uncensored Narrative of the Battle of the Washita and Custer's Southern Campaign,* by Charles J. Brill (Oklahoma City: Golden Saga Publishers, 1938); and *Custer's Battle of the Washita and a History of the Plains Indian Tribes,* by Jess C. Epple (New York: Exposition Press, 1970).

The Joel Elliott Controversy

The circumstances surrounding the deaths at Washita of Maj. Joel H. Elliott and a small detachment of troopers was an open wound that festered within the 7th Cavalry long after Custer's demise almost eight years later.

While the battle along the Washita River raged, Elliott, without informing Custer, rallied a group of volunteers to follow him downstream to chase Indians escaping from Black Kettle's village.

The exact number of troopers who accompanied Elliott has been a matter of debate. Custer, in *My Life on the Plains,* stated that the detachment comprised nineteen enlisted plus Elliott. De B. Randolph Keim, who accompanied the expedition, reported in *Sheridan's Troopers on the Border* that the bodies of Elliott and sixteen troopers were later found. Other sources have set the number as sixteen, eighteen, or nineteen.

As Elliott and his volunteers galloped past Lt. Owen Hale, the major called out, "Here goes for a brevet or a coffin!" Later that day, when the village had been captured and the troops were re-forming, Elliott had not returned. Custer dispatched Capt. Edward Myers to scout downstream for any sign of the missing men. Myers reported that he ventured about two miles without success.

By this time, Custer's outnumbered 7th Cavalry was under attack by swarms of Indians from the villages downstream, and it was necessary to withdraw. It was assumed that Elliott had simply become lost and would eventually find his own way back to the supply train. That, however, was not the case.

Sheridan and Custer returned to the Washita battlefield in early December, and on the tenth, they discovered the mutilated bodies of Elliott and his volunteers some miles downstream.

Although Custer clearly had acted prudently by withdrawing his command after making an attempt to locate the missing troopers, the tragic death of the popular Elliott provided the major's friend and former Civil War superior, Capt. Frederick Benteen—already a notorious Custer critic—with fuel to fan the flames of controversy.

In a letter to a friend in St. Louis, Benteen accused Custer of abandoning Elliott and included an evaluation of Custer's conduct at Washita that could only be called slanderous. This letter was published, anonymously and apparently without Benteen's permission, in the *St. Louis Democrat* newspaper and was reprinted by the *New York Times* on February 14, 1869.

A copy of the newspaper found its way to Custer, who had officers' call sounded and threatened to horsewhip the author of the letter. When Benteen readily admitted that he had written the letter, Custer was surprised and somewhat befuddled. He reportedly dismissed his officers without another word.

Benteen related a different version of the incident in Custer's tent. The captain allegedly shifted his revolver to a ready position on his belt. "At a pause in the talk I said, 'Gen. Custer, while I cannot father all the blame you have asserted, I guess I am the man you are after, and I am ready for the whipping promised.' He stammered and said, 'Col. Benteen, I'll see you again, sir!'"

Whatever the circumstances, some scholars have reasoned that Custer backed off his threat for the good of the outfit; others have questioned Custer's fortitude.

Benteen claimed that he later returned to Custer's tent with newspaperman and author De B. Randolph Keim as a witness and that Custer "wilted like a whipped cur."

Perhaps Benteen's accusation of abandonment was misdirected. No evidence exists, and the theory has not before been proposed to afford historians ample opportunity for debate, but there is a possibility that Capt. Edward Myers was the officer responsible for leaving Elliott and his men at the mercy of the Indians. It is known that Myers was dispatched by Custer to search for Elliott and the missing troopers. The report by Myers that he rode two miles without observing any sign of them has been taken for granted. Elliott was likely within two miles of the battlefield, either pinned down or already dead and the subject of Indian interest. Could Myers have ridden two miles without noticing anything suspicious—no heavy firing, no assemblage of aroused Indians?

Myers had been known to disobey orders in the past and had, in fact, been convicted a year earlier at a court-martial and sentenced to be dismissed from the service but was later restored to duty. Could Myers, in the face of an overwhelming number of Indians advancing from that direction, have failed to ride those two miles or adequately search for Elliott and simply reported that he had?

If that were the case, then why would Benteen have chosen to ignore Myers and placed the blame on Custer? Perhaps Ben-

Hunt" on page 107). That same year, Buntline coaxed Cody into portraying himself in a melodrama—*The Scouts of the Plains*—in Chicago, which launched his performing career. Cody then scouted or guided hunting parties in the summer and returned to the stage each winter.

Cody's most famous, or perhaps infamous, performance for the army came several weeks following the battle of the Little Bighorn. On July 17, 1876, Cody was scouting for Col. Wesley Merritt and his 400-man 5th Cavalry when he came upon thirty Cheyenne—out of an estimated 800 that had left Red Cloud Agency—at Warbonnet, or Hat, Creek. In what was later reported as a duel to the death, Cody shot the pony out from beneath a subchief named Hay-o-wai, or Yellow Hair, then killed and scalped the defenseless Indian. A reenactment of the "duel" became a popular play, *The Red Right Hand; or, Buffalo Bill's First Scalp for Custer.*

In 1883, Cody organized his first Wild West Show as part of a Fourth of July celebration in North Platte, Nebraska. His exhibitions of Western drama played throughout the United States and Europe for the next twenty-five years. The show featured rodeo events, as well as reenactments of Pony Express relays, stagecoach and wagon train attacks by Indians, Custer's Last Stand, the battle of Summit Springs, and the first scalp for Custer. Notable performers over the years included Annie Oakley, Wild Bill Hickok, Frank North and his Pawnee, and Sitting Bull.

It has been estimated that Ned Buntline made Cody the hero of over 1,700 novels. In addition, Prentiss Ingraham wrote countless other heroic novels and stories, as well as serving as ghostwriter for Cody as a published author. One of the more absurd novels was *Buffalo Bill with General Custer,* written by Ingraham, in which the famous scout was depicted as the lone survivor of the battle of the Little Bighorn.

In December 1890, Cody attempted to meet with Sitting Bull to solicit the chief's help in calming the uprising caused by the Ghost Dance. Sioux agent James McLauglin refused Cody access to the Hunkpapa leader, and within days, Sitting Bull had been killed in prelude to the Wounded Knee incident.

In 1898, Cody founded a town bearing his name in scenic northwestern Wyoming. The downtown Irma Hotel features a $100,000 bar that was a gift from Queen Victoria to Buffalo Bill in appreciation of his Wild West Show. The Buffalo Bill Historical Center in Cody offers four magnificent museums that display personal belongings of Cody, a fabu-

(continued on following page)

lous collection of more than 5,000 firearms, an extensive collection of Plains Indian artifacts, and paintings by many famous Western artists.

Cody made his final show appearance in 1916 and died on January 10, 1917, in Denver. He had requested burial on Cedar Mountain, Wyoming, but his wife, for financial considerations, permitted him to be interred atop Lookout Mountain above Denver.

📖 Cody boasts a rather extensive bibliography, with many books containing questionable information culled from a combination of Ned Buntline's fiction, Cody himself, associates and family members, and Wild West Show press releases. Perhaps the best biography is Don Russell's *The Lives and Legends of Buffalo Bill* (Norman: University of Oklahoma Press, 1973). *Buffalo Bill Cody,* by Robert A. Carter (New York: Wiley, 2000) places more emphasis on Cody's exploits in the West.

Other notable sources include *The Life of Hon. William F. Cody, Known as Buffalo Bill, the Famous Hunter, Scout and Guide: An Autobiography,* by Frank E. Bliss (1879); *Buckskins, Bullets, and Business: A History of Buffalo Bill's Wild West,* by Sarah J. Blackstone (Westport, CT: Greenwood, 1986; *First Scalp for Custer: The Skirmish at Warbonnet Creek,* by Paul L. Hedren (Lincoln: University of Nebraska Press, 1987).

✸ George Alexander "Sandy" Forsyth
Major, U.S. Army

Forsyth was born in Muncy, Pennsylvania, on November 7, 1837. In April 1861, he enlisted as a private in the 8th Illinois Cavalry. During the course of the war, he rose to the rank of major with brevets to brigadier general. Forsyth participated in eighty-six engagements, including those in the Shenandoah as a member of Gen. Phil Sheridan's staff—accompanying the general on his famous ride from Winchester—and was wounded four times.

Forsyth was a bright, capable officer, and after the war, he won an appointment as major in the 9th Cavalry and later joined Sheridan's staff. He craved field duty, however, and in 1868 was chosen by Sheridan to command an elite company of fifty scouts to protect the Kansas Pacific Railroad from hostile Indians. His company was pinned down on the Arikaree Fork of the Republican River in eastern Colorado for nine days by Cheyenne under Tall Bull and Sioux led by Pawnee Killer in the September 17–25 battle of Beecher Island. Forsyth was wounded three times and nearly died, but he maintained steady command

(continued on following page)

teen chose his commander for practical reasons. Myers was known to be a hot-tempered man who had once pulled his pistol on a fellow officer. To add to the intrigue, Myers had been the officer who rushed into Custer's tent on June 8, 1867, to report that Capt. Wickliffe Cooper had just taken his own life. That ruling of suicide was years later changed to "died by hand of person or persons unknown." Could it be that Benteen wanted no part of the dangerous Captain Myers, and instead found an easy target in Custer, whom he already hated and whom it could be presumed—in the name of proper military order—would not publicly confront Benteen?

Regardless, Benteen's accusations that Custer had abandoned Elliott created dissension for years to come among the officers of the regiment, who chose sides along loyalty lines.

📖 The text of Benteen's letter can be found in *The Custer Myth: A Source Book of Custeriana,* by W. A. Graham (Harrisburg, PA: Stackpole Books, 1953). Benteen's explanation of the incident in Custer's tent is described in his letter of February 22, 1896, to Theodore Goldin in *The Benteen-Goldin Letters on Custer and His Last Battle,* edited by John M. Carroll (Lincoln: University of Nebraska Press, 1974).

The best accounts of the Joel Elliott affair can be found in *Cavalier in Buckskin: George Armstrong Custer and the Western Military Frontier,* by Robert M. Utley (Norman: University of Oklahoma Press, 1988); *Custer Legends* by Lawrence A. Frost (Bowling Green, OH: Bowling Green University Popular Press, 1981); *The Battle of the Washita: The Sheridan-Custer Indian Campaign of 1867–69,* by Stan Hoig (Garden City, NY: Doubleday, 1976); and *Sheridan's Troopers on the Borders: A Winter Campaign on the Plains,* by De B. Randolph Keim (Lincoln: University of Nebraska Press, 1985). Keim, the reporter whom Benteen noted as being a witness to a later confrontation with Custer, makes no mention of that incident in his coverage of Elliott's tragic fate, although he did write that he reported the reason for Custer's officers' call to Sheridan.

🐎 Custer and Mo-nah-se-tah

One of the most enduring and debated rumors about Custer's personal life concerns the nature of his relationship with Mo-nah-se-tah, a Cheyenne Indian girl taken captive during the battle of the Washita who served as his interpreter and intermediary with the hostiles for the remainder of the campaign. The question under debate is whether this teenage daughter of Chief Little Rock (who was killed in the battle) also served as Custer's mistress and perhaps bore him a son.

Mo-nah-se-tah, also known as Me-o-tzi, which translated means "Young Grass That Shoots in Spring," was strikingly beautiful. Custer described her in the most glowing of terms.

She was about seven months pregnant at the time of the Washita battle and gave birth to a son on January 14, 1869, which assuredly could not have been Custer's. Cheyenne oral tradition, however, contends that Mo-nah-se-tah gave birth to another child in the fall of 1869, a boy named either Yellow Tail or Yellow Swallow—common names among the Cheyenne—and that Custer was the father. No documentation of this birth exists in reservation records at Fort Cobb.

The accusations of Custer's infidelity have been based solely on the assertions of notorious Custer critic Capt. Frederick W. Benteen; Ben Clark, who blamed Custer for his dismissal as an army scout; and Cheyenne Indian oral tradition. Oddly enough, apparently no other written source at that point bothered to document what would appear to be an exceedingly titillating and noteworthy allegation.

Benteen's hatred of Custer would make anything he wrote, which was for the most part merely a repeating of camp gossip, highly suspect. The memories of Clark, who did not refer to Mo-nah-se-tah by name, could be dismissed for the same reason. Therefore, it would seem that the credibility of the story hinges on Cheyenne oral tradition.

Plains Indian oral tradition has provided many valid details about nineteenth-century events but must be viewed under the same scrutiny as the writings of whites, which were often tainted by prejudices, failing memories, or other human factors, such as camp gossip—boastful, malicious, or otherwise. Indian testimony was also occasionally swayed by a willingness to say what someone would want to hear or by inaccurate or biased translation. And in the case of Custer and Mo-nah-se-tah, there are known discrepancies in the Cheyenne stories. In fact, an opposing view within Cheyenne oral tradition is presented by John Stands in Timber and Margot Liberty in *Cheyenne Memories* (New Haven: Yale University Press, 1967), which dismisses any notion of a liaison between Custer and the girl.

Most Custer scholars—Frost, Monaghan, Connell, Ambrose, and Wert, to name a few—deem the Cheyenne account nonsense. Evidence that would point to Custer's paternity would never stand up in court. Testing DNA from an alleged Cheyenne descendant of Custer with that of a known Custer descendant would be inconclusive—even if it matched. Another Custer, Tom, could have been the culprit, if indeed Mo-nah-se-tah gave birth to a fair-skinned child in the fall of 1869. Tom noted that Mo-nah-se-tah was "a great favorite with the entire command," and Benteen contemptuously wrote that Custer "winks at being cuckolded by his kid-brother," who relieved Armstrong of "blanket duty."

Additionally, Custer was said to have been sterile, which was the reason he and Libbie were childless.

Another factor, given Custer's known moral discipline in other areas, was that his marriage to Libbie—based on their letters—was one of the great romances of all time, and it likely

of his men until rescued. He was promoted to the regular rank of lieutenant colonel and breveted brigadier general for his bravery (see "The Battle of Beecher Island" on page 98).

Forsyth served as military secretary to Sheridan from 1869 to 1873 and participated in the Russian grand duke's Kansas buffalo hunt (see "The Russian Grand Duke's Buffalo Hunt" on page 107). He also accompanied Custer on his Black Hills expedition of 1874 as a battalion commander, with instructions from Sheridan to keep a daily log, which was published in the *Chicago Tribune* on August 27 and 28, 1874. Between 1875 and 1876, he was a member of a board of officers that inspected armies in Europe and Asia. He resumed duties with Sheridan as aide-de-camp from 1878 to 1881. The following year, Forsyth was transferred to the 4th Cavalry to campaign under Col. Ranald S. Mackenzie against Apache in Arizona and New Mexico. He participated in the battle of Horseshoe Canyon on April 23, 1882, and with six troops of the 4th Cavalry futilely chased Apache leader Geronimo into Mexico—until told to withdraw from Mexican soil. In 1887, he served as commander of Fort Huachuca, Arizona. He retired as a colonel in 1890 and died at his retirement home in Rockport, Massachusetts, on September 12, 1915.

📖 Forsyth wrote two autobiographies detailing his exploits: *Thrilling Days of Army Life* (New York: Harper & Brothers, 1900); and *The Story of a Soldier* (New York: Appleton, 1900), in which he defended Custer's actions at Little Bighorn. An excellent biography is *Hero of Beecher Island: The Life and Military Career of George A. Forsyth,* by David Dixon (Lincoln: University of Nebraska Press, 1994).

✹ Owen Hale
First Lieutenant, 7th U.S. Cavalry

This descendant of American patriot Nathan Hale was born in Troy, New York, on July 23, 1843. During the Civil War, he served first as sergeant major with the 1st New York Mounted Rifles and later the 7th New York Cavalry until May 8, 1863, when he received a commission as second lieutenant. Hale was promoted to first lieutenant on October 19, 1864, and breveted captain on March 13, 1865.

Hale was one of the original officers in the 7th Cavalry when he was appointed a first lieutenant on July 28, 1866. He became known as "Holy Owen" due to his personification of the ideal army officer. Hale commanded a troop in the Washita campaign and was the last officer to see Maj. Joel Elliott alive. Elliott was said to have called out to

(continued on following page)

Hale in passing, "Here goes for a brevet or a coffin" (see "The Joel Elliott Controversy" on page 90). He was promoted to captain in 1869 and participated in every major 7th Cavalry campaign—as commander of Company K—until the Little Bighorn, which he missed while on detached duty at Jefferson Barracks, Missouri.

In September 1877, Hale and the 7th Cavalry accompanied Gen. Nelson Miles in pursuit of Nez Perce chief Joseph. The inclement weather on the morning of September 30 led Hale to say: "My God! Have I got to go out and be killed in such cold weather!" Later that day, Hale led a squadron on the first charge into Chief Joseph's encampment at Snake Creek near the Bear Paw Mountains. He was within twenty yards of the Indians when he was killed by a bullet in the neck.

Hale, who never married, was buried in Oakwood Cemetery in Troy. His obituary was printed in the *Bismarck Tribune* on October 15, 1877. The post at Lower Brule Agency, Dakota Territory, was named Fort Hale in his honor in January 1879.

📖 *Northwestern Fights and Fighters,* by Cyrus T. Brady (Garden City, NY: Doubleday, Page, 1923).

"We have cleaned Black Kettle and his band out so thoroughly that they can neither fight, dress, sleep, eat or ride without sponging upon their friends. It was a regular Indian 'Sailor's Creek.'"

—CUSTER IN A NOTE TO PHIL SHERIDAN THE MORNING AFTER THE WASHITA BATTLE, REFERRING TO THE DEFEAT OF THE CONFEDERATES PRIOR TO APPOMATTOX IN WHAT WAS CALLED "BLACK THURSDAY" IN THE SOUTH

✸ William Babcock Hazen
Colonel, U.S. Army

Hazen was born into a farming family on September 27, 1830, in West Hartford, Vermont. In 1833, the family moved to Hiram, Ohio, where Hazen became friends with future president James A. Garfield. He entered the U.S. Military Academy at West Point in 1851 and became known as an independent-minded perfectionist with great ambition, although upon his graduation four years

(continued on following page)

would have taken more than a comely Indian girl to cause him to compromise his vows.

📖 Cheyenne oral tradition contending that Custer and Mo-nah-se-tah were an item can be found in *Cheyenne Autumn,* by Mari Sandoz (New York: Hastings House, 1953); *Custer on the Little Bighorn,* by Thomas Marquis (Lodi, CA: Kain Publishing Co., 1969); *Custer's Fall: The Indian Side of the Story,* by David Humphreys Miller (New York: Duell, Sloan & Pierce, 1957); and "She Watched Custer's Last Battle," by Kate Bighead as told to Thomas B Marquis, in *The Custer Reader,* edited by Paul A. Hutton (Lincoln: University of Nebraska Press, 1992).

Benteen's allegations are contained in his letters of February 14 and 17, 1896, in *The Benteen-Goldin Letters on Custer and His Last Battle,* edited by John M. Carroll (Lincoln: University of Nebraska Press, 1974). Ben Clark's memories were recorded in a 1910 interview with Walter Camp (Field Notes, Folder 4, Box 2, Walter Camp Papers, Lilly Library, Indiana University).

An analysis by Custer scholars includes *General Custer's Libbie,* by Lawrence A. Frost (Seattle: Superior Publishing Co., 1976); *Custer: The Life of General George Armstrong Custer,* by Jay Monaghan (Lincoln: University of Nebraska Press, 1971); *Son of the Morning Star,* by Evan S. Connell (San Francisco, North Point Press, 1984); Stephen E. Ambrose's *Crazy Horse and Custer: The Parallel Lives of Two American Warriors* (Garden City, NY: Doubleday, 1975); and Jeffry D. Wert's *Custer: The Controversial Life of George Armstrong Custer* (New York: Simon & Schuster, 1996).

One noted historian, Robert M. Utley, in his biography, *Cavalier in Buckskin: George Armstrong Custer and the Western Military Frontier* (Norman: University of Oklahoma Press, 1988), leaves the door open a crack to the possibility that another child was born late in 1869 and that Custer could have been the father. Mo-nah-se-tah is a prominent figure in Custer's memoirs, *My Life on the Plains; or, Personal Experiences with Indians* (Norman: University of Oklahoma Press, 1962); and Elizabeth Bacon Custer's *Following the Guidon* (New York: Harper and Brothers, 1890). See also: "Mo-nah-se-tah: Fact or Fiction," by Barbara Zimmerman, *4th Annual Symposium Custer Battlefield Historical and Museum Assn.,* 1990.

🐎 The 19th Kansas Volunteer Cavalry

When planning the Washita campaign, Phil Sheridan requested assistance from Kansas governor Samuel J. Crawford in providing additional troops. The Kansas militia was already serving on garrison duty in eastern Kansas and therefore was not available. Within days of Sheridan's request, however, a war party of hostiles committed atrocities in Ottawa County, killing, raping, and taking women captives. Crawford and the incensed Kansans were anxious to exact revenge and perhaps rescue the captives. The former Civil War general resigned his office, appointed himself colonel, and within three weeks had formed a 1,200-man regiment called the 19th Kansas Volunteer Cavalry.

On November 5, Colonel Crawford led his regiment from Topeka toward Indian Territory. The Kansas volunteers were expected to rendezvous with Custer's 7th Cavalry and Sheridan's other troops at a stockaded supply depot known as Camp Supply, which had been established at the point where Wolf and Beaver Creeks met to form the North Canadian River. The combined force of over 2,000 men would then commence offensive operations.

Sheridan had designated Crawford's command to accompany Custer, who had been issued orders to proceed toward the Washita River, where the winter camps of the Indians were thought to be located. The Kansas cavalry failed to arrive in a timely fashion, however, and Custer, impatient for action, departed on November 23 to lead his 7th Cavalry toward Black Kettle's village.

The Kansas horsemen had encountered problems along the way with inadequate supplies and forage, then lost 100 horses when 600 of their mounts somehow stampeded through camp. To add to the misery, the hungry men became lost in a blizzard. Crawford's column eventually straggled into Camp Supply between November 28 and December 1, and required time to recuperate from their ordeal.

Ten companies of Crawford's rejuvenated cavalry were part of a force of 1,700 men fielded by Sheridan and Custer on December 7 when operations in the Washita River area resumed. The Kansans then endured several months of campaigning under miserable conditions—poor rations, severe weather, and the indignity of marching instead of riding, due to a lack of horses—but had yet to locate any captives or exact satisfactory revenge for the atrocities committed on their soil.

On March 15, 1869, however, Custer's and Crawford's men happened upon the Indians that were believed to be the culprits of the Kansas raids, including the capture and captivity of two white women—one, Anna Morgan, the sister of Kansas trooper Daniel Brewster. The volunteers cried for immediate vengeance and wanted to charge the village. Custer refused and endured taunts of cowardice for his inaction, but he managed to successfully negotiate the release of the captives (see "The Rescue at Sweetwater Creek" on page 96).

Col. Samuel J. Crawford and his 19th Kansas Volunteer Cavalry saw little further action of consequence before being mustered out on June 4, 1869, at which time the regiment ceased to exist.

later, he ranked twenty-eighth in a class of thirty-four due to excessive demerits (150 in his senior year) and poor grades in his military courses.

His initial assignment took him to various frontier posts in the Oregon Territory until 1858, when he was transferred to Texas. In 1859, Hazen was severely wounded during a skirmish with the Comanche when struck by a bullet that entered his left hand, passed through the right side of his chest, and lodged in his rib cage. The bullet was never removed and rendered him permanently—albeit slightly—disabled.

In early 1861, Hazen was transferred to West Point as an assistant instructor of infantry tactics and was promoted to first lieutenant in April. It was at West Point that Hazen and George Armstrong Custer first crossed paths. When cadet Custer was arrested for condoning a fight between two other cadets, Hazen, who was Custer's commander, acted as a character reference at the court-martial. Hazen attested to Custer's good conduct, which may have helped save Custer's military career when he received only a reprimand rather than dismissal.

With the assistance of James A. Garfield, his boyhood friend, Hazen was appointed colonel of the 41st Ohio Volunteers at the outbreak of the Civil War. In November 1861, he took command of a brigade in General Buell's Army of the Ohio. At the April 1862 battle of Shiloh, he led a charge on the second day that succeeded in protecting Brig. Gen. William Nelson's division on the right wing. Hazen was promoted brigadier general of volunteers in November 1862. He once again distinguished himself at Stone's River by repulsing a series of assaults, which cost his brigade one-third of its strength. Hazen later erected a monument at Stone's River in memory of those who had lost their lives, which became the first Civil War battlefield monument.

Although his attitude was somewhat contentious and critical of army policy, particularly toward whiskey rations, which he considered too costly and injurious to military effectiveness, Hazen continued to impress his superiors. He served with distinction during the siege of Chattanooga and routed the enemy in November 1863 at Missionary Ridge.

At the latter engagement, Hazen developed a feud with Gen. David S. Stanley that would continue throughout their careers. Stanley had previously accused Hazen of cowardice at Shiloh and now attempted to have Hazen court-martialed for falsely claiming the capture of some cannons at

(continued on following page)

Missionary Ridge in November 1863. Gen. Phil Sheridan was drawn into the controversy and refused to court-martial Hazen.

Hazen joined Sherman's March to the Sea and commanded a division of the XV Corps under Gen. John A. Logan. In the December 1864 siege of Savannah, he captured Fort McAllister and earned a promotion to major general of volunteers.

After the war, Hazen commanded the XV Corps from May to August 1865. He mustered out and reverted to the rank of colonel with the 38th Infantry, subsequently serving as assistant inspector general of the Department of the Platte. In the fall of 1868, he was in command of Fort Cobb and was named agent of the southern of two large Indian districts, responsible for arranging the settlement of 6,000 members of various Plains Indian tribes at his post. He also had the unenviable task of determining which tribes were peaceful.

Prior to the battle of the Washita, Black Kettle and other chiefs met with Hazen, who informed them that they must make peace with General Sheridan to ensure their safety. On November 27, Custer and his 7th Cavalry attacked Black Kettle's village. Black Kettle was killed, which outraged Hazen, who had determined the chief to be peaceful. Later in the campaign, General Sheridan and Custer discovered the bodies of Clara Blinn and her son in a village downstream from the Washita battlefield that reportedly belonged to Satanta's Kiowa (see "Indian Captives Clara Blinn and Her Son" on page 84). Hazen dispatched a messenger to notify Sheridan that Satanta, whom Sheridan was convinced was responsible for the murders as well as other atrocities, could not be guilty of such a crime and was deemed friendly. The message infuriated Sheridan, who later captured Satanta and forced his people to submit to the Fort Cobb Reservation. Hazen's duty in this capacity concluded on June 30, 1869. He was then named the southern superintendent of Indian affairs, and he formed an intertribal government for the Five Civilized Tribes in Indian Territory.

Hazen served briefly in 1870 as a military observer in Europe, then, perhaps as retribution for his actions at Fort Cobb, was assigned duty as colonel of the 6th Infantry at remote Fort Buford in 1872. In 1874, Hazen resumed his reputation as a critic by engaging in a public literary duel with George Armstrong Custer over the merits of the Northern Pacific Railroad. The controversy also revived differences stemming from the treatment of Satanta and the Kiowa (see "The Custer-Hazen Fued" on page 135).

(continued on following page)

The best accounts of the march of the Kansas cavalrymen can be found in *Campaigning with Custer and the Nineteenth Kansas Volunteer Cavalry on the Washita Campaign, 1868–69*, by participant David L. Spotts, edited by E. A. Brininstool (Lincoln: University of Nebraska Press, 1988); "Winter Campaigning with Sheridan and Custer: The Expedition of the Nineteenth Kansas Volunteer Cavalry," by Lonnie J. White, *Journal of the West* 6 (July 1966); "The Nineteenth Kansas Cavalry in the Indian Territory, 1868–69: Eyewitness Accounts of Sheridan's Winter Campaign," edited by Lonnie J. White, *Red River Valley Historical Review* 3 (Spring 1978); and *The Battle of the Washita: The Sheridan-Custer Indian Campaign of 1867–68*, by Stan Hoig (Garden City, NY: Doubleday, 1976).

Other helpful sources include "The Nineteenth Kansas Cavalry and the Conquest of the Plains Indians," by James A. Hadley, *Transactions of the Kansas State Historical Society* 10 (1908); "The Nineteenth Kansas Cavalry in the Washita Campaign," by Colonel Horace L. Moore, *Chronicles of Oklahoma* 2, no. 4 (December 1924); "Medical Sketch of the Nineteenth Regiment of Kansas Cavalry Volunteers," by Mahlon Bailey, *Kansas Historical Quarterly* 6 (1937); and Paul A. Hutton's *Phil Sheridan and His Army* (Lincoln: University of Nebraska Press, 1985).

The Rescue at Sweetwater Creek

On March 15, 1869, while campaigning with elements of the 7th Cavalry reinforced by the 19th Kansas Volunteer Cavalry (see "The 19th Kansas Volunteer Cavalry" on page 94), Custer was notified by his scouts that they had located two Cheyenne villages consisting of a combined 260 lodges under chiefs Medicine Arrow and Little Robe at Sweetwater Creek, Texas.

The Kansans were certain that these were the Indians who held two white women, Mrs. Anna Belle Morgan and Miss Sarah C. White, whose rescue was a major reason the unit had mobilized the previous fall. Mrs. Morgan, a bride of one month, had been taken from James Morgan's homestead on the Solomon River near Delphos. Her brother, Daniel Brewster, had accompanied the expedition to search for her. Eighteen-year-old Sarah White had been seized at her family homestead on Granny Creek near Concordia at the same time that her father was killed.

In advance of his weary command, Custer, in the company of only 1st Lt. William W. Cooke, brazenly entered the Cheyenne village unannounced and was escorted to the chief's lodge. Custer shared the pipe ritual with the chief and was the subject of incantations and ceremonies by a holy man that, unknown to Custer, were intended to signify that if he acted treacherously toward the Indians, he and his command would be killed. In spite of this attempted intimidation, which ended with ashes from the pipe bowl being dropped on Custer's boot, he confirmed that the two white women in question were indeed captives in the village.

Custer returned to announce the news to his command. The Kansas cavalrymen were elated and demanded that an immediate attack be launched. The fate of Clara Blinn and her son (see "Indian Captives Clara Blinn and Her Son" on page 84), however, was foremost on Custer's mind, and he feared that these captives would also be killed if he initiated an attack. Much to the outrage of the Kansans—many even branding Custer a coward and a traitor—he decided that they would attempt to parley for the release of Mrs. Morgan and Miss White before taking any military action. It was all Custer could do to restrain the irate volunteers from taking matters into their own hands.

Opportunity arose, however, when Chief Little Robe and a delegation visited the cavalry bivouac under a flag of truce. Custer ignored the flag, seized three minor chiefs as hostages, and threatened to hang them if the white women were not released.

Three days later, when intense negotiation failed to break the stalemate and a battle loomed, Custer looped three ropes over the limb of a large willow tree and paraded his hostages beneath. At that point, the Cheyenne relented and released their white captives.

Custer also demanded that the Indians report to Camp Supply, but the chiefs argued that their ponies were too weak and could not travel. Instead, they would report when their ponies grew stronger. Custer reluctantly agreed and offered as an incentive for compliance the release of the women and children captured at Washita.

The incident serves as an example of Custer's growing maturity as an Indian fighter, realizing that bloodshed was not always the correct course when dealing with the enemy.

📖 Custer's own fascinating account can be found in *My Life on the Plains; or, Personal Experiences with Indians* (Norman: University of Oklahoma Press, 1962). His wife, Libbie, adds her perspective to the story in *Following the Guidon* (New York: Harper and Brothers, 1890). Participant David Spotts gives an eyewitness account in *Campaigning with Custer and the Nineteenth Kansas Volunteer Cavalry on the Washita Campaign, 1868–69* (Reprint. New York: Argonaut Press, 1965).

For two other interesting versions, see *California Joe: Noted Scout and Indian Fighter,* by his grandson, Joe E. Milner, and Earle R. Forrest (Lincoln: University of Nebraska Press, 1987); and chapter 11, "Deliverance by Deception," in Stan Hoig's *The Battle of the Washita: The Sheridan-Custer Indian Campaign of 1867–69* (Garden City, NY: Doubleday, 1976).

Hazen was also an outspoken critic of Secretary of War William W. Belknap, who had been accused of selling post traderships. Hazen had prepared a list of possible witnesses for the secretary's 1876 impeachment trial, which happened to include Custer's name. Custer was sent a summons to testify, which subsequently placed him in an unfavorable light with President Grant (see "Custer and the Belknap Hearings" on page 171).

In 1879, Gen. David Stanley renewed his feud when he accused Hazen of perjury in the Belknap impeachment trial. Hazen retaliated by charging Stanley with slander. Stanley was court-martialed and found guilty of "conduct to the prejudice of good order and military discipline." Phil Sheridan had testified against Hazen to no avail.

"Tom has just come in. He is cuter than ever, but he is becoming more profane, and a little vulgar. I have not spoken to him about it, but am leaving that pleasant duty to you."

—CUSTER TO LIBBIE, WITH RESPECT TO HIS BROTHER TOM, FEBRUARY 1869

In spite of his combative personality, Hazen was promoted to the rank of brigadier general in December 1880 and appointed chief signal officer of the army. Another controversy erupted in 1883, when Secretary of War Robert T. Lincoln refused Hazen's request to send an additional relief vessel to join other relief vessels attempting to rescue the Lady Franklin meteorological expedition, which had set out for the Arctic two years earlier. When relief finally did arrive in 1884, eighteen of the twenty-four men had died. Hazen was court-martialed and reprimanded for publicly criticizing Lincoln.

Hazen died suddenly on January 16, 1887, while on active duty in Washington, D.C., of what was reported as kidney poisoning—with complications perhaps caused by the moving within his body of the bullet he had carried since 1859. His obituary was published the next day in the *New York Times*.

📖 For a biography of Hazen, see *Great Plains Command: William B. Hazen in the Frontier West,* by Marvin E. Kroeker (Norman: University of Oklahoma Press, 1976). The Custer-Hazen feud

(continued on following page)

over the Northern Pacific Railroad is covered in *Penny-an-Acre Empire in the West*, edited by Edgar I. Stewart (Norman: University of Oklahoma Press, 1968). The Stanley feud and Hazen's actions during the winter campaign of 1868–69 are detailed in *Phil Sheridan and His Army*, by Paul Andrew Hutton (Lincoln: University of Nebraska Press, 1985). Hazen's "Some Corrections of 'Life on the Plains'" can be found in *My Life on the Plains; or, Personal Experiences with Indians*, by George Armstrong Custer (Norman: University of Oklahoma Press, 1962).

✷ Henry Lippincott
First Lieutenant and Assistant Surgeon, 7th U.S. Cavalry

Lippincott was born in New Glasgow, Nova Scotia, on September 22, 1839. After completing his studies in medicine, he entered the U.S. Army in 1863 as an acting medical cadet. The following year, he was assigned to the 6th California Volunteers as regimental surgeon. In March 1867, Dr. Lippincott was appointed first lieutenant and assistant surgeon of the 7th Cavalry and served in that capacity until November.

The following October, he was attached to the 7th Cavalry for the winter campaign. At the battle of the Washita, Lippincott was afflicted with snow blindness, which to some degree affected his ability to administer to the wounded. Lippincott returned to the Washita battlefield with Sheridan and Custer in early December. He examined by firelight the frozen bodies of Maj. Joel Elliott and his detachment and wrote graphic descriptions of the multiple wounds suffered by each man. This information can be found in his report, File F, 421, Old Military Records, National Archives, with excerpts reprinted in appendix D of Stan Hoig's *The Battle of the Washita: The Sheridan-Custer Indian Campaign of 1867–69* (Garden City, NY: Doubleday, 1976) and in Custer's *My Life on the Plains; or, Personal Experiences with Indians* (Norman: University of Oklahoma Press, 1962).

Lippincott also accompanied Custer into the Texas Panhandle when white captives Anna Morgan and Sarah White were liberated (see "The Rescue at Sweetwater Creek" on page 96). He served with the 7th Cavalry until March 1871, then continued with the Medical Department, assigned as the first chief surgeon of the Pacific and the 8th Army Corps, as well as in Manila. He rose to the rank of colonel and assistant surgeon general before retiring in 1903. He died in Brooklyn on January 24, 1908.

⬦ The Battle of Beecher Island

One of the most heroic episodes in Western history took place on September 17, 1868, when fifty-one soldiers commanded by Maj. George A. "Sandy" Forsyth were trapped for nine days on a tiny island in the Republican River by nearly 900 Sioux, Arapaho, and Cheyenne led by war chiefs Pawnee Killer and Roman Nose.

In August, Gen. Phil Sheridan had created an elite force of seasoned scouts under trusted aide Sandy Forsyth, giving them orders to guard the railroad up the Smoky Hill Road. On September 16, the command, which had been following the Arikaree Fork of the Republican River, camped for the night. At dawn, they mounted to resume their patrol when without warning, hundreds of Indians attacked from the nearby hills. Forsyth led his men to refuge on a timbered island, or sandbar, about 200 feet long by 40 feet wide.

The scouts frantically dug entrenchments as best they could in the soft sand as the Indians raked the position with deadly rifle fire, inflicting numerous casualties and killing all the horses. When the Indians charged, Forsyth coolly directed the fire of his men, who carried seven-shot Spencer carbines, and repulsed the attack.

The Sioux and Cheyenne resorted to long-range sniping, and Forsyth was struck by two bullets—one in the thigh, the other shattering a bone in his left leg. Forsyth refused immediate medical attention and was once again hit. This time the bullet fractured his skull. Dr. John H. Mooers rushed to treat Forsyth and was himself struck in the head and severely wounded.

The Indians charged three more times that day, but the firepower of the Spencers prevailed. During one assault, second in command Lt. Frederick H. Beecher was shot in the spine; he died at sunset. Four scouts had been killed and nineteen others wounded when darkness brought welcome rain to cool the exhausted soldiers. Although a total of probably only about nine Indians would be killed by the desperate frontiersmen (Forsyth reported thirty-two), one casualty was Roman Nose, who was cut down in the afternoon and died that evening.

That night, Forsyth, despite his near delirium, had the presence of mind to dispatch two volunteers to attempt to reach Fort Wallace, about eighty-five miles away. The remainder of the detachment settled in to endure a frightening night as the sound of war cries, pounding drums, and the death wail of mourners echoed from the nearby Indian camp.

The attack resumed the following morning without much damage sustained by either side. At nightfall, Forsyth sent out two more men to summon aid.

The Indians attempted several unsuccessful assaults on the third day, then hid behind rifle pits to snipe at the soldiers. On the fourth day, Dr. Mooers succumbed to his wound. At about the same time, Major Forsyth dug the bullet out of his leg with a razor. The Indians, apparently frustrated by the accuracy of the Spencers, vanished after the sixth day.

The departure of the Indians was a welcome but small consolation to Forsyth's desperate command. By this time, many of the wounded men were in near-death agony, the stench of rotting horse carcasses was unbearable, and the threat of starvation became a reality. Doubts about whether the messengers had succeeded in reaching Fort Wallace haunted the minds of the survivors.

Forsyth's first couriers had reached Fort Wallace in five days, however, and on September 25, the ninth day, a detachment of the 10th Cavalry—black Buffalo Soldiers (see "Buffalo Soldiers" below)—arrived to rescue Forsyth and his beleaguered men and escort them to Fort Wallace for treatment of their wounds.

It took Maj. George A. "Sandy" Forsyth two years to recover. He received a brevet to brigadier general in recognition of his gallantry. The tiny speck of land situated in the Arikaree would become known as Beecher Island in honor of Frederick H. Beecher, who had been killed on the first day of the battle.

📖 The best contemporary account is John H. Monnett's *The Battle of Beecher Island and the Indian War of 1867–69* (Niwot: University of Colorado Press, 1992). George A. Forsyth's own romanticized version of the battle can be found in "A Frontier Fight," *Harper's New Monthly Magazine* 91 (June 1895), and in his autobiographies, *Thrilling Days in Army Life* (New York: Harper & Brothers, 1900) and *The Story of a Soldier* (New York: Appleton, 1909). Eyewitness accounts by participants John Hurst and Sigmund Shlesinger appear in "The Beecher Island Fight," in *Collections of the Kansas Historical Society,* 15 (1919–22). The rescue by the 10th Cavalry is detailed in *The Buffalo Soldiers: A Narrative of the Negro Cavalry in the West,* by William H. Leckie (Norman: University of Oklahoma Press, 1967).

Other notable sources include *Hero of Beecher Island: The Life and Military Career of George A. Forsyth,* by David Dixon (Lincoln: University of Nebraska Press, 1994); *The Beecher Island Battle,* by Fred H. Werner (Greeley, CO: Werner Publications, 1989); "The Battle of Beecher Island: The Scouts Hold Fast on the Arickaree," by Lonnie J. White, *Journal of the West* 5 (January 1966); *The Fighting Cheyennes,* by George B. Grinnell (Norman: University of Oklahoma Press, 1962); and *Indian Fights and Fighters,* by Cyrus T. Brady (New York: McClure, Phillips, 1904).

🐎 Buffalo Soldiers

In 1866, Congress authorized four regiments—two cavalry (the 9th and 10th) and two infantry (the 24th and 25th)—comprising African-Americans to assist with hostilities in the

✺ Little Robe
Southern Cheyenne

Little Robe (Ski-o-mah), who was born in about 1828, became a noted young warrior during combat against traditional enemies. His first tribal distinction came after a battle with Pawnee in Kansas in 1852, when he was given the honor of carrying from camp to camp the pipe of mourning in memory of those lost in the engagement. He became a chief around 1863. Col. John Chivington claimed to have killed Little Robe at Sand Creek, but reports of his death were greatly exaggerated.

That massacre compelled Little Robe to wage war against whites, but he soon came to the conclusion that such actions were hopeless. He participated in the April 1867 council with General Hancock at Fort Larned, then worked with Black Kettle in an effort to persuade militant brethren to join them in signing the Medicine Lodge Treaty of 1867.

In November 1868, Little Robe accompanied Black Kettle to Fort Cobb to talk peace with Col. William Hazen, but they were told to contact Gen. Phil Sheridan to ensure their safety. The two chiefs returned to their camp on the Washita and were subsequently attacked by Custer's 7th Cavalry. When Black Kettle was killed at that battle, Little Robe initially supported the hostiles. In March 1869, he was camped at Sweetwater Creek, Texas, and met with Custer, who was attempting to secure the release of two white women from a nearby village. In the spring, Little Robe surrendered at Fort Cobb and assumed the role of principal chief of the peace faction (see "The Rescue at Sweetwater Creek" on page 96).

Little Robe was a member of delegations that toured Washington and other eastern cities in both 1871 and 1873. He met President Grant on the second trip. He once again was a voice for peace during the Red River War of 1874–75, refusing to leave his reservation home in Indian Territory on the North Canadian River. Although he was a proponent of peace with whites, Little Robe would not send children from his tribe to white schools. He died peacefully in 1886.

📖 See *The Southern Cheyennes,* by Donald J. Berthrong (Norman: University of Oklahoma Press, 1963); and *The Fighting Cheyennes,* by George B. Grinnell (Norman: University of Oklahoma Press, 1956).

✸ Lone Wolf
Kiowa

Lone Wolf (Guipago or Quirl-Parko), a principal chief during the Kiowa Wars of the 1870s, was born about 1820. He quickly proved himself as a warrior and became one of the most respected in his tribe. In 1863, he was a member of a delegation to Washington, D.C., that met with President Abraham Lincoln.

In 1866, his tribe was wary about choosing as chief either Satanta, head of the war faction, or Kicking Bird, head of the peace faction, and Lone Wolf became the compromise choice. He signed the Medicine Lodge Treaty of 1867 but refused to comply with its provisions and submit to the reservation. During the Washita campaign, Sheridan and Custer seized Lone Wolf and Satanta and threatened to hang them unless their tribe submitted to the reservation. The Kiowa people grudgingly straggled in to Fort Cobb, and the two chiefs' lives were spared.

Lone Wolf returned to Washington as part of a delegation in 1872 and pledged peace with the whites. In 1873, however, after his son and nephew were killed by soldiers, he went back on the warpath. He fought Texas Rangers as well as troops under Miles and Mackenzie during the Red River War of 1874–75, participating in battles at Adobe Walls in June 1874 and three months later in the defense of Palo Dura Canyon. He surrendered at Fort Sill in February 1875 and was chosen by fellow Kiowa Kicking Bird to be exiled to Fort Marion, Florida. In 1878, Lone Wolf contracted malaria and was permitted to return to Indian Territory, where he died the following year. He was buried on the north shoulder of Mount Scott.

📖 See *Bad Medicine and Good: Tales of the Kiowas,* by Wilbur S. Nye (Norman: University of Oklahoma Press, 1962); *Plains Indian Raiders: The Final Phases of Warfare from the Arkansas to the Red River,* by Wilbur S. Nye (Norman: University of Oklahoma Press, 1968); *The Kiowas,* by Mildred P. Marshall (Norman: University of Oklahoma Press, 1962); and *Satanta and the Kiowas,* by F. Stanley (Borger, TX: Jim Hess Printers, 1968).

West. Most were former slaves and illiterate, which made them dependent upon white leadership, but they were known for their discipline, good humor, physical endurance, sobriety, and ability to face adversity. These units served in a variety of capacities: keeping order among settlers, chasing rustlers, guarding stagecoaches, protecting survey parties, maintaining peace during railroad and mine strikes, construction (building Fort Sill), and the endeavor for which they gained the most fame—fighting Indians.

The black units were commanded by white officers and segregated from the rest of the army, whose members called their fellow soldiers Brunettes. The Plains Indians used the respectful term Buffalo Soldiers to describe the black cavalrymen, believing their short, curly hair resembled the coat of a buffalo, which to them was a sacred animal. The Buffalo Soldiers made a buffalo the central figure on their regimental crest. The black infantrymen were called "Walk-a-Heaps," the customary infantry nickname in recognition of the long distances they marched. Another nickname of historical note associated with the Buffalo Soldiers was Black Jack, which was bestowed upon John J. Pershing by his fellow officers when the future commander of American forces in World War I was a lieutenant serving with the 10th Cavalry.

Although contemporary culture has ignored the fact, the two black cavalry regiments accounted for about 20 percent of the total cavalry strength in the West. Black cavalrymen served in desolate posts under more primitive conditions than whites and were issued secondhand gear and worn-out horses—castoffs from white regiments—but stood fewer court-martials for drunkenness and had one of the lowest rates of desertion in the cavalry. The Buffalo Soldiers viewed the army as a career, which instilled unit pride and made their retention rate much higher than that of whites. A total of eighteen black soldiers were awarded the Medal of Honor for their bravery fighting Indians.

Buffalo Soldiers served with the U.S. Army in battles throughout the West, including the Mexican border campaigns, the Red River War, the campaigns against Apache chiefs Victorio and Nana, and the Ghost Dance troubles. One of the most celebrated episodes was when the 10th Cavalry—while serving with Sheridan on the winter campaign of 1868–69—rushed to the rescue of Maj. George A. Forsyth's beleaguered command at Beecher Island on September 25, 1868 (see "The Battle of Beecher Island" on page 98).

📖 The best account of the black cavalry units in the West is *The Buffalo Soldiers: A Narrative of Negro Cavalry in the West,* by William H. Leckie (Norman: University of Oklahoma Press, 1967). Also see "Colonel Grierson in the Southwest," by Frank M. Temple, *Panhandle-Plains Historical Review* 30 (1957).

🦌 The Battle of Summit Springs

Sheridan's winter campaign on the plains officially ended on April 6, 1869, but many Cheyenne Indians had procrastinated about submitting to the reservation, which was a blemish on the intended result of the operation. That failure to corral the hostiles brought about the fear that there would be another summer of raiding. That fear was realized when Chief Tall Bull and his Cheyenne Dog Soldiers resumed hostile activities against railroads and settlements along the Republican River.

While Custer and his 7th Cavalry remained in garrison at Fort Hays, eight companies of the 5th Cavalry under Maj. Eugene A. Carr, accompanied by a battalion of Frank and Luther North's Pawnee scouts and guided by William F. "Buffalo Bill" Cody, marched from Fort McPherson on June 9 to pursue the raiders.

After a monthlong hunt, Carr located a recent trail on the Arikaree Fork of the Republican not far from the Beecher Island battlefield. Tall Bull's Cheyenne had apparently decided to abandon their traditional range and joined a group of Sioux and Arapaho led by Oglala Pawnee Killer. On July 11, Pawnee scouts came to the end of the trail at a village in a narrow valley known as Summit Springs, some sixty miles upstream from Fort Sedgwick on the South Platte River near present-day Sterling, Colorado. Tall Bull, with eighty-four lodges, had camped at Summit Springs while waiting for the water to subside before continuing across the swollen river.

Major Carr with about 250 troopers and 50 Pawnees, swept down on the unsuspecting encampment. The surprised Cheyenne dashed from their lodges, many running to reach the cover of nearby ravines, while others were cut down in the initial charge. When the battle had ended, fifty-two Indians had been killed, among them Chief Tall Bull. Seventeen women and children were taken prisoner, including Tall Bull's wife.

The 5th Cavalry suffered the loss of only one wounded soldier. A pony and mule herd estimated at 400 was confiscated, then the entire village—including weapons, food, and clothing—was destroyed. The village also revealed the presence of two white women who had been captured on May 30 on the Saline. One of them, Mrs. Susanna Alderice, was killed when Carr charged; the other, Mrs. Maria Weichell, was severely wounded but survived.

One controversy arising from the battle centers around the identity of the person who killed Tall Bull. Various conflicting accounts attribute the killing of the chief to either "Buffalo Bill" Cody or Frank North. In an April 21, 1917, interview with Walter Camp, Luther North, Frank's brother, related that the fight was over by the time Cody arrived at the village, and Frank North was in fact the one who had killed Tall Bull. Luther North went on to say that dime novelist Ned Buntline (actually E. C. Z. Judson) wrote a purely

⊛ Moses Embree "California Joe" Milner
Army Scout and Adventurer

Milner was born near Stanford, Kentucky, on May 8, 1829. He departed home at the age of fourteen to head west and become a mountain man. His army service began during the Mexican War years of 1846–48, when he scouted for Kearny and Col. Alexander W. Doniphan, commander of the Missouri Mounted Volunteers, in New Mexico and Chihuahua. He reportedly was captured by Utes in 1849 but soon escaped. Milner returned home in 1850 and married thirteen-year-old Nancy Watts, with whom he had four children. The couple honeymooned by crossing 2,000 miles of prairie and mountains in a wagon train to prospect for gold in California. He was moderately successful, and in 1853, he established a cattle ranch in Oregon.

———◆———

"[Chief] Little Rock's daughter was an exceedingly comely squaw, possessing a bright, cheery face, a countenance beaming with intelligence, and a disposition more inclined to be merry than one usually finds among the Indians. Added to the bright, laughing eyes, a set of pearly teeth, and a rich complexion, her well-shaped head was crowned with a luxuriant growth of the most beautiful silken tresses, rivaling in color the blackness of the raven and extending, when allowed to fall loosely over her shoulders, to below her waist."

—CUSTER DESCRIBING MO-NAH-SE-TAH, THE CHEYENNE GIRL CAPTURED DURING THE BATTLE OF THE WASHITA WHO SERVED AS HIS INTERPRETER AND LIAISON THROUGHOUT THE REMAINDER OF THE CAMPAIGN, AND TO WHOM HE WAS ROMANTICALLY LINKED BY RUMOR

———◆———

Domestic life, however, did not suit Milner, and he was soon off adventuring. He prospected in Idaho and Montana and traveled throughout the southern plains. During this time it was said that he killed several men—one claim jumper in

(continued on following page)

Bannack, Montana; another in Virginia for kicking Milner's dog; and one in Texas.

At some point, Milner hired on as a scout and guide for the U.S. Army. He served briefly as chief scout for Custer on the Hancock expedition, becoming at that time a good friend of fellow scout "Wild Bill" Hickok, but was demoted to common scout after a bout with the bottle. He was once again hired on to scout for the Sheridan-Custer winter campaign of 1868–69. Following the battle of the Washita, Milner and another scout traveled 100 miles in two days through hostile territory to report the result to Sheridan at Camp Supply.

The loquacious, humorous Milner, who always rode a mule and sported a briar pipe stuck between his tangled red whiskers, became a favorite of Custer during his tenure with the 7th Cavalry.

In the early 1870s, Milner returned to prospecting, ran a cattle ranch near Pioche, Nevada, scouted for the Jenny expedition of 1875, then remained in the Black Hills near Rapid City to prospect. He was working as a scout for Gen. George Crook's 5th Cavalry when, on October 29, 1876, at Fort Robinson, he was murdered—shot in the back by Thomas Newcomb, a man with whom he had quarreled, perhaps over Milner's public statement that gamblers had arranged the death of his friend Hickok three months earlier.

"California Joe" Milner, one of the most colorful characters on the frontier, was buried with full military honors in the post cemetery.

📖 Milner's grandson, Joe E. Milner, along with Earle R. Forrest, wrote a romanticized biography titled *California Joe, Noted Scout and Indian Fighter* (Caldwell, ID: Caxton Printers, 1935).

✺ Edward Myers
Captain, 7th U.S. Cavalry

Myers was born in Germany in 1830. He emigrated to the United States, and in 1857, he enlisted in the 1st Dragoons, which became the 1st Cavalry in 1861. Myers was commissioned a second lieutenant in 1862 and promoted a year later to first lieutenant. He distinguished himself at Todd's Tavern and Five Forks and earned brevets up to lieutenant colonel.

Myers joined the newly formed 7th Cavalry in 1866 as a captain in command of E Troop. From all accounts, Myers was an ill-tempered officer whose personal actions stretched the limits of military discipline. He was known to disobey orders upon occasion; had refused to submit

fictional story about how Cody discovered the village, charged into it, and killed Tall Bull. Carr's official report, however, confirms that Cody was involved in the battle. Several notable historians have contradicted North by stating that Cody was indeed the killer of the Cheyenne chief. Other scholars have made the case for Frank North. With such vehement opinions on both sides of the debate, the final verdict would likely result in a hung jury, and the killer of Tall Bull will remain unknown.

More important than counting coup (the act of closing with an enemy and touching them with a lance or other weapon), however, was that Carr's smashing victory effectively disorganized the Cheyenne and their allies and brought to an end their cohesiveness and ability to mount a unified resistance. The Plains Indians had little choice but to straggle onto their reservations, which satisfied the goals of Sheridan's winter campaign of clearing the Republican River country of Indians.

Although the battle at Summit Springs was similar in most respects to Custer's victory at Washita, there was no public outcry condemning the destruction of this Cheyenne village or employing the term "massacre" to describe the incident.

📖 The best version of the battle of Summit Springs can be found in a biography of Major Carr by James T. King, *War Eagle: A Life of General Eugene Carr* (Lincoln: University of Nebraska Press, 1963). *The Summit Springs Battle,* by Fred H. Werner (Greeley, CO: Werner Publications, 1991), includes copies of Carr's official reports and several interesting maps. Luther North's interview with Walter Camp about the battle can be found in *Camp on Custer,* edited by Bruce R. Liddic and Paul Harbaugh (Spokane: A. H. Clark Co., 1995).

Don Russell gives an in-depth analysis with respect to who actually killed Tall Bull—in his opinion, Buffalo Bill—in *The Lives and Legends of Buffalo Bill* (Norman: University of Oklahoma Press, 1973). For support for Frank North as the slayer of Tall Bull, as well as coverage of the battle, see both *Two Great Scouts and Their Pawnee Battalions,* by George B. Grinnell (Lincoln: University of Nebraska Press, 1973); and Donald F. Danker's *Man of the Plains: Recollections of Luther North, 1856–1882* (Lincoln: University of Nebraska Press, 1961).

Other notable sources for the battle include *Summit Springs,* by Capt. Charles King (Fort Collins, CO: Old Army Press, 1984); *Across the Continent with the Fifth Cavalry,* by George F. Price (New York: Antiquarian Press, 1959); Phil Sheridan's *Record of Engagements with Hostile Indians within the Military Division of the Missouri, from 1868 to 1882, Lieutenant-General P. H. Sheridan, Commanding* (Fort Collins, CO: Old Army Press, 1972); and *The Fighting Cheyennes,* by George B. Grinnell (Norman: University of Oklahoma Press, 1956).

(continued on following page)

🐎 Benteen's Battlefield Duel

George Armstrong Custer, in his book *My Life on the Plains; or, Personal Experiences with Indians* (Norman: University of Oklahoma Press, 1962), related the story of an unavoidable duel between Capt. Frederick W. Benteen and an Indian boy. The incident casts considerable favor upon the humanitarian aspects of the captain, who has become known as Custer's most bitter critic.

Before the battle of the Washita, Custer had issued orders for his troopers to avoid killing anyone but warriors. When the charge was sounded, Captain Benteen rode with the lead squadron. Upon entering Black Kettle's village, he was boldly confronted by a mounted Indian whom Custer described as "scarcely fourteen years of age." The youngster, armed with a pistol, appeared to invite Benteen to engage in a personal duel. Benteen admirably resisted the boy's entreaties and instead made "peace signs" in an attempt to encourage the boy to surrender.

The youthful warrior refused to do so, however, and spurred his horse toward Benteen while discharging his revolver. The bullet whistled past the captain's head. The boy closed the distance, again firing, with the same result. Benteen maintained his discipline as a third round was fired at him, this one passing through the neck of his horse.

Benteen, who had been dumped onto the snowy ground, made one final appeal for his antagonist to surrender. The determined boy answered by leveling his revolver for another shot. Regretfully, Benteen had no other choice but to shoot and kill the brave young warrior.

Later, a trooper retrieved from the boy's saddle a small pair of moccasins, elaborately ornamented with beads, and presented the trophy to Benteen. Custer wrote that the moccasins "furnished the link of evidence by which we subsequently ascertained who the young chieftain was—a title which was justly his, both by blood and bearing."

This statement has prompted most historians to regard the boy as the son of Black Kettle. This may or may not be true. According to George E. Hyde in *The Life of George Bent: Written from His Letters* (Norman: University of Oklahoma Press, 1968), Bent, the half-breed son of trader William Bent who married Black Kettle's niece, identified this young duelist as a twenty-one-year-old named Blue Horse who was a nephew of Black Kettle.

The true age and identity of Benteen's opponent will never be known. But tribute must be paid to the courage and discipline of Captain Benteen, whose restraint could have cost him his life, and respect is due for the determination of the warrior who may have looked younger than he actually was when he bravely rode out to defend his village.

to arrest; twice drew his pistol and challenged another officer to a duel; and countermanded an order from Dr. I. T. Coates to send an ill trooper back to duty. He stood a court-martial at Fort Leavenworth in December 1867 and was sentenced to be dismissed from the service. That sentence, however, was rejected by the judge advocate general, and Myers was returned to duty in June 1868.

During the battle of the Washita on November 27, 1868, Myers and his command—in direct disobedience of Custer's orders—were observed firing into a group of women and children. Later that day, Custer ordered Myers to ride downstream and search for Maj. Joel Elliott and his men, who were missing. Myers reported that he rode two miles without locating Elliott. Taking into consideration his tendency to disregard orders, it could be speculated that—in the face of an overwhelming number of Indians advancing from that direction—he may have failed to ride those two miles or adequately search for Elliott, whose death became a source of controversy (see "The Joel Elliott Controversy" on page 90).

Myers, who had been in declining health, died on July 11, 1871, at Spartanburg, South Carolina, where his troop was stationed.

⊛ Frank Joshua North
Scout and Plainsman

Frank North was born on March 10, 1840, at Ludlowville, Tompkins County, New York, but spent his boyhood in Richland County, Ohio, before moving to Omaha in 1858. While breaking land for new settlers near Columbus, Nebraska, North became acquainted with the local Pawnee Indians and learned their language. In 1859, he began hauling freight to the Colorado goldfields and between Omaha and Fort Kearny, then returned home to work as interpreter and clerk for the Indian agent at the Pawnee reservation near Fullerton, Nebraska.

In 1864, North was guiding army troops when Maj. Gen. Samuel R. Curtis suggested that he organize a company of Pawnee Indians—the natural enemy of the Lakota Sioux—for service on the plains. In January 1865, Company A, composed of 100 Pawnee, was formed with North as captain. The Company saw action in several skirmishes on the Tongue River in the Dakota Territory. The scout battalion gained recognition on one occasion by killing 34 Sioux and Cheyenne and on another by locating an army column that had been separated from the main force and was

(continued on following page)

near starvation in harsh weather. In the fall of 1865, North and his company returned to the reservation, and on Christmas Day, he married twenty-year-old Mary Louise Smith, with whom he had one daughter.

In March 1867, he was directed to enlist a Pawnee battalion—200 men divided into four companies, with North as "major" and his younger brother, Luther, a company commander—for the purpose of protecting the Union Pacific Railroad. The battalion participated in a number of engagements, including the July 11, 1869, battle of Summit Springs, which crushed Cheyenne resistance on the plains. The death of Chief Tall Bull in that battle is attributed to either North or "Buffalo Bill" Cody (see "The Battle of Summit Springs" on page 101).

"Not even the proverbial stoicism of the red man was sufficient to conceal the chagrin and disappointment recognizable in every linament [sic] *of the countenances of both Satanta and Lone Wolf when they discovered that all their efforts at deception had not only failed, but left them prisoners in our hands."*

—CUSTER UPON SEIZING THE TWO CHIEFS IN DECEMBER 1868 AND THREATENING TO HANG THEM IF THEIR FOLLOWERS DID NOT REPORT TO THE RESERVATION

The Pawnee battalion—and its commander—grew in fame while continuing to serve on the frontier. In 1873, North claimed the title of best revolver shot on the plains when he beat "Wild Bill" Hickok and others in a competition. After the June 1876 Little Bighorn battle, North raised another company of 100 Pawnee to accompany Gen. George Crook, which culminated with North leading his men on the November 1876 attack by Col. Ranald S. Mackenzie on Dull Knife's Cheyenne village. In the spring of 1877, North and his Pawnee were mustered out of service.

At that time, the North brothers became partners with Cody in a cattle-ranching operation on the Dismal River, northwest of North Platte,

(continued on following page)

Another excellent version of the incident appears in Stan Hoig's *The Battle of the Washita: The Sheridan-Custer Indian Campaign of 1867–68* (Garden City, NY: Doubleday, 1976).

The Sand Creek Massacre

Almost four years to the day before the battle of the Washita, in which he lost his life, Chief Black Kettle barely escaped during another conflict with soldiers. This one, however, was not by any means a battle, but a massacre that enraged the Plains tribes as well as many whites.

Throughout the summer of 1864, hostile Indians had initiated a reign of terror on the plains—attacking wagon trains and robbing stagecoaches, burning ranches and settlers' cabins, stealing stock, and committing atrocities upon the white populace.

Consequently, most Westerners were of the opinion that the Indians must be dealt with severely. Newspapers adopted that battle cry, calling for extermination of the red man and chiding the army for timidity. In August, the governor of the Colorado Territory, John Evans, issued a proclamation that urged citizens to hunt down and kill every hostile Indian they could find. This policy endangered innocent Indians, many of whom were killed by white war parties.

In order to protect the friendly tribes, Governor Evans invited all Plains Indians in the area to demonstrate their peaceful intentions by moving their camps to locations near forts, where they could be protected by the army. At the urging of Maj. Edward W. Wynkoop of the Colorado Volunteers, who was serving as commander of Fort Lyon, Black Kettle and his band of about 700 Cheyenne agreed to trust the army. The tribe presented itself at Fort Lyon and were treated to a generous amount of supplies, then directed by Wynkoop to camp for the winter at a place about forty miles away called Sand Creek, where it was promised that they would be unmolested.

Some Coloradoans, however, chose not to distinguish between friendly and hostile Indians. One of those was Methodist preacher and militia colonel John M. Chivington, who believed that it was honorable under God's law to kill any Indian. At dawn on November 29, 1864, Chivington led 600 troops of the 3rd Colorado Cavalry in an attack on Black Kettle's unsuspecting village at Sand Creek. His orders: "Kill and scalp all, big and little. Nits make lice."

In a deliberate and indiscriminate slaughter, the militia killed, mutilated, and scalped at least 150 Cheyenne—two-thirds of them women and children—then burned the village and its contents to the ground and captured several hundred ponies. The triumphant militiamen were hailed as heroes in Denver when they later displayed Indian scalps and other trophies to an appreciative audience between acts at a theatrical performance.

Plains Indian tribes lashed out at this flagrant betrayal and intensified their raiding, an ongoing rebellion costly in both resources and lives that would not abate for many years to come.

📖 The best account of the massacre can be found in *The Fighting Cheyennes,* by George Bird Grinnell (Norman: University of Oklahoma Press, 1956). Another excellent work is *The Sand Creek Massacre,* by Stan Hoig (Norman: University of Oklahoma Press, 1961). Helen Hunt Jackson was a resident of Colorado Springs when she wrote *A Century of Dishonor* (1881; reprint, Norman: University of Oklahoma Press, 1995), which describes the massacre in great detail and quotes liberally from testimony given before a Congressional committee. The report of the U.S. War Department was published in 1975 by the Library of Congress under the title *Report of the Secretary of War Communicating, in Compliance with a Resolution of the Senate of February 4, 1867: Copy of Evidence Taken at Denver and Fort Lyon, Colorado by a Military Commission Ordered to Inquire in the Sand Creek Massacre, November 1864.*

Other helpful sources include *Life of George Bent, Written from His Letters,* by George E. Hyde (Norman: University of Oklahoma Press, 1967); *Blood at Sand Creek: The Massacre Revisited,* by Robert Scott (Caldwell, ID: Caxton Printers, 1994); *The Tall Chief: The Unfinished Autobiography of Edward Wynkoop, 1856–1866,* edited by Christopher B. Gerboth (Denver: Colorado Historical Society, 1994); *Song of Sorrow: Massacre at Sand Creek,* by Patrick Mendoza (Denver: Willow Word Publishing Co., 1993); *Month of the Freezing Moon: The Sand Creek Massacre,* by Duana Schultz (NY: St. Martin's Press, 1990); "The Military Investigation of Col. John M. Chivington Following the Sand Creek Massacre," by William J. Mellor, *Chronicles of Oklahoma* 16, no. 4 (1938); "Chivington's Raid—a Black Day in Colorado," by Robert L. Perkin, *Rocky Mountain News* (January 20, 1957); and "Sands of Sand Creek Historiography," by Michael Sievers, *Colorado Magazine* (Spring 1972). For an opposing view that defends Chivington's actions, see *I Stand by Sand Creek,* by William R. Dunn (Fort Collins, CO: Old Army Press, 1985).

🦌 The Stevens Lode Mine

By 1871, the monotony of frontier duty had taken its toll on George Armstrong Custer. He craved more action than was afforded by escort duty and the rare, brief skirmish with Indians. And when the reassignment of the 7th Cavalry in detachments across the South became imminent, the Custers discussed the prospect of retirement from the service.

Rather than make a hasty decision, Custer decided to obtain a leave of absence in order to investigate opportunities in New York, where he was a known and popular figure. On

Nebraska. In 1882, Frank North was elected to one term in the Nebraska legislature. The following year, he began touring with Cody's Wild West Show, leading his Pawnee in exhibitions of Indian warfare. In 1884, at Hartford, Connecticut, he was thrown from a horse and hospitalized for several months, but he recovered enough to briefly continue touring. His various injuries and the years that he had suffered from asthma, however, had taken a toll on him. North died in Columbus, Nebraska, on March 14, 1885, preceded in death by his wife two years earlier.

📖 An interesting account of North's exploits, although greatly exaggerated, can be found in *Two Great Scouts and Their Pawnee Battalion,* by George B. Grinnell (Lincoln: University of Nebraska Press, 1973). Excerpts from a field diary kept by North in 1869 can be found in "The Journal of an Indian Fighter," by Donald F. Danker, *Nebraska History* 39, no. 2 (June 1958).

Also notable are *Man of the Plains: Recollections of Luther North, 1856–1882,* edited by Donald F. Danker (Lincoln: University of Nebraska Press, 1961); *The Fighting Norths and Pawnee Scouts,* by Robert Bruce (New York: Brooklyn Eagle Press, 1932); and *The Lives and Legends of Buffalo Bill,* by Don Russell (Norman: University of Oklahoma Press, 1973).

⚜ Alfred Sully
Lieutenant Colonel, U.S. Army

Sully was born in 1821 in Philadelphia, the son of famed painter Thomas Sully. Although he showed artistic ability in his youth, Sully chose to embark on a military career. He graduated from West Point in 1841 and was commissioned a second lieutenant in the 2nd Infantry. He fought in the Seminole and Mexican Wars and served in Oregon, California, and on the northern plains. During the Civil War, he was appointed colonel of the 1st Minnesota Infantry and was promoted to brigadier general in 1862. After distinguishing himself at South Mountain, Second Bull Run, Antietam, Fredericksburg, and Chancellorsville, Sully was sent in 1863 to the District of Dakota, where he proved himself a skillful Indian fighter.

In the September 1863 battle at White Stone Hill, Dakota Territory, against the Sioux, his command killed or wounded 300 Indians and captured about the same number, while losing only 30 soldiers killed and 38 wounded. His most famous operation was in the summer of 1864, when he led some 3,400 men into Sioux country on a four-month, 1,600-mile expedition. At the

(continued on following page)

battle of Killdeer Mountain, Sully's men killed as many as 150 Indians, while suffering only 2 killed and a handful wounded.

After the war, Sully remained in the West as a lieutenant colonel with the 3rd Infantry and, contrary to his previous accomplishments, gained a reputation as an "ambulance" general, one who was excessively slow and cautious. In September 1868, Sully was serving as commander of the District of the Upper Arkansas when he led his 3rd Infantry and the 7th Cavalry—while George Armstrong Custer was serving his suspension—on an expedition into Indian Territory. In one engagement, his men killed or wounded thirty-four Indians, while losing only three troopers killed and five wounded. Much of his campaigning, however, was quite timid and predictably cautious. When Custer returned to duty, the two men clashed over this deliberate manner. In November 1868, Gen. Phil Sheridan was called upon to decide which officer would be field commander for the Washita campaign. Little Phil chose the more aggressive Custer to replace Sully, who was sent back to Fort Harker to command his district.

"Few wealthy people seem to enjoy their married life. Only think, little one, how much pleasure we have, planning to procure this or that article, make this or that journey. I have yet to find husband and wife here who enjoy life as we do."

—CUSTER TO LIBBIE FROM NEW YORK CITY, JULY 1871

In 1869, Sully was appointed superintendent of Indian Affairs for Montana, and the following year, he became embroiled in a controversy over the massacre of 170 Piegan of the Blackfoot Confederacy. He was promoted to colonel in 1873 and commanded the 21st Infantry in several Indian operations.

Over the years, Sully, an accomplished artist, painted many Western landscapes, specializing in views of forts. At some point, he married a Spanish-Mexican woman at Monterey and fathered a

(continued on following page)

January 11, 1871, he sent Libbie to Monroe by way of Topeka and traveled east on a leave that would extend until September of that year.

Custer quickly cultivated friendships with wealthy investors such as John Jacob Astor, August Belmont, and Jay Gould. He traveled comfortably in this circle of high financial and influential political society and had soon developed an idea that would interest these men—and, he hoped, make himself rich.

The lure of silver and gold from rich strikes in Western mines had been the reason for many of the desertions that had plagued the 7th Cavalry from its inception. For Custer, these mines held the prospect of an investment that could reap great rewards. He had at one point taken the time to investigate the potential of one such silver mine, the Stevens Lode, which was located about ten miles from Georgetown, Colorado.

Custer, whose famous name gained him entrée to the most reclusive tycoon, pitched his confidence in the Stevens Lode to potential investors with the fervor of one of his frontal assaults. Two thousand shares of stock were issued at $50 a share with a valuation of $100 each. Astor handed over $10,000, Belmont was in for $15,000, others chipped in thousands more, and Custer subscribed to $35,000, although likely not in cash but rather a promoter's share.

While in New York promoting his silver mine, Custer dressed in Brooks Brothers suits and was a welcome guest at fashionable dinner parties and other events reserved for the social elite. He mingled with celebrities and dignitaries at Delmonico's and other fine restaurants, attended gala affairs at local mansions, frequented the opera and theatrical performances (Custer loved the theater throughout his life), sailed on private yachts, and traveled to Saratoga for the horse races.

When September arrived, however, Custer chose the army over civilian life and reported to Elizabethtown, Kentucky, for duty with the 7th Cavalry. At that time, he sold his shares in the Stevens Lode and sent the money to his brother Nevin to use as a down payment on a farm near his parents—a most prudent decision. His investors never realized a profit from the silver mine. The enterprise collapsed after several years of assaying and mining.

A detailed account of Custer's investment venture and his New York socializing can be found in *General Custer's Libbie*, by Lawrence A. Frost (Seattle: Superior Publishing Company, 1976). Correspondence on the subject between and by Custer and Libbie has been reprinted in *The Custer Story: The Life and Letters of General George A. Custer and His Wife Elizabeth*, by Marguerite Merington (New York: Devin-Adair Co., 1950). Another notable source is Robert M. Utley's *Cavalier in Buckskin: George Armstrong Custer and the Western Military Frontier*

(Norman: University of Oklahoma Press, 1988), which suggests that Custer's practices in promoting the mine, although common for the time, were less than honorable.

The Russian Grand Duke's Buffalo Hunt

In January 1872, George Armstrong Custer enjoyed a respite from duty in Kentucky when he was summoned to Nebraska by Phil Sheridan to be part of an escort for Russian grand duke Alexis Romanov. The visiting nineteen-year-old third son of Russian czar Alexander II, who spoke excellent English, had been receiving royal treatment from the government and the military in the form of lavish banquets, flowery speeches, and rifle salutes, but the highlight of his trip would be a buffalo hunt, the most famous sport in the United States at that time.

In addition to Custer, Sheridan, Russian admirals, various other dignitaries, and a flock of reporters, the Nebraska hunting entourage would include William F. "Buffalo Bill" Cody and about 100 Lakota Sioux Indians led by Spotted Tail, who brought along his comely, flirtatious sixteen-year-old niece (the first cousin of Crazy Horse), whom the others called Miss Spotted Tail. Another invited guest—a questionable choice, to say the least—was Lakota Sioux war chief Pawnee Killer, Custer's nemesis from the Hancock expedition who had murdered Lieutenant Kidder's detachment and later was an enemy participant in the Beecher Island and Summit Springs battles.

The hunting party established a base camp, dubbed Camp Alexis, on Red Willow Creek. The camp had been furnished with plush accoutrements, featuring forty of the army's best wall tents, two elegantly carpeted hospital tents, Chinese lanterns hanging from trees, and meals served with caviar, champagne, and other delicacies. The guests were entertained with singing and dancing and by exhibitions of Indian war dances, horse races, and prowess with bow and arrow.

On January 14, Custer, who had been appointed to lead the hunt, and Cody, accompanied by Spotted Tail and eight warriors, led the grand duke through snow that rose to eighteen inches deep in search of their prey. Cody located a small herd, and Custer and Alexis charged. The grand duke twice emptied his six-shot revolver without success. Finally, Alexis brought down his first buffalo with a well-placed pistol shot to the head. A courier was immediately dispatched to North Platte,

Custer with Grand Duke Alexis, 1872. *Courtesy Little Bighorn Battlefield National Monument.*

child. Sully died on April 27, 1879, at Fort Vancouver, Washington.

📖 Sully's paintings and letters, published by his grandson in *No Tears for the General: The Life of Alfred Sully, 1821–1879*, edited by Langdon Sully (Pala Alto, CA: American West, 1974), provide an excellent record of mid-nineteenth-century military life. Also see "The Sully Expedition of 1864 Featuring the Killdeer Mountain and Badlands Battles," by Louis Pfaller, *North Dakota History* 31, no. 1 (January 1964).

❀ William Thompson
Captain, 7th U.S. Cavalry

Thompson held the distinction of being the oldest officer in the 7th Cavalry. He was born in Fayette County, Pennsylvania, on November 13, 1813, which made him twenty-six years older than field commander George Armstrong Custer. Thompson studied law in Mount Vernon, Ohio, and was admitted to the bar in 1837. He moved to Mount Pleasant, Iowa, in 1839 and served as chief clerk of the territorial legislature, secretary of the 1846 state constitutional convention, and a U.S. representative from 1847 to 1850. He then opened a law office and became editor of the *Iowa State Gazette*.

"To-day is our wedding anniversary. I am sorry we cannot spend it together, but I shall celebrate it in my heart."

—CUSTER TO LIBBIE, FEBRUARY 1869

Thompson was appointed a captain in 1861, and later a colonel, in the 2nd Iowa Cavalry, which patrolled Missouri and Arkansas. By war's end, he had been breveted up to brigadier general of volunteers. Following the war, he served with Custer on Reconstruction duty in Texas and received a captaincy in the newly formed 7th Cavalry in 1866. Thompson, who had commanded a mutinous regiment while in Texas, was referred to by Libbie Custer as her husband's worst enemy at Fort Riley.

At the November 1868 battle of the Washita, Thompson commanded a squadron that consisted of Troops B and F, which attacked Black Kettle's village from the south. Due to difficulties traversing the terrain, Thompson's unit was the last to reach the village, and his inability to connect with Elliott's flank afforded the Indians an avenue of escape.

He retired on disability at age sixty-two in December 1875 and returned to his position as editor of the *Iowa State Gazette*. He died in Tacoma, Washington, on October 6, 1897.

fifty miles away, to cable the czar in Russia with the triumphant news. That day Alexis killed eight buffalo, and the same number the next day.

When camp broke up two days later, the grand duke, who had taken quite a fancy to Custer, received permission from Sheridan to allow his newfound friend to accompany him on the remainder of his tour. Custer and Alexis boarded the Union Pacific to visit Denver and engaged in another buffalo hunt before heading east. Libbie Custer joined them at Louisville and marveled at the royal treatment at each stop, which consisted of grand balls, elegant restaurants, receptions, shopping, and even coffee and rolls served in bed in a suite adjacent to that of the grand duke. The entourage traveled by steamboat down the Ohio to the Mississippi and on to New Orleans, where Alexis boarded a Russian warship for a trip to Havana before heading home.

The Custers went to Monroe, Michigan—in decidedly less lavish style—to attend the wedding of Custer's sister Maggie to James Calhoun before returning to mundane duty at Elizabethtown, Kentucky.

📖 Perhaps the best account of the grand duke's entire U.S. visit, which was compiled from newspaper stories, can be found in *The Grand Duke Alexis in the United States,* by William Tucker and Jeff C. Dykes (1872; reprint, New York: Interland Publishing, 1972). For an excellent overview, see "When the Czar and Grant Were Friends," by William F. Zornow, *Mid-America* 43 (July 1961). An excerpt from Libbie Custer's diary can be found in *The Custer Story,* by Marguerite Merington (New York: Devin-Adair, 1950). Two versions by participants are Cody's *The Life of Hon. William F. Cody, Known as Buffalo Bill* (Lincoln: University of Nebraska Press, 1978); and "A Royal Buffalo Hunt," in *Transactions of the Kansas State Historical Society* 10 (1907–08), by James Albert Hadley, a scout who also had been an officer in the 19th Kansas Volunteer Cavalry during the winter campaign of 1868–69.

Other notable sources include "Red Carpet for a Romanoff," by John I. White, *American West* 9 (January 1972); and "Custer, Cody and the Grand Duke Alexis," by Elizabeth Bacon Custer and John Manion, *Research Review: The Journal of the Little Bighorn Associates* 4 (January 1990).

EPILOGUE

The winter campaign of 1868–69 established George Armstrong Custer as the premier Indian fighter in the land. He and Libbie settled in for the summer at the regimental campsite at Big Bend, two miles east of Fort Hays. Much of the time was whiled away entertaining a succession of guests—including P. T. Barnum—who wanted to meet Custer and perhaps accompany him on a buffalo hunt. Detachments of the 7th Cavalry were stationed at various posts along the Kansas Pacific Railway, and though Custer occasionally accompanied patrols, for the most part his summer was leisurely, with evenings spent enjoying horseback rides with Libbie.

After wintering at Fort Leavenworth, Custer returned to the field. The summer of 1870 was somewhat bloody in Kansas, and he was kept busy chasing marauding Indians.

The monotony of military life gnawed at him, however, and he had begun to question his future in the army. The 7th Cavalry was scheduled to be dispatched in small units on Reconstruction duty to various areas of the South, and Custer desired to test the civilian waters before that assignment. On January 11, 1871, he was granted a furlough that would extend until September, and he traveled to New York City in pursuit of business and employment prospects (see "The Stevens Lode Mine" on page 105).

Custer failed to find his fortune in the big city and returned to duty with a two-company detachment of the 7th Cavalry that had been stationed in Elizabethtown, Kentucky, a quiet community not far from Louisville known as E-Town or Betseytown by the locals. His duties included assisting Federal marshals in keeping track of the activities of the Ku Klux Klan and moonshiners and purchasing horses for the army. Otherwise, his days were marked by boredom, except perhaps for a stimulating game of chess with a local judge, an afternoon at the racetrack, discussing horses at a local farm, or hunting with hounds, of which he had about eighty. Custer also owned a number of Thoroughbreds that he raced, the best being Don Juan and Frogtown (see "Custer, the Sportsman" on page 132).

In January 1872, he was afforded a respite from his inactivity when Sheridan invited him to participate in a Nebraska buffalo hunt that had been arranged for Russian grand duke Alexis (see "The Russian Grand Duke's Buffalo Hunt" on page 107).

Finally, in February 1873, his dreaded duty in Kentucky came to an end. The War Department had agreed to continue providing protection to engineering parties of the Northern Pacific Railroad that were exploring and mapping the Yellowstone region in Montana and Wyoming. The 7th Cavalry would be reunited, and Custer would be part of that summer's expedition.

📖 Between 1867 and 1875, Custer—under the pseudonym "Nomad"—wrote fifteen letters describing his adventures with horses, hounds, and hunting, which were published in *Turf, Field and Farm*. Five of these stories relate his experiences in Kentucky. The entire collection has been published, along with informative anecdotes, by editor Brian W. Dippie in *Nomad: George Armstrong Custer in Turf, Field and Farm* (Austin: University of Texas Press, 1980). A chapter in Lawrence A. Frost's *General Custer's Libbie* (Seattle: Superior Publishing Co., 1976) has been dedicated to the Custers' rather uneventful stay in Kentucky.

Other notable sources include *General Custer's Thoroughbreds: Racing, Riding, Hunting, and Fighting,* by Lawrence A. Frost (Bryan, TX: J. M. Carroll, 1986); "The Two-Year Residence of General George A. Custer in Kentucky," by R. G. McMurtry, *Kentucky Progress Magazine* (Summer 1933); and "Custer's Kentucky: General George Armstrong Custer and Elizabethtown, Kentucky, 1871–1873," by Theodore J. Crackel, *Filson Club History Quarterly* 49 (April 1974).

CHAPTER FIVE

The Yellowstone Expedition

OVERVIEW

In 1870, the Northern Pacific Railroad had commenced laying tracks and was moving steadily westward from its eastern terminus in Duluth, Minnesota. In order to continue plotting the route of the line west of the Missouri River into Montana, however, the survey crews would be venturing into land that was home to hostile Indians. Fortunately for the railroad, the army regarded the completion of rails across this relatively unexplored region of great national strategic importance and was enthusiastic about offering protection for the engineering work (see "The Northern Pacific Railroad" on page 119).

The first Yellowstone expedition, designed to determine the Northern Pacific's route between Bismarck, Dakota Territory, and Bozeman, Montana, was undertaken in 1871 and lasted only one month. The following year, Col. David S. Stanley's infantry provided escort for the survey crews and faced fierce opposition from hostile Sioux Indians. The expedition was forced to con-

"I am told no country equals this region in the number and character of its petrifications, animal and vegetable. What would you think of passing through acres of petrified trees, some with trunks several feet in diameter, and branches perfect? I intend to make a collection of petrifications, fossils, &c. and present it to Ann Arbor University."

—CUSTER TO LIBBIE, JULY 1873

Custer, with guide Bloody Knife kneeling at left. *Courtesy Little Bighorn Battlefield National Monument.*

BIOGRAPHIES

✵ Augustus "Gus" Baliran
Sutler

Baliran was born in France in about 1843. At some point, he immigrated to the United States. In July 1861, at age eighteen, he enlisted as a private in Company I, 10th Regiment of the Louisiana Volunteers. Two years later, he deserted that infantry unit to join the more glamorous Confederate cavalry. He apparently settled in Memphis after the war, where he married a woman named Lizzie, with whom he had two children.

According to Capt. Frederick Benteen, Baliran "was the proprietor of a restaurant and gaming establishment, doing a good business, and a gambler by profession," asserting that this information came from 1st Lt. Carlo DeRudio. He said that Custer induced Baliran into joining the 7th Cavalry's Yellowstone expedition by "telling him the officers of the regiment were high players and he could make a big thing." Whether this account holds any merit, with its implication that Custer was somehow involved in a financial scheme, should be suspect, considering the source. Baliran did, however, attach himself to the 7th Cavalry at Memphis, and he accompanied the unit on the Yellowstone expedition as a sutler.

Shortly after the expedition was under way, Col. David Stanley, who had invited another sutler along for his infantry, confronted Baliran. The colonel, who was drunk, berated Baliran with foul language and ordered that he return to Fort Rice by that evening or face death by hanging. The frightened sutler reported the incident to Custer, who advised Baliran to move his wagons just outside of camp until the matter could be straightened out. Custer then reminded Stanley that permission had been given Baliran to accompany the 7th Cavalry, even though it placed Baliran in competition with Stanley's sutler. The vindictive Stanley then ordered Col. Fred Grant to destroy Baliran's stock of whiskey. Instead of carrying out the order, either Custer or Grant advised the popular sutler to temporarily empty his wagons by distributing his stores to various 7th Cavalry officers for safekeeping. Stanley sobered up and, perhaps realizing that he would be jeopardizing his own liquor supply, rescinded his order.

On August 4, 1873, Baliran and Dr. John Honsinger, the regimental veterinarian, were riding ahead of the main column to join Custer when they were ambushed by about thirty Sioux. The men took refuge in some bushes near a stream and were subsequently killed. Baliran, who wore his hair close-cropped, was not scalped or muti-

(continued on following page)

clude when the foot soldiers were unable to contend with Sioux attacks. To remedy that situation, cavalry support would accompany Stanley's infantry on the next expedition. George Armstrong Custer and the 7th Cavalry would be part of the campaign scheduled for the summer of 1873.

The 7th Cavalry regiment, which had been spread out around the South on Reconstruction duty, assembled during the last week of March 1873 in Memphis. At Sioux City, Iowa, Custer led ten companies up the Missouri toward Dakota Territory to prepare for the expedition. Meanwhile, Maj. Marcus Reno, with Capt. Thomas B. Weir's Company D and Capt. Myles W. Keogh's Company I, would continue by rail to Fort Snelling, Minnesota, where they would participate in the Northern Boundary Survey (see "The Northern Boundary Survey" on page 121).

Col. David S. Stanley's expedition marched from Fort Rice on June 20. The column comprised nineteen infantry companies; two cannons; ten companies of the 7th Cavalry—over 1,500 soldiers; about 350 civilians, including the engineering and scientific parties and the teamsters; a detachment of white and Indian scouts; a herd of nearly 450 cattle; and a train of 275 wagons. Two steamboats—the *Far West* and the *Josephine*—had been chartered to haul supplies on the Yellowstone River (see "Table of Organization of the 7th Cavalry for the Yellowstone Expedition of 1873" on page 118).

Custer had endured three years of inactivity and was thrilled to be out in the field once again. He joyously roamed ahead of the column, acting as scout, and led daily hunting parties that kept the messes in fresh meat. Custer also collected fossils and practiced taxidermy, working late into the night preparing game for mounting (see "Custer, the Sportsman" on page 132).

In spite of traveling through hail, rain, and windstorms, the initial portion of the trek heading west across Dakota toward Montana could be described as an extended party, with the regimental band furnishing musical accompaniment. Custer occupied his time with outdoor-related activities and writing letters to Libbie—including one that was forty-two pages long—that described the remarkable terrain and detailed his hunting exploits. A number of others in the group, however, let their vices get the best of them.

Capt. George Yates, fretting over the poor health of his wife, who had endured a difficult pregnancy, went on a binge and remained intoxicated for days, while losing hundreds of dollars playing cards. First Lt. James Calhoun, Custer's brother-in-law, lost all of his money playing poker and could not find anyone who would trust him with a loan. Lt. Col. Frederick Grant, the president's son, who was attached as an observer for Gen. Phil Sheridan, also drank to excess—although Custer found Grant to be a fine companion. Tom Custer had a streak of losing card hands and had been borrowing money in order to continue playing.

One member of the expedition whose company Custer particularly enjoyed was former Confederate general Thomas L. Rosser, Custer's closest West Point friend. Rosser was in charge of the surveying crews as chief engineer of the Northern Pacific Railroad's Dakota Division. Custer and Rosser had faced each other numerous times on Civil War battlefields and now whiled away many hours swapping war stories. Rosser readily admitted that his worst defeat had come at the hands of Custer at Tom's Brook, Virginia (see "Custer and Confederate Friends" on page 27).

It was inevitable, however, that the headstrong Custer and Colonel Stanley, who has been described as "a squat, humorless, peevish alcoholic . . . the antithesis of Custer," would come to loggerheads. Neither man had much respect for the other.

Shortly after the expedition was under way, a drunken Stanley, who had invited another sutler along for his infantry, ordered that Augustus Baliran, a sutler attached to the cavalry, return to Fort Rice by that evening or face death by hanging. The incident was reported to Custer, who reminded Stanley that permission had been given Baliran to accompany the 7th Cavalry. Stanley relented but ordered Col. Frederick Grant to destroy Baliran's stock of whiskey. Instead of carrying out the order, the kindhearted Grant advised the sutler to temporarily distribute his stores to various 7th Cavalry officers for safekeeping. Stanley rescinded the order when he sobered up.

lated, but the $100 he carried was taken. Sioux warrior Rain-in-the-Face later bragged about killing Baliran and Honsinger and was arrested for the crime (see "The Arrest and Revenge of Rain-in-the-Face" on page 129).

The sutler was buried on the banks of the Yellowstone River with full military honors similar to those accorded high-ranking officers. Libbie Custer wrote an expression of sympathy to Baliran's wife, who, three years later, responded in kind and requested a photograph of the general.

📖 The most information about Baliran can be found in Lawrence W. Frost's *Custer's 7th Cavalry and the Campaign of 1873* (El Segundo, CA: Upton & Sons, Publishers, 1985). The late Frost was also in possession of Baliran's ledger book for the expedition, which lists the names of the various officers and men and the amounts that each owed. The ledger book was said to have been found stored in the attic of the Custer farmhouse in Monroe, Michigan. Benteen's account is contained in *The Benteen-Goldin Letters on Custer and His Last Battle,* edited by John M. Carroll (Lincoln: University of Nebraska Press, 1974). Also see Libbie Custer's *"Boots and Saddles"; or, Life in Dakota with General Custer* (New York: Harper & Brothers, 1913).

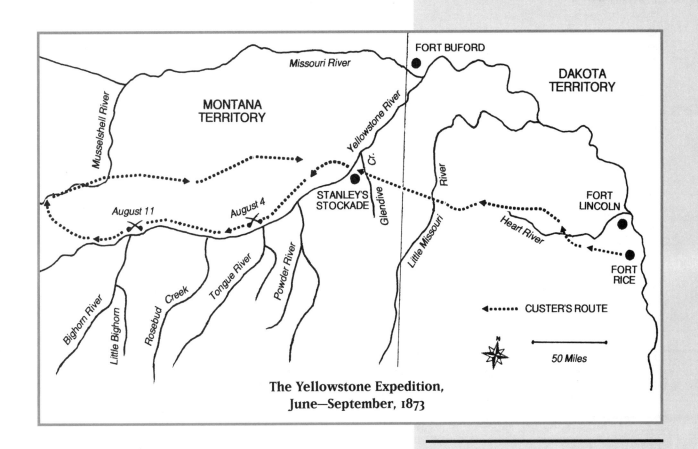

**The Yellowstone Expedition,
June—September, 1873**

✿ Bloody Knife
Arikara-Sioux Scout

Bloody Knife (Arikara name Nee si Ra Pat; Sioux name Tamina Wewe) was born sometime between 1837 and 1840 in Dakota Territory to a Hunkpapa Sioux father and Arikara (Ree) mother. He lived with the Sioux, who were traditional enemies of the Arikara, and was discriminated against and treated as an outcast due to his mixed blood. This resulted in a deep hatred for that tribe and, in particular, one of his peers, Gall, with whom he developed a feud that endured for years. Sitting Bull, who had adopted Gall as a younger brother, also subjected the mixed-blood boy to abuse.

When Bloody Knife was about fifteen years old, his mother left her husband and returned to her people at Fort Clark, an American Fur Company trading post on the Upper Missouri near present-day Stanton, North Dakota. He was able to make good use of his multicultural background in the early 1860s, when he carried mail between Fort Totten and other Missouri forts. Many mail carriers were killed by Sioux on this route, which made it difficult to employ riders, but Bloody Knife almost always got the mail through on time. He also occasionally worked as an army scout and as a runner and hunter for the American Fur Company.

The animosity between Bloody Knife and Gall nearly resulted in Gall's death during the winter of 1865–66. Bloody Knife was serving as a scout with a detachment of soldiers that went to arrest Gall, who was visiting a Sioux camp south of Fort Berthold. Gall attempted to escape and was bayoneted. Bloody Knife stepped forward with the intention of shooting his enemy in the head, but he was stopped by an officer who believed that Gall was already dead. Gall miraculously survived and became a war chief with whom to be reckoned.

In 1866, Bloody Knife married an Arikara woman named either She Owl or Owl Woman, who gave birth to at least one daughter and one son. The daughter evidently died young, according to a grave marker at Fort Buford that bears the inscription: "Daughter of Bloody Knife, December 28, 1870, Disease." The son was said to have been murdered by his wife in 1904.

Bloody Knife enlisted as a corporal with the U.S. Army's Indian scouts at Fort Stevenson in May 1868. He soon acquired a serious drinking problem, which may have contributed to his desertion that September. He was, however, promoted to lance corporal in 1872.

Another matter of contention concerned the presence of Custer's black cook, Mary Adams, and the cast-iron stove he had brought along. Mary's preparation of wild game made Custer's mess extremely popular, and this apparently did not set well with Stanley. The colonel ordered that Custer rid himself of the stove, which was nonmilitary equipment, but it survived several attempts to have it abandoned.

The column halted on July 1 at Muddy Creek, which was overflowing and would require the infantrymen to construct a makeshift bridge in order to cross. Custer, whose troops Stanley had expected to assist with the crossing, had—under his own initiative—marched a detachment of his cavalry some distance ahead of the main body. He then dispatched a messenger requesting that Stanley send him forage and rations. An angry Stanley ordered that Custer return at once and consider himself under arrest.

The 7th Cavalry with its insolent commander was exiled to march at the rear of the column. Tom Rosser reasoned with Stanley, advising that common sense dictated that the cavalry lead the way. A sober Stanley agreed and not only lifted the arrest, but also apologized to Custer, asked his forgiveness, and vowed to quit drinking. Regardless of promises, Stanley remained in an intoxicated state, which for all intents and purposes permitted Custer to assume leadership of the expedition.

In mid-July, Custer led two companies on a treacherous march through the Badlands to reach the Yellowstone River, where the steamer *Far West* waited with provisions and mail. They constructed a supply depot on the south bank of the Yellowstone, about eight miles above the mouth of Glendive Creek, and left Capt. Frederick W. Benteen and two companies behind to guard "Stanley's Stockade."

The party was over when the expedition moved into the Yellowstone Valley, an area known to be populated by Lakota Sioux. The order of march was Custer's cavalry, followed by the surveyors with their transits and maps, and the infantry bring up the rear. Custer, along with his favorite scout, Bloody Knife, and a small detachment, normally rode in advance of the column. Bloody Knife became concerned by the frequency of fresh Indian sign and warned Custer to be prepared for an attack. By early August, the expedition was deep into hostile territory, camped on the Yellowstone several miles downstream from the Tongue River.

"General Stanley is acting very badly, drinking, and I anticipate official trouble with him. I should greatly regret this, but fear it cannot be avoided."

—CUSTER TO LIBBIE, JUNE 1873

(continued on following page)

At noon on August 4—with the temperature hovering around 110 degrees—Custer, Capt. Myles Moylan, 1st Lt. Tom Custer, 1st Lt. James Calhoun, and 2nd Lt. Charles Varnum, with about ninety cavalrymen from Companies A and B, had taken a break from a scout to halt in a grove of cottonwood trees near the mouth of the Tongue River (the site of present-day Miles City, Montana). The horses had been turned out to graze, the men were lazing around, and Custer was taking a nap when pickets shouted, "Indians!" The cavalrymen began firing at the small group of warriors that were attempting to scatter the horses.

Custer, with his brother and Calhoun, mounted twenty men and gave chase. Moylan was ordered to advance more slowly with the main body. After riding about two miles up the valley, Custer became suspicious and halted his squadron. Accompanied by two orderlies, he cautiously continued after the Sioux, in his words, "to develop their intentions." Those intentions quickly became known when 300 mounted warriors burst from a stand of timber and charged.

Custer wheeled his Thoroughbred, Dandy, and easily outdistanced the Indians to arrive back where he had left his small detachment. Moylan brought up the remainder of the squadron, and the troopers were formed into a skirmisher line in the cottonwoods behind the bank of a dry streambed. The men would rise up to fire point-blank into the onrushing warriors with effective volleys that discouraged each advance. The Sioux pulled back, dismounted, and began to creep through the tall grass toward the position of the cavalrymen.

Custer and his troopers spent the long, hot afternoon defending their position against repeated assaults. The Sioux eventually set fire to the grass and advanced behind the smoke, but they were repulsed each time.

By late in the afternoon, ammunition was running low, when—just as in a Western movie—the rest of the cavalry could be observed riding to the rescue. A confident Custer mounted his men and surprised the Sioux by executing a counterattack. The Indians broke and ran, and the cavalrymen chased them several miles down the valley. Custer lost only one man and two horses in the skirmish.

While Custer had been pinned down, about thirty Sioux had happened upon veterinarian John Honsinger and sutler Augustus Baliran as the two men, unaware of danger, rode ahead of the main body to join Custer. Honsinger and Baliran were brutally murdered. Most accounts relate that Pvt. John H. Ball was also killed, although evidence exists to suggest that he had deserted. Sioux warrior Rain-in-the-Face later bragged about killing these men and was arrested and confined for the crime (see "The Arrest and Revenge of Rain-in-the-Face" on page 129).

The command pushed up the Yellowstone until—on August 8—Bloody Knife, riding with Custer in the advance, discovered the site of a recently abandoned Indian village. The

When Fort Abraham Lincoln was established in June 1872, Bloody Knife was a leader of the Arikara scouts attached to it. He was hired for the Yellowstone expedition of 1873 and at this point met George Armstrong Custer for the first time. He quickly became Custer's favorite scout by proving himself a faithful companion and invaluable at reading sign. The scout located the site of a recently abandoned Sioux village, which he estimated at perhaps 500 lodges, with as many as 1,000 warriors. The fleeing Indians' trail was followed and led to the battle at the Yellowstone.

In May 1874, Bloody Knife enlisted for six months' duty as chief scout—reportedly in charge of as many as 100 Indian scouts—with Custer's Black Hills expedition. When most of his Arikara and Santee scouts refused to enter this sacred Sioux reservation, Bloody Knife agreed to accompany Custer and was considered a "personal aide." Bullets from the Indian's rifle contributed to Custer's bringing down his first grizzly during that expedition. The scout also thrust his knife into the bear's jugular to finish the job. He was discharged as a private of excellent and reliable character on November 30.

Bloody Knife reenlisted as a guide with the 7th Cavalry in March 1876 for duty in the Little Bighorn campaign. On the morning of the famous battle, Bloody Knife advised Custer from a lookout known as Crow's Nest that there were more Indians ahead than the soldiers had bullets. Bloody Knife was attached to Maj. Marcus A. Reno, whose battalion swept across the valley toward the Indian village to initiate the battle. When the battalion retreated into the timber, Bloody Knife was shot in the head, his blood and brains splattering onto the face of Major Reno. This caused Reno to lose his nerve and panic, which set in motion a series of actions by Reno that led to the death of many troopers.

Bloody Knife's remains were buried on the battlefield by Col. John Gibbon's troops on June 27. It has been reported that one of Gibbon's officers found a scalp in a deserted Sioux lodge that the Arikara identified by the gray streaks as belonging to Bloody Knife. She Owl presented herself to Fort Berthold in April 1879 and collected almost $100 in pay that had been due her husband.

   📖 See *Bloody Knife: Custer's Favorite Scout*, by Ben Innis, edited by Richard E. Collin (Bismarck, ND: Smoky Water Press, 1994); "Bloody Knife: Custer's Favorite Scout," by Richard E. Collin, *Greasy Grass* 13 (May 1997), a publication of the Custer Battlefield Historical and Museum

(continued on following page)

Association; "Bloody Knife, Ree Scout for Custer," by John Gray, *Chicago Westerners Brand Book* (February 1961); and "Bloody Knife and Gall," by Joseph Taylor, *Frontier and Indian Life* (1932).

✳ Charles Braden
Second Lieutenant, 7th U.S. Cavalry

Braden was born in Detroit on November 23, 1847. He entered West Point in 1865 and graduated four years later, ranked nineteenth in a class of thirty-nine. Braden was commissioned a second lieutenant in the 7th Cavalry on June 15, 1869, and was initially stationed at Fort Hays, Kansas. In 1871, he was temporarily assigned to accompany an expedition commanded by Col. Richard I. Dodge for the purpose of locating a road from Fort Lyon, Colorado, to Fort Union, New Mexico. Braden then joined his unit in South Carolina until April 1873, when the regiment assembled for the Yellowstone expedition.

During that expedition, Braden participated in skirmishes with the Sioux on August 4 and 11. In prelude to the second battle, Braden manned an observation post on a high bluff and reported to Custer the approach of the Sioux. He was in command of a twenty-man detachment deployed on a benchland rising from the valley when hundreds of Indians commenced their assault. His small unit successfully repelled four concerted efforts by the superior force to breach their line. During the battle, however, Braden's left thigh was shattered by a bullet, and he fell critically wounded. He was removed by a crude litter—described by Custer as not an ambulance, but "a long stretcher on wheels, pushed and pulled by men on foot"— and carried nearly 400 miles over rough country for twenty-eight days, nearly dying en route. He was finally sent to Fort Abraham Lincoln aboard the steamer *Josephine* for treatment of the severe wound. He remained at that post until October, when he was moved to St. Paul, then went on permanent sick leave, returning only briefly to the 7th Cavalry for a month in 1876.

Braden was promoted to first lieutenant on December 9, 1875, and retired on June 28, 1878, due to the wound that had incapacitated him. On June 5, 1879, he married Jeanette E. Devin, daughter of Gen. Thomas C. Devin, with whom he had two children. He resided at West Point and taught at a school that prepared candidates for admission to the U.S. Military Academy. Braden served as secretary of the Association of Graduates of West Point for thirty-one years. He died at Highland Falls, New York, on January 15, 1919,

(continued on following page)

scout estimated that it consisted of 500 lodges, which would indicate the presence of perhaps as many as 1,000 warriors. Custer received permission from Stanley to follow this hot trail and immediately dashed off with eight companies and the Arikara Indian scouts.

After a thirty-six-hour march, the trail led to the banks of the Yellowstone near the mouth of the Bighorn River. Bloody Knife swam across to determine that the tracks continued on the south side, but the river at this point was too deep and swift for the cavalry to cross. Custer decided to camp for the night, planning to resume attempts to cross the following morning, August 11.

At daybreak, however, the Sioux made their presence known. Hundreds of Indians hidden in the cottonwoods on the opposite bank opened up with withering rifle fire and a torrent of arrows. While the women and children gathered on the bluffs to watch, hundreds more warriors began swimming the river above and below Custer's position.

Custer reacted quickly and deployed sharpshooters to engage and try to pin down the entrenched warriors. To counter the threat from the flanks, he dispatched two companies commanded by Capt. Thomas French down the valley and two companies under Capt. Verlin Hart up the valley. Hart posted twenty men under 2nd Lt. Charles Braden in a forward position on a benchland rising from the valley.

Braden's detachment bore the brunt of the initial assault. His small unit bravely repelled four concerted efforts by the superior force to breach their line. During the battle, Braden's left thigh was shattered by a bullet, and he fell critically wounded.

Custer was seemingly everywhere, handling his command with the calm deliberation and battlefield instincts that he had developed in the Civil War. He rode along his line, shifting companies to meet each attack or to flush out groups of warriors from nearby ravines, all the while exposing himself to a vicious onslaught of bullets and arrows.

Finally, Stanley arrived on the field and began lobbing artillery shells into the timber across the river. Custer decided to seize the initiative. He mounted his entire 450-man command, signaled for the band to strike up "Garry Owen," and ordered a charge. He once again surprised his enemy with this bold tactic. The Sioux responded by scattering and racing away as fast as their ponies could run. The cavalrymen chased the fleeing Indians for nine miles before losing the trail.

The 7th Cavalry had suffered three men killed, four wounded, and eight horses lost during the engagement. Custer estimated that about forty Indians had been killed in both August battles. The identity of the Indians that attacked the 7th Cavalry has been a matter of speculation, although Frank Grouard, a future army scout who was known to have been adopted by Sitting Bull, had participated (see "Who Were Those Sioux That Attacked Custer?" on page 128).

The survey moved up the Yellowstone another thirty miles before halting on August 15 at Pompey's Pillar, a solitary sandstone landmark some 380 miles west of Fort Rice that had been named by Lewis and Clark. The column had settled in to rest for the day when a group of Sioux warriors opened fire on some swimming soldiers, who were scared and scattered but were otherwise unharmed. Custer chose not to pursue the hostiles.

The following day, the column headed east on a difficult yet uneventful return march overland to the Musselshell River and down the Missouri, finally reaching Fort Abraham Lincoln on September 21—several days before Stanley's plodding foot soldiers and wagon train made their appearance. Stanley estimated that the expedition had covered 935 miles in ninety-five days.

Ironically, on the day that Custer reached Fort Lincoln, Jay Cooke and Company, the sponsor of bonds for the Northern Pacific Railroad, collapsed, bankrupting the railroad. The demise of that firm was followed by numerous banks and even caused the temporary closure of the New York Stock Exchange in what became known as the Panic of 1873. The end of track would be stalled at Bismarck for six years until the Northern Pacific could raise the resources to resume operations westward.

📖 The best source in this rather lean bibliography is *Custer's 7th Cav and the Campaign of 1873,* by Lawrence A. Frost (El Segundo, CA: Upton & Sons, 1986). Accounts by participants include "Battling with Sioux on the Yellowstone," by George Armstrong Custer, *Galaxy* 22 (July 1876), which has been reprinted in *The Custer Reader,* edited by Paul A. Hutton (Lincoln: University of Nebraska Press, 1992); and "Expedition to the Yellowstone River in 1873: Letters of a Young Cavalry Officer," by Charles W. Larned, edited by George F. Howe, *Mississippi Valley Historical Review* 39 (December 1952), also reprinted in *The Custer Reader.* The appendix of David S. Stanley's *Personal Memoirs of Major General David S. Stanley* (Cambridge, MA: Harvard University Press, 1917) contains Stanley's official report and extracts from letters to his wife relating to the expedition.

Another interesting source, which provides excerpts from fifteen of Custer's letters to his wife, is *The Custer Story: The Life and Intimate Letters of General George A. Custer and His Wife Elizabeth,* edited by Marguerite Merington (New York: Devin-Adair, 1950). For Libbie's personal account and a reprint of Custer's report, see her *"Boots and Saddles"; or, Life in Dakota with General Custer* (New York: Harper and Brothers, 1913). See also "The Yellowstone Expedition of 1873," by Alan Rolston, *Montana* 20 (April 1970).

and was posthumously awarded the Distinguished Service Cross for his actions during the Yellowstone expedition.

📖 For his observations on the expedition, see Braden's "The Yellowstone Expedition of 1873," *Cavalry Journal* (October 1905).

✸ John W. Burkman
Private, 7th U.S. Cavalry

Burkman, the Custers' loyal orderly, or striker, was born on January 10, 1839, apparently in Allegheny County, Pennsylvania—although his autobiography states that he was an immigrant from Germany and his death certificate lists Missouri as his birthplace. He worked as a teamster for trader William Bent before enlisting in the 5th Missouri Volunteer Mounted Infantry and fighting in the August 1861 Civil War battle of Wilson's Creek. At some point in the early 1860s, he joined Brig. Gen. Henry H. Sibley's troops in Minnesota and campaigned against the Sioux.

Burkman enlisted in Company A, 7th Cavalry, in August 1870 and was soon detailed as an orderly to George Armstrong Custer. The two men shared a common love of animals, and Burkman lovingly cared for Custer's horses and dogs until the general's death. Burkman, who was bestowed with the nickname "Old Neutriment" for his insatiable appetite, was illiterate and slow of speech and movement, but he became indispensable to the Custers. Libbie Custer wrote in *"Boots and Saddles"; or, Life in Dakota with General Custer* (New York: Harper and Brothers, 1885), "My husband and I were so attached to him, and appreciated so deeply his fidelity, we could not thank the good fortune enough that gave us one so loyal to our interests."

Burkman served Custer in both the Yellowstone expedition of 1873 and the Black Hills expedition of 1874. At the Little Bighorn battle, he was detailed to the pack train, where he tended Custer's horse Vic. He so devoutly worshiped Custer that he agonized for the rest of his life that he had not died at the side of his idol. On the night of the battle, Burkman was assigned to guard Maj. Marcus Reno's tent. He claimed late in life that Reno "had a keg, and he was drinkin' considerable." It must be taken into consideration that at the time of his statement, Burkman was an eccentric, cranky recluse who was becoming senile.

Burkman participated in the 1877 Nez Perce campaign. He was discharged from the army in May 1879 for disability after falling off a horse in Nebraska. He resided briefly at the National

(continued on following page)

Military Home in Los Angeles, then, in order to remain close to the place where Custer had perished, eventually moved to Billings, Montana, where he lived for thirty years. Burkman attended the dedication of the Custer Monument on June 4, 1910, in Monroe, Michigan, and was one of the first to visit Libbie Custer, who had come from New York and was staying at the home of her niece.

On November 6, 1925, at age eighty-six, Burkman committed suicide at his boardinghouse—a gun in one hand, a bag of candy in the other. He was buried in Custer National Cemetery. His obituary was published in the November 7, 1925, *Billings Gazette.*

📖 Burkman's biography, *Old Neutriment,* by Glendolin Damon Wagner (Lincoln: University of Nebraska Press, 1989), was based for the most part on Burkman's reminiscences. His memories provide an excellent, if not emotional, insight into the personal life of the Custers and associated events from the viewpoint of an enlisted man.

✸ Frederick S. Calhoun
First Lieutenant, 14th Infantry

This younger brother of 7th Cavalry officer 1st Lt. James Calhoun was born on April 19, 1847, in Cincinnati. He attended school until the age of fourteen, when he was sent to Iowa to learn the hardware business. In May 1864, he enlisted in the 137th Ohio Infantry, a volunteer regiment organized to protect the nation's capital, and served in that capacity until August, when he returned to Cincinnati. Calhoun soon headed west and was, in his words, "employed at various times as clerk in the Quartermaster Department."

Calhoun accompanied the Yellowstone expedition of 1873 as a civilian employee of Custer's former West Point friend Tom Rosser, who was chief surveyor for the Northern Pacific Railroad. He became embroiled in a controversy when Custer loaned him the use of a horse belonging to Company H—over protests of company commander Capt. Frederick Benteen. Colonel Stanley later placed Custer under arrest for this unauthorized use. The incident was soon forgotten, perhaps by all but Benteen, who despised those counted among what he called the "Custer Clan," which now included Calhoun.

Calhoun spent the winter of 1873–74 residing with his brother at Fort Abraham Lincoln and apparently impressed Custer and other members of the unit. When a vacancy in the officer ranks of 7th Cavalry opened up, he was encouraged to

(continued on following page)

SIDEBARS

Table of Organization of the 7th Cavalry for the Yellowstone Expedition of 1873

Field and Staff:
Lt. Col. George Armstrong Custer, commanding in the field
Lt. Col. Frederick D. Grant, acting aide
1st Lt. James M. Bell, acting quartermaster
1st Lt. James Calhoun, acting adjutant
1st Lt. Algernon E. Smith, acting commissary
Dr. James P. Kimball, chief surgeon
John Honsinger and John Tempany, veterinarians

Company A	Capt. Myles Moylan; 2nd Lt. Charles A. Varnum
Company B	1st Lt. Edward G. Mathey; 2nd Lt. Benjamin H. Hodgson
Company C	Capt. Verlin Hart; 2nd Lt. Henry Harrington
Company E	1st Lt. Thomas M. McDougall; 2nd Lt. John Aspinwall
Company F	Capt. George W. Yates; 2nd Lt. Charles W. Larned
Company G	1st Lt. Donald McIntosh, 2nd Lt. George D. Wallace
Company H	Capt. Frederick Benteen, 1st Lt. Francis M. Gibson; 2nd Lt. Charles C. DeRudio
Company K	Capt. Owen Hale; 1st Lt. Edward S. Godfrey
Company L	Capt. John F. Weston; 1st Lt. Charles Braden
Company M	Capt. Thomas French; 1st Lt. Thomas W. Custer

Detached Service: Col. Samuel D. Sturgis; Capt. William Thompson; Capt. Michael V. Sheridan; Capt. Charles S. Ilsley; Capt. John E. Tourellotte; 1st Lt. Henry Jackson; 1st Lt. Henry J. Nowlan; 2nd Lt. William T. Craycroft

Northern Boundary Survey:
Maj. Marcus A. Reno, commanding

Company D	Capt. Thomas Weir; 2nd Lt. Winfield S. Edgerly; 2nd Lt. Richard H. L. Alexander
Company I	Capt. Myles Keogh; 1st Lt. James E. Porter

Leave of Absence: Maj. Joseph G. Tilford; Maj. Lewis Merrill; 1st Lt. William W. Cooke

Sick: 2nd Lt. Andrew H. Nave

"I have told Satan to get behind me as far as poker goes."

—CUSTER COMMENTING ABOUT WATCHING BROTHER-IN-LAW JAMES CALHOUN AND OTHERS LOSING THEIR MONEY IN CARD GAMES

🐎 The Northern Pacific Railroad

The Northern Pacific Railroad came about as a result of the Pacific Railway Act of July 2, 1864, in which Congress granted railroad entrepreneurs 25,600 acres of public land for each mile of track laid. The sale of this land, which amounted to twenty sections per mile within the states and forty sections per mile in the territories, held the promise of an excellent investment return.

Preliminary plans for this railroad, the most northern of the transcontinental transportation projects, began in May 1866, when the board of directors authorized the commencement of a survey. Financing, however, delayed the project when Congress refused aid. Revenue could be raised by offering land for people to own and settle, but first an exact route had to be determined. And that survey work would cost quite a sum of money to conduct.

In 1869, the famous Philadelphia firm of Jay Cooke and Company, which had negotiated government war loans during the Civil War, was brought in to provide financial backing. Cooke's banking firm undertook the sale of $5 million of Northern Pacific bonds for 12 percent of the principal, which paid each $100 bond $7.30 annual interest in gold. Cooke lauded the prospects of this line to the Pacific Ocean, which would greatly enhance trade with the Orient, and in two years had sold over $30 million worth of bonds.

Construction on the railroad commenced in the summer of 1870. Its eastern terminus was located near Duluth on Lake Superior, which supported all the lake commerce, and the intended western terminal, Puget Sound, Washington, would offer a shorter route to the Far East than any other railroad line. (Cooke, by the way, possessed advance information and invested heavily in land around Duluth.)

The railroad survey crews would be venturing into regions of the country that had yet to be fully explored and were known to be home to hostile Indians. Fortunately for the railroad, the army—from General Sherman on down—viewed the laying of tracks across these uninhabited areas as being of strategic importance. The transcontinental lines served a national purpose by facilitating the opening of the West and, with that, the eventual conquest of the Indian. The army, therefore, pledged to serve as a guardian as the tracks moved westward.

The first Yellowstone expedition to determine the Northern Pacific's route between Bismarck and Bozeman, Montana, was undertaken in 1871. The command of Col. J. N. G. Whistler escorted former Confederate general Thomas L. Rosser and his surveying party on a 600-mile trip that left Fort Rice in September, marched to the confluence of the Yellowstone and Powder Rivers, and returned the next month.

In 1872, Col. David S. Stanley's infantry provided escort for the Northern Pacific survey crew. The expedition left Fort Rice on July 19 and was ultimately forced to conclude just east of

seek an army commission—with the enthusiastic endorsement of Custer and other officers. Predictably, Benteen refused to sign the petition that twelve officers submitted to the secretary of war attesting to Calhoun's fitness. While awaiting word on his appointment, Calhoun accompanied Custer's Black Hills expedition of 1874 as a civilian employee.

At Custer's urging, a board of examiners met at Fort Lincoln in January 1875 to examine Calhoun and found him "a proper person, morally, mentally and physically to be commissioned in the Army." When his commission arrived on March 10, 1875, however, it was not for the 7th Cavalry, but for the 14th Infantry. He was ordered to duty at Corinne, Utah, to protect Mormon settlers from Shoshone Indians.

After his brother was killed with Custer at the Little Bighorn, Calhoun's unit began campaigning with Gen. George Crook and participated in the "Starvation March" and the September 1876 battle of Slim Buttes. The 14th Infantry reported to Camp Robinson, and Calhoun was serving as post adjutant on May 6, 1877, when Crazy Horse surrendered. The Sioux warrior was subsequently shot by a member of Calhoun's Company F and taken to Calhoun's office. He later died in the building next door.

On February 20, 1879, Calhoun married Emma Reed, the daughter of Custer's half-sister, Lydia, and her husband, David. Emma, the sister of Harry Armstrong Reed, who had perished with Custer, had visited the Custers at Fort Lincoln in 1876 and accompanied her aunts—Libbie and Maggie Calhoun—with the 7th Cavalry column for the march on the first day of the Little Bighorn campaign. The Calhouns had one daughter, Emma May.

Calhoun served in various frontier posts and was promoted to first lieutenant in February 1887. He became ill in 1888 with what was diagnosed as a disorder of the nervous system and was medically retired in 1890. The Calhouns resided in Monroe, Michigan, before moving to Wellesley, Massachusetts, to be close to their daughter, who was attending Wellesley College. Calhoun died at Wellesley on March 20, 1904, from a variety of ailments and was buried in Cincinnati.

📖 An excellent biographical article, "Frederick Calhoun: A Little-Known Member of the 'Custer Clique,'" by Tom Buecker, can be found in *Greasy Grass* 10 (May 1994), which is published by the Custer Battlefield Historical and Museum Association.

BIOGRAPHIES

✹ James "Jimmy" (or "Jimmi") Calhoun
First Lieutenant, 7th U.S. Cavalry

This older brother of Frederick S. Calhoun was born on August 24, 1845, in Cincinnati. He graduated from Mt. Pleasant Academy in Ossining, New York, in June 1860 and spent the initial years of the Civil War traveling through Europe. In January 1864, Calhoun enlisted as a private in the 14th Infantry. He was promoted to first sergeant in February 1865. He applied for a commission in May 1865 but was found unqualified by an examining board. Calhoun remained a first sergeant until July 1867, when he was appointed second lieutenant, 32nd Infantry, at Camp Warner, Oregon. He served with his unit in Arizona and Camp Grant for two years before being transferred to the 21st Infantry in July 1869.

1st Lt. James Calhoun. *Courtesy Little Bighorn Battlefield National Monument.*

When the army was reorganized in 1870, Calhoun was unassigned and awaiting orders. At this time, he apparently was present at Fort Leavenworth, Kansas, where he met Margaret Emma "Maggie" Custer, the younger sister of George Armstrong Custer, with whom he became romantically involved. Custer must have taken to Calhoun as well: Calhoun, along with 1st Lt. W. W. Cooke, witnessed Custer's April 1870 last will and testament. In January 1871, with assistance from Custer, Calhoun was appointed first lieutenant and assigned to the 7th Cavalry. He reported for Reconstruction duty at Bagdad, Kentucky, as commander of Company L. Calhoun expressed his appreciation of Custer's help in a letter dated April 23, 1871:

> I have just received my commission as 1st Lt. in the 7th Cavalry, and it reminds me more vividly than ever how many, many times I am under obligations to you for your very great kindness to me in my troubles. I shall do my best to prove my gratitude. If the time comes you will not find me wanting.

The man who was relentlessly teased because of his seriousness and nicknamed "Adonis" due to his good looks, blond hair, and six-foot, one-inch height married Maggie Custer on March 7, 1872, in the Methodist Church in Monroe, Michigan. The couple had no children.

Calhoun served ably as Custer's regimental adjutant during the Yellowstone expedition of 1873, but his behavior during off hours was less

Pompey's Pillar in October, when the foot soldiers were unable to contend with attacks by hostile Sioux.

It was decided that cavalry support was required to adequately protect Rosser's surveying crews. Stanley's infantry, this time supported by ten troops of George Armstrong Custer's 7th Cavalry, returned to the Yellowstone in the summer of 1873. The Sioux once again strongly opposed the surveying effort, but they were chased away by the cavalry.

The country's economic boom, however, soon dipped sharply downward as the market for stocks and bonds dried up. Jay Cooke's firm failed, which plunged the railroad into bankruptcy. Cooke's failure caused scores of securities companies, manufacturing plants, banks, and other railroads to close their doors—even the New York Stock Exchange closed for ten days—in what would be known as the Panic of 1873. Track on the Northern Pacific was halted after 450 miles, reaching almost to the Missouri River at Bismarck, Dakota Territory.

The only way in which the Northern Pacific could attain financial solvency and resume laying track would be to sell the land along its route to farmers and settlers. This region between the Missouri River and the Rocky Mountains, however, was known as the "Great American Desert." Jay Cooke made an effort to change that image with promotional literature extolling the wonderful climate and fertile soil. One of his pamphlets found its way into the hands of Col. William B. Hazen, commander of Fort Buford. D. T. Hazen took exception to Cooke's glowing description, and a literary feud over the potential of the railroad land ensued between Hazen and Custer, who had been encouraged by the railroad to respond (see "The Custer-Hazen Feud" on page 135).

The discovery of gold in the Black Hills by Custer's 1874 expedition proved quite beneficial to the Northern Pacific. Bismarck was the ideal place to outfit and set off for the goldfields, and coincidentally, the railroad was the best way to reach that city. When several members of the expedition commented that they had not observed gold in the Black Hills, some eastern newspapers speculated that the alleged discovery had been simply a promotional scheme by the railroad. That pessimistic view, however, did not deter the horde of prospectors who raced to stake claims. This invasion infuriated the Sioux, who already greatly resented the presence of the railroad.

The downfall of Custer at the Little Bighorn and the subsequent subduing of hostile Indians played a dominant role in opening up the West for expansion. The sale of large lots of the railroad's enormous land grant spawned many Minnesota and Dakota wheat farms. Steamboats were purchased by the

(continued on following page)

railroad in 1879 and 1881, and they were deployed on the Yellowstone to link the various ends of track with upstream destinations. By July 1881, the Northern Pacific had reached Glendive, Montana Territory, and the first locomotive arrived at Billings in August 1882.

The Northern Pacific then made an agreement with the Benton and Coulson steamboat lines that they would not haul freight on the Yellowstone during 1883 in exchange for preferred freight rates on the railroad, which would eliminate any competition.

In 1883, Henry Villard took over development of the line, linking it with the Oregon Steam Navigation Company, which was operating on the Columbia River. Villard organized a pool of investors and poured $8 million into the line. At that time, the Northern Pacific was connected in Montana with the Utah and Northern from Salt Lake City. But this venture failed in 1884, due to an inability to control costs. Villard was reportedly bailed out by German investors, and the Northern Pacific tracks finally reached their intended destination, Seattle, in 1887.

📖 An excellent source for the casual reader is Lawrence A. Frost's *Custer's 7th Cav and the Campaign of 1873* (El Segundo, CA: Upton & Sons, 1986). Also see *Penny-an-Acre Empire in the West,* by Edgar I. Stewart (Norman: University of Oklahoma Press, 1968); *History of the Northern Pacific Railroad,* by Eugene B. Smalley (New York: G. P. Putnum's Sons, 1883); Smalley's *Guide to the Northern Pacific Railroad and Its Allied Lines* (St. Paul: 1886); *Guidebook of the Western United States. Part A. The Northern Pacific Route,* by Marius Campbell et al. (Washington, DC: Government Printing Office, Bulletin 611, 1916). For the role of steamboats in the progress of the line, see "Steamboats on the Yellowstone," by William E. Lass, in *The Great Sioux War, 1876–77,* edited by Paul L. Hedren (Helena: Montana Historical Society, 1991). Information and documents pertaining to the Northern Pacific are contained in the collection of the Minnesota Historical Society.

🐎 The Northern Boundary Survey

The Northern, or International, Boundary Survey Commission was a joint British-American operation organized to map the border between the United States and Canada. An accurate survey of the boundary line was required in order to determine responsibility for raids by Indians and crimes by outlaws, as well as whether settlers were establishing themselves in the United States or Canada. Two companies of the 7th Cavalry under the command of Maj. Marcus A. Reno were

than commendable. His penchant for card playing became quite a concern to his family members. Calhoun lost heavily and could not be discouraged from playing until all of his money was gone. He approached his brother-in-law Tom Custer about a loan, to which Tom reportedly replied: "Relationships don't count in poker. Bunkey or no bunkey, keep your hand out of my haversack." Calhoun also served as Custer's adjutant during the Black Hills expedition of 1874, during which he kept a diary that provides interesting insights.

Calhoun commanded Company L during the 1876 Little Bighorn campaign and stayed up all night on June 21, the night before his regiment marched, playing cards on board the docked steamer *Far West* with Maj. Marcus Reno, Capt. Myles Keogh, Tom Custer, and steamer captain Grant Marsh. On June 25, Calhoun's company was eventually deployed at the south end of Battle Ridge on a hill above Deep Coulee—perhaps acting as rear guard—while Custer and his detachment rode north. Calhoun and his men were killed when the combined forces of Crazy Horse from the north and Gall from the south crushed his company between them. The location of his death would become known as Calhoun Hill. His body was identified by a distinctive dental filling.

In 1877, Calhoun's remains were removed from the battlefield and reinterred on August 3 at Fort Leavenworth, Kansas. Several years after the battle, Frederick Calhoun recovered his brother's watch from an Indian and sent it to Maggie. Calhoun's saber, which had been stored at the Powder River depot, is on display at the Little Bighorn Battlefield National Monument museum.

📖 A most fascinating romantic version of the death of Calhoun can be found in Frederick Whittaker's imaginative biography of Custer, *A Complete Life of Gen. George Armstrong Custer* (New York: Shledon, 1876). Calhoun's diary kept during the Black Hills expedition of 1874 was published in book form, titled *With Custer in '74: James Calhoun's Diary of the Black Hills Expedition,* edited by Lawrence Frost (Provo, UT: Brigham Young University Press, 1979).

❋ Thomas Henry "Tucker" French
Captain, 7th U.S. Cavalry

French was born on March 5, 1843, in Baltimore. His father passed away from a fever when he was fifteen. In January 1864, French enlisted in the 10th Infantry. He quickly rose in rank, becoming a second lieutenant on May 18 and first lieutenant the following month. He fought in the Petersburg

(continued on following page)

siege and the battle of Weldon Railroad and was wounded at Chappell House, Virginia. He was breveted captain on August 18, 1864.

In 1866, French declined an appointment as captain, 44th Infantry, but later accepted a captaincy in the 19th Infantry on March 26, 1868. When the army was reorganized, he was eventually assigned to the 7th Cavalry on January 1, 1871, and gained a reputation as a crack shot with the .50-caliber Springfield "Long Tom" infantry rifle that he carried.

1st Lt. Thomas French. *Courtesy Little Bighorn Battlefield National Monument.*

French distinguished himself on August 11 during the Yellowstone expedition of 1873, while commanding two companies dispatched by Custer to thwart an attempt by the Sioux to cross the Yellowstone River. His detachment successfully prevented the Indians from crossing and closing with the main body. French commanded Company M during the Black Hills expedition of 1874.

At the battle of the Little Bighorn, French was in command of Company M, which was attached to Maj. Marcus Reno's battalion, and participated in the valley fight and later defended the south side of the perimeter on the bluffs. He reportedly exposed himself time and again to enemy fire while assisting troopers whose rifles had jammed. At one point, a bullet passed through his hat without striking him. He continued his service with the 7th Cavalry in the Nez Perce campaign in 1877 and was slightly wounded in the September 13 Canyon Creek fight.

French, himself no stranger to the bottle, told a *New York Times* reporter on January 19, 1879, that Major Reno had been drunk during the hilltop fight and had hidden himself from the command from the evening of June 25 until noon on June 26. French could not testify at the 1879 Reno Court of Inquiry, however, because at that time he was confined while facing a court-martial. On January 13, 1879, he was sentenced to be dismissed from the service for drinking on duty and violating terms of his close arrest at Camp Ruhlen, Dakota Territory. President Hayes— on the recommendation of Gen. George Crook— commuted the sentence to suspension of rank and half pay for a year.

French retired from the service on February 5, 1880, and fifteen days later, his house in Bismarck burned to the ground. The cause of the fire was listed as of a suspicious incendiary origin. Per-

designated to provide an escort for the American portion of this survey team during the summers of 1873 and 1874.

In the spring of 1873, the 7th Cavalry companies that had been spread around the South on Reconstruction duty assembled in Memphis. At Sioux City, Iowa, Custer led ten companies up the Missouri toward Dakota Territory. Field headquarters would be established at Fort Abraham Lincoln, where the regiment would prepare for an expedition that summer into the Yellowstone region as protection for surveyors and workers on the Northern Pacific Railroad.

Meanwhile, Major Reno, with Capt. Thomas B. Weir's Company D and Capt. Myles W. Keogh's Company I, continued by rail to Fort Snelling, Minnesota, arriving on April 11. Reno's battalion would depart June 3 by rail to Breckenridge, Minnesota, and from there march through Fort Abercrombie to Fort Pembina. Upon arrival on June 22, the cavalry battalion was joined by two infantry companies from Fort Totten. The combined unit headed west to rendezvous with surveyors working in the Turtle Mountains, where a temporary supply base had been established.

British and American surveyors worked on alternate boundary segments, passing each other while moving in a westward direction. The British employed about thirty scouts for protection, with instructions not to use force should Indians attack. The Americans, with about 70 infantry and 150 cavalrymen, were prepared to fight should hostiles appear.

The men of the 7th Cavalry occasionally provided labor for the railroad surveyors and were often called upon to carry flags to distant positions for sightings, a practice that Major Reno disliked. He preferred that his men and horses be kept fresh in case of an Indian attack. The Minnesota Sioux, however, were not observed until late in the summer, apparently at that time with white women as captives, but a confrontation was avoided.

In early October, snow and blizzard conditions shut down work for the season. The two companies of the 7th Cavalry moved into winter quarters with the infantry at Fort Totten. Duty at this remote post, which was known as "a powderkeg of alcoholism and desertion," was a monotonous routine of hauling hay and firewood, and caring for the horses, broken only by sleigh rides, tobogganing, and dogsled races.

The following summer, while Custer led the 7th Cavalry through the Black Hills, Reno's battalion once again spent an uneventful summer as escort for the surveyors. Companies D and I, without Major Reno, who had taken a one-year leave of absence, remained at Fort Totten during the winter of 1874–75 before rejoining the regiment at Fort Lincoln in May 1875.

(continued on following page)

🐎 Regimental Battle Song
"Garry Owen"
(Composer Unknown)

Gaelic for "Owen's Garden," this distinctive, jaunty, Irish quick-step tune became synonymous with Custer's 7th Cavalry, although when and by whom it was introduced to the unit has been the subject of much conjecture.

Several Irish regiments, including the 5th Irish Lancers, had embraced it as a rowdy drinking song. Enigmatic 7th Cavalry officer Capt. Myles W. Keogh, whose father may or may not have been a member of the 5th Irish Lancers, traditionally has been credited with introducing the tune to Custer. Some researchers have disputed much of Keogh's heretofore accepted biography, which casts doubts about whether his father in fact ever served in that particular unit. Libbie Custer, however, was under the impression that Keogh had indeed introduced her husband to "Garry Owen" shortly after the formation of the 7th Cavalry at Fort Riley. The tune, which apparently dates from the Revolutionary War, could have been known to Custer as early as his school days at West Point.

"Garry Owen" became the battle song of the 7th Cavalry and was played during expeditions, campaigns, battles, and ceremonies, to the delight of its members and onlookers alike. It was the final song heard by Custer and his cavalry before marching to the Valley of the Little Bighorn. The regimental band, positioned on a knoll overlooking the Powder River,

Music to "Garry Owen." *Courtesy Little Bighorn Battlefield National Monument.*

haps French was too outspoken in his criticism of Reno, which cast his unit in a bad light.

The torching of his house could not quiet French, if it indeed had been intended to do so. In June 1880, he wrote a letter to the wife of Dr. A. H. Cooke in which he stated that he would have considered himself fully justified had he shot Reno when the major ordered the disastrous retreat from the timber to the bluffs.

French died on March 27, 1882, at the age of thirty-nine in Leavenworth, Kansas, and was buried in Fort Leavenworth National Cemetery. His obituary was published in the April 14, 1882, edition of the *Bismarck Tribune*. His body was reinterred on March 4, 1891, in Holy Road Cemetery, Washington, D.C.

📖 French is the subject of "A Captain of Chivalric Courage," by Barry Johnson, English Westerners' Society *Brand Book* (1988); and articles in two newspapers: "The Man in Buckskin," in the *Bismarck Tribune*, April 11, 1877; and "Tracking a Custer Indian Fighter" in the *Washington Post*, March 27, 1980. His letter to the wife of Dr. A. H. Cooke has been reprinted in *The Custer Myth: A Source Book of Custeriana*, edited by W. A. Graham (Harrisburg, PA: Stackpole, 1953).

❋ Frederick Dent Grant
Lieutenant Colonel, 4th Cavalry

Grant, the oldest son of President U.S. Grant, was born in St. Louis on May 30, 1850. His childhood was relatively normal until the outbreak of the Civil War. Although he did not serve as a soldier, young Fred was permitted to accompany his father during various campaigns—including Vicksburg in 1863—where he came under enemy fire and was awarded an honorary staff appointment.

Grant's adventures in the war and a series of illnesses had interrupted his schooling. After being tutored at an academy in New Jersey, however, he entered the U.S. Military Academy at West Point on July 1, 1866. His career as a cadet was marred by low academic scores, excessive demerits, and several widely publicized scandals, including a hazing incident involving the first black cadet, James Webster Smith. He graduated on June 12, 1871, thirty-seventh in a class of forty-one.

He was appointed second lieutenant in the 4th Cavalry, but the influence of his father—who was now president—obtained him leave to work as a civil engineer on the Union Pacific Railroad. In 1872, Grant accompanied Gen. William T. Sherman on a tour of Europe and was embarrassed by his hosts, who assumed that he was the principal

(continued on following page)

member of the party. Upon his return, he joined the staff of Gen. Philip Sheridan as an aide-de-camp with the rank of lieutenant colonel.

In June 1873, Grant accompanied Col. David Stanley's Yellowstone expedition as an acting aide. One incident occurred that endeared him to the officers of Custer's command. When ordered by Colonel Stanley to destroy sutler Augustus Bali-ran's stock of whiskey, he instead preserved Bali-ran's investment by distributing the spirits with various officers until Stanley rescinded the order. Custer and Grant, who both had come close to dismissal from West Point, became fast friends while discussing their experiences there. "I find him most congenial," Custer wrote to Libbie, "so modest and unassuming, withal sensible and manly." Grant departed the expedition early to head east upon hearing about the death of his grandfather. Custer wrote Libbie: "If he—Col. Grant—goes to Long Beach from Chicago by way of Monroe to see you, you will, of course, do all in your power to make his stay agreeable. Have his father's picture hung in the parlor in compliment to him."

Following duty with Sheridan in Chicago, Grant accompanied Custer's 1874 Black Hills expedition, once again as an observer for Sheridan with instructions to keep a daily log. From all accounts, he served no vital function and drank to excess, and on one occasion Custer was obliged to place him under arrest for intoxication. Grant caused a public furor upon his return by stating that he had seen no gold, which compelled the *New York Times* to speculate that the information about gold having been discovered was simply a ruse to further the ambitions of those promoting the Northern Pacific Railroad. "We had several miners along," he wrote in his journal, "who had nothing to lose and everything to gain; they all lived together and could concoct any plan they wished. After we got to Harney's Peak they said they found gold. . . . I don't believe that any gold was found at all."

Custer's arrest of Grant apparently engendered no animosity. In October 1874, the Custers attended his marriage to Ida M. Honore, the daughter of a wealthy businessman. The couple had two children.

After participating in the 1878 Bannock Indian war, Grant took leave to accompany his parents on a tour of Asia and, at Sherman's direction, observed the British Army in India. He returned in September 1879. In October 1881, he resigned from the army to pursue business opportunities.

Grant was bankrupted in May 1884, when the financial firm owned by his brother, Grant and

(continued on following page)

performed the tune to a chorus of hearty cheers from the troops as they forded the river. In 1905, the 7th Cavalry's chief musician J. O. Brockenshire penned lyrics to the tune.

The Original 5th Lancer Lyrics

1.
Let Bacchus' sons be not dismayed
    But join with me each jovial blade;
Come booze and sing, and lend you aid,
    To help me with the chorus.

Chorus
Instead of spa we'll drink down ale,
    And pay the reck'ning on the nail
No man for debt shall go to gaol
    From Garryowen in glory.

2.
We are the boys that take delight in
    Smashing the Limerick lights when lighting;
Through the streets like sporters fighting
    And clearing all before us.

3.
We'll break windows, we'll break doors
    The watch knock down by threes and fours;
Then let doctors work their cures,
    And tinker up our bruises.

4.
We'll beat the bailiffs out of fun
    We'll make the Mayors and Sheriffs run;
We are the boys man dares dun,
    If he regards a whole skin.

5.
Our hearts so stout have got us fame
    For soon 'tis known from whence we came;
Where'er we go they dread the name,
    Of Garryowen in glory.

The 7th Cavalry Lyrics

1.
We are the pride of the army,
    And a regiment of great renown,
Our name's on the pages of history
    From sixty-six on down.
If you think we stop or falter
    While into the fray we're goin'
Just watch the steps with our heads erect,
    When our band plays "Garry Owen."

Chorus
In the fighting Seventh's the place for me
    It's the cream of all the cavalry;
No other regiment ever can claim
    It's pride, honor, glory and undying fame.

2.
We know no fear when stern duty
    Calls us away from home,
Our country's flag shall safely o'er us wave,
    No matter where we roam.
'Tis the gallant Seventh Cavalry
    It matters not where we're goin'
Such you'll surely say as we march away;
    And our band plays, "Garry Owen."

3.
Then hurrah for our brave commanders!
    Who lead us into the fight.
We'll do or die in our country's cause,
    And battle for the right.
And when the war is o'er,
    And to our home we're goin'
Just watch the step, with our heads erect,
    When our band plays, "Garry Owen."

The Buffalo: A Four-Legged Commissary

Had the Indians known that cheap transportation provided by new railroads would eventually lead to the extermination of the buffalo, they might have offered more resistance to the Yellowstone expedition. By this time, the southern herds were steadily being decimated, and the northern herds were soon to follow. By 1883, all but a few small herds had vanished, and

"My Precious Darling—Well, here we are at last, at the far-famed—and to you far-distant—Yellowstone. How I have longed for you during our march in what seems a new world, a Wonderland. . . . No artist could fairly represent the wonderful country we passed over, while each step of our progress was like each successive shifting of the kaleidoscope, presenting to our wondering gaze views which almost apalled us by their sublimity."

—CUSTER TO LIBBIE, JULY 1873

Ward, collapsed. Upon learning that his father was dying of throat cancer, he volunteered to assist in the writing of the former president's *Personal Memoirs.* When his father died, Grant entered politics. He ran unsuccessfully for New York secretary of state in 1887, then accepted the position as minister to Austria-Hungary in March 1889, where he spent four years. He returned to New York City and in 1895 joined Theodore Roosevelt as a police commissioner. In 1897, he resigned in protest over the issue of using regular police for undercover work in brothels.

In April 1897, Grant returned to military service, and one month later, he received a commission as brigadier general of volunteers. He became district commander in San Juan, Puerto Rico, and later fought on the island of Luzon in the Philippines. In 1902, he was given command of the Department of Texas, leaving two years later to command the Department of the East in New York City. He was promoted to major general in February 1906.

Grant died from heart failure on April 12, 1912, and was buried at West Point. His obituary was published in the *New York Times* and *Chicago Tribune* on April 12 and 13, 1912.

    Grant wrote two notable articles: "My Father as I Knew Him," *New York World Sunday Magazine,* (April 25, 1897); and "With Grant at Vicksburg," *Outlook* (July 2, 1898). Biographical information can be found in *The Personal Memoirs of Julia Dent Grant,* written by Grant's mother (New York: Putnam, 1975); and *In the Days of My Father General Grant,* by his brother, Jesse R. Grant (New York: Harper & Brothers, 1925). His Black Hills journal can be found in Grant to Acting Adjutant General, Division of the Missouri, September 7, 1874, LR, Division of the Missouri, no. 4385 (1874), RG 98, NA.

Frank Grouard
Renegade and U.S. Army Scout

This controversial frontier character was born about 1850 on the Polynesian Island of Tubuai to a Mormon missionary named Benjamin F. Grouard and a native girl named Nahina—although some accounts record his father as a black steamboat cook and his mother as an American Indian. The elder Grouard moved to Utah in 1852, then withdrew from the church and settled in San Bernardino, California. Frank remained in Utah, where he was raised as a foster child in the family of Addison Pratt in Beaver. In about 1865, Grouard was said to have killed a

(continued on following page)

classmate and ran away to Montana Territory. He worked as a teamster and later a mail carrier before either stealing some mail horses and fleeing or being captured by Sioux Indians in 1869 or 1870.

Grouard apparently lived with the Assiniboine and the Yankton Sioux, until finally being adopted into the family of Hunkpapa Sioux leader Sitting Bull, perhaps after being captured by the tribe and accepted due to his dark complexion. Grouard at that time was given the name Standing Bear and became a trusted counselor to Sitting Bull. In 1873, he participated in the Sioux attacks against George Armstrong Custer's 7th Cavalry during the Yellowstone expedition. Shortly after, he had a falling out with Sitting Bull and joined Crazy Horse's band. He became known as "The Grabber" and continued to fight against whites.

Perhaps due to in-law problems, he defected from the Sioux in 1875 and appeared at Camp Robinson. Grouard was known as a crack shot and skilled plainsman. General George Crook was impressed with Grouard's credentials and hired him as an army scout. His first mission was to accompany Federal Indian commissioners to a peace council with Sitting Bull, who refused to negotiate and instead made a declaration of war. In March 1876, Grouard led an advance party to the Sioux camp on the Powder River, which was attacked by Col. Joseph Reynolds, who withdrew and later was subjected to a court-martial for his indecision. Grouard then located Crazy Horse's village on Rosebud Creek, which led to the June 17 battle in which Crook claimed victory but had actually fought to a stalemate.

At the time of the Little Bighorn battle, Grouard was said to have read smoke signals and informed some officers about Custer's defeat but was not believed. He dressed like an Indian and rode off to investigate—likely passing near Reno's beleaguered troops on the hilltop without noticing them—and confirmed the story, which would explain why Crook's scouts were aware of Custer's fate before Crook was informed. He also participated in the September 9–10 skirmish at Slim Buttes. Crook later said that "he would rather lose one-third of his command" than lose the services of Grouard.

Grouard indirectly contributed to the untimely death of one of the greatest Sioux warriors. When Crazy Horse surrendered in May 1877, Grouard, who had reason to fear the wrath of his former comrade, reportedly disappeared. The scout,

(continued on following page)

with them the fortunes of the Plains Indian tribes, who were dependent on this beast for life itself.

The Plains Indians not only regarded the buffalo as sacred, but these nomadic hunters viewed a herd of these shaggy animals with the same prospects that modern consumers might contemplate a spacious shopping mall. There, in one centralized location, was nearly every item required not solely for basic survival, but as a dependable source for those luxuries that provided a comfortable standard of living.

Best of all, this shaggy beast had covered the plains in abundance. During the early nineteenth century, buffalo herds were estimated to total upward of seventy-five to one hundred million, an impressive figure, considering that each animal weighed around a ton, with most bulls tipping the scale at a ton and a half. Nowhere else in the annals of food resources can such an infinite provider of sustenance be documented.

There has been a continuing debate about whether the by-products derived from the buffalo were indeed vital to the health and welfare of the average Plains Indian. Granted, there was an abundance of other wild game, and those animals were assuredly a part of the menu and wardrobe. But these nomadic people sustained a thriving self-sufficiency by ingeniously utilizing every portion of the buffalo but the bellow.

The most obvious, and important, benefit was food. The buffalo was truly a four-legged commissary. The muscle was high in protein, and other parts supplied more than the daily requirements of vitamins and minerals. What was not readily consumed could be preserved for the long winter months. One manner was by drying the meat under the sun. The Indians pounded berries and fruit into the dried meat to create pemmican—a treat that provided every element necessary for a balanced diet.

Within the village proper, the first thing to catch the eye would be the structures—the lodges or tepees—which were

---

"Much as I dote on my profession and am devoted to it, yet, should accident cut me adrift, I have no fear but that energy and a willingness to put my shoulder to the wheel would carry me through to a resonable success. In this country no man of moderate education need fail if determined to succeed, so many opportunities for honorable employment."

—CUSTER TO LIBBIE, JULY 1873

constructed mainly from buffalo hides. Inside those lodges were warm coats and sleeping robes also fashioned from those same hairy hides, and summer blankets made soft by scraping off the hair and tanning both sides. These dressed hides were also sewn into shirts, leggings, moccasins, and women's dresses.

Green skins made serviceable kettles for drinking and cooking. Buffalo hair was braided into ropes, lariats, and reins for ponies. Horns were used for ladles, cups, and other containers. Bull boats to traverse the rivers were made watertight with stretched hides. Hooves were boiled down to make glue for many applications. Bones could be carved into arrowheads, spear tips, or needles. Other uses included bowstrings from sinew; skin battle shields; axes and hoes from shoulder blades; sledge runners from ribs; paint from blood; hair-stuffed pillows; fly swatters and whisk brooms from tails; black beards adorning clothing; fuel for campfires from buffalo chips, the dried droppings; primitive toys, including baby rattles, from various parts; and the list goes on and on.

Another advantage was that the buffalo was relatively easy to kill in whatever numbers were desired. As white hunters quickly discovered, when one animal fell, the others simply continued grazing, and if the herd should happen to stampede, the animals could be directed toward a cliff and chased over to plunge to their death.

Other game may have collectively provided the bulk of the above-mentioned products, but the buffalo offered everything in one specially packaged container. It was the difference between a shopping trip to a mall and a visit to the corner convenience store.

Thus the destruction of the great buffalo herds assuredly led to the demise of this major aspect of traditional Plains Indian lifestyle. And the railroads, which brought the hunters and made it easy to ship millions of hides to Eastern tanners, were largely responsible for those huge piles of weathered bones that were scattered about the plains as a tragic reminder of man's greed and disregard for other cultures.

📖 *The Buffalo: The Story of American Bison and Their Hunters from Prehistoric Times to the Present,* by Francis Haines (New York: Thomas Y. Crowell, 1976); "Bison Ecology and Bison Diplomacy: The Southern Plains from 1800 to 1850," by Dan L. Flores, *Journal of American History* 78 (September 1991); *The Buffalo Hunters: The Story of the Hide Men,* by Mari Sandoz (New York: McGraw-Hill, 1954); *The Buffalo Book: The Full Saga of the American Animal,* by David A. Dary (Chicago: Swallow Press, 1974); *The Great Buffalo Hunt,* by Wayne Gard (Lincoln: University of Nebraska Press, 1959); and "Indians as Buffalo Hunters," by Carl Coke Rister, *Frontier Times* 5 (September 1928).

however, was later called in by the army to interpret during the questioning of Crazy Horse. The Sioux warrior had been asked if he would recruit scouts among his people to help fight the Nez Perce Indians. Crazy Horse's spokesman, Touch-the-Clouds, apparently replied that the Sioux leader would consider fighting against the Nez Perce. Grouard deliberately misinterpreted Crazy Horse's words to the effect that the Sioux were ready to fight against the *white men.* General Crook had Crazy Horse arrested, and he was subsequently killed.

Grouard resumed his scouting career in the Dakota Territory with Gen. Nelson A. Miles and spied for the army against the Sioux during the Ghost Dance episode in 1890–91 that led to the Wounded Knee engagement. He then assisted law enforcement officers by tracking down horse thieves and other outlaws before his death in 1905.

📖 An autobiography, which was written with the assistance of newspaperman Joe DeBarthe in 1894, does not mention Grouard's involvement in the death of Crazy Horse and occasionally suffers from historical inaccuracies, but nonetheless offers a fascinating insight into the life and exploits of this colorful character: *Life and Adventures of Frank Grouard,* by Joe DeBarthe, edited by Edgar I. Stewart (Norman: University of Oklahoma Press, 1958). Grouard's family and early life, including the death of his classmate, are discussed in "Frank Grouard: Kanaka Scout or Mulatto Renegade?" by John S. Gray, *Chicago Westerners Brand Book* 16, no. 8 (October 1959).

For details on his association with Crazy Horse, see Grouard's "An Indian Scout's Recollections of Crazy Horse," *Nebraska History* 12 (January–March 1919); and the less flattering *Crazy Horse: The Strange Man of the Oglalas,* by Mari Sandoz (Lincoln: University of Nebraska Press, 1942).

An in-depth account of Grouard's participation in the death of Crazy Horse appears in *The Killing of Chief Crazy Horse,* by Robert Clark and Carroll Friswold (Glendale, CA: Arthur H. Clark Co., 1976); *McGillycuddy Agent,* by Julia B. McGillycuddy (Stanford, CA: Stanford University Press, 1941); and "The Death of Crazy Horse," in *Custer and Company: Walter Camp's Notes on the Custer Fight,* edited by Bruce R. Liddic and Paul Harbaugh (Spokane, WA: Arthur H. Clark Co., 1995).

BIOGRAPHIES

✷ Dr. John Honsinger
Veterinarian, 7th U.S. Cavalry

Honsinger, about whom scant information is available, was reportedly born around 1824, perhaps in New York. He apparently served in the Civil War and had accompanied General Fremont on several expeditions. His home was said to be Adrian, Michigan, where an 1870 census of Lenawee County listed him as a stock dealer. Col. David Stanley mentions in the appendix of his *Personal Memoirs of Major-General D. S. Stanley, U.S.A.* (Cambridge, MA: Harvard University Press, 1917) that Honsinger (whom he refers to as "Housinger" and calls him a "fine old man of sixty") was a widower with two sons. Honsinger has also been referred to as "Holzinger" in other accounts, which poses the question of whether any of the above personal information pertains to our subject.

At some point, however, a man named John Honsinger signed on with the army as a veterinary surgeon at $75 a month, a position that carried the rank of sergeant major but held no authority over enlisted men and provided no military benefits. He was a member of the 7th Cavalry for Yellowstone expedition of 1873, which would prove tragic for him.

On August 4, Honsinger and Augustus Baliran, a sutler, rode ahead of the column in an effort to catch up with George Armstrong Custer. Thirty Sioux warriors appeared, and the two men took refuge in a grove of trees near a stream. The Indians attacked, and Honsinger and Baliran were killed as they fled. The doctor was bald and therefore not scalped, nor was he mutilated. His gold watch was taken from him and displayed by his assassin, Sioux warrior Rain-in-the-Face, who was later arrested for the crime (see "The Arrest and Revenge of Rain-in-the-Face" on page 129).

Honsinger was buried on the banks of the Yellowstone River with full military honors similar to those accorded high-ranking officers. The September 8, 1873, edition of the *New York Herald* had picked up a wire copy of the murders and reported that Honsinger "had been a long time connected with the 7th Cavalry and was greatly esteemed by officers and men for his personal and professional qualities."

📖 The speculative information about Honsinger's early life, as well as details of his death, can be found in Lawrence W. Frost's *Custer's 7th Cav and the Campaign of 1873* (El Segundo, CA: Upton & Sons, Publishers, 1985).

⌁ Who Were Those Sioux That Attacked Custer?

There has been some question regarding the identity of the Lakota Sioux Indians who attacked Custer's cavalry in the engagements of August 4 and 11, 1873.

There are those, including author Stephen Ambrose in *Crazy Horse and Custer: The Parallel Lives of Two American Warriors* (Garden City, NY: Doubleday, 1975), supported by Mari Sandoz in *Crazy Horse: The Strange Man of the Oglalas* (Lincoln: University of Nebraska Press, 1942), who have written that famed warrior Crazy Horse and medicine man Sitting Bull probably participated in at least the first skirmish, if not both.

The tactics employed in that initial skirmish on August 4 certainly resembled those that Crazy Horse had first displayed to the white man during Red Cloud's War (see "Red Cloud's War" on page 68). He was a master of the decoy tactic, which he had used to lure an unsuspecting Capt. William J. Fetterman and his eighty men to their death on December 21, 1866. Ambrose makes the case that Crazy Horse was likely a member of the decoy party that attempted to deceive Custer's tiny command into an ambush during the August 4 skirmish.

Ambrose writes that as the two sides halted and the Indians made an effort to tempt Custer to follow them into an ambush:

> For a brief instant the two parties stared at each other, there beside the Yellowstone. Did Crazy Horse and Custer see each other? There is no direct evidence, but certainly Custer stood out; even without his red shirt he would have caught Crazy Horse's eye. Crazy Horse would have been less likely to catch Custer's eye—with his single feather in his hair and his unpainted body, he paled beside his resplendent fellow warriors.

Ambrose's narrative goes on to describe the command decisions allegedly made by both Crazy Horse and Sitting Bull as the action played out and finally ended with the Indians breaking contact.

One piece of evidence that may point to Sitting Bull having a hand in the attacks was the presence of Frank Grouard

---

"Writing to others seems difficult, but to you not so. When other themes fail we still have the old story which in ten years has not lost its freshness . . . indeed its [sic] newer than when, at the outset we wondered if it would endure in its first intensity."

—CUSTER TO LIBBIE, JULY 1873

with the Sioux. This future army scout, whose treachery indirectly contributed to the death of Crazy Horse, at that time was known to have been a member of Sitting Bull's family by adoption.

Custer noted in his report that was reprinted in his wife's book, *"Boots and Saddles"; or, Life in Dakota with General Custer* (New York: Harper & Brothers, 1913), that "The Indians were made up of different bands of Sioux, principally Uncpapas [*sic*], the whole under command of 'Sitting Bull,' who participated in the fight, and who for once has been taught a lesson he will not soon forget."

Custer, however, does not repeat that assertion in his article "Battling with the Sioux on the Yellowstone," published in *Galaxy Magazine* 22 (July 1876), reprinted in *The Custer Reader*, edited by Paul A. Hutton (Lincoln: University of Nebraska Press, 1992). It would seem odd that Custer did not mention Sitting Bull or Crazy Horse, if indeed these by then famous warriors had participated.

Also, another article reprinted in Hutton's *Custer Reader*, "Expedition to the Yellowstone River in 1873: Letters of a Young Cavalry Officer," by Charles W. Larned, a 7th Cavalry officer who was a member of the expedition, failed to name any of the Indians who attacked the cavalry.

Custer scholar Lawrence A. Frost, in his *Custer's 7th Cav and the Campaign of 1873* (El Segundo, CA: Upton & Sons, 1986), related the Indian fights without identifying any of the Sioux participants. In his notes, however, Frost quotes Col. David Stanley as stating that upon the colonel's arrival at Fort Sully, he spoke to a man named Antoine Clement, who had learned from a Sioux chief named Little White Swan that the leaders in the attacks were Red Ears' son, a Brule, and Bull Without Hair, a Minniconju. Clement said that "Long Dog, an Uncpapa [*sic*], went to see Sitting Bull, who refused to join the war party, saying his promise to [missionary] Pere de Smet was 'medicine,' and he would not fight unless attacked."

In the absence of definitive sources, perhaps the romantic view that the eyes of Custer and Crazy Horse had briefly met in prelude to their meeting at the Little Bighorn add to the drama and create a more stirring picture of those two battles on the Yellowstone.

🐎 The Arrest and Revenge of Rain-in-the-Face

The killing by the Sioux of sutler Augustus Baliran and veterinarian John Honsinger, which occurred on August 4, 1873, during the Yellowstone expedition, was not on anyone's mind until scout Charley Reynolds visited Standing Rock Agency during the winter of 1874. While observing a scalp dance, Reynolds overheard Sioux warrior Rain-in-the-Face brag to a

✹ Charles William Larned
Second Lieutenant, 7th U.S. Cavalry

Larned was born on March 9, 1850, in New York City. He attended Racine College before being appointed to the U.S. Military Academy at West Point on July 1, 1866. Larned graduated—in the same class as future fellow 7th Cavalry officers Winfield S. Edgerly and Benjamin H. Hodgson— four years later, ranked twenty-eighth in a class of fifty-eight. He joined the 3rd Cavalry on June 15, 1870, and was assigned to the 7th Cavalry at Fort Leavenworth on October 10 of that same year. From that time until April 1873, Larned served with his unit in Kansas and Louisville, Kentucky.

Beginning in May 1873, Larned was a member of the Yellowstone expedition as second in command of F Company and also represented the Chicago *Inter-Ocean* as a correspondent. He participated in the August 11 battle against the Sioux and dispatched several special telegrams describing his version of events.

On that expedition, Larned had been looking forward to viewing Pompey's Pillar, expecting to see "some monumental rock perched on the summit of a towering peak." Instead, he disgustedly wrote, it was "a wicked swindle; in fact, a dump rock seated on a sand bar in the middle of the Yellowstone River." He did write with enthusiasm about the scenery when reaching the Musselshell River, but his final dispatch was not so glowing: "Truth compels me to state, however, that the general resources of the whole country as regards to agriculture, minerals or timber are, to use an expressive phrase, very slim."

Larned, who in a series of letters to his mother described George Armstrong Custer as an egotistical, petty tyrant, went on leave in September 1873. He never returned to duty with the 7th Cavalry. From December 1873 to July 1874, he was on detached duty with the War Department, serving part of the time as aide-de-camp to President Grant. In August, he was assigned as assistant professor of drawing at West Point. Larned was promoted to first lieutenant, 7th Cavalry, on June 25, 1876, and one month later was appointed professor of drawing, replacing Robert Weir, who had been with the Drawing Department for forty-two years. He married Louise Hoffman on August 14, 1884, in St. Paul. The couple had four children.

Larned died on June 19, 1911, at Danville, New York, and was buried at West Point.

📖 A compilation of Larned's letters, "Expedition to the Yellowstone River in 1873: Letters of a Young Cavalry Officer," edited by George F. Howe,

(continued on following page)

was first published in the *Mississippi Valley Historical Review* (December 1952) and reprinted in *The Custer Reader*, edited by Paul A. Hutton (Lincoln: University of Nebraska Press, 1992).

✳ Myles Moylan
Captain, 7th U.S. Cavalry

Moylan was born in Amesbury, Massachusetts, on December 17, 1838. He enlisted as a private in Company C, 2nd Dragoons, on June 8, 1857, listing his birthplace as Galway, Ireland, and served in Utah and Nebraska. Moylan was promoted to corporal on October 1, 1858, sergeant exactly one year later, and first sergeant on May 17, 1861. He fought with his unit, now the 2nd Cavalry, in Civil War battles at Wilson's Creek, Fort Henry, Fort Donelson, Shiloh, and the 1862 siege of Corinth. In February 1863,

Capt. Myles Moylan. *Courtesy Little Bighorn Battlefield National Monument*

while stationed at Memphis, Moylan was commissioned a second lieutenant in Company D, 5th Cavalry, and saw action at Aldie, Middleburg, Snicker's Gap, Ashby's Gap, Beverly Ford, and Gettysburg. In October 1863, however, he faced a court-martial for an unauthorized visit to Washington and was cashiered from the service. He promptly enlisted in the 4th Massachusetts Cavalry under the name Charles E. Thomas. In January 1864, he was commissioned a first lieutenant, and in December, he was promoted to captain while serving on the staff of Maj. Gen. John Gibbon.

In January 1866, Moylan enlisted in the mounted service under his real name. He was promoted to corporal in March. On August 20, Moylan was assigned to the newly formed 7th Cavalry. He quickly caught the eye of Custer, who appointed Moylan sergeant major of the regiment on September 1 and encouraged him to seek a commission. His application was endorsed by several officers, including Col. A. J. Smith, and Moylan was subsequently appointed first lieutenant to date from July. The awarding of the bars was premature, however, because Moylan failed the examination. Custer begged for another opportunity for Moylan to take the test and set about tutoring his protégé, which proved successful and resulted in the commission.

Moylan subsequently was ostracized by some of the junior officers, including use of the bachelor officers' mess. This prejudice, according to Libbie

large audience of his peers that he had killed the two men. Reynolds immediately relayed that information to George Armstrong Custer at Fort Abraham Lincoln.

Custer summoned Capt. George Yates and ordered him to assemble fifty men for an unspecified detail. This detachment from Companies F and L, along with 1st Lt. Tom Custer, proceeded to Fort Rice, where it was joined by another fifty-man detachment from the 7th Cavalry, commanded by Capt. Thomas H. French.

On December 13, 1874, the temperature was 54 degrees below zero as the column moved along the frozen Missouri River. After traveling twenty miles as instructed, Yates opened the sealed envelope that contained Custer's orders. Yates was directed to Standing Rock Agency to arrest Rain-in-the-Face for the murders of Baliran and Honsinger. Total secrecy was to be maintained; Custer feared that if the Indian agent learned of the mission, he would warn the Sioux warrior. Charley Reynolds would travel ahead of the column to ascertain the whereabouts of the fugitive.

After arriving at Standing Rock that evening and spending a freezing night in an unheated warehouse, Yates learned that Rain-in-the-Face was located in a Hunkpapa Sioux camp some three miles away. It was ration day, however, and all the Indians would be visiting the Hatch Trading Store at the agency to draw provisions. As a diversion, a forty-man detachment was dispatched to another Indian camp ten miles away to inquire about some other Sioux who were wanted for depredations on the Red River. Yates and the remaining men then rode to the trader's store.

Tom Custer, Charley Reynolds, and several others entered the store while the remaining troopers waited outside the entrance. Reynolds pointed out Rain-in-the-Face to Custer, who grabbed the surprised warrior and threw him to the floor. Rain-in-the-Face's hands were bound, and he was escorted outside and strapped on a waiting horse.

Due to the lateness of the hour, the cavalrymen and their captive remained at the agency that night. They departed on the morning of December 15 and struggled through eighteen-inch-deep snow to arrive at Fort Lincoln the next day.

Rain-in-the-Face was confined in the wooden guardhouse in the company of a civilian caught stealing grain from the government. Custer, through an interpreter, patiently interrogated his prisoner for hours. Finally, Rain-in-the-Face confessed to the murders in the presence of all the officers, his account matching the conclusions of the military.

Rain-in-the-Face and the white thief remained chained together in the guardhouse for several months until friends of the thief tore through the wall one night and freed them both. Rain-in-the-Face later said that he had been released by a sym-

(continued on following page)

pathetic "old soldier," who had waited until he was safely away before firing his weapon to sound the alarm. Whatever the circumstances, the Sioux warrior fled to Sitting Bull's camp, where he vowed revenge for his arrest—promising to someday cut out Tom Custer's heart and eat it.

Both Rain-in-the-Face and Tom Custer were on the field at the 1876 battle of the Little Bighorn. Custer was killed and so badly mutilated that he could be identified only by his tattoos. This has caused some to speculate that Rain-in-the-Face had exacted revenge.

Capt. Frederick W. Benteen, who examined Custer's body on the battlefield, swore that his heart had not been removed. But Libbie Custer, Tom's sister-in-law, believed that the Sioux warrior had indeed made good on his promise, writing in *"Boots and Saddles"; or, Life in Dakota with General Custer* (New York: Harper and Brothers, 1885): "The vengeance of that incarnate fiend was concentrated on the man who had effected his capture. It was found on the battlefield that he had cut out the heart of that gallant, loyal, and lovable man, our brother Tom."

A drunken Rain-in-the-Face at one point admitted to killing and mutilating Tom Custer when he told reporters at Coney Island in 1894: "The long sword's blood and brains splashed in my face. . . . I leaped from my pony and cut out his heart and bit a piece out of it and spit it in his face."

But his startling confession was likely nothing more than a flippant response to the badgering of sensationalism-seeking reporters. There exists no evidence to suggest that Rain-in-the-Face cut out, ate, or in any other way disturbed the heart or any other body part of Tom Custer. Mutilations were normally reserved for boys, women, and old men. The warriors would have already left the field to celebrate by the time that took place. And cannibalism was just as repugnant to the Indian as it was to the white man.

Another myth surrounding the revenge of Rain-in-the-Face has been debated for years—whether he killed George Armstrong Custer. The details of that legend are contained in the Sioux warrior's biography.

  📖 The most complete account of Rain-in-the-Face's arrest and escape can be found in *Custer's 7th Cav and the Campaign of 1873*, by Lawrence A. Frost (El Segundo, CA: Upton & Sons, 1986). Various versions of the event attributed to Rain-in-the-Face are in "Rain-in-the-Face: The Story of a Sioux Warrior," by Charles A. Eastman, *Outlook* (October 1906); Eastman's *Indian Heroes and Great Chieftains* (Boston: Little, Brown and Co., 1929); "The Personal Story of Rain-in-the-Face," by Cyrus T. Brady, which appears in *Indian Fights and Fighters* (New York: McClure, Phillips, 1904); and "Custer and Rain-in-the-Face," by E. L. Huggins, *American Mercury* 9, no. 35 (November 1926). Rain-in-the-Face's statement that he bit into Tom

Custer, was based on the fact that he had previously served as an enlisted man. Another version states that Moylan was judged simply too vulgar and unpolished for polite company. In spite of such alleged faults, Custer invited Moylan to dine with him and in March 1872 promoted him to captain over other eligible officers. Moylan's ties to Custer became even closer when he married Charlotte Calhoun, the sister of 1st Lt. James Calhoun, who was married to Custer's half-sister. The couple had no children.

Moylan served as regimental adjutant in the winter campaign of 1868–69 and as commander of Company A on the Yellowstone expedition of 1873 and the Black Hills expedition the following year. On the Yellowstone expedition, he was involved in two engagements with the Sioux. The August 4 skirmish pitted Moylan as commander of a squadron, the Custer brothers, and his ninety troopers against an overwhelming number of warriors that had sprung an ambush. He also participated in the August 11 battle at the Yellowstone River.

Moylan commanded Company A at the battle of the Little Bighorn and participated in Reno's valley fight and the Reno-Benteen defense on the bluff. He was seriously wounded in the September 1877 battle of Bear Paw Mountain against the Nez Perce, saw action against Crow Indians in Montana in late 1887, and was involved in the 1890 Wounded Knee incident. In 1890, Moylan received the Medal of Honor for his "distinguished gallantry" in the Nez Perce campaign. In April 1892, he was promoted to major and assigned to the 10th Cavalry.

He retired in April 1893 and settled in San Diego, where he died of stomach cancer on December 11, 1909. He was buried in that city's Greenwood Memorial Park. His obituary was printed in the *San Diego Union* on December 12, 1909.

  📖 Numerous references to Moylan, including an excerpt from a letter defending Reno's actions written to fellow 7th Cavalry officer Edward S. Godfrey, appear in *The Custer Myth: A Source Book of Custeriana*, edited by W. A. Graham (Harrisburg, PA: Stackpole Books, 1953). See also *Life in Custer's Cavalry: Diaries and Letters of Albert and Jennie Barnitz, 1867–68*, edited by Robert M. Utley (New Haven, CT: Yale University Press, 1977); and Libbie Custer's *Tenting on the Plains; or, General Custer in Kansas and Texas* (New York: Charles L. Webster & Co., 1889).

BIOGRAPHIES

✸ Rain-in-the-Face
Hunkpapa Sioux

Sioux warrior Rain-in-the-Face. *Courtesy Little Bighorn Battlefield National Monument.*

Rain-in-the-Face (Iromagja, Iromagaju, or Amarazhu, meaning "Face Raining") was born about 1835 at the forks of the Cheyenne River in present-day North Dakota. The origin of his unusual name is difficult to confirm. James McLaughlin, an Indian agent at Standing Rock Reservation, claimed that as an infant, Rain-in-the-Face received his name when raindrops fell on his face while he hung from a tree branch in his cradle and streaked a nosebleed. Dr. Charles Eastman, a fellow Sioux who interviewed Rain-in-the-Face, reported that the name resulted from two childhood incidents. The first occurred when Rain-in-the-Face was about ten years old, and blood washed away his paint during a fight with a Cheyenne boy. The second incident happened when he was a youth fighting the Gros Ventre and was described by Rain-in-the-Face:

> I had wished my face to represent the sun when half covered with darkness, so I painted it half black, the other half red. We fought all day in the rain, and my face was partly washed and streaked with red and black: so again I was christened Rain-in-the-Face. We considered it an honorable name.

Rain-in-the-Face gained a reputation as a fierce warrior during Red Cloud's War over the Bozeman Trail in 1866–68. Along with fellow warriors Gall and Crazy Horse, he participated in the December 1866 Fetterman Fight. He was possibly wounded

(continued on following page)

Custer's heart is in *Custer and the Great Controversy: The Origin and Development of a Legend,* by Robert M. Utley (Los Angeles: Westernlore Press, 1962). See also "Custer Throws a Boomerang," by John S. Gray, *Montana: The Magazine of Western History* 11 (April 1961); *Son of the Morning Star,* by Evan S. Connell (San Francisco: North Point, 1984); *Ten Years with General Custer among the American Indians,* by John Ryan, edited by John M. Carroll (Bryan, TX: n.p., 1980); and "Captain Yates' Capture of Rain-in-the-Face," by Cyrus T. Brady, *The Tepee Book* (Sheridan, WY, 1916).

🦌 Custer, the Sportsman

Popular culture has created an image that frontier military posts were hubs of exciting activity as the cavalrymen mounted up and bravely rode off to the sound of the bugle to engage in one thrilling skirmish after another with hostile Indians. Nothing could be further from the truth. For the most part, these isolated posts—and even campaigns and expeditions—were a constant routine of boredom and monotony. The officers and men, therefore, were compelled to find diversions to entertain themselves. Many turned to the bottle—alcoholism was rampant. Others took advantage of the plentiful wildlife on the plains and hunted for pleasure—and for a change of menu.

It could be said that the most enthusiastic hunter in the West was George Armstrong Custer. But his passionate outdoor interests went beyond simply killing animals. He was like a child in a playground of nature. His correspondence never failed to mention the beauty of his surroundings and his fascination with the flora, fauna, fossils, or natural wonders that he had happened upon. On numerous occasions, he captured live game and donated it to zoos, and his study of animals led him to taxidermy—perhaps an attempt to preserve the moment. And no one was more fond of good horseflesh or a well-bred leash of hounds than Custer. Over the years, his horses and hounds became famous and, combined with his hunting prowess, gained him a reputation as the finest sportsman in the army.

Custer's first buffalo hunt, however, proved to be somewhat embarrassing, although he related the episode with good humor. He was out hunting during the Hancock expedition of 1867, accompanied only by several English greyhounds, when he sighted a buffalo—the first he had ever observed. He chased the beast with his horse and brought up his pistol to shoot. At that moment, the buffalo wheeled around and charged. Custer's horse reared as he pulled the trigger. The bullet went into the horse's brain, killing the animal and sending Custer toppling head over bootheels. He was stranded in hostile Indian country until a detail of the 7th Cavalry happened upon him.

On that same expedition, he went beaver hunting with guide Will Comstock and, believing that he was aiming at a beaver in tall grass, shot a wildcat that he had mistaken for a beaver. Later, he engaged in several shooting contests with the son of Kiowa warrior Satanta, a future nemesis, and prevailed in each one.

While camped on Big Creek, near Fort Hays, in the summers of 1869 and 1870, Custer added to his growing reputation as a hunter. He was much in demand by dignitaries—including political leaders, Eastern industrialists, English noblemen, and even P. T. Barnum—who traveled on the Kansas Pacific Railroad to visit the Wild West and hoped to participate in a buffalo hunt accompanied by the famous General Custer.

In preparation for the 7th Cavalry's assignment on Reconstruction duty throughout the South in 1871, Custer donated a pet bear that he had captured to the Central Park Zoo. His subsequent duty at Elizabethtown, Kentucky, consisted mainly of purchasing horses for the army. He also owned a number of Thoroughbreds, which he rode while hunting small game with his Russian wolfhounds and English staghounds. Custer's pack of dogs at that time was said to number about eighty, and he assigned orderly John Burkman the duty of caring for his animals. The dogs were a constant source of trouble, often killing other people's pets, but the Custers owned up to their responsibility and sympathetically compensated each owner. Custer spent much of his time at horse-breeding farms and racetracks, but he longed for action on the frontier.

That respite from Kentucky came in January 1872, when Custer was asked by Phil Sheridan to serve as an escort for the Russian grand duke Alexis on a Nebraska buffalo hunt. Custer and Alexis became fast friends, and at the grand duke's request, the Custers accompanied him on the remainder of his U.S. trip. (see "The Russian Grand Duke's Buffalo Hunt" on page 107).

The Yellowstone expedition of 1873 afforded Custer an opportunity to hunt in new territory. He led hunting parties nearly every day, bagging deer, elk, pronghorn antelope, buffalo, geese, ducks, prairie chickens, and sage hens, which kept

---

"I was up, the Indians were up, and for a little while, I thought it was 'all up' with me. It was a dash race. I'm glad it wasn't heats. I won the dash, but might have lost the second heat."

—CUSTER DESCRIBING HIS AUGUST 4 ENCOUNTER WITH THE SIOUX, WHICH WAS THE NARROWEST ESCAPE HE EVER EXPERIENCED WITH INDIANS

---

in a raid on Fort Totten in 1868 (see "Red Cloud's War" on page 68).

In 1874, Rain-in-the-Face became involved in a controversy resulting from the death of sutler Augustus Baliran and veterinarian John Honsinger during the Yellowstone expedition of 1873. The two men had been ambushed by a party of Sioux while riding alone on August 4. The murders were unsolved until early December 1874, when scout Charley Reynolds visited Standing Rock Agency and overheard Rain-in-the-Face bragging about killing the men the previous summer. Rain-in-the-Face was subsequently arrested by a detail commanded by Tom Custer and was imprisoned at Fort Abraham Lincoln to await a trial. Apparently a sympathetic guard allowed Rain-in-the-Face to escape. At that time, legend has it that he vowed revenge on Tom Custer for his arrest—promising to cut out his heart and eat it.

Rain-in-the-Face was present at the battle of the Little Bighorn, although his actual role has not been determined. Tom Custer was killed in this battle and singled out for the most brutal of mutilations. This has caused some to speculate that Rain-in-the-Face had made good on his vow, but few scholars believe that to be true (see "The Arrest and Revenge of Rain-in-the-Face" on page 129).

Other, more widespread stories attribute the killing of George Armstrong Custer to Rain-in-the-Face, which was not true. This myth was perpetrated by Henry Wadsworth Longfellow in his popular poem "The Revenge of Rain-in-the-Face." Who can forget those stirring words:

"Revenge!" cried Rain-in-the-Face,
"Revenge upon all the race
Of the white chief with yellow hair!"

Another interesting yet absurd interpretation of that myth was a three-reel film released in 1912. Thomas Ince's *Custer's Last Fight,* which starred Francis Ford, the brother of director John Ford, depicted Rain-in-the-Face stalking George Armstrong Custer on the battlefield to avenge his arrest.

Rain-in-the-Face may have indeed boasted at one time or another about being the one who had killed Custer, but only because he knew the futility in denying it. Prior to his death, he said to Dr. Eastman, "Many lies have been told of me."

After the Little Bighorn battle, Rain-in-the-Face fled with Sitting Bull's band to Canada. He finally surrendered at Fort Keogh, Montana, in 1880 and settled on the Standing Rock Reservation in North Dakota. At some point, he had received injury to his leg that left him crippled and kept him on

(continued on following page)

crutches for much of his life. One account claims that he was wounded at the Little Bighorn and operated on himself with a razor taken from a dead soldier. Another source states that the injury occurred when he shot himself in the leg during a buffalo hunt in 1880.

The Sioux warrior, who reportedly had seven wives during his life, was stabbed in 1890 by one of them in a jealous rage but survived and asked that he be punished rather than his wife. It was said that his last wife was found with her throat slashed.

Rain-in-the-Face sought the limelight and became a feature attraction at the 1893 World's Fair, billed as the most famous Sioux survivor of the Little Bighorn battle. He also briefly toured with Buffalo Bill's Wild West Show and later cashed in on his fame by learning how to write his name and signing autographs at Coney Island, New York.

He eventually retired to the reservation and became a source of material—much of it contradictory or far-fetched—for any interviewer who wanted to discuss the Custer battle. Rain-in-the-Face died on September 14, 1905, and was buried near Aberdeen, South Dakota.

📖 See "Rain-in-the-Face: The Story of a Sioux Warrior," by Charles A. Eastman, *Outlook* 84 (October 27, 1906). Events surrounding the killing of Baliran and Honsinger on the Yellowstone and the arrest of Rain-in-the-Face are best told in *Custer's 7th Cav and the Campaign of 1873,* by Lawrence A. Frost (El Segundo, CA: Upton and Sons, 1986). Rain-in-the-Face is the subject of a handful of references with respect to his actions at Little Bighorn in *The Custer Myth: A Source Book of Custeriana,* edited by W. A. Graham (Harrisburg, PA: Stackpole, 1953). The origin of his name and other material appear in *My Friend the Indian,* by James McLaughlin (Boston: Houghton Mifflin, 1910); and *Indian Heroes and Great Chieftains,* by Charles A. Eastman (Boston: Little, Brown, 1929).

See also "The Personal Story of Rain-in-the-Face," in *Indian Fights and Fighters,* by Cyrus T. Brady (New York: McClure, Phillips & Co., 1904); *Rain-in-the-Face and Curly, the Crow,* by Thomas B. Marquis (Hardin, MT: Custer Battlefield Museum, 1934); *Red Cloud's Folk: A History of the Oglala Sioux,* by George E. Hyde (Norman: University of Oklahoma Press, 1937); *Campaigns of General Custer in the North-West, and the Final Surrender of Sitting Bull,* by Judson Elliott Walker (New York: Jenkins and Thomas, 1881); and "Custer and Rain-in-the-Face," by Eli L. Huggins, *American Mercury* 9, no. 35 (November 1926).

the messes in fresh meat. He also shot two white wolves and a red fox. He wrote to Libbie on June 26 from camp at Heart River, "Such hunting I have never seen." Other wildlife was captured, including rattlesnakes, a badger, a wildcat, two marsh hawks, a jackrabbit, and a porcupine, which were later donated to the Central Park Zoo. During this trip, taxidermy became an obsession for Custer, who worked in his tent late into the night under the tutelage of C. W. Bennett, a taxidermist who had accompanied the column. Custer learned to mount many species, including a complete elk, which he donated to the Detroit Audubon Club.

He also spent much of his time hunting during the Black Hills expedition of 1874 and accumulated a menagerie of snakes, rabbits, and birds. He proudly reported to Libbie that he had achieved the greatest feat attainable by a hunter: He had killed a grizzly bear. The killing of that grizzly, however, had been a team effort, with bullets also supplied by scout Bloody Knife and Col. William Ludlow. A photograph of Custer posing with the bear became quite popular in Eastern stationery shops. It required an ambulance detail of twelve men to transport the flora, fauna, and fossils that Custer collected in the Black Hills. He donated much of this collection—including game heads, horns, and hides that he had personally mounted—to the Audubon Club.

While stationed at Fort Abraham Lincoln, Custer practiced his marksmanship on targets set up outside the post. Richard A. Roberts, who briefly served as a civilian secretary for Custer, observed that Custer, "shooting under the greatest possible difficulties for a marksman," hit the bull's-eye ten out of ten times at 500 yards, eight out of ten at 750, and seven out of ten at 1,000. George B. Grinnell, however, described an incident in the Black Hills when Custer engaged in a shooting contest with Luther North. North blew the heads off three ducks with three shots, but Custer's shots completely missed his targets.

Custer's fame as a dead-eyed marksman and all-around sportsman can be attributed in large part to his own considerable promotion. His articles in *Galaxy* magazine and the sportsmen's journal *Turf, Field and Farm* record many memo-

"Mounted and caparisoned with all the flaming adornments of paint and feathers . . . [the Sioux] displayed unusual boldness, frequently charging up to our line and firing with great deliberation and accuracy."

—CUSTER DESCRIBING THE INDIAN ATTACK OF AUGUST 4 THAT PINNED DOWN HIS DETACHMENT FOR THREE HOURS

rable hunts and days spent with Thoroughbred horses in Kentucky. The *Galaxy* articles were compiled into Custer's book, *My Life on the Plains; or, Personal Experiences with Indians* (Norman: University of Oklahoma Press, 1962). The *Turf, Field and Farm* articles have been reprinted in *Nomad: Custer in Turf, Field and Farm,* edited by Brian W. Dippie (Austin: University of Texas Press, 1980).

📖 In addition to the sources given above, also see *General Custer's Thoroughbreds: Racing, Riding, Hunting, and Fighting,* by Lawrence A. Frost (Bryan, TX: J. M. Carroll Co., 1986); "Buffalo Hunting with Custer," by Frank Talmadge, *Cavalry Journal* (January 1929); "Big Game Hunting with the Custers," by Minnie Dubbs Millbrook, *Kansas Historical Quarterly* 41 (Winter 1975); "A Hunt with General Custer," by J. B. Irvine, Jr., *Outdoor Life* (May 1923); "Custer's Kentucky: General George Armstrong Custer and Elizabethtown, Kentucky, 1871–73," by Theodore J. Crackel, *Filson Club Historical Quarterly* 48 (April 1974); and General Custer and His Sporting Rifles, by C. V. Haynes, Jr. (Tuscon, AZ: Westernlore Press, 1995).

Many of Custer's hunts and observations are noted by his wife in her three books: *"Boots and Saddles"; or, Life in Dakota with General Custer* (New York: Harper and Brothers, 1885); *Tenting on the Plains; or, General Custer in Kansas and Texas* (New York: Harper and Brothers, 1887); and *Following the Guidon* (New York: Harper and Brothers, 1890). John Burkman's recollections about tending Custer's hounds is in *Old Neutriment,* by Glendolin Damon Wagner (Lincoln: University of Nebraska Press, 1989).

🐎 The Custer-Hazen Feud

Custer's exploits during the Yellowstone expedition had further endeared him to the public and earned him the gratitude of the Northern Pacific Railroad. He also commanded Fort Abraham Lincoln, which had been established for the express purpose of protecting railroad interests. Custer, as was the case with most army officers, believed that the railroad had a strategic importance—that the future of the West was dependent on the ability of the railroad to spread its tracks across the great expanse. What was good for the railroad was good for the country, especially considering its significance in the eventual conquest of the Indian.

By 1874, however, the Northern Pacific had fallen on hard times. Jay Cooke's banking house had failed, which bankrupted the railroad and touched off the Panic of 1873. The financial future of the railroad depended on settling the millions of acres of land granted by the Federal government through which its tracks ran. The railroad could profit only

⚙ David Sloan Stanley
Colonel, U.S. Army

Stanley was born on June 1, 1828, in Cedar Valley, Ohio. He briefly apprenticed in medicine, then entered West Point in 1848, graduating four years later ninth in a class of forty-three that would include fifteen future generals. (Stanley's classmate Phil Sheridan, with whom he traveled to West Point from Ohio, had been set back a year due to a suspension.) The newly commissioned second lieutenant was assigned to the 2nd Dragoons and served as quartermaster and commissary for a railroad survey from Fort Smith, Arkansas, to Los Angeles. In March 1855, he was transferred to the 1st Cavalry, and while stationed on the frontier, he was promoted to first lieutenant. Two years later, he married Anna Maria Wright, with whom he had seven children. That same year, he engaged in battle under Col. Edwin V. Sumner with the Cheyenne on the Solomon River—nine Indians were killed, while the army lost two killed and ten wounded. Stanley was promoted to captain in March 1861.

At the outbreak of the Civil War, the Confederacy offered Stanley a colonelcy of a regiment, which he declined. Instead, he joined Union brigadier general Nathaniel Lyon in Missouri and participated at Wilson's Creek. In September 1861, Stanley was appointed a brigadier general of volunteers. He subsequently fought in the campaigns for New Madrid, Island Number Ten, Shiloh, and Fort Pillow. In November 1862, he was promoted to major general and appointed chief of cavalry for the Army of the Cumberland. In September 1863, Stanley assumed command of the 1st Division, IV Corps, which he led through the Atlanta campaign. He was promoted to corps commander in July 1864 and came under fire for his slowness at Jonesborough. Four months later, however, Stanley regained his reputation when he was severely wounded by a bullet in the neck while leading the decisive assault at the battle of Franklin. He would be awarded the Medal of Honor in 1893 for his bravery.

During the war, Stanley developed a feud with Col. William B. Hazen (who also later feuded with George Armstrong Custer) that continued throughout their careers. Stanley had accused Hazen of cowardice at Shiloh and attempted to have Hazen court-martialed for falsely claiming the capture of some cannons at Missionary Ridge in November 1863. Phil Sheridan, who opposed a court-martial, became involved in the controversy, which no doubt contributed to the bad

(continued on following page)

blood between the general and Hazen in later years during the winter campaign of 1868–69.

Following the Civil War, Stanley briefly served in Texas, supporting diplomatic moves against the French in Mexico, then in July 1866 received the colonelcy of the 22nd Infantry Regiment. In 1872, he provided escort for a survey by the Northern Pacific Railroad, which was terminated due to frequent skirmishes with superior forces of hostile Sioux led by Hunkpapa chief Gall.

In 1873, Stanley was chosen to command another, larger expedition with the mission of protecting surveyors and scientists with the Northern Pacific Railroad. During this Yellowstone expedition of 1873 (June 20 to September 23, 1873), the colonel, who displayed a severe drinking problem, was constantly at odds with his subordinate, Lt. Col. George Armstrong Custer, who wished to operate free of supervision.

The Stanley-Hazen feud erupted once again in 1879, when Stanley accused Hazen of perjury in the 1876 Belknap impeachment trial. Hazen retaliated by charging Stanley with slandering a fellow officer. Stanley was court-martialed and, in spite of Phil Sheridan's testimony against Hazen, was found guilty of "conduct to the prejudice of good order and military discipline."

Stanley's 22nd Infantry Regiment was transferred to Texas in 1879. He was promoted to brigadier general in 1884 and commanded the Department of Texas from that time until his retirement in 1892. He served as governor of the Washington, D.C., Soldiers' Home from 1893 until 1898 and died in that city on March 13, 1902.

📖 Stanley covers the scope of his military career in his *Personal Memoirs of Major-General D. S. Stanley, U.S.A.* (Cambridge, MA: Harvard University, 1917). The appendix of this book includes his official report: *Report on the Yellowstone Expedition of 1873* (Washington, DC: Government Printing Office, 1874), as well as extracts from Stanley's letters to his wife during the Yellowstone expedition, which convey his low opinion of Custer. Custer's vacillating opinion of Stanley can be found in his correspondence with Libbie in Marguerite Merington's *The Custer Story: The Life and Letters of General George A. Custer and His Wife Elizabeth* (New York: Devin-Adair, 1950). More about the Stanley-Hazen feud can be found in *Great Plains Command: William B. Hazen in the Frontier West,* by Marvin E. Kroeker (Norman: University of Oklahoma Press, 1976); and *Phil Sheridan and His Army,* by Paul Andrew Hutton (Lincoln: University of Nebraska Press, 1985).

when this land was sold to immigrants who would plow and plant and create a thriving agricultural business. In an effort to encourage settlement, Cooke produced promotional literature portraying the region as a "Fruitful Garden" of fertile soil with an agreeable climate.

There was one army officer, however, who held a contrary opinion about the prospects for agricultural success as described in the railroad's literature. Col. William B. Hazen, who had been involved in controversies with Sheridan during the Civil War and with Sheridan and Custer during the winter campaign of 1868–69, had been banished by Sheridan to remote Fort Buford in northwest Dakota Territory in 1872. His dreary assignment far from civilization perhaps fueled his already contentious nature.

After reading a promotional brochure published by the Northern Pacific Railroad about the agricultural possibilities of the Dakota Territory and Montana, Hazen responded in a letter to the *New York Tribune* on February 7, 1874, with a pessimistic view claiming that the land in that region was not worth "a penny an acre."

Northern Pacific representative Tom Rosser contacted his friend Custer and asked him to write a rebuttal to Hazen's widely publicized letter. "A line or two from your pen," Rosser wrote, "will render us a great service."

Custer obliged with an April 17 letter published in the *Minneapolis Tribune* that refuted Hazen's assertions and presented a glowing picture of the future of the railroad and the agricultural opportunities along its route. He added:

> The beneficial influence which the Northern Pacific Railroad, if completed, would exercise in the final and peaceable solution of the Indian question, and which in this very region assumes its most serious aspect, might well warrant the general Government in considering this enterprise one of National importance, and in giving to it, at least, its hearty encouragement.

Custer's letter was reprinted in a booklet published by the railroad and widely circulated.

Hazen fought back with an article in the January 1875 issue of the *North American Review* and later that year with a book, *Our Barren Lands.* In an effort to add further insult, he privately published a pamphlet, "Some Corrections of 'My Life on the Plains,'" which criticized Custer's contention in his recently published book that Satanta and certain other chiefs deserved punishment for their depredations.

Custer wisely ignored Hazen's later writings and declined to engage in a full-scale literary duel. Instead, he relied on the public to determine whose opinion was more credible.

The railroad treated Custer like a VIP and richly rewarded him for his loyalty. He was presented with a spacious wall tent, on which was stenciled "NPRR." Custer and Libbie traveled on the Northern Pacific compliments of free passes, occasionally in a private coach, and were once provided a special train.

📖 The Custer-Hazen feud is covered in *Penny-an-Acre Empire in the West,* edited by Edgar I. Stewart (Norman: University of Oklahoma Press, 1968); *Great Plains Command: William B. Hazen in the Frontier West,* by Marvin E. Kroeker (Norman: University of Oklahoma Press, 1976); "Deceit about the Garden: Hazen, Custer, and the Arid Lands Controversy," by Marvin E. Kroeker, *North Dakota Quarterly* 38 (Summer 1970); and "A Short Evaluation of the Custer-Hazen Debates," in *4 On Custer by Carroll,* by John M. Carroll (Bryan, TX: Guidon Press, 1976).

Hazen's "Some Corrections of 'Life on the Plains'" and Custer's opinion of Hazen can be found in *My Life on the Plains; or, Personal Experiences with Indians,* by George Armstrong Custer (Norman: University of Oklahoma Press, 1962). An attack on Hazen's position, *Major General Hazen on His Post of Duty in The Great American Desert* (New York: G. P. Putnum's Sons, 1874), was written by former U.S. surveyor general John O. Sargeant. Excerpts of letters written by Hazen and Custer, as well as others involved, are contained in *Custer's 7th Cav and the Campaign of 1873,* by Lawrence A. Frost (El Segundo, CA: Upton & Sons, 1986). Rosser's letter of February 16, 1874, which requests that Custer respond to Hazen, is in the E. B. Custer Collection, Little Bighorn National Battlefield Monument.

Custer's relationship with the railroads is discussed in "Fort Desolation: The Military Establishment, the Railroad, and the Settlement on the Northern Plains," by Paul A. Hutton, *North Dakota History* 56 (Spring 1989).

"In regard to my arrest and its attendant circumstances, I am sorry it ever reached your ears, as I hoped—not for myself, but for those who were the cause of it, that the matter should end here. Suffice to say that I was placed under arrest for acting in strict conscientious discharge of what I knew to be my duty. Within forty-eight hours Genl. Stanley came to me, and apologized in the most ample manner . . . and promising to turn over a new leaf."

—Custer to Libbie, September 1873, responding to her concern about his problems with General Stanley

---

✳ Samuel Davis Sturgis
Colonel, 7th U.S. Cavalry

Sturgis was born in Shippensburg, Pennsylvania, on June 11, 1822. He entered the U.S. Military Academy at West Point in July 1842 and graduated four years later, ranked thirty-second in a class of fifty-nine. His classmates included future Civil War notables John Gibbon, Jesse Reno, George Stoneman, and George B. McClellan on the Union side and Confederates Ambrose Powell Hill, George Pickett, and Thomas "Stonewall" Jackson. The new second lieutenant was assigned to the 2nd Dragoons in the Mexican War and fought in the battles at Palo Alto and Resaca de la Palma. He was captured while on a reconnaissance mission prior to the battle of Buena Vista. Sturgis was held for eight days and returned with valuable information. After the war, he was assigned to West Ely, Missouri. On July 5, 1851, he married Jerusha "Judie" Wilcox, with whom he had four children.

Sturgis was promoted to first lieutenant in July 1853 and assigned to the 1st Cavalry. Two years later, he was promoted to captain. He participated in campaigns against Jicarilla Apache in New Mexico, then moved on to take part in the 1857–58 "Mormon War" in Utah. In 1860, Sturgis served as a liaison between white settlers and Kiowa and Comanche Indians in the "neutral lands" on the Cherokee border.

At the outbreak of the Civil War, Sturgis commanded Fort Smith, Arkansas, which lost nearly all its officers to the Confederacy. He succeeded in fleeing the post with most of the property entrusted him, which gained him a promotion to major. At the August 1861 battle of Wilson's Creek, Sturgis assumed command when Nathaniel Lyon was killed and was promoted to major general for his bravery. He commanded the District of Kansas for the next year before being sent to support General Pope's army at Second Bull Run. Sturgis became known for his colorful response when told that Pope wanted him to wait for troops and supplies before going forward: "I don't care for John Pope one pinch of owl dung!"

Sturgis commanded a division with the 9th Army Corps at the September 1862 battle of South Mountain, and three days later, he led a charge across the famous Burnside Bridge at Antietam. After the debacle at Fredericksburg, where Sturgis led a charge that carried the bridge, he accompanied Burnside into eastern Tennessee. In 1863, he commanded a small cavalry brigade that captured the entire Confederate command of Gen. Robert B. Vance.

(continued on following page)

At Brice's Crossroads, Mississippi, on June 10, 1864, Sturgis suffered an embarrassing defeat at the hands of Nathan Bedford Forrest, which led to his being relieved of duty. He faced an inquiry and spent the remainder of the war awaiting assignment. He was mustered out of the army on August 24, 1865.

After the war, Sturgis reverted to his Regular army rank of lieutenant colonel and commanded the 6th U.S. Cavalry in Texas. He was promoted to colonel and assigned command of the 7th U.S. Cavalry in May 1869, stationed during Reconstruction at Louisville. Sturgis and his immediate subordinate, George Armstrong Custer, had a contentious relationship that escalated during duty together in Texas and Kentucky. Phil Sheridan solved that problem by giving the fifty-four-year-old Sturgis a desk and Custer the field command. Sturgis remained in an administrative role in St. Louis and did not participate in any of the regiment's campaigns or battles while Custer was alive.

Sturgis's son, 2nd Lt. James G. "Jack" Sturgis, was killed with Custer at the Little Bighorn. Sturgis reacted to the news of his son's death with predictable animosity toward Custer when he wrote of him: "His experience was exceedingly limited, and that he was overreached by Indian tactics, and hundreds of valuable lives sacrificed thereby, will astonish those alone who may have read his writings—not those who were best acquainted with him and knew the peculiarities of his character." Sturgis assumed field command of the regiment in October 1877 and successfully pursued the Nez Perce Indians. In 1888, he designated special attention for Myles Keogh's horse, Comanche, which had survived the Little Bighorn battle (see "Comanche" on page 238).

In 1881, he was named governor of a soldiers' home in Washington, D.C., and remained in that capacity until 1885, when he commanded Fort Meade, Dakota Territory. He retired on June 11, 1886. Sturgis died from diabetes in St. Paul on September 28, 1889, and was buried at Arlington National Cemetery. His obituary was published in the *St. Paul Pioneer Press* on September 29, 1889, and in the *Army and Navy Journal* on October 5, 1889.

📖 Sturgis's miscellaneous papers, edited by Dumas Malone, can be found at the Library of Congress. *The Colonel Sturgis Collection,* prepared by Mamie Sturgis, is in the William Robertson Coe Collection at Yale University Library. The Sturgis Family Papers are located at the U.S. Military Academy at West Point.

EPILOGUE

George Armstrong Custer was showered with further accolades as the country's premier Indian fighter for his actions during the Yellowstone expedition—not to mention strengthening his relationship with the Northern Pacific Railroad. His official report of the campaign, which was published by the *New York Times* and the *Army and Navy Journal,* was well received by an adoring public.

Upon his return, he was issued orders from the War Department assigning him command of the newly established Fort Abraham Lincoln, five miles south of Bismarck, which was still under construction when the 7th Cavalry arrived. Six companies of the 7th and three infantry companies would be posted at the fort, while the four additional cavalry companies, under the command of Maj. Joseph G. Tilford, would be stationed at Fort Rice, twenty-five miles downstream. Maj. Marcus Reno and Companies I and D were wintering at Fort Totten, where they would resume escort duty for the Northern Boundary Survey in the spring.

Almost immediately, Custer departed for Monroe, Michigan, and returned with Libbie to their new duty station in November. The couple was greeted by the regimental band, which struck up "Home Sweet Home" then "Garry Owen" as the officers and wives welcomed them. The Custers settled into their quarters and presided over the busy winter social season at the isolated fort. There were drama performances to participate in and attend, hunts, sleigh rides, monthly company balls, and nightly gatherings for conversation, charades, and card games. On many occasions, guests would assemble around the piano that had been rented in St. Paul to sing all the favorites. Custer spent much time reading and volunteered to tutor several children inasmuch as Fort Lincoln had no school.

From all accounts, the atmosphere that winter at Fort Lincoln was quite congenial, which was rare at military posts, where petty jealousies were known to disrupt harmony. One visitor to the Custer home said:

> One was permitted to receive the courtesies of the happiest home I ever saw, where perfect love and confidence reigned. The whole regiment with one or two exceptions seemed imbued with the spirit of its commander, and in fact so close was he to his officers, that when off duty one would be led to think that all were brothers, and happy brothers at that.

Perhaps that cordiality could be attributed to the fact that notorious Custer critic Capt. Frederick W. Benteen, as well as Majors Reno and Tilford, with whom Custer shared cool relations, were stationed elsewhere.

That happy home suffered tragedy on the night of February 6, 1874, when the Custer residence burned to the ground.

The attic had been insulated with "warm paper," a petroleum-based product, which caught fire and consumed the entire house. Carpenters began work on a new two-story house that included Libbie's request for a bay window in the parlor.

While Custer waited for the completion of his new quarters, he became embroiled in a literary feud with Col. William Hazen over the merits of the land that the Northern Pacific Railroad was attempting to sell along its route. The sale of this property was vital to the future of the railroad, and Custer obliged a request from Tom Rosser to aid the cause (see "The Custer-Hazen Feud" on page 135).

Fort Abraham Lincoln was located on the fringes of Sioux country and therefore was rarely threatened. An Indian raiding party in April, 1874, stampeded a herd of civilian mules, which Custer and all six companies recovered after a chase—meanwhile leaving the fort defenseless. Again in May, Custer rode out in an effort to prevent a Sioux attack against the Arikara and Mandan, but he was unable to make contact. Otherwise, duty settled into the typical monotonous routine of an isolated frontier post that was known to provoke troopers into desertion, bad behavior, or drowning themselves with whiskey.

While Fort Lincoln shivered in the arctic blasts, Gen. Phil Sheridan was in Chicago making plans. He had set his sights on establishing a post that would be strategically located near the Red Cloud and Spotted Tail Agencies for the purpose of discouraging the Sioux from raiding into Nebraska and the travel routes to the south. Ideally, this fort would be located somewhere in the western portion of the Great Sioux Reservation, in the vicinity of the Black Hills—territory that had been given to the Indians by provisions of the Fort Laramie Treaty of 1868 (see "The Fort Laramie Treaty of 1868 and the Black Hills Expedition" on page 158).

♦•♦

"I suppose you think I am of a very forgiving disposition.
Well, perhaps I am. I often think of the beautiful
expression uttered by President Lincoln—
'With malice toward none; with charity toward all . . .'
and I hope this may ever be mine to say."

—Custer to Libbie, September 1873, remarking about
his opinion that when sober, General Stanley
was an agreeable and considerate officer

♦•♦

✸ George Wilhelmus Mancius Yates
Captain, 7th U.S. Cavalry

Capt. George Yates. *Courtesy Little Bighorn Battlefield National Monument.*

Yates was born on February 26, 1843, in Albany, New York. His father was a Princeton graduate, and other ancestors included a mayor of Albany and a governor of New York. Yates's father died in 1855, and at that time, his mother relocated to Lansing, Michigan, with three of her four sons, leaving George behind to live with an uncle in Ontario County, New York. In 1860, at age seventeen—with $500 from his uncle—he traveled to Texas and became involved in horse trading. He returned penniless to his mother's home in February 1861.

In June 1861, Yates enlisted in Company A, 4th Michigan Volunteer Infantry, and participated in the battle of Bull Run. He was appointed first lieutenant and regimental adjutant in September 1862 and served with his unit at Beverly Ford, Sharpsburg, Antietam, and Fredericksburg, where he was wounded when a shell exploded beneath his horse. While recuperating in Michigan, Yates struck up a friendship with George Armstrong Custer. In May 1863, Custer persuaded his superior, Gen. Alfred Pleasanton, to add Yates to the general's staff. In this capacity, Yates participated in engagements at Chancellorsville, Brandy Station, Aldie, Middleburg, Upperville, and Gettysburg. He also accompanied General Custer as Pleasanton's liaison on the February 1864 raid to Charlottesville.

In March 1864, when Pleasanton was removed from his cavalry command, Yates accompanied the general to the Department of the Missouri in St. Louis. In June 1864, he was mustered out of the 4th Michigan, and two months later, he obtained a commission as first lieutenant, 45th Missouri Infantry, while remaining on Pleasanton's staff. On January 5, 1865, Yates married nineteen-year-old Lucretia Beaumont "Lily" Irwin, who was from a prominent St Louis family. In November 1866, Yates filed for divorce on the grounds that Lily had abandoned him. Rumors circulated, however, that it was Yates's interest in other women that doomed the marriage. Lily died in 1916, never having remarried.

In May 1866, Yates was appointed second lieutenant, 2nd Cavalry, and reported to Fort McPherson, Nebraska. One year later—with assistance from his friend Custer—he was appointed cap-

(continued on following page)

tain, 7th Cavalry, and joined the regiment in November 1867 at Fort Leavenworth as commander of Company F, which became known as the "Band Box Troop" for its smart appearance. Yates led his company at the November 1868 battle of Washita. On February 12, 1872, he married Annie Gibson Roberts, a refined and well-educated young lady whose grandfather had served as chief justice of the Pennsylvania Supreme Court and whose father was chief engineer of the Northern Pacific Railroad. The couple had three children.

Yates served on Reconstruction duty in Kentucky from the day after his marriage until the regiment was reunited for the Yellowstone expedition of 1873. During this expedition, Yates, whose wife had endured a difficult pregnancy, stepped out of character and was constantly drunk while playing cards and losing over $400. He did, however, lead a squadron in the August 11 fight against the Sioux, escaping injury when his horse was shot in the neck. His conduct apparently was back to normal when he participated in the Black Hills expedition of 1874. In December 1875, Yates commanded the detail that arrested Sioux warrior Rain-in-the-Face for two murders during the Yellowstone expedition (see "The Arrest and Revenge of Rain-in-the-Face" on page 129).

During the 1876 Little Bighorn campaign, Yates and Company F accompanied Maj. Marcus Reno on the Powder River scout (see "Reno's Powder River Scout" on page 192). He was assigned to Custer's command on June 25 and possibly led a battalion consisting of his company and Company E on a probe of Medicine Tail Coulee in the initial stages of the battle but was driven back. Yates's body was found downslope from that of his friend Custer on Custer Hill. On August 3, 1877, his remains were reinterred at Fort Leavenworth, Kansas.

📖 "Colonel George W. Yates," by Annie Roberts Yates, *Research Review* (September 1981), a publication of the Little Big Horn Associates; "George Yates: Captain of the Band Box Troop," by Brian Pohanka, in *Greasy Grass* (May 1992), a publication of the Custer Battlefield Historical and Museum Association; "Captain Yates' Capture of Rain-in-the-Face," by Cyrus T. Brady, in *The Tepee Book* (Sheridan, WY: n.p., 1916); and *A Summer on the Plains, 1870: From the Diary of Annie Gibson Roberts,* by Brian Pohanka (Bryan, TX: J. M. Carroll & Company, 1983).

Sheridan was granted permission from William Sherman for a reconnaissance to determine a precise location. In June 1874, George Armstrong Custer was advised that he would command an expedition into the Black Hills to assess the potential of establishing a post in that region—and perhaps to verify claims of valuable mineral deposits.

📖 The best account of the Custers' life at Fort Abraham Lincoln can be found in Libbie's *"Boots and Saddles"; or, Life in Dakota with General Custer* (New York: Harper and Brothers, 1885). Another interesting source is chapter 24 of *General Custer's Libbie,* by Lawrence A. Frost (Seattle: Superior Publishing Co., 1976). Also see *Custer's Seventh Cavalry Comes to Dakota,* by Roger Darling (El Segundo, CA: Upton & Sons, 1989).

Into the Black Hills

OVERVIEW

Lt. Col. George Armstrong Custer marched out of Fort Abraham Lincoln on July 2, 1874, at the head of a column composed of 10 companies of the 7th Cavalry, 2 infantry companies, a train of 110 wagons, 3 gatling guns, scouts, interpreters, a scientific corps, 2 professional miners, and numerous journalists—more than 1,000 participants (see "Table of Organization of the 7th Cavalry for the Black Hills Expedition of 1874" on page 149).

His mission was to explore the Black Hills region of Dakota Territory, land that had been granted the Sioux as part of their reservation in the Fort Laramie Treaty of 1868. The published purpose of this controversial reconnaissance was to identify likely locations for a military post. It was a poorly kept secret,

"The expedition is entirely peaceful in its object, it being the intention to explore the country known as the Black Hills. The Indians have long opposed all effort of white men to enter the Black Hills and I feel confident that the Sioux will combine their entire strength and endeavor to oppose us."

—Custer to actor Lawrence Barrett, May 1874

Custer with the first grizzly he killed, August 1874. From left: Scout Bloody Knife; Custer; Private Noonan; Capt. William Ludlow. *Courtesy Little Bighorn Battlefield National Monument.*

✹ George Crook
Brigadier General, U.S. Army

Crook was born on a farm near Dayton, Ohio, on September 8, 1828. He graduated from the U.S. Military Academy at West Point in 1852, near the bottom of his class, and was assigned to an infantry regiment in the Pacific Northwest. In addition to escort duty and building military posts, Crook was involved in the Yakima War of 1855–56 in eastern Washington Territory, as well as the simultaneous Rogue River War in southern Oregon. He received a poisoned arrow in the hip during one engagement with the Pitt Indians.

At the outbreak of the Civil War, Crook was made colonel of the 36th Ohio Infantry, which was assigned to western Virginia, and by applying lessons learned on the frontier, he successfully fought guerrilla actions. In May 1862, he was wounded at Lewisburg, and three months later, he was promoted to brigadier general. Crook commanded the Kanawha Division at South Mountain and the September 1862 battle of Antietam. He was then placed in command of the 2nd Cavalry Division and participated in the heavy fighting of the August–September 1863 Chickamauga campaign. In February 1864, Crook assumed command of the Kanawha District and led a series of raids between Lynchburg, Virginia, and eastern Tennessee. He was given command of the Department of Western Virginia in the summer of 1864 and was part of Maj. Gen. Phil Sheridan's Shenandoah Valley campaign, where he distinguished himself on numerous occasions and became known as "Uncle George." Crook was promoted to major general in October 1864 and was at his headquarters at Cumberland, Maryland, on February 21, 1865, when he and Brig. Gen. Benjamin F. Kelly were captured by Southern partisans. He was released just prior to the end of hostilities.

Crook returned to the regular rank of lieutenant colonel after the war. He commanded the 23rd Infantry in Idaho Territory, where he fought against Northern Paiutes during the Snake River War of 1866–68 in the deserts of southern Idaho and eastern Oregon—finally forcing a surrender. In 1871, at the request of President U. S. Grant, he was placed in command of the Department of Arizona to contend with Chiricahua Apache. Crook won great acclaim by developing a successful strategy of using small, mobile detachments and recruiting surrendered Apache to track renegade Apache. By 1873, the Apache had been rela-

however, that Custer was also interested in verifying claims of valuable mineral deposits—gold in particular—within the Black Hills.

After a march of about 300 miles, Custer and his column entered the northwestern edge of the Black Hills on July 20 by traveling along a well-worn Indian trail. Two days later, at Inyan Kara, an extinct volcano, some of his Arikara and Santee scouts warned him that if he did not turn back, there would be severe retaliation from the Sioux. Custer ignored their protests and, perhaps because these scouts had never been to the region before and would have little to offer with respect to information, released them. Those Indians who did remain with the column included Bloody Knife, Custer's favorite scout.

Before leaving Inyan Kara, Custer, accompanied by chief engineer William Ludlow, botanist A. B. Donaldson, and several others, climbed to the 6,500-foot summit of this mountain. Ludlow, or perhaps Lt. Col. George A. "Sandy" Forsyth, used hammer and chisel to create a monument of sorts, chipping an inscription into a rock that read: '74 CUSTER.

Without capable scouts to guide them, Custer personally rode ahead of his column and blazed the trail, which eventually gained him the reputation of always being able to locate a passage through even the most difficult terrain. He would assume this responsibility throughout the remainder of the expedition.

On July 24, Custer entered a resplendent valley surrounded by pines that overwhelmed everyone with its beauty and provided the botanists a virtual field day. Calling it "an Eden in the clouds," correspondent Samuel Barrows of the *New York Tribune* wrote, "How shall I describe it! As well try to paint the flavor of a peach or the odor of a rose." A. B. Donaldson, who collected fifty-two varieties of flowers in bloom, raved: "It is hardly possible to exaggerate in describing this flowery richness. Some said they would give a hundred dollars just to have their wives see the floral richness for even one hour."

Neither did Custer exaggerate when he chose the name Floral Valley for the area of which he wrote: "In no private or public park have I ever seen such a profuse display of flowers." Nearly every diary, letter home, or report contained a glowing description of this wondrous valley that teemed with wildflowers and offered a mystical serenity. Hard-bitten troopers decorated mule harnesses and hats with flowers, and preserved blossoms as gifts for wives, girlfriends, and family members. Custer noted that while seated at the mess table, they could pick up "seven beautiful varieties" of flowers within reach. The column camped in Floral Valley for two days before moving on.

George Armstrong Custer, as had been his habit on previous expeditions, spent much of his free time along the way enjoying outdoor activities and indulging his curiosity about nature by exploring. He would frequently ride off with a detachment to hunt game, climb hills, or explore caves or other intriguing terrain. One notable cave shown him by a scout

(continued on following page)

named Goose extended for 400 feet, with provocative carvings and drawings on the walls and eerie shrieks and howls emanating from within its depths.

Custer also accumulated his customary wildlife menagerie. This one consisted of, among other species, a jackrabbit, an eagle, two prairie owls, several toads, rattlesnakes, and a number of birds. Unfortunately, two badgers had been accidentally smothered to death. These specimens, as well as generous samples of flora and fossils, including a petrified tree trunk, required an ambulance detail of twelve men under Fred "Antelope" Snow for transport.

tively subdued, and the following year, Crook was rewarded with a brigadier general's star.

In 1875, he was given command of the Department of the Platte and assigned the dubious task of removing the miners who had been trespassing in the Black Hills to prospect for gold. Late in July, Crook called a meeting with the miners and issued an ultimatum that diplomatically suggested that the miners likely would have an opportunity to prospect the area once it had been opened in the near future, but for the present, they

(continued on following page)

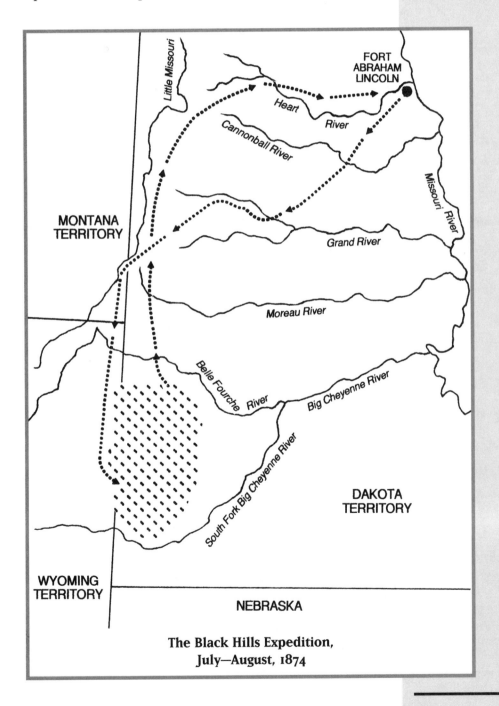

**The Black Hills Expedition,
July–August, 1874**

must depart. Most of the miners, who were quite impressed with Crook's forthrightness, agreed to comply. They even drew up a proclamation that thanked the general for "the kind and gentlemanly manner with which his command have executed his [the President's] order." Crook's ability to rea-

(continued on following page)

Custer also quite often served as a host, inviting guests to his large hospital tent, perhaps with the regimental band supplying entertainment. His brothers, Tom and Boston, were always present, along with favorites Fred Grant, the president's son, who was Sheridan's personal observer; "Sandy" Forsyth; William Ludlow, who was one of the cadets involved in the

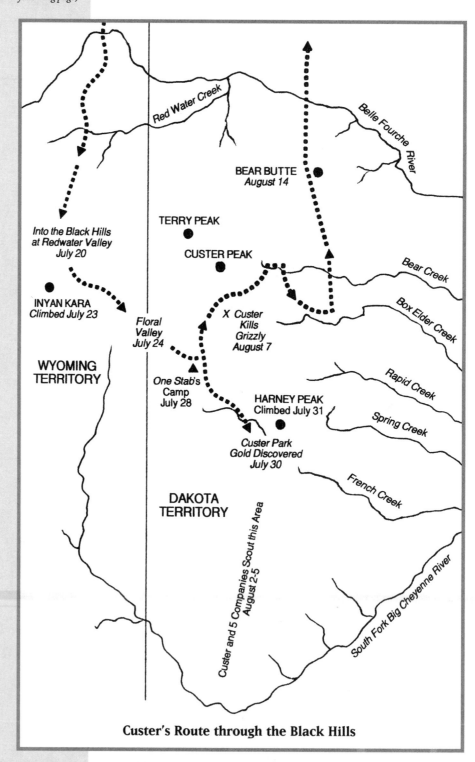

Custer's Route through the Black Hills

fight that nearly caused Custer's dismissal from West Point years earlier; George Bird Grinnell, the young osteologist, and his assistant; scout Luther North; and scout Charley Reynolds, with whom Custer shared much in common.

Although Custer, a noted teetotaler, assured his wife in a letter that there were no incidences of intoxication on the march, just the opposite was true. The sutler's wagon carried an ample supply of liquor, which was freely consumed by those who so desired. It has been reported that Fred Grant "was drunk nearly all the time," which sounds like an exaggeration, except that Custer did at one point place Grant under arrest for drunkenness.

Another incident that points to frequent alcohol abuse by those in authority involved the entire medical staff. An ill trooper, Pvt. John Cunningham, apparently died when the three doctors that had accompanied the column—A. C. Bergen, S. J. Allen, Jr., and chief medical officer J. W. Williams—were all too drunk to adequately care for the man and prescribe proper medicine.

In spite of these moments of indiscretion, there can be no doubt that the march through the Black Hills was as pleasant as any ever experienced by the participants—especially for the officers, if not the enlisted men, who were often assigned undesirable duty (see "The Journal of Pvt. Theodore Ewert" on page 155). Lt. James Calhoun perhaps summed up the sentiments of his peers when he wrote: "The air is serene and the sun is shining in all its glory. The birds are singing sweetly, warbling their sweet notes as they soar aloft. Nature seems to smile on our movement. Everything seems to encourage us onward."

The Sioux had thus far chosen not to interfere with this, to them, insulting invasion of troops, but they indicated with smoke signals that they were aware there had been an intrusion upon their land.

On July 28, however, the column happened upon a small hunting party of five lodges and twenty-seven occupants under Oglala Chief One Stab (or Stabber) in Castle Creek Valley. According to one account, the wife of One Stab was the daughter of Red Cloud. These particular Indians, from the Red Cloud and Spotted Tail Agencies, apparently had not noticed the smoke signals and were quite surprised to encounter the soldiers. Custer, under a flag of truce, smoked the peace pipe with One Stab and graciously invited the chief and several of his people to visit the army camp for coffee, sugar, and bacon, a courtesy that was gratefully accepted.

The Indian scouts that had remained with the column were not as gracious as their commander and wanted to kill their traditional enemy. Due to the threat of hostilities, Custer assigned a detail of fifteen troopers to escort his Sioux guests back to their lodges and protect them through the night. In spite of that precaution, the wary Sioux abruptly galloped away, with the soldiers and scouts in hot pursuit. During the chase—

son with the miners can be attributed in part to his folksy, if not somewhat eccentric, personality. He was an imposing man, standing well over six feet, who braided his parted blond whiskers, wore canvas coveralls rather than a uniform, and preferred riding a mule rather than a horse.

Crook attended a high-level meeting at the White House in November 1875—likely in proper uniform—when it was decided that the army would no longer stem the flow of miners into the Black Hills, and that military force would contend with the opposition of hostile Indians—an edict that led to the Great Sioux War of 1876–77.

"The expedition has surpassed most sanguine expectations. We have discovered a rich and beautiful country. We have had no Indian fights. We have found gold and probably other valuable metals."

—CUSTER TO LIBBIE, JULY 1874

In the 1876 Little Bighorn campaign, Crook was assigned command of a 1,200-man column that was part of General Sheridan's three-pronged offensive against hostile Sioux. He was marching northward from Fort Fetterman when, on March 17, the column, headed by Col. Joseph Reynolds, encountered Sioux Indians under Crazy Horse on the Powder River in southeastern Montana. Reynolds attacked and held the village, until Crazy Horse counterattacked and routed the cavalrymen. Crook was furious and filed court-martial charges against Reynolds, who was subsequently found guilty of neglect (see "Prelude to Little Bighorn: The Powder River and Rosebud Engagements" on page 189).

Crook marched again in May, and on June 17, he was attacked by Crazy Horse at Rosebud Creek. The fight was for all intents and purposes a stalemate. Crook, however, claimed victory when the Indians broke contact and he was left holding the field. The battle was a great embarrassment for Crook, who retreated to his camp on Goose Creek (see "Prelude to Little Bighorn: The Powder River and Rosebud Engagements" on page 189). While the other two

(continued on following page)

columns marched toward a rendezvous with Sitting Bull and Crazy Horse on the Little Bighorn, Crook remained in camp, licking his wounds and fishing, and inexplicably failed to inform anyone of his whereabouts. Many scholars believe that Crook's failure to resume his march northward to execute the three-pronged pincer movement was a contributing factor to Custer's defeat.

After Custer's June 25 battle at the Little Bighorn, Crook—although Terry had called an end to the campaign—continued to doggedly pursue the hostiles. He turned his column toward the Black Hills on a forced march that became known as the "Starvation March." His exhausted troops resorted to eating mules and horses due to the lack of food. He scored a victory at the battle of Slim Buttes on September 9, when Col. Anson Mills routed a village of thirty-seven lodges and killed Chief American Horse. In November, his forces defeated Cheyenne Dull Knife's 200-lodge village in the Bighorn Mountains. Crook then marched east in search of more Indians, but he ended his campaign in late December without further contact.

In 1882, when the Chiricahua Apache under Geronimo left the reservation to raid, Crook was once again assigned command of the Department of Arizona. The next four years were spent pursuing the renegades, until he finally forced Geronimo's surrender in March 1886. When Geronimo escaped, Crook was returned to the Department of the Platte, replaced in Arizona by Gen. Nelson A. Miles, who managed the final capture of the Apache chief.

In 1888, he was promoted to major general and assumed command of the Division of the Missouri, which comprised most of the Great Plains. Crook, who believed that Indian hostilities were caused by the government's failure to live up to the terms of its treaties, campaigned on behalf of Indian-rights groups until his death in 1890.

Every book about the Apache Wars in Arizona contain references to Crook. An autobiography is *General George Crook: His Autobiography* (Norman: University of Oklahoma Press, 1946). Other excellent sources include *Campaigning with Crook,* by Capt. Charles King (Norman: University of Oklahoma Press, 1964); *With Crook at the Rosebud,* by J. W. Vaughn (Harrisburg, PA: Stackpole, 1956); and *Battle of the Rosebud: Prelude to the Little Bighorn,* by Neil C. Mangum (El Segundo, CA: Upton and Sons, 1987).

although Custer had ordered that there be no violence—one of the Sioux was shot by one of the Santee scouts. The troops arrived at the Indian camp to find that it had been abandoned.

Custer, however, had detained Chief One Stab, either as a hostage or guest. Custer wrote, perhaps with tongue in cheek: "I have effected arrangements by which the Chief One Stab remains with us as a guide." Whatever the circumstances, the chief, who was greatly distressed by his captivity, guided the expedition for several days into the southern hills. During this time, rumors had spread throughout the reservations that One Stab had been killed. His eventual safe release likely prevented any retaliation by the Sioux.

On July 30, about 100 miles into their reconnaissance, the column camped in a glade that Custer modestly named Custer Park, which was near the site of present-day Custer City, South Dakota. While the troops passed the time playing cards, writing letters, catching up on their sleep, or exploring their new surroundings, miners Horatio Ross and William McKay discovered some "color" along the upper part of French Creek. Which one of the miners actually was the first to recognize gold has been a matter of speculation. Ross generally receives credit for the discovery. McKay, however, noted in an undated journal entry:

> In the evening I took a pan, pick and shovel, and went out prospecting. The first panful was taken from the gravel and sand obtained in the bed of the creek; and on washing was found to contain from one and a half to two cents, which was the first gold found in the Black Hills.

Regardless of who struck color first, the two miners wrapped the few specks of gold in a piece of paper and together presented their findings to Custer that night. Ross and McKay were skeptical about the prospects of a big strike but vowed to continue panning in the morning.

At dawn, the miners returned to French Creek, while Custer and an escort commanded by Lt. Charles Varnum rode to 7,200-foot Harney's Peak, the highest point in the Black Hills. Custer, along with Forsyth, Ludlow, Donaldson, Winchell, and topographer W. W. Wood, climbed the summit and pointed out two other distinctive peaks that he named for Gen. Alfred Terry and himself. The members of the climbing party wrote their names and the date on a piece of paper, then rolled it up, inserted it into a copper cartridge casing, and slipped it into a crevice. The casing was found sixty years later, but the message was missing.

During Custer's absence, the troops engaged in a rousing game of baseball: The Actives of Fort Lincoln defeated the Athletes of Fort Rice 11 to 6 in a disputed game (see "The Benteen Base Ball Club" on page 157). That was followed by a champagne dinner for some of the officers hosted by Maj. Joseph G. Tilford.

Outing at the Heart River, 1875. From left: 1st Lt. James Calhoun; Mr. Leonard Swett; Capt. Stephen Baker; Boston Custer; 2nd Lt. Winfield S. Edgerly; Miss Emily Watson; Capt. Myles W. Keogh; Mrs. Margaret Custer Calhoun; Mrs. Elizabeth "Libbie" Custer; Dr. Holmes O. Paulding; Lt. Col. George Armstrong Custer; Mrs. Nettie Smith; Dr. George E. Lord; Capt. Thomas B. Weir; 1st Lt. William W. Cooke; 2nd Lt. Richard E. Thompson; Miss Nellie Wadsworth; Miss Emma Wadsworth; 1st Lt. Thomas W. Custer; 1st Lt. Algernon E. Smith. *Courtesy Little Bighorn Battlefield National Monument.*

On August 1, Custer moved the camp three miles away to a better grazing area and named the site Agnes Park after Agnes Bates, a friend of Libbie's. The miners tested the loose soil around the creek and were impressed with the results. They speculated that under the right conditions, a miner could expect to reap perhaps as much as $150 a day. French Creek was soon lined with ambitious soldiers who sought their fortunes digging with shovels, picks, knives, pothooks, plates, cups, and any other implement that could penetrate dirt. Twenty troopers later staked a claim under the name Custer Park Mining Company.

On August 2, Custer decided that the outside world should be notified of this gold discovery. He prepared a dispatch to Gen. Phil Sheridan, which read in part, "Gold has been found in several places, and it is the belief of those who are giving their attention to this subject that it will be found in paying quantities." This message was entrusted to scout Charley Reynolds, who had been engaged for such a purpose. Reynolds traveled ninety miles in four days through hostile territory to deliver Custer's dispatch to Fort Laramie (see "The Midnight Ride of Charley Reynolds" on page 169).

The expedition moved onward, following its old trail in a northerly direction. On August 7, Custer attained what he considered his greatest feat as a hunter: He killed a grizzly bear, although bullets from the rifles of Ludlow and Bloody Knife contributed to the demise of the beast (see "Custer, the Sportsman" on page 132), and others, most notably George Bird Grinnell, diarist Theodore Ewert, and even Bloody Knife, remarked that this particular griz was less than fearsome, being an old male with teeth reduced to mere stumps, many incisors missing, and claws severely worn down.

✸ A. B. Donaldson
Botanist

Donaldson was born in Ohio in 1831. He graduated from Ohio Wesleyan College and subsequently taught in various Ohio schools for twenty years.

The sponsorship of his participation in Custer's Black Hills expedition of 1874 has never been determined. He was listed as a botanist but contributed little to further knowledge in that area. Donaldson collected only 75 of the more than 1,000 plant species available in the Black Hills. These he sent for identification to Professor John M. Coulter at Hanover, Indiana. Although he was thought to have been working for the University of Minnesota, it has been speculated that Donaldson was primarily sponsored by the *St. Paul Daily Pioneer* newspaper, to which he submitted lengthy

(continued on following page)

dispatches. That theory might explain his meager efforts at collecting.

He also reportedly had a bad back, but he was fit enough on July 23 to accompany Custer, William Ludlow, and several others to the 6,500-foot summit of Inyan Kara Mountain. And on August 14, Donaldson and geologist Newton Winchell traversed old deer and antelope trails to climb Bear Butte, an extinct volcano on the northern fringe of the Black Hills that rose 1,200 feet above the prairie floor.

"You may judge how fertile the country when I tell you that our mules, also our beef herd, are in better condition than when we started."

—Custer to Libbie, July 1874

Donaldson apparently was popular with his companions. *Chicago Inter-Ocean* correspondent William Elroy Curtis, in a dispatch dated July 23 and published on August 17, described him as follows:

> A big-bodied, big-hearted old fellow, a professor in a western college, who is doing the botany. His character is noble, yet funny, for in it are mixed the most generous, manly emotions, and a simple childishness it does one good to see. The professor—he alone, of the titled scientists, is exclusively known as such—is doing the botany; and to see him come in from a long day's march, with a benevolent smile playing over his sun-burned, half-peeled face, and wreathing itself in his whiskers, and a huge nosegay of flowers in his hand—to see him lower his corpulent form from the back of "Dobbin," slowly and carefully, so as not to jar the sensitiveness of his rheumatic back, and to hear his sigh of relief, breathed secretly under a cheerful, hearty greeting, is as good as a tonic.

Donaldson's love of writing evidently compelled him to forsake botany in 1875, when he purchased the Alexandria, Minnesota, *Post,* which he published until his death in 1883.

📖 Donaldson's dispatch of July 25, first published in the *St. Paul Daily Pioneer* on August 15, is reprinted in *South Dakota Historical Collections*

On August 14, Custer chose Bear Butte, an isolated granite laccolith rising 1,200 feet above the prairie on the northern fringe of the Black Hills, as the location to halt his column and prepare his official report. Ironically, Bear Butte was a special place to the Sioux Nation, where, for a century, they had gathered to trade, share news, and participate in religious ceremonies.

The column marched east from Bear Butte through the hot, dusty plains, with Custer pushing the troopers hard. With the band striking up "Garry Owen," the column triumphantly paraded into Fort Abraham Lincoln on August 30, after a march of 60 days and 883 miles.

📖 Perhaps the best account, which provides an excellent overview of this expedition and contains interesting anecdotes, is *Custer's Gold: The United States Cavalry Expedition of 1874,* by Donald Jackson (New Haven, CT: Yale University Press, 1966). Newspaper coverage, Custer's reports, and journals maintained by Forsyth and Grant can be found in *Prelude to Glory: A Newspaper Accounting of Custer's 1874 Expedition to the Black Hills,* by Herbert Krause and Gary D. Olson (Sioux Falls: Brevet Press, 1974). For Custer's official report, see *Report of the Expedition to the Black Hills under Command of Brevet Major General G. A. Custer,* 43 Cong., 2 sess., Sen. Exec. Doc. 32, which is also in South Dakota Department of History, *Collections,* VII, 583–94.

Two military participants—one officer and one enlisted—kept diaries on this expedition: *With Custer in '74: James Calhoun's Diary of the Black Hills Expedition,* edited by Lawrence A. Frost (Provo, UT: Brigham Young University, 1979); and *Private Theodore Ewert's Diary of the Black Hills Expedition of 1874,* edited by John M. Carroll and Lawrence A. Frost (Piscataway, NJ: CRI Books, 1976). Another participant's view is in *The Passing of the Great West: Selected Papers of George Bird Grinnell,* edited by John F. Reiger (New York: Winchester Press, 1972). For a modern-day photographic reconstruction of Custer's route, see *Following Custer,* by Donald R. Progulske and Frank J. Shidler (Brookings: Agricultural Experiment Station, South Dakota State University, 1974).

Also see *Gold in the Black Hills,* by Watson Parker (Lincoln: University of Nebraska Press, 1982); *Black Hills/White Justice: The Sioux Nation versus the United States, 1775 to the Present,* by Edward Lazarus (New York: HarperCollins, 1991); "The Red Man and the Black Hills," by Charles F. Bates, *Outlook Magazine* 27 (July 1927); "The Black Hills Expedition of 1874: A New Look," by Max E. Gerber, *South Dakota History* 8 (June–July 1970); and *The Fatal Environment: The Myth of the Frontier in the Age of Industrialization, 1800–1890,* by Richard Slotkin (New York: Antheneum, 1985).

(continued on following page)

SIDEBARS

Table of Organization of the 7th Cavalry for the Black Hills Expedition of 1874

Field and Staff:
Lt. Col. George Armstrong Custer, commanding
Lt. Col. Frederick D. Grant, 4th cavalry, acting aide
Maj. George A. Forsyth, 9th Cavalry, battalion commander
Maj. Joseph G. Tilford, battalion commander
1st Lt. James Calhoun, adjutant
1st Lt. Algernon E. Smith, quartermaster and commissary
2nd Lt. George D. Wallace, commanding Indian scouts

Company A	Capt. Myles Moylan; 2nd Lt. Charles Varnum
Company B	1st Lt. Benjamin H. Hodgson
Company C	Capt. Verlin Hart; 2nd Lt. Henry M. Harrington
Company E	1st Lt. Thomas M. McDougall
Company F	Capt. George W. Yates
Company G	1st Lt. Donald McIntosh
Company H	Capt. Frederick W. Benteen; 1st Lt. Francis M. Gibson
Company K	Capt. Owen Hale; 1st Lt. Edward S. Godfrey
Company L	1st Lt. Thomas W. Custer
Company M	Capt. Thomas French; 1st Lt. Edward G. Mathey

Medical Staff:
Dr. John W. Williams, chief medical officer
Dr. S. J. Allen, Jr., acting assistant surgeon
Dr. A. C. Bergen, acting assistant surgeon

Engineering:
Capt. William Ludlow, chief engineer
W. H. Wood, civilian assistant

Mining Detachment:
Horatio Nelson Ross
William McKay

Scientists:
George Bird Grinnell
Newton H. Winchell
A. B. Donaldson
Luther North

Photographer:
William H. Illingworth

Correspondents:
William E. Curtis, *Chicago Inter-Ocean*
Samuel J. Barrows, *New York Tribune*
Nathan H. Knappen, *Bismarck Tribune*

7 (1914). An excerpt from his dispatch of August 15, which appeared in the *St. Paul Daily Pioneer* on August 26 and describes an elk dance held by the Arikara, has been reprinted in *Custer's Gold: The United States Cavalry Expedition of 1874,* by Donald Jackson (New Haven, CT: Yale University Press, 1966).

⊛ George Bird Grinnell
Naturalist, Historian, and Ethnologist

This advocate of the Plains Indians and founder of the North American conservation movement was born in Brooklyn on September 20, 1849. His interest in nature began at an early age, when his neighbor, Lucy Audubon, widow of John James Audubon, and her son introduced him to the wonders of the outdoors. He graduated from Yale University in 1870, with a degree in zoology, and that same year participated in a student paleontology expedition led by Professor O. C. Marsh to study fossil beds in Wyoming and Utah. Grinnell was fascinated by the region and headed west in 1872 to participate in the Pawnee's last great buffalo hunt, where he met Frank and Luther North. He returned the following year to again hunt buffalo. On one occasion, Grinnell hunted with William F. "Buffalo Bill" Cody.

In 1874, while on the staff of the Peabody Museum of Natural History at Yale, Grinnell served as naturalist and paleontologist for George Armstrong Custer's Black Hills expedition. The expenses of Grinnell and his novice assistant, Luther North, who had been his guide on his 1873 buffalo hunt, were paid by Yale. Grinnell, although hurried across the plains by the steady itinerary of the expedition, collected numerous specimens and compiled lists of indigenous birds and mammals, including jackrabbits, prairie dogs, mule deer, elk, mountain lion, grizzly bear, bighorn sheep, and 110 species of birds. He saw no live buffalo but did find the skull of an old bull. Grinnell was amazed to observe a pronghorn antelope with two broken legs outdistance Charley Reynolds on horseback for more than two miles. The leg bone of an animal that he speculated to be a dinosaur was found at Castle Butte, about six miles north of Prospect Valley. Most of the fossils, however, consisted of marine specimens, mainly shells.

While working on his doctorate degree in 1875, which he received five years later, Grinnell accompanied Col. William Ludlow's reconnaissance

(continued on following page)

team from Carroll, Montana, through the Yellowstone region. Because of a heavy workload, he declined an invitation from Custer to accompany the 7th Cavalry on the Little Bighorn campaign. Grinnell became editor in 1876 of *Forest & Stream* magazine, which was devoted to encouraging sportsmen to support regulations and conserve wildlife, and its owner in 1880, a tenure that lasted until 1911.

Although he made his home in New York, Grinnell bought a Western ranch, which afforded him a base of operations from which to explore Wyoming and Montana. He founded the Audubon Society for the Protection of Birds in 1886 and served on its board of directors for twenty-six years. Grinnell organized the Boone and Crockett Club with his friend Theodore Roosevelt and others in 1887 and served as its president from 1918 to 1937. He assisted with drafting plans for the New York Zoological Park and was a naturalist for Edward H. Harriman's 1899 Alaskan expedition.

Grinnell was a prolific writer, writing or editing countless articles and dozens of books—including a juvenile fiction series—about Indian folklore, hunting, and conservation. He fought to prevent hunting in national parks, helped create Glacier National Park in 1910 (having discovered Grinnell's Glacier in 1885), and became president of the National Parks Association in 1925.

George Bird Grinnell, an intriguing man of many talents and conservation concerns, died on April 11, 1938, in New York City.

📖 Grinnell's descriptive books and articles about the Cheyenne, Pawnee, and Blackfoot remain an excellent source of information. Most notable are *The Cheyenne Indians,* 2 vols. (New Haven: Yale University Press, 1923); *The Fighting Cheyennes* (Norman: University of Oklahoma Press, 1962); and *The Passing of the Great West* (New York: Winchester Press, 1972). Grinnell's *Two Great Scouts and Their Pawnee Battalion* (Lincoln: University of Nebraska Press, 1973) provides a sympathetic portrayal of his friends, Frank and Luther North, but contains many inaccuracies.

See also *Grinnell's Glacier: George Bird Grinnell and the Founding of Glacier National Park,* by Gerald A. Diettert (Missoula, MT: Mountain Press, 1992); "A Dedication to the Memory of George Bird Grinnell," by John F. Reiger, *Arizona and the West* 21, no. 1 (Spring 1979); and *American Sportsmen and the Origins of Conservation,* by John F. Reiger (Norman: University of Oklahoma Press, 1986).

Guides:
Louis Agard
Boston Custer
Charles Reynolds

Detached Service: Col. Samuel D. Sturgis; Maj. Lewis Merrill; Capt. Michael V. Sheridan; Capt. William Thompson; Capt. Charles S. Ilsley; Capt. John E. Tourtellotte; 1st Lt. William W. Cooke; 1st Lt. Henry J. Nowlan; 1st Lt. John Weston; 1st Lt. Henry Jackson; 1st Lt. James M. Bell; 2nd Lt. Charles W. Larned; 2nd Lt. Charles C. DeRudio; 2nd Lt. Richard H. L. Alexander

Northern Boundary Survey:
Maj. Marcus A. Reno, commanding

Company D   Capt. Thomas Weir; 2nd Lt. Winfield S. Edgerly
Company I   1st Lt. James E. Porter

Leave of Absence: Capt. Myles W. Keogh; 2nd Lt. William T. Craycroft; 2nd Lt. Andrew H. Nave

Sick Leave: 2nd Lt. Charles Braden

 President Grant's Indian Policy

Prior to the Civil War, the government had established an Indian policy that called for removing offending tribes to the Great Plains, where they could live on one big reservation in a region where the whites had no interest. After the war, however, whites became interested in the plains—both for crossing to points west and for settling—and Indian resistance was dealt with by military force. At that point, the government had two choices when setting policy with respect to the Indian: annihilation or assimilation. The public seemed to feel that enough blood had been shed during the recent war and favored a peaceful approach. By the time Ulysses S. Grant won the election of 1868, major treaties had been negotiated and reservations set aside.

Grant, a man of unquestionable personal integrity whose administration would be plagued with numerous cases of corruption, made an admirable effort to treat the Indian with fairness. In his 1869 inauguration speech, he stated: "The proper treatment of the original occupants of this land—the Indians—is one deserving of careful study. I will favor any course towards them which tends to their civilization and ultimate citizenship."

Shortly thereafter, he announced his Federal Indian policy, which endorsed his goal of acculturating the Indians and eventually inviting them to become U.S. citizens. His plan of action became known as the "peace policy," due to its intended mission, which was "the hitherto untried policy in connection with Indians, of endeavoring to conquer by kindness." Grant affirmed his intentions by appointing as commissioner of Indian affairs, Ely Parker, a full-blooded Seneca who had become his friend in Illinois, the first Indian to hold that post.

Grant had initially assigned mainly army officers for duty as Indian agents, but in 1870, Congress banned military personnel from serving in civil-service positions. At that time, Grant refused to make patronage appointments and instead chose Indian agents from Christian denominations, which then set to work implementing the process of peacefully relocating tribes to reservations where they could be protected by the army. Grant believed that his "Quaker policy," as it was called, would pacify the Indians and encourage them to accept his policies. The churchmen had final authority on the reservations, but Grant warned that "a sharp and severe war policy" would face those tribes that would not submit to the reservation.

The president personally assisted in the effort by entertaining many tribal leaders in the White House over the years, including Lakota Sioux chiefs Red Cloud and Spotted Tail. Many of the chiefs toured various cities, and the U.S. Indian Commission organized Indian lectures in New York and Boston.

Grant also helped raise funds—both public and private—for the assimilation of Indians into white society. "Friends of the Indian" reform groups also were established and raised a considerable amount of money for education and other expenses necessary to bridge the cultural gap.

Politics, however, played a major role in Grant's Indian policy. The Interior Department and the army, which claimed that they could police Indian agencies better than could government bureaucrats, waged a behind-the-scenes battle over the direction of Indian affairs. Even Grant's old military colleagues were surprised and angered by the president's decision to favor civilian control over that of the military.

Unfortunately for all concerned, Grant's compassionate approach toward the Indian failed to bring an end to Indian hostilities on the plains. In late 1875, the public was clamoring for the government to acquire the Black Hills, where gold deposits had been found. Grant had by then lost patience with the peace policy and was persuaded by Generals Sherman and Sheridan to permit the military to find a solution. This decision set in motion events that led to the Great Sioux War of 1876–77.

After Custer's defeat at Little Bighorn, the *New York Herald* answered the question posed in its headline "Who Slew Custer?" by writing:

> The celebrated peace policy of General Grant, which feeds, clothes and takes care of their noncombatant force while the men are killing our troops—that is what killed Custer. . . . That nest of thieves, the Indian Bureau, with its thieving agents and favorites as Indian traders, and its mock humanity and pretense of piety—that is what killed Custer.

BIOGRAPHIES

✺ William H. Illingworth
Photographer

Illingworth was born in England and as a child immigrated with his family to Philadelphia. The family moved to St. Paul in 1850, where Illingworth apparently helped his father, who was a jeweler and clockmaker. He studied photography in Chicago and in 1866 accompanied the Fisk emigrant expedition from St. Paul to Montana. His thirty stereoscopic photographs from that expedition were published by John Carbutt of Chicago and became the main attraction for a studio and gallery that he opened in St. Paul the following year.

⬥━━━◆━━━⬥

"Three days ago we reached the cave referred to by the Indian called 'Goose.' It is about 400 feet long, its walls covered with drawings of animals, and prints of hands and feet. I cannot account for the drawings of ships."

—CUSTER TO LIBBIE, JULY 1874

⬥━━━◆━━━⬥

In 1874, Illingworth was hired—on the rolls as a teamster—by Col. William Ludlow to accompany Custer's Black Hills expedition. Ludlow provided the camera and necessary chemicals and equipment, rations, and a wagon and horse, and paid all his expenses. In return, Illingworth promised to deliver six sets of prints to Ludlow, but he could retain the negatives for his own purposes. At that time, he may have been representing another St. Paul photographer, Charles J. Huntington—pictures later published in newspapers bore the imprint "Published by Huntington & Winn."

Illingworth photographed dozens of scenes as the expedition wound its way through the Black Hills. He also found time to hunt, returning to camp on July 6 with two pronghorn antelope he had shot from a herd that he estimated at 300. The photographer was called when Custer shot his first grizzly and recorded the scene; this picture later gained popularity in stationery shops throughout the East.

When it was time to deliver the prints to Ludlow, however, Illingworth failed to live up to his

(continued on following page)

terms of the contract. Ludlow received only one incomplete set of prints. When the colonel complained, Illingworth claimed that he did not have the financial resources to produce more. Complete sets at that time, much to Ludlow's chagrin, were being offered for sale commercially through Huntington & Winn. An angry Ludlow made a futile effort to prosecute Illingworth in St. Paul for embezzlement of government property and later requested that the War Department take action.

Illingworth married three times. His first two wives died, and he divorced the third. Shortly after that divorce, perhaps because of ill health, he committed suicide by shooting himself on March 17, 1893.

📖 See "Restless, Troubled Opportunist: Portrait of a Pioneer Photographer," by Henry Wall, *Ramsey County History* 4, no. 1 (January 1968). Illingworth's photographic record of early life in Minnesota is located in the collection of the Minnesota Historical Society.

✴ William Ludlow
Engineer and Army Officer

Ludlow was born on November 27, 1843, in Islip, Long Island, the second of six children to William H. Ludlow, who would distinguish himself as a Civil War general. He was educated at Burlington Academy in New Jersey and the University of the City of New York (later NYU). Ludlow entered the U.S. Military Academy at West Point in 1860. The following year, he was involved in an incident that nearly ended the military career of George Armstrong Custer. On June 29, 1861, Custer was appointed officer of the day while awaiting assignment. Cadet Ludlow and another cadet taunted a plebe named Peter Ryerson, who called Ludlow a coward. Ludlow punched Ryerson, and a fight ensued. Rather than break up the fight in accord with regulations, Custer called out, "Stand back boys, let's have a fair fight." Two officers appeared, and Custer was subsequently placed under arrest. Ludlow testified at Custer's court-martial that the fight had been simply an insignificant "scuffle." Custer was found guilty but—likely because the Union needed every available officer—was only reprimanded.

Upon his 1864 graduation from West Point, Ludlow became chief engineer, XX Army Corps. In July 1864, he won the brevet of captain for his actions during the battle of Peach Tree Creek, Georgia. He participated in the siege and capture

📖 "The Celebrated Peace Policy of General Grant," by Robert M. Utley, *North Dakota History* 20 (July 1953); "Indian Fighters and Indian Reformers: Grant's Indian Peace Policy and the Conservative Consensus," by Richard R. Levine, *Civil War History* 31, no. 4 (December 1985); "The Argument over Civilian or Military Indian Control, 1865–1880," by J. D'Elia, *The Historian* 24 (February 1962); and *The Military and United States Indian Policy, 1865–1903,* by Robert Wooster (New Haven, CT: Yale University Press, 1988).

🐎 The Lakota Sioux and the Black Hills

The white man was engaged in fighting his war to gain independence from England when a small band of Lakota Sioux led by warrior Standing Bear—prompted by their nomadic instinct—had walked from their homeland in Minnesota to visit for the first time the Black Hills, a wilderness region along the South Dakota–Wyoming border that runs roughly 100 miles north to south and 60 miles east to west.

The members of Standing Bear's Lakota Sioux hunting party were not by any means the first American Indians to view the Black Hills, for its dominion had been the matter of contention among a number of tribes for centuries. These particular explorers, however, regarded their discovery as if it had been preordained by their Creator. There was apparently an awakening within their souls that spoke to tell them that the innate spirits that dwelled within the Black Hills had reserved that place for them—as if some mystical magnet was calling home those who had wandered for so long. Although other tribes may have discovered this place before them, the Lakota were the first to speak of it as sacred land.

Standing Bear returned home from his trek and spoke in glowing terms about his wondrous discovery. His assessment of the Black Hills affected his people with such a seductive force that they abandoned the North and journeyed en masse to that unknown territory to establish a homeland for the Lakota Sioux Nation. The Dakota and Nakota remained in Minnesota.

The emigrating Lakota Sioux declined to settle permanently inside the boundaries of the Black Hills, on what they considered sacred land. For three-quarters of a century, they rarely made camp out of sight of this place they now called Paha Sapa—"Hills That Are Black"—entering only to hunt, cut lodgepoles, hide out after raiding parties, or perform ceremonies.

The seven principal Lakota Sioux bands—the Blackfeet, Brule, Hunkpapa, Minniconjou, Oglala, Sans Arc, and Two Kettle—thus became the final group of Indians to arrive in that part of the country (see "The Seven Principal Lakota Sioux Bands" on page 154). Each autonomous band established its own territory throughout Montana, Wyoming, Kansas, Nebraska, and

(continued on following page)

Custer's Camp along French Creek where gold was discovered, July 1874. *Courtesy Little Bighorn Battlefield National Monument.*

the Dakota Territory, but together the Lakota enjoyed greater numbers than their rivals due to a supportive alliance and became the strongest tribe on the Great Plains. They used force to acquire proprietorship of the area from the Cheyenne, who years earlier had pushed aside the Comanche, who themselves still earlier had pushed aside the Crow.

The Fort Laramie Treaty of 1868 (see "The Fort Laramie Treaty of 1868 and the Black Hills Expedition" on page 158), which ended Red Cloud's War (see "Red Cloud's War" on page 68), included the Black Hills within the boundaries of the Great Sioux Reservation. The Panic of 1873, however, compelled the U.S. government to view the Black Hills in terms of its valuable resources. Public outcry for admittance to this forbidden territory became overwhelming following Custer's 1874 Black Hills expedition. It was reasoned that the Sioux were not settled within the hills, and the area should therefore be opened to settlers, miners, loggers, and any other practical purpose.

The government began making overtures toward the Lakota Sioux to sell the Black Hills, and that was the beginning of the end. In a series of unscrupulous actions by the U.S. government, which led to the Great Sioux War of 1876–77, ownership of Paha Sapa, the sacred Black Hills, was removed from the Lakota Sioux.

The U.S. Supreme Court ordered in 1980 that the Lakota be compensated for the loss of their land, but the tribe has refused to accept nothing less than the land itself.

The Black Hills region has become a popular tourist destination and recreation area, featuring such attractions as Mount

of Atlanta and the remainder of the Georgia and Carolinas campaigns, breveted major in December 1864 and lieutenant colonel in March 1865—quite a remarkable record for a young man not yet one year removed from West Point.

Ludlow married Genevieve Almira Sprigg of St. Louis in 1866. The couple had one daughter.

In March 1867, Ludlow was commissioned a captain and served as assistant to the chief of engineers, stationed at Staten Island and Charleston, South Carolina. In late 1872, he became chief engineer of the Department of the Dakotas. The following year, Ludlow surveyed what would later become Yellowstone National Park.

Ludlow accompanied Custer's Black Hills expedition of 1874 as chief engineer, responsible for mapping the route. From all accounts, Ludlow, although aligned with the bug hunters, was respected by the 7th Cavalry officers, many of whom he had met the preceding summer, on account of his previous military service.

Custer held no grudge or hard feelings toward Ludlow for the earlier episode at West Point. In a

(continued on following page)

letter to wife Libbie on July 15, he mentioned that "Col. Ludlow is a great favorite." Ludlow was a frequent guest for various social functions at Custer's huge headquarters tent. On July 23, Ludlow, Custer, botanist A. B. Donaldson, and several others climbed to the 6,500-foot summit of Inyan Kara Mountain. Ludlow with hammer and chisel created a monument by etching into a rock '74 CUSTER. Ludlow also accompanied Custer in climbing the 7,200-foot Harney Peak, the highest in the Black Hills. He witnessed Custer killing his first grizzly—and may have contributed to its death—then posed with the general for the famous picture. Ludlow had a hand in hiring a number of participants for the expedition, including photographer William H. Illingworth.

Ludlow remarked in his report that the Black Hills region was "admirably adapted to settlement," but he qualified that statement by saying, "It is probable that the best use to be made of the Black Hills for the next 50 years would be as the permanent reservation of the Sioux." It was his opinion that the region was cherished by the tribe, and that any occupation by whites would be met with aggression. He admitted that gold had been discovered but deferred to the scientists to predict whether prospectors would locate it in paying quantities.

Ludlow made another surveying trip to the Yellowstone area in 1875, then returned east. It has been widely written that Ludlow happened upon Custer in May 1876 on a street in Washington. Custer at that time told Ludlow that during the upcoming Little Bighorn campaign, he would "cut loose and make [his] operations independent of General Terry" in the same manner as he had from Gen. David Stanley in 1873. Custer marched from Fort Abraham Lincoln a week later.

Ludlow meanwhile became involved in river and harbor work in Philadelphia and was promoted to major in June 1880. He served as engineer secretary of the Light House Board in Washington until March 1883. At that time, Ludlow was hired as chief engineer of the Philadelphia water department, responsible for rejuvenating the city's inadequate water system. He held that position until 1886, when the president appointed him engineer commissioner of the District of Columbia, where he accomplished the same task as in Philadelphia. Ludlow was military attaché to London from 1893 to 1896, during

Rushmore, the Crazy Horse Memorial, Custer State Park, and the historic gambling town of Deadwood, South Dakota.

📖 Excellent sources for the arrival and domination of the Lakota Sioux in the Black Hills area can be found in *Red Cloud's Folk: A History of the Oglala Sioux Indians,* by George E. Hyde (Norman: University of Oklahoma Press, 1937); *Spotted Tail's Folk: A History of the Brule Sioux,* by George E. Hyde (Norman: University of Oklahoma Press, 1957); *The Sioux: Life and Times of a Warrior Society,* by Royal B. Hassrick (Norman: University of Oklahoma Press, 1964); and "The Intertribal Balance of Power on the Great Plains, 1760–1850," by Colin G. Calloway, *Journal of American Studies* 16 (1982). The best source for the complete history of the fight over the Black Hills by the Lakota Sioux is *Black Hills/White Justice: The Sioux Nation versus the United States, 1775 to the Present,* by Edward Lazarus (New York: HarperCollins, 1991).

🐎 The Seven Principal Lakota Sioux Bands

Blackfeet (Sihasapa). This band, which should not be confused with the Blackfoot tribe to the north, related to the eastern Algonquins, was said to have received its name because its members wore black moccasins, perhaps discolored by camping near ashes and soot. Another story, told by Standing Rock Agency agent James McLaughlin, centers around a family who arrived in camp with blackened feet after walking through a burnt prairie. Notable chiefs or war leaders included Kill Eagle and Scabby Head.

Brule. Fire also played a part in the naming of this band. Several people were burned to death in a prairie fire sometime during the mid-1700s, and others escaped by jumping into a lake but emerged with burnt legs and backsides. This disfigurement apparently caused them to be called Cu Brule, roughly meaning "Burnt Buttocks." Notable chiefs or war leaders included Crazy Bull and Crow Dog.

Hunkpapa (Unkpapa, Uncpapa). Roughly translated, Hunkpapa means an edge or border, or "They Camp by Themselves," which apparently was why this band traditionally camped near the entrance to a village. Notable chiefs and war leaders included Sitting Bull, Gall, Rain-in-the-Face, Crow King, Black Moon, Buffalo Calf Moon, and Knife Chief.

Minniconjou. The rough translation of the name of this band means "People Who Planted Crops beside Water." At some point in time, this tribe imitated the lifestyle of their Arikara neighbors and attempted to become farmers, but they soon realized that they were not suited for agriculture. Notable chiefs and war leaders included Big Foot, White Bull, Hump, Iron Plume (American Horse), Fast Bull, and Black Shield.

(continued on following page)

Oglala. This band's name apparently means scattered or divided, perhaps because of their ostracism during the 1700s due to their notion to raise crops, which was contemptuous to other tribes, who called them "dust-scatters." Notable chiefs and war leaders included Red Cloud, Crazy Horse (half Brule), Pawnee Killer, Black Elk, One Stab, He Dog, Big Man, Big Road, Black Twin, and Low Dog.

Sans Arc. This band, known as "Those without Bow" or "No Bows," were at first thought to possess great powers and were consulted on matters of importance. Then, at some point, they set aside their weapons at the behest of a hermaphroditic (bisexual) prophet while he contemplated and were subsequently caught unarmed and massacred by an enemy war party. Foolish people were then called "Sans Arc" in memory of this act, which was quite humorous to the Sioux. Notable chiefs or war leaders included Old Eagle, Two Eagles, Fast Bear, High Elk, Red Bear, Black Eagle, and Spotted Eagle.

Two Kettle (Oo-hen-on-pa). This band's name was apparently derived from "Two Cookings," for the fact that their hunters bragged that they could provide meat enough for two meals from one hunting trip. A notable war leader was Runs the Enemy.

🦌 The Journal of Pvt. Theodore Ewert

Theodore Ewert was born in 1847 in Prussia. He immigrated with his family to Chicago in 1857. He enlisted in the cavalry at age fourteen and eventually served as an artillery second lieutenant near the end of the Civil War. He was a member of the 36th Infantry from 1867 until his discharge as a corporal two years later. Ewert subsequently enlisted in 1871 as a private in the 7th Cavalry.

Ewert is notable for the journal he kept during the Black Hills expedition of 1874 while serving as Custer's orderly trumpeter. His record of events provides interesting and relevant information not available in official reports or articles submitted by correspondents. His descriptions of the daily routine include amusing observations and complaints that have been expressed by enlisted men throughout military history. He also had the freedom to state opinions that may have been contrary to those of his superiors, the public, and the mainstream press.

He apparently maintained a low opinion of Custer, whom he believed was seeking a "star" with "fresh laurels" gained from the expedition. His view evidently associated Custer with higher authority, of which he wrote: "The United States Government forgot its honor, forgot the sacred treaty in force between itself and the Dakota Sioux, forgot its integrity, and ordered the organization of an Expedition for the invasion of the Black Hills."

which time he inspected the Suez, Keil, Corinth, and other deep-water canals. He was promoted to lieutenant colonel in April 1895 and two years later was placed in charge of improvements in the New York Harbor.

Ludlow was appointed brigadier general of volunteers in May 1898 at the outbreak of war with Spain. He commanded the 1st Brigade of the V Corps in Santiago-de-Cuba. In September 1898, he was commissioned major general of volunteers for his meritorious service, and in December, he was made military governor of Cuba. He became president of the Army War College in 1900 and embarked that summer on an inspection tour of training methods in France and Germany.

In April 1901, Ludlow was ordered to duty in the Philippines, but he was taken ill and died on August 30 at the home of his daughter in Convent Station, New Jersey. He was buried with full military honors at Islip. His ashes were later removed to Arlington National Cemetery.

———◆◆◆———

"I am more than ever convinced of the influence a commanding officer exercizes [sic] for good or ill. There has not been a single card party, not a single drunken officer, since we left Ft. Lincoln. But I know that did I play cards and invite the officers to join there would be playing every night."

—CUSTER TO LIBBIE, JULY 1874

———◆◆◆———

📖 Ludlow's official report, *Report of a Reconnaissance of the Black Hills of Dakota,* was published by the Government Printing Office in 1875. His preliminary report was published in the *Annual Report* of the Chief of Engineers, 1874, as well as in several other publications, including the September 14, 1874, edition of the *New York Tribune* and the *Army and Navy Journal* on September 19. Ludlow's May 1876 meeting with Custer can be found in *Custer's Luck,* by Edgar I. Stewart (Norman: University of Oklahoma Press, 1955).

BIOGRAPHIES

✴ Luther Heddon North
Scout and Plainsman

Luther North was born on March 6, 1846, in Richland County, Ohio. He moved to Omaha at age ten. Luther tagged along with his older brother, Frank, as the elder North worked at clearing land for new settlers and hauling freight, which by 1861 brought them to the Pawnee reservation near Columbus, Nebraska. In 1863, North enlisted in the 2nd Nebraska Cavalry and accompanied Gen. Alfred Sully's Sioux expedition in Minnesota. The following year, he hauled freight between Columbus and Fort Kearny, then signed on to scout for the army—nearly losing his life in a skirmish with the Sioux.

In 1866, North joined his brother on a scout with the Pawnee Battalion; the following year, he became captain of one of its companies. The Pawnee scouts were involved in numerous battles and skirmishes over the ensuing years, including the battle of Summit Springs in July 1869, which ended Cheyenne hostilities on the southern plains (see "The Battle of Summit Springs" on page 101). North then guided Easterners on hunts throughout the West, and in the fall of 1873, he headed a fossil-collecting expedition east of Greeley, Colorado.

In 1874, North participated in George Armstrong Custer's Black Hills expedition as an assistant zoologist to George B. Grinnell, his way paid for by Yale University. He had worked as a guide for Grinnell on a buffalo hunt in 1872 but had no training whatsoever in zoology. His primary responsibility was to serve as Grinnell's guide and assist in collecting specimens.

After the June 1876 Little Bighorn battle, North once again joined his brother's Pawnee Battalion and served with Gen. George Crook, taking part in Ranald Mackenzie's November 1876 fight with Dull Knife's Cheyenne. He was mustered out of service with his brother and the battalion in May 1877.

The North brothers at that time entered into a partnership with William F. "Buffalo Bill" Cody to run a cattle ranch northwest of North Platte, Nebraska. Luther eventually relocated to the Black Hills of South Dakota and was involved in ranching and farming in that region until 1890, when he moved to Omaha, where he worked as a deputy collector for the Internal Revenue Service. In 1898, he married Elvira S. Coolidge. The couple, who had no children, moved to Columbus, Nebraska, in 1917, where Luther died on April 18, 1935.

📖 Luther North's relationship with George B. Grinnell remained close through the years. Grin-

(continued on following page)

Ewert's attitude toward Indian policy was extremely bitter, however.

> How is it that many red murderers are not punished according to our laws? How is it that the Sioux chief "Red Cloud," the cause, author and instigator of the Fort Phil Kearny massacre, is received at, and allowed to go about, certain frontier posts without being apprehended?

He blamed this on the "Almighty Dollar" that Indian agents would lose "were every red scamp punished."

He resented, as soldiers have for eternity, the privileges afforded officers. In one instance, he complained:

> The men raised no tents, as it was near midnight ere the horses were fed and groomed and the men got their supper, but the Officers, oh these gentlemen, they could not sleep these few hours without having their large wall-tents pitched, they did not have to put them up and the poor men, well what does an Officer care how tired or worn out, or even how ill a man is, their imperial will would at all times, have to be obeyed, humanity is something that is foreign to their feelings and a little kindness is but seldom or never shown to one of the rank and file.

That basic sentiment was echoed on another occasion, when he wrote:

> You may ask "Did the Officers stand exposed to these storms and rains as well as the rank and file?" I answer emphatically, No! As soon as a storm was seen approaching, four, six or eight men were called upon to stretch the Captains or Lieutenants tent, and as soon as the first pins were driven these would step inside dry and comfortable, while poor Pat, Hans, or Dick could stand in the storm and finish driving the pins, and then, already wet through and through, he could go and pitch his own little dog-tent, under which he would be shelter'd hardly better than under the sky.

Ewert assumed a novelist's approach when describing the funeral service for Pvt. James King, who had taken ill and died.

> In the grey twilight of morning, the men with bowed heads, tears trickling down the sunburnt cheeks, the dead body suspended over the grave, the Captain [Benteen] with his grey hair reading the service, the silence, all are impressed on my memory never to be erased.

Ewert evidently was a fan of baseball and not only mentioned a game in his journal, but also wrote an insightful commentary about the Benteen Base Ball Club for a local newspaper in early 1876 (see "The Benteen Base Ball Club" on page 157). He was discharged from the army on April 10, 1876, and therefore did not march with the 7th Cavalry to the Little Bighorn.

📖 *Private Theodore Ewert's Diary of the Black Hills Expedition of 1874,* edited by John M. Carroll and Lawrence A. Frost (Piscataway, NJ: CRI Books, 1976). Many extracts from Ewert's journal can be found in *Custer's Gold: The United States Cavalry Expedition of 1874,* by Donald Jackson (New Haven, CT: Yale University Press, 1966).

The Benteen Base Ball Club

The Benteen Base Ball Club was an athletic organization composed of 7th Cavalry enlisted men that played competitive baseball against both civilian and military teams in Dakota Territory between 1873 and 1876.

Theodore Ewert, whose journal provided much information about the Black Hills expedition (see "The Journal of Pvt. Theodore Ewert" on page 155), wrote of the origins of the club in a letter that appeared in the February 25, 1876, Yankton *Press and Dakotaian:*

> On the first day of March, 1873, "H" company, seventh cavalry, stationed at Nashville, Tennessee, resolved to organize a club with the view of having games, sports and exercises to be known as the "Benteen base ball and gymnasium club" (in honor of our company commander, captain F. W. Benteen, Brevet Colonel U.S.A.).

Fifty-four men signed up for the club, Ewert stated, and a variety of athletic and recreational items were purchased, including "one-and-a-half dozen base ball bats and one dozen base balls." Ewert went on to write, "By continuous and strenuous effort the base ball club was practiced and exercised till our captain [Joseph McCurry] believed us able to compete with the average amateur 'nines' then in the league."

Ewert added thumbnail sketches of the team's starting lineup that showed an intimate knowledge of the players, in both talent and disposition. An extract:

> JOSEPH McCURRY—captain and pitcher of the nine. Delivers a swift and correct ball, generally to suit the batter, is a sure baserunner, briskly if it pays, earns his runs, and is a gentlemanly player withal. He is undoubtedly the stay and prop of the club, is also the best player.

> WILLIAM DAVIS—third base, a sure catch, poor thrower, fair at the bat, slow runner, and he has the worst fault imaginable, wishing to play "fancy," thereby weakening his already very weak place.

> CHARLES H. BISHOP—plays remarkably fine game anywhere, though needing continually the sharp eye of the captain, not being exactly lazy, but born woefully tired. He is one of the best in the nine, heavy hitter with the willow, tricky base runner, and an aggravating sure catcher.

> ALONZO PLUMB—right field, the "funnyman," don't profess to play base ball, but thinks he can keep the "nine" in a good humorous vein, thus in a good working condition.

Ewert noted in his Black Hills journal one particular game that was played on July 31, 1874, during the expedition. The

nell's *Two Great Scouts and Their Pawnee Battalion* (Lincoln: University of Nebraska Press, 1973) is a glowing account of the North brothers, but it unfortunately contains many inaccuracies. Also notable are *Man of the Plains: Recollections of Luther North, 1856–1882,* edited by Donald F. Danker (Lincoln: University of Nebraska Press, 1961); *The Fighting Norths and Pawnee Scouts,* by Robert Bruce (New York: Brooklyn Eagle Press, 1932); *The Lives and Legends of Buffalo Bill,* by Don Russell (Norman: University of Oklahoma Press, 1973); and "Interview with Luther H. North, April 21, 1917," in *Camp on Custer,* edited by Bruce R. Liddic and Paul Harbaugh (Spokane: A. H. Clark Co., 1995).

Charles Alexander Reynolds
Scout

Scout "Lonesome Charley" Reynolds, 1874. *Courtesy Little Bighorn Battlefield National Monument.*

"Lonesome Charley" Reynolds was most likely born on a farm near Stephensburg, Hardin County, Kentucky, on March 20, 1842, although some accounts question that date and note the place of his birth as Warren County, Illinois. His father, a farmer and physician, moved the family at some point to Abington, Illinois—where Reynolds attended Abington College—and in 1859 to Pardee, Atchison County, Kansas. In 1860, Reynolds heeded the call "Pikes Peak or Bust" and headed west on a wagon train to the Colorado goldfields. The emigrant train was attacked and looted by Cheyenne. The survivors fled to Fort Kearny, where Reynolds joined a mountain man to run a trap line along the Platte.

(continued on following page)

In July 1861, he returned home and enlisted in Company E, 10th Kansas Infantry. He served primarily on border duty in Missouri and Kansas, participating in the battle of Prairie Grove, then on escort duty along the Santa Fe Trail to Fort Union, Mexico. One account states that Reynolds scouted against Confederate general Sterling Price on what became known as Price's Missouri Raid in the fall of 1864. If so, he would have been a civilian—he was mustered out of the service in August 1864 at Fort Leavenworth, prior to Price's October raid.

In 1865, Reynolds decided to establish a trading venture in New Mexico, but the enterprise ended when his partner was killed by Cheyenne on Rabbit Ears Creek in southwestern Kansas. Reynolds wintered in Santa Fe—reportedly having a failed romance with a Mexican girl—then embarked on several years as a buffalo hunter on the Republican River, furnishing game for military posts. During the winter of 1866–67, he shot and wounded a drunk and abusive army officer from Fort McPherson at Jack Morrow's ranch on the Platte. Reynolds then traveled to Dakota Territory on the upper Missouri to hunt and trap; he became known to the local Indians around Fort Rice as "White Hunter Who Never Goes Out for Nothing." His initial work as a scout for the army came when he hired on for Col. David Stanley's Yellowstone expedition of 1872.

Reynolds by this time not only was familiar with the territory, but also understood the Sioux tongue and Indian sign language. He was said to be quite reticent of speech and by nature reserved, hence the nickname "Lonesome Charley." He was never heard to brag about his exploits, but he was highly regarded by both Indians and whites for his skill as a hunter, courage, endurance, and resourcefulness. He preferred to spend his free time hunting alone or in a small party rather than frequenting bars or playing cards. These traits and extraordinary talents elevated him to the highest level of Western scouts.

Reynolds first became acquainted with George Armstrong Custer when he was engaged as a scout for Stanley's Yellowstone expedition of 1873. The well-educated Reynolds had a lot in common with Custer, including interests in geology, zoology, and reading—not to mention hunting—and neither man drank or smoked. On August 19, Reynolds and another scout, Gilman Norris, were dispatched by Colonel Stanley to carry orders requesting boat transportation as well as to provide an escort for two Englishmen to Fort Benton.

(continued on following page)

Actives of Fort Lincoln, chosen from members of the regimental band and right wing, beat the Athletes of Fort Rice, composed of men from Companies C, H, and K, by a score of 11 to 6. It was alleged, however, that the umpire, whom Ewert identifies as "Mr. Tenpenny, Vetinary Surgeon," favored the Fort Lincoln team.

The chronicle of the Benteen Base Ball Club for the years 1875–76 can be attributed to T. O. Dore, another 7th Cavalry enlisted man, who evidently acted as a "stringer" for the Yankton *Press and Dakotaian* newspaper. In a series of colorfully written articles, Dore reported on games played at various forts and against a civilian team in Yankton, where in May 1875, the 7th Cavalry's "McDougall nine" defeated the Yanktons 24 to 17, although the loss could be attributed to the fact that one of Yankton's "best men was sick and could not do himself justice."

The activities of the club were drastically curtailed after the battle of the Little Bighorn, due in part to the escalated campaign against the Indians and perhaps on account of casualties. First Sgt. Joseph McCurry, who is also notable as the likely author of the Enlisted Men's Petition (see "The Enlisted Men's Petition" on page 242), was wounded in the left shoulder. Cpl. Alexander B. Bishop and Pvt. Charles H. Bishop both suffered wounds in the right arm. Pvt. William C. Williams was wounded in the left leg, but apparently not badly enough to be evacuated. Pvt. William Davis, riding with Company E in Custer's column, was killed.

📖 Additional information and specific dates for a number of Dore's articles in the Yankton *Press and Dakotaian* can be found in "The Benteen Base Ball Club: Sports Enthusiasts of the Seventh Cavalry," by Harry H. Anderson, *Montana, the Magazine of Western History* 20, no. 3 (Summer 1970).

🐎 The Fort Laramie Treaty of 1868 and the Black Hills Expedition

This treaty of April 29, 1868, negotiated between U.S. commissioners and the chiefs and subchiefs of various bands of the Sioux Nation at Fort Laramie, Wyoming, ended hostilities over the Bozeman Trail known as Red Cloud's War (see "Red Cloud's War" on page 68). More than 200 Sioux signed the treaty at Fort Rice on July 2, but Red Cloud waited until November 6—after army forts along the Bozeman had been burned to the ground. The treaty was ratified by the U.S. Congress on February 24, 1869.

Basic provisions of the treaty called for the U.S. Army to abandon Forts Phil Kearny, Reno, and C. F. Smith; establish a

Sioux reservation, which would encompass nearly all of present-day South Dakota west of the Missouri River, including the region known as the Black Hills; grant hunting rights to certain areas; and provide buildings, medical care, education, seeds and agricultural supplies, money, and support personnel. In return, the Sioux agreed to withdraw all opposition to the construction of railroads not passing through their reservation and to cease attacks against white travelers and settlers.

The treaty represented a victory for the Sioux, and a majority of the tribe—about 15,000—settled on the reservation, where they would gradually become dependent on government rations.

Sioux leaders Sitting Bull, Crazy Horse, and Gall—all of whom had not "touched the pen" to the treaty—refused to report to the reservation and found a haven in the unceded territory, considered traditional buffalo hunting grounds, designated in the treaty. This area, which was roughly east of the Bighorn Mountains and north of the North Platte River (known as the Powder River Basin), had been reserved for Indians only. In summer months, other Indians would leave the reservation to join bands of their "free" kinsmen in the unceded territory to live the old way of life. This land separate from the reservation would later pose a problem with respect to exact boundaries—and by the presence of Indians hostile to whites.

In 1874, there was vocal opposition when an expedition into the Black Hills region was proposed by the military. According to the Fort Laramie Treaty, it was argued, the Sioux Reservation was strictly off-limits to whites. Therefore, a reconnaissance through this area would constitute a violation.

The army position on the legality of the Black Hills expedition was summed up by Gen. Alfred H. Terry, a member of the treaty commission, who wrote in a letter to Gen. Phil Sheridan:

> I am unable to see that any just offense is given to the Indians by the expedition to the Black Hills. From the earliest times the government has exercised the right of sending exploring parties of a military character into unceded territory, and this expedition is nothing more.

Terry backed up his interpretation by stating his belief that provisions in the treaty never intended to exclude military forces, and he was certain that the Indians understood that as well.

Gen. William T. Sherman concurred and wrote in his endorsement of Terry's statement: "I also was one of the commissioners to the treaty of 1868, and agree with General

Fort Laramie Treaty of 1868 negotiations. Commissioner Gen. Alfred Terry, second from right. Gen. William T. Sherman, fifth from right. *Courtesy Little Bighorn Battlefield National Monument.*

Stanley's orders stated, "They will each be paid ($100) One Hundred Dollars for the trip." The two scouts swiftly and safely traversed the 150 miles from the Musselshell River to Fort Benton.

In 1874, Reynolds hired on as a scout for Custer's Black Hills expedition. On August 2, he was entrusted with Custer's message that told about the discovery of gold. Reynolds traveled over 100 miles alone though hostile territory to Sioux City to deliver the message (see "The Midnight Ride of Charley Reynolds" on page 169).

Reynolds happened to be visiting Standing Rock Agency in December 1874, when he overheard Sioux warrior Rain-in-the-Face brag about killing two men from Custer's command on the Yellowstone during the summer of 1873. The scout informed Custer, who sent a detail that included his brother Tom and Reynolds to arrest the warrior for the murders. The alleged revenge of Rain-in-the-Face created a controversy that continues to this day (see "The Arrest and Revenge of Rain-in-the-Face" on page 129).

In 1875, Reynolds was chief scout and hunter for Capt. William Ludlow's expedition into Yellowstone Park and Judith Basin.

On April 3, 1876, Reynolds was employed as a civilian guide for the Little Bighorn campaign by the 7th Cavalry quartermaster, with monthly pay set at $100. On June 25, the morning of the

(continued on following page)

famous battle, he was one of the scouts who visited the promontory known as Crow's Nest, and he pointed out to Custer what he believed was the biggest Indian village he had ever seen. Reynolds, who was suffering from an infected hand, had a premonition that he was going to die that day and gave away all of his possessions. He was a member of Reno's detachment that charged down the valley toward the village and subsequently retreated to take refuge in the timber near the Little Bighorn. Reynolds was one of the last to leave the timber when Reno's troops commenced an every-man-for-himself dash for the bluffs across the river. His horse was shot out from under him, and he made a gallant stand either pinned under his mount or using the animal for breastworks before eventually being killed. One report—likely an exaggeration—states that fifty-eight spent cartridge shells were found near his body.

Reynolds, who never married, was buried in grave no. 260 on the field. The August 27, 1877, edition of the *Bismarck Tribune* reported that Col.

(continued on following page)

Terry, that it was not intended to exclude the United States from exploring the Reservation for Roads, or for any other national purpose."

An extract from Article II of the treaty, which, for the most part, concerned the establishment of precise boundaries of the Great Sioux Reservation, states:

> The United States now solemnly agrees that no persons except those herein designated and authorized so to do, and except such officers, agents, and employees of the government as may be authorized to enter upon Indian reservations in discharge of duties enjoined by law, shall ever be permitted to pass over, settle upon, or reside in the territory described in this article.

It would appear from the above wording that by splitting legal hairs, it could be interpreted to favor the military with its belief that a military expedition through the Black Hills was within its rights.

The Indians, however, thought otherwise and would dub Custer's route through the Black Hills the "Thieves' Road." This intrusion onto sacred land would not be the primary reason that the Sioux would go on the warpath in the future, but it served as an additional insult, another threat that they

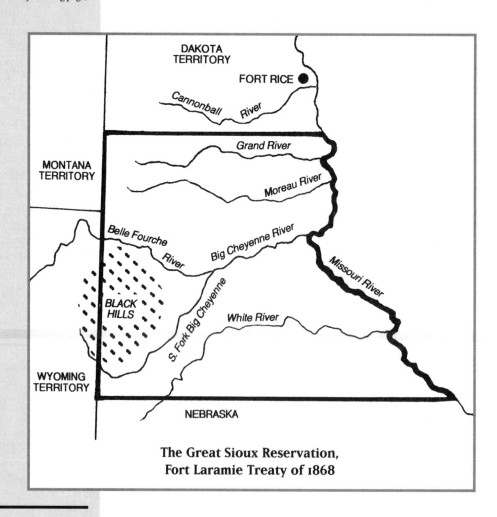

The Great Sioux Reservation, Fort Laramie Treaty of 1868

could lose more of their land and culture—regardless of treaty provisions.

📖 Text of the Fort Laramie Treaty of 1868 (from *U.S. Statutes at Large* 15, pp. 635–40) can be found in *Custer's Gold: The United States Cavalry Expedition of 1874,* by Donald Jackson (New Haven, CT: Yale University Press, 1966); and in *Indian Affairs: Laws and Treaties,* vol. 2, compiled by Charles J. Kappler (Washington, DC: Government Printing Office, 1904–41). An excellent account of the treaty and its aftermath, based on Indian and white sources, is *Red Cloud and the Sioux Problem,* by James C. Olson (Lincoln: University of Nebraska Press, 1965).

Also see *Fort Laramie in 1876: Chronicle of a Frontier Post at War,* by Paul L. Hedren (Lincoln: University of Nebraska Press, 1988); *Phil Sheridan and His Army,* by Paul A. Hutton (Lincoln: University of Nebraska Press, 1985); and *Frontier Regulars: The United States Army and the Indian, 1866–1890,* by Robert M. Utley (New York: Macmillan Publishing Co., 1973).

🐎 Military Forts on the Northern Plains

FORT ABERCROMBIE, DAKOTA TERRITORY

Established in August 1857, this fort, located on the left bank of the Red River about thirty-two miles south of Fargo, was the first permanent military post in Dakota Territory. Fort Abercrombie had originally been built in the traditional manner, without a stockade, but after 2nd U.S. Infantry troops commanded by Lt. Col. John J. Abercrombie—for whom the fort was named—were pinned down for five weeks during the Sioux uprising of 1862, ten acres were enclosed as soon as reinforcements arrived.

The fort was called the "Gateway to the Dakotas" for settlers heading to the Northwest. To the rank and file, however, the fort became known as the "Armpit of the Dakotas," a most undesirable duty station. The wagon trains and mule teams that accompanied the Yellowstone expedition of 1873 were assembled at this location. Maj. Marcus A. Reno was assigned duty at the fort, and in 1877, he faced a court-martial and was convicted of making improper advances toward a woman. The buildings were sold when Fort Abercrombie was abandoned on October 23, 1878. The fort has been partially rebuilt and is presently owned by the North Dakota State Historical Society.

📖 "Fort Abercrombie, 1857–1877," by Thomas Forsyth, *Collections of the State Historical Society of North Dakota* 2, part 2 (1908); "Fort Abercrombie," by Linda W. Slaughter, *Collections of the State Historical Society of North Dakota* 1 (1906), pp. 412–23.

P. W. Norris, a friend who was superintendent of Yellowstone National Park, removed the remains of Reynolds from the field and apparently had them reinterred in his family plot at Norris, a suburb of Detroit. Reynolds Island on the Missouri River was named in his honor.

An enduring tribute to Reynolds by Libbie Custer is in her *"Boots and Saddles"; or, Life in Dakota with General Custer* (New York: Harper & Brothers, 1913). She wrote, in part, of Reynolds:

"My darling Sunbeam—I cannot tell you how hard and earnestly I have worked to make this expedition a success. I have been, not only Commanding Officer, but also guide among other things. I have the proud satisfaction of knowing that our explorations have exceeded the most sanguine expectations."

—CUSTER TO LIBBIE, AUGUST 1874

My husband had such genuine admiration for him that I soon learned to listen to everything pertaining to his life with marked interest. He was so shy that he hardly raised his eyes when I extended my hand at the General's introduction. He did not assume the picturesque dress, long hair, belt full of weapons that are characteristic of the scout. His manner was perfectly simple and straightforward, and he would not be induced to talk of himself. He had large, dark blue eyes, and a frank face.

📖 Reynolds's diary, with entries from May 17 to June 22, 1876, is in the archives of the Minnesota State Historical Society, St. Paul. The text of the diary can be found in Mike Koury's *Diaries of the Little Big Horn* (Fort Collins, CO: Old Army Press, 1968). Notable books and articles about Reynolds include the definitive biography *Charley Reynolds: Soldier, Hunter, Scout and Guide,* by John E. and George J. Remsburg (Kansas City, MO: H. M. Sender Co., 1931); *Recollections of Charley Reynolds:* "The Return of a War Party: Reminiscences of Charley Reynolds," by George B. Grinnell, *Forest & Stream Magazine,* December 26, 1896, and January 30, 1897; "Charley Reynolds, Hunter

(continued on following page)

BIOGRAPHIES

& Scout," by E. A. Brininstool, *North Dakota Historical Quarterly* (July 1930); "Charley Reynolds Honored" and "A Trooper with Custer," *Winners of the West,* November 1938 and June 1941; "On the Trail of Lonesome Charley Reynolds" by John S. Gray, *Chicago Westerners Brand Book* 16, no. 8 (1959); and Gray's "Last Rites for Lonesome Charley Reynolds," *Montana* 13, no. 3 (July 1963).

✹ Spotted Tail
Brule Sioux Chieftain

Spotted Tail (Sinte Gleska) was born in the winter of 1823–24, either near Fort Laramie, Wyoming Territory, or along the White River in present-day South Dakota. He was known as Jumping Buffalo as a youth and received the name Spotted Tail when a trapper gave him a striped raccoon pelt. He quickly established himself as a notable warrior in battle with his tribe's traditional enemy, the Pawnee, and by age thirty was chosen as a "Shirt Wearer," or war chief. In 1854, Spotted Tail participated in the Grattan incident, and the following year, he defended his tribe's territory at Ash Hollow against Gen. William S. Harney (see "The Initiation of Warfare between the Plains Indians and the U.S. Army" on page 49). Subsequently, word

(continued on following page)

FORT ABRAHAM LINCOLN, DAKOTA TERRITORY

This fort was established on June 14, 1872, by Lt. Col. Daniel Huston, 6th Infantry, at a location three miles from Bismarck on the west bank of the Missouri River at the mouth of the Heart River. It was originally named Fort McKean in honor of Col. Henry McKean, who was killed in the Civil War battle of Cold Harbor, but was renamed on November 19, 1872, in honor of the assassinated president. The fort was established to garrison troops whose duty was to protect workers on the Northern Pacific Railroad. Custer and his 7th Cavalry were assigned to the fort on September 23, 1873, upon their return from the Yellowstone expedition of 1873.

The fort had been built with three barracks that could house six cavalry companies, seven officers' quarters, various storehouses, six stables that could accommodate 600 horses, and the other necessities—including a guardhouse. One portion of the post, located on the level river plain near the mouth of the Heart River, was reserved for infantry. The Custer residence burned to the ground in February 1874, when insulation in the attic caught fire, but a new home for the commanding officer was immediately put under construction. Custer and ten troops of the 7th Cavalry marched from the fort on July 2, 1874, on the Black Hills expedition and returned on August 30. On May 17, 1876, Custer and his command departed the

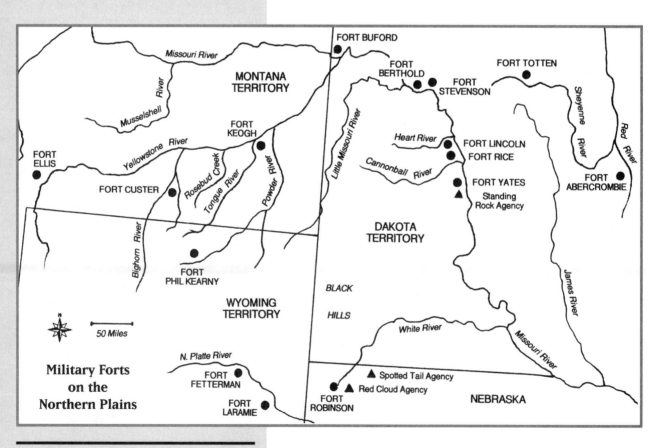

Military Forts on the Northern Plains

fort to march to the Valley of the Little Bighorn. Fort Lincoln was abandoned on July 22, 1891, and has been partially restored as part of Fort Lincoln State Park.

📖 An interesting perspective of army life at Fort Abraham Lincoln can be found in Libbie Custer's *"Boots and Saddles"; or, Life in Dakota with General Custer* (New York: Harper and Brothers, 1885). Also see "The Historical Significance of Ft. Lincoln State Park," by A. O. Goplen, *North Dakota History* 13, no. 4 (October 1946).

FORT BERTHOLD INDIAN AGENCY, DAKOTA TERRITORY

This fort at Like-a-Fishhook, a bend on the Missouri River, was founded by Bartholomew Berthold in 1845 as Fort Atkinson, a trading post for the American Fur Company. It was here during the winter of 1865–66 that Hunkpapa Sioux chief Gall, who was visiting friends, was thought to have been mortally wounded by troops from Fort Stevenson that had been dispatched to arrest the warrior for some unknown offense. Gall, however, miraculously survived his wounds and vowed vengeance. The post was evacuated in June 1867 and the following year became home to Arikara (Ree), Mandan (hereditary enemies of the Sioux), and Gros Ventre tribes, including many of the Ree scouts that participated in the Little Bighorn campaign. It continued to operate as a trading post until 1874. The site of Fort Berthold has been covered by the Garrison Reservoir.

📖 *A History of Old Fort Berthold,* by Adrian R. Dunn (Bismarck, ND: n.p., 1964).

FORT BUFORD, DAKOTA TERRITORY

This fort, established in June 1866 by Capt. William G. Rankin, 31st Infantry, under orders from Maj. Gen. Alfred H. Terry, was named for Civil War hero John Buford. Located on the Missouri River across from the mouth of the Yellowstone, the post protected the emigrant route from Minnesota to Montana—including navigation along the Missouri River. From the day it was founded, due to its location in the middle of prime buffalo hunting country, Fort Buford was a target of the Sioux—Sitting Bull in particular—who repeatedly ran off cattle and mules and attacked patrols. Outspoken Col. William B. Hazen was "banished" by Gen. Phil Sheridan to serve as commander of this isolated post from 1872 to 1877 and was denied any part in operations of the Department of Dakota. Several thousand Sioux that had fled to Canada after the Little Bighorn battle were placed on a temporary reservation at Fort Buford when they surrendered in 1880. It was here that Sitting Bull and 187 of his followers also surrendered on July 19, 1881, symbolically ending the Great Sioux War. The fort

was passed that certain chiefs—including Spotted Tail—would be required to surrender or their tribes would be severely punished. In October 1855, Spotted Tail surrendered at Fort Laramie, fully expecting to be killed. But after being moved around to various Kansas forts, he was released a year later. During this captivity, he reportedly learned how to speak and write English and became aware of the might of the U.S. Army.

"I have upon my table 40 or 50 small particles of pure gold, in size averaging that of a small pinhead, and most of it obtained today from one panful of earth."

—DISPATCH TO SHERIDAN, AUGUST 2, 1874

Spotted Tail's act of courage for enduring imprisonment gained him further prestige among his tribe. In the early 1860s, the tribal council ignored the hereditary line and elevated him to chief of the Brule band. He responded to the Sand Creek massacre (see "The Sand Creek Massacre" on page 104) by leading raids on Julesburg, Colorado. Spotted Tail then sought peace and advised accommodation with the whites. He met with a government commission during Red Cloud's War over the Bozeman Trail (see "Red Cloud's War" on page 68) and later signed the Fort Laramie Treaty of 1868 (see "The Fort Laramie Treaty of 1868 and the Black Hills Expedition" on page 158).

In 1870, Spotted Tail traveled to Washington, D.C., the first of many trips to negotiate for his tribe. He was a guest—along with George Armstrong Custer—on the January 1872 Nebraska buffalo hunt organized for Grand Duke Alexis of Russia (see "The Russian Grand Duke's Buffalo Hunt" on page 107). The following year, the agency bearing his name was established in Nebraska.

Spotted Tail was among the chiefs who were invited to Washington in 1875 under the pretense of discussing agency business but instead were asked to sell the Black Hills, which were part of the Great Sioux Reservation. He was in favor of the sale and was given the responsibility of setting the price, much to the ire of hostile factions. But

(continued on following page)

his price was refused by the government, and war was at hand. In 1876, Spotted Tail was appointed agency chief of the Sioux—over Red Cloud—and embarked on a personal fifty-five-day journey to persuade militant bands to submit to the reservation. His efforts failed, and the Great Sioux War of 1876–77 ensued.

Spotted Tail's leadership was constantly questioned, especially when he encouraged four of his sons, two grandchildren, and forty others from the reservation to attend Carlisle Indian School in Pennsylvania. Within months, the students had converted to the Episcopal faith, adopted Christian names, and were working on farms and in industrial settings. He removed his family members in 1880 but became a target for his opponents because of the incident. Throughout the 1870s, Red Cloud accused him of stealing money from the sale of tribal land, but his primary nemesis was chief of police Crow Dog.

Crow Dog encouraged the tribal council to replace Spotted Tail with Yellow Hair but was refused. He then wrote a letter to the secretary of the interior making charges against Spotted Tail. In a confrontation between the two men on July 4, 1881—perhaps a dispute over a woman—Crow Dog drew a gun. Spotted Tail dared him to shoot, but Crow Dog backed down. On August 5, however, Crow Dog ambushed Spotted Tail, killing him with a rifle shot.

In accordance with tribal custom, Crow Dog was punished locally for his crime—ostracism of himself and his family for generations, along with a penalty of eight horses, a blanket, and $50 cash. Publicity over the murder, however, caused Crow Dog to be arrested by civilian authorities and jailed in Deadwood. A jury trial in March 1882 found him guilty of murder. But there was a question concerning proper jurisdiction. In 1883, the U.S. Supreme Court—in a landmark case—reversed the conviction, ruling that state and Federal courts had no jurisdiction on Indian land. Crow Dog was freed.

A small memorial marks the gravesite of Spotted Tail near Rosebud Agency. A more significant tribute to this warrior-diplomat, however, is a tribal college, Sinte Gleska University, on the Rosebud Reservation in South Dakota, which was chartered in 1971 and named in his honor.

📖 The most detailed account of Spotted Tail's life, although little is recorded for the years 1841 to 1854, is George E. Hyde's *Spotted Tail's Folk: A History of the Brule Sioux* (Norman: University of Oklahoma Press, 1961). Other notable sources include *A Sioux Chronicle,* by George E. Hyde (Norman:

(continued on following page)

was abandoned in October 1895, and the buildings were sold at auction.

📖 *Tales from Buffalo Land: The Story of Fort Buford,* by Usher L. Burdick (Baltimore: Wirth Brothers, 1940); and "Fort Buford," by James P. Kimball, *North Dakota Historical Quarterly* 4 (January 1930).

FORT CUSTER, MONTANA TERRITORY

This fort was originally named Big Horn Post or Big Horn Barracks when it was established on July 4, 1877, by Lt. Col. George P. Buell, 11th U.S. Infantry, under orders from Gen. Nelson Miles on a bluff above the confluence of the Bighorn and Little Bighorn Rivers—eleven miles from the famous battlefield. On November 8, 1877, it was renamed in honor of George Armstrong Custer. This permanent base denied the Sioux and Cheyenne free reign over what had been their principal domain, the Yellowstone Basin, which led to their eventual submission. The fort became a steamboat destination for the delivery of building materials, grain for animals, and other provisions. Troops from Fort Custer were charged in 1882 with helping protect wild game from poachers in Yellowstone National Park and also put down a religious uprising by the traditionally friendly Crow Indians in 1887. The fort was garrisoned until April 1898. At that time, the structures were sold at auction and used to build the nearby town of Hardin, Montana. Nothing remains of Fort Custer except a marker placed at the site by the Daughters of the American Revolution.

📖 *Fort Custer on the Big Horn, 1877–1898,* by R. Upton (Glendale, CA: Arthur H. Clark Co., 1973).

FORT ELLIS, MONTANA TERRITORY

This post was established by Capt. Robert S. LaMotte, 13th U.S. Infantry, under orders from Brig. Gen. Alfred H. Terry in August 1867. It was named in honor of Col. Augustus Van Horn Ellis, who was killed at Gettysburg. It was located three miles west of present-day Bozeman, on the left bank of the East Gallatin River, in a strategic position from which to command Bozeman, Bridger, and Flathead Passes—by which the Powder River Sioux were terrorizing mining settlements in the Gallatin Valley. This military presence failed to discourage raids by the Sioux under Sitting Bull, however, and the area was in a constant state of siege. On March 30, 1876, Col. John Gibbon, with post commander Maj. James S. Brisbin and 450 men from the 7th Infantry and 2nd Cavalry, marched from Fort Ellis as part of the Little Bighorn campaign. The Montana Column had orders to patrol the north bank of the Yellowstone and intercept any hostile Indians that fled northward. Following the Little Bighorn battle, scout H. M. "Muggins" Taylor was dispatched to Fort Ellis by Gen. Alfred Terry with news of Custer's defeat. Taylor arrived on July 3, and the temporary commanding officer, Capt. D. W. Benham, turned over the dispatches to the *Bozeman Times,* which broke the story. In 1882, troops from Fort Ellis were assigned to help protect wild game from poachers in Yellowstone National Park. It was abandoned in 1886 and transferred to the Interior Department.

FORT FETTERMAN, WYOMING

This fort was established in July 1867 by Maj. William McEntyre, 4th U.S. Infantry, near the mouth of La Prele Creek at the point where the Bozeman Trail veered northward from the North Platte River. It was named in honor of Capt. William J. Fetterman, who had been killed by Sioux during Red Cloud's War over the Bozeman Trail (see "Red Cloud's War" on page 68). Fort Fetterman was used primarily as a supply base for operations against the Sioux. On March 1, 1876, Gen. George Crook and his Wyoming Column marched from the fort as part of the Little Bighorn campaign. The troops limped back to the fort after one detachment under Col. Joseph J. Reynolds mismanaged a March 17 battle on the Powder River. On May 29, Crook marched out of Fort Fetterman, this time destined to face defeat, or at least a stalemate, at Rosebud Creek. Crook, replenished with supplies, departed the fort for the third time that year on November 14 to resume his chase of Crazy Horse and the Sioux. The fort was abandoned by the military in November 1882, when the buildings were sold. A cattle town grew up around the site but was eventually deserted, leaving several buildings still standing.

FORT KEOGH, MONTANA TERRITORY

This fort, originally named "Cantonment on Tongue River," "New Post on the Yellowstone," and "Tongue River Barracks," was established by Gen. Nelson Miles in August 1876 on the south bank of the Yellowstone River two miles above the mouth of the Tongue River (near present-day Miles City). The post was intended to serve as a supply base in the heart of Sioux country. In November 1877, it was renamed in honor of Capt. Myles W. Keogh, who had perished in the Little Bighorn battle. Operations conducted by Miles from the fort, which kept the Indians away from buffalo herds, forced the final surrender of the Sioux and the Cheyenne. In 1877, Miles marched from Fort Keogh to engage Chief Joseph and the Nez Perce in the crucial battle of Bear Paw Mountain. In 1880, Sioux that had fled to Canada after the Little Bighorn battle, as well as those who had submitted earlier, were transferred from Fort Keogh to Standing Rock Agency—against the protests of Miles City residents who wanted the Indians to remain as a boost to the local economy. Fort Keogh was gar-

University of Oklahoma Press, 1956); *The Last Days of the Sioux Nation,* by Robert M. Utley (New Haven, CT: Yale University Press, 1963); "Spotted Tail: Warrior, Diplomat," by Donald E. Worcester, *American West* 1, no. 4 (1964); "The Murder of Spotted Tail," by William Seagle, *Indian History* 3, no. 4 (Fall 1970); "Spotted Tail the Strategist," by Mildred Fielder, in *Sioux Indian Leaders* (Seattle: Superior Publishing Co., 1975); "Sioux Response to Non-Indian Intrusion: Sitting Bull, Spotted Tail, and Crazy Horse," by Richmond Lee Clow, in *South Dakota Leaders: From Pierre Chouteau, Jr., to Oscar Howe,* edited by Herbert T. Hoover and Larry J. Zimmerman (Vermillion: University of South Dakota Press, 1989); and "History of Sinte Gleska (Spotted Tail)," by Victor Douville, *Sinte Gleska University Catalog,* 1990–93, Rosebud Sioux Reservation, South Dakota.

> *"My Darling Sunbeam—I calculate on one week more here. Should I be detained longer I should give up all thought of a summer campaign and send for my Bunkey. Many would rejoice at a summer in the east. . . . But not I.*
>
> —Custer to Libbie from Washington, April 1876

Alfred Howe Terry
Brigadier General, U.S. Army

Terry was born on November 10, 1827, in Hartford, Connecticut. At the age of twenty-one, he briefly attended Yale Law School, but he withdrew after a year. Terry became fluent in French and German and traveled in Europe on an inheritance. In 1858, he became clerk of the New Haven County Superior Court, a position he held until the outbreak of the Civil War.

Terry became colonel of the 2nd Connecticut, a ninety-day militia regiment, which he commanded at First Bull Run. He then recruited the 7th Connecticut and led this regiment to share the capture of the important naval base at Port Royal, South Carolina, in November 1861. In April of the following year, Terry's regiment helped take Fort Pulaski, Georgia, which led to his promotion that month to brigadier general.

(continued on following page)

Gen. Alfred H. Terry. *Courtesy Little Bighorn Battlefield National Monument.*

In the fall of 1863, he assumed command of X Corps in the Army of the James, which operated against Petersburg and Richmond. He participated in Maj. Gen. Benjamin F. Butler's ill-fated attempt to capture Fort Fisher, North Carolina, in December 1864. When Butler was recalled, Terry replaced him and personally led the storming and capture of Fort Fisher in January 1865, which sealed off Wilmington, the last Confederate port on the East Coast. For this accomplishment, he received the rarely awarded "Thanks of Congress," a coveted citation published in the *Congressional Record,* and was promoted to major general of volunteers and brigadier in the Regular army, as of January 15, 1865. He ended the war in the Carolinas as part of the Army of the Ohio under Maj. Gen. William T. Sherman.

(continued on following page)

risoned until 1908, when the Interior Department converted the post for use as a Range and Live-stock Experiment Station. It was used as a quartermaster's depot during World War II. Several of the original buildings on officers' row are presently in use.

FORT LARAMIE, WYOMING

This fort, on the west bank of the Laramie River, about one mile above its juncture with the North Platte River, was established in 1834 by fur trappers William Sublette and Robert Campbell. It was originally named Fort William, then Fort John. In March 1849, the fort was sold to the U.S. government and converted into a military post, renamed Fort Laramie after the river, which was named after French trapper Jacques Laramie, who was killed by Arapaho in 1821. It was garrisoned to protect travelers on the Oregon Trail and monitor the Plains Indians, and countless emigrants prepared for the long upgrade haul to the mountains at the fort. The Fort Laramie Treaty of 1851 with the Sioux brought about a somewhat shaky peace that fell apart in 1854 with death of Lt. John Grattan and thirty troopers in a dispute over the killing of an ox (see "The Initiation of Warfare between the Plains Indians and the U.S. Army" on page 49). The Fort Laramie Treaty of 1868 was negotiated at this site (see "The Fort Laramie Treaty of 1868 and the Black Hills Expedition" on page 158). Fort Laramie remained an important northern plains fort until 1890, when it was abandoned. Most of the buildings were dismantled or sold, but some of the old structures have been preserved as the Fort Laramie National Historical Site.

📖 *Fort Laramie and the Pageant of the West, 1834–1890,* by LeRoy R. Hafen and Francis Marion Young (Glendale, CA: Arthur H. Clark Co., 1938); *Fort Laramie and the Changing Frontier,* by David Lavender (Washington, DC: U.S. Department of the Interior, 1983); *Fort Laramie in 1876: Chronicle of a Frontier Post at War,* by Paul L. Hedren (Lincoln: University of Nebraska Press, 1988).

FORT PHIL KEARNY, WYOMING

This fort was established by Col. Henry B. Carrington, 18th U.S. Infantry, on July 13, 1866, on Big Piney Fork at the foot of the Bighorn Mountains, about fifteen miles from present-day Buffalo. The stockaded post was the largest and most important of the forts constructed to protect the Bozeman

Trail leading to the Montana mines. It was named in honor of Maj. Gen. Phil Kearny, who was killed in the September 1862 battle of Chantilly, Virginia. Much of Red Cloud's War was waged within the vicinity of the fort, including the Fetterman massacre and the Wagon Box fight (see "Red Cloud's War" on page 68). The fort was abandoned, according to provisions of the Fort Laramie Treaty of 1868, and was subsequently burned to the ground by the Sioux.

📖 *Fort Phil Kearny: An American Saga,* by Dee Brown (New York: G. P. Putnam's Sons, 1962).

FORT RICE, DAKOTA TERRITORY

This fort, the buildings of which were initially constructed from cottonwood logs with earth roofs, was established on July 7, 1864, by Gen. Alfred Sully during his expedition against the Sioux west of the Missouri River. Named in honor of Brig. Gen. J. C. Rice, who was killed in the May 1864 battle of Laurel Hill, Virginia, the fort was located on the west bank of the Missouri River near the mouth of Long Lake Creek. Fort Rice suffered from primitive conditions, and eighty-one members of the U.S. Volunteers (Galvanized Yankees) died from scurvy and other diseases between October 1864 and May 1865. The fort served as the base for Sully's 1865 expedition to Devil's Lake and was intended to protect emigrants traveling from Minnesota to Montana, as well as navigation on the Missouri River. The Fort Laramie Treaty of 1868 was signed by more than 200 chiefs and subchiefs at Fort Rice on July 2, 1868. The post was the staging area for expeditions into the Yellowstone Valley during the early 1870s by Maj. Joseph Whistler and Col. David S. Stanley—including the Yellowstone Expedition of 1873, when Custer's 7th Cavalry assembled there from various other posts for the march. Upon returning from that expedition, four companies of the 7th Cavalry under Maj. Joseph G. Tilford—and Custer nemesis Capt. Frederick Benteen—were assigned to Fort Rice, while Custer remained at Fort Abraham Lincoln. Fort Rice was abandoned in 1878, when Fort Yates was established downriver. The site of the post is presently part of a state park.

FORT (CAMP) ROBINSON, NEBRASKA

This post, located at the junction of White River and Soldier Creek, west of present-day Crawford City, was established on March 8, 1874, by Gen. Phil Sheridan to monitor activities at Red Cloud and Pine Ridge Agencies. It was named in honor of 1st Lt. Levi H. Robinson, who had been killed by Indians in Wyoming in January 1874. Troops from this post unsuccessfully tried to prevent miners from invading the Black Hills in 1874. Sioux warrior Crazy Horse was killed at the fort in 1877, when soldiers tried to arrest him. In 1879, more than

Terry remained in the army as a brigadier general and was given command of the Department of Dakota, which included Minnesota and parts of the Dakota and Montana Territories. He served on the commission that condemned the Sand Creek massacre (see "The Sand Creek Massacre" on page 104) and was a member of the presidential peace commission that negotiated the Medicine Lodge Treaties in 1867 (see "The Medicine Lodge Treaties" on page 65). In 1869, he was transferred to the Department of the South to contend with Reconstruction. He returned to Dakota as department commander in 1872.

The general was a strong advocate of Indian rights and a proponent of arming Indians with weapons for hunting purposes, which was a controversial position within the army. In 1872, Terry also sat on the board that selected the Model 1873 Springfield carbine for use by the army, a decision that garnered much criticism following the Little Bighorn battle (see "Weapons Carried by the Cavalrymen" on page 195). He opposed any intrusion by whites into the Black Hills region, but nonetheless served as supervisor for Custer's Black Hills expedition of 1874 and the subsequent Jenny expedition of 1875. Terry was also involved in the joint American-British Northern Boundary Survey that marked the Canadian border in 1873–74 (see "The Northern Boundary Survey" on page 121). He was a member of the Allison Commission, which met with the Sioux at Red Cloud Agency in June 1875 to try to negotiate the purchase of the Black Hills but was unsuccessful.

In the spring of 1876, Terry was assigned command of the Dakota Column, part of the three-pronged approach for the upcoming Little Bighorn campaign. After George Armstrong Custer was denied permission by President Grant to accompany that expedition, Terry, who was known as a kind man, interceded on Custer's behalf (see "Custer and the Belknap Hearings" on page 171). There were also personal motives for Terry's actions. He had no experience fighting Indians and certainly desired that Custer be in command of the 7th Cavalry in the field.

One of the major controversies surrounding the Little Bighorn battle was whether Custer willfully disobeyed Terry's orders and thereby brought about the loss of his command (see "Did Custer Disobey Orders?" on page 208). In addition to his written order, which was issued on June 21 aboard the steamer *Far West,* Terry reportedly said, "Use your own judgment and do what you think best if you strike the trail." Terry later told a reporter that

(continued on following page)

Custer would have faced a court-martial for disobedience of orders had he survived—perhaps because Terry was also under fire for Custer's defeat. At least one newspaper stated that he should stand a court-martial for his actions. It was the Terry-Gibbon column that arrived on the battlefield on June 27 to discover Custer's annihilated command and rescued Reno's men on the hilltop.

In the fall of 1877, Terry met with Sitting Bull at Fort Walsh in Canada, but his offer of amnesty was refused. He also authorized the two courts-martial of Maj. Marcus A. Reno, the second resulting in Reno's dismissal from the service. Terry was promoted to major general in 1886—one of few non–West Pointers to become a major general of volunteers and later attain the same rank in the Regular army—and at that time assumed command of the Department of the Missouri.

*"I have reached the hunter's
highest round of fame. . . .
I have killed my grizzly."*

—CUSTER TO LIBBIE, AUGUST 1874

Terry retired at his own request due to poor health in 1888. He died on December 16, 1890—one day after Sitting Bull was shot and killed.

Nearly every volume published about the U.S. Army's campaigns against the Indians on the northern plains include references to Terry. His official report of the Little Bighorn campaign can be found in 44 Cong., 2 sess., *House Exec. Doc. 1*, part 2, and *Annual Report, 1876*, United States War Department. Notable sources include *Pacifying the Plains: General Alfred Terry and the Decline of the Sioux, 1866–1890*, by John W. Bailey (Westport, CT: Greenwood, 1979); *The Field Diary of General Alfred H. Terry: The Yellowstone Expedition—1876* (Bellevue, NE: Old Army Press, 1970); and *The Terry Letters: The Letters of General Alfred Howe Terry to His Sisters during the Indian War of 1876*, edited by James Willert (La Mirada, CA: James Willert, 1980).

sixty Northern Cheyenne that had fled from Indian Territory and had been confined at Fort Robinson were killed during an escape attempt. Troops from the post were among the first to arrive at Pine Ridge during the Sioux Ghost Dance uprising of 1890. The post served as a quartermaster remount depot during World War I and a K-9 dog training center and P.O.W. camp during World War II. It was abandoned in 1948, and the site is presently a part of Fort Robinson State Park and Museum.

Outpost of the Sioux Wars, by Frank N. Schubert (Lincoln: University of Nebraska Press, 1993), and "Fort Robinson, Outpost on the Plains," by Roger T. Grange, *Nebraska History Magazine* 39 (September 1958).

FORT STEVENSON, DAKOTA TERRITORY

This fort, named for Brig. Gen. Thomas G. Stevenson, who had been killed in the May 1864 battle of Spotsylvania, was established in June 1867 by Maj. Joseph N. G. Whistler, 31st U.S. Infantry, at a site selected in 1864 by Brig. Gen. Alfred Sully on the east bank of the Missouri River at the mouth of Douglas Creek. It was intended as a supply base for Fort Totten, protection for emigrants traveling from Minnesota to Montana, as well as navigation on the Missouri River, and to monitor Indians at the Fort Berthold Agency. The post was abandoned in August 1883 and turned over to the Fort Berthold Indian Agency. It was used as an Indian school until 1894. The site is presently covered by the Garrison Reservoir.

"Old Fort Stevenson—A Typical River Military Post, by Ray H. Mattison, *North Dakota History* 18 (April 1951).

FORT TOTTEN, DAKOTA TERRITORY

This fort, located on the south shore of Devil's Lake, was established on July 17, 1867, by Capt. Samuel A. Wainwright, 31st U.S. Infantry, under orders from Brig. Gen. Alfred Terry. It was named in honor of Brig. Gen. Joseph G. Totten, who had served as chief engineer of the army and died during the Civil War. The purpose of the fort was to protect travelers en route from Minnesota to Montana. The temporary log buildings were in the process of being replaced by permanent frame buildings by the time Companies D and I of the 7th Cavalry, under Captains Thomas Weir and Myles Keogh, were quartered there during the winters of 1873–74 and 1874–75 while on detached duty with the International Boundary Survey. The lonely outpost was said to be "a powderkeg of alcoholism and desertion." Fort Totten was abandoned in 1890 and later became an Indian agency and industrial school. It is presently a subagency of the Turtle Mountain Indian Agency and has been preserved by the North Dakota Historical Society.

📖 "Soldiers and Sioux: Military Life among the Indians at Fort Totten," by J. Michael McCormack, in *Fort Totten Military Post and Indian School, 1867–1959,* edited by Larry Remele (Bismarck: State Historical Society of North Dakota, 1986); and "The History of Fort Totten," by Charles de Noyer, *Collections of the State Historical Society of North Dakota* 3 (1910).

FORT YATES, DAKOTA TERRITORY

This fort, which was established on the west bank of the Missouri River on December 23, 1874, was originally named Standing Rock Agency for the Indian agency that it guarded. On December 30, 1878, it was designated Fort Yates in honor of Capt. George Yates, who was killed with Custer at Little Bighorn. It was here on December 15, 1890, that Sioux chief Sitting Bull was killed by Indian police. The fort was abandoned in 1903 but remains as the headquarters for the Standing Rock Reservation.

📖 General-interest sources include *Forts of the West: Military Forts and Presidios and Posts Commonly Called Forts West of the Mississippi to 1898,* by Robert W. Frazer (Norman: University of Oklahoma Press, 1965); *A Guide to the Military Posts of the United States, 1789–1895,* by Francis Paul Prucha (Madison: State Historical Society of Wisconsin, 1964); *Outline Descriptions of the Posts in the Military Division of the Missouri,* by Philip H. Sheridan, facsimile edition (Fort Collins, CO: Old Army Press, 1972); *Forts of the Upper Missouri,* by Robert G. Athearn (Englewood Cliffs, NJ: Prentice Hall, 1967); and "The Army Fort of the Frontier (1860–70)," by Raymond L. Welty, *North Dakota Historical Quarterly* 2 (April 1928).

🐎 The Midnight Ride of Charley Reynolds

On July 30, gold deposits, albeit mere flecks, were discovered by the miners accompanying the expedition in the upper reaches of French Creek along the narrow valley that had been named Custer Park. Two days later, George Armstrong Custer was sufficiently assured that the deposits held prospects of gold in payable quantities. At that time, he wrote a dispatch to Phil Sheridan about the find that would forever change history in the Black Hills region. He turned to his trusted scout, Charley Reynolds, who by prearrangement had been engaged to carry this important message to the outside world.

Custer's Special Order No. 26, dated August 2, 1874, read:

> Government scout Charles Reynolds will accompany the five companies of cavalry which leave camp tomorrow morning and at a point hereafter to be designated will proceed with dis-

✴ **Joseph Greene Tilford**
Major, 7th U.S. Cavalry

Tilford was born on November 26, 1828, in Georgetown, Kentucky, the son of Col. Alexander Tilford, a veteran of the War of 1812. He entered the U.S. Military Academy at West Point on July 1, 1847, and graduated four years later ranked fortieth in a class of forty-two. Tilford joined the Mounted Rifles and was assigned to the cavalry school. He served at various posts in Texas in 1855, participated in the Utah expedition in 1858, and later took part in the Navajo expedition. He was promoted to first lieutenant in June 1858.

At the outbreak of the Civil War, Tilford was sent to Fort Union, New Mexico Territory, and was promoted to captain, 3rd Cavalry, in July 1861. He saw action against Confederates at Albuquerque, Peralta, and Parugo and was breveted major in February 1862 for action in the battle of Valverde. He later fought at Cherokee Station; the capture of Tuscumbia, Alabama; and the campaigns at Lookout Mountain and Missionary Ridge, Tennessee. He took time off from the war to marry Cornelia Van Ness Dean on February 9, 1864, in St. Louis. The couple had two children.

Tilford was breveted lieutenant colonel in March 1865 and commanded Fort Seldon, New Mexico. He was appointed major, 7th Cavalry, in November 1867. He was constantly in ill health and had a disagreeable temperament, and he despised his commander, George Armstrong Custer. Custer thought little of the major as a commander of troops, and the two endured a cool relationship.

Tilford had, for one reason or another, been absent from all the field operations of the 7th Cavalry until the Black Hills expedition of 1874. Even then, he had chosen to remain at Fort Rice but was pressed into duty as a battalion commander when no other officer was available.

In early August, while Custer and five companies scouted the South Fork of the Cheyenne, Tilford assumed temporary command back at Custer Park. He immediately exerted his authority by changing the time of reveille from 2:45 to 4 A.M. Pvt. Theodore Ewert wrote in his journal about this change: "I scarcely think that he done this for the benefit of the men, but simply because he wanted to change existing orders." Custer returned on August 5, and reveille was changed back to 2:45. Before departing the Black Hills, Tilford hosted a champagne supper for some of the officers. It is not

(continued on following page)

known whether Custer, a teetotaler, attended. On the march back to Fort Abraham Lincoln, Tilford broke a standing order and lost a wagon. Custer dispatched a note dated August 25 to the major written by adjutant James Calhoun, which read:

> The General directs that you at once turn over your wagon to the Qrmster as it was hauling water for K & H Companies. He also directs me to say that he considers your allowing your wagon to carry Water Kegs a direct violation of existing orders on your part and the part of the two Company Commanders.

Apparently no disciplinary action was taken. Tilford was on a leave of absence during the 1876 Little Bighorn campaign. One year later, however, he wrote a letter to Libbie Custer that was certainly magnanimous and highly out of character for a well-known Custer antagonist. Libbie had fretted about the identification of her husband's remains when they were exhumed from the battlefield and shipped to West Point for burial. Tilford responded on July 28, 1877:

"I expect to be in the field, in the summer, with the 7th, and think there will be lively work before us. I think the 7th Cavalry may have its greatest campaign ahead."

—CUSTER TO BROTHER TOM, JANUARY 1876

On yesterday I shipped by U.S. Express via Chicago, the remains of your heroic husband Genl. Custer to West Point, N.Y., care of the Commanding Officer at that post. Those were my instructions from Genl. Sheridan. I presume an officer will accompany the remains from Chicago on. It may be some consolation for you to know that I personally superintended the transfer of the remains from the box in which they came from the battlefield to the casket which conveys them to West Point. I enclose you a lock of hair taken from the remains which are so precious to you. I also kept a few hairs for myself as having been worn by a man who was my beau ideal of a soldier and honorable gentleman.

patches to Fort Laramie reporting upon his arrival to the commanding officer of that post. On arrival he will deposit in the mail such dispatches and letters as are intended for transmission by mail and should there be a telegraph station at Fort Laramie he will deliver to the operator such dispatches as may be intended for telegraph. Should there be no telegraph he will proceed to the nearest telegraph station, taking with him all mail and telegraph matter consigned to his care. On completing this duty he will proceed to Fort Lincoln and await the arrival of this command. Upon arrival at Fort Laramie he will turn in the public horse ridden by him to the post quartermaster at Fort Laramie, which officer is requested to receipt for the same.

In other words, when Reynolds separated from the cavalry detachment, he would be required to travel alone about ninety miles through hostile country in order to reach Fort Laramie.

Custer provided Reynolds with a canvas mailbag that had been inscribed: "Black Hills Express. Charley Reynolds, Manager. Connecting with All points East, West, North, South. Cheap rates; Quick Transit; Safe Passage. We are protected by the Seventh Cavalry."

Reynolds galloped away from the column with the awareness that his route would intersect several Indian trails and there was a distinct possibility that he would be discovered by hostiles.

The most stirring account of his ride was provided by Libbie Custer in her *"Boots and Saddles"; or, Life in Dakota with General Custer* (New York: Harper and Brothers, 1885). Although somewhat embellished, Libbie wrote in part:

> During the day he hid as well as he could in the underbrush, and lay down in the long grass. In spite of these precautions he was sometimes so exposed that he could hear voices of Indians passing near. The last nights of his march he was compelled to walk, as his horse was exhausted and he found no water for hours. His lips became so parched and his throat so swollen that he could not close his mouth. In this condition he reached Fort Laramie and delivered his dispatches.

Reynolds fulfilled his mission in four days of hard riding, then moved on to Sioux City, where his swollen throat apparently healed. While in that fair city, he gave an interview to the editor of the *Sioux City Journal,* which was published on August 19. Although he said that he personally had not found any gold, he admitted to having seen specks of the mineral washed from surface dirt that would likely yield 2 or 3 cents a pan. He then set out for Bismarck and Fort Lincoln, leaving behind the spark that helped ignite a gold rush in the Black Hills.

📖 In addition to the above source, see those following the biography of Reynolds on page 157.

(continued on following page)

🐎 Custer and the Belknap Hearings

It had been a dirty little open secret for years around the War Department and Western military posts that certain high-ranking government officials were profiting from kickbacks in the awarding of post traderships. Those who had suspicions or were aware of this corruption simply looked the other way—with one exception.

George Armstrong Custer refused to ignore this criminal activity. He had investigated circumstances at Fort Abraham Lincoln and concluded that this corruption went right to the top—Secretary of War William W. Belknap was conspiring with a local trader in a kickback scheme. Custer, disgusted by his findings, had in effect snubbed the secretary when he visited Fort Lincoln during the summer of 1875.

The manner in which information of this sort found its way to the *New York Herald* newspaper, an ardent Grant administration critic, would be a matter of speculation. Rumor points to the likelihood that Custer, who was a political friend of James G. Bennett, Jr., the newspaper's publisher, had been supplying details as an informant—perhaps paid for his material. Regardless of the source, the February 10, 1876, edition of the *Herald* accused Secretary Belknap of selling traderships and receiving kickbacks, and further implicated Orville Grant, the president's brother.

This scandal was not particularly new, but revelations in this particular editorial were seized upon by the Democrat-controlled Congress as an ideal opportunity to embarrass Republican president Grant. Heister Clymer, chairman of the House Committee on Expenditures in the War Department, announced that hearings would be held to investigate the matter, which could possibly result in the impeachment of Belknap.

Belknap, without admitting guilt, resigned as secretary of war on March 2, but Clymer continued his hearings. On March 9, Orville Grant admitted that his brother had given him license to four posts in 1874, and that he had acted as a middleman in awarding these traderships. In addition, supplies that were supposed to have been delivered to authorized recipients had been diverted and resold elsewhere. The profits had been split; Belknap's share was funneled to his wife.

Custer would have preferred not to testify at the hearing, but he was a high-profile witness whose presence would generate great publicity for the Democrats. His popularity in early 1876 can be evidenced by the fact that the Redpath Lyceum Bureau, a Boston talent agency, had offered him a contract calling for lectures five nights a week for four to five months at $200 per night. He could earn more than ten times his annual army salary in less than half a year merely by speaking—not to mention adding to his fame as the country's premier Indian fighter. Custer turned down the lucrative offer, however,

Tilford was post commander at Fort Rice in 1876, Fort Abraham Lincoln the following year, and Fort Buford, Dakota Territory, in 1882. He was appointed lieutenant colonel, 9th Cavalry, in April 1889 and retired on July 1, 1891. While residing in New York City, Tilford was advanced to brigadier general in April 1904.

He died of pneumonia on February 24, 1911, in Washington, D.C., and was buried in Arlington National Cemetery. Tilford, South Dakota, was named in his honor.

📖 The letter to Libbie Custer was quoted from *General Custer's Libbie,* by Lawrence A. Frost (Seattle: Superior Publishing, 1976). The original was part of Frost's personal collection.

✹ Newton Horace Winchell
Geologist

Winchell was born on December 17, 1839, in Northeast, Dutchess County, New York. He was educated at the academy of Salisbury, Connecticut, and began teaching school in Northeast at the age of sixteen. In 1858, Winchell enrolled at the University of Michigan—where his brother was a professor of geology—and graduated six years later, after taking time off during his studies to become the school superintendent in St. Clair, Michigan. In August 1864, he married Charlotte S. Imus of Galesburg, Michigan, with whom he had five children.

Winchell taught school in Adrian, Michigan, for a period of three years. From 1869 to 1870, he served as an assistant to his brother on the Michigan state geological survey, and from 1870 to 1872, he assisted in the geological survey of Ohio. In 1872, Winchell became Minnesota state geologist and embarked on a survey that would not be completed until 1900. Also, beginning in 1874, he was a professor of geology at the University of Minnesota, a tenure that lasted until 1900.

Winchell served under William Ludlow in George Armstrong Custer's Black Hills expedition of 1874 and was paid $450. He was most concerned with the geological formations in the region and had little interest in finding gold, which dismayed Custer. Winchell, who complained that the expedition moved too quickly for him to reliably and adequately study the terrain, maintained a journal but noted few significant contributions to geology. He climbed Harney Peak on August 1, and on August 14, Winchell and botanist A. B. Donaldson, traversing old deer and

(continued on following page)

antelope trails, climbed Bear Butte, an extinct volcano on the northern fringe of the Hills.

Winchell returned from the Black Hills and addressed the Academy of Natural Sciences in Minneapolis. He stated during his lecture that he had not personally observed any gold in the Black Hills, nor had a sample of this mineral been brought to him for identification. Furthermore, he doubted that any gold existed within that region. Predictably, inasmuch as the discovery of gold had been widely reported, his speech created quite a controversy. The *New York Times* on September 14, 1874, reported his words as fact. The *Bismarck Tribune* responded on September 16, attacking the source: "If Professor Winchell has made such reports . . . he has written himself an ass." The paper went on to quote members of the expedition who recalled that the geologist had been away—climbing Harney Peak and on a scout—when the gold was found. Custer later entered the fray, writing to the *New York World* on December 13, "Why Professor Winchell saw no gold was simply due to the fact that he neglected to look for it."

Winchell resumed his dual jobs as college professor and geologist for the Minnesota state survey. He was one of the founders of the Minnesota Academy of Sciences and was widely published in not only geology, but also botany, ethnology, and archaeology. His theory, after studying the recession of the falls at St. Anthony at Minneapolis, that man had lived on this continent during the most recent ice age has finally gained modern acceptance. He also founded the American Geological Society and its magazine *American Geologist,* the first of its kind in this country, and served as editor from 1888 to 1905. Winchell died on May 2, 1914, in Minneapolis.

📖 Some of Winchell's manuscripts are located in the collections of the Minnesota Historical Society.

because it would interfere with preparations for the upcoming campaign against hostile Sioux and Cheyenne Indians.

Custer was called before the committee for the first time on March 29 and related how after he had assumed command at Fort Lincoln, he had requested the removal of the trader, S. A. Dickey, for various infractions, including introducing alcohol to the Indians. The new trader, Robert C. Siep, subsequently had confessed to Custer that he had been delivering two-thirds of his profits to Belknap. Custer's concern was that this practice resulted in increased prices on goods at frontier posts, which caused a hardship on the troops. Contrary to popular belief, an examination of the transcript does not show that Custer implicated Orville Grant in the scheme. His hearsay testimony concluded on April 4. Custer at that time expected to return to Fort Lincoln and prepare for the Little Bighorn campaign.

Although Custer's testimony predictably provided more in publicity than in substance, he was not without critics. Cynics pointed out that Custer saw nothing contradictory about fighting Indians as well as those who cheated them. The most damaging blow, however, was delivered by his commander-in-chief. President Grant was infuriated by Custer's testimony—Belknap was a close personal friend of his. Grant decided to punish his impudent officer by denying him permission to lead the 7th Cavalry on the spring campaign.

Custer was devastated by the decision. While the 7th Cavalry prepared for the march—temporarily under the command of Maj. Marcus A. Reno—Custer visited the White House on three occasions hoping for an audience with Grant, but the president refused to see him. On May 6, he sent the following telegram to the president:

> I have seen your order transmitted through the General of the Army directing that I not be permitted to accompany the expedition to move against hostile Indians. As my entire regiment forms a part of the expedition and I am the senior officer of the regiment on duty in this department I respectfully but most earnestly request that while not allowed to go in command of the expedition I may be permitted to serve with my regiment in the field. I appeal to you as a soldier to spare me the humiliation of seeing my regiment march to meet the enemy and I not share its dangers.

Generals Sherman, Sheridan, and especially Terry, who realized the need for an experienced Indian fighter in his Dakota Column, interceded on Custer's behalf. On May 8, the president grudgingly relented and gave permission for Custer to join the march for the Little Bighorn campaign.

Grant's remarks in the public debate following the battle of the Little Bighorn perhaps reflected his malice toward Custer over the Belknap affair when he said: "I regard Custer's Massacre as a sacrifice of troops brought on by Custer himself, that was wholly unnecessary—wholly unnecessary."

Many of the pro-Custer faction, however, blamed Grant indirectly for Custer's defeat, maintaining that his humiliation of Custer undermined the 7th Cavalry commander's authority and set the stage for Benteen and Reno to disregard orders.

📖 The best readily available account of the Belknap impeachment hearings and Custer's involvement can be found in *Custer's Luck*, by Edgar I. Stewart (Norman: University of Oklahoma Press, 1955). The official report is "Report on Management of the War Department, Rep. Heister Clymer, Chairman of Committee," *House Reports* no. 79, 44th Congress, 1st Session, serial no. 1715 (1876).

Other notable sources include *Testimony: Custer on the Sale of Post Traderships, The Clymer Committee* (Brooklyn: Arrow & Trooper, n.d.); *Nation* (New York), March 16, 1876; *Army and Navy Journal,* April 1, April 8, April 15, and May 27, 1876; *New York Herald,* May 2, May 6, May 10, and June 6, 1876; *New York World,* May 1, 2, and 6, 1876; *New York Times,* May 1, 1876; *Cincinnati Inquirer,* April 5, 1876; *Cincinnati Commercial,* April 5, 1876; and "Campaign against the Sioux in 1876," by Col. Robert P. Hughes, *Journal of the Military Service Institution of the United States* 18 (January 1896), reprinted in *Story of the Little Bighorn,* by William A. Graham (New York: Century Co., 1926).

For more about Custer's snub of Belknap, see "Custer's Last Meeting with Secretary of War Belknap at Fort Abraham Lincoln," by Eric Brigham, *North Dakota History* (August 1952). The kickback scheme by Belknap and Grant is detailed in *Tales from Buffalo Land: The Story of Fort Buford,* by Usher L. Burdick (Baltimore: Wirth Brothers, 1940); and "The Malfeasance of William Worth Belknap, Secretary of War," by Robert C. Prickett, *North Dakota History* (January 1950).

Interesting information about Custer's activities in Washington, including extracts from letters he wrote to Libbie, is contained in *The Custer Story: The Life and Intimate Letters of General George A. Custer and His Wife Elizabeth,* edited by Marguerite Merington (New York: Devin-Adair, 1950).

EPILOGUE

The Panic of 1873 had plunged the nation into a deep economic depression, and the news that Custer's expedition had found gold in the Black Hills aroused the poverty-stricken public's imagination. Adventurers immediately made plans to journey to the Black Hills to prospect for gold. Naturally, word of this potential intrusion into Lakota Sioux land infuriated many tribal leaders. The Lakota called Custer's route through the Black Hills the "Thieves Road" and prepared for war.

Custer, meanwhile, visited Monroe, Michigan, for six weeks before settling in for another winter at Fort Abraham Lincoln. The social season was once again quite agreeable to the Custers, as the post maintained its normal routine of drills and monotony.

One notable event occurred during this time: Custer's series of magazine articles about his exploits on the Hancock expedition of 1867 had been compiled into a book, *My Life on the Plains; or, Personal Experiences with Indians,* and its release established him as a best-selling author (see "Custer's Literary Career" on page 69).

The only other excitement was the arrest, capture, and escape of Sioux warrior Rain-in-the-Face, who had boasted about killing sutler Augustus Baliran and Dr. John Honsinger during the Yellowstone expedition of 1873 (see "The Arrest and Revenge of Rain-in-the-Face" on page 129).

In spite of government warnings to the contrary, by the summer of 1875, more than 800 prospectors had invaded the Black Hills to seek their fortune. This provoked the Sioux, led by Sitting Bull and Crazy Horse, to retaliate by attacking these invaders and raiding wagon trains, mail routes, and settlements in the unceded territory. Soon the miners were demanding that the government protect them from Indian attacks.

Gen. George Crook was dispatched to uphold the provisions of Fort Laramie Treaty of 1868 and chase off the miners. Late in July, Crook called a meeting with the miners and issued an ultimatum, in his folksy manner, diplomatically suggesting that the miners likely would have an opportunity to prospect the area once it had been opened in the near future, but for the present they must depart. Most of the miners, who were quite impressed with Crook's forthrightness, agreed to comply.

Nevertheless, newspapers, especially those from nearby Dakota towns, ignored the ban on mining and jumped on the golden bandwagon, promoting their towns as the ideal places to outfit and enter the Black Hills.

There remained skepticism in some circles over the validity of Custer's discovery, however, especially when high-profile people like geologist Newton Winchell and Fred Grant, the president's son, had claimed not to have personally observed any gold. The government therefore authorized another expedition into the Black Hills in the summer of 1875 to confirm Custer's conclusions.

This expedition was headed by New York School of Mines geologist Walter P. Jenny, with escort provided by six cavalry and two infantry companies under Lt. Col. Richard I. Dodge. Jenny reported that although it would be difficult for individual miners to extract enough gold with primitive pan and rocker to make it worth their while, the Black Hills did indeed hold rich mineral deposits that could be profitable with sophisticated mining equipment. Jenny's guarded opinion meant little to the public. Gold had been confirmed, and the rush to strike it rich commenced in earnest.

Red Cloud, Spotted Tail, and other chiefs were invited to Washington, D.C., that summer of 1875. They had been led to believe that the meeting would pertain to agency business, but to their surprise, the government requested that they sign over title to the Black Hills. The chiefs refused, saying they lacked authority to make such a decision.

The government promised to reward the Lakota well should they sell the Black Hills. Spotted Tail was asked to estimate the worth of the region, which he subsequently set at $7 million to $40 million dollars and enough provisions to provide for seven generations of Sioux.

The tribe was split over the proposal to sell the Black Hills to the U.S. government. Those members who resided on the reservation approved of the idea, thinking only of the rewards that they would receive. Another faction, led by Sitting Bull and Crazy Horse, vowed that this sacred land would be sold only over their dead bodies.

The Allison Commission, named for its chairman, Iowa senator William B. Allison, convened near Red Cloud Agency in September 1875 to discuss the sale. The commission members were greeted with a show of hostility from the younger warriors, who disrupted the proceedings and threatened severe reprisals against any chief who dared sign a treaty giving away the Black Hills. Senator Allison proposed that the Sioux accept $400,000 a year for mining rights, or the U.S. would buy the Black Hills for $6 million. The offer was declined. The commission returned to Washington empty-handed and recommended that Congress simply offer whatever value they judged was fair. If the Lakota refused to sell at that price, rations and other provisions should be terminated.

The frustration over the Black Hills and Indian raids in the unceded territory finally came to a head when President Grant, after consulting government officials and military leaders, issued an order on December 6 stating that all Indians must report to the reservation by January 31, 1876. Otherwise, the Interior Department would assign disposition of the hostiles to the War Department.

This ultimatum was carried by runners to those Sioux and Cheyenne known to be camped along the Yellowstone River and thereabouts. In all fairness, it would have been extremely difficult for the Indians to move at that time of year, even if they had wanted to comply with the order: Ponies were weak from lack of forage, and winter travel could be hazardous to families. It was evident, however, that Sitting Bull and his kinsmen never intended to obey the order.

On February 1, 1876, those Indians were deemed hostile, and Gen. Phil Sheridan set in motion plans for an immediate campaign designed to catch the Indians in their vulnerable winter camps.

George Armstrong Custer meanwhile became embroiled in Washington politics, which placed his career in jeopardy. Custer testified at an impeachment hearing for former Secretary of War William W. Belknap—hearsay evidence but nonetheless damaging to the secretary (see "Custer and the Belknap Hearings" on page 171). This very public opinion by Custer enraged President Grant, who decided to punish Custer by forbidding him to participate in the upcoming campaign against the hostile Sioux and Cheyenne. Finally, Generals Sherman, Sheridan, and Terry interceded on Custer's behalf, and Grant relented.

On May 8, Custer rushed to Fort Abraham Lincoln to lead the 7th Cavalry on what would be his final campaign.

📖 The best sources for the Allison Commission's attempt to purchase the Black Hills and ensuing events leading to hostilities include Allison's report, *Annual Report to the Commissioner of Indian Affairs, 1875; Red Cloud's Folk: A History of the Oglala Sioux,* by George E. Hyde (Norman: University of Oklahoma Press, 1937); George E. Hyde's *Spotted Tail's Folk: A History of the Brule Sioux* (Norman: University of Oklahoma Press, 1961); *A History of the Dakota or Sioux Indians,* by Doane Robinson (Minneapolis: Ross and Haines, 1904); "The Majors and the Miners: The Role of the U.S. Army in the Black Hills Gold Rush," by Watson Parker, *Journal of the West* 11 (January 1972), pp. 99–113; *Centennial Campaign: The Sioux War of 1876,* by John S. Gray (Fort Collins, CO: Old Army Press, 1976).

Walter P. Jenny's *Report on the Mineral Wealth, Climate and Rainfall and Natural Resources of the Black Hills of South Dakota,* which covers his 1875 expedition, can be found in 44 Cong., 1 sess., *Exec. Doc. 51.* Grant's edict of December 6, 1875, to the Lakota Sioux in the unceded territory is contained in *Report of the Secretary of War, 1876,* p. 28. The instructions to the various Indian agents are in 44 Cong., 1 sess., *Sen. Exec. Doc. No. 52,* pp. 5–6, and 44 Cong., 1 sess., *House Exec. Doc. No. 184,* pp. 14–15.

Custer's duty at Fort Lincoln during this period is chronicled in *"Boots and Saddles"; or, Life in Dakota with General Custer,* by Elizabeth B. Custer (New York: Harper and Brothers, 1885). Sources for Custer's testimony at the impeachment hearings can be found in "Custer and the Belknap Hearings" on page 171.

CHAPTER SEVEN

Custer's Last Stand

OVERVIEW

The strategy for the Little Bighorn campaign, designed by Generals Alfred H. Terry and George Crook, called for three columns to converge on the Indians—whose exact location was unknown—and catch them within this three-pronged movement. Gen. George Crook would command one column, which would march north from Fort Fetterman, Wyoming. The Montana Column would be led by Col. John Gibbon and would march east down the Yellowstone River from Fort Ellis. The third column, which was commanded by General Terry and included Lt. Col. George Armstrong Custer and the 7th Cavalry, would march west from Fort Abraham Lincoln.

The first column to take to the field was the one commanded by Crook, which set off in early March. On March 16, a detachment of Crook's column, led by Col. Joseph J. Reynolds, encountered an Indian village on the Powder River. Reynolds quickly routed the Indians, but Crazy Horse mounted a fierce counterattack, which forced the troops to abandon the field (see "Prelude to Little Bighorn: The Powder River and Rosebud Engagements" on page 189).

On April 3, Gibbon marched from Fort Ellis with six companies of his own regiment and the 2nd Cavalry under Maj. James Brisbin—about 450 troops. The Dakota Column—nearly 1,000 men—had been delayed by poor weather, which prevented the receipt of supplies, but finally marched on May 17 from Fort Abraham Lincoln (see "Table of Organization and Casualty Report of the 7th Cavalry for the Little Bighorn Campaign" on page 187).

The various Indian bands in the vicinity—Sioux and Northern Cheyenne—were aware that the army was on their trail and began to assemble under Sitting Bull's command. Perhaps as many as 400 lodges—some 3,000 people—steadily moved toward a gathering point in the Rosebud River Valley.

"I guess we'll get through them in one day."

—CUSTER'S REPLY ON THE MORNING OF JUNE 25 TO HIS SCOUT'S ASSERTION THAT THERE WERE ENOUGH SIOUX TO KEEP THEM FIGHTING TWO OR THREE DAYS

George Armstrong Custer, March 1876. *Courtesy Little Bighorn Battlefield National Monument.*

BIOGRAPHIES

✳ Minton "Mitch" Bouyer
Guide and Interpreter

Bouyer (or Boyer, or Bouer) was born about 1837 to John Baptiste Bouyer, a Frenchman, and a full Santee Sioux woman. Known as "Chopper," "Hammering Out," "Man Wearing Calfskin Vest," Michael, Mitch, or Minton Bouyer had access to both white and Indian cultures, and could speak English, Sioux, and Crow. His father, a blacksmith, was killed by Indians in 1863 while trapping near Fort Laramie.

Mitch Bouyer. *Courtesy Little Bighorn Battlefield National Monument.*

Bouyer became a protégé of Jim Bridger at some point and explored much of the West with the famous mountain man. He served as a guide for the Sir George Gore hunting expedition from 1854 until 1857, then moved to the Yellowstone region and operated a ferry on the river crossing of the Bozeman Trail. In 1865, he guided Gen. Patrick Conner's expedition from Fort Laramie to the Tongue

(continued on following page)

Scouts under Col. George Gibbon had noticed this activity as early as May 16 but failed to inform General Terry until his column arrived in early June at the mouth of the Powder River, where the steamer *Far West* was docked. On June 7, Terry dispatched Maj. Marcus Reno and six companies of the 7th Cavalry to scout the Powder and Tongue River Valleys (see "Reno's Powder River Scout" on page 192).

On June 17, while Reno was on his scout, Gen. George Crook's column had halted for a mid-morning coffee break on upper Rosebud Creek, and was attacked by a large force of the Indians led by Crazy Horse. Crook battled the Indians for about six hours, until his enemy finally broke contact. Crook, proclaiming victory, immediately fell back to his camp on Goose Creek without informing anyone of his whereabouts or intentions—effectively removing his command from the operation (see "Prelude to Little Bighorn: The Powder River and Rosebud Engagements" on page 189).

Reno returned from his scout, and although he had disobeyed orders by venturing to the Rosebud, he had gathered valuable information. He had located a large, abandoned vil-

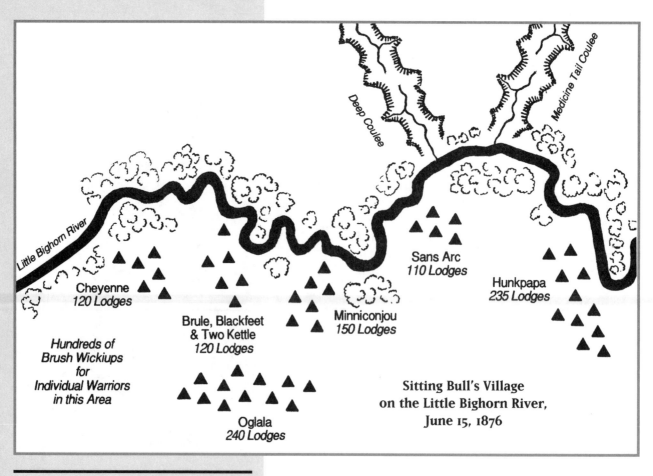

Cheyenne
120 Lodges

Hundreds of Brush Wickiups for Individual Warriors in this Area

Brule, Blackfeet & Two Kettle
120 Lodges

Oglala
240 Lodges

Minniconjou
150 Lodges

Sans Arc
110 Lodges

Hunkpapa
235 Lodges

Sitting Bull's Village on the Little Bighorn River, June 15, 1876

lage, with a trail that indicated which direction the Indians had gone. Terry could now assume that the hostiles he sought were in the vicinity of the Valley of the Little Bighorn.

The Indians had indeed moved their village to that location, and their numbers had grown. Bolstered by those Indians who had left the reservations for a summer of freedom, the village had swelled to about 1,000 lodges—some 7,000 people, including perhaps 2,000 or more warriors.

On June 21, aboard the *Far West,* which was moored on the Yellowstone at the mouth of the Rosebud, Terry issued orders for Lt. Col. George Armstrong Custer and his 7th Cavalry to follow the Indian trail that Reno had found. These orders later created a controversy when some—including Terry—contended that Custer had disobeyed them (see "Did Custer Disobey Orders?" on page 208).

Custer's command covered over seventy miles in the next three days, locating and following the Indian trail on the second day out. On the morning of June 24, Custer had passed the limits of Reno's scout and happened upon a large abandoned village where the Indians had recently held a Sun Dance. The column followed the fresh trail from the village and camped at dusk on Mud Creek, after a march of about twenty-eight miles. Scouts under 2nd Lt. Charles Varnum, who had been dispatched earlier to gather information, returned to report that the Indians were likely on the lower Little Bighorn River. Custer marched at 11 P.M. and paused three hours later, in the wee hours of June 25, for a brief rest before resuming the march.

At 8 A.M., Custer was summoned to a promontory called Crow's Nest—a traditional Plains Indian lookout—that afforded a fair view of the Valley of the Little Bighorn, although the river, the bordering trees, and the Indian village located there some fifteen miles distant were not visible. The scouts—Varnum, Charley Reynolds, Mitch Bouyer, and a number of Arikara and Crow—had observed some smoke in that direction, as well as what they believed to be a sizable pony herd grazing in the valley. By the time Custer arrived at about 9 A.M., a haze had settled over the hilly terrain that made it impossible for him to recognize anything that far away. He did, however, accept the assessment of his scouts that a huge Indian village lay ahead.

Custer returned to camp, where he was informed by his brother Tom that Capt. Myles Keogh, whose battalion had been detailed with the pack train, reported that a troubling incident had occurred. Troopers with Company F had been sent back to retrieve a box of hardtack that had fallen off a mule during the night march. When the detail located the box, it was surrounded by several Indians, who had been sampling the contents and raced away as the soldiers approached.

This information convinced Custer that the hostiles were now aware of the presence and location of his command. This would necessitate immediate action, or—as was the custom

River. He later hired on as a guide and interpreter at Fort C. F. Smith and then Fort Phil Kearny. In late 1869, Bouyer married Magpie Outside, known as Mary, with whom he had two children.

In the summer of 1870, Bouyer began working for a trader among the Mountain Crow, and by the time he had moved on two years later, he had been adopted as a member of that tribe. For the next six years, he was employed in various capacities, including guide for the military escort for the 1872 Northern Pacific Railroad Survey; post guide at Fort Ellis in 1872; and from 1873 as interpreter, laborer, or messenger at the Crow Agency.

Bouyer was employed in April 1876 for $150 a month as a guide for the Montana Column, which was part of the Little Bighorn campaign. On June 22, he was attached to the 7th Cavalry due to his extensive knowledge of the Rosebud and Little Bighorn Valleys. He accompanied Lt. Charles Varnum to the observation point known as Crow's Nest on the morning of June 25 and warned George Armstrong Custer that they would find more Indians than they could handle in the distant camp. Custer reputedly told Bouyer that he could stay behind if he was afraid. Bouyer replied that he would go wherever Custer went, and thus he became the only army scout killed with Custer's detachment.

In 1987, it was announced that bone fragments discovered on the battlefield had been identified as belonging to Bouyer. Those remains were buried at the Little Bighorn National Monument Cemetery on July 25 of that year.

📖 Excellent information about Bouyer can be found in John S. Gray's classic *Custer's Last Campaign: Mitch Boyer and the Little Bighorn Reconstructed* (Lincoln: University of Nebraska Press, 1991). Also see *Memoirs of a White Crow Indian,* by Thomas B. Marquis (New York: The Century Co., 1928); "Mitch Bouyer . . . A Scout for Custer," by R. G. Hickox, *Gun Report* (March 1980); "Nameless Faces of Custer Battlefield, *Greasy Grass* (1988), Custer Battlefield Historical and Museum Association; and a letter from W. B. Logan, Fort Belknap Agency to Walter Camp, dated May 17, 1909, in the Walter Camp Collection, Lee Library, Brigham Young University.

BIOGRAPHIES

⚙ Crazy Horse
Oglala-Brule Sioux

Crazy Horse (Tashunka Witco or Tashunca-Uitco, meaning "His Horse Is Crazy") was born about 1842 on the eastern edge of the Black Hills near the site of present-day Rapid City, Sioux Dakota. His mother was a member of the Brule tribe, reportedly the sister of Spotted Tail, and his father was an Oglala medicine man. His mother died when he was quite young, and his father took her sister as a wife and raised the child in both Brule and Oglala camps. He had a fair complexion, as well as light, curly hair, for which he was called Curly. He killed a buffalo when he was twelve and received a horse for his accomplishment. At about that time, he witnessed the Grattan massacre while residing in Conquering Bear's camp. He also viewed the destruction of the Indian village at Ash Hollow caused by Gen. William Harney's punitive expedition (see "The Initiation of Warfare between the Plains Indians and the U.S. Army" on page 49). Those experiences made an indelible impression on him and helped shape his militant attitude toward white men.

Not long after the Grattan affair, Curly sought guidance and underwent a vision quest by meditating on a mountaintop. He experienced a vivid dream depicting a mounted warrior in a storm who became invulnerable by following certain

(continued on following page)

of the Indians when discovered by the army—the village would vanish into the hills. Time was now of the essence. The column would march at once in the direction of the presumed location of the village. Custer would formulate his battle plan as events warranted.

At about noon, the 7th Cavalry paused at the head of Reno Creek. Custer's first move was to separate his regiment into battalions. Maj. Marcus A. Reno would command one battalion, consisting of Companies A, G, and M—about 140 men. Capt. Frederick W. Benteen was assigned Companies D, H, and K—about 125 men. Capt. Myles W. Keogh would command C, I, and L, and Capt. George Yates, E and F—about 225 men—under Custer's direct control. Capt. Thomas McDougall was placed in charge of the pack train, which consisted of his Company B, an escort of troopers from various companies, and the civilian packers—about 85 men (see "Should Custer Have Separated His Command?" on page 211).

Captain Benteen's battalion was detailed on a reconnaissance to the west along a series of ridges that overlooked the Little Bighorn River for the purpose of thwarting an Indian escape in that direction. It would later catch up with the main column farther down Reno Creek.

The remainder of the regiment—with McDougall's pack train quickly falling behind—marched eight miles toward the village before halting when they came upon another abandoned village site. Only a lone tepee with the body of a dead warrior inside was left standing. The Arikara scouts were setting fire to the tepee as scout Fred Girard galloped up. "Here are your Indians, General!" he shouted, "Running like devils."

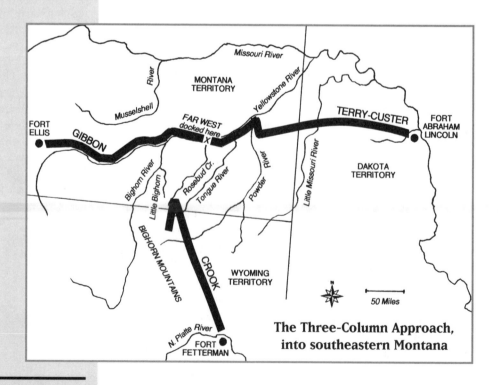

The Three-Column Approach, into southeastern Montana

Plumes of dust could be observed rising from beyond the distant hills. Custer understood that he must act immediately or the Indians would escape. The regiment was moved another two miles before halting on a fork of Reno Creek.

It was here that 1st Lt. William W. Cooke, Custer's adjutant, relayed orders to Major Reno. Custer directed Reno to move rapidly forward toward the village "and charge afterward," telling him that he would be supported by the whole outfit. Reno's three companies immediately moved out and crossed the creek a short distance upstream from where it flowed into the Little Bighorn River (see "Custer's Battle Plan" on page 205).

It was just after 3 P.M. when Major Reno and his three companies of cavalrymen advanced steadily toward their objective, which lay about two miles directly ahead.

By this time, Custer had maneuvered his battalion onto the high ridge on the eastern side of the Little Bighorn River. From this vantage point, he could view the Indian village as well as assess the terrain and select suitable routes by which to send his men down the various ravines toward the village on the opposite side of the river. Custer dispatched Sgt. Daniel Kanipe with orders to tell Captain McDougall to hurry the pack train, which was laden with ammunition.

rituals, such as wearing long, unbraided hair; painting his body with white hail spots; tying a small stone behind each ear; and decorating his cheek with a zigzag lightning bolt. Curly's father interpreted the dream as a sign of his son's future greatness in combat.

The following year, Curly was said to have killed his first human. He was in the company of a small band of Sioux warriors who were attempting to steal Pawnee horses when they happened upon some Osage buffalo hunters. In the midst of a fight, Curly spotted an Osage in the bushes and killed this person, which, to his surprise, turned out to be a woman. It was not shameful in Sioux culture to kill a woman, but he was so upset that he refused to take her scalp and left it for someone else.

When he was sixteen years old, Curly proved his worth as a warrior during a battle with Arapaho. Decorated like the warrior in his dream, he was in the thick of the fighting, scoring coup after coup, taking many scalps, but to his dismay, he was

(continued on following page)

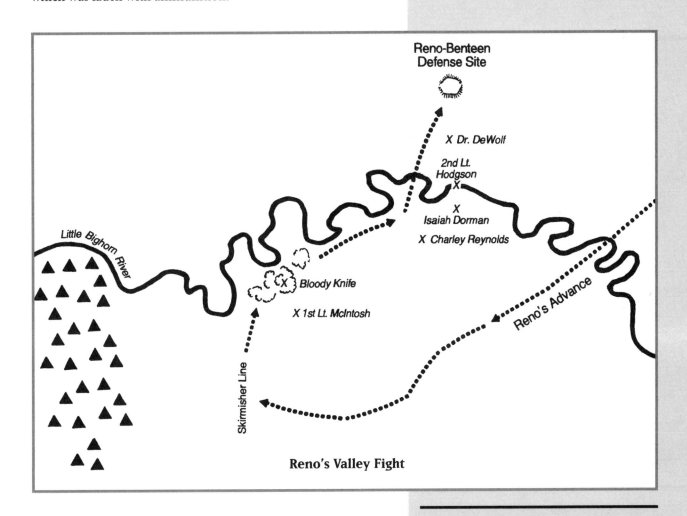

Reno-Benteen Defense Site

X Dr. DeWolf

2nd Lt. Hodgson
X

X
Isaiah Dorman

X Charley Reynolds

Little Bighorn River

X Bloody Knife

X 1st Lt. McIntosh

Skirmisher Line

Reno's Advance

Reno's Valley Fight

struck by an arrow in the leg. Curly wondered why he had been wounded when the rituals he had imitated from the warrior he saw in his vision had promised protection. He finally realized that his dream warrior had taken no scalps, and he had. From that day forward, Curly never again scalped an enemy.

He received a great tribute after that battle. His father sang a song that he had composed for his son and announced that the boy would now be known by a new name—Crazy Horse. That name, by the way, was nothing special, rather an old, common name among the Sioux tribes.

Throughout the ensuing years, Crazy Horse built a reputation among his people as a crafty, fearless warrior. He participated in many successful raids against traditional Indian enemies and the occasional small party of whites traveling through Sioux country but had not faced the might of the U.S. Army. In 1865, that dramatically changed when an endless stream of whites—gold seekers headed for Montana—flooded the Bozeman Trail, and the army garrisoned several forts to protect them.

In 1866–67, during what became known as Red Cloud's War, Crazy Horse was instrumental in rallying his fellow warriors and displaying an almost mythical courage and tactical craftiness. Along with Red Cloud's leadership and the efforts of Crazy Horse, Hump, Gall, and Rain-in-the-Face, the army finally admitted defeat and negotiated a treaty to end hostilities (see "Red Cloud's War" on page 68).

Crazy Horse, however, refused to "touch the pen" to the Fort Laramie Treaty of 1868, disdained the reservation, and chose instead to freely roam traditional Sioux hunting grounds and wage war against the Crow and Shoshone. It was said that during this time of wandering, he married a Northern Cheyenne woman, which gained him friends and followers from that tribe. His interest in a certain Lakota Sioux woman, however, nearly cost him his life.

Crazy Horse, who was known as introverted and eccentric, had ten years earlier vigorously courted Black Buffalo Woman, Red Cloud's niece. At that time, she had spurned Crazy Horse in favor of a warrior named No Water. Gossip spread that Crazy Horse had continued to visit Black Buffalo Woman when her husband was away. In 1871, Crazy Horse persuaded her to run away with him. No Water was incensed and set out on the trail, finally finding the couple together in a tepee. He shot Crazy Horse, the bullet entering at the nostril, fracturing his jaw, and nearly killing him. Crazy

(continued on following page)

Kanipe raced off as Reno's men thundered down the widening valley on a collision course with the village. About a quarter mile from the village, however, Reno inexplicably aborted his charge and halted the battalion. Reno had suffered no casualties and had faced little opposition, yet, in his first meaningful encounter with hostile Plains Indians, he had countermanded Custer's orders and called for a halt short of his objective.

Indian testimony later stated that the unexpected appearance of Reno's troops had them preparing the village for flight—until Reno stopped his charge. That pause in the action permitted the Indians time to assemble a defense and, subsequently, a counterattack on Reno. The presence of Custer's command remained unknown to the Indians at this time.

Reno dismounted his troopers and formed a skirmish line a few hundred yards in length across the prairie. The horse holders (every fourth man) led the mounts to the protection of the underbrush by the riverbank fifty yards to the east. The troopers could observe the Indians gathering in force and, although they were somewhat out of range, began firing in earnest into the village. Reno to that point had lost only two men whose horses had bolted and carried them into the village.

It is unknown whether Custer was aware of Reno's actions. He may have noticed that the village was not being disassembled, which meant that the Indians, for some reason, intended to stand and fight. He likely headed north at a trot, halting his command a short distance down Cedar Coulee. It may have been Custer that Reno's men thought they observed at about this time on the ridge watching them before he moved on to Weir Point, either alone or in the company of other officers. Custer, now able to view the entire village, sent orderly Pvt. John Martin with a hastily scribbled order written by Cooke to locate Benteen and urge the captain to hurry his troops and bring the ammunition packs with him.

Meanwhile, Reno was informed that a group of Indians was maneuvering down the gully toward the horses. Company G was ordered to the river, which left the skirmisher line spread out much too thinly to be effective.

Reno was now uncertain about what course of action to take, and either he ordered a retreat or the battalion simply executed one of its own accord. Regardless, no tactical covering fire was employed for the impulsive movement that led to

"Bloody Knife looks on in wonder at me because I never get tired, and says no other man could ride all night and never sleep."

—CUSTER TO LIBBIE, MAY 1876

a crescent-shaped stand of timber near the river, and the Indians took advantage of that by surrounding the position.

It was now about 3:30 P.M. Reno's command had lost only several killed and wounded from snipers to this point. The position in the timber was an excellent site to defend, due to its density and thick underbrush. Additionally, it posed no direct threat to the village, inasmuch as it was lower in elevation. The Indians could now pack up and depart if they so desired. Reno could simply hunker down in a defensive position and await the arrival of Custer and Benteen.

But Major Reno, instead of being satisfied with his relative safety, decided that he would move the command to the high bluffs across the Little Bighorn River. Rather than executing a bugle call that could have been heard above the din, he issued a verbal command ordering his men to mount and prepare to move out. The troopers near Reno understood the order and mounted, but others were too distant to hear or had problems controlling or catching their excited mounts, which caused mass confusion.

In their haste to assemble, the soldiers' firing had almost completely ceased. This allowed a party of Indians to approach the gathered troops and fire their weapons at close range. The deadly volley dropped a number of troopers. One casualty was Bloody Knife, Custer's favorite scout, who had been conferring with Reno when a bullet struck him between the eyes, sending blood and brains splattering onto the major's face.

The shocked Reno panicked. He ordered the troops to dismount, then ordered them to remount. Then, without regard for the men in the timber, Reno put the spurs to his horse and dashed for the river. The disorganized command trailed along behind their leader. A number of troopers and scouts—1st Lt. Charles DeRudio, Pvt. Thomas O'Neill, Billy Jackson, George Herendeen, and Fred Girard—found themselves abandoned during the retreat and remained trapped in the timber while the rest of the command raced for the river. Military discipline had broken down, and it was every man for himself.

The river was one-half to one mile of open terrain away. No effort had been made to cover the retreat with a base of covering fire, and the fleeing soldiers could offer little resistance. The warriors, seizing the opportunity, rode within fifty feet on the flanks of the loose formation and opened fire, easily picking off the exposed troopers one by one, then closing in to kill the wounded or those whose horses had faltered.

The Little Bighorn River offered further obstacles to Reno's panicked command. The water itself was a hindrance, but on the far side awaited a steep and slippery eight-foot-high riverbank. Numerous cavalry horses balked and lost their footing, and when the command bunched up, the warriors closed in and clubbed the soldiers off their mounts.

Those troopers who managed to reach the eastern shore and scramble up the bluff provided no assistance to their

Horse gradually recovered from this serious wound. Black Buffalo Woman returned to No Water, but some months later, she gave birth to a sandy-haired child that suspiciously resembled Crazy Horse. The Sioux warrior licked his romantic wounds, and in the summer of 1872 married Black Shawl, with whom he had a daughter, They-Are-Afraid-of-Her.

The military had been encroaching on Sioux buffalo hunting grounds for some time, and when George Armstrong Custer's Yellowstone expedition of 1873 served as escort for the Northern Pacific Railroad survey crews, it has been said that Crazy Horse may have participated in the violent opposition (see "Who Were Those Sioux That Attacked Custer?" on page 128).

The discovery of gold during Custer's Black Hills expedition the following year brought hordes of miners into that sacred Sioux region, which had been promised them by the provisions of the 1868 Fort Laramie Treaty. Negotiations by the U.S. government to buy the land angered Crazy Horse and other free-roaming Sioux. The bodies of many miners—unscalped—began turning up in the Black Hills. Although no direct evidence exists, it has been widely speculated, even by his own people, that Crazy Horse was behind these brutal acts.

Another incident occurred about this time that had a profound effect on Crazy Horse. He was out fighting Crow Indians when his daughter died of cholera. The village had moved about seventy miles from the location of the burial scaffold on which lay They-Are-Afraid-of-Her. Crazy Horse tracked down the site and lay for three days beside his daughter's body.

The U.S. government issued an edict in late 1875 demanding that all Indians in the vicinity of the Yellowstone Valley report to the reservation by January 31, 1876, or face severe military reprisals. Crazy Horse, Sitting Bull, and others ignored the demand and remained free. The first indication that the army meant business came in mid-March, when troops under Gen. George Crook attacked and destroyed a Sioux-Cheyenne village on the Powder River. Crazy Horse came to the rescue of his people that night in the midst of a raging snowstorm to recapture the pony herd (see "Prelude to Little Bighorn: The Powder River and Rosebud Engagements" on page 189).

Three months later, Crook marched again, this time headed down Rosebud Creek—unbeknownst to Crook, directly toward Sitting Bull's huge camp. Concerned about the welfare of their families, it was decided that Crazy Horse would attack this col-

(continued on following page)

umn. Crazy Horse struck at midmorning on June 17 and, in a three-hour battle that demonstrated his masterful decoy tactics, fought Crook to a stalemate (see "Prelude to Little Bighorn: The Powder River and Rosebud Engagements" on page 189).

On the afternoon of June 25, when Custer's 7th Cavalry attacked Sitting Bull's village on the Little Bighorn River, Crazy Horse, his body painted with white hail spots, the zigzag lightning bolt on his cheek, and a brown pebble tied behind each ear, led a group of warriors that delivered the final, murderous charge into the cavalrymen. He rode down the valley below the village, crossed the river, and swept along the ridge south from Custer Hill, killing as he went and forcing the remaining soldiers on Calhoun Hill into the clutches of Gall and his warriors, who had attacked from the west.

After the battle, Crazy Horse and 600 of his followers spent about a month celebrating their victory with feasts and dances. He then returned to the Black Hills to harass prospectors. While other Sioux bands split up and apparently had lost their lust for war, Crazy Horse waged what amounted at times to a one-man fight to regain the land promised to his people.

On September 9, a detachment from Crook's column happened upon a Sioux village at Slim Buttes and quickly routed the residents. Crazy Horse, who was nearby, was notified and arrived with his warriors about noon to mount a counter-

(continued on following page)

comrades. There was no organized covering fire to assist the soldiers, who then became easy prey for Indians firing from both banks.

Major Reno was reportedly among the first to arrive safely at the top of the bluff across the river. The remnants of his command had straggled up the cliff and began forming a defensive position. Reno had lost at least forty killed and thirteen wounded in the action. The dead bodies of both men and horses marked the route Reno had taken in his retreat from the timber to the river.

Dr. Henry Porter, the acting assistant surgeon, approached Reno on the bluff and mentioned that the troops were quite demoralized by the retreat. Reno replied irritably, "That was a cavalry charge, sir!"

It was about 4 P.M., and remarkably to those on the hilltop, the Indians broke contact with them and could be noticed riding toward the north. The troops were too involved in their own preservation to consider the reason for this sudden departure. They were not aware that another force of Sioux and Cheyenne had encountered Custer's command on the barren grassland some four miles away, and that their tormentors were hurrying to join that fray.

Perhaps Custer had noticed only Reno's initial skirmisher line, not the retreat, and believed that Reno would be fighting his way toward the village as ordered. Regardless, instead of retreating, Custer chose to strike the village with his battalion. He moved his command down Cedar Coulee to upper Medicine Tail Coulee, perhaps pausing for a few moments to adjust equipment as well as allow Benteen additional time to arrive.

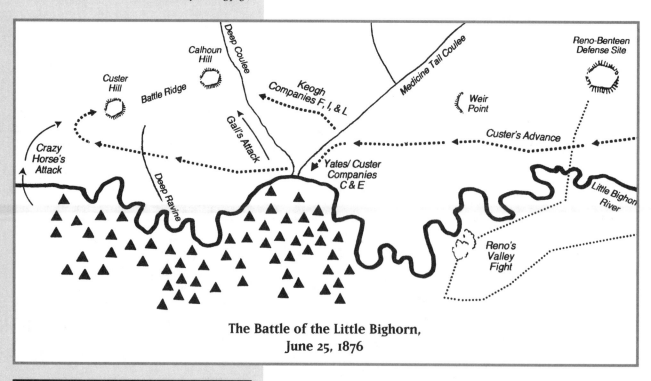

**The Battle of the Little Bighorn,
June 25, 1876**

Orderly John Martin, who looked back as he rode off, claimed that his last sight of Custer's command was the Gray Horse Troop—Capt. George Yates with Companies E and F—galloping down Medicine Tail Coulee, heading toward the center of the village, perhaps personally led by Custer. This action may have been intended as merely a feint or decoy to distract the attention of the enemy from the other battalion. Capt. Myles Keogh, with Companies C, I, and L, by this time would have ascended the slope to higher ground, likely with orders to ride toward the north end of the village and seek a suitable striking point along the way.

The Indians who had routed Reno, however, could now concentrate on this new threat—joined by their brethren who had been tending the pony herd. Yates was met with fierce resistance as he approached the village, which lay across the river, and took enough casualties to force him to pull back and head for higher ground.

attack. The battle raged throughout the afternoon, until Crook arrived with reinforcements and Crazy Horse was forced to break contact.

Gen. Nelson A. Miles and his infantry then commenced a relentless pursuit of the hostile Sioux and Cheyenne. The winter of 1876–77 had taken its toll, and many fugitive Indians, weary of running and near-starvation conditions, were surrendering. Crazy Horse, however, continued to fight. On January 8, 1877, he led 500 warriors in a surprise attack on Miles at Wolf Mountain on the Tongue River in southern Montana. Miles had disguised his howitzers as wagons and opened up on Crazy Horse's force, which retreated to some bluffs. The soldiers counterattacked, and Crazy Horse prudently withdrew under the cover of a snowstorm.

(continued on following page)

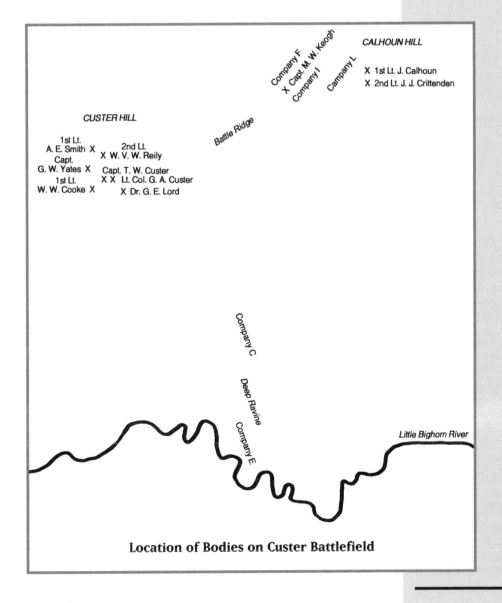

Location of Bodies on Custer Battlefield

By that time, Crazy Horse's defiance had begun to waver. His people were starving, and his wife had contracted tuberculosis. General Crook had promised Crazy Horse a reservation of his own if he would submit. On May 5, 1877, the legendary warrior led 800 to 900 of his brethren in a parade two miles long, guided by Red Cloud, into Fort (Camp) Robinson.

His presence at Red Cloud Agency had a great effect on young braves, who worshiped him; the older chiefs, who resented him; and the army, which distrusted him. The reservation that Crook had promised him apparently had been simply a ruse to encourage him to surrender. He was asked by Crook to visit Washington but refused. Crook, through interpreter Frank Grouard, asked Crazy Horse if he would help the army fight against the Nez Perce. Grouard reportedly misinterpreted the response on purpose to indicate that Crazy Horse wanted to fight whites, which led Crook to believe that the Sioux warrior intended to lead his people in a rebellion.

Crazy Horse requested that he be allowed to take the ill Black Shawl to Spotted Tail Agency, but that was viewed as a threat and he was denied permission. He went anyway, chased by soldiers who failed to catch him. He did, however, agree to return and did so—to his surprise, as a prisoner—on September 5.

Crazy Horse was being led to the stockade at Fort Robinson when he panicked at the thought of incarceration and tried to escape. Little Big Man and several other Indian guards grabbed him, and Pvt. William Gentiles stepped forward to run his bayonet through Crazy Horse's body.

According to *The Killing of Crazy Horse*, by Robert A. Clark (Lincoln: University of Nebraska Press, 1976), Crazy Horse said as he lay on his deathbed:

> I was not hostile to the white man. . . . We had buffalo for food, and their hides for clothing and our tipis. We preferred hunting to a life of idleness on the reservations, where we were driven against our will. At times, we did not get enough to eat, and we were not allowed to leave the reservation to hunt. We preferred our own way of living. We were no expense to the government then. All we wanted was peace, to be left alone. . . . They tried to confine me, I tried to escape, and a soldier ran his bayonet through me. I have spoken.

Crazy Horse died later that day. His father buried the body of his son at some secret location in his homeland—legend has it near Wounded

There has been speculation that Custer was struck down on this assault down Medicine Tail Coulee. Although no definitive evidence exists to prove this theory, dead or alive, Custer would have been transported by his troopers to the high bluffs. Had he been killed, Captain Keogh as senior officer would have assumed command, and adjutant Cooke would have moved to Keogh's side. Cooke's body, however, was found with Custer on Custer Hill, while Keogh was some distance away.

Keogh's command had taken a position on the high ridge—known as Battle Ridge—between Medicine Tail and Deep Coulee and formed a skirmisher line. Company L under 1st Lt. James Calhoun assumed the position farthest south on what would be known as Calhoun Hill, likely acting as rear guard waiting for the expected arrival of Benteen and the pack train.

It is entirely possible that portions or all of Custer's command had continued beyond Custer Hill to the north, where they were forced by the enemy to fall back to that "last stand" position.

The Indians would not have immediately charged into the beleaguered troops along Battle Ridge, but remained at a safe distance—hidden in the tall buffalo grass, bushes, and rugged terrain—firing an endless stream of arcing arrows and rifle fire at their pinned-down prey. Some warriors would have sneaked up close to wave blankets and pick off horse holders in an attempt to stampede the cavalry mounts, which carried precious ammunition in their saddlebags. Captured horses were then stampeded through the various positions. The desperate cavalrymen shot the remaining horses for breastworks, but one by one the soldiers fell, until each pocket of resistance was weakened by loss of manpower. Eventually, as defenses became vulnerable, incidences of hand-to-hand combat became commonplace as the Sioux and Cheyenne came forward with hatchets, clubs, and coup sticks.

The end came within a hour's time, or, according to Gall, "about as long as it takes a hungry man to eat dinner." The troopers were running out of ammunition, and additional warriors had entered the fray. The fatal blow was administered by Crazy Horse and Two Moons, who led a large force of warriors down the valley above the village, crossed the river, and attacked those left alive on Custer Hill. Custer was later found with two wounds—a bullet hole in the left breast at or near the heart and one in the left temple.

Then, continuing south, the warriors swept the eastern slope, crushing what remained of Keogh and Calhoun's troops against Gall's warriors, who had attacked from the direction of the village.

Immediately following the battle, the warriors left the field to the women, old men, and children and rode four miles north, where the remnants of Maj. Marcus Reno's command had taken refuge on a high bluff above the Little Bighorn River.

📖 See sources listed after chapter 8.

(continued on following page)

SIDEBARS

Table of Organization and Casualty Report of the 7th Cavalry for the Little Bighorn Campaign

Nearly every source about the battle differs in estimated casualty totals. This table was compiled from the official 7th Cavalry muster rolls dated June 30, 1876. Those troopers from companies attached to Custer's battalion listed as "wounded in action" or "died of wounds" either were serving with another company or were with the pack train at the time of the battle. Therefore, it is extremely difficult to calculate exact strength numbers for individual companies. Although identification was impossible in some cases due to mutilation, 208 or 210 bodies, depending on the account, were said to have been found and buried on June 27, 1876, on the Custer battlefield. This figure may not account for an undetermined number that may have been missing from the field—excluding Lieutenants Henry M. Harrington, James E. Porter, and James G. Sturgis, who were presumed to have been killed but whose bodies were never found.

Code: KIA: killed in action; WIA: wounded in action;
DOW: died of wounds

Headquarters:
Lt. Col. George Armstrong Custer, commanding (KIA)
1st Lt. William W. Cooke, adjutant (KIA)
Lt. George E. Lord, assistant surgeon (KIA)
Mitch Bouyer, interpreter (KIA)
Marcus H. Kellogg, correspondent (KIA)
Harry Armstrong Reed, attached civilian (KIA)
Boston Custer, forage master (from pack train—KIA)
(3 officers, 2 enlisted, and 4 staff members KIA)

Custer's Battalion:

Company C	Capt. Thomas W. Custer (KIA); 2nd Lt. Henry M. Harrington (KIA) (2 officers and 36 enlisted KIA; 4 enlisted WIA; 1 enlisted DOW)
Company E	1st Lt. Algernon E. Smith (KIA); 2nd Lt. James G. Sturgis (KIA) (2 officers and 37 enlisted KIA; 2 enlisted WIA)
Company F	Capt. George W. Yates (KIA); 2nd Lt. William V. W. Reilly (KIA) (2 officers and 36 enlisted KIA)
Company I	Capt. Myles W. Keogh (KIA); 1st Lt. James E. Porter (KIA) (2 officers and 36 enlisted KIA; 1 enlisted WIA; 1 enlisted DOW)
Company L	1st Lt. James Calhoun (KIA); 2nd Lt. John J. Crittenden (KIA) (2 officers and 44 enlisted KIA; 1 enlisted WIA)

Knee—which has yet to be discovered by the white man.

The late Boston-born sculptor Korszak Ziolkowski, who helped carve Mount Rushmore, began a project in 1948 to sculpt a likeness of Crazy Horse on a mountainside in the Black Hills near the town of Custer. Ziolkowski died in 1982, but his vision has been carried on by other members of his family. The task of creating an exact likeness of the Lakota warrior may be difficult, however, inasmuch as no known photo of him exists.

📖 Perhaps the most famous and interesting account of Crazy Horse's life is the fictionalized *Crazy Horse: The Strange Man of the Oglalas,* by Mari Sandoz (New York: Alfred A. Knopf, 1942). Another fascinating biography, which fills in the blanks with dramatic and believable speculation, is *Crazy Horse and Custer: The Parallel Lives of Two American Warriors,* by Stephen E. Ambrose (Garden City, NY: Doubleday, 1975).

Also see *Crazy Horse: The Life behind the Legend,* by Mike Sajna (New York: John Wiley & Sons, 2000); *Red Cloud's Folk: A History of the Oglala Sioux,* by George E. Hyde (Norman: University of Oklahoma Press, 1937; *Spotted Tail's Folk: A History of the Brule Sioux,* by George E. Hyde (Norman: University of Oklahoma Press, 1961); *Crazy Horse,* by E. A. Brininstool (Los Angeles: Wetzel Publishing Co., 1949); *A Sioux Chronicle,* by George E. Hyde (Norman: University of Oklahoma Press, 1980); "Crazy Horse's Story of the Custer Battle," edited by Doane Robinson, *South Dakota Historical Collections* 12, no. 1 (1929); "Chief Crazy Horse, His Career and Death," by E. A. Brininstool, *Nebraska History* 12, no. 1 (1929); "Oglala Sources on the Life of Crazy Horse," by Eleanor Hinman, *Nebraska History* 57, no. 1 (1976); "An Indian Scout's Recollections of Crazy Horse," by Frank Grouard, *Nebraska History,* no. 12 (January–March, 1929); "The Man Who Killed Crazy Horse," by John M. Carroll, *Old West* 27, no. 4 (Summer 1991); "The Death of Crazy Horse," chapter 5 of *Camp on Custer,* edited by Bruce R. Liddic and Paul Harbaugh (Spokane: A. H. Clark Co., 1995). An excellent chronicle of Crazy Horse's last days can be found in *The Surrender and Death of Crazy Horse,* by Richard G. Hardorff (Spokane, WA: Arthur H. Clark, 1998).

BIOGRAPHIES

✺ James Madison DeWolf
*Acting Assistant Surgeon,
7th U.S. Cavalry*

DeWolf was born into a farming family on January 14, 1843, in Jenningsville, Pennsylvania. On August 1, 1861, he enlisted in the 1st Pennsylvania Light Artillery. He participated in the Peninsula campaigns, including the battles of Mechanicsville and Gaines Mill, and was wounded in the arm at the August 1862 second battle of Bull Run. In October of that year, he was medically discharged because of his injury as a corporal. DeWolf regained partial use of his arm and reenlisted in his artillery unit in September 1864. He was discharged on June 14, 1865.

Dr. James M. DeWolf. *Courtesy Little Bighorn Battlefield National Monument.*

DeWolf enlisted in Company E, 14th Infantry, in October 1865 and served most of the time as a hospital steward until his discharge on October 5, 1868. That same day, at Camp Lyon, Idaho, DeWolf enlisted under the name "James DeWall." He was discharged three years later and reenlisted once more, this time under his real name. On October 31, 1871, at Camp Warner in Oklahoma Territory, DeWolf married Fannie J. Downing, who served as a hospital matron at the post. In September 1873, he was transferred to Watertown Arsenal, Massachusetts, in order to attend Harvard University School of Medicine. He graduated on June 26, 1875, but subsequently failed the army medical examination for assistant surgeon. In October, however, while at Forkston, Pennsylvania, DeWolf managed to secure a position as contract surgeon with the army and was sent to Fort Totten, Dakota Territory. He assisted the post surgeon until March 1876, when he was sent to Fort Abraham Lincoln.

On June 21, 1876, DeWolf was assigned temporary duty with the 7th Cavalry as acting assistant surgeon. He was attached to Maj. Marcus Reno's command and accompanied the other troopers on their flight from the timber to the bluffs across the Little Bighorn River. DeWolf and his orderly made it to the bluffs but chose the wrong ravine to climb; they were halfway to the top when they were cut down by the Indians. It has been speculated that the doctor had possibly stopped to administer to a wounded soldier when he was killed. His death came by a gunshot wound to the abdomen and six wounds to the head and face,

(continued on following page)

Reno's Battalion:

Maj. Marcus A. Reno, commanding

2nd Lt. Benjamin H. Hodgson, adjutant (KIA)

Company A	Capt. Myles Moylan; 1st Lt. Charles DeRudio (8 enlisted KIA; 7 enlisted WIA; 1 enlisted DOW)
Company G	1st Lt. Donald McIntosh (KIA); 2nd Lt. George D. Wallace (1 officer and 13 enlisted KIA; 6 enlisted WIA)
Company M	Capt. Thomas H. French (12 enlisted KIA; 11 enlisted WIA; 1 enlisted DOW)

James M. DeWolf, acting assistant surgeon (KIA)
Henry R. Porter, acting assistant surgeon
2nd Lt. Charles A. Varnum (WIA), commanding Indian scouts
2nd Lt. Luther R. Hare, with Indian scouts
(2 scouts KIA; 2 scouts WIA)
Bloody Knife, scout (KIA)
Isaiah Dorman, interpreter (KIA)
Frederic Girard, interpreter
George B. Herendeen, scout
Billy Jackson, scout
Charles Reynolds, scout (KIA)

Benteen's Battalion

Capt. Frederick W. Benteen, commanding (WIA)

Company D	Capt. Thomas B. Weir; 2nd Lt. Winfield S. Edgerly (3 enlisted KIA; 3 enlisted WIA)
Company H	1st Lt. Francis M. Gibson (2 enlisted KIA; 20 enlisted WIA; 2 enlisted DOW)
Company K	1st Lt. Edward S. Godfrey (5 enlisted KIA; 3 enlisted WIA)

Pack Train:

1st Lt. Edward G. Mathey, commanding
(1 civilian packer KIA; 1 civilian packer WIA)

| Company B | Capt. Thomas M. McDougall (2 enlisted KIA; 5 enlisted WIA) |

Detached Service: Col. Samuel D. Sturgis; Maj. Lewis Merrill; Capt. Michael V. Sheridan; Capt. Charles S. Ilsley; Capt. John E. Tourtellotte; Capt. Owen Hale; 1st Lt. Henry J. Nowlan (with Terry); 1st Lt. William T. Craycroft; 1st Lt. Henry Jackson; 2nd Lt. Charles W. Larned

Leave of Absence: Maj. Joseph G. Tilford; 1st Lt. James M. Bell; 2nd Lt. Ernest A. Garlington

Sick Leave: 2nd Lt. Charles Braden; 2nd Lt. Andrew H. Nave

Total Casualties
KIA: 263
WIA: 68
DOW: 6

📖 Two excellent volumes are Richard G. Hardorff's *Custer Battle Casualties I* and *II* (El Segundo, CA: Upton and Sons, 1991 and 2000).

🐎 Prelude to Little Bighorn: The Powder River and Rosebud Engagements

Gen. George Crook and 800 men departed Fort Fetterman in early March 1876 and encountered a savage adversary in the Wyoming winter. Nevertheless, they pushed north toward known hostile country. On March 16, Crook's scouts located a Sioux-Cheyenne village of about 100 lodges, with perhaps as many as 250 warriors, on the Powder River. Colonel Joseph Reynolds, with six companies of the 3rd Cavalry—about 300 men—was issued orders to attack the unsuspecting village the following morning.

At dawn, Reynolds's men charged into the village and, without much opposition, quickly routed the surprised warriors—losing four soldiers killed and six wounded in the process. The cavalrymen took control of the village and commenced destroying everything of value, including a large quantity of beef that the poorly supplied army could have used for themselves. This loss of provisions and lodges, however, was a far greater blow to the Indians than the reported one killed and one wounded during the brief fight.

By early afternoon, during a raging snowstorm, Sioux warrior Crazy Horse, who had been camped downstream, had rallied the warriors and initiated a counterattack from the nearby bluffs. Reynolds, perhaps panicking, ordered an immediate withdrawal, abandoning several dead soldiers and at least one wounded man. The soldiers also left behind the Indian pony herd, which was easily recaptured by Crazy Horse.

General Crook was furious with Reynolds for not holding the village. When the command returned to Fort Fetterman on March 26, Crook filed court-martial charges against Reynolds, who was subsequently found guilty of neglect of duty. Reynolds was punished with a one-year suspension from duty, which was eventually commuted by his former West Point classmate, President U.S. Grant. Reynolds, however, would be quietly retired on disability the following year.

On May 29, Crook and a column consisting of fifteen companies of cavalry and five of infantry—more than 1,000 men—once again departed Fort Fetterman as part of Gen. Alfred H. Terry's three-pronged approach designed to close in around the hostile Indians. The men reached the head of the Tongue

and he was said to have been scalped in plain view of Reno's troops.

DeWolf was initially buried on the battlefield where he fell. His body was exhumed in July 1877 and reinterred in Woodlawn Cemetery at Norwalk, Ohio.

📖 "The Diary and Letters of Dr. James M. DeWolf, Acting Assistant Surgeon, U.S. Army: His Record of the Sioux Expedition of 1876 as Kept until His Death," by Edward S. Luce, *North Dakota History* 25, nos. 2 and 3 (April and July 1958). A notebook belonging to DeWolf was stolen while on display in the museum at Little Bighorn Battlefield National Monument and has never been recovered.

✴ Isaiah Dorman
Interpreter

Dorman, whose date and place of birth are unknown, was likely a runaway slave, possibly from the D'Orman family of Louisiana and Alabama, who reported the escape of a male slave named Isaiah. At some point, Dorman headed west and moved in with the Sioux tribe, who called him a *wasicum sapa,* or black white man. He married a Santee Sioux girl, Visible, from Inkpaduta's band and lived in a cabin near Fort Rice. The couple had two sons. He was said to have become friends during this time with Sitting Bull.

Dorman, whose Sioux names were Black Hawk, Azimpi, and Teat, worked as a woodcutter until signing on in 1865 to carry the mail between Forts Rice and Wadsworth, an ideal job for one whose relationship with the Sioux permitted him to travel through Indian country unmolested. In 1867, he vanished from the public record until resurfacing as a guide for the Yellowstone expedition in 1871. He subsequently served as an interpreter at Fort Rice.

Dorman was employed by the 7th Cavalry on May 14, 1876, as a guide for the Little Bighorn campaign. On June 25, he was attached to Maj. Marcus A. Reno's battalion and was killed in the valley fight, during the retreat from the timber to the river.

Circumstances surrounding his death have fostered a number of stories. One such story portrayed Dorman lying near death on the field when his friend Sitting Bull found him. He asked the Sioux medicine man for a cup of water, which was provided. It is doubtful, however, that Sitting Bull was even on the field that day. Other accounts claim that Dorman was singled out for special torture for betraying the Sioux.

(continued on following page)

Painting "Custer's Last Fight" by Cassilly Adams. This painting was later re-created by Otto Becker for a famous advertisement by Anheuser-Busch that adorned saloon walls in the late nineteenth century. *Courtesy Little Bighorn Battlefield National Monument.*

Sioux chief Runs-the-Enemy described the death of Dorman in *The Vanishing Race*, by Joseph K. Dixon (Garden City, NY: Doubleday, 1913):

We passed a black man in a soldier's uniform and we had him. He turned on his horse and shot an Indian right through the heart. Then the Indians fired at this one man and riddled his horse with bullets. His horse fell over his back and the black man could not get up. I saw him as I rode by. I afterward saw him lying there dead.

Eyewitnesses from the 7th Cavalry stated that Dorman had been badly mutilated. Pvt. William C. Slaper said Dorman was "found with many arrows shot in his body and head, and badly cut and slashed, while unmentionable atrocities had been committed." Custer's striker, John Burkman, added that Dorman had at least a dozen arrows in him, and a picket pin had been driven through his private area. According to scout George B. Herendeen: "I saw Indians shooting at Isaiah and squaws pounding him with stone hammers. His legs below the knees were shot full of bullets."

(continued on following page)

River near the Wyoming-Montana border on June 9, where they established a base camp on Goose Creek while waiting for about 260 Shoshone and Crow who wanted to take part in the campaign against their traditional enemies.

At about this time, the Sioux held a Sun Dance on the Rosebud, and Sitting Bull experienced a vision of dead soldiers falling from the sky into their camp, which was interpreted to mean that they would be victorious in a fight against the army.

Unknown to Crook, his presence was being closely monitored by Cheyenne scouts led by Wooden Leg. And when Crook broke camp on June 16, those scouts determined that the army was following a trail that would lead them directly to Sitting Bull's village, located a few miles north of present-day Busby, Montana. The Indians, concerned about the well-being of their families, held a council and decided that they would not wait for the army; Crazy Horse with as many as 1,000 Sioux and Cheyenne warriors would attack Crook's column.

On June 17, Crook called a halt at midmorning for coffee and to graze the horses in a valley of the Rosebud short of Big Bend. This cul-de-sac-shaped valley with steep walls was made up of broken terrain dotted with trees, bushes, ridges, and rock formations. It was sometime between 8 and 10 A.M. when Crow scouts raced into this camp from the north to spread the alarm that they had spotted a large body of hostile Indians.

Crook, however, would not be afforded the opportunity to assemble his troops in a battle formation or employ effective military tactics. Crazy Horse had departed from his customary tactic of circling around his prey from a distance, and instead immediately following the Crow scouts over the hills to lead his warriors on a charge into the surprised cavalrymen.

Because of the terrain, the fighting was reduced to small, hastily organized units engaging the determined warriors—at times hand-to-hand—at various locations around the three-mile-long field of battle. The Indians would hit and run, riding in and out among the troops, who attempted to hold their positions against each onslaught.

As the battle ensued, Crook decided that the best defense was an offense. In an effort to divert the warriors, he ordered that a detachment led by Capt. Anson Mills ride downstream and attack the Indian village that he incorrectly presumed was just a few miles away. Mills, with the promise that Crook would be following with the main column, rode down the valley, which, as he progressed, became narrower. He correctly assumed that Crazy Horse, the master of decoy, had deployed warriors in ambush along this route, so he proceeded with caution. Mills eventually turned back from his harrowing ride, either of his own accord or perhaps with recall orders from Crook, and thereby escaped disaster.

The fierce battle had raged for perhaps as long as six hours, or until midafternoon, when the Indians began massing for one final concentrated attack. Crook, however, recognized the strategy and ordered Mills to maneuver his cavalry behind the Indians. Crook's tactic was successful—the Indians broke contact and left the field to the cavalrymen, effectively ending the battle. The Indians later claimed that the reason they had fled at that point in time was because they were low on ammunition and their horses were worn out.

Crook proclaimed victory because his troops held the field at the end, but he had in truth fought to a stalemate at best. His fate might have been even worse had not the Shoshone and Crow saved the day on more than one occasion with bold feats of bravery.

The army's casualty figures have become a matter of controversy. Crook's official report stated that he suffered ten killed and twenty-one wounded. Scout Frank Grouard's estimate of twenty-eight killed and fifty-six wounded is probably closer to the truth. Crazy Horse later acknowledged that he had lost thirty-six killed and sixty-three wounded.

Rather than resume his pursuit of the hostiles, Crook chose to countermarch and return to his camp on Goose Creek to lick his wounds. Without notifying the other columns with whom he was expected to rendezvous in the Valley of the Little Bighorn, Crook had of his own accord taken his command out of action. Had he aggressively followed the fresh Indian trail, Crook would have likely arrived at Sitting Bull's village

The descriptions of the manner in which Dorman was mutilated, however, do not differ enough from those of others to state that he had been singled out by the Sioux on account of his race or previous relationship with the tribe.

Dorman, who is listed only as Isaiah on the monument at the battlefield, died leaving behind a paycheck for $62.50 that went unclaimed until 1879, when a man named Isaac McNutt presented a voucher for the money. His claim was denied. Dorman's Sioux wife, who was entitled to the back pay, apparently could not be located.

📖 "Isaiah Dorman and the Custer Expedition," by Ronald C. McConnell, *Journal of Negro History* 33 (July 1948); "Custer's Negro Interpreter," by Robert Ege, *Negro Digest* (February 1965); Ege's "Braves of All Colors: The Story of Isaiah Dorman Killed at the Little Big Horn," *Montana* (Winter 1966); *Custer's Black White Man,* by William Boyes (Washington, DC: South Capitol Press, 1972). Also see *Troopers with Custer: Historic Incidents of the Battle of the Little Bighorn,* by E. A. Brininstool (Harrisburg, PA: Stackpole, 1952).

✳ Gall
Hunkpapa Sioux Chieftain

Sioux chief Gall. *Courtesy Little Bighorn Battlefield National Monument.*

Gall (Pizi, "The Man Who Goes in the Middle," or "Red Walker") was born about 1840 along the Moreau River in present-day South Dakota. His unusual name was said to have been given him by his mother when he ate the gallbladder of an animal. He was orphaned as a child and, after proving his worthiness as a warrior, was adopted by Sitting Bull as a younger brother.

His earliest recorded relations with the white man occurred when he was visiting friends near Fort Berthold during the winter of 1865–66. Some unknown crime had been committed, and authorities presumed that Gall was responsible—which probably was not the case. Nevertheless, a reward was placed on him, dead or alive. Soldiers from Fort Stevenson came to arrest Gall at Fort Berthold, and he attempted to escape by slashing his way through the back of his tepee. Unfortunately for him, this move had been anticipated, and soldiers were stationed on the

(continued on following page)

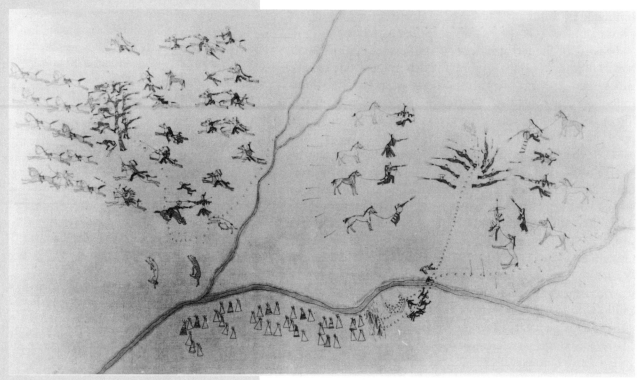

Painting, "Battle of the Little Big Horn" by Cheyenne White Bird. *Courtesy Little Bighorn Battlefield National Monument.*

other side. Gall was said to have been bayoneted, perhaps so severely that the bayonet passed through him and a soldier had to place one foot on Gall's chest to remove it. Some accounts claim that he was shot and stabbed numerous times.

Another story states that future Custer scout Bloody Knife was prepared to shoot the severely wounded Gall with a shotgun but was thwarted by an officer who believed that the Sioux warrior was already dead. Bloody Knife may have grown up with Gall and perhaps sought revenge for being picked on during childhood because he was only half Sioux.

Whatever the specific circumstances, Gall was not dead when the soldiers departed. He purportedly crawled away—perhaps twenty miles through the snow—to the cabin of a friend, variously said to be Hairy Chin, a medicine man named Padanegricka, or a nameless old woman, who nursed him back to health.

In 1866, Gall and other Sioux warriors joined Red Cloud when war was waged against the U.S. Army over the intrusion of the Bozeman Trail (see "Red Cloud's War" on page 68). Gall claimed that he had not signed the Fort Laramie Treaty of 1868, which ended hostilities. One biographer of Sitting

(continued on following page)

on the Little Bighorn either before Custer's 7th Cavalry or in coordination with the other two columns, which had been General Terry's plan.

📖 Perhaps the best source is *Battle of the Rosebud: Prelude to the Little Bighorn,* by Neil C. Mangum (El Segundo, CA: Upton and Sons, 1987). See also *The Reynolds Campaign on the Powder River,* by J. W. Vaughn (Norman: University of Oklahoma Press, 1961); *Campaigning with Crook,* by Capt. Charles King (Norman: University of Oklahoma Press, 1961); and *With Crook at the Rosebud,* by J. W. Vaughn (Harrisburg, PA: Stackpole, 1956). For the Indian account, see *Soldiers Falling into Camp: The Battles of the Rosebud and the Little Bighorn,* by Frederick Lefthand, Joseph Marshall, and Robert Kammen (Encampment, WY: Affiliated Writers of America, 1991). Newspaper accounts from reporters with Crook can be found in Robert Legoski's *General Crook's Campaign of 1876* (Sheridan, WY: Robert Legoski, 2000).

🐎 Reno's Powder River Scout

As early as May 16, Col. John Gibbon, commanding the Montana Column, was told by his scouts that a large Indian village was located somewhere in the Valley of the Little Bighorn. For reasons known only to himself, Gibbon inexplicably failed to notify anyone in authority about this information provided by his Crow scouts until June 9, when he arrived at the mouth of the Powder River and reported to Gen. Alfred H. Terry, who maintained his headquarters aboard the steamer *Far West.*

At that time, Terry decided that a reconnaissance was in order to verify Gibbon's assertion. Custer was opposed to the scout of an area with no evidence of the enemy. He argued that such a plan was a waste of time and believed that the entire force should move forward to locate and engage the enemy before they could flee. Although voicing his disapproval of the scout, Custer half-heartedly volunteered to lead the operation. Terry instead chose Maj. Marcus A. Reno for the command. The general evidently was certain that Reno would not encounter hostile Indians on his scout and simply wanted to make sure that the area was free of Indians; otherwise, he assuredly would have chosen Custer as the commander.

Reno and six troops of the 7th Cavalry moved out on the afternoon of June 10, with a definite route provided by Terry to scout the Powder and Tongue River Valleys.

Terry meanwhile had decided to move his supply depot from Stanley's old stockade on Glendive Creek to the mouth of the Powder. On June 11, Custer arrived at that location with his left wing. He was disappointed that wife Libbie was not aboard the *Far West,* and also that the steamer had brought a sutler, who spent the afternoon serving whiskey to the regiment over a makeshift bar of planks and barrels.

By June 13, Reno was camped on the upper Mizpah Creek, a waterway that was part of his assigned scout. Rather than inspect that creek, however, Reno determined that he could see far enough in that direction from a promontory on the western divide and decided that a scout was unnecessary.

On June 16, Reno came upon an abandoned Indian village estimated at 400 lodges with perhaps 1,000 warriors. In direct

---

"The success of the reservation system depends on the Government keeping its promises. . . . The Indians have a strong attachment for the lands containing the bones of their ancestors and dislike to leave it. Love of country is almost a religion with them. It is not the value of the land that they consider; but there is a strong local attachment that the white man does not feel, and consequently does not respect. . . . He [the Indian] keenly feels the injustice that has been done him and, being of a proud and haughty nature, he resents it."

—Custer voicing his opposition to taking the Black Hills away from the Sioux by force, in a 1875 article in the *New York Herald*

Bull, however, believed that he had signed and has Sitting Bull stating: "You must not blame Gall. Everyone knows he will do anything for a square meal." At this time, as throughout his life, Gall was a physically imposing man who weighed well over 200 pounds. Whether or not he signed, Gall refused to report to the reservation and continued to enjoy the traditional Sioux nomadic lifestyle.

Gall possibly was involved in the Sioux attacks on Custer's 7th Cavalry during the Yellowstone expedition of 1873, although no confirming evidence exists (see "Who Were Those Sioux That Attacked Custer?" on page 128). He did, however, play a major role as a field commander on June 25, 1876, when Custer attacked Sitting Bull's village on the Little Bighorn River.

According to Gall, orders were given to tear down the village when troops commanded by Maj. Marcus Reno were observed charging. But Reno came so quickly that the Indians were compelled to fight. Gall, whose Hunkpapa band was camped in their traditional place at the vulnerable edge of the village, rallied a small group of warriors to engage Reno. Gall said that during this initial assault, two of his wives and three of his children were killed by Reno's men firing into the village. The Sioux and their allies—led by Gall—counterattacked and routed Reno and his troops, killing many of them, before turning their attention to Custer's detachment, which was threatening the village from the eastern bluffs.

Gall claimed that Custer's cavalrymen—likely a detail from the Gray Horse troop, commanded by Capt. George Yates or 1st Lt. Algernon Smith—attempted to cross the river at Medicine Tail Coulee but were forced to retreat. During the ensuing battle, warriors led by Gall swept up that coulee from the village and overwhelmed the commands of Capt. Myles Keogh and 1st Lt. James Calhoun on the eastern slope of Battle Ridge as Crazy Horse attacked from the north.

In later interviews, Gall, who credited the soldiers with great bravery, said that all of Custer's men had been killed by the time Capt. Thomas Weir arrived at the location known as Weir Point. He estimated that the battle itself lasted only half an hour. He also revealed that the Indians believed they were fighting Gen. George Crook rather than Custer that day.

Gall fled to Canada with Sitting Bull following the battle, but after the two men quarreled, he surrendered on January 1, 1881, with about 300 of his followers at the Poplar River Agency in Montana. He then settled peacefully at the Standing Rock

(continued on following page)

Agency in present-day North Dakota. This war chief, who possessed great intellect, became an influential voice for the good of his people and served as a judge of the Court of Indian Offenses. Indian agent James McLaughlin described Gall as "a man of noble presence and much esteemed for his candor and sagacity by the whites with whom he came in contact."

Gall attended the tenth reunion of the famous battle and, through an interpreter, captivated the audience with his colorful account. He traveled to Washington in 1889 as a member of a delegation to discuss treaties. He was said to have been at that time given spending money and, when asked about how it was used, stated that he gave the money to beggars on the street—chiding the listeners by saying that Indians feed their poor. He remained neutral during the Ghost Dance uprising that led to the 1890 Wounded Knee affair.

Gall died at Oak Creek, South Dakota, on December 5, 1894—what would have been George Armstrong Custer's fifty-fifth birthday. His death has been variously attributed to falling out of a wagon, an overdose of patent medicine, or the effects of those bayonet wounds received in the winter of 1865–66.

📖 A chapter devoted to Gall, "The Story of War Chief Gall of the Uncpapas," is contained in *The Custer Myth: A Source Book of Custeriana*, edited by W. A. Graham (Harrisburg, PA: Stackpole, 1953). That chapter is followed by "General Godfrey's Comment on Gall's Story."

Also see *The Lance and the Shield: The Life and Times of Sitting Bull*, by Robert M. Utley (New York: Henry Holt, 1993); *Sitting Bull: Champion of the Sioux*, by Stanley Vestal (Norman: University of Oklahoma Press, 1957); *Indian Notes on the Custer Battle*, by David F. Barry (Baltimore: Proof Press, 1939); "Custer's Last Battle," by Edward S. Godfrey, originally published in *Century Magazine* and reprinted in *The Custer Reader*, edited by Paul A. Hutton (Lincoln: University of Nebraska Press, 1992); and "Gall: Sioux Gladiator or White Man's Pawn?" by Neil Mangum, *5th Annual Symposium Custer Battlefield Historical and Museum Association*, 1991.

Little Bighorn Battlefield: View looking northwest toward Custer Hill from the position of Company I. *Courtesy Little Bighorn Battlefield National Monument.*

disobedience of Terry's orders, Reno chose to follow the trail of those who had departed this village down the Rosebud. Unknown to him, on June 17 he came within forty miles of Gen. George Crook, who was engaged in the battle of the Rosebud (see "Prelude to Little Bighorn: The Powder River and Rosebud Engagements" on page 189).

On June 19, Reno camped at the mouth of the Rosebud, upriver from Col. John Gibbon, and notified Terry by courier of his present position. Reno informed Terry that he not only had scouted the Powder and Tongue River Valleys, but also had entered the Rosebud Valley while following the fresh Indian trail. He had traversed more than 240 miles, when his itinerary had been set by Terry at about 175 miles.

Terry and Custer were both furious with Reno, for different reasons. Terry had explicitly warned Reno not to go to the Rosebud for fear that the action would alert the Indians to their presence and jeopardize the movement of the three columns. The commanding general certainly would have preferred charges against Reno had he not been the only major in Custer's command. Custer, on the other hand, believed that Reno should have pursued and attacked the hostiles he had trailed.

But Reno, to his credit, had provided vital information by identifying that the Indians were not on the lower section of Rosebud Creek. General Terry could now assume that the hostiles were moving toward the Valley of the Little Bighorn and formulate his plans accordingly.

📖 "The Reno Scout," by Edgar I. Stewart and E. S. Luce, *Montana: The Magazine of Western History* 10, no. 3 (July 1960); and *To the Edge of Darkness,* by James Willert (El Segundo, CA: Upton and Sons, 1998), which covers both Gibbon's Montana Column and the Reno Scout.

🦌 Weapons Carried by the Cavalrymen

In the early 1870s, the army's Ordnance Department staged field trials of prospective rifles and carbines for use by the troops. The army was seeking a weapon that could take a beating yet remain reliable, and one that used a single-shot system rather than a repeating system because of its lower manufacturing cost. The rifles were tested for every factor, from defective cartridges to the effects of rust and dust. In the end, about ninety entries by such makers as Elliot, Freeman, Mauser, Peabody, and Spencer were winnowed down to four finalists: the Remington rolling-block; the vertically sliding breech-block Sharps; the trapdoor Springfield; and the Ward-Burton bolt-action. The final selection was made in 1872 by a board of officers that was presided over by Gen. Alfred Terry and included Maj. Marcus A. Reno as a member.

On May 5, 1873, the winner of the rifle competition was announced in the board's final report to the secretary of war. The Model 1873 Springfield .45/.55-caliber, single-shot, breech-loading carbine had emerged on top. The Springfield weighed about 6.9 pounds and was 41.3 inches long. It fired a .45-caliber copper-cased cartridge with 55 grains of black powder and had an effective range of about 250 to 300 yards, although it could shoot as far as 1,000 yards. A properly trained rifleman could fire his weapon up to seventeen times a minute with accuracy. The 7th Cavalry was issued the Springfield just prior to the Black Hills expedition of 1874.

At the battle of the Little Bighorn, each trooper with the 7th Cavalry carried 100 cartridges for his Springfield carbine— half in his cartridge belt and half in his saddlebags. This would have afforded Custer's detachment more than 20,000 available rounds of ammunition. After the battle, however, there was some question about whether a known defect of the Springfield to extract the spent copper cartridge casings attributed to Custer's defeat (see "Malfunction Allegations Concerning the Springfield Carbine" on page 196). The Springfield remained the army's weapon of choice until 1892, when it was replaced by the Krag-Jorgensen magazine rifle.

The troopers also carried a Model P 1872 Colt single-action revolver, which had been chosen over the Smith and Wesson Schofield primarily because of its simpler operation, stronger parts, and dependability. The army placed an initial order of 13,000 in 1873–74, then bought about 1,000 a year thereafter until 1891. Called a "thumb-buster" by the troops, this .45-

⚜ John Gibbon
Colonel, 7th U.S. Infantry

Gibbon was born on April 20, 1827, near Holmesburg, Pennsylvania, and during his childhood, the family moved to Charlotte, North Carolina. He graduated—with future generals Ambrose E. Burnside and Ambrose P. Hill—from the U.S. Military Academy at West Point in 1847, ranking twentieth in his class. Gibbon was commissioned a second lieutenant in the 4th Artillery and assigned to duty in Mexico after hostilities had ceased. Two years later, he took part in operations against the Seminole Indians in Florida. He was promoted to first lieutenant in 1850. From May 1853 to August 1854, he assisted in the removal of the Seminole from Florida to Indian Territory. His next assignment was as an artillery instructor at West Point, where he spent five years. While at West Point, Gibbon wrote the basic *Artillerist's Manual,* which was published by the War Department. Gibbon then served briefly in Utah and as captain of the 4th U.S. Artillery at Fort Leavenworth until the outbreak of the Civil War.

Although three of his brothers chose to serve in the Confederate army, Gibbon remained with the North, where he was made chief of artillery in October 1861. He was promoted to brigadier general in May 1862 and at that time given command of a brigade consisting of the 6th Indiana and 2nd, 6th, and 7th Wisconsin regiments—which initially became known as the Black Hat Brigade for the morale-boosting tall, black, felt hats that Gibbon provided them. After the unit's heroic action at South Mountain in September 1862, it became known as the Iron Brigade of the West. Gibbon, now commanding I Corps, was wounded at Fredericksburg and returned to duty as commander of the 2nd Division of the II Corps. He was severely wounded once again at Gettysburg and thereafter walked with a decided limp. Gibbon was promoted to major general in June 1864 and assumed command of the XXIV Corps in January 1865. He was one of the commanders who accepted Lee's surrender at Appomattox.

Gibbon became colonel of the 36th Infantry in July 1866 and colonel of the 7th Infantry at Fort Ellis, Montana, in March 1869. Known to the Plains Indians as "No Hip Bone" or "One Who Limps," he then commanded the District of Montana from Fort Shaw.

On March 21, 1876, Gibbon assumed command of the Montana Column, which was part of the three-pronged attack designed to trap the hostile Indians gathered in the Valley of the Little

(continued on following page)

Bighorn. He marched from Fort Ellis on April 3, east down the Yellowstone River, with six companies of his own regiment and the 2nd Cavalry under Maj. James Brisbin. Perhaps as early as May 16, Gibbon was aware of the location of Sitting Bull's village, but he informed no one until June 9, when he met with Gen. Alfred Terry aboard the steamship *Far West* near the mouth of Rosebud Creek. That set in motion Maj. Marcus Reno's Powder River Scout to confirm the information (see "Reno's Powder River Scout" on page 192).

Gibbon was summoned to the *Far West* on June 21 for a meeting with Terry and Custer. At that time, orders were issued for Custer to lead the march and strike from the south. Terry would accompany Gibbon's column, which would act as a blocking force at the mouth of the Little Bighorn River. The Terry-Gibbon column, having heard rumors of Custer engaging the Indians, arrived at the battlefield on June 27 to discover the annihilated command and rescue Reno's beleaguered troops on the nearby hilltop. Gibbon's men spent two days assisting in the hasty burial of the dead, then transported the wounded to the *Far West* for evacuation.

In the summer of 1877, Gibbon commanded a battalion that attacked Nez Perce chief Joseph in the August 9 battle of Big Hole, where the colonel was severely wounded in the thigh. The Nez Perce counterattacked, and the fight was at best a standoff—Gibbon losing two officers, six civilians, and twenty-one enlisted killed and another five officers, four civilians, and thirty-one enlisted wounded, while Indian losses were estimated to be between sixty and ninety.

Gibbon commanded the Department of Dakota in 1878–79; Fort Snelling, Minnesota, in 1879; and the Department of the Platte in 1884. He was promoted to brigadier general in July 1885 and at that time assumed command of the Department of the Columbia until April 30, 1891, when he retired. He died on February 6, 1896, in Baltimore.

📖 *Gibbon on the Sioux Campaign of 1876,* by John Gibbon (Bellevue, NE: Old Army Press, 1970), which includes reprints of articles from the April and October 1877 *American Catholic Quarterly Review;* and *On Time for Disaster: The Rescue of Custer's Command,* by Edward J. McClerand (Lincoln: University of Nebraska Press, 1889). Generous mentions about Gibbon's role in the Little Bighorn campaign can be found in *Custer's Luck,* by Edgar I. Stewart (Norman: University of Oklahoma Press, 1955); and *Custer and the Great Controversy,* by Robert M. Utley (Los Angeles: Westernlore Press, 1962).

caliber revolver, with a 7.5-inch barrel, fired six metallic cartridges with 28 grains of black powder and had an effective range of about 60 yards. At the battle of the Little Bighorn, each man carried twenty-four rounds for his Colt. This popular revolver, known as the "Peacemaker" to frontier lawmen, was manufactured by the Colt Company into the 1980s.

Some of the officers and men, however, chose to carry personal weapons. George Armstrong Custer went into the battle with a .50-caliber Remington sporting rifle with an octagonal barrel, as well as two self-cocking white-handled British Webley Bulldog double-action revolvers. Capt. Thomas A. French was widely known for his marksmanship with his .50-caliber Springfield rifle, known as "Long Tom." Sergeant John Ryan took along a specially made .45-caliber, 15-pound Sharps rifle with a telescopic sight.

Contrary to depictions by some artists, the 7th Cavalry—with perhaps the exception of Europeans 1st Lt. Charles DeRudio and 1st Lt. Edward Mathey—did not carry their sabers into the battle. These heavy, cumbersome, noisy weapons, which were for the most part merely an ornament for inspection and parade, had been intentionally left behind at the Powder River base camp.

📖 *Custer Battle Guns,* by John S. duMont (Fort Collins, CO: Old Army Press, 1974); *The Springfield Carbine on the Western Frontier,* by Kenneth Hammer (Fort Collins, CO: Old Army Press, 1971); *Firearms in the Custer Battle,* by John E. Parson and John S. duMont (Harrisburg, PA: Stackpole, 1953); "The Army's Search for a Repeating Rifle," by Pierce Chamberlain, *Military Affairs* 32 (1968); "Firearms at Little Bighorn," by John S. duMont, *Greasy Grass* (May 1990), a publication of the Custer Battlefield Museum and Historical Association; and "Cavalry Firepower: Springfield Carbine's Selection and Performance," by Ron Nichols, *Greasy Grass* (May 1999).

🐎 Malfunction Allegations Concerning the Springfield Carbine

A debate has ensued for years over whether the Model 1873 Springfield carbines that the cavalrymen carried into battle on June 25, 1876, malfunctioned and hereby contributed to the defeat.

The controversy stems from the fact that this weapon was known after firing to frequently fail to properly extract its spent .45/.55-caliber copper cartridge casing, which expanded when hot. That failure, combined with a faulty extractor mechanism and common dirt, could cause the head of the cartridge to be torn away when the block was opened. This would have left the cartridge cylinder remaining inside the chamber, requiring manual removal with a pocketknife before reloading and firing. This extraction malfunction problem had been noted in 1872 by the board of officers who selected the carbine for use by the army, but at that time, it was not considered a serious enough reason not to choose this firearm.

There is no doubt that if this malfunction occurred with enough frequency during the battle, the troopers would have been seriously affected in firepower. Therefore, the question that must be posed is, with what frequency did this defect occur on June 25, 1876, when it really mattered?

Rather than cite sources by those historians who can only advance an opinion based on speculation, this question requires solid statistics to substantiate an answer. And these facts have been uncovered and analyzed by Dr. Richard A. Fox in his excellent *Archaeology, History, and Custer's Last Battle* (Norman: University of Oklahoma Press, 1993).

Fox found during the study of items from excavations on the battlefield that very few .45/.55-caliber cartridge casings displayed any evidence of pry or scratch marks, such as those by a pocketknife, which would have permanently scarred a hot casing. On the Custer portion of the field, only three of eighty-eight casings could have been involved in an extraction jam. Seven out of 257 fit this category on the Reno-Benteen defense site. If these are representative numbers, and there is no reason to believe otherwise, it would appear that malfunction of the carbine from that cause was minimal and could not be considered a factor in the defeat.

Both sides did, however, mention that some weapons either malfunctioned or were discarded for other reasons. Maj. Marcus Reno used the extraction problem as one excuse for the defeat, perhaps to avert blame from himself. Sioux chief Gall mentioned that he witnessed soldiers throwing away their long guns in favor of their short guns.

There is a possibility that the men had simply run out of ammunition for their carbines. Each cavalryman carried only fifty .45/.55 cartridges in his cartridge belt. The fifty additional rounds located in his saddlebags would have been lost when the Indians stampeded the horses. Fifty rounds fired in the frantic heat of battle could be expended in a very short period of time. The Colt revolvers, for which the men each

Frederic Francis Girard
Interpreter

Girard (or Gerard, the Canadian spelling of his name) was born on November 14, 1829, in St. Louis to a Canadian father and American mother. He attended St. Xavier Academy for four years and was employed by the *St. Louis Republic*. In September 1848, he headed up the Missouri River to Fort Pierre, Dakota Territory, where he was hired as a clerk for the American Fur Company. Girard moved on to Fort Clark the following year. Over the next few years, he became fluent in the Arikara and Sioux languages. In 1855, he traveled to the headwaters of the Platte, and two years later, he became a trader for the American Fur Company at Fort Berthold. Shortly thereafter, Girard married an Arikara (Ree) woman, Helena Catherine, with whom he had three daughters.

Girard was working at Fort Berthold on Christmas Day 1863 when it was attacked by 600 Yankton Sioux. Girard and seventeen others defended the fort and claimed to have killed at least 40 Indians while wounding 100 in seven hours of fighting. The Sioux were driven off by the Assiniboine, and the whites all left—except Girard, who remained alone at the fort for ten days.

In 1869, he became a trader in his own right at Forts Buford and Stevenson. Three years later, he was employed as post interpreter for the Arikara and Sioux scouts at Fort Abraham Lincoln. Girard, who lived near the fort on a farm (present-day Mandan), apparently fathered a son in 1872 with a full-blooded Piegan woman. He raised corn, potatoes, beans, radishes, and other vegetables and supplied milk to the fort.

In May 1876, Girard accompanied the Dakota Column on the Little Bighorn campaign as an interpreter at $75 a month. He was assigned to Maj. Marcus A. Reno's column on June 25 and, as the 7th Cavalry approached the Valley of the Little Bighorn, he had ridden ahead to scout. Custer had paused at a lone tepee that contained the body of a dead Indian to confer with Reno, when Girard raced toward them and excitedly yelled, "Here are your Indians, General, running like devils!" Clouds of dust could

Frederic F. Girard. Courtesy Little Bighorn Battlefield National Monument.

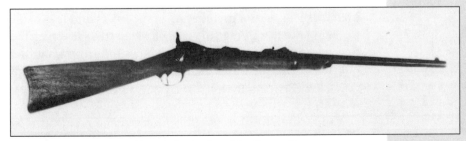

Springfield Model 1873 .45-caliber, single-shot, breech-loading carbine. *Courtesy Little Bighorn Battlefield National Monument.*

(continued on following page)

be observed from beyond the high bluffs between them and the valley.

When Reno aborted his charge into the Indian village and retreated, Girard, along with scout Billy Jackson, was stranded in the timber beside the Little Bighorn River while the rest of the command frantically made their way to the high bluffs. Girard remained hidden throughout the night of June 25, finally rejoining Reno on the hilltop the following evening.

On November 15, 1877, Girard married twenty-year-old Ella Scarborough Waddell of Kansas City, with whom he had four children.

In 1878, Girard became county assessor of Morton County, Dakota Territory. He testified against Reno at the 1879 court of inquiry and later remarked of some officers that he was "amused to see how bad their memories became" with respect to the events at Little Bighorn. In 1880, he became post interpreter at Fort Stevenson, and three years later, he opened a store in Mandan. He moved to Minneapolis in 1890 and was employed as a salesman or advertising agent for Pillsbury Mills.

In 1908, Girard was paralyzed in a freak accident while lifting a trunk. He lived briefly with his son in Seattle, then moved in with his daughter in St. Cloud, Minnesota, where he died at St. Joseph's Home on January 13, 29, or 30, 1913. His gravestone at St. Benedict's Convent (present-day College of St. Benedict) reads, "January 29, 1913."

📖 "Interview with Frederic F. Gerard, January 22 and April 3, 1909," in *Custer in '76: Walter Camp's Notes on the Custer Fight,* edited by Kenneth Hammer (Provo, UT: Brigham Young University, 1976); "F. F. Girard, Scout and Interpreter," by Clement Lounsberry, *The Record* (July 1896); and "F. F. Gerard's Story of the Custer Fight," in *The Custer Myth: A Source Book of Custeriana,* edited by W. A. Graham (Harrisburg, PA: Stackpole, 1953). Girard's criticism of Major Reno at Little Bighorn can be found in the February 22, 1879, *Bismarck Tribune.*

❀ Henry Moore Harrington
Second Lieutenant, 7th U.S. Cavalry

Harrington was born on April 30, 1849, in Albion, New York. At some point during his childhood, his family moved to Coldwater, Michigan. He entered the U.S. Military Academy at West Point in July 1868 and graduated four years later, ranked nineteenth in a class of fifty-seven. Harrington was appointed second lieutenant, 7th Cavalry, on June 14, 1872. On November 15 of that year, he married

(continued on following page)

carried twenty rounds, may have been more effective at short range, but again, twenty rounds would not have lasted long.

Custer had dispatched an urgent message to Capt. Frederick Benteen that emphasized bringing up the ammunition packs in a hurry. Benteen dawdled along the trail, never arriving to assist Custer. There is a distinct possibility that rather than any malfunction of the carbine having caused the defeat, a more logical explanation would be that the cavalrymen simply ran out of ammunition and were overwhelmed by their enemy.

Perhaps that also explains why Custer's command was strung out along Battle Ridge rather than formed in a tight defensive position. The companies to the south, led by 1st Lt. James Calhoun, may have been sent to escort Benteen and the ammunition.

📖 In addition to the above-mentioned book by Fox, also see "Carbine Extractor Failure at the Little Big Horn," by Paul L. Hedren, *Military Collector and Historian* 25 (1973); and "The Cartridge Case Evidence on Custer Field," by Bruce A. Trinque, *5th Annual Symposium Custer Battlefield Historical & Museum Association,* 1991.

🐎 Weapons Carried by the Indians

At the battle of the Little Bighorn, the Sioux and Cheyenne were armed with weapons that included everything from primitive clubs, bows and arrows, lances, knives, and hatchets to an array of new and old firearms. The Indians obtained their firearms, which the Lakota called *maza wakan* or "holy iron," through trade, gunrunning, capture from enemies, or from the U.S. government for hunting purposes in fulfillment of annuities.

Archaeological excavations of the battlefield, which began in 1983, recovered cartridge casings from at least forty-five different makes of firearms used by about 371 different individuals. That evidence indicated that the Indians were in possession of Spencers, Sharps, Smith and Wessons, Evans, Forehand and Wadworths, Remingtons, Henrys, Starrs, Winchesters, Maynards, and Enfields, as well as many Springfields and Colt revolvers taken that day from dead cavalrymen.

Perhaps the most accurate analysis by percentage of the weapons comes from Pvt. Charles Windolph, who won the Medal of Honor as a member of Company H and is notable for being the last living survivor of the battle. He estimated that at least half the warriors carried bows and arrows, another quarter were armed with old muzzleloaders and single-shot rifles, and the rest, perhaps as many as 300 to 500 Indians, were armed with modern repeaters.

The weapon most frequently observed and mentioned by the soldiers was the Winchester repeating rifle. Maj. Marcus Reno later said that "the Indians had Winchester rifles and the column made a large target for them and they were pumping bullets into it." This was the weapon of choice for the Indians, when they could get their hands on it.

The Model 1866 Winchester fired a .44-caliber rimfire cartridge, used a 200-grain bullet with 28 grains of powder, had a capacity of seventeen cartridges, and was deadly accurate at 100 yards but fell off dramatically at longer distances. The Winchester was similar to the 1860 Henry, which fired the same .44-caliber rimfire cartridge, with a 216-grain bullet and 25 grains of powder. The Winchester had a spring cover on the right side of the receiver; cartridges were inserted into the front of the Henry magazine. The archaeological digs revealed evidence of at least sixty-two .44-caliber Henry cartridge casings within range of Custer's detachment.

2nd. Lt. Henry M. Harrington. *Courtesy Little Bighorn Battlefield National Monument.*

It has been debated whether the Indians were better armed than the cavalrymen, which might have contributed to the defeat. There can be no question that the cavalry was outgunned by the Indians that day, but this was not necessarily due to better firearms, but simply by sheer numbers. A minimum of 134 Indian firearms, as opposed to 81 for the soldiers, were found on the Custer portion of the battlefield. Customary Indian tactics called for the warriors to remain a safe distance away—hidden by tall grass, bushes, and terrain features—while they fired an endless stream of arcing arrows at the pinned-down cavalrymen. Add to that arrow barrage the fifty or so more firearms possessed by the Indians than the soldiers had at their disposal, and the all-important fire superiority certainly favored the Indians in a battle of attrition.

There can also be no doubt that the modern repeaters made quite a difference. Gen. George Crook, in a September 25, 1876, report, stated:

> Of the difficulties with which we have had to contend, it may be well to remark, that when the Sioux Indian was armed with a bow and arrow he was more formidable, fighting as he does most of the time on horseback, than when he got the old fashioned muzzle loading rifle. But when he came into possession of the breech loader and metallic cartridge, which allows him to load and fire from his horse with perfect ease, he became at once ten thousand times more formidable.

📖 The best source for this subject is *Archaeology, History and Custer's Last Battle: The Little Bighorn Reexamined,* by Richard A. Fox, Jr. (Norman: University of Oklahoma Press, 1993). Also see *Archaeological Insights into the Custer Battle: A Preliminary Assessment,* by Douglas D. Scott and Richard A. Fox, Jr. (Norman: University of Oklahoma Press, 1987); and *Archaeological Perspectives on the Battle of the Little Bighorn,* by Douglas D. Scott, Richard A. Fox Jr., Melissa A. Conner, and Dick Harmon (Norman: University of Oklahoma Press, 1989).

Grace Bernard of Highland Falls, New York. The couple had two children.

Harrington participated in the Yellowstone expedition of 1873 and the following year's Black Hills expedition, both with Company C. It is possible that Harrington was in command of that company during the Little Bighorn battle, if Tom Custer was serving as an aide-de-camp to his brother, as has been suggested. It has been said that he had a premonition before the battle and drew a sketch that he mailed to a friend that depicted himself tied to a tree surrounded by hostile Indians. Harrington was killed along with the rest of his company somewhere along Battle Ridge, but his remains have never been located.

Sioux chief Gall informed Walter Camp that four eyewitnesses had told him about a soldier who "rode through the Indians on a very swift horse which they could not catch. They told that after chasing him for about a mile or two the soldier drew his pistol and killed himself. This they could not understand because the man's horse was swifter than theirs and was continually getting farther away from the pursuers." Custer scholar Kenneth Hammer speculated that this soldier may have been Harrington, a theory that could be reinforced by the lieutenant's obvious fear of capture, as evidenced by the sketch he made prior to the battle.

Stranger yet, however, was the legend of Harrington's wife, who was said to have mysteriously vanished at some point after the battle. She was found two years later in Texas, suffering from amnesia. An attack of pneumonia restored her mind, but she recalled nothing about the missing two years. Her daughter stated that the Indians told of a woman dressed in black who had been seen several times on the Little Bighorn battlefield during that two-year period, and she believed this to have been her mother.

📖 *Custer in '76: Walter Camp's Notes on the Custer Fight,* edited by Kenneth Hammer (Provo, UT: Brigham Young University Press, 1976); "Another Custer Mystery," *Pony Express Courier,* Placerville, CA (August 1936); "Echoes of the Custer Tragedy," by Elmo Scott, *Winners of the West* (July 1936). Another version of Gall's story about a trooper committing suicide was told by Charles King in "Custer's Last Battle," originally

(continued on following page)

published in *Harper's New Monthly Magazine* 81 (August 1890), pp. 378–87, and reprinted in *The Custer Reader,* edited by Paul A. Hutton (Lincoln: University of Nebraska Press, 1992). King stated that a year after the battle, one of the Sioux pursuers of this rider pointed out a skeleton to officers of the 5th Cavalry. King also wrote that three years after the battle, Harrington's watch was returned to his father after being traded by a Sioux who had fled to Canada.

✽ Benjamin Hubert Hodgson
Second Lieutenant, 7th U.S. Cavalry

Hodgson was born on June 30, 1848, in Philadelphia. He entered the U.S. Military Academy at West Point in July 1865 and graduated five years later, ranked forty-fifth in a class of fifty-eight. He was commissioned a second lieutenant, 7th Cavalry, on June 15, 1870, and joined his unit on scouting duty in Colorado. Hodgson served with Company B in South Carolina from March 1871 until the command was reassembled in March 1873 to participate in the Yellowstone expedition. He commanded his company during the Black Hills expedition of 1874.

2nd Lt. Benjamin H. Hodgson. *Courtesy Little Bighorn Battlefield National Monument.*

Hodgson then served for the better part of the next two years on detached duty in Shreveport, Louisiana, until rejoining the 7th Cavalry in May 1876 for the Little Bighorn campaign. At that time, he was said to have decided to resign his commission, but 2nd Lt. Charles Varnum, his best friend, apparently persuaded him to remain for one more campaign.

Hodgson was assigned temporary duty as adjutant to another friend, Maj. Marcus A. Reno. During Reno's disorganized retreat from the timber, Hodgson's horse was killed, and he was wounded in the leg while attempting to cross the Little Bighorn River. According to Pvt. James Darcy (also known as James Wilber), in *Of Garry Owen in Glory: The History of the 7th U.S. Cavalry,* by Melbourne C. Chandler (Annandale, VA: Turnpike, 1960): "Right at the Little Big Horn a trooper was shot down in front of me and Lieutenant Hodgson got his first wound.... Hodgson hung on to the stirrup of Bugler [Frank] Myers and got over the river and part way up the hill, but received another wound and was killed."

A more flowery version was written by Charles King in "Custer's Last Battle," originally published

(continued on following page)

Indian Strength and Casualties

The question of how many warriors were present in Sitting Bull's village was bandied about even before the smoke on the battlefield had cleared. Unfortunately, no definitive answer has been agreed upon to this day, although there has been no lack of those who have speculated on the figure.

It is known that the village had grown considerably in size from earlier in the year. Families had left the reservation to join their brethren for a summer of freedom—just how many would be a matter of speculation. The Indian agent would have underreported these defections in order to receive supplies for a higher number, then disposed of the surplus, with the profits going into his own pocket. An article in the *Army and Navy Journal,* dated October 21, 1876, states that at Standing Rock Agency, "Out of 7,000 [Indians]—the basis upon which supplies have sent out by the Bureau for the last year or two—only 2,300 are now present."

A year after the battle, Lt. H. L. Scott visited the site of the village and quit counting lodge circles when he arrived at 1,500. His effort proved little, as families often moved several times, on each occasion leaving an empty circle. In addition, the village also contained hundreds of wickiups, brush shelters that would have blown away without a trace.

The following are estimates of the number of warriors by army personnel who participated in the battle or examined the site: Col. John Gibbon, 2,500; 2nd Lt. Luther Hare, 4,000; scout George Herendeen, 3,000; 1st Lt. Charles DeRudio, 3,000 to 4,000; Capt. Myles Moylan, 3,500 to 4,000; and 2nd Lt. Charles Varnum, not less than 4,000. Second Lt. George D. Wallace at first estimated the number at 3,000, then at the 1879 Reno Court of Inquiry testified that there were 9,000. Capt. Frederick Benteen initially set the number at 1,500, then in later years arrived at a figure of 8,000 to 9,000.

It might be thought that the Indians themselves could have provided an exact number of warriors, but that was not the case. Gall was unable to offer any estimate. Numbers given by other Indian participants varied: Flat Iron, 8,000; Chief Runs-the-Enemy, 2,000; Flying Hawk, 1,000; and Crazy Horse, at least 7,000. Nonparticipant Red Cloud set the figure at 2,000. Allegedly, Indians believed that the number was inconsequential, and that anyone who counted higher than 1,000 must be dishonest.

Estimates from historians include the following: Stanley Vestal, 2,500; Frazier Hunt, 1,800 to 2,000; Lewis Crawford, 2,000 to 2,500; Fred Dustin, 3,000 to 3,500; full-blooded Sioux Dr. Charles Eastman, not more than 1,411; Edgar I. Stewart,

3,000; Robert M. Utley, 2,000; Jeffry D. Wert, 2,000; and George B. Grinnell, 4,500 to 6,000.

Perhaps the best estimate of the number of lodges has been provided by John S. Gray in his classic *Centennial Campaign: The Sioux War of 1876* (Fort Collins, CO: Old Army Press, 1976):

Northern Cheyenne: 120
Oglala Sioux: 240
Blackfoot, Brule, and Two Kettle Sioux: 120
Sans Arc Sioux: 110
Minniconjou Sioux: 150
Hunkpapa Sioux: 235
Yanktonnais and Santee Sioux: 25

Gray estimated the total number of lodges at 1,000 but does not include any Arapaho, members of which tribe were known to be in the village.

It has been said that each lodge would be home to two warriors, perhaps more if the older boys were involved. Add to that the wickiups on the north end of the village, which housed young warriors who did not live with their families; subtract those men who had reached "retirement" age, which was said to be sometime before their fortieth birthday.

Whatever the exact number of warriors, it would be safe to say that their number far exceeded Custer's troops that day.

As far as Indian losses go, most estimates are that only thirty or forty were killed. As Custer once said, "The Indians invariably endeavored to conceal their exact losses." The only Indian casualties that were found after the battle consisted of eight bodies located in two lodges—five in one, three in the other—within the abandoned village. These dead warriors were dressed in their finest clothing and were lying on scaffolds.

Few Indian participants offered an opinion with respect to casualties. Red Horse did later say that "the soldiers killed 136 and wounded 160 Sioux." It would stand to reason that the allied Indians likely lost that many, perhaps more, although David Humphreys Miller, who consulted dozens of Indian participants for *Custer's Fall: The Indian Side of the Story* (New York: Duell, Sloan & Pearce, 1957), lists the names of only twelve Cheyenne and twenty Lakota Sioux who were said to have been killed. And one, Cheyenne chief Lame White Man, was shot and scalped by a Sioux who mistook him for an Arikara or Crow, perhaps because he was wearing a captured cavalry uniform.

📖 In addition to the above sources, an excellent commentary with plentiful references can be found in *Custer's Luck,* by Edgar I. Stewart (Norman: University of Oklahoma Press, 1955). Also see *Hokahey! A Good Day to Die!: The Indian Casualties of the Custer Fight,* by Richard G. Hardorff (Spokane: Arthur H. Clark Co., 1991).

in *Harper's New Monthly Magazine* 81 (August 1890) and reprinted in *The Custer Reader,* edited by Paul A. Hutton (Lincoln: University of Nebraska Press, 1992):

> In vain had Donald McIntosh and "Benny" Hodgson, two of the bravest and best-loved officers in the regiment, striven to rally, face about, and fight with the rear of column.... Hodgson, shot out of the saddle, was rescued by a faithful comrade, who plunged into the stream with him; but close to the farther shore the Indians picked him off, a bullet tore through his body, and the gallant little fellow, the pet and pride of the whole regiment, rolled dead into the muddy waters.

Hodgson's death greatly affected Major Reno. In fact, a shaken Reno left Capt. Frederick Benteen in charge during the crucial initial stages on the hilltop while he embarked on a futile search for Hodgson's body.

Capt. Thomas M. McDougall testified at the 1879 Reno Court of Inquiry that:

> On the night of the 26th of June, 1876, I took privates Ryan and Moore of my company, and we went and got Lieut. Hodgson's body and carried it to the breastworks and kept it until the next morning, the 27th. After sewing him up in a blanket and a poncho, I proceeded with those two men to bury him.

According to the November 25, 1876, edition of the *Bismarck Tribune,* a watch belonging to Hodgson was found by Indians in Sitting Bull's camp and turned over to military authorities.

Hodgson's remains were exhumed in July 1877 and reinterred in October in Philadelphia's Laurel Hill Cemetery.

📖 "In Memoriam Lieutenant Benjamin H. Hodgson," by Mrs. Gustavus Remak, *Army and Navy Journal* (July 29, 1876); and "Who Buried Lieutenant Hodgson?" by Jud Tuttle, *4th Annual Symposium Custer Battlefield Historical and Museum Association,* 1990.

✸ Daniel Alexander Kanipe
Sergeant, 7th U.S. Cavalry

Kanipe was born into a farming family on April 15, 1853, near Marion, McDowell County, North Carolina. He enlisted in the army in August 1872 and was assigned to Company C, 7th Cavalry. He participated in the Yellowstone expedition in 1873 and the Black Hills expedition the following year, and he rode out with his unit in May 1876 on the Little Bighorn campaign.

Kanipe accompanied Maj. Marcus A. Reno on his controversial Powder River Scout (see "Reno's Powder River Scout on page 192), and was a mem-

(continued on following page)

ber of Custer's command when the 7th Cavalry approached the Valley of the Little Bighorn. When the strength of the enemy in Sitting Bull's village was determined, Kanipe was ordered by Custer to carry a message to Capt. Thomas McDougall, who was in the rear with the pack train, which read in part: "Bring the pack train straight across to high ground—if packs get loose don't stop to fix them, cut them off. Come quick. Big Indian camp." As Kanipe rode off, he heard Custer order the men to hold their horses, "there are plenty of them down there for us all."

Sgt Daniel A. Kanipe. *Courtesy Little Bighorn Battlefield National Monument.*

On his ride to deliver the message, Kanipe encountered Capt. Frederick W. Benteen and informed him about the impending fight. Evidently the news did not impress Benteen, who did not hasten his leisurely pace to come to the aid of Custer. Kanipe remained with Reno on the hilltop and thereby did not suffer the fate of his company, which was wiped out. He later offered the opinion that if Reno and Benteen had followed orders, Custer's plan of attack would have been successful.

In April 1877, Kanipe married Ann Wycoff Bobo, the widow of 1st Sgt. Edwin Bobo, who had perished with Custer. The couple had two daughters, in addition to raising the two sons from Ann's previous marriage.

Kanipe was discharged from the service in 1882 and worked for the U.S. Revenue Service for twenty years. He became a captain in the 19th North Carolina Militia during World War I. Kanipe died on July 18, 1926, in Marion, North Carolina, and was buried in Oak Grove Cemetery in that city. He apparently had been married before his union with Ann—he was said to have been survived by three sons, five daughters, and the two stepsons.

📖 In 1908, Kanipe accompanied historian Walter Camp on a tour of the battlefield, which resulted in "Daniel A. Kanipe's Account of Custer Fight Given to Me on June 16 and 17, 1908," in *Custer in '76: Walter Camp's Notes on the Custer Fight,* edited by Kenneth Hammer (Provo, UT: Brigham Young University Press, 1976). Letters written by Kanipe to Camp are in the Walter Camp Collection, Lee Library, Brigham Young University. See also "A New Story of Custer's Last

(continued on following page)

🐎 Battlefield Terrain Features

BATTLE RIDGE

This half-mile-long elevation above the eastern side of the Little Bighorn River, bordered by Custer Hill on the north and Calhoun Hill on the south, was where most of the troops in Custer's five companies fought and died. Crazy Horse was said to have rallied a group of warriors in the village, crossed the river to the north, and swept down Battle Ridge from Custer Hill to Calhoun Hill, killing everyone in his path.

CALHOUN HILL

This hill overlooking Deep Coulee constitutes the southern end of Battle Ridge and is notable as the place where 1st Lt. James Calhoun and his Company L made their last stand against Gall and perhaps Crazy Horse.

COMPANY I POSITION

This area, located along the eastern slope of Battle Ridge between Custer Hill and Calhoun Hill and just north of Deep Coulee, indicates the location where Capt. Myles Keogh with his Company I and elements of Companies C and F fought their last stand against Crazy Horse.

CUSTER HILL

This hill, which was on the northern end of Battle Ridge, was the location where George Armstrong Custer and about forty others made their last stand behind a breastwork of dead horses. The location is presently marked by marble slabs

Little Bighorn Battlefield: View of Custer Hill looking west toward the Little Bighorn River. Black marker denotes position of Custer's body. *From author's collection.*

depicting where these men fell. A monument erected in 1881 bearing the names of all the officers and enlisted killed in the battle stands atop the hill.

DEEP COULEE

This ravine, which led to the Little Bighorn River near the center of the Indian village, was located at the northern end of Nye-Cartwright Ridge, just south of Calhoun Hill. Smith's Gray Horse troop may have retreated to Battle Ridge up this ravine after descending Medicine Tail Coulee and encountering fierce opposition. Gall and a group of warriors may have ridden up this coulee to strike Battle Ridge near Calhoun Hill.

DEEP RAVINE

This drainage, also known as North Medicine Tail Coulee, was located near the end of the slope that ran from Custer Hill west to the Little Bighorn River. It was the scene of heavy fighting. Testimony from soldiers on the field two days after the battle indicated that twenty-eight members of Company E were located at a point some 2,000 feet from Custer Hill near the Little Bighorn River. The bodies of these men were at that time buried where they fell but, perhaps because of a change in the course of the river, have to this day eluded detection.

MEDICINE TAIL COULEE

This coulee sloped from north of Weir Point on Battle Ridge about 300 yards to the river at the southern end of the Indian village, which was on the opposite bank. It has been theorized

Stand, by the Messenger Boy Who Survived," by Will Aiken, *Montana Historical Society Contributions* 4 (1923); and "The Story of Sergeant Kanipe, One of Custer's Messengers," by Kanipe, in *The Custer Myth: A Source Book of Custeriana*, edited by W. A. Graham (Harrisburg, PA: Stackpole, 1953).

✹ Marcus Henry "Mark" Kellogg
Newspaper Correspondent

Kellogg, the third of ten children, was born on March 31, 1833, in Brighton, Ontario, Canada. The family moved quite often during his childhood—to Toronto; Watertown, New York; Bowmanville, Ontario, Canada; Marengo and Waukegan, Illinois; and finally to LaCrosse, Wisconsin. While living in Waukegan, Kellogg learned the telegrapher's trade, and when the family settled in LaCrosse, he worked for the Northwestern Telegraph Company and later the old Atlantic and Pacific Telegraph Company. In May 1861, he married Martha L. Robinson, with whom he had two daughters. He was a reporter for the *LaCrosse Democrat* during the Civil War years. His wife died in 1867, and his daughters were subsequently raised by an aunt. In 1868, Kellogg became assistant editor of the Council Bluffs, Iowa, *Daily Democrat*.

(continued on following page)

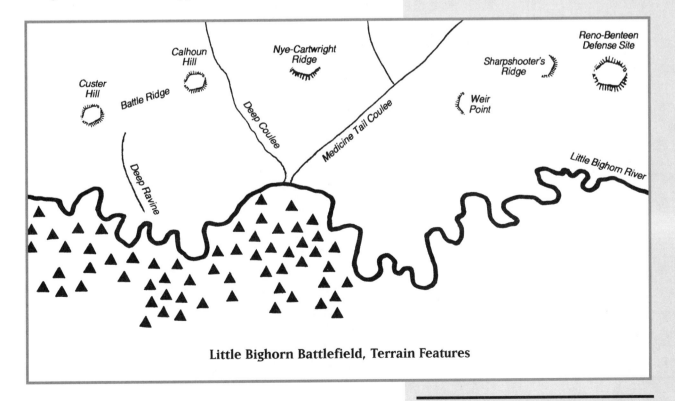

Little Bighorn Battlefield, Terrain Features

His whereabouts are somewhat of a mystery from that point, except for a short stint as a train dispatcher in Brainard, Minnesota, from sometime in 1872 until May 1873, when he surfaced as an editorial assistant for the *Bismarck Tribune.* He apparently worked only part-time for the newspaper; in the summer of 1974, he ran a hay camp north of Bismarck while studying law. He then went east and returned to Bismarck in early 1876 aboard the same train as the Custers. The train became snowbound, and Kellogg was said to have fashioned a telegraph key that summoned Tom Custer to the rescue with a sleigh.

Mark Kellogg. *Courtesy Little Bighorn Battlefield National Monument.*

Kellogg, likely working only part-time for the *Tribune,* was not scheduled to accompany Custer's 7th Cavalry on the Little Bighorn campaign, but at the last moment, he replaced his employer, Clement A. Lounsberry, whose wife had become ill. During the march, he submitted three dispatches, dated May 31, June 12, and June 21, the final one from the mouth of the Rosebud.

Kellogg was killed with Custer's column on June 25, his body apparently found in the ravine with those of Company E. Col. John Gibbon, in an 1877 article for the *American Catholic Quarterly Review,* stated that he happened upon a body at that location that was missing an ear and had been scalped but not stripped. "The clothing was not that of a soldier, and, with the idea of identifying the remains, I caused one of the boots to be cut off and the stockings and drawers examined for a name." No name was found, but the boots were later identified as Kellogg's.

📖 Kellogg's battlefield notes (May 17 to June 9), which were delivered to Bismarck druggist John P. Dunn, with whom Kellogg played chess, are in the possession of the North Dakota State Historical Society. His final dispatch, published in the *New York Herald,* July 11, 1876, has been reprinted in *The Custer Myth: A Source Book of Custeriana,* edited by W. A. Graham (Harrisburg, PA: Stackpole, 1953). For a well-researched chronicle of the life and death of Kellogg, including a reprinting of his diary, see *I Go with Custer,* by Sandy Barnard (Bismarck, ND: *Bismarck Tribune,* 1997).

See also "Custer's 'Mysterious Mr. Kellogg' and the Diary of Mark Kellogg," by John C. Hixon, *North Dakota History* 17, no. 3 (1950); "The Mark Kellogg Story," by J. W. Vaughn, *Westerners New*

(continued on following page)

that in the initial stages of the battle, Custer dispatched a battalion of the Gray Horse troop—Company E, commanded by 1st Lt. Algernon Smith—down this ravine either as a feint or in an attempt to attack the village. Those troops were met with fierce opposition and retreated north and east, perhaps up Deep Coulee, to Battle Ridge. It also has been speculated that Custer was either killed or wounded during this assault.

NYE-CARTWRIGHT RIDGE

This ridge, which forms part of the divide between Medicine Tail and Deep Coulees, was named for two students of the battle who located firing positions in the vicinity. It has been speculated that troopers were deployed at this position to guard Custer's right flank and cover the approach of the pack train. Another theory suggests that those troops had simply become separated from the command.

RENO-BENTEEN DEFENSE SITE

Seven companies of the 7th Cavalry—about 400 men—under the command of Maj. Marcus Reno assumed a defensive position on this bluff on the eastern side of the Little Bighorn River after retreating from the valley and subsequently being joined by Capt. Frederick Benteen's battalion.

SHARPSHOOTER'S RIDGE

This hill, 500 yards north of the Reno-Benteen Defense Site, was the location where one day after the battle an Indian sharpshooter killed and wounded a number of the pinned-down cavalrymen with his accurate fire. He gained a grudging respect for his marksmanship before either being killed or breaking contact when the troopers concentrated fire at him.

Calhoun Hill marker. *From author's collection.*

WEIR POINT

This promontory above Medicine Tail Coulee was the location to which Capt. Thomas Weir advanced without orders. From here, he observed Indians in the distance firing at objects on the ground at Custer Hill. Weir was subsequently driven back from this point to the Reno-Benteen Defense Site.

Custer's Battle Plan

Contrary to the assumption of many historians and casual observers that Custer's plan of attack was hastily devised, reckless, and destined to fail, his battle plan was in fact well thought out, logical, and could have—should have—succeeded. But how do we know what he intended when apparently no one who survived the fight was told the specific details? It does not take a military genius to understand exactly how Custer envisioned the unfolding of his plan. Plenty of evidence exists to support a strategy that was nothing less than brilliant, especially given the terrain.

Major Reno was ordered by Custer in the person of adjutant W. W. Cooke to cross the river and charge the Indian village, allegedly with the parting words: "You will be supported by the whole outfit." That was all Reno was told. He had no other knowledge of Custer's overall plan, only his part in it. And Reno's part in the plan was to charge the village, not to wonder about Custer's location or how his battalion would be supported by Custer.

From all indications, during the charge, Reno kept looking around for any sign of reinforcement by Custer's command, which, to his dismay, did not appear. This led Reno to believe that Custer had abandoned him and he must fend for himself. Therefore, he inexplicably aborted his charge one-quarter mile from the village.

It is quite obvious, however, that Custer never intended his command to appear behind or beside Reno. Custer never intended to follow or join Reno's charge into the village with reinforcements, as Reno might have presumed. Reno was part diversion, part strike force. The Indians in the village were unaware of Custer's presence on the eastern bluffs. He had the all-important element of surprise in his favor. Custer meant to support Reno when the two commands rendezvoused inside the Indian village.

This had been Custer's customary tactic during the Civil War and again at Washita. He would execute a frontal assault with one detachment while sending one or two other detachments on a flanking movement.

When Reno charged into that village, it would have caused great chaos within, as well as prevented the Indians from organizing any defense or mounting a counterattack. Then individual units from Custer's command would have descended within

York Posse Brand Book 7, no. 4 (1961); "Colonel Custer's Copperhead, The Mysterious Mark Kellogg," by Lewis O. Saum, *Montana* (Autumn 1978); "Mark Kellogg Telegraphed for Custer's Rescue," by Oliver Knight, *North Dakota Historical Society* 27, no. 2 (1960); and "The Custer Campaign Diary of Mark Kellogg," by Elmo Watson, *Westerners Brand Book, 1945–46,* Chicago (1947).

✳ Myles Walter Keogh
Captain, 7th U.S. Cavalry

Capt. Myles W. Keogh. *Courtesy Little Bighorn Battlefield National Monument.*

Keogh was born at Orchard House, Leighlinbridge, County Carlow, Ireland, on May 25, 1840. Some accounts list the year of his birth as 1839 or 1842. Keogh later stated on his application for a commission in the U.S. Army that he had attended Carlow College until the age of sixteen, when he quit to tour Europe for six months. He claimed to have joined the French Foreign Legion at that time and participated in the closing stages of the Algerian campaign.

In August 1860, Keogh was appointed second lieutenant in the Battalion of St. Patrick, a volunteer unit that went to Italy to fight for Pope Pius IX when the Papal States were being threatened by Napoleon II and the Piedmontese. About one month later, Keogh distinguished himself at the Adriatic port of Ancona, when his outgunned battalion was attacked by a superior force of Piedmontese supported by artillery. Keogh's unit repulsed several bayonet charges and drove back the enemy. For his extraordinary gallantry during

(continued on following page)

this battle, Keogh was awarded the coveted Pro Petri Sede medal and the Ordine di San Gregorio (Cross of the Order of St. Gregory the Great). After the flag of the Papal States was lowered in defeat the following month, Keogh remained to serve for two years in the Papal Guard.

This routine duty was contrary to Keogh's adventurous nature, and in March 1862, he resigned his commission and sailed for the United States. On April 1, he arrived in New York City and offered his services to the Union army. Keogh was commissioned a captain on April 9 and assigned as acting aide-de-camp to Brig. Gen. James Shields, another Irish immigrant. Keogh's soldierly qualities soon came to the attention of Gen. George B. McClellan, and he was assigned to the staff of the army commander. He subsequently served as an aide-de-camp to various generals and participated in such engagements as Cedar Mountain, Second Bull Run, South Mountain, Antietam, Brandy Station, Aldie, Gettysburg, and Mine Run.

Keogh was promoted to major in April 1864. Three months later, he was on the staff of Gen. George Stoneman during a raid to liberate Andersonville prison, when his 700-man unit was captured at Sunshine Church, near Macon Georgia. His confinement was brief. He was exchanged for Confederate prisoners two months later. Keogh went on to distinguish himself in operations in southwest Virginia, North Carolina, and Georgia and was breveted lieutenant colonel in March 1865. He was mustered out of the service on September 1, 1865, after having participated in over thirty engagements.

With recommendations from several generals, Keogh was appointed second lieutenant, 4th Cavalry, in May 1866 and joined the 7th Cavalry on July 28 as a captain and commander of Company I. Some accounts state that Keogh was a favorite of George Armstrong Custer, others dispute this, but one fact is certain: He was known to habitually drink to excess, and during those times, his mood became dark and combative. Keogh also has been mentioned as the person who introduced Custer to the 7th Cavalry marching song, "Garry Owen" (see "Regimental Battle Song 'Garry Owen'" on page 123).

In 1867, Keogh was assigned command of Fort Wallace, the westernmost post in Kansas, which was said to have had miserable, primitive conditions and was under constant siege by Indians. He was absent for the Washita campaign the following year while serving on the staff of Gen. Alfred Sully as acting inspector general. In 1870, Keogh

the several ravines on the field or down Medicine Tail Coulee and spread out from there to strike the village at several places at once—without having any concentrated opposition. Perhaps all or part of Keogh's detachment would have ridden to strike the village from the north. That coordination would have created a massive one-two-three punch that would have made it virtually impossible for the Indians to escape and would have inflicted devastating casualties.

It has been suggested that the Indians that day were just so furious and fed up with the white man that they decided to make a stand, and that spelled Custer's doom. The facts fail to support this theory. Chief Gall, perhaps the fiercest of all Sioux warriors, stated that when Reno's troops were observed approaching, orders were given to tear down the village in preparation for flight. Packing up and running always had been the custom of the Indians when soldiers attacked, and that was by all accounts their intention on that day as well—no matter how many warriors were present to fight. In fact, the greatest fear of most officers of the regiment was that the Indians would flee before the soldiers could strike.

Reno and others have made the case that to have charged into the village would have been tantamount to suicide. First of all, there was no discretion given in Reno's orders. He was not told to use his best judgment on whether to charge the village. Subordinates obey orders from their superior officers—without question—or face punishment. Many a soldier throughout history has charged the cannon's mouth under more desperate circumstances. Reno was told to charge. It was not by any stretch of the imagination his prerogative to consider the odds before carrying out his orders. Even so, those odds were decidedly in his favor.

Reno, who had never witnessed an arrow fired in anger, had every advantage—the upper hand on his charge and afterward. This can be evidenced by the fact that he had not lost even one man up to the time he aborted his charge. Not one

"If I were an Indian, I often think I would greatly prefer to cast my lot among those of my people adhered to the free open plains rather than submit to the confined limits of a reservation, there to be the recipient of the blessed benefits of civilization, with its vices thrown in without stint or measure."

—CUSTER FROM *MY LIFE ON THE PLAINS; OR, PERSONAL EXPERIENCES WITH INDIANS,* 1874

(continued on following page)

cavalryman had been shot from his horse by a bullet or an arrow on the approach. Gall had rallied a handful of warriors as a delaying tactic while the women packed the village, and there was some return fire, but there had not been time for the Indians to mount a concerted effort to repulse Reno.

If these Indians at the edge of the village were such a threat, why was it that Reno subsequently lost only two men, whose horses had bolted and taken them into the village during his presence in the valley, before retreating and during his indecisive wait in the timber? He suffered no other losses until he failed to maintain control of his command in the timber.

Reno's disregard for Custer's orders, perhaps motivated by cowardice, which compelled him to halt his charge and form a line of dismounted skirmishers, afforded the Indians an opportunity to assemble in numbers sufficient to counterattack. Had Reno carried out his orders and charged the village, Custer's troops would have been there to joyfully greet him—just as Cooke had indicated. Reno would have been supported by the whole outfit.

Instead, when Custer made an attempt to probe the village with a detachment sent down Medicine Tail Coulee, it was forced back by warriors who would not have been available for defense had Reno penetrated the village as ordered. Custer's other detachments were forced to retreat to or remain on the eastern bluffs, as sitting ducks, when Reno left Custer's command high and dry.

Also, had Benteen ridden to the rescue immediately instead of dawdling along the trail, another 125 troopers would have roared into this chaotic village to wreak havoc upon their enemy. But Benteen, for reasons known only to himself, chose to disobey Custer's order as well. And when Benteen later met Reno, his order from Custer would have become Reno's order. In other words, both men should have immediately led their commands to the aid of Custer. Instead, they cowered on the hilltop and accused Custer of abandoning *them.*

The outcome of the battle also probably would have been different had Captain Benteen, rather than Reno, been in command of the battalion in the valley. In spite of his hatred for Custer, Benteen, a fearless soldier, would have slammed into that village as ordered, which would have permitted Custer's strategy to proceed as planned. But Custer evidently had been obliged to place Reno, his second in command, at the head of the valley charge.

No other theory about this battle makes any sense whatsoever. Reno charges the village in the valley. Custer stealthily descends from the eastern bluffs and wades into the village. Benteen rushes up with reinforcements and ammunition packs. It was a brilliant plan by Custer, using the terrain like a chessboard and moving his pieces masterfully to checkmate his enemy.

rejoined his unit, which was transferred to Kentucky on Reconstruction duty from 1871 to 1873. He missed the Yellowstone expedition of 1873 and the Black Hills expedition the following year when his company was assigned as part of an escort for the Northern Boundary Survey (see "The Northern Boundary Survey" on page 121).

During the June 25, 1876, Little Bighorn battle, Keogh commanded a three-company battalion that was part of Custer's detachment. He was killed along with his troops on the eastern slope of Battle Ridge, within half a mile of Custer Hill. Keogh's actions that day make him a candidate for the "Bravest Man the Sioux Ever Fought," the last soldier to die (see "The Bravest Man the Sioux Ever Fought" on page 217). His trusted horse, Comanche, was the only living thing found on the battlefield after the fight (see "Comanche" on page 238). Keogh's best friend in the regiment, 1st Lt. Henry J. Nowlan, who had been on temporary duty with Terry's column, took charge of Comanche. Nowlan was also the recipient of Keogh's will, which had been drawn up just days before the battle.

Keogh's remains were removed from the battlefield in July 1877 and reinterred in the Martin family plot at Fort Hill Cemetery, Auburn, New York. One legend has it that Keogh had a love affair with Nellie Martin, but the two never married, for whatever reasons. It has been said that Nellie never married, and fifty years later, she was buried beside Keogh. The inscription on Keogh's marble monument reads:

> Sleep soldier!
> Still in honored rest
> Your truth and valor wearing
> The bravest are the tenderest
> The loving are the daring

Fort Keogh, named in his honor, was established in 1877 at the confluence of the Tongue and Yellowstone Rivers.

📖 Perhaps the most accurate book about Keogh's career is *Myles Keogh: The Life and Legend of a Irish Dragoon in the Seventh Cavalry,* edited by John P. Langellier, et al. (El Segundo, CA: Upton and Sons, 1990). The most romantic and thought-provoking account is *Keogh, Comanche and Custer,* by former battlefield superintendent Edward S. Luce (St. Louis: John S. Swift and Co., 1959). Also see *The Honor of Arms,* by Charles L. Convis (Tucson: Westernlore, 1990); *Captain Myles Walter Keogh, United States Army, 1840–1876,* by G. A. Hayes-McCoy (Dublin: National University of Ireland, 1965); "Captain Myles Walter Keogh, the Irish

(continued on following page)

Sword," by G. A. Hayes-McCoy, *Journal of the Military Historical Society of Ireland* (1951); "The Man Who Rode Comanche, Sidelights of the Sioux War," by Francis B. Taunton, *English Westerners, Special Publication No. 2;* and "Myles Keogh from the Vatican to the Little Big Horn," by Brian Pohanka, *Military Images* (September–October 1986).

✹ George Edwin Lord
Assistant Surgeon, 7th U.S. Cavalry

Lord was born on February 17, 1846, in Boston and was subsequently adopted by Rev. Thomas N. Lord, a Congregationalist minister. At some point during his childhood, the Lord family moved to West Auburn, Maine. He attended Lewiston Falls Academy in Danville and Bowdoin College, from which he graduated in 1866. Lord served as a high school principal in South Abington, Massachusetts, before enrolling the following year in Chicago Medical School (now Northwestern University), graduating in March 1871.

Dr. George E. Lord. *Courtesy Little Bighorn Battlefield National Monument.*

In April 1871, Lord became a contract surgeon with the army and served at Fort Ripley; Leech Lake, Minnesota; and Fort Randall, Dakota Territory. His contract was canceled at his request in November 1873, and at that time, he returned to Limerick, Maine. The following May, he accepted another contract and was assigned to Dakota Territory, where he worked with the Northern Boundary Survey (see "The Northern Boundary Survey" on page 121). After a brief visit to New York City, Lord signed another contract and was sent to St. Paul. In June 1875, at Fort Snelling, he was appointed assistant surgeon with the army rank of first lieutenant. Lord was serving at Fort Buford when he was attached to the 7th Cavalry at Fort Lincoln just prior to the Little Bighorn campaign.

Lord became ill on the march up the Rosebud on the 7th Cavalry's approach to the Little Bighorn Valley and halted some distance behind the column to rest. He straggled to Custer's camp the night of June 24 and was too weary and sick to eat. At that time, Custer advised Lord to remain behind with the pack train, but the doctor refused. He was killed the following day in the battle, his body found on Custer Hill. Officers and men from various companies were also found at that location, and it has been speculated that they had been wounded and brought there for the doc-

(continued on following page)

The 7th Cavalry would have routed the Indians that day, killing and capturing great numbers of them, destroying a huge village, its valuable contents, and the pony herd, which would have crippled those who escaped to the extent that eventual surrender would have been their only alternative.

The portrayal of Custer as a bumbling tactician who led his men into certain death due to his ego is simply not supported by the evidence. The outcome of the battle assuredly would have been different—regardless of the number of Indians—had Custer's subordinate officers obeyed their orders to the letter.

🦌 Did Custer Disobey Orders?

> Camp at Mouth of Rosebud River
> Montana Territory
> June 22nd, 1876

Lieut.-Col. Custer 7th Cavalry
Colonel:

The Brigadier-General Commanding directs that, as soon as your regiment can be made ready for the march, you will proceed up the Rosebud in pursuit of the Indians whose trail was discovered by Major Reno a few days since. It is, of course, impossible to give you any definite instructions in regard to this movement, and were it not impossible to do so the Department Commander places too much confidence in your zeal, energy, and ability to wish to impose upon you precise orders which might hamper your action when nearly in contact with the enemy. He will, however, indicate to you his views of what your actions should be, and he desires that you should conform to them unless you shall see sufficient reasons for departing from them. He thinks that you should proceed up the Rosebud until you ascertain definitely the direction in which the trail above spoken of leads. Should it be found (as it appears almost certain that it will be found) to turn towards the Little Horn, he thinks that you should still proceed southward, perhaps as far as the headwaters of the Tongue, and then turn toward the Little Horn, feeling constantly, however, to your left, so as to preclude the possibility of the escape of the Indians to the south or southeast by passing around your left flank. The column of Colonel Gibbon is now in motion for the mouth of the Big Horn. As soon as it reaches that point it will cross the Yellowstone and move up at least as far as the forks of the Big and Little Horns. Of its future movements must be controlled by circumstances as they arise, but it is hoped that the Indians, if upon the Little Horn, may be so nearly enclosed by the two columns that their escape will be impossible.

The Department Commander desires that on your way up the Rosebud you should thoroughly examine the upper part of Tulloch's Creek, and that you should endeavor to send a scout through to Colonel Gibbon's column, with information of the result of your examination. The lower part of the creek will be examined by a detachment from Colonel Gibbon's command. The supply steamer will be pushed up the Big Horn as far as the forks if the river is found navigable for that distance, and the Department Commander, who will accompany the column of Colonel Gibbon, desires you to report to him not later than the expiration of time for which your troops are rationed, unless in the meantime you receive further orders.

> Very respectfully your obedient servant
> E. W. Smith
> Captain 18th Infantry
> Acting Assistant Adjutant General

Surprisingly, the above order issued by Brig. Gen. Alfred H. Terry to George Armstrong Custer on June 22, 1876, ignited a major controversy over whether Custer willfully disobeyed Terry's instructions.

After reading the text, which includes such phrases as "It is, of course, impossible to give you any definite instructions in regard to this movement" and "the Department Commander [Terry] places too much confidence in your zeal, energy, and ability to impose upon you precise orders which might hamper your action," no fair-minded person could make the accusation that Custer was guilty of disobedience. It must also be remembered that Terry had no practical experience fighting Indians; Custer had. Therefore, it would have been logical for him to allow Custer to take his own initiative, depending on what he found in front of him.

Yet after the battle and through the ensuing years, mainly fueled by statements from defensive military personnel, people have come to the conclusion that Custer brought about the loss of his command by disregarding those orders. This accusation was more likely an attempt to make the dead Custer a scapegoat.

In addition to his official report outlining the facts of the battle, General Terry wrote a "confidential" report on July 2, 1876. This second, explosive report, which was leaked to the press by Gen. William T. Sherman, implied that Custer had disobeyed orders by not following Terry's "plan." Headlines in newspapers revealed this shocking story under headlines such as "Custer's Blunder" and "Custer's Fault."

Terry also told Charles S. Diehl, a reporter for the *Chicago Times,* in an article published September 16, 1876, that had Custer survived, he would have faced a court-martial for disobeying orders. To be fair, it must be noted that at the time, Terry was fighting for his military life. His own competence in the matter was being questioned, with at least one newspaper calling for his court-martial.

tor's attention. Lord's surgical case was discovered two days later in the abandoned Indian village.

Dr. Lord was initially buried on the battlefield. His body was exhumed in July 1877 and reinterred in Custer National Cemetery. Lord, whose marital status has been somewhat of a mystery, may have left behind a widow.

📖 "Dr. George E. Lord, Regimental Surgeon," by J. W. Vaughn, *New Westerners Brand Book,* 1962; "Surgeon George Lord: A Brief History," *Research Review,* Little Big Horn Associates (September 1984); and "Custer's Surgeon, George Lord, among the Missing at Little Bighorn Battle," by C. Lee Noyes, *Greasy Grass* 16, a publication of the Custer Battlefield Historical and Museum Association (May 2000).

✸ Donald "Tosh" McIntosh
First Lieutenant, 7th U.S. Cavalry

1st Lt. Donald McIntosh. *Courtesy Little Bighorn Battlefield National Monument.*

McIntosh was born on September 4, 1838, at Jasper House, Montreal, Quebec, Canada. His father was an agent with the Hudson's Bay Company, and his mother a direct descendant of Red Jacket, a chief of the Six Nations. When McIntosh was fifteen, his father was killed by Indians, and in the ensuing years, the family resided at various frontier posts in Canada, Oregon, and Washington. In 1861, he moved to Washington, D.C., and served as chief clerk for Col. Daniel Rucker, a position he held throughout the Civil War. On October 13, 1866, McIntosh married Mary (Molly) Garrett in Baltimore. The couple had no children. Molly's sister, Katherine, later married McIntosh's future 7th Cavalry comrade Francis M. Gibson.

McIntosh was appointed a second lieutenant, 7th Cavalry, on August 17, 1867, and joined his regiment at Fort Harker, Kansas, in October. He missed the Washita battle while on sick leave and was promoted to first lieutenant in March 1870. His promotion, however, could be considered surprising, given the report of commanding officer Col. Samuel Sturgis, who wrote about McIntosh five months later:

> Eminently inefficient through ... extreme indifference to his official duties, giving him the appearance of desiring to render the smallest possible service compatible with absolute security of his commission. If he were an enlisted man he would pass as a malingerer.

(continued on following page)

McIntosh was acting commander of Company G during the Yellowstone expedition of 1873 and the Black Hills expedition the following year, and he was serving in that capacity when the 7th Cavalry departed Fort Abraham Lincoln in May 1876 on the Little Bighorn campaign.

On June 25, while in the process of directing his men from the timber in Reno's retreat from the valley to the bluffs above the Little Bighorn River, McIntosh was shot off his horse. A trooper provided him with another, and he was eventually surrounded by an overwhelming number of Indians. McIntosh was dragged from his horse and struck with a tomahawk, his scalp torn from the forehead to the neck. Capt. Frederick W. Benteen remarked, "I am inclined to think that had McIntosh divested himself of that slow poking way which was his peculiar characteristic, he might have been left in the land of the living."

McIntosh's mutilated body, identified by the distinctive sleeve buttons on his shirt, was buried on the battlefield. His remains were exhumed in July 1877 and reinterred the following month at Fort Leavenworth National Cemetery. His remains were once again exhumed in October 1909 and reinterred in Arlington National Cemetery. Although certainly not flawless as an officer, McIntosh was well educated, and his obituary called him "a gentleman of culture."

📖 "Donald McIntosh: First Lieutenant, 7th U.S. Cavalry," by Juana Fraser Lyon, *Clann Chatain* 5, no. 2 (1965). He is also the subject of numerous references in *The Custer Myth: A Source Book of Custeriana*, edited by W. A. Graham (Harrisburg, PA: Stackpole, 1953).

✸ John Martin
Trumpeter and Orderly, 7th U.S. Cavalry

John Martin was born Giovanni Martini in January 1853 in Sola Consalina, Italy. At age fourteen, he was a drummer boy in the Italian Army, and he may have fought at Custoza against the Austrians in 1866. Martin immigrated to the United States in 1873 and enlisted in the army on June 1, 1874, in New York City. He was assigned to Capt. Frederick W. Benteen's Company H, 7th Cavalry, and arrived at Fort Lincoln, Dakota Territory, in time to accompany his unit on the Black Hills expedition.

Pvt. John Martin. *Courtesy Little Bighorn Battlefield National Monument.*

(continued on following page)

In addition to the top brass circling the wagons, Custer critic Capt. Frederick W. Benteen, no stranger himself to disobeying orders, wrote to his wife on July 4, 1876:

> Had Custer carried out order he got from Genl. Terry the command would have formed a junction exactly at the village—and have captured the whole outfit of tepees, etc. and probably any quantity of squaws, papooses &c. &c. but Custer disobeyed orders from the fact of not wanting any other command—or body to have a finger in the pie, and thereby lost his life.

It is doubtful that by the time this letter was written that Benteen had been privileged to read the order that Custer received to have enough knowledge to determine whether the orders had been disregarded. Perhaps it had been written from the position that the best defense is a good offense.

Benteen's letter, Terry's order, and other statements have led some historians to suggest that Custer was scheduled to rendezvous with the Terry-Gibbon column on June 26, or at least was required to send a messenger when he found a village and wait for the other column to arrive before attacking. But Terry had written in his order that "its [Gibbon's column's] future movements must be controlled by circumstances as they arise." That column, by the way, did not arrive at the battlefield until the twenty-seventh.

In his defense, Custer was under the impression that his column had been discovered by the Sioux, when the box of hardtack that had been lost was subsequently surrounded by Indians. Knowing that it was the Indian custom to flee from a large detachment of approaching soldiers, that would have made it seem imperative that he immediately attack.

Similar views were later expressed by many army officers, including Generals Nelson Miles and Phil Sheridan, who were experienced in the ways of the hostiles. The real concern of the campaign participants, which was summed up in the June 20, 1876, edition of the *St. Paul Pioneer Press* was that "there is not much probability of these cunning rascals being caught by our more slow-moving forces, for they can break up and fly in a thousand different directions and hide among the hills and gullies, every foot of which is to them familiar ground." This certainly was Terry's concern as well. He wrote to Sheridan on June 21, "My only hope is one of the two columns will find the Indians."

Custer's cook, Mary Adams, who had accompanied him on the campaign, claimed in an affidavit dated January 16, 1878, that she had overheard Terry tell Custer, "Use your own judgment and do what you think best if you strike the trail."

Blame for Custer's defeat at one time or another has been placed on Custer, Reno, Benteen, Terry, Sheridan, Crook, the

Little Bighorn Battlefield: View looking south from Medicine Tail Coulee. *Courtesy Little Bighorn Battlefield National Monument.*

War Department, the Bureau of Indian Affairs, President Grant, and combinations of the above.

The man who has shouldered the most blame, the "scapegoat," is the only one on that list who could not defend himself against the charges. Therefore, the accusation that Custer disobeyed orders and thereby lost his command has been a convenient excuse for those who may have played a part in the defeat but lived to tell their stories. Those orders, however, tell a different story and serve to clear him of that charge.

📖 *Did Custer Disobey Orders at the Battle of the Little Bighorn?,* by Charles Kuhlman (Harrisburg, PA: Stackpole, 1937); *"Sufficient Reason?" An Examination of Terry's Celebrated Order to Custer,* by Francis B. Taunton (London: English Westerners' Society, 1977); *Indian Fights and Fighters,* by Cyrus T. Brady (New York: McClure, Phillips, 1904); *The Custer Myth: A Source Book of Custeriana,* by W. A. Graham (Harrisburg, PA: Stackpole, 1953); *Custer and the Great Controversy: The Origin and Development of a Legend,* by Robert M. Utley (Pasadena, CA: Westernlore, 1980); "A Modern Look at Custer's Orders," by Thomas E. O'Neil and Hoyt S. Vandenberg, *Research Review: The Journal of the Little Big Horn Associates* 8, no. 2 (June 1994); and *General Terry's Last Statement to Custer,* by John S. Manion (El Segundo, CA: Upton and Sons, 2000).

🐎 Should Custer Have Separated His Command?

There has been much to-do about Custer's decision to separate his command into three battalions at the mouth of Reno Creek prior to his advance toward the Indian village. Some scholars have argued that Custer's total command of about

On June 25, 1876, Martin was detailed as an orderly to George Armstrong Custer. He carried Custer's last known order—thereby giving him the distinction of being the last cavalryman to see Custer alive. The hastily scribbled message, written by Adj. William W. Cooke to Captain Benteen, read: "Benteen. Come on. Big Village. Be Quick. Bring Packs. W. W. Cooke. P. bring pacs."

Martin told Benteen that as he rode off, he heard Custer, who had been studying the village through field glasses he had borrowed from 1st Lt. Charles DeRudio, exclaim, "Hurrah, boys, we've got them!" Martin could have been confused by the unfamiliar English language, or Custer may have believed that victory was at hand. Martin said that his last sight of Custer's detachment was of the Gray Horse Troop, 1st Lt. Algernon Smith's Company E, as it was galloping down Medicine Tail Coulee toward the Indian village on the other side of the river. Martin also told Benteen that the village was the largest he had ever seen, and that Reno's troops had charged and were killing everybody, which was not true. Those positive statements by Martin, however, may have contributed to Benteen's subsequent inaction, when he dawdled along the trail instead of obeying orders to "Be Quick."

Benteen later referred to Martin as a "thickheaded, dull-witted Italian, just as much cut out for a cavalryman as he was for a king." Martin remained with his company and participated in the hilltop fight.

In 1877, Martin fought in the Nez Perce campaign, including the September Canyon Creek fight. He also testified at the January 1879 Reno Court of Inquiry. Martin reenlisted in June 1879 and was assigned to Company G, 3rd Artillery. On October 7 of that year, he married Julia Higgins in Westchester, New York. The couple had five children.

Martin remained in various artillery units, including service in the Spanish-American War, until September 1900, when—as a corporal—he once again joined Company H, 7th Cavalry. One month later, he transferred to Company 90, Coast Artillery Corps, at Fort McHenry near Baltimore. He retired as a sergeant on January 7, 1904. Martin lived in Brooklyn and worked as a subway ticket agent for the New York City Transportation Company, until dying from bronchopneumonia on December 24, 1922. He was buried in Cypress Hills National Cemetery in Brooklyn. His obituary appeared in the December 27, 1922, edition of the *New York World.*

(continued on following page)

BIOGRAPHIES

📖 "Interviews with John Martin, October 24, 1908 and May 10, 1910," in *Custer in '76: Walter Camp's Notes on the Custer Fight,* edited by Kenneth Hammer (Provo, UT: Brigham Young University Press, 1976); "John A. Martin—Custer's Last Courier," by Raymond J. Ross, *The West* (April 1967); and "Custer's Battle Plan," by W. A. Graham, *Cavalry Journal* (July 1923). A letter from Martin to D. R. Barry, dated April 7, 1907, can be found in the collection at the Little Bighorn Battlefield National Monument. Numerous references to Martin, including his own story, are in *The Custer Myth: A Source Book of Custeriana,* edited by W. A. Graham (Harrisburg, PA: Stackpole, 1953).

✳ James Ezekiel Porter
First Lieutenant, 7th U.S. Cavalry

Porter was born on February 2, 1847, in Strong, Maine. He entered the U.S. Military Academy at West Point from that state in September 1864. He graduated five years later, ranked sixteenth in a class of thirty-nine, which included future 7th Cavalry officers Charles Braden and William Craycroft. On July 27, 1869, Porter married Eliza Frances Westcott in Portland, Maine, with whom he had two sons.

1st. Lt. James E. Porter. *Courtesy Little Bighorn Battlefield National Monument.*

He joined the 7th Cavalry at Fort Leavenworth in October 1869 and served in Kansas throughout the following year. From 1871 to 1873, he served on Reconstruction duty in various Southern cities. He was appointed first lieutenant, Company I, on March 1, 1872, to fill the vacancy created by the promotion of Myles Moylan. For the next two years, Porter served with his unit on the Northern Boundary Survey (see "The Northern Boundary Survey" on page 121).

Porter was second in command of Company I during the 1876 Little Bighorn campaign. On June 25, he was evidently killed along with other members of his company on the southern slope of Battle Ridge. His body either was too mutilated to be recognized or was not on the field, for it was never found. His bloody coat, containing two bullet holes, was discovered two days later in the abandoned Indian village site.

500 fighting men would have been quite a formidable force had it swept into the village. By separating his command, Custer weakened his ability to contend with the overwhelming number of warriors. This poor judgment on Custer's part has been said to have been a contributing factor in his downfall.

The subject, however, is irrelevant inasmuch as Maj. Marcus A. Reno and Capt. Frederick Benteen failed to execute Custer's orders and therefore the outcome of the battle cannot be fairly assessed. It would seem that this issue falls into the category of simply another smokescreen to generate excuses for the malfeasance of Reno and Benteen and to place the blame on Custer, who was not available to defend his true intentions (see "Custer's Battle Plan" on page 205).

It must also be noted that Custer traditionally separated his command before charging into the enemy. He had employed this tactic with great success in the Civil War and again at Washita in 1868. He would dispatch one strike force on a frontal assault of his objective while sending one or more detachments on a flanking movement.

Custer's battle plan was devised with the belief—and rightly so—that the Indians would flee, as had been their custom. Had he charged into the village with his entire command from the south, where Reno had been ordered to enter, the thousands of occupants would have raced through the maze of lodges toward the north, and many would have escaped. Besides that, the warriors could have organized a solid defense and effective counterattack if afforded the opportunity to gather on the north end. Those cavalrymen who successfully threaded their way through the time-consuming maze would have been met with much resistance. Either way, the women and children would have escaped, and there is a good chance that the cavalrymen would have been driven from the village.

With that in mind, it would appear that the only logical method of attacking the village was by separating the command. When Reno charged from the south, escape routes to the west would have been covered by Benteen and to the north and east by Custer's detachment.

According to Custer's battle plan, Reno's charge into the village would have caused the Indians to flee blindly into the hands of Custer's command, which had ridden to the east and north. It then would have been a matter of securing the village and deploying a number of men to guard against a counterattack from hostiles who had slipped through the seams, while other troopers chased down the stragglers. By that time, Benteen and his battalion, along with the pack train of ammunition and an additional eighty-five men, would have arrived as reinforcements. Captured Indian women and children could have been held as hostages with which to bargain and assure that a counterattack in force would not be forthcoming for fear of harming the captives. Systematic destruction of the village, its valuable contents, and pony herd could then have taken place. Messengers could have been dispatched to hurry the Terry-Gibbon column. Even if Custer had become surrounded, he had enough firepower to maintain his position until Terry arrived.

In the above scenario, it would not have mattered how many Indians had escaped Custer's trap. They would have been demoralized, split into small bands running for their lives, and on the verge of poverty, which would have encouraged many to submit to the reservation.

Readiness of the Cavalrymen

The question regarding the readiness, or lack thereof, of the cavalrymen to effectively fight on June 25, 1876, was a matter of discussion after the battle, but it was first brought to the forefront during testimony at the 1879 Reno Court of Inquiry. Theories that many of the troopers were untrained raw recruits and that the unit as a whole had succumbed to fatigue by the time they reached the battlefield have been posed as reasons for the 7th Cavalry's poor showing against the enemy.

The first matter of contention pertains to new recruits who lacked proper training and were said to have been called upon to fight alongside seasoned veterans. There can be no question that poorly trained troops are more vulnerable under combat conditions. The ability to fight effectively is dependent upon learning the skills necessary to be proficient in the ways of warfare. Lessons in weaponry and military discipline are essential in order to engender personal confidence and unit cohesiveness when facing the enemy. This requires intense training over a period of time.

Records show that about 150 recruits joined the 7th Cavalry in 1875, with about 60 of them having had prior service. Another 62 new men were said to have joined the unit in early 1876, although only 54 could be verified from regimental rosters on June 25 of that year. These men were more than likely untrained in the ways of a cavalryman; their daily activities had consisted mainly of guard duty, fatigue duty, and the monotonous post routine. This lack of training for the new recruits can be placed on the shoulders of Maj. Marcus A. Reno, who commanded the 7th Cavalry in Custer's absence during preparations for the campaign. Reno neglected to schedule target practice training or the rudiments of cavalry tactics. Granted, it did not take an expert to figure out how to aim and fire the Springfield Model 1873 or the Colt .45 revolver. But with

❋ William Van Wyck Reilly
Second Lieutenant, 7th U.S. Cavalry

2nd Lt. William V. W. Reilly. Courtesy Little Bighorn Battlefield National Monument.

Reilly was born on December 12, 1853, in Washington, D.C. About nine months later, on September 21, 1854, his naval officer father was lost in the China Sea while stationed aboard the USS *Porpoise*. His mother then married Col. L. M. Johnson, whose influence assisted Reilly in gaining an appointment to the U.S. Naval Academy in September 1870. He resigned in October 1872 and joined an eight-month surveying expedition to Nicaragua, then, for the next two years, superintended the breakup of old warships.

Reilly's military service began when he was commissioned a second lieutenant in the 10th Cavalry on October 15, 1875. Three months later, in January 1875, he transferred to the 7th Cavalry. During the 1876 Little Bighorn campaign, Reilly was on temporary duty from Company E as second in command of Capt. George Yates's Company F. He was killed on June 25. His body was found and buried on Custer Hill. Reilly's remains were exhumed in July 1877 and reinterred in Mount Olive Cemetery, Washington, D.C. A ring that he wore when he was killed is on display at the Smithsonian Institution.

📖 "Profile: Lieutenant William Van Wyck Reilly, 7th Cavalry," by Brian Pohanka, *Greasy Grass* (1986), a publication of the Custer Battlefield Historical and Museum Association.

❋ Marcus Albert Reno
Major, 7th U.S. Cavalry

Reno was born on November 15, 1834, in Carrollton, Illinois. He entered the U.S. Military Academy at West Point in 1851 and was scheduled to graduate with the class of 1855. Due to excessive demerits (he allegedly set the record with 1,031), however, Reno finally graduated in 1857, ranked twentieth in a class of thirty-eight. He was commissioned a brevet second lieutenant in the 1st Dragoons in July 1857 and second lieutenant in June 1858. Reno served with his unit on frontier duty at forts in Dalles, Oregon, and Walla Walla, Washington Territory, until the outbreak of the Civil War.

Reno was appointed first lieutenant, 1st Dragoons, in April 1861 and captain, 1st Cavalry, in November. In March 1863, at Kelly's Ford, he was cited for bravery and breveted major for his actions

(continued on following page)

Maj. Marcus A. Reno. *Courtesy Little Bighorn Battlefield National Monument.*

when he led a charge against the Rebels and his horse fell, pinning him beneath with an injury.

On July 1, 1863, Reno married Mary Hannah Ross, the daughter of a Pennsylvania banker and industrialist, in Harrisburg. The couple had one son.

At the October 1864 Cedar Creek battle, Reno once again distinguished himself and was breveted lieutenant colonel. He also fought at Gaines Mill, Beverly Ford, Upperville, and on the Peninsula. Reno was appointed colonel of the 12th Pennsylvania Cavalry from January until July 1865, when he was mustered out. On March 13, 1865, he was breveted colonel, USA, and brigadier general, USV, in recognition of his exemplary record.

After the war, Reno served briefly as an infantry tactics instructor at West Point, then was assigned as provost marshal in New Orleans until he requested frontier duty, which took him to Fort Vancouver, Washington, as acting assistant inspector general of the Department of the Columbia. He was appointed major, 7th Cavalry, in December 1868 but apparently did not report for duty until late the following year. Reno was stationed at Fort Hays, Kansas, from December 1869 to July 1871, when he was assigned to New York City as a member of the Small Arms Board for two years. It was during this time that the army adopted the

(continued on following page)

respect to the Springfield trapdoor carbine, there was a technique of loading and extracting that required proper learning and practice in order to fire the maximum number of rounds per minute (see "Weapons Carried by the Cavalrymen" on page 195). Training in horsemanship—other than feeding, grooming, and mucking out stalls—had been lacking as well.

At first glance, it would appear that these new recruits were a detriment to the efficiency of the 7th Cavalry against the Sioux and Cheyenne—if indeed they had been called upon for a combat role—as was stated at the 1879 Reno Court of Inquiry.

The controversy arises when considering information presented in "Varnum, Reno and the Little Bighorn," an article by W. J. Ghent in *Winners of the West* (April 30, 1936). In this article, battle participant 2nd Lt. Charles Varnum alleges that the number of recruits participating in the battle was greatly exaggerated at the court of inquiry in order to aid Reno's case. Varnum claimed that most of the new recruits had been left back at the Powder River base camp, and that no company had more than two recruits on the march.

A check of regimental rosters confirms Varnum's assertion. At the time of the battle, a total of thirty-seven new recruits—those who signed up in 1876—were on detached duty at the Powder River base camp. One was at Fort Abraham Lincoln, another was in confinement, and two were en route. Nine were detailed with the pack train escort, and only four remained with companies assigned to Reno's battalion—including Pvt. Theodore Goldin, who was awarded the Medal of Honor, and two others who had years of prior service with the infantry. No new recruits were members of the companies that made up Custer's command. Therefore, the charge that untrained recruits contributed to Custer's defeat can be readily dismissed.

Another problem that has plagued cavalry units throughout history is the number of "green" horses experiencing combat for the first time. It has been estimated that as many as 50 per-

Little Bighorn Battlefield: View of Custer Hill looking east. *Courtesy Little Bighorn Battlefield National Monument.*

cent of the 7th Cavalry mounts were newly acquired. The reactions of these animals to the sounds, smells, and chaos of battle also may have had an effect on the ability of troopers to fight.

The second allegation concerning readiness charges that the cavalrymen were too fatigued to fight by the time they had arrived in the Valley of the Little Bighorn. The regiment had traveled about 113 miles, with little sleep or nourishment, between June 22 and June 25. A long, hard march such as this can certainly create a state of tiredness that would prevent anyone from functioning at peak performance. Field rations during the previous month had consisted mainly of hardtack and bacon, with the occasional supplement of wild game. Fatigue and malnourishment unquestionably sap the spirit and can result in a breakdown of discipline and morale.

These cavalrymen, however, were proud professionals in an elite unit and were expected to perform under the most adverse conditions. Soldiers have traditionally gone into battle under less-than-ideal circumstances—a number of these troopers had braved freezing temperatures and a blizzard to successfully attack Black Kettle's village at the battle of the Washita in November 1868.

There is another element that must be considered when judging a person's readiness to fight. The one factor that can overcome fatigue and hunger is experiencing shots fired in anger. As anyone who has endured combat is aware, adrenaline-fueled energy plays a major role in quickly readying the body and mind for battle. Like a slap in the face, senses and concentration are heightened, and although fatigue may become a factor during a prolonged battle, men trained to fight usually respond in an admirable fashion in the short term. Whether Custer's men could have fared better had they enjoyed a good night's sleep and a full belly is a matter of conjecture.

It can be concluded that there were more relevant reasons than readiness—such as a battle plan gone awry, which placed the command in jeopardy—that can be cited for Custer's defeat.

"We are now in a country hitherto unvisited by white men. [Charley] Reynolds had been guiding the column, but had lost his way and General Terry did not know what to do about finding a road. . . . I told him I thought I could guide the column. And when, after a hard day's work we arrived here the General was delighted and came to congratulate me."

—CUSTER TO LIBBIE, JUNE 9, 1876,
FROM CAMP ABOUT TWENTY MILES
FROM THE MOUTH OF THE POWDER RIVER

Model 1873 Springfield .45/.55-caliber, single-shot, breech-loading carbine, which became a source of controversy following the Little Bighorn battle (see "Weapons Carried by the Cavalrymen" on page 195, and "Malfunction Allegations Concerning the Springfield Carbine" on page 196).

In 1873, Reno returned to the 7th Cavalry, but he did not participate in the Yellowstone expedition that year or the Black Hills expedition the following year. Instead, he was in command of a two-company detachment that provided an escort for the Northern Boundary Survey (see "The Northern Boundary Survey" on page 121).

His wife unexpectedly passed away on July 10, 1874. Reno requested permission from headquarters to attend her funeral and received the reply: "While fully sympathizing with your affliction, the Department Commander feels it is imperative to decline to grant you leave." To add insult to injury, his wife's family denied him a share of the family fortune.

In November 1875, Reno returned from leave in Europe to become temporary commander of the 7th Cavalry while Custer was embroiled in Washington politics. He requested that the position be permanent, but Gen. Alfred H. Terry delayed making a decision until Custer's fate had been determined. When Custer returned in time to assume command for the Little Bighorn campaign, Reno was without question quite resentful—an attitude that had festered from the day Reno had been assigned to the 7th Cavalry. This resentment—not unlike that of Capt. Frederick W. Benteen—stemmed from professional jealousy over the fact that the younger Custer had reaped glory during the Civil War and was a national hero. Although Reno was not outwardly antagonistic toward Custer, his opinion of his superior officer was decidedly less than complimentary. This opinion was said to be mutual, which had made Reno's lengthy absences beneficial to Custer and the morale of the regiment.

Reno was not without his detractors. It has been said that he was not liked, and even despised, by many of his contemporaries. Gen. Hugh Scott, then a young second lieutenant, "disliked him intensely." Lieutenant Francis M. Gibson was "wary of Reno and considered him to be arrogant and vicious." First Lt. Edward S. Godfrey (the future general) wrote in his journal, "Reno's self important rudeness makes him unbearable." Even Captain Benteen, who shared a common dislike of Custer, once slapped Reno in public, called him an "S.O.B.," and challenged him to a fight. Reno prudently declined the invitation.

(continued on following page)

Reno's controversial, and perhaps disgraceful, actions during the Little Bighorn campaign began when he disobeyed General Terry's orders on a scout of the Powder River (see "Reno's Powder River Scout" on page 192), escalated on June 25, when he disobeyed Custer's orders to charge the Indian village and instead sacrificed much of his command on a disorganized retreat to the bluffs across the Little Bighorn River, and culminated when he lost control of his command, possibly while drunk, while pinned down on the hilltop (see "The Conduct of Maj. Marcus A. Reno on the Hilltop" on page 245).

After the battle, Reno was the subject of immediate and intense criticism from the officers and men who had witnessed his actions, as well as public condemnation. He was subsequently assigned (or exiled) to Fort Abercrombie, known as the armpit of the Dakotas. Shortly after arriving, he was accused of cavorting with a fellow 7th Cavalry officer's wife—Emeline Bell, wife of Capt. James M. Bell. He faced a general court-martial on March 8, 1877, on the charges of "conduct unbecoming an officer and gentleman" and being drunk on duty. Reno claimed that the charges were simply post politics and that Mrs. Bell had been the aggressor, but he was found guilty as charged. He was sentenced to be dismissed from the service, but President Rutherford B. Hayes, citing Reno's exemplary record, commuted the punishment to two years suspension, effective May 1, 1877. At that time, other 7th Cavalry officers, McDougall, Moylan, DeRudio, and Bell, charged Reno with striking a junior officer and being drunk on duty, but the charges were eventually dropped.

Due to public fervor over Reno's actions at Little Bighorn, he requested a court of inquiry to investigate his conduct. The informal proceedings convened in January 1879 in Chicago and could be likened to a song-and-dance performance by officers who closed ranks and did not desire to bring disgrace on the elite 7th Cavalry. The inquiry, which ostensibly "cleared" Reno's name, was more farcical than factual (see "The Conduct of Maj. Marcus A. Reno on the Hilltop" on page 245).

Reno was restored to duty at Fort Meade and soon found himself in more trouble. A drunken Reno struck another officer over the head with a pool cue and was confined to quarters when he was accused of a "Peeping Tom" incident. The subject was Ella Sturgis, the twenty-year-old daughter of Col. Samuel Sturgis, with whom Reno was said to have had a one-sided interest. While strolling on the parade ground on November 10, 1879, Reno inexplicably peered into the window of the Sturgis parlor, then, upon seeing Ella, tapped on the window. Ella screamed bloody murder, and Colonel Sturgis left his bed to chase Reno with his cane.

Reno's court-martial convened on November 28, and he was once again found guilty and sentenced to be dismissed from the service. This time President Hayes refused to commute the sentence—in spite of a petition for clemency from Generals Terry and Sherman—and Reno was dishonorably discharged on April 1, 1880, after twenty-three years in the army.

Reno, who for the rest of his life tried unsuccessfully to clear his name, fell on hard times in civilian life. He married for a second time, but his wife left him after only a few months. Newspaper and magazine editors were not interested in his accounts of the famous battle. He even lacked the funds to travel to his son's wedding. Reno eventually landed a job as a clerk with the Bureau of Pensions in Washington, but that apparently did not last long.

Reno had cancer of the tongue and developed complications following surgery. He died on March 30, 1889, at Providence Hospital in Washington. His brief obituary in the *Washington Star* read: "Reno—In this city died, Marcus A. Reno, late major and Brevet Lt. Col., U.S. Army."

In the mid-1960s, Reno's great-nephew, backed by the American Legion, asked the army to reexamine the final court-martial charges. The judge advocate general's office concluded that Reno had been improperly dismissed from the service, and his records were corrected to reflect an honorable discharge.

On September 9, 1967, Reno was reinterred with full military honors in the Custer National Cemetery, thus making him the only battle participant honored with such pomp and circumstance.

Two sympathetic biographies of Reno are *In Custer's Shadow: Major Marcus Reno,* by Ronald Nichols (Norman: University of Oklahoma Press, 2000), and *Faint the Trumpet Sounds,* by John Upton Terrell and George Walton (New York: David McKay, 1966). Author Walton joined with Reno's great-nephew and the American Legion in 1967 in the successful petition to have Reno's record reviewed. The result of that review can be found in the June 1, 1967, edition of the *New York Times.* Reno presents his side of the story in "The Custer Massacre," *Americana Magazine* 7 (March–April 1912). The effort by Reno's relatives to reopen his case is in *Reno and Apsaalooka Survive Custer,* by Ottie W. Reno (NY: Cornwall Books, 1997). A literary duel between Reno and Custer's friend Tom Rosser, as well as a statement by Reno and other material, can be found in *The Custer Myth: A Source Book of Custeriana,* edited by W. A. Graham (Harrisburg, PA: Stackpole, 1953).

Also see: "Case of Marcus Reno," by Barry Johnson, English Westerners' Society *Special Publication No. 3;* Johnson's "Reno as Escort Commander," English Westerners' *Brand Book* (September 1972); *The Reno Court of Inquiry: The* Chicago Times *Account* (Fort Collins, CO: Old Army Press, 1972); *Abstract of the Official Record of Proceedings of the Reno Court of Inquiry,* by W. A. Graham (Harrisburg, PA: Stackpole, 1954); "The Reno Court Martial," *Bismarck Tribune* (March 21, 1877); "Major Reno's Affair," by Roy Paul Johnson, *Fargo* (North Dakota) *Forum* (December 23, 1956); "Major Marcus A. Reno at the Little Bighorn," by Lee Noyes, *North Dakota History* 28, no. 1 (1961); "Marcus Albert Reno," by Ronald Nichols, *Greasy Grass* (1986), a publication of the Custer Battlefield Historical and Museum Association; *The Reno Court of Inquiry,* by Ronald Nichols (Hardin, MT: CBHMA, 1994).

Reno's Valley Fight: View from bluffs showing position of first skirmish line. *Courtesy Little Bighorn Battlefield National Monument.*

The Bravest Man the Sioux Ever Fought

Custer's men, according to the consensus opinion of the Sioux and Cheyenne, fought with great courage and bravery. Sitting Bull perhaps summed up that sentiment when he later stated: "I tell no lies about dead men. Those men who came with the 'Long Hair' were as good men as ever fought." None of the soldiers attempted to surrender, and there was no mention of anyone committing suicide by the Sioux, though the Cheyenne did tell of several suicides. Those interested in delving into that subject, an argument advanced by Dr. Thomas B. Marquis, can find his flawed theory in *Keep the Last Bullet for Yourself: The True Story of Custer's Last Stand* (New York: Reference Publications, 1976).

At least one soldier was singled out by the Indians for extraordinary bravery. Perhaps the most intriguing and difficult puzzle to solve with respect to the battle is the identity of this cavalryman who distinguished himself as the bravest man the Sioux ever fought.

The controversy was ignited by an interview on February 27, 1877, in which Sioux chief Red Horse said:

> Among [the soldiers] was an officer who rode a horse with four white feet. The Indians have fought a great many tribes of people, and very brave ones, too, but they all say that this man was the bravest man they have ever met. I don't know whether this man was Gen. Custer or not; some say he was. I saw this man in the fight several times, but did not see his body. It is said that he was killed by a Santee, who still holds his horse. This officer wore a large-brimmed hat and a buckskin coat. He alone saved his command a number of times by turning

⊛ Sitting Bull
Hunkpapa Sioux Medicine Man and Chief

Sitting Bull (Tatanka Yotanka, "A Large Bull Buffalo at Rest") was born about 1830 at a supply site the Hunkpapa called Many Caches along the Grand River, near present-day Bullhead, South Dakota. He was the son of a chief named either Four Horn or Sitting Bull, and his boyhood name was "Slow" or "Jumping Badger." At age ten, he killed his first buffalo. Four years later, he counted coup on an enemy Crow, an act that prompted his father to change the boy's name to Sitting Bull. Also at about that time, he went on a vision quest and was accepted into the Strong Hearts warrior society. Sitting Bull proved himself a fierce warrior, gaining the utmost respect of his peers for his daring exploits, especially after he sustained a wound in battle with the Crow that forced him to limp for the rest of his life. He assumed leadership of the Strong Hearts at age twenty-two.

Sitting Bull subsequently led raiding parties of his warriors against traditional Sioux enemies, such as the Crow, Blackfeet, Shoshone, and Arapaho. He eventually became known as someone special, a warrior whose medicine was good, and became a *Wichasha Wakan*—a man of mystery, or medicine man. He also became legendary for practicing the "Sash Dance"—in the face of the enemy, he would pin himself to the ground to indicate that he would never retreat.

Sitting Bull, who did not "touch the pen" to the Fort Laramie Treaty of 1851, avoided any confrontation with the U.S. Army until the early 1860s, when Gen. Alfred Sully encroached on Hunkpapa territory in the Dakotas while pursuing Santee Sioux fugitives. He carried out hit-and-run raids on small army detachments and led his Strong Hearts at the July 28, 1864, battle of Killdeer Mountain.

During the 1866–67 conflict known as Red Cloud's War (see "Red Cloud's War" on page 68), Sitting Bull's band roamed farther north, where he led attacks in northern Montana and Dakota Territory, particularly in the vicinity of newly constructed Fort Buford at the confluence of the Missouri and Yellowstone Rivers. Many Sioux moved onto the reservation when Red Cloud negotiated the Fort Laramie Treaty of 1868. Sitting Bull refused to submit and continued to follow the traditional nomadic lifestyle of his people. He and his

(continued on following page)

Sioux Sitting Bull, 1881. *Courtesy Little Bighorn Battlefield National Monument.*

band, however, would occasionally visit the reservation to obtain supplies and spread discontent among their brethren. His warriors were said to have been the Sioux who aggressively protested the presence of the army during Custer's Yellowstone expedition of 1873 (see "Who Were Those Sioux That Attacked Custer?" on page 128).

When Custer marched through the Black Hills the following year, Sitting Bull considered this intrusion and the prospectors who later came to dig for gold to be tantamount to a declaration of war. He assumed the position as head of the war council and gathered around him allies from the Northern Cheyenne and a few other tribes.

For all intents and purposes, war was declared by the U.S. government when an edict was issued requiring all Indians in the Yellowstone Valley to report to the reservation by January 31, 1876, or face the consequences. To be fair, it would have been quite difficult at that time of year for Sitting Bull and his followers to comply. It is evident, however, that this defiant spiritual leader had no intention of obeying the order.

The first indication that the government meant business came in mid-March, when troops under Gen. George Crook attacked and destroyed a Sioux-Cheyenne village on the Powder River. It was evident that the gauntlet had been thrown, and the Sioux would have to contend with the might of the U.S. Army in order to survive.

In early June, while camped in the Rosebud Valley, Sitting Bull's people held a Sun Dance. Sitting Bull did not participate in this ritual, in which warriors had strips of rawhide attached to a stick and inserted into their chests, then dangled in the air from a center pole. Instead, he directed his adopted brother to slice strips of flesh from his arms, then commenced dancing until he passed out. When Sitting Bull was revived, he told of a vision that he had experienced: dead soldiers falling from the sky into their camp. This vision was interpreted to mean that they would be victorious in battle against their enemy.

The first opportunity to verify this vision came in mid-June, when General Crook's troops were observed approaching on a route that would take them directly into the Sioux village. Sitting Bull remained behind, while Crazy Horse rallied the warriors and attacked Crook on June 17. Although the battle on the Rosebud was a stalemate and Crook held the field when Crazy Horse broke contact, enough soldiers were killed to encourage the Indians that they could not be defeated (see "Prelude to Little Bighorn: The Powder River and Rosebud Engagements" on page 189).

Two days later, Sitting Bull moved his village into the Valley of the Little Bighorn. During the previous week, the population of the village had been increased by brethren who had left the reservation to enjoy a summer of freedom. By June 25, when Custer's 7th Cavalry attacked, the village had more than doubled in size—from 400 lodges to over 1,000—with perhaps as many as 2,000 warriors available to fight.

Sitting Bull did not actively participate in the battle against the cavalry; that was the responsibility of the young warriors. His place as an older chief and counselor was to remain in the village to protect the women and children from harm. He did at one point ride onto the field to encourage his braves for a short time before returning to his duties across the river. By late afternoon, Sitting Bull's vision of soldiers falling into camp had come true.

The huge village on the Little Bighorn broke up the following day, and the various bands separated. Sitting Bull and his people headed southwest into the Bighorn Mountains, where they celebrated their victory with dances and feasts. The army, however, remained relentlessly on the trail of the hostiles. On October 21, Sitting Bull had a parley with Gen. Nelson Miles, and although many Sioux by then were surrendering, the defiant medicine man refused. A fight at Clear Creek, Montana, ensued, which caused more Sioux to submit to the reservation. Sitting Bull, along with Chief Gall and the rest of his followers, fled northward and remained around the upper Missouri for some time before finally withdrawing into Canada.

The Canadian government refused to provide supplies, and life became hard for Sitting Bull's band. On July 19, 1881, under a pledge of amnesty, he led 200 of his people to Fort Buford. Sitting Bull was held a virtual prisoner for nearly two years at Fort Randall in present-day Gregory County, South Dakota, before being permitted in May 1883 to settle at the Standing Rock Indian Agency.

In June 1885, Sitting Bull signed a four-month contract with Buffalo Bill's Wild West Show for $50 a week and a bonus of $125, along with the rights to sell his photograph and autograph. His reception by Eastern audiences, who frequently

(continued on following page)

on his horse in the rear in the retreat. In speaking of him, the Indians call him "The man who rode the horse with four white feet." There were two men of this description, looking very much alike, both having long yellowish hair.

From the context of Red Horse's statement, which can be found in *The Custer Myth: A Source Book of Custeriana*, edited by W. A. Graham (Harrisburg, PA: Stackpole, 1953), it would seem that this action occurred during Reno's retreat from the timber to the hilltop. Former battlefield superintendent Edward S. Luce, writing in *Keogh, Comanche and Custer* (St. Louis: John S. Swift Co., 1939), claims that only four officers wore buckskin that day—both Custer brothers, W. W. Cooke, and Capt. Myles Keogh. Edgar I. Stewart, in *Custer's Luck* (Norman: University of Oklahoma Press, 1955), adds to that list Capt. George Yates, 1st Lt. James Calhoun, 1st Lt. Algernon Smith, and 1st Lt. James E. Porter, none of whom were members of Reno's battalion, but who were with Custer.

Oddly enough, in spite of the glaring discrepancies, many believe that the officer alluded to by Red Horse was Capt. Thomas French, although he was one of the first officers to reach the bluffs and could not have covered his men, apparently was not wearing buckskin, did not have long yellowish hair, and was not killed.

Tactics employed by Indians on the field of battle make it quite difficult to piece together one consistent story from various eyewitness accounts. Indians did not fight as an organized unit; once the battle commenced, they were free to fight as individuals, and for that reason, they generally had no idea regarding specific time frames, places, movements of their comrades, or an overall perspective of events.

hissed when this Indian villain appeared, was quite disrespectful, which was a source of displeasure to the Sioux medicine man. During the tour, he also met President Cleveland and a number of the army officers who had futilely chased him around the northern plains.

When the Sioux embraced the Ghost Dance religion in late 1890, Sitting Bull apparently did not participate. Nevertheless, it was said that he clearly enjoyed and encouraged the turmoil this ritual had provoked. Indian agent James McLaughlin, who had always regarded Sitting Bull as a threat to good order, believed that the Sioux leader was indeed inciting members of his tribe to defy the government. McLaughlin ordered that Sitting Bull be arrested.

On December 15, Indian police went to serve the arrest warrant. A confrontation between more than 40 Indian police and about 150 Ghost Dancers ensued outside Sitting Bull's cabin. In the resultant melee, the Sioux medicine man was shot and killed by Indian policemen Lieutenant Bullhead and Sergeant Red Tomahawk. Sitting Bull's seventeen-year-old son, Crow Foot, and six other Ghost Dancers were killed, along with six Indian policemen. This act led Minniconjou chief Big Foot to flee the reservation, which culminated in the December 29 Wounded Knee massacre.

McLaughlin, in an obituary, wrote that "the shot that killed [Sitting Bull] put a stop forever to the domination of the ancient regime among the Sioux of the Standing Rock Reservation." And that

(continued on following page)

Reno's Valley Fight: View from bluffs, dotted line shows Reno's retreat route. *Courtesy Little Bighorn Battlefield National Monument.*

was likely the true reason for the murder of Sitting Bull. He had married as many as nine wives and had fathered about the same number of children.

📖 Two excellent biographies are at the top of the list: *The Lance and the Shield: The Life and Times of Sitting Bull,* by Robert M. Utley (New York: Henry Holt, 1993); and *Sitting Bull: Champion of the Sioux,* by Stanley Vestal (Norman: University of Oklahoma Press, 1957). Also see *Sitting Bull,* by Alexander B. Adams (New York: Putnam and Sons, 1973); *Sitting Bull,* by Bill Dugan (San Francisco: HarperCollins, 1994); *Cry of the Thunderbird,* by Charles Hamilton (Norman: University of Oklahoma Press, 1972); *A Sioux Chronicle,* by George E. Hide (Norman: University of Oklahoma Press, 1956); *My Friend, the Indian,* by James McLaughlin (New York: Houghton-Mifflin, 1926); "The True Story of the Death of Sitting Bull," by E. G. Fechet, *Proceedings and Collections of the Nebraska State Historical Society,* 2nd ser., 2 (1898); "Surrender of Sitting Bull," by E. H. Allison, *South Dakota Historical Quarterly* 6 (1912); "Sitting Bull and the Mounties," by Ian Anderson, *Wild West* (February 1998); and *Sitting Bull: The Collected Speeches,* by Mark Diedrich (Rochester, MN: Coyote Books, 1998).

✹ Algernon Emory "Fresh" Smith
First Lieutenant, 7th U.S. Cavalry

Smith was born on September 17, 1842, in Newport, New York, and attended Hamilton College. His Civil War service began in June 1862, when he enlisted in Company K, 7th Infantry. Two months later, he was appointed second lieutenant, 117th New York Infantry, and commanded Company G from February to October 1863, when he was assigned as an aide-de-camp to Gen. Alfred H.

1st Lt. Algernon E. Smith. *Courtesy Little Bighorn Battlefield National Monument.*

Terry. Smith was promoted to first lieutenant in April 1864 and saw action as a staff officer during the battle of Cold Harbor, the siege of Petersburg, and Drury's Farm. He was promoted to captain in October 1864. In the January 1865 assault on Fort Fisher, North Carolina, Smith was severely wounded in the shoulder while leading a charge. He was hospitalized for two months and had limited use of this arm for the remainder of his life. Smith could not even put on his coat without assistance. He was brevetted major in March 1865 for his bravery at Fort Fisher.

Smith was appointed second lieutenant, 7th Cavalry, in August 1867 and two months later married Nettie B. Bowen in Newport, New York. He participated in the 1868–69 Washita campaign and in December 1868 was promoted to first lieutenant. Smith applied for disability retirement in 1870 due to his arm injury but withdrew the request. That same year,

when Benzine review boards were formed to reduce the officer corps, commanding officer Col. Samuel Sturgis recommended that Smith be discharged, calling him "wanting in integrity." The board did not approve that recommendation, however, and Smith remained on duty as second in command of Company A. During this time, Smith's wife became one of Libbie Custer's closest friends, and evidently Custer must have thought highly of Smith. In 1872, the two families shared a house in Elizabethtown, Kentucky, with the two wives alternating weekly housekeeping chores. Smith was with Company A for the Yellowstone expedition of 1873 and served as acting assistant quartermaster and acting commissary of subsistence for the Black Hills expedition of 1874.

In the spring of 1876, when the 7th Cavalry marched out of Fort Lincoln on the Little Bighorn campaign, Smith assumed temporary command of Company E, known as the Gray Horse Troop, named for the color of its mounts. It has been theorized that on June 25, during the opening stages of the Little Bighorn battle, Smith's troop was deployed down Medicine Tail Coulee to probe the Indian village. The company was apparently forced to retreat and was subsequently annihilated, the bodies later buried in Deep Ravine, where they have thus far eluded detection. Smith's body, however, was the only one of his company found on Custer Hill, which leads to speculation that he had perhaps been wounded and taken to that location for medical treatment or was responding to officers' call by whoever was in command at that time.

Smith was buried on the battlefield. His remains were exhumed in July 1877 and reinterred in Fort Leavenworth National Cemetery.

📖 The Nettie Bowen Smith scrapbook is in the collection at Bancroft Library, University of California, Berkeley.

✹ James Garland "Jack" Sturgis
Second Lieutenant, 7th U.S. Cavalry

Sturgis was born on January 24, 1854, in Albuquerque, the son of Col. Samuel D. Sturgis, who would command the 7th Cavalry. He entered the U.S. Military Academy at West Point in July 1871 and graduated four years later, ranked twenty-ninth in a class of forty-three. Sturgis was appointed second lieutenant, 7th Cavalry, in June 1875 and, after temporary court-martial duty, joined

2nd Lt. James G. Sturgis. *Courtesy Little Bighorn Battlefield National Monument.*

his unit in late October at Fort Rice, Dakota Territory.

Sturgis was the youngest and final Regular officer assigned to the regiment before it marched in May 1876 on the Little Bighorn campaign. He had initially been assigned as third in

(continued on following page)

Although Red Horse's statement would lead us to believe that the "bravest man" was with Reno, no one in that command comes close to fitting the description. Perhaps another officer, this one in Custer's battalion, was actually the subject of the Indians' admiration—as the last man to die.

In "Custer's Last Fight as Seen by Two Moon," an article by Hamlin Garland in *McClure's Magazine* (September 1898), Cheyenne chief Two Moon described this bravest man, who would have been on the Custer battlefield while the Cheyenne rode up the ridge.

> We circled all around him—swirling like water around a stone. We shoot, we ride fast, we shoot again. Soldiers drop, and horses fall on them. Soldiers in line drop, but one man rides up and down the line—all the time shouting. He rode a sorrel horse with white face and white forelegs. I don't know who he was. He was a brave man. . . . He wore a buckskin shirt, and had long black hair and mustache. . . . His men were all covered with white dust."

In *Wooden Leg, a Warrior Who Fought Custer,* by Thomas B. Marquis (Lincoln: University of Nebraska Press, 1931), Cheyenne warrior Wooden Leg described the last man killed: "It appeared that all of the white men were dead. But there was one of them who raised himself to a support on his left elbow." Wooden Leg told how this man was finally killed, then said:

> I think he must have been the last man killed in this great battle where not one of the enemy got away. This man had a big strong body. His cheeks were plump. All over his face was a stubby black beard. His mustache was much longer than his other beard, and it was curled up at the ends.

Similar statements by Indian eyewitnesses have led many historians, including two excellent researchers, Edward S. Luce and Charles Kuhlman, in *Legend into History: The Custer Mystery* (Harrisburg, PA: Stackpole, 1952), to conclude that this brave officer was Capt. Myles W. Keogh. Bruce A. Rosenberg, in *Custer and the Epic of Defeat* (University Park: Pennsylvania State University Press, 1974), also suggested that Keogh was this man, quoting Capt. Will A. Logan, who was with Gibbon's column, as saying that an "Irish or Irish-American" officer was the last to die.

David H. Miller, who interviewed seventy-one Indian survivors of the battle for *Custer's Fall: The Indian Side of the Story* (New York: Duell, Sloan & Pearce, 1957), described the bravest man—whose white metal bars, captain's bars, had little meaning to the Indians—in terms similar to those of Wooden Leg, writing: "He was the last man of Custer's command to be killed on the ridge. This brave man may well have been Cap-

command of Company M, where it was said that he was very popular with the troops, but he was transferred to Company E as second in command just before the march. Sturgis was killed during the June 25 battle, perhaps in Deep Ravine, where many of his company's troopers were said to have been found and buried. These bodies, including that of Sturgis, have thus far eluded detection.

A blood-soaked undergarment belonging to Sturgis was discovered in the abandoned Indian village site two days after the battle. In the archives of the U.S. Signal Corps, there is a photograph taken on the battlefield depicting a primitive monument made of stones, with a board lettered, "Lt. STURGIS, 7th CAV JUNE, '76." That photo, however, was staged in an effort to mislead Sturgis's mother, who had not been informed that her son's remains had not been found. In July 1878, Camp J. G. Sturgis, located on the northwest slope of Bear Butte on the edge of the Black Hills, was named in his honor. It was abandoned in late August of that year.

✸ Two Moons
Northern Cheyenne

Cheyenne Two Moons. *Courtesy Little Bighorn Battlefield National Monument.*

Two Moons (or Two Moon, Ishi'eyo Nissi) was born about 1857, but little else is known about his early life. His uncle, Chief Two Moon, led Cheyenne warriors on an 1866 attack of Fort Phil Kearny, which contributed to the success of Red Cloud's War over the Bozeman Trail (see "Red Cloud's War" on page 68).

On March 17, 1876, Two Moons' village on the Powder River was attacked by Col. Joseph J. Reynolds. The Cheyenne were reinforced by Crazy Horse and their Sioux allies and managed to save the pony herd, but the village and its valuable contents were destroyed (see "Prelude to Little Bighorn: The Powder River and Rosebud Engagements" on page 189). Two Moons and the homeless Cheyenne took refuge with Sitting Bull and on June 25, 1876, participated in the defeat of the 7th Cavalry on the Little Bighorn River—accompanying Crazy Horse on his attack from the north. In early 1877, Two Moons was persuaded by Gen. Nelson Miles to surrender and subsequently became an army scout for that year's Nez Perce campaign.

In the ensuing years, Two Moons became a valuable source of information about the Little Bighorn battle. He became chief of the Northern Cheyenne

(continued on following page)

reservation and traveled to Washington, D.C., to advance his people's cause, meeting with President Woodrow Wilson in 1914. Two Moons served as the model for James Fraser, who designed the Indian head or buffalo nickel, which was circulated in 1913. The Northern Cheyenne warrior died in 1917.

📖 "General Custer's Fight as Seen by Two Moon," by Hamlin Garland, *McClure's Magazine* 11 (May–October 1898), which has been reprinted in *The Custer Myth: A Source Book of Custeriana*, edited by W. A. Graham (Harrisburg, PA: Stackpole, 1953).

✳ Charles Albert Varnum
Second Lieutenant, 7th U.S. Cavalry

2nd Lt. Charles A. Varnum. *Courtesy Little Bighorn Battlefield National Monument.*

Varnum was born on June 21, 1849, in Troy, New York. He was raised in Dracut, Maine, where he lived until 1866, when his family moved to Florida. Varnum worked as paymaster aboard the USS *Tallapoosa*, which sailed from Florida to Tampico, Mexico, in August 1866 and returned the following spring. In June 1868, he entered the U.S. Military Academy at West Point. He graduated four years later, ranked seventeenth in a class of fifty-seven, which included future fellow 7th Cavalry officer George D. Wallace. Varnum was appointed second lieutenant, 7th Cavalry, in June 1872 and reported for duty with Company A at Elizabethtown, Kentucky. He participated in the Yellowstone expedition of 1873 and was involved in the August 4 and August 11 battles with the hostile Sioux. Varnum was second in command of Company A during the Black Hills expedition of 1874. The following year, he served on temporary duty as a scout assigned to Fort Randall, Dakota Territory.

Varnum was on temporary duty as chief of the Crow and Arikara scouts during the 1876 Little Bighorn campaign and led the advance up the Rosebud following an Indian trail into the Little Bighorn Valley. Early on the morning of June 25, he led a party of scouts to a traditional Indian lookout called Crow's Nest, which, unknown to them, was located some fifteen miles from Sitting Bull's village. The village itself could not be observed, but the scouts recognized smoke and what they believed to be a sizable pony herd. Varnum summoned Custer, but by the time he arrived at about 9 A.M., a haze had settled over the area to obliterate any sign of the village. Custer, however, accepted his scouts' assessment that a huge village lay ahead and prepared his attack plan. Varnum was attached to Maj. Marcus A. Reno's battalion during the battle and suffered a leg wound.

Varnum was promoted to first lieutenant effective June 25, 1876, and transferred to Company C. In 1877, he served in the Nez Perce campaign, but he did not encounter the hostiles. Varnum was regimental quartermaster until 1879 and also participated in several scouting operations. In January 1879, he testified at the Reno Court of Inquiry. He was promoted to captain the following July while commanding Company B at Fort Riley.

Varnum participated in the December 29, 1890, affair at Wounded Knee, where he had his pipe shot out of his mouth. The following day, in action at White Clay Creek, Varnum refused to withdraw his troops when ordered to do so, which, in his estimation, would have left another command exposed. Instead, he held his position until both commands could safely pull back. He was awarded the Medal of Honor in September 1897 for his distinguished gallantry that day at White Clay Creek.

In 1895, Varnum was on detached service at the University of Wyoming as professor of military service. At the outbreak of the Spanish-American War, he purchased horses for Teddy Roosevelt's Rough Riders, then rejoined the 7th Cavalry and sailed for Cuba in January 1899. He became ill with typhoid fever and returned home in May. Varnum then served in Denver as adjutant general, Department of Colorado, and was appointed major in February 2, 1901. That promotion was followed four years later with an appointment to lieutenant colonel in April 1905. He was retired for disability on October 31, 1907.

From 1907 to 1909, Varnum was an instructor for the Idaho National Guard, then moved on to the University of Maine, where he was professor of military science and tactics until 1912. For the next six years, he was on recruiting duty in Portland, Oregon, and Kansas City. Varnum was appointed colonel, retired, in July 1918 and served for a year as disbursing officer at Fort Mason, California.

Varnum attended the fiftieth anniversary of the Little Bighorn battle in 1926. When he died on February 26, 1936, he was the last surviving officer who participated in the famous battle. He was buried in San Francisco National Cemetery. His obituary appeared in the February 27, 1936, edition of the *San Francisco News* and the same day in the *New York Herald Tribune*. Varnum was survived by a wife, Mary, and a daughter.

📖 Varnum's unfinished memoir was published as *I, Varnum: Autobiographical Reminiscences of Custer's Chief of Scouts*, edited by John M. Carroll and Charles K. Mills (Glendale, CA: Arthur H. Clark Co., 1982); and *Custer's Chief of Scouts: The Reminiscences of Charles A. Varnum*, edited by John M. Carroll (Lincoln: University of Nebraska Press, 1987). Varnum wrote "I was There: Colonel Charles A. Varnum's Experience," *Winners of the West* (April 1936); and "Fighting the Indians," which first appeared in the Lowell, Massachusetts, *Weekly Journal* (August 1876) and has been reprinted, along with numerous other references to him, in *The Custer Myth: A Source Book of Custeriana*, edited by W. A. Graham (Harrisburg, PA: Stackpole, 1953).

Also see "Interview with Charles A. Varnum, May 1909," in *Custer in '76: Walter Camp's Notes on the Custer Fight,* edited by Kenneth Hammer (Provo, UT: Brigham Young University

(continued on following page)

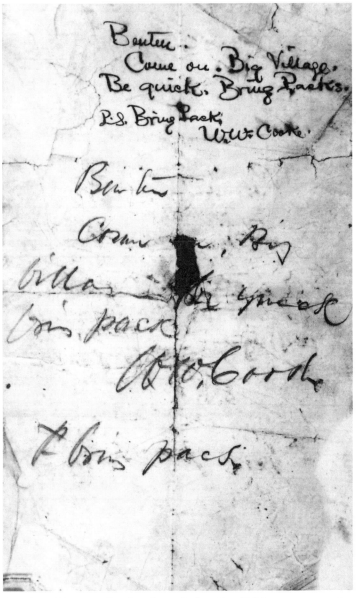

Custer's Last Message, written by adjutant Cooke to Capt. F. W. Benteen. Courtesy Little Bighorn Battlefield National Monument.

tain Myles Keogh, gallant Irish soldier of fortune, former papal guardsman and Civil War hero."

Of the officers wearing buckskin, those on Custer Hill—the Custer brothers, Yates, Cooke, and Smith—must be ruled out, if not for any other reason, because of where their bodies were found on the field. The body of Porter, who was Keogh's second in command, was never found. Calhoun was killed nearby, but as was the case with Porter, he was a lieutenant, not a captain. In addition, most of the above do not fit the consensus description—the black hair and mustache in particular.

Every description, except for the fact that his horse, Comanche, did not have white feet, would seem to point to

Press, 1976); and "Varnum: The Later Years of Custer's Last Lieutenant," by Jay F. Kanitz, *5th Annual Symposium Custer Battlefield Historical and Museum Association,* 1991.

⊛ Wooden Leg
Northern Cheyenne

Wooden Leg (Kummok'quiviokta, meaning "Good Walker") was born about 1858 along the Cheyenne River in present-day South Dakota. He was a member of the village on the Powder River that was attacked by Col. Joseph J. Reynolds in March 1876 and subsequently joined Sitting Bull and fought in the Little Bighorn battle. Wooden Leg surrendered in the spring of 1877 and was sent along with other tribesmen, including Dull Knife, to a reservation in Indian Territory. He declined to join Dull Knife and Little Wolf when the two chiefs decided to flee to the north in 1878.

About six years later, Wooden Leg was permitted to return to Montana, where he scouted for the army throughout the 1880s, and eventually became a tribal judge. In his capacity as judge, he was ordered by the Bureau of Indian Affairs to enforce the rule that Indian men could not have more than one wife. This edict was in response to a government offensive against polygamy, which also affected the Mormons in Utah and was not well received by the Cheyenne men. The men initially resisted, then invented reasons for the extra wives to circumvent the law, such as claiming that the other households were actually in-laws. Wooden Leg himself was forced to abandon one of his two wives.

Wooden Leg had participated in the Ghost Dance movement in 1890, converted to Christianity in 1908, and died in 1940. He is notable for the information he related about the Little Bighorn battle, as well as Cheyenne culture and customs, telling his story for the most part in sign language.

📖 Wooden Leg's eyewitness testimony became the basis of a memoir, *Wooden Leg: A Warrior Who Fought Custer,* as told to researcher Thomas B. Marquis (Lincoln: University of Nebraska Press, 1931). Excerpts can be found in *The Custer Myth: A Source Book of Custeriana,* edited by W. A. Graham (Harrisburg, PA: Stackpole, 1953).

*"My darling—I have but a few moments to write as
we start at twelve, and I have my hands full of preparations for the scout.
Do not be anxious about me. You would be surprised how closely I obey
your instructions about keeping with the column. I hope to have a good
report to send you by the next mail. A success will start
us all toward [Fort] Lincoln.*

—CUSTER'S LAST LETTER TO LIBBIE, JUNE 22, 1876

Keogh as the last man to die that day. But more than one eyewitness described the dust on the field, which could have coated Comanche's sweaty forelegs and perhaps given the impression of white feet.

Whether Myles Keogh was the celebrated bravest man the Sioux ever fought, as described by Chief Red Horse, there is more than enough evidence to indicate that Keogh fought with a courage that distinguished him in the eyes of his enemies, and that he was probably the last man killed at the battle of the Little Bighorn.

CHAPTER EIGHT

The Reno-Benteen Hilltop Fight

OVERVIEW

While Maj. Marcus Reno's command had been battling the hostiles, the 125-man battalion led by Capt. Frederick Benteen had reconnoitered ten grueling miles along ridges and ravines of broken terrain without observing anything of interest. Benteen considered his march a wild goose chase and finally decided to return to the main trail and follow Custer, Reno, and the pack train. Benteen had called a halt of perhaps twenty minutes to water the horses, when his command heard the faint sound of firing—likely Reno's men engaged in the valley fight. Benteen's officers wanted to move out immediately, but the captain ignored their requests for some time before finally mounting the battalion and riding out at a slow trot.

They had gone three miles when they met Sgt. Daniel Kanipe, who carried orders from Custer to Capt. Thomas McDougall ordering the pack train of ammunition to be brought up. "We've got them, boys!" Kanipe hollered as he rode past. Most of the battalion took that to mean that Custer had engaged the hostiles, but still Benteen refused to hurry. About a mile farther, within a mile or so of Reno's men on the hilltop, Benteen again halted to water the horses.

It was there that Pvt. John Martin, Custer's orderly, who was riding a wounded horse, arrived from the north. Martin presented Benteen a message that had been hastily scribbled by Adj. William W. Cooke, which was in effect Custer's last known order. The message read: "Benteen. Come on. Big Village. Be Quick. Bring Packs. W. W. Cooke. P. bring pacs." Martin, a recent Italian immigrant who spoke broken English, made a remark that could have been interpreted to mean that Custer had charged the village and the situation was in hand. Boston Custer, who had been with the pack train, waved as he hurried to catch up with his brother.

Benteen discussed the message with his officers, until the unmistakable sound of firing was heard. The battalion moved out at a gallop and topped a ridge to view the valley below, where Reno's men were in the process of crossing the river and scrambling up the bluffs on the other side. Benteen estimated that at least 1,500 Indian warriors were in the river bottom and farther upstream. He turned his troops and rode for the bluffs on the eastern side of the Little Bighorn River.

Standard battlefield marker: "U.S. Soldier, 7th Cavalry, Fell here, June 25, 1876." *From author's collection.*

BIOGRAPHIES

✷ Black Elk
Oglala Sioux

Black Elk (Hehaka Sapa or Ekhaka Sapa), one of the most written about and studied experts on Sioux culture, was born about 1853 along the Little Powder River in northeast Wyoming. He experienced his first vision at age five and another at age nine—the second one an event that he later interpreted to mean that his mission in life was to preserve the Sioux religion. At age thirteen, he participated in the June 25, 1876, Little Bighorn battle and claimed to have scalped a soldier who was still alive. "He had short hair and my knife was not very sharp," Black Elk said. "He ground his teeth. Then I shot him in the forehead and got his scalp." He presented the trophy to his mother, who honored him with a shrill tremolo.

Black Elk had been a student of Crazy Horse, and when that revered warrior was killed in 1877, he fled with his family to join Sitting Bull's band in Canada. Black Elk became a respected shaman among his people during his time north of the border. In 1881, he returned with Sitting Bull and settled on the reservation, where tribal leaders consulted him. Black Elk became a member of Buffalo Bill Cody's Wild West Show in 1886 and remained with it for three years, once performing for Queen Victoria in England.

He then returned to the Pine Ridge Reservation and became an ardent supporter of the 1890 Ghost Dance movement. The killing of Big Foot's band at Wounded Knee, however, had a sobering effect. He grieved that his once-proud people were now impoverished prisoners penned up on various reservations. "The nation's hoop is broken and scattered," he lamented. "There is no center anymore, and the sacred tree is dead."

According to Michael Steltenkamp, who wrote *Black Elk: The Holy Man of the Oglala* (Norman: University of Oklahoma Press, 1993), a daughter of Black Elk related that at some time after 1900, Black Elk became a Roman Catholic missionary—odd for someone who believed that his mission was to preserve the Sioux religion. Lucy Looks Twice, who died in 1978, said: "The Jesuits took my father to other different tribes—even though he couldn't understand their languages. He instructed Arapaho, Winnebago, Omaha, and others—teaching them the Catholic faith with the help of an interpreter.... He converted a lot of these people." The church was said to have also sent Black Elk to various Eastern cities, where he professed his faith.

(continued on following page)

The Benteen battalion was within 200 yards of Reno's position when the major rode out to meet them. "For God's sake, Benteen," Reno implored, "halt your command and help me! I've lost half my men!"

Benteen produced Custer's order, which, according to the military chain of command, was now Reno's to obey. Reno, however, ignored the order and requested that Benteen join his command on the hilltop. When Benteen asked about Custer's whereabouts, he was informed that Custer had started downstream with five companies.

The distinct clamor of a battle in progress could be heard from that direction. Some officers suggested to Reno that they should ride to Custer's support—that in the absence of direct orders, they should march to the sound of firing. The major replied that they could not leave because their supply of ammunition was low, which, according to later testimony, was not true—plenty of ammo was available.

Capt. Thomas Weir, commander of Company D, lost patience with Reno's timidity and requested that Reno at least permit a detail to scout downstream. Permission was denied, and a heated exchange ensued. Weir then blatantly disobeyed orders and rode off to the north on his own. Weir's second in command, 2nd Lt. Winfield Edgerly, was under the impression that Weir had obtained permission to move and began following him with Company D. Weir rode forward about a mile or so to a promontory now known as Weir Point. His vision was obscured by dust and smoke, but he nonetheless could recognize what he believed to be Indians riding around in the distance shooting at objects in an area that later would be known as Custer Hill. Weir then observed another group of warriors advancing toward Edgerly and his company, who were moving along a ravine, and ordered them to high ground.

Reno, perhaps having had a change of heart, dispatched a courier to inform Weir that the rest of the command would soon follow and directed the captain to attempt to open communication with Custer. It was too late. The firing downstream had for the most part ceased, and a huge force of Indians was riding toward Weir Point.

Weir's company had been followed by the remainder of Reno's disorganized command. Most of the troops had halted at Weir Point when they became aware of the large force of onrushing hostiles. An impromptu retreat ensued, as the troops hastened back to the more defensible position where they had initially arrived on the bluffs.

It was perhaps nearing 7 P.M. when the defensive perimeter, consisting of seven companies, including Captain McDougall's pack train, had been firmly established on the hilltop. This defensive position above the Little Bighorn River was formed by two parallel ridges running east and west, with a depression between. It resembled a horseshoe or a saucer with one edge broken off. The troops ringed the crests of the ridges, and the horses, mules, and a field hospital for the wounded were placed in the low-lying portion.

The Sioux and Cheyenne, fresh from the beating of Reno and the annihilation of Custer and his men, unleashed a furious barrage of arrows and rifle fire from the surrounding bluffs and ravines, which pinned down the cavalrymen in their vulnerable, makeshift rifle pits.

The Indians broke contact as darkness fell, returning to their village for a night of feasting, dancing, and recounting their individual exploits of counting coup from the day's victories.

Meanwhile, the fatigued, desperate cavalrymen attempted to fortify their positions. The soil was maddeningly porous, and they had few shovels with which to dig, so they resorted to fashioning breastworks with packs, saddles, hardtack boxes, and a picket line of dead horses and mules.

The night was soon transformed into a living nightmare for the troopers. Sitting Bull's village had erupted in clamorous celebration. The darkness reverberated with pounding war drums,

BIOGRAPHIES

Nebraska poet John G. Neihardt visited Pine Ridge in 1930 and met Black Elk. Neihardt returned the following year to record Black Elk's oral history, which he chronicled in a book-length poem first published in 1932 called *Black Elk Speaks: The Life Story of a Holy Man of the Oglala Sioux* (Lincoln: University of Nebraska Press, 1961).

Black Elk confirmed his strong belief in Catholicism when he complained after the publication of Neihardt's book that not enough had been written about his conversion. "My family is all baptized," Steltenkamp quotes him as saying. "All my children belong to the Black-gown church and I am glad of that and I wish that all should stay in that holy way.... I will never fall back from the true faith in Christ." Steltenkamp wrote that Black Elk saw no contradiction in his beliefs.

Black Elk, who had two wives and an unknown number of children, spent his later years as a mis-

(continued on following page)

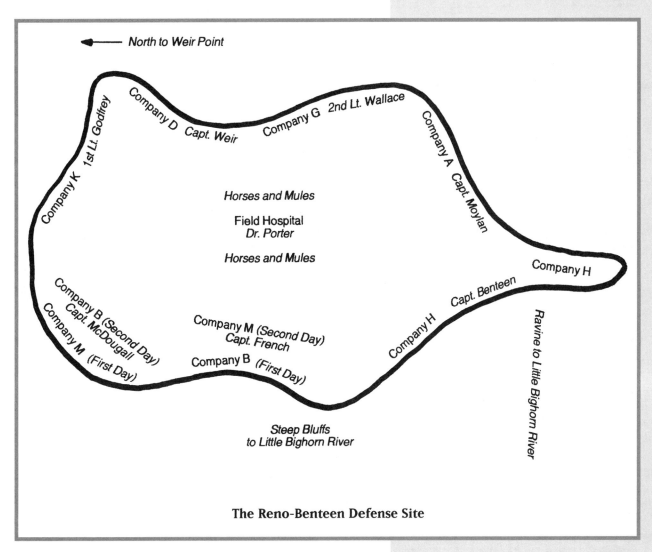

The Reno-Benteen Defense Site

The Ravine leading from the Reno-Benteen Defense Site to the Little Bighorn River. *From author's collection.*

sionary and an occasional showman at South Dakota attractions. He once said that there would be lights in the sky when he died. The vicinity of the Pine Ridge Reservation was illuminated by a bright meteor shower on the night he died in 1950 at the age of eighty-seven.

In addition to the above sources, see *The Sacred Pipe: Black Elk's Account of the Seven Rites of the Lakota Sioux,* edited by Joseph Epes Brown (New York: Penguin, 1973); *Black Elk and Flaming Rainbow: Personal Memories of the Lakota Holy man,* by Hilda Neihardt (Lincoln: University of Nebraska Press, 1995); and *Black Elk's Story,* by Julian Rice (Albuquerque: New Mexico University Press, 1991).

✺ James Howard Bradley
First Lieutenant, 7th U.S. Infantry

Bradley was born on May 25, 1844, in Sandusky County, Ohio. At the outbreak of the Civil War, he enlisted at age seventeen in the 14th Ohio Infantry, later served in the 45th Ohio, and was discharged four years later as a sergeant. He was appointed second lieutenant, 18th U.S. Infantry, in February 1866 and was promoted five months later to first lieutenant and transferred to the 7th Infantry.

Bradley became a footnote in history while serving as chief of scouts for the Terry-Gibbon column during the 1876 Little Bighorn campaign. At about 9 A.M. on the morning of June 27, while in advance of the column, he had the dubious distinction of being the man who discovered the

(continued on following page)

the exultant war cries of the warriors, and the terrifying wails of the women who mourned their dead—all set in eerie shadows from the bouncing flames of huge bonfires.

It was thought at one point that columns of cavalry could be recognized in the distance, which caused the trumpeters to alert those soldiers to the presence of Reno's hilltop position. It was soon determined, however, that the "cavalry" was likely Indians wearing army uniforms and riding cavalry mounts.

One effort was made during the night to make contact with Custer or Gen. Alfred H. Terry, who was with Col. John Gibbon's Montana Column, by sending several Indian scouts outside the lines. They were fired upon and quickly returned to safety.

There was much speculation that night regarding the whereabouts of Custer's command. One faction, led by Captain Benteen, was of the opinion that Custer had abandoned them. Another group refuted that idea and stated that Custer would be there if it were humanly possible. Apparently neither faction seriously considered that Custer and his command had been wiped out by the Indians.

The conduct of Maj. Marcus Reno during that night has been the subject of controversy. A number of officers later recalled that Reno had hidden himself in a protected position and issued no orders from darkness until dawn; other witnesses claimed that Reno gave the appearance of being under the influence of alcohol (see "The Conduct of Maj. Marcus A. Reno on the Hilltop" on page 245).

Another matter of contention arose when Reno suggested to Benteen that they mount the command and make a forced march back to the base camp on the Powder River. The wounded who could travel would accompany them; those who could not would be left behind. Benteen, to his credit, rejected the idea. Rumors of this plan, however, spread to the wounded and understandably caused anxiety among them.

It should be noted that Captain Benteen displayed great courage throughout the ordeal, as he constantly exposed himself to enemy fire. Reno apparently was willing to relinquish *de facto* command of the unit to Benteen, while the major made himself scarce.

Hostilities resumed at daybreak. Throngs of Indians had crept close to the lines during the night, and immediate action was required to prevent the position from being overrun. Benteen led a detail of troopers that brazenly counterattacked and pushed back the surprised hostiles. Subsequently, lone warriors or a small group of warriors would from time to time charge on foot or on horseback, only to be repulsed by volleys of fire from the perimeter. It became clearly evident that it would have been possible for the Indians to mount one concerted attack and overwhelm the hilltop defenders. Chief Gall later explained that the medicine man did not consider the medicine right for such an attack.

In any event, the troopers remained surrounded by as many as 2,000 warriors, who sustained a withering fire from nearby ridges that were of a higher elevation than the defensive position. One particular Indian sharpshooter on a hilltop about 500 yards to the north picked off a number of troopers with his accurate fire, until he either lost interest or was silenced by a bullet.

The cavalrymen had been without water for quite some time and were in desperate need—especially the wounded. The Little Bighorn River flowed about 600 yards away, down a ravine presently occupied by the enemy. Captain Benteen assembled a detail and led a charge down the ravine that drove the Indians away. Volunteers were requested, and every pot, pan, canteen, and other suitable container was collected. Sharpshooters were deployed to provide covering fire, and many successful trips to the river were accomplished with only two fatalities. Those sharpshooters and others who participated in the dangerous mission were later awarded Medals of Honor for their bravery (see "Medals of Honor Awarded" on page 241).

The fire from the Indians considerably slackened by about noon on the twenty-sixth. Some soldiers thought it was a trick to lure them out of their positions, so they could be more easily picked off. It has been theorized that it was at this point that the Terry-Gibbon column had entered the valley and was noticed by the Indians, who began packing up their village. One pocket of Indian snipers, however, remained to devastate the position of Captain McDougall's Company B. Another detail was formed and executed a charge on foot to rout those hostiles.

In late afternoon, a column of Sioux and Cheyenne men, women, and children could be viewed marching southwest toward the Bighorn Mountains. Benteen observed:

> It started about sunset and was in sight till darkness came. It was in a straight line about three miles long, and I think a half mile wide, as densely packed as animals could be. They had an advance guard and platoons formed, and were in as regular order as a corps or division.

Major Reno was suspicious—a few snipers had remained to nag them—and decided to remain in position for the time being. Nevertheless, the men on the line relaxed, the cooks prepared a meal, and the horses and mules were taken to the river to drink and then put out to graze. Eventually those troopers and scouts who had been trapped in the timber below straggled onto the bluffs and joined their comrades to relate their harrowing experience.

The night passed without incident. On the morning of June 27, a long, winding column of blue could be observed approaching from the south. The Terry-Gibbon column, following rumors that Custer had engaged the Indians, made contact with the survivors of Reno's beleaguered command.

bodies of Custer's command. Bradley also reportedly was the first to notify Reno's command on the hilltop of the tragedy.

Bradley was killed while commanding a mounted detachment at the August 9, 1877, battle of Big Hole during the Nez Perce campaign. He left behind a wife and two daughters.

Bradley also was a prolific writer, maintaining journals of various military operations in which he participated. His most famous work is an account of Gibbon's Montana Column in 1876, which has been published as *The March of the Montana Column: A Prelude to the Custer Massacre,* edited by Edgar I. Stewart (Norman: University of Oklahoma Press, 1961). Other narratives by Bradley have appeared over the years in issues of *Contributions to the Historical Society of Montana.*

✹ James Sanks Brisbin
Major, 2nd U.S. Cavalry

Brisbin was born on May 23, 1837, in Boalsburg, Pennsylvania. He studied law and edited a newspaper until enlisting in the army as a private at the outbreak of the Civil War. Brisbin was soon commissioned and was wounded at First Bull Run. He served with various cavalry regiments in the Peninsular campaign and at Gettysburg, and by war's end, he had received brevets to major general of volunteers and Regular army colonel.

Brisbin remained in the army as a captain with the 6th Cavalry and later the 1st Cavalry, then was assigned command of the 2nd Cavalry at Fort Ellis, Montana. In February 1876, he led four of his troops to the relief of Fort Pease, where civilians had taken refuge from hostile Indians.

During the 1876 Little Bighorn campaign, Brisbin's unit was part of Col. John Gibbon's Montana Column. Just prior to Custer's fatal march, he had argued with Gen. Alfred H. Terry that his troops with Gatling guns should be permitted to accompany that column. Brisbin, however, did not want to serve under Custer and requested that Terry assume command. Custer refused assistance from Brisbin, and Terry abided by his wishes. Brisbin also was present aboard the steamer *Far West* when Terry issued his orders to Custer. Brisbin later stated that Custer had disobeyed those orders (see "Did Custer Disobey Orders?" on page 208).

After the battle, Brisbin ghost-wrote a widely published "first-person" account of the battle under the byline 1st Lt. Charles DeRudio of the 7th Cavalry. DeRudio claimed that the article greatly embellished his role and disavowed any participation in its writing.

(continued on following page)

Brisbin was called "Grasshopper Jim," a nickname good-naturedly bestowed upon him for his frequent analyses and numerous pamphlets extolling the agricultural possibilities of Montana and the Northwest. His only work of lasting significance was *The Beef Bonanza; or, How to Get Rich on the Plains* (Philadelphia: 1881. Reprint. Norman: University of Oklahoma Press, 1959).

In 1892, Brisbin wrote a letter to Gen. Edward S. Godfrey that was quite critical of a popular article the general had written about the famous battle that had been published in *Century* magazine. Brisbin believed that the article was too pro-Custer. His letter has been included in *Troopers with Custer: Historic Incidents of the Battle of the Little Big Horn,* by E. A. Brininstool (Harrisburg, PA: Stackpole, 1952).

Brisbin died on January 14, 1892.

✸ John Jordan Crittenden
Second Lieutenant, 20th Infantry

Crittenden was born on June 7, 1854, in Frankfort, Kentucky. His namesake grandfather was governor of Kentucky, a three-term U.S. senator, and U.S. attorney general. His father, Thomas L., was a lawyer who served as an aide to Gen. Zachary Taylor at the Mexican War battle of Buena Vista and rose to the rank of Union major general in the Civil War. An uncle, George B., became a major general in the Confederate army.

Crittenden entered the U.S. Military Academy at West Point in July 1871—a classmate of 2nd Lt. James Sturgis—but was discharged in June 1874, at the end of his junior year, because of academic deficiency. He petitioned President Grant for a Regular army commission and was appointed second lieutenant, 20th Infantry, on October 15, 1875. Crittenden was assigned to Fort Abercrombie. Ten days later, he suffered an injury when a shotgun cartridge exploded and a piece struck his left eye. The eye was removed during treatment in Cincinnati a month later, but he subsequently managed to resume his military career.

Crittenden—with his father's influence—was assigned to detached service with the 7th Cavalry in May 1876 for the Little Bighorn campaign. He reported for duty as second in command of 1st Lt. James Calhoun's Company L. Crittenden was killed during the June 25 battle, his mutilated

2nd Lt. John J. Crittenden. *Courtesy Little Bighorn Battlefield National Monument.*

(continued on following page)

The troops who had endured two days pinned down by hostile Indians on the hilltop were at this time informed of the fate of Custer's command. The entire outfit then moved from the hilltop to a more defensible position in the valley near the abandoned Indian village.

The next morning, June 28, Reno and his troops visited the site of Custer's annihilation for the grisly task of burying their 7th Cavalry comrades (see "Interment and Reinterment of Little Bighorn Dead" on page 232). Litters were prepared for Reno's nearly sixty wounded men, and an evacuation march was conducted to the steamer *Far West,* which waited to transport them to Fort Abraham Lincoln (see "Grant Marsh and the *Far West*" on page 237).

The battle of the Little Bighorn had come to an end—but it was far from concluded in the minds of the public or future historians.

📖 There is no lack of material about this famous battle for the serious researcher or casual reader. In fact, the bibliography is one of the most voluminous in American history. A number of books, however, rise to the top of the list. Perhaps the best single volume, although it may be somewhat studious for the beginner, is John S. Gray's *Centennial Campaign: The Sioux War of 1876* (Fort Collins, CO: Old Army Press, 1976; Norman: University of Oklahoma Press, 1988). Gray's well-researched study uses time lines, detailed documentation, and careful reasoning and analysis to reconstruct the battle. Gray expanded on his earlier work in *Mitch Boyer and the Little Bighorn Reconstructed* (Lincoln: University of Nebraska Press, 1991).

Another notable book—a personal favorite—that will satisfy both the researcher and casual reader is *Custer's Luck,* by Edgar I. Stewart (Norman: University of Oklahoma Press, 1953). A must-have volume for students at any level is *The Custer Myth: A Source Book of Custeriana,* edited by W. A. Graham (Harrisburg, PA: Stackpole, 1953). Graham's work offers eyewitness testimony from both white and Indian participants, letters, reports, and other fascinating miscellany, including a comprehensive bibliography—albeit outdated. Other invaluable sources of testimony are *Custer in '76: Walter Camp's Notes on the Custer Fight,* edited by Kenneth Hammer (Provo, UT: Brigham Young University Press, 1976), and to a lesser extent, *Camp on Custer,* edited by Bruce R. Liddic and Paul Harbaugh (Spokane: Arthur H. Clark Co., 1995).

Other reminiscences of note from soldiers can be found in *Troopers with Custer: Historic Incidents of the Battle of the Little Big Horn,* by E. A. Brininstool (Harrisburg, PA: Stackpole, 1952); *Diaries of the Little Big Horn,* by Michael J. Koury (Bellevue, NE: Old Army Press, 1968); *I Fought with Custer: The Story of Sergeant Windolph, Last Survivor of the Battle of* the *Little Big Horn,* by Robert W. Frazier and Robert Hunt (Lincoln: University of Nebraska Press, 1987); and *I Buried Custer: The Diary of Pvt. Thomas W. Coleman, 7th U.S. Cavalry,* edited by Bruce R. Liddic (College Station, TX: Creative Publishing Co., 1979). An interesting memoir written by Richard A. Roberts, who was Capt. George Yates's brother-in-law and accompanied the campaign as a youngster, is *Custer's Last Battle: Reminiscences of General Custer* (Monroe, MI: Monroe County Library Systems, 1978).

For accounts by Indian eyewitnesses, as well as the Indian side of the story, see *Custer's Fall: The Indian Side of the Story,* by David Humphreys Miller (New York: Duell, Sloan and Pearce, 1957); *Soldiers Falling into Camp: The Battles at the Rosebud and the Little Bighorn,* by Frederick Lefthand, Robert Kammen, and Joseph Marshall (Encampment, WY: Affiliated Writers of America, 1991); *Warpath: The True Story of the Fighting Sioux Told in a Biography of Chief White Bull,* by Stanley Vestal (Boston: Houghton Mifflin, 1934); *David F. Barry's Indian Notes on the Custer Battle,* edited by U. L. Burdick (Baltimore: Wirth Brothers, 1949); *My Friend the Indian,* by James McLaughlin (Lincoln: University of Nebraska Press, 1989); *Custer on the Little Bighorn,* by Thomas B. Marquis (Lodi, CA: Kain Publishing Co., 1969); and *Killing Custer: The Battle of the Little Bighorn and the Fate of the Plains Indians,* by James Welch, with Paul Stekler (New York: W. W. Norton & Co., 1994).

The official documents can be found in *General Custer and the Battle of the Little Big Horn: The Federal View,* edited by John M. Carroll (New Brunswick, NJ: Garry Owen Press, 1976); and *The Little Big Horn 1876: The Official Communications, Documents, and Reports,* by Loyd J. Overfield II (Glendale, CA: Arthur H. Clark Co., 1971).

An examination of the day-by-day activities leading up to the battle is the subject of *Little Bighorn Diary: Chronicle of the 1876 Indian War,* by James Willert (La Mirada, CA: James Willert, Publisher, 1977). See also: *Benteen's Scout,* by Roger Darling (El Segundo, CA: Upton and Sons, 2000).

The best analyses of the legends created by the battle appear in *Custer's Last Stand: The Anatomy of an American Myth,* by Brian W. Dippie (Missoula: University of Montana Press, 1976); *Custer and the Great Controversy: The Origin and Development of a Legend,* by Robert M. Utley (Los Angeles: Westernlore Press, 1962); and *Custer and the Epic of Defeat,* by Bruce A. Rosenberg (University Park: Pennsylvania State University Press, 1974).

Other worthwhile sources not listed elsewhere include (in alphabetical order by author) *The Custer Mystery,* by Charles G. du Bois (El Segundo, CA: Upton & Sons, 1986); *Kick the Dead Lion: A Casebook for the Custer Battle,* by Charles G. du Bois (El Segundo, CA: Upton & Sons, 1987); *The Custer Tragedy: Events*

body found at the southern end of Battle Ridge. His father requested that his son be interred where he fell, which made him the only officer buried in a marked grave on the field. On September 11, 1931, however, his remains were exhumed and reinterred with full military honors in the nearby Custer National Cemetery.

📖 *The Crittenden Memoirs,* by H. H. Crittenden (New York: Putnam's Sons, 1936); "Lt. Crittenden: Striving for the Soldier's Life," by Jerry Cecil, *Greasy Grass* 11 (May 1995), a Custer Battlefield Historical and Museum Association publication.

☸ Curly
Crow Indian Scout

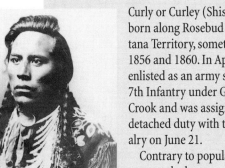

Curly. *Courtesy Little Bighorn Battlefield National Monument.*

Curly or Curley (Shishi'esh) was born along Rosebud Creek, Montana Territory, sometime between 1856 and 1860. In April 1876, he enlisted as an army scout for the 7th Infantry under Gen. George Crook and was assigned on detached duty with the 7th Cavalry on June 21.

Contrary to popular belief, Curly was not the lone survivor of the June 25 Little Bighorn battle. Many stories over the years have been told, most of them by Curly, about his harrowing escape that day, but none of them were true (see "Alleged Survivors of the Battle" on page 251).

Curly and the other Crow scouts—whose job was finding the Sioux, not fighting them—were likely released by George Armstrong Custer well before the battle began. According to the July 15, 1876, edition of the *Helena Herald,* Curly admitted that his army commanders had told him to go home after locating Sitting Bull's camp. There certainly exists the possibility that Curly, while departing the area, could have witnessed the beginning of the battle and was able to speculate about the eventual result. Regardless, he arrived two days later at the Yellowstone River, where the steamship *Far West* was docked. Without an interpreter present, Curly allegedly reported Custer's annihilation by using hand signals and drawings, which were not understood. Despite the lack of evidence, he was hailed by some imaginative writers as the only one to have escaped the battle. To his credit, Curly did upon occasion deny that he had participated in the fight.

Curly left the army on September 30, 1876, and became a rancher near Crow Agency, Montana—

(continued on following page)

just miles below the battlefield. At least one account indicates that he had married a Crow woman named Takes a Shield before the Little Bighorn battle; others claim that he had been married to Bird Woman and divorced her in 1886 to marry Takes a Shield. The latter version is probably correct. Curly and Takes a Shield were said to have had two children.

In 1886, Curly attended the tenth reunion of the battle and was confronted by Hunkpapa Sioux chief Gall. The chief called Curly a coward for departing before the fight and told him that had he stayed, he would be dead. Curly apparently remained silent in the presence of the imposing Gall.

Curly carried on a long battle with the government over his right to a pension, which was finally granted in December 1920. He died of pneumonia on May 21, 1923, at Crow Agency and was buried in the cemetery at Custer National Monument. His reservation log cabin is on display at an attraction called Trail Town in Cody, Wyoming.

📖 "Interview with Curly, September 18, 1908," in *Custer in '76: Walter Camp's Notes on the Custer Fight,* edited by Kenneth Hammer (Provo, UT: Brigham Young University Press, 1976); "Curley the Crow Scout Once More," in *Winners of the West* (St. Joseph, MO: National Indian Wars Veterans, 1924); "Statement of Curley the Scout," *The Tepee Book* (June 1916 and June 1926); "The Custer Massacre: Narrative of Curley, A Crow Scout," by Lt. Charles Roe, interpreted by Thomas LeForge, *Army and Navy Journal* (March 25, 1882), p. 761; chapter 3 of *The Custer Myth: A Source Book of Custeriana,* edited by W. A. Graham (Harrisburg, PA: Stackpole, 1953); "The Truth about Curley, Crow Scout," by Harry Chatfield, *Real West* (May 1963); "A Personal Look at Curley's Life after the Battle of the Little Bighorn," by Mardell Plainfeather, *Greasy Grass* (1988), a Custer Battlefield Historical and Museum Association publication; and "A Vindication of Curly," by John S. Gray, *4th Annual Symposium Custer Battlefield Historical and Museum Association,* 1990.

⚜ Charles Camilius DeRudio
First Lieutenant, 7th U.S. Cavalry

DeRudio was born Carlo Camilio di Rudio on August 26, 1832, in Belluno, Venetia Province, Austria, into a family with royal roots, making him a minor nobleman. He graduated from the Royal Austrian Military Academy and subsequently held a commission in Emperor Franz Josef's army. On December 9, 1855, DeRudio married Eliza Booth, reportedly an illiterate eighteen-year-old confectioner's assistant, at Parish Church,

(continued on following page)

Leading Up to and Following the Little Big Horn Campaign of 1876, by Fred Dustin (Ann Arbor, MI: Edwards Brothers, 1939); *War-Path and Bivouac; or, The Conquest of the Sioux,* by John Finerty (Norman: University of Oklahoma Press, 1961); *The Story of the Little Big Horn: Custer's Last Fight,* by W. A. Graham (New York: Century Co., 1926); *Evidence and the Custer Enigma: A Reconstruction of Indian-Military History,* by Jerome A. Greene (Kansas City, MO: Kansas City Posse of Westerners, 1973); *Custer and the Little Big Horn: A Psychobiographical Inquiry,* by Charles Hofling (Detroit: Wayne State University Press, 1981); *Legend into History: The Custer Mystery,* by Charles Kuhlman (Harrisburg, PA: Stackpole, 1952); *Custer to the Little Big Horn: A Study in Command,* by Thomas E. O'Neil (Brooklyn: Arrow & Trooper, 1991); *Decision at Little Bighorn: A Custer Retrospective,* by Thomas E. O'Neil (Brooklyn: Arrow & Trooper, 1994); *The Little Bighorn Campaign,* by Wayne Michael Sarf (Conshohocken, PA: Combined Books, 1993); and *To Hell With Honor: Custer and the Little Bighorn,* by Larry Sklenar (Norman: University of Oklahoma Press, 2000).

SIDEBARS

🐎 Interment and Reinterment of Little Bighorn Dead

By the time the survivors of the battle marched the four miles north to view Custer's annihilated command, the more than 200 mutilated bodies—along with many horse carcasses—had been decomposing in the summer heat for two days. First Lt. Edward S. Godfrey described the scene as they approached: "We saw a large number of objects that looked like white boulders scattered over the field . . . and it was announced that these objects were the dead bodies." Capt. Thomas Weir exclaimed: "Oh, how white they look! How white!" First Lt. Francis M. Gibson sadly said, "It was the most horrible sight my eyes rested on." Capt. Frederick Benteen looked down at Custer's body and said, with emotion, "There he is, God damn him, he will never fight anymore."

The gruesome task of burying the dead began soon after the rescue of Reno's command on the hilltop and continued until at least the evening of June 28, when the regiment marched away with the wounded on litters toward the mouth of the Little Bighorn River.

The soldiers on the burial detail, many of whom were quickly overcome with nausea and vomiting, did not possess proper digging implements. Only a dozen or so spades, shovels, and picks—found in the rubble of the Indian village—were available, so they used anything that could scoop away the dirt to hasten the job. The soil was dry and porous, described as resembling sugar, so burial was simply a token gesture. The men basically left the bodies lying where they fell and covered them as best they could with sagebrush and dirt or rolled them into shallow trenches. They identified the officers by writing their names on slips of paper, which they then stuffed into cartridge cases and hammered into crude cedar stakes placed near the gravesites.

The bodies at the various locations were counted—42 on Custer Hill, 28 in Deep Ravine—208 or 210 on the Custer portion of the field, and an approximate total of 263 when all the officers, enlisted, civilians, and scouts had been tallied.

On June 25, 1877—one year to the day after the battle—Capt. Henry Nowlan and the newly recruited Company I of the 7th Cavalry arrived at the battlefield for the purpose of collecting the remains of the officers who had fallen. Nowlan was accompanied by Lt. (later Maj. Gen.) Hugh L. Scott; Col. Michael V. Sheridan, brother of Gen. Phil Sheridan; and all the Crow scouts that had gone with Custer the year before. Fortunately, there would be no need for guesswork to identify the dead officers. Nowlan had been provided a chart that designated where each officer was buried.

Only one officer was reburied on the field. The father of 2nd Lt. John J. Crittenden, an infantry colonel, had said, "Let my boy lie where he fell." Crittenden's body was placed in a coffin and reinterred where he had been found. In September 1931, his remains were moved to the nearby Custer National Cemetery.

The remains of the other officers from both the Custer and Reno battlefields were gathered up and transferred into pine boxes for transport to cemeteries designated by the next of kin. Apparently, at that time, many of the enlisted men were reburied either individually where they were found or together in mass graves on the field. One group of twenty-eight or twenty-nine bodies from Company E has never been located on the field.

George Armstrong Custer had told wife Libbie that when the time came, he wanted to be buried at the U.S. Military Academy at West Point, and she was determined to honor his wishes. She had been assured by Maj. Joseph G. Tilford of the 7th Cavalry that the remains being sent east were indeed those of her husband. Libbie was advised to wait until fall to hold the funeral, as West Point was relatively vacant during the summer. Custer's remains were stored in a Poughkeepsie, New York, vault owned by Philip Hamilton, whose son Louis had fallen at the 1868 battle of the Washita.

On October 10, 1877, crowds lined the Hudson River as the bunting-draped *Mary Powell*, her flags flying at half-mast, brought Custer's remains to the south dock of the academy. The casket, which was adorned with a flag belonging to Captain Hamilton, was escorted by a cavalry detachment to the chapel.

Shortly before 2 P.M., Maj. Gen. John M. Schofield, commandant of the Military Academy, escorted Libbie into the

1st Lt. Charles C. DeRudio. *Courtesy Little Bighorn Battlefield National Monument.*

Godalming, Surrey, England. The couple had four children, all born in the United States.

At some point, DeRudio decided to became a revolutionary activist. He was involved in a January 14, 1858, plot planned by Felice Orsini to assassinate Napoleon III and Empress Eugenie at the Paris Opera. Orsini held Napoleon responsible for the failure of the Italian revolutions of 1848–49. Napoleon and the empress arrived outside the opera house that evening as the orchestra inside struck up the William Tell Overture. Three bombs exploded nearby, killing several guards and a horse. Napoleon narrowly escaped injury when a piece of metal struck his hat, and Eugenie suffered a cut eyelid.

Orsini and his three accomplices were captured and convicted. One man received life imprisonment; the others, including DeRudio, were sentenced to execution by guillotine. Orsini and another man met that fate. DeRudio received a last-minute reprieve when his wife appealed to Empress Eugenie. His sentence was commuted to life on Devil's Island penal colony in French Guiana. In the fall of 1858, however, DeRudio and about a dozen other men hollowed out a log to fashion a canoe and sailed to freedom in British Guiana, then traveled by more conventional means to England.

In February 1864, DeRudio and his family migrated to the United States. He enlisted in the army as a private and served with Company A, 79th New York (Highlander) Infantry, from August to October 1864. The following month, he was appointed second lieutenant, Company D, 2nd U.S. Colored Infantry. He was mustered out at Key West, Florida, in January 1866.

On August 31, 1867, DeRudio received an appointment as second lieutenant, 2nd Infantry, but it was held up while the government investigated his European criminal background. The appointment was restored on October 25, 1867, and he remained unassigned until joining the 7th Cavalry in July 1869. The following year, DeRudio was placed in temporary command of Company K and assigned duty escorting settlers across the Kansas plains.

He participated in the Yellowstone expedition of 1873 as a member of Company H but missed the Black Hills expedition the following year while on

(continued on following page)

detached service at Fort Rice. DeRudio was appointed first lieutenant in December 1875. At that time, he was in line to assume command of Company E but was passed over by George Armstrong Custer in favor of Algernon E. Smith, an act that to some extent soured his previously good relationship with Custer.

Just prior to the May 1876 march to the Little Bighorn, DeRudio was assigned as assistant commander of Company A. The night before the famous battle, he and several other officers—Benteen, Keogh, and Porter—were swapping stories of thrilling escapades and escapes, and DeRudio's tale of his escape from Devil's Island certainly topped the list. Little did he know that he would add another to his resumé the following day.

DeRudio's predicament began during Maj. Marcus Reno's disastrous retreat from the timber to the bluffs across the river. DeRudio, scouts Fred Girard and Billy Jackson, and Pvt. Thomas O'Neil were cut off by the Indians and trapped in the timber while the remainder of the command scrambled in an attempt to reach safety, many of their bodies left strewn across the bloody route. After dark, the four men caught two horses and were riding upstream when they were challenged by an Indian. The two scouts galloped away, while DeRudio and O'Neil hid on a small island. At dawn, DeRudio thought he observed soldiers approaching and called out to one, thinking it was Tom Custer. But it was apparently an Indian riding Custer's horse, and the warriors fired at the two cavalrymen. DeRudio and O'Neil fired back, then scampered away into the brush, breathing a sigh of relief when the Indians broke contact. The two men remained hidden, watching the following day as a long procession of Indians, mostly women and children, passed within fifty yards of their position on their way to the Bighorn Mountains. That night, while DeRudio contemplated walking to the Rosebud, he heard the braying of a mule and realized that soldiers must be nearby. He and O'Neil investigated and soon approached Reno's perimeter on the bluffs. They identified themselves and were saved. Scouts Jackson and Girard had presented themselves earlier.

Prior to the battle, the troops had left their sabers with the pack train, but DeRudio reportedly hung on to his blade, as perhaps did 1st Lt. Edward G. Mathey. It has been said that European soldiers did not consider themselves properly dressed without a saber. This saber may have been the gold-mounted one that he had received as a gift from members of his company in 1870 at

(continued on following page)

chapel. Other close family members in attendance were Emanuel Custer and Margaret "Maggie" Custer Calhoun. Classes had been suspended, and the cadets crowded into the chapel to witness the event. The West Point chaplain, Dr. John Forsyth, conducted an Episcopal service, concluding with Psalm 19. Afterward, cadets carried the casket to a caisson, which bore it to the cemetery. A lone horse displaying a pair of cavalry boots with spurs, with the toes pointed to the rear, followed the caisson. The procession halted at the cemetery, the chaplain spoke, three volleys were fired, and George Armstrong Custer was laid to rest. In 1933, Libbie Custer was buried beside her husband.

In 1881, the remains of the enlisted men were removed from the scattered graves on the battlefield and reinterred in a common grave under the base of an imposing granite monument that was erected on Custer Hill. The names of the dead, a number of which were incorrectly spelled, were inscribed on the monument. Marble headstones were placed around the battlefield to provide a rough guide as to where the soldiers had been killed.

The final resting places of the officers who were killed on June 25, 1876, are as follows:

1st Lt. James Calhoun—Fort Leavenworth National Cemetery, August 3, 1877

1st Lt. William W. Cooke—Hamilton Cemetery, Hamilton, Ontario, Canada

2nd Lt. John J. Crittenden—Custer National Cemetery, September 11, 1931

Lt. Col. George A. Custer—U.S. Military Academy at West Point, New York, October 10, 1877

Capt. Thomas W. Custer—Fort Leavenworth National Cemetery, August 3, 1877

Dr. James M. DeWolf—Woodlawn Cemetery, Norwalk, Ohio, August 1, 1877

2nd Lt. Henry M. Harrington—body never found

2nd Lt. Benjamin H. Hodgson—Laurel Hill Cemetery, Philadelphia, October 1877

Capt. Myles W. Keogh—Fort Hill Cemetery, Auburn, New York, October 25, 1877

Dr. George E. Lord—Custer National Cemetery

1st Lt. Donald McIntosh—Arlington National Cemetery, July 28, 1909

1st Lt. James E. Porter—body never found

2nd Lt. William V. W. Reilly—Mount Olivet Cemetery, Washington, D.C., August 3, 1877

1st Lt. Algernon E. Smith—Fort Leavenworth National Cemetery, August 3, 1877

2nd Lt. James G. Sturgis—body never found

Capt. George W. M. Yates—Fort Leavenworth National Cemetery, August 3, 1877

Perhaps the best source is *The Custer Battle Casualties: Burials, Exhumations and Reinterments,* by Richard G. Hardorff (El Segundo, CA: Upton & Sons, 1989). *The Custer Myth: A Source Book of Custeriana,* edited by W. A. Graham (Harrisburg, PA: Stackpole, 1953), includes an excerpt from Edward S. Godfrey's article "Custer's Last Stand," first published in *Century Magazine* 43 (January 1892) and reprinted in *The Custer Reader,* edited by Paul A. Hutton (Lincoln: University of Nebraska Press, 1992), as well as Col. Michael Sheridan's official report and other material. *The Mystery of E Troop: Custer's Gray Horse Company at the Little Bighorn,* by Gregory Michno (Missoula, MT: Mountain Press Publishing Co., 1994), speculates about the missing troopers of Company E.

See also "The Funeral of General Custer," *Harper's Weekly* (October 27, 1877); "After the Custer Battle," by Albert J. Partoll, *Frontier and Midland* 19, no. 4 (1938–39); *I Buried Custer: The Diary of Pvt. Thomas W. Coleman, 7th U.S. Cavalry,* edited by Bruce R. Liddic (College Station, TX: Creative Publishing Co., 1979); *Custer Soldiers Not Buried,* by Thomas B. Marquis (Hardin, MT: privately printed, 1933); "With Indian and Buffalo in Montana," by Edward J. McClernand, an officer with Gibbon's column who witnessed the burials, in *Cavalry Journal* 36 (January and April 1927); and "Custer's Burial Revisited: West Point, 1877," by Sandy Barnard, *6th Annual Symposium Custer Battlefield Historical and Museum Association* (1992).

Mutilation of the Dead Cavalrymen

After all the cavalrymen had been killed, the Sioux and Cheyenne women, and perhaps a number of children and older men, descended on the field like a flock of ravenous locusts on a fresh crop to help their warriors mutilate the bodies in every conceivable manner, quite a few beyond recognition. The extent of the mutilation has been a subject of debate, with many eyewitnesses claiming that there was very little and an equal number taking the opposite view that it was widespread. This disparity of opinion could be explained by the fact that each troop was assigned a different area of the field to bury the dead, and certain portions may have received more postdeath violence than others.

The acts of mutilation that can be documented include dismemberment of arms, legs, hands, fingers, and penises; decapitation; scalping, lacerations, and slashes from butcher knives, tomahawks, and axes; skulls crushed with stone mallets; and multiple gunshots and arrows fired from close range. The field was said to have been littered with hands, heads, feet, and legs that had been removed. 1st Lt. Edward S. Godfrey said that "many faces had a pained, almost terrified expression."

Ellsworth, Kansas. DeRudio had also had a pair of expensive European binoculars, which he loaned Custer before the battle; he never saw them again.

After the battle, the story of DeRudio's life and daring escapes was widely published under his name. DeRudio claimed that he had not written the article, but that it was the work of Maj. James S. Brisbin, who greatly embellished the events.

DeRudio was promoted to captain in December 1882 and subsequently served at Fort Meade, Fort Sam Houston, and Fort Bayard, New Mexico, until his retirement in August 1896. He was advanced to major, retired, in June 1909 and died on November 1, 1910, in Los Angeles. His remains were cremated and interred in San Francisco National Cemetery.

According to DeRudio, the following article attributed to him was actually written by Maj. James S. Brisbin: "My Personal Story," *New York Herald* (July 30, 1876), reprinted in the *Chicago Times* (August 2, 1876) and the *Frontier and Midland Magazine* (Missoula: Montana State University, January 1934). Also see *Charles C. DeRudio,* by Charles K. Mills (Bryan, TX: J. M. Carroll, 1983); "Interview with Charles DeRudio, February 2, 1910," in *Custer in '76: Walter Camp's Notes on the Custer Fight,* edited by Kenneth Hammer (Provo, UT: Brigham Young University Press, 1976); "Carlo di Rudio, 1st Lt. 7th U.S. Cavalry," by Melville Stone, *Collier's Weekly* (May 15, 1920); "With Reno at the Little Big Horn," by E. A. Brininstool, *Hunter-Trader-Trapper* (March–April 1924); and "Charles DeRudio: European Assassin," by Dale Shoenberger, *Little Big Horn Associates Research Review* (September 1980).

Winfield Scott Edgerly
Second Lieutenant, 7th U.S. Cavalry

2nd Lt. Winfield Edgerly. *Courtesy Little Bighorn Battlefield National Monument.*

Edgerly was born into a farming family on May 29, 1846, in Farmington, New Hampshire. He entered the U.S Military Academy at West Point in July 1866 and graduated four years later, ranked fiftieth in a class of fifty-eight. Edgerly was appointed a second lieutenant and assigned to Company D, 7th Cavalry, at Fort Riley, Kansas, in June 1870. From 1871 to 1873, he served with his unit on Reconstruction duty in the South. While the 7th Cavalry participated in the Yellowstone and Black Hills expeditions during 1873 and 1874, he remained with Company D as part of the escort for the Northern Boundary

(continued on following page)

Survey (see "The Northern Boundary Survey" on page 121).

On October 27, 1875, Edgerly married eighteen-year-old Grace Cory Blum of Cooperstown, New York, in St. Paul. The couple had one daughter, who died at Fort Leavenworth in 1885 at age three and a half.

Edgerly served as second in command of Capt. Thomas Weir's Company D during the 1876 Little Bighorn campaign. On June 25, that company was assigned to Capt. Frederick Benteen's scout while the remainder of the regiment rode toward the Indian village. When Benteen later rendezvoused with Reno's command on the bluffs, Weir, after being denied permission, defiantly rode toward the sound of firing some miles ahead. Edgerly, believing that Weir was under orders, moved their company to join him at a location on the field now known as Weir Point. The company was soon pushed back by advancing Indians and retreated to the defensive position on the hilltop. Edgerly was forced to leave a man behind, whom he had promised to later rescue, but he was refused permission by Weir, and the man was subsequently killed.

Edgerly, who was promoted to first lieutenant effective June 25, 1876, held the opinion that the 7th Cavalry would have been successful that day had Reno charged the village. He wrote a letter to Libbie Custer on October 10, 1877, to "share some personal recollections of your husband which I wrote at the time after the battle, and which I didn't have the heart to send you until I waited so long I was ashamed to write."

In 1883, Edgerly was assigned to recruiting duty in Cincinnati. He was appointed captain in October of that year. He returned to the 7th Cavalry in 1884 and participated in the 1890 affair at Wounded Knee. Edgerly moved on to Texas, where he lived from 1892 to 1895, served for a year as an instructor at Maine State College at Orono, and followed that with two years as a National Guard instructor at Concord, New Hampshire, and one year as inspector general.

He was appointed major, 6th Cavalry, in July 1898 and was transferred back to the 7th Cavalry in January 1899, joining the regiment in Cuba. Edgerly was appointed lieutenant colonel in 1901 and colonel the following year, when he commanded the 2nd Cavalry in the Philippines. He was appointed brigadier general in June 1905, and two years later, he went to Germany to serve as an observer of army maneuvers. Edgerly returned to command the Department of Dakota and the Cavalry and Artillery School at Fort Riley until his

(continued on following page)

Those lying facedown were likely killed by a Cheyenne, a tribe that may have believed that it was bad luck to leave an enemy facing the sky. The Sioux traditionally marked a dead enemy with a slashed thigh. The Indians even went as far as to mutilate some of the dead horses. For reasons unknown, the names had been cut out of the few items of clothing—an undershirt or pair of socks—not stripped from the bodies and taken away. Everything of value—money, watches, rings, and so on—had been stolen from the dead cavalrymen.

Capt. Tom Custer was singled out for perhaps the worst treatment and was identified only by tattoos on one arm. Godfrey described Custer's body thus:

> [It was] lying downward, all the scalp was removed, leaving only tufts of his fair hair on the nape of his neck. The skull was smashed in and a number of arrows had been shot into the back of the head and in the body . . . the features where they had touched the ground were pressed out of shape and were somewhat depressed. In turning the body, one arm which had been shot and broken, remained under the body; this was pulled out and on it we saw "T. W. C." and the goddess of liberty and the flag. His belly had been cut open and his entrails protruded.

The extent of Tom Custer's abuse has caused some to believe that Sioux warrior Rain-in-the-Face made good on his threat to cut out Custer's heart and eat it as revenge for the Indian's 1875 arrest (see "The Arrest and Revenge of Rain-in-the-Face" on page 129). Capt. Frederick Benteen, however, stated that Custer's heart had not been cut out.

The naked body of George Armstrong Custer, from all accounts, had not been mutilated. He was found in a sitting position leaning against and between two troopers, his face said to be wearing the expression of a man who "had fallen asleep and enjoyed peaceful dreams." Custer was found with two wounds—a bullet in front of the left temple and another in the left breast.

Chief Gall said in 1886 that Custer had not been scalped "because he was the big chief and we respected him," which seems ludicrous, inasmuch as they did not know they had been fighting Custer. Cheyenne Kate Bighead stated that Custer had not been mutilated out of respect for their tribal sister, Mo-nah-se-tah, who they believed had gained Custer's affection while working as his translator following the 1868 battle of the Washita (see "Custer and Mo-nah-se-tah" on page 92). Kate did say that the women thrust a sewing awl into each of Custer's ears to "improve his hearing," because he had not heard when he smoked the pipe with them in 1867. Some scholars have speculated that Custer had indeed been mutilated but the truth was deliberately withheld out of respect for the feelings of Libbie Custer.

The reason for the mutilations of the cavalrymen cannot be adequately explained. Perhaps the Indians committed the acts out of rage for their plight or in grief after losing a relative in this or a previous battle.

📖 Edward S. Godfrey's article "Custer's Last Stand," first published in *Century Magazine* 43 (January 1892) and reprinted in *The Custer Reader*, edited by Paul A. Hutton (Lincoln: University of Nebraska Press, 1992); "After the Custer Battle," by Albert J. Partoll, *Frontier and Midland* 19, no. 4 (1938–39); *I Buried Custer: The Diary of Pvt. Thomas W. Coleman, 7th U.S. Cavalry*, edited by Bruce R. Liddic (College Station, TX: Creative Publishing Co., 1979); *Custer Soldiers Not Buried*, by Thomas B. Marquis (Hardin, MT: privately printed, 1933); *She Watched Custer's Last Battle*, by Thomas B. Marquis (Hardin, MT: privately printed, 1933); *Two Days After the Battle*, by Thomas B. Marquis (Hardin, MT: privately printed, 1935); and "With Indian and Buffalo in Montana," by Edward J. McClernand, *Cavalry Journal*, 36 (January and April 1927).

🦌 Grant Marsh and the Far West

The steamship *Far West*, along with the *Josephine*, both owned by the Coulson Line, was awarded the contract to haul supplies for the Little Bighorn campaign. The *Far West*, built in 1870, was 190 feet in length, with a beam of 33 1/2 feet, and could accommodate more than 200 tons of cargo. She had been designed to operate in the shallow and hazardous Western rivers and had power to spare—two 15-inch-diameter engines of 5-foot piston stroke and a steam capstan on each side of her bow to pull her through the strongest of rapids.

The captain of the *Far West* was forty-two-year-old Grant Marsh, who began his career at age twelve as a cabin boy on a Pittsburgh steamer. He had begun navigating the Missouri River in 1864 and quickly became known as the premier navigator on that river—so expert that it was said he could "navigate a steamer on a light dew." Marsh and his steamship had transported supplies for the Yellowstone expedition of 1873. On June 7, 1875, Marsh, piloting the *Josephine*, had gained fame by ascending from the mouth of the Yellowstone River to the highest point ever reached by a steamship, near present-day Billings, surpassing the previous record by 250 miles.

During the Little Bighorn campaign, the column under Gen. Alfred H. Terry that had marched from Fort Abraham Lincoln depended on the *Far West* for the 200 tons of cargo that she carried—including forage, ammunition, medicine, and general supplies. The Quartermaster Department had established a supply depot on the Yellowstone River near the mouth of Glendive Creek. When Terry had reached that point,

retirement on December 29, 1909, after forty-three years of service.

Edgerly died on September 10, 1927, in Farmington, New Hampshire, and was buried in Arlington National Cemetery.

📖 The letter to Libbie Custer, in addition to other material pertaining to Edgerly, including his "An Account of the Custer Battle," originally published in the *St. Paul Pioneer Press* (August 14, 1881), has been reprinted in *The Custer Myth: A Source Book of Custeriana*, edited by W. A. Graham (Harrisburg, PA: Stackpole, 1953). "Interview with Winfield S. Edgerly" can be found in *Custer in '76: Walter Camp's Notes on the Custer Fight*, edited by Kenneth Hammer (Provo, UT: Brigham Young University Press, 1976).

✴ Francis Marion Gibson
First Lieutenant, 7th U.S. Cavalry

1st Lt. Francis M. Gibson. *Courtesy Little Bighorn Battlefield National Monument.*

Gibson was born on December 14, 1847, in Philadelphia. He entered military service with an appointment as second lieutenant, Company A, 7th Cavalry, in October 1867. Gibson was on temporary duty as second in command of Company F during the November 1868 Washita battle. He was promoted to first lieutenant in July 1871 and served with his unit on Reconstruction duty in the South until 1873. Gibson was second in command of Company H during the 1873 Yellowstone expedition and the Black Hills expedition the following year. He was on scouting duty at Fort Randall from May 1875 to May 1876.

Gibson served as second in command of Company H during the 1876 Little Bighorn campaign and on June 25 was part of Capt. Frederick Benteen's scout while the other battalions headed toward the Indian village. He was in charge of a small detachment that rode in advance of Benteen's battalion to reconnoiter the hilly terrain but found nothing of interest. Gibson subsequently participated in the hilltop fight—at one point bravely holding the line with little ammunition under an intense Indian attack. He called Benteen, his commander, "one of the coolest and bravest men I have ever known." He assumed temporary command of Company H in August, with duty involving disarming and dismounting agency Indians.

Gibson was involved in the 1877 Nez Perce campaign. He was appointed captain in February

(continued on following page)

Steamer *Far West*. *Courtesy Little Bighorn Battlefield National Monument.*

1880. He remained in the army on field duty until December 1891, when he was retired for disability. Gibson was married to Katherine Garrett, whose sister married 1st Lt. Donald McIntosh of the 7th Cavalry.

Gibson's daughter, Katherine Gibson Fougera, wrote an account of her mother's frontier experiences, *With Custer's Cavalry: From the Memoirs of the Late Katherine Gibson* (Caldwell, ID: Caxton Printers, 1940). The Gibson-Fougera Collection, composed of papers, photos, and memorabilia, was donated to the collection at Little Bighorn Battlefield National Monument. Gibson's personal account can be found in *Custer in '76: Walter Camp's Notes on the Custer Fight,* edited by Kenneth Hammer (Provo, UT: Brigham Young University Press, 1976).

✺ Edward Settle Godfrey
First Lieutenant, 7th U.S. Cavalry

Godfrey was born on October 9, 1843, in Kalida, Putnam County, Ohio, and attended Vermillion Institute, Harpsville, Ohio. In April 1861, he enlisted in Company D, 21st Ohio Infantry, and fought in the July action at Scary Creek, Virginia. He was discharged in August of that year. Godfrey entered the U.S. Military Academy at West Point in July 1863 and graduated four years later, ranked fifty-third in a class of sixty-three.

(continued on following page)

Captain Marsh and the *Far West* began shuttling supplies and troops upstream to the mouth of the Powder River. Terry wanted to keep the steamship as close to the troops as possible and directed Marsh to reach the juncture of the Bighorn and Little Bighorn Rivers.

On June 21, 1876, General Terry, George Armstrong Custer, Col. John Gibbon, and Maj. James Brisbin held a strategy meeting onboard the *Far West* in which the order that Terry would issue the following day for Custer's march into the Valley of the Little Bighorn was discussed. That night—on the eve of the 7th Cavalry's march—Captain Marsh, Maj. Marcus Reno, Captains Tom Custer and Myles W. Keogh, and 1st Lt. James Calhoun, along with several infantry officers, stayed up all night drinking and playing cards onboard the ship.

The steamship was moored about a half mile above the mouth of the Little Bighorn River on June 27 when the first word arrived about the fate of Custer's command. Marsh hurriedly converted the area between the stern and the boilers into a hospital, covering the planks with fresh grass, then spreading tarpaulins over that to create a soft mattress for the wounded. On June 30, about thirty (or perhaps as many as fifty-two, as Terry had stated in a note to Marsh) wounded cavalrymen, as well as Myles Keogh's horse, Comanche, were transported from the battlefield on crude litters to the *Far West*.

Marsh was cleared to leave shortly after 5 P.M. on July 3. The *Far West,* her colors at half-mast and decks draped in black mourning cloth, made the 710-mile trip to Bismarck, with only two brief stops, in a record-setting time of fifty-four hours, arriving at 11 P.M. on July 5. This heroic feat made Marsh the most hailed and famous steamboat captain in the history of navigation on the Yellowstone. When Marsh arrived at Fort Lincoln, Custer's widow sent her carriage and a note requesting that the captain visit her. Marsh, however, cited pressing duties elsewhere.

The *Josephine,* skippered by Matt Coulson, replaced the departed *Far West* to provide vital supplies for the remainder of the troops.

Conquest of the Missouri: Being the Story of the Life and Exploits of Captain Grant Marsh, by J. M. Hanson (New York: Murray Hill Books, 1946).

🐎 Comanche

This claybank sorrel or buckskin gelding that has gone down in legend as being the only living thing found on the field following the Little Bighorn battle was destined to become one of the most famous horses in history.

Comanche's cavalry career began on April 3, 1868, when he was part of a herd of forty-one mustangs purchased by 1st Lt. Tom Custer for the army from a St. Louis trader. Upon arrival at Fort Leavenworth, Kansas, for processing, which included branding the distinctive "US" on his shoulder, he was listed as five years old, stood fifteen hands, weighed 925 pounds, and was described as being a cross, 75 percent American and 25 percent Spanish.

The horse quickly caught the attention of Capt. Myles W. Keogh, commander of Company I, who was known to be an excellent judge of horseflesh. Although officers normally bought their horses from private traders rather than the army, Keogh decided that this particular horse would make an ideal second mount and purchased him for $90.

It has been said that Comanche received his name following a skirmish with Indians on September 13, 1868, near the Cimarron River in southwest Kansas. Keogh noted that the horse had been somewhat skittish during the brief yet furious fight but continued to perform admirably. He discovered upon returning to camp that the animal had been struck in the right quarter by an arrow during the encounter. The arrow shaft had broken off, leaving the flint inside, which was removed by the farrier. A soldier volunteered the information that he had witnessed the horse being struck by the arrow and it had squalled as loud as a Comanche Indian. Fittingly, Keogh named his brave horse Comanche.

Comanche was wounded by an arrow once again in June 1870 and received an injury to his right shoulder in January 1871 while with Keogh on Reconstruction duty in Kentucky.

From all accounts, Keogh was shot off Comanche's back during the June 1876 Little Bighorn battle. The bullet was said to have passed through the forequarters of the horse and emerged to shatter Keogh's left leg. Keogh, although severely wounded, apparently declined to shoot his horse for breastworks and may have been found by the Indians near death still clutching Comanche's reins.

On the morning of June 27, while the remnants of Reno's command and the Terry-Gibbon column examined the battlefield, several cavalry horses were found wandering about. First Lt. Henry Nowlan, who had been Keogh's best friend, apparently recognized Comanche and decided to save the horse, although the animal had been wounded perhaps as many as seven times and was in extremely poor condition. The other horses were either too badly wounded to rescue and were shot or simply left behind.

Comanche was transported by wagon fifteen miles to the steamship *Far West*. A stall had been provided between the rudders, and the horse was supported within by a sling. At Fort Abraham Lincoln, he was diligently nursed back to health

1st Lt. Edward S. Godfrey. *Courtesy Little Bighorn Battlefield National Monument.*

Godfrey was appointed second lieutenant, Company G, 7th Cavalry, in June 1867 and assigned to Fort Harker, where he performed scouting and escort duties. He was promoted to first lieutenant in February 1868 and commanded Company K during the November 1868 Washita battle. On June 15, 1869, Godfrey married Mary J. Pocock in Harpsville, Ohio. The couple had four children. The following year, 7th Cavalry commander Col. Samuel Sturgis submitted Godfrey's name to the "Benzine Board," which was in the process of reducing the officer corps by discharging undesirables. Sturgis, however, later withdrew recommendation of Godfrey.

Godfrey served with his company on Reconstruction duty in Yorkville and Chester, South Carolina, from 1871 to 1873. He was second in command of Company K during the Yellowstone expedition of 1873 and was assigned as assistant engineering officer for the Black Hills expedition of 1874. He was on detached duty as commander of the post at Colfax, Louisiana, from 1874 to 1876.

Godfrey commanded Company K during the Little Bighorn campaign. On June 25, his unit was part of Capt. Frederick Benteen's scout and subsequently participated in the hilltop fight. He was promoted to captain in December 1876 and at that time assumed command of Company D. Godfrey led his company during the 1877 Nez Perce campaign, including the Snake Creek fight, where he was severely wounded in the hip. In November 1894, he was awarded the Medal of Honor for "most distinguished gallantry" during that fight. Godfrey also was breveted major, U.S.A., in February 1890 for his actions that day.

In July 1879, Godfrey was appointed instructor in cavalry tactics at West Point; he served in that capacity until 1883. His wife passed away in February 1883 at West Point.

In 1890, Godfrey commanded D Troop during the battles at Wounded Knee and Drexel Mission, South Dakota. He was injured in a train wreck while returning from this campaign and never fully recovered. In October 1892, Godfrey married Ida De La Mothe Emley in Cookstown, New Jersey. He was appointed major, 1st Cavalry, effective December 1896 and returned to the 7th Cavalry the following month for duty as commander of H Troop at Fort Apache, Arizona, and in New Mexico.

(continued on following page)

Comanche as he presently stands in the Museum of Natural History at Dyche Hall on the campus of the University of Kansas at Lawrence. *Courtesy University of Kansas Museum of Natural History.*

In February 1901, Godfrey was appointed lieutenant colonel, 12th Cavalry, and after briefly serving in Cuba, he was assigned to Fort Sam Houston. In June 1901, he was appointed colonel, 9th Cavalry, and was in command of that unit in the Philippines. From 1904 to 1907, Godfrey commanded the Mounted Service School at Fort Riley, Kansas. He was promoted to brigadier general in January 1907 and was assigned command of the Department of the Missouri. His promotion, however, was held up by President Theodore Roosevelt, who considered Godfrey partially responsible for the killing of women and children at Wounded Knee. When his rank was finally confirmed in October 1907, he retired from the service after forty years.

Godfrey died at age eighty-eight in Cooksville, New Jersey, on April 1, 1932, and was buried in Arlington National Cemetery.

📖 Perhaps the best account of the Little Bighorn battle by a white participant is "Custer's Last Battle," taken from a lecture by Godfrey at West Point, which was published in *Century Magazine* 43 (January 1892). Lengthy extracts of that

(continued on following page)

by blacksmith Gustave Korn. At that time, the famous horse became a favorite for a young ladies' riding mount—so much so that his use caused a bitter rivalry among the young ladies at the fort. This problem was solved by Col. Samuel D. Sturgis, commanding officer of the 7th Cavalry, who on April 10, 1878, issued General Order No. 7:

1. The horse known as "Comanche" being the only living representative of the bloody tragedy of the Little Big Horn, Montana, June 25, 1876, his kind treatment and comfort should be a matter of special pride and solicitude on the part of the 7th Cavalry, to the end that his life may be prolonged to the utmost limit. Though wounded and scarred, his very silence speaks in terms more eloquent than words of the desperate struggle against overwhelming odds, of the hopeless conflict, and heroic manner in which all went down that day.

2. The commanding officer of "I" troop will see that a special and comfortable stall is fitted up for Comanche. He will not be ridden by any person whatever under any circumstances, nor will he be put to any kind of work.

3. Hereafter upon all occasions of ceremony (of mounted regimental formation), Comanche, saddled, bridled, and led by a mounted trooper of Troop I, will be paraded with the regiment.

Thereafter, Comanche lived a life of privilege as the "2nd commanding officer" of the 7th cavalry. He roamed the post at will, rooting through garbage pails and begging for buckets of beer at the enlisted men's canteen. Comanche would follow Private Korn around like a puppy, once trailing the blacksmith into town and creating a jealous ruckus on the front lawn of a home Korn was visiting. When Korn was killed in 1890 at Wounded Knee, Comanche became quite despondent, and his health began to fail. He died on November 6, 1891, at age twenty-eight.

Professor L. L. Dyke, a naturalist at the University of Kansas, volunteered to have Comanche mounted if the animal would be donated to the University Museum at Lawrence. His offer was accepted. Comanche was exhibited at the 1893 Chicago World's Fair, then went on display at the museum. He presently stands in a humidity-controlled glass case designed to discourage souvenir hunters—including students wishing for good luck on a test—from plucking hair from him.

📖 *Comanche (The Horse That Survived the Custer Massacre),* by Anthony A. Amaral (Los Angeles: Westernlore, 1961); *Comanche of the Seventh,* by Margaret Leighton (New York: Berkley, 1959); *His Very Silence Speaks: Comanche—The Horse Who Survived Custer's Last Stand,* by Elizabeth Atwood Lawrence (Detroit: Wayne State University Press, 1989); and *Keogh, Comanche and Custer,* by Edward S. Luce (Ashland, OR: Lewis Osborne, 1947).

🐎 Medals of Honor Awarded

By the morning of June 26, the lack of water to quench the thirst of the troops dug in on the hilltop became a serious problem. The men had carried full canteens when the siege began, but much of that water had been depleted, and most of them—particularly the wounded—were now suffering severely under the hot sun on the barren hill. "Our throats were parched," wrote Pvt. Edward H. Pickard of Company F, "the smoke stung our nostrils, it seemed as if our tongues had swollen so we couldn't close our mouths, and the heat of the sun seemed fairly to cook the blood in our veins."

Perhaps this condition was one reason that the Indians chose not to attack the hilltop en masse. Not only would a frontal assault cost many Indian lives, but it was evident that sooner or later the troops would need water to survive. In order to procure any water, the cavalrymen would have to traverse a 600-yard ravine that led to the river from the hilltop—and that ravine was presently occupied by armed Indians.

Capt. Frederick Benteen, acting on his own without consulting Maj. Marcus Reno, decided to drive the Indians from their positions in the ravine. He led a charge of troops toward the surprised Indians, killing several of them and chasing away the others, without losing a man until returning to the line, where one man was shot and killed. This action had cleared the ravine itself, but anyone attempting to reach the river at

article, as well as considerable other material by and about Godfrey, can be found in *The Custer Myth: A Source Book of Custeriana,* edited by W. A. Graham (Harrisburg, PA: Stackpole, 1953).

A revised version of the *Century Magazine* article written by Godfrey in 1908 can be found in *The Two Battles of the Little Big Horn,* edited by John M. Carroll (New York: Liveright, 1974); and *The Custer Reader,* edited by Paul A. Hutton (Lincoln: University of Nebraska Press, 1992). Godfrey's diary covering the Little Bighorn campaign from May 17 to September 24 was published posthumously as *The Field Diary of Lt. Edward Settle Godfrey, Commanding Co. K, 7th Cavalry under Lt. Colonel George Armstrong Custer in the Sioux Encounter at the Battle of the Little Bighorn,* edited by Edgar and Jane Stewart (Portland, OR: Champoeg Press, 1957).

Also see "Interview with Edward S. Godfrey," in *Custer in '76: Walter Camp's Notes on the Custer Fight,* edited by Kenneth Hammer (Provo, UT: Brigham Young University Press, 1976). His diary and papers have been preserved in the Library of Congress and the U.S.A. Military History Institute, Carlisle Barracks, Pennsylvania.

✳ Theodore W. Goldin
Private, 7th U.S. Cavalry

Goldin, whose real name was John Stillwell, was born on July 25, 1858, in Avon Township, Wisconsin, and subsequently was adopted by the Goldin family. He was working as a brakeman until enlisting in the army in April 1876, when he was assigned to Company G, 7th Cavalry, at Fort Abraham Lincoln.

Goldin's company was part of Maj. Marcus Reno's battalion during the June 25, 1876, Little Bighorn battle. He was said to have been wounded twice while retreating from the valley across the river to the bluffs and during the two-day siege of the hilltop. Goldin participated in the 1877 Nez Perce campaign until November, when he was discharged as a private of good character because he had concealed that he was too young to enlist.

He returned to Wisconsin and on February 23, 1881, married Laura Belle Dunwiddie in Beloit. The couple had one son. In 1882, Goldin was elected clerk of the Green County circuit court. He resigned in 1885 to serve as assistant chief clerk of the Wisconsin Assembly. During this time, he had been studying law, and after being admitted to the bar in 1885, he moved to Janesville, where he practiced law with his brother-in-law.

(continued on following page)

In May 1888, Goldin enlisted as a private in Company A, 1st Wisconsin Infantry, and was soon promoted to sergeant major. Then, in January 1889, he was made colonel and appointed aide-de-camp to the governor. He entered the Wisconsin National Guard in 1890 and was promoted to captain the following year.

Goldin is notable due to his correspondence with former 7th Cavalry officer Capt. Frederick W. Benteen. Between the fall of 1891 and the summer of 1896, the two men traded letters that recorded gossip, innuendo, opinion, and memories about the 7th Cavalry, with emphasis on the famous battle. Benteen, who addressed Goldin as "Colonel," perhaps his National Guard rank, would not have remembered the former enlisted man and likely would not have corresponded with him had he known that Goldin had not been a former Regular army officer. These fascinating accounts bear further witness to the dark side of Benteen, who revealed a startling bitterness and sarcasm toward his former comrades, especially Custer. These letters were compiled by historian John M. Carroll and published as *The Benteen-Goldin Letters on Custer and His Last Battle* (New York: Liveright, 1974).

Goldin applied for the Medal of Honor, claiming that he had been among the volunteers who had risked their lives to carry water to the wounded while trapped on the hilltop in June 1876. He was awarded the medal on December 21, 1895—nineteen years after the battle—probably with some assistance from Benteen.

Goldin served as chairman of the Republican Central Committee in 1904. He moved to Kansas City in 1907 and spent the next four years associated with the YMCA. His wife died in July 1911 in Oklahoma City. In 1917, Goldin moved on to Texas, where he lived until he retired to the Wisconsin Masonic Home in 1924. On June 20, 1929, he married Sarah J. Patterson Murphy in Waukegan, Illinois. Goldin died on February 15, 1935, at the Wisconsin Veterans Home in King, and was buried in that institution's cemetery.

✺ Luther Rector Hare
Second Lieutenant, 7th U.S. Cavalry

Hare was born on August 24, 1851, in Noblesville, Indiana. His father, a lawyer, moved the family to Sherman, Texas, where in September 1870, Luther was appointed to the U.S. Military Academy at West Point. He graduated four years later, ranked twenty-fifth in a class of forty-one. Hare

(continued on following page)

the bottom would be required to cross about thirty feet of open space, with Indian sharpshooters firing from the opposite bank.

Benteen declined to order any of the troops to make the perilous journey down the ravine; rather, he asked for volunteers. After the volunteers had collected every possible container that could hold water, four of the best shots available—George H. Geiger, Henry Meckling, Otto Voit, and Charles Windolph—were deployed in a skirmish line and ordered to lay down a base of fire into the bushes across the river. The mission was relatively successful, although one man was killed and six or seven wounded. Subsequent water carriers acted of their own accord until about noon, when the Indian firing decreased and additional troops were dispatched to fill their canteens and other receptacles.

For their bravery, twenty-four 7th Cavalry troopers were awarded the Medal of Honor, the highest number cited in any one engagement in U.S. history. These men were as follows:

Company A:	Pvt. Neil Bancroft; Pvt. David W. Harris; Sgt. Stanislas Roy
Company B:	Pvt. Thomas J. Callan; Sgt. Benjamin C. Criswell; Pvt. Charles Cunningham; Sgt. Rufus D. Hutchinson; Sgt. Thomas Murray; Pvt. James Pym
Company C:	Sgt. Richard P. Hanley; Pvt. Peter Thompson
Company D:	Pvt. Abram B. Brant; blacksmith Frederick Deetline; Pvt. William M. Harris; Pvt. Henry Holden; Pvt. George D. Scott; Pvt. Thomas W. Stivers; Pvt. Frank Tolan; Pvt. Charles H. Welch
Company G:	Pvt. Theodore W. Goldin
Company H:	Sgt. George Geiger; blacksmith Henry W. B. Mechlin; Pvt. Otto Voit; Pvt. Charles Windolph

📖 "Account of Edward Pickard," *Oregon Journal* (July 31–August 4, 1923); "Custer Battle Water Party," by E. A. Brininstool, *Hunter-Trader-Trapper* 65 (August 1932); *Army and Navy Journal* (July 15, 1876); *Winners of the West* (June 24, 1926); "A Survivor's Story of the Custer Massacre on the American Frontier," by Jacob Adams, *Journal of American History* 3 (1909); and *Indian Fights and Fighters,* by Cyrus T. Brady (New York: McClure, Phillips, 1904).

🦌 The Enlisted Men's Petition

The smoke had barely cleared on the field when a curious document dated July 4, 1876, signed by 236 of the cavalry survivors of the Little Bighorn battle, approximately 80 percent of the survivors of Reno's and Benteen's commands, was sent

"To His Excellency the President and the Honorable Representatives of the United States." The text read as follows:

> We, the enlisted men the survivors of the battle of the Heights of Little Big Horn River, on the 25th and 26th of June 1876, of the 7th Regiment of Cavalry who subscribe our names to this petition, most earnestly solicit the President and Representatives of our Country, that the vacancies among the Commissioned Officers of our Regiment, made by the slaughter of our brave, now heroic, now lamented Lieutenant Colonel George A. Custer, and the other noble dead Commissioned Officers of our Regiment who fell close by him on the bloody field, daring the savage demons to the last, be filled by the Officers of the Regiment only.
>
> That Maj. M. A. Reno, be our Lieutenant Colonel vice Custer, killed; Captain F. W. Benteen our Major vice Reno, promoted.
>
> The other vacancies to be filled by officers of the Regiment by senority.
>
> Your petitioners know this to be contrary to the established rule of promotion, but prayerfully solicit a deviation from the usual rule in this case, as it will be conferring a bravely fought for and justly merited promotion on officers who by their bravery, coolness, and decision on the 25th and 26th of June 1876, saved the lives of every man now living of the 7th Cavalry who participated in the battle, one of the most bloody on record and one that would have ended with the loss of life of every officer and enlisted man on the field only for the position taken by Major Reno, which we held with bitter tenacity against fearful odds to the last.
>
> To support this assertion—had our position been taken 100 yards back from the brink of the heights overlooking the river, we would have been entirely cut off from water; and from those heights the Indian demons would have swarmed in hundreds picking off our men by detail, and before midday June 25th not an officer or enlisted man of our Regiment would have been left to tell of our dreadful fate as we then would have been completely surrounded.
>
> With prayerful hope that our petitions be granted, we have the honor to forward it through our commanding officer.
>
> Very Respectfully,
> [236 signatures]

At face value, this petition appears innocent enough. The enlisted survivors of the battle—at least 236 of them—in appreciation of the gallant efforts of their senior officers for saving their lives and perhaps in an effort to maintain continuity within the regiment, had formally requested that Maj. Marcus A. Reno and Capt. Frederick W. Benteen be rewarded with promotions.

2nd Lt. Luther R. Hare. *Courtesy Little Bighorn Battlefield National Monument.*

was appointed second lieutenant, 7th Cavalry, in June 1874, but he had not joined the regiment in time to participate in the Black Hills expedition.

Hare was initially assigned to the Indian scouts during the 1876 Little Bighorn campaign, but he rejoined his own Company K as second in command on June 25 and participated in Maj. Marcus A. Reno's ill-fated charge of the Indian village and subsequent retreat. He remarked about the mad dash to the bluffs across the Little Bighorn River: "The crossing was not covered and no effort was made to hold the Indians back. If the Indians had followed us in force to the hilltop, they would have got us all."

Hare was assigned as Reno's acting adjutant on the hilltop and was dispatched to hurry the pack train. Upon his return, he claimed to have heard firing from the direction of Custer Hill and observed Capt. Thomas Weir's company advancing that way. Reno, who had denied Weir permission for the move, dispatched Hare to tell Weir to attempt, if possible, to open communications with Custer. That detachment, however, was forced back to the hilltop defensive position by the Indians. Hare later carried a message to 1st Lt. Edward Godfrey, his company commander, and made the decision on his own to remain with his unit rather than serve any longer as Reno's adjutant.

Hare was appointed first lieutenant effective June 25, 1876, and commanded Company L in the latter stages of the campaign. He served as the regimental engineering officer on the 1877 Nez Perce campaign, including the September 13 Canyon Creek fight.

On June 21, 1878, Hare married Virginia Hancock, the niece of Gen. Winfield S. Hancock. The couple had three children.

Hare served as regimental quartermaster from August 1886 to July 20, 1887, and missed the affair at Wounded Knee while on sick leave at Fort Riley. He was promoted to captain effective December 1890. Hare commanded K Troop at Fort Huachuca, Arizona Territory, in the Apache campaign of 1896. He was appointed lieutenant colonel, 1st Texas Cavalry, in May 1898 and colonel one month later while briefly serving in Cuba. In July 1899, Hare was appointed colonel, 33rd U.S. Volunteer Infantry, and took his regiment to the Philippines, where he fought in the

(continued on following page)

BIOGRAPHIES

Spanish-American War battles of San Fabian, Mangatani Bridge, San Jacinto, and San Quentin, Luzon. He was awarded two Silver Star Medals in 1924 for gallantry in action at San Jacinto on November 11, 1899, and in Northern Luzon from December 4 to 18, 1899.

Hare was appointed brigadier general, U.S.V., in June 1900 and commanded the 1st District, Department of Southern Luzon. In February 1901, he was appointed major, 12th Cavalry. He retired for disability in July 1903 but returned to active service in October of that year and spent two years as inspector instructor of militia at Austin, Texas. He served as professor of military science and tactics at the University of Texas from May 1908 to January 1911, when he again retired. Hare was advanced to colonel, retired, in July 1916. Two years later, he served for a year as commander of the Student Army Training Corps at Simmons College in Abilene, Kansas.

Hare died of throat cancer at Walter Reed Hospital on December 22, 1929, and was buried in Arlington National Cemetery.

📖 Hare's lone biography is *Luther Rector Hare: A Texan with Custer: Biography of an American Hero,* by Ray Meketa (Mattituck, NY: Mad Printers, 1983). Also see "Interview with Luther Hare, February 7, 1910," in *Custer in '76: Walter Camp's Notes on the Custer Fight,* edited by Kenneth Hammer (Provo, UT: Brigham Young University Press, 1976); "A Gallant American Officer: Luther Hare," by Frederic Remington, *Colliers Weekly* (April 7, 1900); and numerous references in *The Custer Myth: A Source Book of Custeriana,* edited by W. A. Graham (Harrisburg, PA: Stackpole, 1953).

✳ George B. Herendeen
U.S. Army Scout

Herendeen was born on November 28, 1846, in Parkman Township, Geauga County, Ohio, and was orphaned at age thirteen. He served in the Civil War, then lived with an uncle in Indiana before heading west to Denver in 1868. Herendeen worked at that time as a cowboy in New Mexico and on cattle trails into Montana. He was on the Yellowstone Wagonroad and Prospecting expedition in 1874, and the following year, he accompanied a forty-three-man party headed by "Major" Fellows Pease, a Crow Indian agent, to help built Fort Pease on the north bank

George B. Herendeen. *Courtesy Little Bighorn Battlefield National Monument.*

Trumpeted by newspapers, the petition was forwarded through military channels until it reached Gen. William T. Sherman, who returned it with his endorsement but, noting the authority of the president and Senate, could not grant the petition. The matter never did reach the White House or Congress, and no further action was taken. At the time of the 1879 Reno Court of Inquiry, there was no reason to assume that the document was not authentic, which was a boost to Reno's case.

The first indication that there could be a question about the validity of petition arose years later, when Gen. Edward S. Godfrey looked into the matter and wrote:

> There were several men of the 7th Cavalry at Soldiers Home and in Washington in 1921 and 1922 who, when asked if they had signed the petition, denied ever having had such a thought, yet their signatures proved genuine. . . . Not one would admit that he had signed, until shown his signature.

Taking into consideration the absolute authority that officers had over enlisted men, perhaps these soldiers had been "ordered" to sign or had signed without knowing the content of the document and had later dismissed the act as inconsequential or were ashamed to admit that they had been coerced.

In 1954, Maj. Edward S. Luce, the superintendent of Custer Battlefield National Monument, became suspicious about certain irregularities within the petition. He noticed that a number of the signees were not on regimental rolls at the time of the battle, and others had always signed the payroll with an "X" but had signed their full names on the document. Luce called in the FBI to determine the authenticity of the signatures in question.

The FBI, although hindered by a lack of handwriting samples from many of the enlisted men, nevertheless concluded that at least seventy-six of the signatures—one-third of the total—were "probable forgeries." Many had purportedly been signed by one man: 1st Sgt. Joseph McCurry of Company H, which was commanded by Capt. Frederick Benteen.

That overwhelming evidence clearly points toward a devious scheme by a person or persons unknown, who perhaps had a desire to head off any potential criticism and validate his conduct on June 25, 1876. The finger of guilt, inasmuch as First Sergeant McCurry was involved, would point directly at Captain Benteen. Furthermore, McCurry could not have accomplished the task without Benteen's knowledge.

To his credit, Benteen was popular with the enlisted men and had distinguished himself during the hilltop fight—although his actions beforehand are a subject of controversy—and possibly in the minds of the troops, he

(continued on following page)

was deserving of a promotion. Reno was not well liked, but the petition would have been far less credible had he been left off.

Without additional evidence—a "smoking gun"—the guilty party or parties will never be revealed. The enlisted men's petition, however, stands as another example of the pattern of deception, which includes the Reno Court of Inquiry, that has created many myths, controversies, and conjectures about the battle, suppressing the facts and hindering the emergence of the truth about the actual events.

A list of the signees can be found in *The Custer Myth: A Source Book of Custeriana,* edited by W. A. Graham (Harrisburg, PA: Stackpole, 1953).

The Conduct of Maj. Marcus A. Reno on the Hilltop

The conduct of Maj. Marcus A. Reno during the period of time that his command remained in a defensive position on the hilltop under siege by the hostile Indians has been the subject of controversy. Some have accused him of cowardice and drunkenness; others claim that his handling of the situation, although not heroic, was quite competent.

One piece of evidence that casts a dark shadow on Reno's conduct is the notable bravery and command presence of his subordinate, Capt. Frederick W. Benteen. The fact that Benteen inspired the men with acts of courage—constantly exposing himself to fire while directing the troops—suggests that Reno was not in control and apparently had permitted Benteen to assume *de facto* command of the unit.

Many members of the 7th Cavalry, most of whom testified at Reno's 1879 Court of Inquiry, have offered their versions of events on the hilltop with respect to Reno's action or inaction.

First Lt. Edward S. Godfrey recalled, "It was evident that Reno carried no vigor of decision and his personal behavior gave us no confidence in him." Godfrey reported that he did not see Reno during the night of June 25, nor did he received any orders from him.

Second Lt. George Wallace testified that he also had not seen Reno from that first night until the next morning, but he did add that Reno was on the line throughout June 26 in a position where the Indians were expected to attack.

Captain Thomas French, who did not testify at Reno's court, claimed that Reno hid himself from the evening of June 25 until the Indian attack had weakened around noon the following day. French, by the way, also wrote in a June 1880 letter to the wife of Dr. A. H. Cooke that he would have been fully justified had he shot Reno when the major ordered the retreat from the timber to the hilltop that caused the majority of his command's casualties.

of the Yellowstone below the mouth of the Bighorn. In February 1876, Herendeen spread the alarm in Bozeman about that fort being under siege by hostile Sioux, which compelled Maj. James Brisbin and his 2nd Cavalry to ride from Fort Ellis to the rescue of those civilians trapped in the fort.

Herendeen was then hired on as a scout and courier for Col. John Gibbon's Montana Column, which was part of the 1876 Little Bighorn campaign. On June 22, he was sent to join Custer's 7th Cavalry as it marched for the Valley of the Little Bighorn, and three days later, he was attached to Maj. Marcus A. Reno's battalion for the ill-fated charge and subsequent retreat. Herendeen became separated from the rest of the cavalrymen during the every-man-for-himself dash from the timber to the bluffs across the Little Bighorn River. He hid in a willow thicket until later in the day, when he was able to safely rejoin Reno's command on the hilltop.

Herendeen served as a scout during the 1877 Nez Perce campaign, then resided in Bozeman, Lewistown, and Great Falls before moving to Harlem in 1889, where he was employed on the Fort Belknap Indian Reservation. He died of pneumonia on June 17, 1918, and was buried in Harlem Cemetery.

"George Herendeen, Montana Scout," by Barry Johnson, English Westerners' *Brand Book* 2, nos. 3 and 4 (April and July 1960). His accounts of the battle, which were originally published in the *New York Herald* on July 8, 1876, and January 22, 1878, have been reprinted in *The Custer Myth: A Source Book of Custeriana,* edited by W. A. Graham (Harrisburg, PA: Stackpole, 1953). Also see "Interview with George Herendeen," in *Custer in '76: Walter Camp's Notes on the Custer Fight,* edited by Kenneth Hammer (Provo, UT: Brigham Young University Press, 1976).

William "Billy" Jackson
Private, 7th U.S. Cavalry

Jackson was born between 1855 and 1860 at Red River Portage, LaPreary, Canada, or perhaps Fort Benton, Montana. His father was a white tailor, his mother a Pikuni Blackfoot, and he was either a half-blood or quarter-blood Indian, named Little Blackfoot (Siksikakoan). His initial military service was as a scout with the 7th Cavalry on the Yellowstone expedition of 1873 and the Black Hills expedition the following year.

Jackson was a member of the scout detachment during the 1876 Little Bighorn campaign. He has

(continued on following page)

been mentioned as a disciplinary problem on the march—one time for firing his revolver at a snake, and another when he was made to stand on a water keg for committing various offenses.

On June 25, he was attached to Maj. Marcus Reno's battalion, and during the every-man-for-himself retreat, he became trapped and was left behind in the timber along with 1st Lt. Charles DeRudio, Pvt. Thomas O'Neil, and fellow scout Fred Girard, while the rest of the command scrambled for the bluffs across the Little Bighorn River. After dark, the four men managed to catch two horses and were riding upstream when they were challenged by an Indian. Jackson and Girard galloped away and subsequently hid in some willows until the following evening, when they made their way safely to Reno's perimeter on the hilltop.

Jackson served as a scout with the 22nd Infantry during the 1877 Nez Perce campaign. Two years later, he built a trading post at Flat Willow near the Snowy Mountains. In the 1880s, he resumed scouting in the Northwest Territories during the Riel rebellion. Jackson returned to his homestead on the Blackfoot Reservation at Cutbank Creek, north of Browning, Montana, where he died on December 30, 1899, leaving behind a widow. Mount Jackson (Siksikakoan) in Glacier National Park was named in his honor.

Jackson's brother, Robert, was also a scout with the 7th Cavalry but was sent back to Fort Abraham Lincoln with a dispatch shortly before the June 25, 1876, battle.

📖 Jackson's biography is *William Jackson, Indian Scout,* by James W. Schultz (Boston: Houghton Mifflin, 1926). His account of the famous battle can be found in *Battles and Skirmishes of the Great Sioux War, 1876–77: The Military View,* edited by Jerome A. Greene (Norman: University of Oklahoma Press, 1993).

✸ Thomas Mower McDougall
Captain, 7th U.S. Cavalry

McDougall was born on May 21, 1845, at Fort Crawford, Prairie de Chien, Wisconsin, the son of brevet Brig. Gen. Charles McDougall, a surgeon with the medical corps. He attended St. Mary's Academy, near Baltimore, and military school in Cornwall, New York. McDougall was in command of a cadet regiment from his school that served as escort for Edward VII, prince of Wales, on a visit to West Point in 1860. In October 1863, he volunteered as an aide-de-camp without pay to Gen. J. P. Hawkins and remained in that capacity until February 1864. At that time, McDougall was commis-

Second Lt. Winfield S. Edgerly testified that he had witnessed Reno asleep on a blanket. Dr. Henry R. Porter reported that he had seen Reno once during the night, but did not elaborate. Captain Benteen testified that he had been in Reno's company for much of that first night, and that the major was decidedly in control of himself and his command.

In addition to Reno's apparent failure to instill confidence in his troops by his presence that first night, there are two incidences of major importance that call into question his ability to command.

First, Reno may have been drunk on the night of June 25. He did admit to having had a drink that night but contended that he was perfectly sober. Many years later, however, Reno was said to have told Rev. Arthur Edwards that his odd actions on the hilltop were because he was drunk.

A number of witnesses had observed Reno drinking but contradicted on the issue of whether he was under the influence. Custer's loyal striker, John Burkman, claimed Reno was drunk. First Lt. Edward Mathey said that he observed Reno drinking on the morning of June 26 but did not consider him drunk.

An encounter with a civilian packer named John Frett that occurred between 9 and 10 P.M. that first night may shed some light on the subject. Frett happened upon Reno at the pack train and was asked a question by the major that he did not understand. An angry Reno slapped Frett, and when doing so, the movement caused a flask in Reno's other hand to spill whiskey on the packer. Reno then became incensed and leveled a carbine at Frett, threatening to shoot him. Another packer, Benjamin F. Churchill, led Frett away, and the major went about his business. Those were not the actions of a man in control of his faculties and certainly could be interpreted as those of a man who had already had too much to drink and became angry when his precious stock spilled.

Another incident during the night of June 25, however, is much more troubling. Reno at some point suggested to Captain Benteen that they destroy all the property that could not be transported, mount the command, and ride for the supply depot on the Powder River. The wounded who were able to ride would be taken along; the others would be abandoned—left behind in the hands of the Sioux. To his credit, Benteen rejected the idea. The rumors of the plan, however, spread to the wounded, who must have endured more than merely physical pain throughout that long night. Had a man of lesser discipline than Benteen been second in command and agreed with Reno's plan, there might have been another bloody retreat similar to one Reno had ordered earlier that night from the timber to the hilltop.

The questions about Reno's conduct will never be resolved to everyone's satisfaction. The Reno Court of Inquiry could have assisted in that endeavor, but the officers by then had

(continued on following page)

chosen to circle the wagons for the good of the unit and were evasive, forgetful, or failed to tell the whole truth.

The evidence that does exist points to Reno as a man either intoxicated by drink or overcome with fright, or both, who had already proven himself a coward by failing to obey orders to charge the village earlier that day. Therefore, there is no reason to believe that Reno was in control of himself or his command on the hilltop, and thankfully for the troops, Benteen was available to take charge.

📖 Eyewitness testimony with respect to Reno's actions on the hilltop can be found in *The Reno Court of Inquiry: The* Chicago Times *Account* (Fort Collins, CO: Old Army Press, 1972); *Abstract of the Official Record of Proceedings of the Reno Court of Inquiry,* by W. A. Graham (Harrisburg, PA: Stackpole, 1954); and *Reno Court of Inquiry,* edited by Ron Nichols (Hardin, MT: Custer Battlefield Historical and Museum Association, 1994). Reno's admission of being drunk is in *Indian Fights and Fighters,* by Cyrus Brady (New York: Doubleday, Page and Co., 1904). Reno's suggestion to abandon the hilltop is discussed at length in *I Fought with Custer: The Story of Sergeant Charles Windolph,* by Frazier and Robert Hunt (New York: Charles Scribner's Sons, 1947).

🐎 First News of Custer's Defeat

Clement A. Lounsberry, publisher of the *Bismarck Tribune,* bragged for many years that his newspaper had scooped the world in its July 6, 1876, edition with the news of Custer's defeat. Lounsberry did score a coup by being the first to publish the names of the presumed dead and wounded, but his paper was not by any means the first to break the news of the Little Bighorn battle.

On June 28, 1876, while the remnants of Maj. Marcus Reno's command were occupied with the unenviable task of burying the dead from Custer's command, Col. John Gibbon stood on the battlefield and scribbled a message in his notebook. "General Custer's command met with terrible disaster here on the 25th," he wrote. "Custer, with five companies, were so far as we can ascertain, completely annihilated. . . . Roughly stated the loss of Custer's command is about one-half, say 250 men." The dispatch most likely would have been written above the signature of Gen. Alfred H. Terry, inasmuch as Terry was the highest-ranking officer present.

Gibbon tore the pages from his notebook and ordered scout H. M. "Muggins" Taylor to carry the message without delay to Capt. D. W. Benham at Fort Ellis, near Bozeman, Montana, the site of the closest telegraph station.

Capt. Thomas M. McDougall. *Courtesy Little Bighorn Battlefield National Monument.*

sioned a second lieutenant in the 10th Louisiana Volunteers of African Descent (renamed the 48th U.S. Colored Infantry). He was severely wounded in a battle at Lakeville, Louisiana.

McDougall was mustered out on June 1, 1865, at Benton Barracks, Missouri, and the following day was appointed captain, Company G, 5th U.S. Volunteer Infantry. Two months later, he was mustered out again. He remained a civilian until May 1866, when he was appointed second lieutenant in the 14th Infantry, which would soon became the 32nd Infantry, and reported to Fort Laramie. McDougall was promoted to first lieutenant in November 1866 and breveted captain in March 1867. He served briefly at Fort Vancouver and Fort Walla Walla, Washington, before moving to Arizona Territory, where he participated in engagements against the Apache Indians at Aravipa Canyon, Tonto Basin, Point of Mountain, and Rock Springs.

McDougall was assigned to the 7th Cavalry in December 1870 and was subsequently stationed with his unit on Reconstruction duty in South Carolina from 1871 to 1873. In May 1872, he married Alice M. Sheldon in Spartanburg, South Carolina. The couple had no children. McDougall commanded Company E in both the Yellowstone expe-

(continued on following page)

dition of 1873, where he was involved in the August 11 battle, and the 1874 Black Hills expedition. He was appointed captain in December 1875 and at that time assumed command of Company B.

McDougall's company was detailed as pack train escort during the 1876 Little Bighorn campaign. The pack train lagged well behind the main column on the June 25 approach toward the Indian village and finally arrived at the hilltop where Maj. Marcus Reno's battered command had taken refuge. On the night of June 26, McDougall, who had been slightly wounded in the fighting, retrieved the body of 2nd Lt. Benjamin H. Hodgson and buried it on Reno Hill. Inasmuch as he previously had been commander of Company E, McDougall was assigned the task of identifying and burying the members of that company who had fallen with Custer. It has been reported that a blood-stained photograph of McDougall's sister, which for some unknown reason had been carried by Capt. Myles Keogh, was found on November 25, 1876, when the Cheyenne village under Dull Knife was attacked and destroyed.

McDougall was on a scouting detail in Montana during the 1877 Nez Perce campaign and later commanded part of the detachment that escorted Chief Joseph and his people from Bear Paw Mountain to Fort Abraham Lincoln. He served in Montana and Dakota Territory until his retirement for disability in July 1890.

McDougall was advanced to major, retired, in April 1904 while residing at Cummings Place, Wellesville, New York. He died on July 3, 1909, at Echo Lake Farm near Brandon, Vermont, and was buried in Arlington National Cemetery.

📖 "Interview with Thomas M. McDougall," in *Custer in '76: Walter Camp's Notes on the Custer Fight,* edited by Kenneth Hammer (Provo, UT: Brigham Young University Press, 1976). A letter about the aftermath of the Little Bighorn battle from McDougall to Gen. Edward S. Godfrey is in the Manuscript Room, New York Public Library. Also see "Thomas M. McDougall," by Charles Mills, in *Custer and His Times, Book Two* (Fort Worth: Little Big Horn Associates, 1984). McDougall is the subject of numerous references in *The Custer Myth: A Source Book of Custeriana,* edited by W. A. Graham (Harrisburg, PA: Stackpole, 1953).

Taylor, who has been described as a gambler and professional hunter, embarked upon a circuitous route to the fort. On the evening of July 2, he arrived in Stillwater, Montana, now present-day Columbus, too exhausted to continue his mission. He stopped in at the general store, owned by William H. Norton and Horace Countryman, and related the news of Custer's fate. Norton, apparently a stringer for the *Helena Herald,* interviewed Taylor and quickly wrote a story that his partner Horace Countryman would deliver to Helena.

Taylor and Countryman departed Stillwater on the morning of July 3 and arrived at Fort Ellis by midafternoon. Taylor delivered Gibbon's dispatch to Captain Benham, who immediately turned it over to the telegraph office for transmission. Inexplicably, the message was not sent out over the wire until after the Fourth of July celebration. Perhaps the operator had been doing too much celebrating.

Horace Countryman resumed his ride toward Helena. Taylor, however, left Fort Ellis and chose as his first stop the offices of the *Bozeman Times.* He told his story to the editor, E. S. Wilkinson, who hurriedly assembled a crew to set type and prepare the presses. By 7 that evening, Wilkinson had scooped the world by publishing an extra that recounted Taylor's slightly embellished tale, which, among a few other altered details, had changed the number of dead to 315. Unfortunately, no copies of this edition are known to presently exist.

On July 4, Horace Countryman delivered a copy of the extra from the *Times* along with Norton's story to coeditor J. A. Fisk at the *Helena Herald.* Fisk immediately published a special edition that made its debut at 6:30 P.M. At that time, Fisk sent the story across the wire to the Associated Press in Salt Lake City. He also informed the governor, who confirmed the news with Captain Benham at Fort Ellis, then telegraphed Commander of the Army William T. Sherman. Sherman and others at the War Department were said to have been skeptical about the validity of the tragic news.

Other Montana newspapers picked up the story from the *Herald* and from independent sources and published their own special editions. The Deer Lodge *New Northwest* released an extra on the evening of July 4, with many other newspapers following suit over the next several days.

Several Eastern newspapers received the Associated Press wire story and included the news in their late editions on July 5. The prestigious *New York Herald* ran the story on July 6—eleven days after Custer's defeat. This story, which was also published in the *Army and Navy Journal* on July 8, cited sources from Salt Lake City (the Associated Press); Stillwater, Montana (William H. Norton); and a special correspondent from the *Helena Herald.* The *New York Herald* then set up telegraph communications with Bismarck, Dakota Territory, and spent upwards of $3,000 receiving information that included additional details of the battle and interviews with members of Reno's command.

📖 Perhaps the best account can be found in "Montana Editors and the Custer Battle," by Rex C. Myers, *Montana: The Magazine of Western History* 26 (Spring 1976), which has been reprinted in *The Great Sioux War 1876–77: The Best from Montana: The Magazine of Western History,* edited by Paul L. Hedren (Helena: Montana Historical Society Press, 1991). Also see "Why Helena Instead of Bozeman Scooped the News in 1876," in *The Custer Myth: A Source Book of Custeriana,* edited by W. A. Graham (Harrisburg, PA: Stackpole, 1953).

Indian Scouts Accompanying the 7th Cavalry

The army had learned over years that the main problem that plagued cavalry columns when fighting hostile Indians was a lack of mobility. Therefore, excellent intelligence from reconnaissance was essential in order to locate and surprise the Indians in their camps, where they were vulnerable. White frontiersmen who were wise in the ways of the Indians were of great help, but Indian scouts—usually bitter enemies of the hunted—who knew the terrain and could assist in bringing the command within striking distance were indispensible.

Fifty-one Indian scouts commanded by 2nd Lt. Charles Varnum accompanied the 7th Cavalry on the Little Bighorn campaign. These scouts rode ahead of the cavalry column on the approach into the Valley of the Little Bighorn and reported about the numerous fresh trails they encountered, which appeared to be leading toward a single objective.

On the morning of June 25, Crow scouts led Varnum, scouts Mitch Bouyer, Charley Reynolds, a handful of Arikara, and later George Armstrong Custer to a lookout called "Crow's Nest," which afforded an excellent view of the valley due to its topography rather than height. It was from this vantage point that evidence of Sitting Bull's huge village, some fifteen miles ahead, was confirmed by the scouts, although haze obscured Custer's view.

At that point, many of the Arikara scouts refused to accompany Custer any farther, and others were dismissed, their job of locating the village accomplished. In the ensuing battle, two Indian scouts were killed and two were wounded.

✹ Edward Gustave Mathey
First Lieutenant, 7th U.S. Cavalry

1st Lt. Edward G. Mathey. *Courtesy Little Bighorn Battlefield National Monument.*

Mathey was born on October 27, 1837, in Besançon, France. In 1845, the family immigrated to the United States, settling in Corydon, Indiana, and later New Albany, where Mathey worked in his brother's saloon and restaurant. He applied for citizenship in April 1859. Two years later, he enlisted as a private in Company C, 17th Indiana Infantry. He was appointed first sergeant of his company in May 1861 and second lieutenant one year later. He resigned from the 17th Indiana in August 1862. The following month, he joined the 81st Indiana Infantry, which had been newly organized in New Albany. Mathey fought with his regiment at Stone River, Tunnel Hill, the skirmish at Liberty Gap, and the battle of Chickamauga. He was appointed first lieutenant in March 1863 and captain eight months later. He was involved in actions at Kenesaw Mountain, Kingston, Marietta, and the siege of Atlanta and commanded his regiment in the battles of Franklin and Nashville. In September 1864, Mathey was appointed major. He was mustered out in June 1865.

Mathey returned to Indiana and worked as a store clerk and farmhand before being appointed second lieutenant, Company M, 7th Cavalry, in September 1867. He allegedly suffered from snow blindness at the November 1868 battle of the Washita and traded places with Capt. Louis Hamilton, who was anxious to see action. Mathey commanded the pack train, while Hamilton was killed on the initial charge into the Indian village.

Mathey was appointed first lieutenant effective May 1870. That same year, Mathey, who has been described as being so addicted to blasphemous language that he was nicknamed "Bible-Thumper," was recommended for discharge by Col. Samuel Sturgis at the "Benzine Board," which was reducing the officer corps. Mathey, however, successfully convinced the board that he was neither incompetent nor undesirable and should be retained. On November 8, 1871, he married Meda Jones, with whom he had a daughter.

Mathey commanded Company B on the Yellowstone expedition of 1873 and was second in command of Company M for the Black Hills expedition the following year.

(continued on following page)

Mathey was on temporary duty during the 1876 Little Bighorn campaign, in charge of a detachment of troops guarding the pack train. He was involved in the two-day hilltop siege and later testified at the 1879 Reno Court of Inquiry that he had observed Maj. Marcus Reno with a flask of whiskey but did not consider him drunk.

Mathey served as second in command of Company B during the 1877 Nez Perce campaign and was appointed captain effective in September. He commanded Company K as part of the escort for the 1878 movement of the Northern Cheyenne in Nebraska. Mathey missed the 1890–91 Wounded Knee campaign while on detached service in Chicago. He retired due to disability as a major in December 1896. From October 1901 to June 1903, he served as professor of military science at Baylor University in Waco, Texas. He was residing in Denver when he was appointed colonel, retired, in April 1904.

Mathey died on July 17, 1915, in Denver and was buried in Arlington National Cemetery.

📖 "Interview with Edward G. Mathey, October 19, 1896," in *Custer in '76: Walter Camp's Notes on the Custer Fight*, edited by Kenneth Hammer (Provo, UT: Brigham Young University Press, 1976); and "Edward Gustave Mathey of Company M," by James Schneider, Little Big Horn Associates *Research Review* (September 1977).

Goes Ahead. *Courtesy Little Bighorn Battlefield National Monument.*

Hairy Moccasin. *Courtesy Little Bighorn Battlefield National Monument.*

White Man Runs Him. *Courtesy Little Bighorn Battlefield National Monument.*

The following is a list of those Indian scouts who accompanied the 7th Cavalry, most of them having enlisted in April or May 1876:

William Baker (tribe unknown)
Barking Wolf (Arikara)
Bear Come Out (Dakota)
Bear Running in the Timber (Dakota)
Bear's Eye (Arikara)
Black Calf (Arikara)
Black Fox (Arikara)
Black Porcupine (Arikara)
Bob Tailed Bull (Arikara) (killed in action)
Bull (Arikara)
Bull in the Water (Arikara)
Bush (Arikara-Sioux)
Climbs the Bluff (Arikara)
William Cross (Teton)
Curly (Crow)
Curly Head (Arikara)
Foolish Bear (Arikara)
Forked Horn (Arikara)
Goes Ahead (Crow)
Good Face (Arikara)
Goose (Arikara) (wounded in action)
Hairy Moccasin (Crow)
Half Yellow Face (Crow)
Horns in Front (Arikara)
Howling Wolf (Arikara)
Robert Jackson (Pikuni)
William Jackson (Pikuni)
Laying Down (Arikara)
Left Hand (Arikara)
Little Brave (Arikara) (killed in action)
Little Sioux (Arikara-Sioux)
Long Bear (Arikara)
One Feather (Arikara)
One Horn (Arikara)
Owl (Arikara)
Red Bear (Arikara)
Red Foolish Bear (Arikara)
Round Wooden Cloud (Dakota)
Running Wolf (Arikara)
Rushing Bull (Arikara)
Soldier (Arikara)
Stab (Arikara)
Strikes the Bear (Arikara)
Strikes the Lodge (Arikara)
Strikes Two (Arikara)
Wagon (Arikara)

White Cloud (Dakota)
White Eagle (Arikara)
White Man Runs Him (Crow)
White Swan (Crow) (wounded in action)
Young Hawk (Arikara)

📖 *Wolves for the Blue Soldiers: Indian Scouts and Auxiliaries with the United States Army, 1860–90,* by Thomas W. Dunlay (Lincoln: University of Nebraska Press, 1982); *The Arikara Narrative of the Campaign against the Hostile Dakotas, June 1876,* by O. G. Libby (New York: Sol Lewis, 1973); "The Crow Scouts: Their Contributions in Understanding the Little Big Horn Battle," by Joe Sills, Jr., *5th Annual Symposium Custer Battlefield Historical and Museum Association* (1991); and "Did Custer Believe His Scouts?" by Robert Church, *5th Annual Symposium Custer Battlefield Historical and Museum Association* (1991).

🐎 Alleged Survivors of the Battle

Predictably, many people over the ensuing years claimed to be the sole survivor of the Little Bighorn battle. Some who basked in this fifteen minutes of fame were said to have gained financially by fleecing gullible tourists or selling their stories to ambitious Eastern journalists. Given the number of alleged survivors, it is a wonder that any bodies were found on the battlefield.

To be fair, the Indians did relate several stories describing soldiers who rode for their lives away from the fighting. These men have never been identified or their freedom substantiated. A couple sets of bones have been found some distance from the fighting, which may explain the fate of those who fled. In one case, however, a dead cavalry horse was found several weeks after the battle above the mouth of Rosebud Creek, which raised speculation that its rider had escaped—but perhaps by deserting when the column passed that point on the approach to the Valley of the Little Bighorn.

The most famous "lone survivor" was Curly, one of Custer's Crow Indian scouts. Curly had been released prior to the battle but may have witnessed the initial stages as he departed. He later returned to the steamship *Far West* and tried to tell about the fate of Custer, but he was not understood. For years, however, Curly encouraged researchers with several tantalizing tales of his harrowing escape that day—how he had fooled the hostiles by stripping off his Crow clothing and fashioning his hair Sioux style, how he had secreted himself inside the carcass of a dead horse, or how he had covered himself with a blanket and hid in a ravine. None of the stories were true. At the tenth reunion of the battle, Curly was confronted by Sioux chief Gall, who stated that had Curly been on the field that day, he would have been dead. The Crow scout did not dare refute Gall's assertion.

⚜ Henry James Nowlan
First Lieutenant, 7th U.S. Cavalry

Nowlan, an Irishman, was born on June 18, 1837, on Corfu in the Ionian Islands, which are located off the western coast of Greece. He graduated from the Royal Military Academy at Sandhurst—the British equivalent of West Point. He was commissioned a lieutenant in August 1854 and served with the 41st Welsh Regiment in the Crimean War, including the siege of Sevastopol, where he was decorated for gallantry. His father was paymaster of the English Army, and he had two other brothers who also served.

In 1862, Nowlan sold his commission and immigrated to the United States. He was commissioned a first lieutenant, 14th New York Cavalry, in January 1863. Nowlan was involved in the Red River campaign and the siege of Port Royal, Louisiana. He was captured in June 1863 and finally escaped in March 1865. Nowlan joined the 18th New York Cavalry in June 1865 and was appointed captain effective in January 1866. He was wounded on a Reconstruction duty expedition to Yorktown, Texas, and was mustered out of the service on May 31, 1866.

Nowlan was appointed second lieutenant, 7th Cavalry, on July 28, 1866—the day the regiment was organized—and was promoted to first lieutenant in December 1866. He participated in the Hancock expedition as commander of Company F, which was garrisoned at beleaguered Fort Wallace. He served as acting commissary of subsistence for the Washita campaign and was regimental quartermaster for the 1873 Yellowstone expedition and the Black Hills expedition of 1874. Nowlan became known as one of the best shots in the regiment and was close friends with fellow Irishman Capt. Myles Keogh, with whom he often hunted.

Nowlan was on detached service with Gen. Alfred H. Terry during the Little Bighorn campaign. When that column arrived on the battlefield, he likely was the one who recognized Myles Keogh's horse, Comanche, and vowed to save him (see "Comanche" on page 238). Nowlan had been given Keogh's will just days before, with instructions to deliver it to the captain's sister.

He was promoted to captain effective June 25, 1876, and assumed command of his late friend's Company I. Nowlan returned to the battlefield in July 1877, in command of the reburial detail (see "Interment and Reinterment of Little Bighorn

(continued on following page)

Dead" on page 232). He participated in that year's Nez Perce campaign, including the Canyon Creek fight, for which he would be breveted major in 1890—the same year that he commanded his company during the Wounded Knee affair.

Nowlan was promoted to major, 7th Cavalry, in July 1895. He died on November 10, 1898, at the Army and Navy Hospital in Hot Springs, Arkansas, and was buried in Little Rock National Cemetery.

📖 Nowlan is the subject of numerous references in *Life in Custer's Cavalry: Diaries and Letters of Albert and Jennie Barnitz, 1867–68,* edited by Robert M. Utley (New Haven, CT: Yale University Press, 1977). Col. Michael V. Sheridan's official report of Nowlan's reburial detail in 1877 can be found in *The Custer Myth: A Source Book of Custeriana,* edited by W. A. Graham (Harrisburg, PA: Stackpole, 1953).

✴ Henry Rinaldo Porter
Acting Assistant Surgeon, 7th U.S. Cavalry

Porter was born on February 3 or 13, 1848, in either New York Mills or Lee Center, New York. In 1872, he graduated from Georgetown University School of Medicine and in June of that year entered into a contract as acting assistant surgeon with the 5th Cavalry at Camp Hualpai, Arizona Territory. He immediately participated in the Apache campaign, including the September 26 fight at Muchos Canyon. Porter was cited by Gen. George Crook for "conspicuous gallantry in the closing campaign against the Tonto Apaches in February and March 1873."

Dr. Henry R. Porter. *Courtesy Little Bighorn Battlefield National Monument.*

He was appointed post surgeon at Camp Grant in July 1873 and served in that capacity until July, when he canceled his contract and moved to San Francisco. In October, he signed another contract and served at Camp Hancock, Dakota Territory, until December 1874. At that time, Porter entered into a partnership called Nicholson & Porter, druggists and stationers, in Bismarck. He returned to Camp Hancock in November 1875 and remained until May 1876, when he entered into a three-month contract to accompany the 7th Cavalry on the Little Bighorn campaign.

Other alleged former members of Custer's command who offered fanciful stories of a daring escape appeared off and on in the press around the country, but only one has been found to have even a shred of credibility. This claimant was Frank Finkel (also known as Frank Hall), a resident of Dayton, Washington, who was the subject of a feature story in the *Walla Walla Bulletin* on March 20, 1921.

Finkel related that he had been wounded several times that day and escaped when his horse bolted. He happened upon a trapper's cabin the following day and was nursed back to health. At that time, he reported to Fort Benton, where an officer in charge did not believe his story. Finkel soon thereafter deserted and became a farmer near St. Louis before moving to Dayton, Washington, where he lived for many years. His description of the terrain was said to have been nearly perfect, and his body did show scars from apparent bullet wounds.

Finkel claimed that he had been a member of Tom Custer's Company C. A check of the official muster rolls reveals a Sergeant George August Finckle, with Company C, born in Berlin, Germany, in 1844, who apparently had been a captain in the German Army before enlisting in the 7th Cavalry in January 1872. Sergeant Finckle was presumed to have been killed in the battle. There were two cavalrymen named Hall, Edward and John; both were with Company D and known to have survived the battle.

Inasmuch as aliases were a common practice at that time, and different spellings of names appeared on various documents, it is virtually impossible to confirm or debunk the claim by Finkel. One curious note: He died in 1930 from a malignancy caused by a bullet in his side that he had received decades before—perhaps from an Indian rifle at the Little Bighorn battle.

Another, more recent claimant to the title of survivor is a farrier with Company L named William H. Heath, an immigrant from Staffordshire, England. His name has been listed as one of the casualties of the battle, but official records in Pennsylvania show that he was buried in Schuylkill County Cemetery on May 2, 1891, after dying of a brain tumor. It has been speculated that Heath in his capacity as a farrier may not have been with Custer's column at all but could have been detailed to care for an injured horse or some other such duty. Heath, who had enlisted in October 1875, may have deserted, leaving behind $1.14 due him for tobacco and $15 for clothing. His personal effects were sold at auction in March 1877 and brought $5. His death at the Little Bighorn, however, has been duly noted in "Britons Who Fell at the Little Big Horn" in the English Westerners' *Tally Sheet* (Summer 1984).

📖 "Was There a Custer Survivor?" by E. A. Brininstool, *Hunter-Trader-Trapper* (April 1922); *Indian Fights and Fighters,* by Cyrus T. Brady (New York: McClure, Phillips, 1904);

(continued on following page)

and "Unwritten Seventh Cavalry History," by E. A. Brininstool, *Middle Border Bulletin* (Spring 1945). A collection of newspaper clippings and personal material about Frank Finkel's claim can be found in the Oshkosh, Wisconsin, Public Museum. The William Heath mystery appears in the June 28, 1999, *Billings Gazette.* Also see Kathryn Wright's "Custer's Last Man," *Guns Magazine* (July 1955).

🐎 Would Gatling Guns Have Saved Custer?

Some military tacticians have suggested that Gatling guns would have provided Custer the firepower necessary to defeat the overwhelming number of Indians that he faced on June 25, 1876. Custer had been offered the use of three Gatling guns by Gen. Alfred H. Terry and Maj. James Brisbin of the 2nd Cavalry prior to his march to the Valley of the Little Bighorn. Custer at first accepted the offer, then about an hour later changed his mind, deciding that the guns would impede his march.

There can be no doubt about the formidable firepower that those guns, which were invented in 1861, could have brought into play. The Gatling gun was a forerunner of the machine gun. It worked on the principle of having a soldier turn a crank that fed ammunition from a hopper into either six or ten barrels and could fire up to 350 rounds per minute.

The downside of their operation was that they had not been modified much since their invention and were known to frequently malfunction, often jamming due to residue from black powder or overheating. Also, they were designed to repel a massed attack of the enemy, such as that customary in European warfare, whereas the Indians would not have marched into the line of fire in the tradition of Redcoats. Another disadvantage was that the guns were mounted on large wheels, which meant that during operation, the gun crew would be standing upright, which would make them sitting ducks to Indian snipers.

But perhaps the most negative aspect of Gatlings in turning the tide of a battle such as the Little Bighorn was the difficulty in simply getting them to the battlefield. The guns were drawn by four condemned horses, no longer suitable for riding, and each obstacle would have required unhitching the horses in favor of manpower to maneuver the guns to an agreeable location, then rehitching the horses in order to continue. Taking into consideration the rugged terrain on Custer's march, the guns would have greatly impeded his progress. This fact can be evidenced by Terry's own battery—the one he had offered to Custer. Gibbon's 20th Infantry was in charge of the guns and were unable keep up with the column.

There are also scholars who suggest that Custer would have fared better had he taken the Gatling guns, but not necessarily on account of their firepower. The guns would have delayed Custer's march to the extent that he would have rendezvoused

Porter was attached to Maj. Marcus A. Reno's battalion and participated in the Powder River scout before marching for the Valley of the Little Bighorn. On June 25, he was involved in Reno's disastrous retreat from the valley to the bluffs. Once atop the bluffs, Porter approached Reno to notify him that the troops were quite demoralized by the bloody retreat. An irritated Reno was said to have replied: "That was a cavalry charge, sir!" The doctor established a makeshift hospital in a shallow area on the hilltop and cared for the wounded as best he could while also rationing out the diminishing water supply. On June 27, Porter supervised the evacuation of the wounded to the steamer *Far West.* He also visited Custer's battlefield and clipped locks of hair from each of the dead officers.

Porter returned briefly to his practice in Bismarck, then signed another contract at Camp Hancock, which ran from December 1876 to February 1877. In September 1877, he married Charlotte Viets in Oberlin, Ohio, with whom he had one son.

Porter served as Burleigh County physician and commissioner for the insane from 1878 to 1882 and also was president of the Medical Society of North Dakota and vice president of the Society of Veterans of Indian Wars. He toured Europe in the summer of 1883 and made subsequent trips to South America, Cuba, Puerto Rico, and Mexico. Porter died of heart disease on March 3, 1903, at the Hotel Metropole in Agra, India, while on a trip around the world. He was buried in Cantonment Cemetery in Agra.

📖 Porter wrote two accounts of the Little Bighorn battle: "The Terrible Sioux: Dr. Porter's Account of the Battle," *New York Herald* (July 11, 1876); and "The Brave Doctor," *Bismarck Tribune* (May 24, 1878). Correspondence between Porter and historian Walter Camp are in the Walter Camp Collection, Lee Library, Brigham Young University. His scrapbook can be found in the North Dakota Historical Society Library.

⚜ George David "Nick" Wallace
Second Lieutenant, 7th U.S. Cavalry

Wallace was born on June 29, 1849, in York County, South Carolina. His father, Alexander, served two terms in the South Carolina legislature. Although he was a slave owner, the elder Wallace supported the Union during the Civil War, which caused the family to be ostracized by vindictive neighbors,

(continued on following page)

who went so far as to destroy the Wallace farm. Alexander Wallace worked to restore his name, but his eventual election to Congress as a Republican in 1868 when his opponent, a former Confederate, was disqualified did little to pacify his neighbors.

Wallace was educated at Langham Academy until September 1868, when he entered the U.S. Military Academy at West Point. He graduated—along with future fellow 7th Cavalry officers Henry Harrington and close friend Charles Varnum—four years later, ranked ninth in a class of fifty-seven. He reported to Company G, 7th Cavalry, in June 1872 and was assigned to Reconstruction duty in Laurensburg, South Carolina, a few miles from his home, reporting in November after a brief illness. Wallace served as second in command of Company G for the Yellowstone expedition of 1873 and commanded the Indian scouts during the 1874 Black Hills expedition. He was then assigned with his company as acting assistant adjutant general for the District of the Red River in New Orleans until April 1876, when he returned to Fort Abraham Lincoln.

Wallace was second in command of Company G for the 1876 Little Bighorn campaign and on the evening of June 24 attended an officers' call at Custer's tent. Afterward, he remarked to 1st Lt. Edward S. Godfrey that he had a premonition that Custer was going to be killed. When Godfrey asked him why, he answered that he had never before heard Custer speak in such a disheartening manner or ask for advice from others. The following day, Wallace was involved in Reno's retreat from the timber to the bluffs across the Little Bighorn River, assuming command of his company after Capt. Donald McIntosh was killed.

Wallace has been identified as the officer who selected the location where Custer was buried on the field and wrote his commanding officer's name on a cartridge case that was placed beside a wooden stake to mark the spot. For his gallant performance during the battle, he was appointed first lieutenant effective June 25, 1876, and named regimental adjutant in August.

Wallace participated in the 1877 Nez Perce campaign, including the Canyon Creek fight, and subsequently served at the Cavalry School at Fort

2nd Lt. George D. Wallace. *Courtesy Little Bighorn Battlefield National Monument.*

with the Terry-Gibbon column and unified their commands to attack the village.

Apparently Custer had discussed artillery with scout Fred Girard prior to the march. Girard was of the opinion that the Indians would not charge the Gatlings or simply stand around getting picked off. The scout told Custer that a twelve-pounder cannon would be a much better choice of artillery. They could destroy a village in quick order by lobbing shells from a mile away.

That theory had already been proven by Col. Kit Carson in early November 1864 at Adobe Walls, Texas. Carson had commanded fewer men than Custer and faced more Indians—in fact, more than anyone ever had or would on the plains—and was able to destroy a large Kiowa-Comanche village and extricate himself from being surrounded by several thousand warriors because of the two twelve-pounder mountain howitzers that he had brought along. Otherwise, Carson assuredly would have suffered Custer's fate.

To be fair, for the disadvantages outlined above, Custer was likely justified in his decision to refuse the Gatlings. It was not his style to allow anything to delay his march to the objective. In his defense, Gen. Nelson Miles wrote to Gen. William T. Sherman on July 8, 1876, that Gatlings "are worthless for Indian fighting."

George Armstrong Custer for President?

Thirty-seven years after the Little Bighorn battle, an Arikara scout named Red Star stated that George Armstrong Custer, through an interpreter, told his Ree scouts before departing Fort Lincoln in May 1876 that a victory against the Sioux would make him the "Great Father" in Washington.

Author Mari Sandoz—known for her fictionalized accounts of history—used Red Star's alleged statement to outline her idea of Custer's plan to gain the nomination of the Democratic party, which was meeting in St. Louis June 27–29, in her *The Battle of the Little Bighorn* (Philadelphia: J. B. Lippincott, 1966). Basically, she theorized, Charley Reynolds would duplicate his Black Hills dash to a telegraph office and relay the news of the victory over the Sioux to the floor of the convention, where Custer's operatives would push for his nomination. With all due respect to Mari Sandoz, who uses this theme throughout her book as Custer's primary motivation for fighting the Sioux, that theory borders on the ludicrous.

These accounts, however, have led some naive historians to assume that Custer intended to use the Little Bighorn campaign as a launching pad into the presidency of the United States—perhaps to the extent that he would become reckless

(continued on following page)

in his zeal to erase Grant's insult over the Belknap scandal and occupy the throne upon which Grant presently sat.

There is no question that at some future date, Custer would have made an attractive candidate to the Democratic party, for which he had performed admirable service over the years. Military commanders traditionally were mentioned as qualified contenders for the presidency after winning a major war. And had Custer defeated the Sioux on June 25, 1876, his already high popularity with the public would have soared to presidential heights.

It is doubtful, however, that Custer at that point in his career even remotely dreamed of the presidency. In fact, it is absurd to believe, given his prior embarrassing dabblings in politics, that he thought himself suited as a politician rather than a soldier.

In 1866, he had accompanied President Andrew Johnson on his "Swing around the Circle," a tour around the country designed to win support for the president's Southern policy. Custer was mercilessly attacked in the North for mingling with Southern traitors, which compelled him to abandon the tour before its end to escape protestors and adverse publicity. Repercussions from his testimony at the Belknap hearings had probably served to further convince him that he presently lacked adequate political skills for national office.

Another problem would be the timing. Word of a victory over the Sioux—much less Custer in person—could not have reached the convention in St. Louis in time to make any impact on the party's nominee, regardless of whether Charley Reynolds had killed several horses in an effort to reach a telegraph.

If Custer indeed had in early 1876 tendered presidential aspirations, the perfect platform for a run had been presented to him. He had been offered a contract by the Redpath Lyceum Bureau, a Boston talent agency, that called for him to make a speech five nights a week for four to five months at an astounding $200 per lecture. Not only could he have earned more than ten times his annual army salary in that short period, but he could have placed his carefully constructed views, thrilling war stories, and considerable charm before an already adoring nationwide audience. Although it had been suggested that the tour would begin in the spring, had Custer been setting his sights on the presidency that year, he could have pushed up the date to suit his ambitions. He almost certainly could have received a leave of absence and not participated in the Little Bighorn campaign in order to fulfill the schedule of speaking engagements.

The lecture tour could have concluded with Custer's triumphant entrance at the Democratic party convention. By that time, he would have gained the admiration and confidence of the public, and that, combined with his influential party benefactors, his friendship with a number of leading Congressmen, his association with New York newspapers, and

Leavenworth and on recruiting duty at Jefferson Barracks. On October 11, 1882, Wallace married Carline "Carrie" Otis, with whom he had a son. He was promoted to captain in September 1885.

Wallace was commanding K Troop on December 29, 1890, when he was killed from gunshot wounds to the head and abdomen during a fight with the Sioux at Wounded Knee Creek, South Dakota. He was buried in the family plot at Rose Hill Cemetery in Yorkville, South Carolina. The inscription on his tombstone reads: "He like a Soldier Fell. Friends, Comrades and Country Unite in Mourning the Loss of an Officer Whose Life Reflected Honor on His Native State. 'Thy Will Be Done, Oh Lord.'"

📖 Wallace maintained a daybook during the Little Bighorn campaign that has been studied with great interest: "March of the Seventh Cavalry, June 22 to June 25, 1876," *Report of Chief of Engineers for Fiscal Year Ending June 30, 1877*, Appendix PP. Also see *Letters From the Field: Wallace at the Little Big Horn*, edited by Douglas Paul Westfall (Orange, CA: Paragon Agency, 1997); and "Lakota Bullet Ends Wallace's Life—14 Years after Little Bighorn," by John MacKintosh, *Greasy Grass* 16 (May 2000), a publication of the Custer Battlefield Historical and Museum Association.

the fact that he had exposed fraud in the hated Grant administration and been punished for his actions, perhaps could have resulted in the nomination. But Custer had turned down this lucrative opportunity to gain publicity for himself in order to remain with the army on active duty.

That appealing scenario of lecturing to help gain the nomination, however, may have been in the back of his mind for the distant future. The lecture tour certainly would have been available as a reward after Little Bighorn and beyond. He was only thirty-six years old, much too young to seriously consider the staid chief executive position, an old man's job. And there is also another relevant consideration: It is doubtful that this man of good humor and sensitivity who craved constant activity could picture himself mired down in the daily partisan bickering and boring policy meetings inherent to that high office. Years later, perhaps, when he was older, but not in 1876, when the West promised excitement for years to come.

If Custer truly had made any statement of that nature to his Arikara scouts before Little Bighorn, it was probably little more than playful banter, an indication of the importance that a victory against the Sioux would hold for his career. More than likely, Custer was envisioning for himself the reward of a brigadier general's star, an appointment made by the president when a vacancy occurred—regardless of seniority—to a worthy recipient.

📖 Red Star's account appears in "The Arikara Narrative of the Campaign against the Hostile Dakotas," edited by Orin G. Libby, *North Dakota Historical Collections* 6 (Bismarck, 1920). Another embellishment of Red Star's alleged statement, in addition to the Sandoz story, can be found in *Custer's Fall: The Indian Side of the Story,* by David Humphreys Miller (New York: Duell, Sloan and Pearce, 1957). Also see *Custer for President?* by Craig Repass (Fort Collins, CO: Old Army Press, 1985).

CHAPTER NINE

After Little Bighorn

OVERVIEW

The nation was understandably horrified and outraged by the Custer disaster. Congress voted to authorize two new forts—Custer and Keogh—on the Yellowstone and recruited an additional 2,500 fresh cavalry troops for duty. Many recruits, calling themselves "Custer's Avengers," enlisted specifically to serve in the 7th Cavalry. The hostile Indians, keenly aware that there would be some sort of retaliation for the battle on the Little Bighorn River, broke up into smaller bands and scattered across the plains.

The conflict that would be known as the Great Sioux War of 1876–77 resumed in early July when 800 Cheyenne warriors fled the Red Cloud Agency and headed for the Powder River country. The 5th Cavalry, now under the command of Lt. Col. Wesley Merritt, intercepted about 30 of the renegades on July 17 at War Bonnet, or Hat, Creek, twenty-five miles northwest of the agency.

Scout William F. "Buffalo Bill" Cody, who had accompanied the column, engaged in a "duel" with a Cheyenne sub-chief named Yellow Hair. Actually, Cody was said to have shot

Present-day view looking northwest from Custer Hill toward museum building. *From author's collection.*

BIOGRAPHIES

✹ Big Foot
Minniconjou Sioux Chieftain

Big Foot, who was born about 1820, was known in his early life as Spotted Elk. He resisted the efforts of whites to civilize him but generally managed to accomplish that in a peaceful manner. Big Foot was a master of diplomacy, who counseled his people to avoid war but also advised them never to turn their backs on Lakota Sioux traditions and culture. Following the surrender of the tribe in 1877, he submitted to the Cheyenne River Reservation and became one of the first of his people to successfully harvest corn. He also was an advocate of education and

(continued on following page)

the Indian off his pony, rode him down, then killed and scalped him. The celebrated scout held up the bloody scalp and announced that this was the "first scalp for Custer." This "duel" became a featured attraction of Cody's Wild West Show and also a play, *The Red Right Hand; or, Buffalo Bill's First Scalp for Custer.*

Merritt chased several dozen Cheyenne back to the agency, then rendezvoused with Gen. George Crook at his base camp on Goose Creek.

On August 5, Crook led nearly 2,300 troops down the Tongue River trailing the Indians, while Gen. Alfred Terry, with Col. John Gibbon and the 7th Cavalry, took another 1,700-man detachment down the Yellowstone to the mouth of the Rosebud. The columns—to their surprise—happened upon each other on August 10 in the Rosebud Valley. The rein-

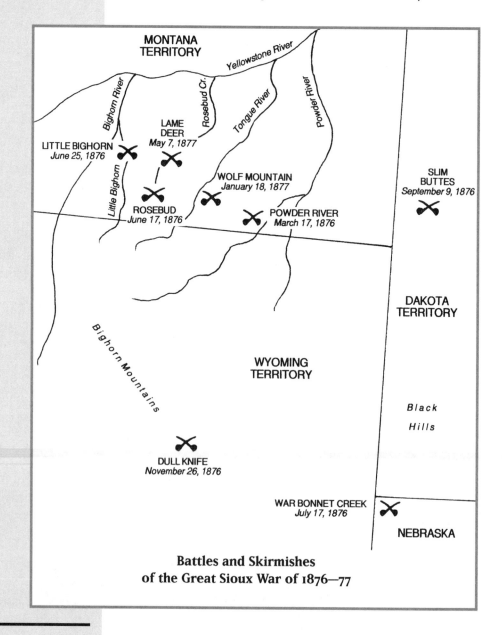

**Battles and Skirmishes
of the Great Sioux War of 1876—77**

forced column then embarked on an arduous march through rain and mud, with many men succumbing to sickness and fatigue. They arrived on August 17 at the mouth of the Yellowstone River, without having come within 100 miles of the hostiles. By this time, Sitting Bull and his band had escaped to the lower Missouri, and Crazy Horse was leading his people toward the Black Hills.

On September 5, General Terry made the decision to disband his portion of the expedition. Gibbon returned to Fort Ellis, and the 7th Cavalry rode for Fort Abraham Lincoln. Crook, however, decided on a forced march to the Black Hills in an effort to overtake those Indians who had earlier embarrassed him on the Rosebud (see "Prelude to Little Bighorn: The Powder River and Rosebud Engagements" on page 189).

Crook was under the impression that he could quickly catch up with the hostiles and ordered that all wagons, extra clothing, tents, and other nonnecessities be abandoned. His column, however, was soon plagued by bad weather and supply problems on what would become known as the "starvation march." Scores of exhausted animals died, and the men were reduced to eating mule and horse meat. Near the town of Deadwood, Crook dispatched Capt. Anson Mills with a detail of 150 cavalrymen to buy rations.

On September 9, Mills happened upon a Sioux camp of thirty-seven lodges near Slim Buttes, a landmark rock formation. The cavalrymen charged and routed the enemy, killing Chief American Horse, and occupied the camp while withstanding heavy fire from warriors who took up a nearby defensive position. At about noon, Crazy Horse and another 200 warriors arrived and attacked. A fierce battle raged without a decision, until Crook and reinforcements reached the field and the Indians broke contact. The army lost three killed and twelve wounded; Indian casualties are unknown. A search of the camp revealed various items taken from Custer's command—clothing, horses and saddles, a guidon, and a gauntlet belonging to Capt. Myles Keogh.

Crook's beleaguered column was finally rescued when wagons laden with supplies accompanied by a herd of cattle reached them on September 13. At that time, he made the decision to abandon his futile search for the hostiles.

The Little Bighorn campaign had come to an inauspicious end, and the U.S. Congress vowed to make the Lakota Sioux tribe pay dearly for its treachery. It was decreed in the annual Indian appropriation act of August 15 that the Sioux would be denied subsistence until the tribe relinquished all claims to hunting rights outside the reservation and signed over ownership of the Black Hills to the government. This ultimatum was delivered to the reservations in September and October, and in order to save their people from starvation, the new treaty was signed by a number of chiefs at the various agencies—instead of the two-thirds of adult males as specified by the

helped build reservation schools for the Lakota. In October 1888, Big Foot represented his tribe on a trip to Washington, D.C.

In 1890, when the Ghost Dance religion, a practice that was forbidden by the Indian Bureau, swept the Lakota Sioux reservations, Big Foot did not embrace this new religion that caused much contention between his people and the army. Nevertheless, Gen. Nelson A. Miles ordered the arrest of this Minniconjou chief, as well as that of Sitting Bull, who resisted and was killed. This act compelled Big Foot to flee the reservation with about 300 of his people. They were overtaken by soldiers from the 7th Cavalry at Wounded Knee Creek and at that time promised to peacefully return to the reservation. The following morning, December 29, 1890, a skirmish broke out that quickly escalated into a one-sided battle, in which the army killed nearly half of Big Foot's band. During the fight, Big Foot was struck in the head by a bullet and died instantly. A photograph of the frozen body of Big Foot contorted in death where he fell has been widely circulated.

📖 The most sympathetic account of Big Foot can be found in *Bury My Heart at Wounded Knee*, by Dee Brown (New York: Holt, Rinehart & Winston, 1970).

✹ Dull Knife
Northern Cheyenne Chief

Dull Knife (or Morning Star; Tash-me-la-pash-me or Wahiev) was born about 1810 on the Rosebud River in Montana. He was known as Dull Knife by the Lakota Sioux and Morning Star by his own people, the former being his most widely accepted name. Dull Knife participated in Cheyenne hostilities in 1864–65, following the Sand Creek massacre, and fought in Red Cloud's 1866–68 war over the Bozeman Trail (see "Red Cloud's War" on page 68). He first became known to the whites when he signed the Fort Laramie Treaty of 1868 as chief of his tribe. Some accounts say that Dull Knife participated in the 1876 Rosebud and Little Bighorn battles, but that has never been verified.

On November 25, 1876, Dull Knife's village was attacked by a detachment of soldiers led by Col. Ranald Mackenzie. The army inflicted many casualties, destroyed the village, and captured the pony herd. Dull Knife escaped, but he grew weary of the constant pursuit and surrendered in May 1877 at Camp Robinson. He and his people were sent to a reservation near Fort Reno, Indian Territory, to live with the Southern Cheyenne—far from their Tongue River homeland.

(continued on following page)

In September 1878, Dull Knife and fellow Cheyenne Little Wolf, homesick and dissatisfied with conditions, fled the reservation with their bands and headed north. More than 10,000 soldiers and civilians took up the pursuit in one of the country's largest manhunts. Dull Knife finally surrendered at Fort (Camp) Robinson and was told he would be imprisoned until he agreed to return to Indian Territory. In January 1879, he and his band broke out of the fort. Dull Knife and his family escaped, but nearly a third of his band was killed by the soldiers. He hid at the Red Cloud Agency and was finally permitted to live on the Pine Ridge Reservation. Dull Knife died on the Rosebud River in 1883—one year before his people were given their own reservation in the Tongue River homeland.

📖 See *Cheyenne Autumn,* by Mari Sandoz (New York: McGraw-Hill, 1953); and *The Fighting Cheyennes,* by George B. Grinnell (Norman: University of Oklahoma Press, 1956).

✹ James William Forsyth
Colonel, 7th U.S. Cavalry

Forsyth was born on August 8, 1835, in Maumee, Ohio. He entered the U.S. Military Academy at West Point in 1852 and graduated four years later, ranked twenty-eighth in his class. Forsyth served in Washington Territory until the outbreak of the Civil War, when he returned to Ohio and instructed recruits at Mansfield. He was promoted to captain in October 1861. The following year, he was given command of a brigade in the Army of Ohio. In March 1862, he was appointed to the staff of army commander Maj. Gen. George B. McClellan and served as inspector general, then provost marshal general. Forsyth was subsequently transferred to the staff of Maj. Gen. Philip Sheridan and served in that capacity for the remainder of the war. He won brevets up to brigadier general of volunteers and Regular army colonel for his service in the Shenandoah Valley.

Forsyth remained in the army after the war and commanded a cavalry brigade for two years, before joining Sheridan's staff as an aide and military secretary. He was promoted to lieutenant colonel in 1878 and, at that time, left Sheridan to command the 1st Cavalry at Fort Vancouver, Washington. In 1886, Forsyth was promoted to colonel and assumed command of the 7th Cavalry. He was instrumental in organizing the School of Cavalry and Field Artillery at Fort Riley, Kansas.

Forsyth was in charge of the detachment of the 7th Cavalry in December 1890, when he was

(continued on following page)

Fort Laramie Treaty of 1868. Regardless, *Paha Sapa,* the land the Lakota believed was sacred, was now officially owned by the United States.

Col. Nelson A. Miles worked throughout the fall building winter quarters at his Tongue River Cantonment, which he used as a supply base from which to chase various Sioux tribes, including that of Sitting Bull, across half of Montana. Skirmishes and negotiations between the two warring factions failed to produce agreeable results, although small bands did occasionally submit to the reservations.

Meanwhile, General Crook, with a column of more than 2,200 men, had marched on November 14 from Fort Fetterman up the old Bozeman Trail to a location near his earlier battle on the Rosebud. At that point, scouts reported finding a large Cheyenne village to the west in the Bighorn Mountains. Crook dispatched Col. Ranald Mackenzie with ten cavalry troops—about 1,100 men—to engage the hostiles.

At dawn on November 25, Mackenzie and his cavalrymen stormed into a canyon of the Red Fork of the Powder River and attacked a 200-lodge village under Chiefs Dull Knife and Little Wolf. The army horsemen quickly routed the surprised occupants. About 400 warriors, however, regrouped within the boulders on a nearby bluff and poured a deadly fire back into the village, while others closed with the soldiers and Indian scouts, fighting hand-to-hand. Chief Little Wolf was said to have been wounded seven times but escaped and survived. It was midafternoon before the cavalrymen had fought off the assault and maintained control of the village. They then set to work destroying everything of value—lodges, clothing, food—and capturing the herd of 700 ponies. Once again, items from Custer's command were found, including a guidon that had been made into a pillowcase.

Mackenzie had lost one officer and five enlisted killed and twenty-six wounded. The Indians suffered about forty dead; other casualties included eleven babies said to have frozen to death that night.

The Cheyenne fled in search of Crazy Horse on the upper Tongue River. Crook determinedly followed, but after enduring low temperatures and blizzards, he ended his campaign in late December without another major engagement.

The military pressure, however, was taking its toll on the renegade Indians. Many of these people submitted to the reservation, and others were prepared to surrender. To that end, communication was opened between the chiefs and Col. Nelson Miles to discuss terms. On December 16, a delegation of Cheyenne approached the Tongue River Cantonment to talk but were attacked by some of Miles's Crow scouts, who killed five of their enemy. The Cheyenne fled, and hostilities resumed.

In early January 1877, Miles and about 350 men set out to search for hostiles up the Tongue River Valley. On January 7, the Indians attempted to lure them into an ambush, but anxious warriors sprang the trap too soon, which enabled Miles to escape and in the process capture a number of Cheyenne women and children. At daybreak the following morning, Crazy Horse and about 500 Sioux and Cheyenne warriors attacked Miles's command with intentions of freeing the captives. The two sides fought fiercely throughout the morning on a battlefield covered with deep snow. Miles was well prepared for the attack and skillfully deployed his artillery and marksmen, which kept the Indians at bay. The battle of Wolf Mountain, or Battle Butte, ended about noon when a blizzard obscured visibility and the Indians withdrew. Miles had intended to continue his campaign, but the difficulty in obtaining supplies forced him to return to the Tongue River Cantonment.

The battle, although each side had sustained only light casualties, convinced many of the hostiles that they could never prevail against the army. Sitting Bull decided to take his band to Canada; other small bands scattered across the plains and mountains; still others chose to straggle onto the reservations. On May 6, Crazy Horse led almost 900 of his brethren into Camp Robinson.

A few bands remained defiant, however, and vowed to continue their resistance. One such group of Sioux under Lame Deer had chosen not to surrender with Crazy Horse. Colonel Miles, acting on information from Indians who had surrendered, marched up the Tongue to search for these hostiles. A village of fifty-one lodges was located on Muddy Creek, a tributary of the Rosebud. At dawn on May 7, Miles, with four cavalry troops, charged into Lame Deer's village. The surprised Indians fled to the hillsides, while the army easily secured the village and commandeered the 450-head pony herd.

One of Miles's scouts persuaded Chief Lame Deer and Iron Shirt, the head warrior, to surrender. Another scout, however, rode up and shot at the two men, who retrieved their weapons and fled toward the high ground while firing. One bullet just missed Miles and struck a trooper to the rear. Both Indians were shot down by a barrage of fire from the troops.

Fourteen Indians had been killed in the assault, while the army lost four enlisted killed and one officer and six enlisted wounded. More than 200 of Lame Deer's band had escaped, and Miles gave chase, without success, before returning to destroy the village. These Indians were followed throughout the summer by Miles—including eleven troops of the 7th Cavalry under Col. Samuel Sturgis—which resulted in most of them eventually surrendering.

Discontent and tension gripped the Lakota Sioux reservations throughout the summer of 1877, which led to the killing of Crazy Horse at Camp Robinson on September 6. The Northern Cheyenne—including Chiefs Dull Knife and Little Wolf—unlike the Sioux, had been denied the right to live on a

ordered to subdue Minniconjou Sioux chief Big Foot and 300 of his people who had fled the reservation. On December 29, Forsyth's blunder in strategy resulted in the death of nearly half of Big Foot's band. He was severely criticized and was subjected to a court of inquiry for his actions, but the matter was eventually dropped.

Forysth was promoted to brigadier general in 1894 and major general three years later when he retired. He died in Columbus, Ohio, on October 24, 1906.

✪ Joseph
Nez Perce Chief

Joseph (Hin-mah-too Yah-lat-kekt, or "Thunder Rolling in the Mountains") was born about 1840 in the Wallowa Valley, Oregon, although one biographer gives the year of his birth as 1832. He assumed leadership of his tribe—in spite of there being five other chiefs—when his father, Old Joseph, a half-Cayuga, died in 1871. About that time, he was said to have reluctantly signed a treaty with the government to move his tribe to a reservation in Lapwai, Idaho. Joseph and his tribe resisted leaving their valley, however, until they were given an ultimatum in 1877. While arrangements for their move were being worked out, a group of settlers stole hundreds of the tribe's prized Appaloosa horses. Young Nez Perce warriors retaliated by killing eighteen settlers.

The army came to arrest the guilty parties, but instead of surrendering them to the authorities, Joseph fled into the mountains with about 650 of his tribe. During the next several months, Joseph led his outnumbered people on a 1,200-mile "Long March" through four states in an attempt to escape army pursuit. Joseph, who was known more for diplomacy than for war, outwitted the army in over a dozen engagements and gained grudging admiration by instructing his people not to take scalps and to avoid killing noncombatants. The Nez Perce escaped from the army time and again, although upon occasion they suffered considerable casualties, losing a total of about 275 warriors, but killing about 266 soldiers.

Finally, on October 5, 1877, Joseph, after being captured and exchanged during talks with Gen. Nelson A. Miles, was forced to surrender to save his fatigued and starving people. In an eloquent speech, he said in part, "I have fought, but from where the sun now stands, Joseph will fight no more forever." Joseph had been promised by Miles that his people could return to their homeland,

(continued on following page)

BIOGRAPHIES

Grave of Maj. Marcus A. Reno in Custer National Cemetery, Little Bighorn Battlefield National Monument. *From author's collection.*

but the government denied that provision and sent them to Indian Territory.

In 1879, Joseph spoke before the full chamber of Congress to plead with them to allow the Nez Perce to return home. The War Department refused and instead imprisoned them at Fort Leavenworth, Kansas, where many died of malaria. Later, Joseph and 150 members of his band were settled on the Colville Reservation in Washington.

Joseph visited Washington, D.C., in 1897 and again in 1903. He had audiences with President McKinley on his first trip and Theodore Roosevelt on the second, but he was never given permission to live in his beloved Wallowa Valley. He died at Nespelem on the Colville Reservation on September 21, 1904, and was survived by two of his three wives.

📖 *I Will Fight No More Forever,* by Merrill D. Beal (Seattle: University of Washington Press, 1963); *Chief Joseph: War Chief of the Nez Perce,* by Russell Davis and Brant Ashabranner (New York: McGraw-Hill, 1962); *A Century of Dishonor,* by Helen Hunt Jackson (Minneapolis: Ross and Haines, 1964); and "An Indian's View of Indian Affairs," by Chief Joseph, *North American Review* 128 (April 1879). The "Long March" is chronicled in Mark H. Brown's *The Flight of the Nez Perce* (Lincoln: University of Nebraska Press, 1982).

reservation located in their own part of the country and had been escorted in August to their new home at Fort Reno in Indian Territory.

Meanwhile, the Nez Perce, a tribe from the Wallowa Valley, Washington, led by the legendary strategic genius Chief Joseph, had gone to war against the U.S. government. The tribe had been pressured to move onto a reservation in Idaho, which would have forced them to reduce the size of their prized herds of Appaloosa horses. Chief Joseph negotiated a peaceful settlement of the dispute, and the tribe was prepared to move when a clash between settlers and young warriors over stock stolen by the settlers left eighteen whites dead. Joseph was compelled to head into the mountains with 650 of his people and was chased by the army.

The outnumbered Nez Perce were caught by surprise on three separate occasions—in White Bird Canyon and Clearwater, Idaho, and by Col. John Gibbon at Big Hole Valley, Montana—but each time fought off the attack of the superior force and escaped. As skirmishes escalated, casualties on both sides mounted, and Chief Joseph decided to make a mad dash to Canada in an attempt to join Sitting Bull's band of Sioux.

On September 13, Col. Samuel Sturgis and 350 troopers of the 7th Cavalry intercepted the Nez Perce at Canyon Creek, Montana, near present-day Billings. In a running battle, Sturgis, who was criticized for his timidity, failed to prevent the tribe from escaping.

Colonel Miles marched with reinforcements and on September 30 attacked Chief Joseph's camp on Snake Creek near the Bear Paw Mountains. In the ensuing bloody battle, the 7th Cavalry bore the brunt of the casualties: Capt. Owen Hale was killed, and Capt. Myles Moylan and 1st Lt. Edward S. Godfrey were wounded. Miles subsequently laid siege to the Indian camp with artillery, until finally, on October 5, Chief Joseph, who had been captured and exchanged, eloquently surrendered the remainder of his people.

The tribe had covered about 1,200 miles on their "Long March" through Washington, Oregon, Idaho, and Montana, losing about 275 warriors and killing about 266 soldiers. The heroic struggle of the Nez Perce, who took no scalps, killed no prisoners, and harmed few noncombatants, gained the sympathy of the American public.

By September 1878, the Cheyenne that had been sent to Indian Territory were beset by hunger, homesickness, and disease. Chiefs Dull Knife and Little Wolf fled the reservation with 300 of their tribe in an effort to return to their Tongue River homeland. More than 10,000 soldiers and civilians followed the renegades, and they engaged in several minor skirmishes. After crossing the North Platte River, however, the two chiefs argued, which divided the tribe. Dull Knife and his band eventually surrendered to a cavalry patrol near Camp (Fort) Robinson on October 23, while Little Wolf resumed his journey north to take refuge at the Red Cloud Agency after a 1,500-mile journey.

Dull Knife's people were held in a barracks at the fort and refused requests to return peacefully to Indian Territory. The post commander attempted to persuade them by cutting off food, water, and fuel. On January 9, 1879, the Cheyenne, who had secreted weapons, were driven by the unbearable conditions to shoot the guards and flee the post. They were chased down, and almost half of them—men, women, and children—were shot down or froze to death. The survivors, which included Chief Dull Knife and his family, took refuge at the Red Cloud Agency, and were later settled on Pine Ridge Reservation.

Little Wolf and his band remained at large throughout the winter, finally surrendering on March 27 to a detachment of the 2nd Cavalry from Fort Keogh. In 1884—one year after Dull Knife had died—the Northern Cheyenne were awarded their own reservation at Tongue River.

During the ensuing years, the Sioux that had fled to Canada straggled into reservations. On July 19, 1881, Sitting Bull and nearly 200 followers surrendered at Fort Buford, Dakota Territory, an act that marked the end of Sioux resistance and opened the plains to the army, the settlers, and the railroad.

That relative peace remained until 1890, when the Sioux became captivated by a new religion. In 1889, a Paiute Indian named Jack Wilson, who called himself Wovoka, claimed to have had a spiritual experience that prompted him to create a religion called the Ghost Dance, which was based on the premise that the white man would disappear and the buffalo would return. Most Western tribes accepted the peaceful doctrine of this Ghost Dance, but the Sioux converted the ceremony to conform to their hostility and began to defy authority. The army feared that there would be an outbreak of war and increased the number of troops at the two Sioux reservations—which included bringing in the 7th Cavalry from Fort Riley.

Sitting Bull did not participate in this ritual, but he clearly enjoyed the turmoil it provoked among his people—as did noted peacemaker Minniconjou chief Big Foot. General Nelson Miles ordered that the two chiefs be arrested. Sitting Bull resisted and was killed by his own tribal police on December 15. This caused Big Foot to subsequently flee the reservation with 300 of his people and head for Pine Ridge. Miles dispatched the 7th Cavalry, commanded by Col. James W. Forsyth, to catch Big Foot and his band and escort them back. Forsyth overtook Big Foot twenty miles from Pine Ridge in the Valley of Wounded Knee Creek, where the two factions camped for the night.

✸ Little Wolf
Northern Cheyenne Chief

Little Wolf (Ohkom Kakit) was born about 1820 near the confluence of the Eel and Blue Rivers in Montana. He established a reputation as a fierce warrior and tactician during his youth in skirmishes against the Comanche and Kiowa and became chief of the Bowstring Society, a tribal military society. He was said to have also been the bearer of the Sacred Chief's Bundle of the Northern Cheyenne, which made him personally responsible for the welfare and preservation of his tribe. Little Wolf and his band eventually joined the Lakota Sioux in fights against the Arapaho and participated in Red Cloud's 1866–68 war over the Bozeman Trail, the chief later signing the Fort Laramie Treaty of 1868 (see "Red Cloud's War" on page 68, and "The Fort Laramie Treaty of 1868 and the Black Hills Expedition" on page 158).

Little Wolf was not present at the June 1876 Little Bighorn battle but paid a price when the army retaliated by attacking Dull Knife's village on the Powder River in November of that year. He was reportedly shot seven times but escaped and survived. Little Wolf surrendered in May 1877 and served briefly as a scout for Gen. George Crook. His tribe was subsequently exiled to a reservation near Fort Reno, Indian Territory, far from their Tongue River homeland.

In September 1878, with the tribe suffering from homesickness, starvation, and illness, Little Wolf—along with Dull Knife—fled the reservation with 300 of their people and headed north. More than 10,000 soldiers and civilians chased the band for 1,500 miles, engaging in several minor skirmishes. After crossing the North Platte River, Little Wolf and Dull Knife argued and the bands split. Dull Knife surrendered at Camp Robinson; Little Wolf made it to Montana, where he wintered at the Red Cloud Agency. He was permitted to remain in Montana after agreeing to scout for Gen. Nelson A. Miles.

In 1880, Little Wolf, who had been drinking, killed a longtime adversary and was removed from a leadership role with the tribe and banished from the reservation. He lived along the Rosebud River until his death in 1904. Little Wolf left behind two wives, two sons, and a daughter.

📖 See *Cheyenne Autumn*, by Mari Sandoz (New York: McGraw-Hill, 1953); and *The Fighting Cheyennes*, by George B. Grinnell (Norman: University of Oklahoma Press, 1956).

BIOGRAPHIES

✹ Ranald Slidell Mackenzie
Colonel, 4th U. S. Cavalry

Mackenzie was born on July 27, 1840, in New York City. He entered the U.S. Military Academy at West Point in 1858 and graduated four years later, ranked first in his class. The newly commissioned officer was immediately thrust into the Civil War with the Corps of Engineers. By the end of the war, Mackenzie, who had been wounded twice, had distinguished himself in numerous major battles and won brevets up to major general of volunteers. U. S. Grant once called him "the most promising young officer in the army."

Following the war, Mackenzie reverted to his Regular army rank of colonel and served with the 41st and 24th Infantry Regiments before assuming command of the 4th Cavalry at Fort Concho in northwestern Texas in February 1871. For the next four years, the colonel and his troops campaigned against Plains and Apache Indians and eventually rid the state of the hostiles. In an 1871 fight against Comanche, Mackenzie was badly wounded when struck by an arrow. In 1873, he crossed the border into Mexico without permission, which became an international incident that was finally resolved by the State Department. He commanded his men during the Red River War of 1874–75 and was able to destroy a large Comanche-Kiowa village located on the Texas Panhandle. His regiment was transferred to Fort Sill, Indian Territory, in 1875.

In 1876, the 4th Cavalry was brought to the northern plains by Gen. Phil Sheridan and stationed at Fort Robinson, Nebraska. On November 25, 1876, Mackenzie led his regiment on a successful attack of Dull Knife's band of Cheyenne at a village on the Red Fork of the Powder River. Early the following year, the regiment was sent to Washington, D.C., to guard against civil unrest resulting from the controversial Hayes-Tilden election of 1876. The regiment was then sent to Fort Clark, Texas, and maintained peace along the Rio Grande. In 1881, Mackenzie and his troops forcefully relocated the Colorado Ute Indians to their new reservation in Utah.

In 1882, Mackenzie was promoted to brigadier general, but soon after, he was stricken with mental illness. He briefly commanded the Department of Texas before being institutionalized in New York City for his growing mental instability. Mackenzie was involuntarily retired from the army in 1884 and died on January 19, 1889, at Staten Island. He was buried at West Point.

The Sioux awoke on the morning of December 29 to find themselves surrounded by 500 troops and four cannons. Colonel Forsyth requested that the Indians hand over their firearms. When they refused, Forsyth ordered that a search be made. One Indian, perhaps Yellow Bird, called for them to resist. A soldier and a warrior engaged in a scuffle, and a weapon was discharged. The young men of the tribe immediately commenced firing into the nearest soldiers. That fire was returned, and in the close-range battle that ensued, with the cavalry supported by artillery, the Indian camp was destroyed and eighty-four Sioux men and boys—including Chief Big Foot—as well as forty-four women and eighteen children, lay dead. In addition, fifty-one Indians were wounded, seven of whom later died. The 7th Cavalry lost one officer, Capt. George D. Wallace, and eighteen enlisted were killed and thirty-three wounded.

On New Year's Day 1891, the Indian bodies were gathered up and buried in a mass grave on the hill from where the artillery had been fired.

The Wounded Knee battle, or massacre, was viewed by the army as a terrible blunder committed by Colonel Forsyth, who was relieved of command and became the subject of a court of inquiry.

The event brought the Ghost Dance ritual to an end, and with it any hope that the Plains Indians had of ever regaining the traditions, land, and culture that had been lost in decades of war against the United States.

📖 The best overall account of the above period is in *Frontier Regulars: The United States Army and the Indian, 1866–1891,* by Robert M. Utley (New York: Macmillan Publishing Co., 1973). The story of Cody's "duel" can be found in *First Scalp for Custer: The Skirmish at Warbonnet Creek, Nebraska, July 17, 1876,* by Paul L. Hedren (Lincoln: University of Nebraska Press, 1987), as well as in other Cody biographies. The Slim Buttes battle is covered nicely in *Slim Buttes, 1876: An Episode of the Great Sioux War,* by Jerome Greene (Norman: University of Oklahoma Press, 1982); and *Campaigning with Crook,* by Charles King (Norman: University of Oklahoma Press, 1964).

The text of the agreement of August 15, 1876, in which the Sioux signed over the Black Hills has been reprinted from the *U.S. Statutes at Large* 19, in the appendix of *Custer's Gold: The United States Cavalry Expedition of 1874,* by Donald Jackson (New Haven, CT: Yale University Press, 1966). The Dull Knife battle is in *Mackenzie's Last Fight with the Cheyennes,* by John G. Bourke (Bellevue, NE: Old Army Press, 1970); *The Fighting Cheyennes,* by George B. Grinnell (Norman: University of Oklahoma Press, 1956); and *The Dull Knife Fight,* by Fred H. Werner (Greeley, CO: Werner Publications, 1981). The best source for the Wolf Mountain battle is "The Battle of Wolf Mountain," by Don Rickey, Jr., *Montana: The Magazine*

(continued on following page)

of Western History 13 (Spring 1963); also see *Faintly Sounds the War-Cry: The Story of the Fight at Battle Butte,* by Fred H. Werner (Greeley, CO: Werner Publications, 1983).

For the Lame Deer fight, see "The Last Fight of the Sioux War of 1876–77," by John F. McBlain, *Journal of the United States Cavalry Association* 10 (1897). The Nez Perce War can be found in *The Flight of the Nez Perce: A History of the Nez Perce War,* by Mark H. Brown (New York: Putnam, 1967). The flight of Dull Knife and Little Wolf has been sympathetically portrayed in *Cheyenne Autumn,* by Mari Sandoz (New York: McGraw-Hill, 1953).

A few of the better sources for the Ghost Dance and Wounded Knee affair are *Eyewitness at Wounded Knee,* by Richard Jensen, R. Eli Paul, and John E. Carter (Lincoln: University of Nebraska Press, 1991); *Wovoka and the Ghost Dance,* edited by Don Lynch (Carson City, NV: Grace Foundation, 1990); *The Ghost Dance Religion and Wounded Knee,* by James Mooney (New York: Dover, 1973); and *Bury My Heart at Wounded Knee,* by Dee Brown (Holt, Rinehart & Winston, 1970).

For a detailed account of Colonel Miles's 1876–77 Campaign, see *Yellowstone Command: Col. Nelson A. Miles and the Great Sioux War,* by Jerome Green (Lincoln: University of Nebraska Press, 1991).

📖 *Ranald S. Mackenzie on the Texas Frontier,* by Earnest Wallace (Lubbock: West Texas Museum Association, 1964); *Mackenzie's Last Fight with the Cheyennes,* by John G. Bourke (Bellevue, NE: Old Army Press, 1970); and *On the Border with Mackenzie; or, Winning West Texas from the Comanches,* by R. G. Carter (New York: Antiquarian Press, 1961).

✸ Wesley Merritt
Colonel, 5th U. S. Cavalry

Merritt was born in New York City on June 16, 1834, and at age three moved with his family to Illinois. He entered the U.S. Military Academy at West Point in 1855 and graduated five years later, ranked twenty-second in his class. Merritt was assigned as a lieutenant with the 2nd Regiment of Dragoons and was promoted to second lieutenant in January 1861. He became a first lieutenant with the 2nd Cavalry in May 1861. Merritt served mostly as a staff officer in Washington, D.C., assigned as an aide to cavalry commander Maj. Gen. George Stoneman, until he was promoted to captain in April 1863 and returned to field duty.

Merritt distinguished himself at the June 1863 cavalry battle at Brandy Station and again at Middleburg, which led to his appointment to brigadier general of volunteers on June 29—the same day that George Armstrong Custer received his appointment to that rank. As commander of the Reserve Cavalry Brigade, he participated in the battle of Gettysburg; the Bristoe, Mine Run, and Overland campaigns; Yellow Tavern; Cold Harbor; and early stages of the Petersburg siege. In August 1864, Merritt assumed command of the 1st Cavalry Division under Gen. Phil Sheridan in the Shenandoah Valley and participated in every major battle until war's end, earning a brevet to major general.

In 1866, Merritt reverted to lieutenant colonel and assumed command of the newly formed 9th Cavalry at San Antonio. He would remain in Texas for the next eight years, leaving only for occasional trips abroad. Merritt was appointed special cavalry inspector for the Division of the Missouri in 1875 and agent at the Red Cloud Agency the following year.

On July 1, 1876, he was promoted to colonel and assumed command of the 5th Cavalry. His first action came when he led a detachment of 400 troops to chase 800 Cheyenne that had bolted from the Red Cloud Agency. On July 17, at War Bonnet, or Hat, Creek, Merritt's troops encoun-

(continued on following page)

tered about thirty renegade Cheyenne, and William F. "Buffalo Bill" Cody engaged in his celebrated "duel" with a subchief, which became known as the "first scalp for Custer." Merritt's cavalry then joined Gen. George Crook and campaigned throughout the remainder of the year, participating in the September Slim Buttes battle. Merritt conducted scouting operations against the Nez Perce in 1877, then took command of Fort D. A. Russell.

In 1879, Merritt was one of the members of the Reno Court of Inquiry. He apparently was responsible for writing the decision that was favorable to Reno, which "cleared" the major of any blame for Custer's defeat at the Little Bighorn. His controversial action was considered a betrayal of Custer by many people, including the general's wife, Libbie (see "The Reno Court of Inquiry," right).

Merritt remained in the West until 1882, when he was appointed superintendent of the U.S. Military Academy at West Point. He was promoted to brigadier general in 1887 and commanded the Department of the Missouri and later the Department of Dakota. In 1895, Merritt was promoted to major general, and three years later, he commanded the expedition to the Philippines. His troops captured Manila in August, and he remained there briefly as governor. Merritt retired in 1900 to Natural Bridge, Virginia, where he died on December 3, 1910. He was buried at West Point.

📖 See *Brandy Station to Manila Bay: A Biography of General Wesley Merritt,* by Don E. Alberts (Austin, TX: Presidial Press, 1980); and *Merritt and the Indian Wars,* by Barry C. Johnson (London: Johnson-Taunton Military Press, 1972). Merritt's "Three Indian Campaigns" appeared in the April 1890 issue of *Harper's New Monthly Magazine.*

✺ Nelson Appleton Miles
Brigadier General, U. S. Army

Miles was born on August 8, 1839, near Westminster, Massachusetts. He moved to Boston at age seventeen in order to further his education and worked as a clerk in a crockery store during the day while attending school at night. Miles at that time also received military instruction from a retired French colonel. At the outbreak of the Civil War, he helped recruit the 22nd Massachusetts Infantry and was commissioned a captain. His superior officers, however, deemed Miles too young to command and assigned him to the staff

(continued on following page)

SIDEBARS

🐎 The Reno Court of Inquiry

Custer's widow, Libbie, and his first biographer, Frederick Whittaker, undertook a relentless effort to persuade the government to hold an official inquiry into the circumstances surrounding the Little Bighorn battle. Libbie wanted to clear her husband's name from blame for the defeat. Whittaker, a former subordinate of Custer's during the Civil War, was involved perhaps both out of loyalty to Custer and to help sales of his recently published biography, *A Complete Life of General George A. Custer.*

Whittaker wrote a letter dated May 18, 1878, to Wyoming congressman W. W. Corlett, demanding an investigation. In the letter, he said that "information from participants in the battle [was] to the effect that gross cowardice was displayed by Major Marcus A. Reno." This letter was leaked to the press, which was the last straw for Reno, who requested that an army court of inquiry to investigate his conduct be convened.

By order of President Rutherford B. Hayes, the court convened at the Palmer House in Chicago on January 13, 1879. The examining committee was composed of three officers: Col. John H. King, 9th Infantry, presiding; Col. Wesley Merritt, 5th Cavalry; and Lt. Col. W. B. Royall, 3rd Cavalry. The court reporter was Lt. Jesse M. Lee, 9th Infantry. Members of the Custer family, including Libbie and Margaret Calhoun, attended every session.

Reno was defended by Lyman Gilbert, the assistant attorney general of Pennsylvania. Reno's primary defense of his actions was to blame Custer for not providing him the complete battle plan. He testified that he had been ordered to charge the village and would "be supported by the whole outfit." He interpreted that to mean that Custer was going to follow him into the village. Instead, Custer employed a strategy that had been successful for him in battles from the Civil War to Washita, which was opening an attack with a frontal assault while later charging from the flank (see "Custer's Battle Plan" on page 205).

An examination of Reno's official report of the battle, however, reveals that he expected Custer to attack on the flank. Therefore, it does not take a lawyer to recognize that Reno's defense was based on a contradiction.

Reno, although evidence indicates otherwise, maintained that his retreat in which about a third of his men became casualties was a "charge." He also was asked whether he had gone into the fight with "confidence or distrust" of Custer. Reno answered, "Well, sir, I had known General Custer a long time, and I had no confidence in his ability as a soldier."

Reno was aided by the fact that fellow officers had closed ranks around the elite 7th Cavalry and did not desire to bring disgrace upon the unit. Stories were carefully altered, and answers were often evasive. Only one officer, 1st Lt. Edward S. Godfrey, supported the charge of cowardice against Reno by stating that the major had displayed "indecision" and "nervous timidity." Testimony for the most part did establish that Benteen had been the true commander on the hilltop. The few disparaging words against Reno came from civilians, scout Fred Girard in particular, who pointed out Reno's mishandling of the retreat, and by two packers who accused Reno of drunkenness (see "The Conduct of Maj. Marcus A. Reno on the Hilltop" on page 245). The inquiry was little more than a dog-and-pony show performed by career military men who understood the politics of their profession.

The testimonies of twenty-three veterans of the battle lasted for twenty-six days and filled 1,300 pages. The finding of the court was as follows: "The conduct of the officers throughout was excellent, and while subordinates, in some instances, did more for the safety of the command by brilliant displays of courage than did Major Reno, there was nothing in his conduct which requires animadversion [criticism or censure] from this Court." Amazingly, given the known facts, Reno had been cleared of any wrongdoing.

Libbie Custer was understandably crushed by the decision, but she said nothing about it in public. Not so with Frederick Whittaker, who wrote a scathing letter to the *New York Sun* that was published on February 26, 1879, in which he called the proceedings a "mockery of justice" and a "whitewash." Whittaker went on to say that Merritt had been "afterward closeted with the Recorder alone for several hours, and, it is understood, did most of the work of the decision, the Recorder having no voice save to present the case on trial."

Libbie expressed her feelings about Merritt in an October 16, 1882, letter to Gen. William T. Sherman, in which she wrote:

> A wife's love sharpens her eyes and quickens her instinct and years ago I knew (not from my husband) that General Merritt was his enemy. On the plains we entertained him and he seemed to have conquered his enmity and jealousy that was so bitter in the Army of the Republic. But when he was placed at the head of the Court of Inquiry that met to investigate Col. Reno's conduct at Chicago, I saw all through the trial how General Merritt <u>still</u> felt toward his dead comrade.

Lieutenant (now Gen.) Jesse M. Lee, the Reno court recorder, wrote a letter to Libbie Custer, dated June 27, 1897, and confessed to having been influenced during the inquiry "by the prejudicial opinions of those whose motive I did not then understand, and whose sources of information I then had no means of testing." Lee went on to offer the opinion that blame for the defeat should have been placed squarely on Reno. This important vindication of Custer, however, had come eighteen years too late.

of Brig. Gen. Oliver Howard. He was wounded at Seven Pines during the Peninsula campaign and distinguished himself enough to be promoted to lieutenant colonel in May 1862 and colonel of the 61st New York Infantry in September.

Miles was wounded at Fredericksburg, where he commanded both the 61st and 64th New York Regiments. He was hit again at Chancellorsville, where he was breveted brigadier general and awarded the Medal of Honor for his bravery. He was wounded for the fourth time at Petersburg and promoted to brigadier general of volunteers in May 1864. At war's end, he was in command of the 1st Division, II Corps. In October 1865, he was promoted to major general.

Miles remained in the army after the war and was appointed colonel of the 40th U.S. Infantry, a black regiment. He then was placed in charge of Fort Monroe, Virginia, where former Confederate president Jefferson Davis was being held. He came under personal criticism for keeping Davis in shackles but likely was under orders from the War Department. Miles assumed command of the 5th Infantry in March 1869 and engaged in numerous campaigns against Indians on the plains and in the Far West. He was commander of the so-called Red River War of 1874–75, which brought peace to the Staked Plain of Texas.

Miles brought his 5th Infantry north during the fall of 1876 and pursued hostile Cheyenne and Sioux, defeating the hostiles in the January 1877 battle of Wolf Mountain and the May 1877 battle of Lame Deer. He then set his sights on Nez Perce chief Joseph and his renegade band, following his enemy to a showdown in the Bear Paw Mountains, where Chief Joseph was forced to surrender in October 1877. The following year, he led his troops in the final stages of the Bannock War. In 1879, Miles pursued Sitting Bull when the Sioux medicine man crossed the border from Canada into Montana to hunt, but he was denied permission to enter Canada to chase the renegades. He was promoted to brigadier general in 1880 and commanded the Department of the Columbia from that time until he assumed command of the Department of the Missouri in 1885.

In 1886, Miles replaced Gen. George Crook as commander of the Department of Arizona and spearheaded the final offensive against Chiricahua Apache, in which Geronimo was persuaded to surrender. He was promoted to major general in 1890 and command of the Department of the Missouri. In that capacity, Miles was faced with the 1890 Ghost Dance uprising on the Sioux reser-

(continued on following page)

vations. He ordered the arrest of Sitting Bull, which led to the death of that medicine man and the Wounded Knee affair, where Chief Big Foot and as many as 150 of his tribe were killed by the 7th Cavalry.

Miles commanded Federal troops in Chicago during the 1894 disturbances resulting from the Pullmen's strike. The next year, he was named commander in chief of the army, but he remained in an administrative capacity and did not lead troops during the Spanish-American War due to a feud with the secretary of war. In 1900, Miles was promoted to lieutenant general. He retired in August 1903.

Miles served as head of numerous veterans' organizations and became a writer of military history. He eventually became embroiled in the debate over the battle of the Little Bighorn. Miles supported Custer's strategy and placed blame for the defeat on Maj. Marcus A. Reno for failing to charge the village as ordered and Capt. Frederick Benteen for not riding to the sound of gunfire. In 1892, he petitioned Congress to allocate sufficient funds for a memorial at the then Custer Battlefield National Monument (see "Establishment of Little Bighorn Battlefield National Monument" on page 268).

Miles died in the District of Columbia on May 15, 1925, during the playing of the national anthem at the Ringling Brothers Circus.

📖 Miles was the author of two autobiographies: *Serving the Republic: Memoirs of the Civil and Military Life of Nelson A. Miles* (New York: Harper & Brothers, 1911); and *Personal Recollections and Observations of General Nelson A. Miles* (New York: Da Capo, 1969). Also see *The Unregimented General: A Biography of Nelson A. Miles,* by Virginia W. Johnson (Boston: Houghton Mifflin Co., 1962); and *Nelson A. Miles: A Documentary Biography of His Military Career, 1861–1903,* edited by Brian Pohanka (Glendale, CA: Arthur H. Clark, 1985).

✺ Anson Mills
Captain, 3rd Cavalry

Mills was born on August 31, 1834, near Thornton, Indiana. He attended the U.S. Military Academy at West Point but dropped out after two years. Mills traveled west in 1857, found work in Texas as a surveyor, and helped lay out the city of El Paso and the boundary line between Texas and New Mexico. He owned a ranch north of El Paso. In 1860, he participated in the gold rush to Pinos Altos, New Mexico, where he used his surveying talents to lay out the camp. At the outbreak of the

(continued on following page)

The Reno Court of Inquiry, which had been convened in order to establish the facts of the battle, was more farcical than credible and simply served to intensify the debate over the conduct of Custer and Reno that continues to this day.

📖 The proceedings can be found in *The Reno Court of Inquiry: The* Chicago Times *Account* (Fort Collins, CO: Old Army Press, 1972); *Abstract of the Official Record of Proceedings of the Reno Court of Inquiry,* by W. A. Graham (Harrisburg, PA: Stackpole, 1954); and *Reno Court of Inquiry: Proceedings of a Court of Inquiry in the Case of Marcus A. Reno Concerning His Conduct at the Battle of the Little Big Horn River on June 25–26, 1876,* edited by Ronald H. Nichols (Crow Agency, MT: Custer Battlefield Historical and Museum Association, 1994).

Two helpful sources are Robert M. Utley's *Custer and the Great Controversy: The Origin and Development of a Legend* (Pasadena, CA: Westernlore Press, 1980); and *The Story of the Little Big Horn: Custer's Last Fight,* by W. A. Graham (New York: Bonanza Books, 1959). Many interesting references can be found in *The Custer Myth: A Source Book of Custeriana,* edited by W. A. Graham (Harrisburg, PA: Stackpole, 1953).

Libbie's letter to Sherman is in the W. T. Sherman Papers, Library of Congress. The letter from Lieutenant Lee to Libbie, which is in the collection at the Little Bighorn Battlefield National Monument, has been reprinted in *General Custer's Libbie,* by Lawrence A. Frost (Seattle: Superior Publishing Co., 1976).

🐎 Establishment of Little Bighorn Battlefield National Monument

The initial interest in establishing a memorial for Custer and his men was created by newspapers that, soon after the battle, began publishing sensational but true stories about half-buried bodies strewn across the barren field. This revelation caused an outcry from the public and high-ranking army officers, who demanded that Congress allocate funds for a cemetery to properly bury the fallen.

Finally, on August 1, 1879, Custer Battlefield National Cemetery was established by General Order No. 78. Troopers from Fort Custer were called upon to make the field more presentable. This included erecting a log memorial on top of Custer Hill and remarking the scattered graves with substantial wooden stakes.

In 1881, the log memorial was replaced by a huge, white granite monument on which the names of the dead—a number of them misspelled—had been inscribed. The remains of the troopers were at that time collected from their various graves and reinterred in a common mass grave at the base of the monument. White marble headstones replaced the wooden markers in 1890 to designate the places where the cavalrymen had fallen. Three years later, the first superintendent was named to oversee the care of the cemetery.

In 1930, the parcel of land that was the location of the Reno-Benteen hilltop fight was added. The two distant battlefields were connected with a right-of-way road between them. Ten years later, the National Park Service of the Interior Department assumed responsibility from the War Department for the area. In 1946, the historic site was renamed Custer Battlefield National Monument, and the principal mission became the study of the battle—primarily from the standpoint of the soldiers, although that gradually changed over the years to include the Indian side of the story.

In 1991, the battlefield was renamed Little Bighorn Battlefield National Monument by an act of Congress, Public Law 102-201, in order to recognize the participation of the Indian in the battle. The mandate also provided that an Indian Memorial was to be built in the vicinity of the 7th Cavalry Monument. This name change and proposed monument created quite a controversy among those who idolized Custer and believed that his name should remain on the battlefield, and that the addition of a monument honoring people hostile to our country would be an insult to the U.S. Army.

Visitors can stroll the battlefield on walkways and drive the road from Custer Hill to the Reno-Benteen defense site. Park personnel are available to provide tour information and offer free lectures during the summer months. The visitor center and historical museum on the grounds features an interesting array of Custer, 7th Cavalry, and Indian artifacts, dioramas, artwork, maps, photographs, books for sale, and an impressive collection of documents. Custer's widow Libbie donated nearly 50,000 letters and papers to the museum. The adjoining Custer National Cemetery holds the remains of such notables as Maj. Marcus A. Reno; Custer's longtime orderly, John Burkman; Lt. John J. Crittenden; Curly, the scout; Dr. George E. Lord; and a mass grave for twenty-one soldiers killed in the 1877 Snake Creek fight against the Nez Perce.

Little Bighorn Battlefield National Monument is located fifteen miles south of Hardin, Montana, off exit 510 of Interstate 90.

📖 The best source is *History of Custer Battlefield,* by Don Rickey, Jr. (Hardin, MT: Custer Battlefield Historical and Museum Association, 1998). Rickey, a former historian at the battlefield, provides answers to just about every possible question. See also Rickey's "Myth to Monument: The Establishment of Custer Battlefield National Monument," *Journal of*

The granite memorial at the crest of Custer Hill. The bodies of the enlisted cavalrymen were buried beneath in a mass grave. *From author's collection.*

Civil War, Mills departed Texas for the Union army, and in May 1861, he was commissioned a first lieutenant in the 18th Infantry. At war's end, he held the rank of captain with brevets to lieutenant colonel.

Mills remained in the army after the war, serving on the Kansas frontier, where he was involved in a number of skirmishes with hostile Indians and became friends with mountain man Jim Bridger. He joined the 3rd Cavalry in late 1870. While in Arizona, he established Fort Reno in the Tonto Basin and operated against the Apache Indians. Mills was a battalion commander during the 1876 Little Bighorn campaign and fought with Reynolds at Powder River in March and with Crook in the June battle of the Rosebud. He was dispatched during the Rosebud battle to attack an Indian village that was presumed to be nearby and avoided a trap set by Crazy Horse, safely returning to the battlefield (see "Prelude to Little Bighorn: The Powder River and Rosebud Engagements" on page 189).

(continued on following page)

Mills continued campaigning with Crook's "starvation march." He commanded a 150-man detachment dispatched by the general to find supplies at Deadwood, South Dakota, when on September 9 he happened upon a thirty-seven-lodge Sioux village near a landmark rock formation named Slim Buttes. Mills routed the warriors and fought off a counterattack by Crazy Horse, until Crook arrived with reinforcements. He was breveted colonel for his actions.

In April 1878, Mills became major of the 10th Cavalry, a black regiment, and later fought against Geronimo. He was promoted to lieutenant colonel of the 4th Cavalry in March 1890 and colonel of the 3rd Cavalry in August 1892. Mills was appointed brigadier general in June 1897 and retired one week later. He established a business that manufactured equipment for soldiers and sportsmen, which made him a wealthy man. Mills sold his business in 1905 and died at Washington, D.C., on November 5, 1924.

📖 Mills wrote *My Story* (Washington, DC: Press of Byron S. Adams, 1918).

the West 7 (April 1969). For material about the name change, see "Whose Shrine Is It? The Ideological Struggle for Custer Battlefield," by Robert M. Utley, in *Montana: The Magazine of Western History* 42 (Winter 1992).

🦌 Archaeological Excavations of Little Bighorn Battlefield

In 1983, a prairie fire swept across 600 grassy acres of the Little Bighorn battlefield, removing much of the obscuring vegetation and making the area suitable for examination. James V. Court, the superintendent at that time, had the foresight to wonder what artifacts might have been exposed that could shed new light on the famous battle and thereby enhance the interpretive programs at the battlefield. Court called in a young archaeologist named Richard A. Fox, Jr., who examined the field and prepared two reports indicating that there was a great potential of uncovering items of significance.

Fox submitted his reports to Douglas D. Scott, chief of the Rocky Mountain Division, Midwest Archaeological Center, National Park Service. Scott also was impressed with the potential and organized a two-year project in which he and Fox would serve as coprincipal investigators.

They obtained National Park Service approval for this dig, but no funding. Then the Custer Battlefield Historical and Museum Association, a nonprofit historical interest group, came forward to finance the project. In 1984, Scott, Fox, and about 100 volunteers embarked on an initial dig that lasted about five weeks.

The following year, the investigators conducted an extensive examination of the field. This time they swept the battlefield with electronic sensing devices—metal detectors—and marked each location of a possible relic with a small plastic flag. The archaeologists then probed these areas with trowels, assigned every item found a number, and recorded and coded them on a computer. Among the 4,000 artifacts that they unearthed were buttons from various types of clothing, pieces of firearms, a watch, coins, a pocketknife, iron arrowheads, horse trappings, bone fragments, and a huge number of bullets and cartridge casings from many different weapons (see "Weapons Carried by the Cavalrymen" on page 195, and "Weapons Carried by the Indians" on page 198). The computer coding assisted in generating a map that detailed battle events from the positions of found bullets and cartridge casings.

One of the more interesting discoveries was that of a nearly complete skeleton they named "Trooper Mike." These remains were examined by famed forensic anthropologist Clyde Snow, who estimated that this trooper was between nineteen and twenty-two years old; stood five feet, eight inches tall; and weighed 150 to 160 pounds. "Mike" had been shot twice in the chest and had a bullet fragment embedded in his left wrist.

Postdeath mutilation was indicated by his shattered skull, knocked-out teeth, and gashed right thighbone from six chopping blows, likely from a hatchet. His remains were reburied in Custer National Cemetery in June 1985.

Subsequent excavations in various areas in and around the battlefield have turned up additional artifacts, but the bodies of about twenty-eight troopers with Company E that were said to have been buried in June 1876 down Deep Ravine have yet to be found.

📖 The best book utilizing information from the archaeological digs, a true classic of the battle—although not for beginners—is *Archaeology, History, and Custer's Last Battle,* by Richard Allan Fox, Jr. (Norman: University of Oklahoma Press, 1993). Dr. Fox combines his extensive knowledge of the battle with his expertise in archaeology to present a fascinating, albeit speculative, glimpse into the unfolding of events on June 25, 1876.

Also see *Archaeological Insights into the Custer Battle: A Preliminary Assessment,* by Douglas D. Scott and Richard A. Fox, Jr. (Norman: University of Oklahoma Press, 1987); *Archaeological Perspectives on the Battle of the Little Bighorn,* by Douglas D. Scott, Richard A. Fox, Jr., Melissa A. Conner, and Dick Harmon (Norman: University of Oklahoma Press, 1989); and *The Mystery of E Troop: Custer's Gray Horse Company at the Little Bighorn,* by Gregory Michno (Missoula, MT: Mountain Press Publishing Co., 1994).

🐎 Historical Interest Groups

Custer Battlefield Historical and Museum Association (P.O. Box 902, Hardin, MT 59034). This educational and research association is dedicated to the study and dissemination of information about the Little Bighorn battle and the Plains Indian Wars.

Custer Battlefield Preservation Committee (P.O. Box 7, Hardin, MT 59034). This organization, founded by former battlefield superintendent James V. Court, uses donated funds to purchase land adjacent to the Little Bighorn Battlefield National Monument for the purpose of protecting the integrity of the area.

Fort Abraham Lincoln Foundation (401 W. Main, Mandan, ND 58554). This organization promotes reconstruction, development, and maintenance of the historic post.

Little Big Horn Associates (105 Bartlett Place, Brooklyn, NY 11229). This interest group is dedicated to seeking the truth about the famous battle and all aspects of the settlement of the West.

Order of the Indian Wars (P.O. Box 7401, Little Rock, AR, 72217). This interest group keeps members informed about events and information, including lectures by noted historians and tours of battlefields, related to the Indian wars.

Index